2002

Deskbook Encyclopedia of

American
School Law

Oakstone

Legal & Business Publishing

FORMERLY DATA RESEARCH, INC.

Oakstone Legal & Business Publishing, Inc.
6801 Cahaba Valley Road
Birmingham, Alabama 35242-2627

First edition 1981
Printed in the United States of America

> "This publication is designed to provide accurate and authoritative information in regard to the subject matter covered. It is sold with the understanding that the publisher is not engaged in rendering legal, accounting or other professional service. If legal advice or other expert assistance is required, the services of a competent professional person should be sought."— from a Declaration of Principles jointly adopted by a Committee of the American Bar Association and a Committee of Publishers and Associations.

ISBN 1-931200-11-4
ISSN 1058-4919

The Library of Congress has cataloged this serial title as follows:
Deskbook Encyclopedia of American school law.— 1980/81— Rosemount, Minn.:
Informational Research Systems, 1981-
                              v.; 23 cm.
Annual.
Published 2001   by: Oakstone Legal & Business Publishing
Prepared by the editors of: Legal Notes for Education,
1980/81-
1. Educational law and legislation—United States—Digests. 2. Educational law and legislation—United States—Periodicals. I. Informational Research Systems (Washington, D.C.) II. Oakstone Legal & Business Publishing (Burnsville, Minn.) III. Legal Notes for Education. IV. Title: Encyclopedia of American School Law.
KF4114.D46   92-054912
                              344.73'07'02638—dc19
                              [347.304702638]
                                        AACR 2#M#MARC-S

Library of Congress   [8704r86]rev

Other Titles Published By
Oakstone Legal & Business Publishing:

Students with Disabilities and Special Education
Private School Law in America
Higher Education Law in America
U.S. Supreme Court Education Cases
Deskbook Encyclopedia of American Insurance Law
Deskbook Encyclopedia of Public Employment Law
U.S. Supreme Court Employment Cases
Deskbook Encyclopedia of Employment Law
Statutes, Regulations and Case Law Protecting
    Individuals with Disabilities
Federal Laws Prohibiting Employment Discrimination

TABLE OF CONTENTS

CHAPTER ONE
Accidents, Injuries and Deaths

TABLE OF CONTENTS

CHAPTER TWO
Freedom of Religion

TABLE OF CONTENTS

CHAPTER THREE
Freedom of Speech and Association

CHAPTER FOUR
Student Rights

TABLE OF CONTENTS

CHAPTER FIVE
Employment Practices

TABLE OF CONTENTS

CHAPTER SIX
Employment Discrimination

CHAPTER SEVEN
Termination, Resignation and Retirement

TABLE OF CONTENTS

CHAPTER EIGHT
Tenure and Due Process

TABLE OF CONTENTS

CHAPTER NINE
Labor Relations

CHAPTER TEN
School Operations

TABLE OF CONTENTS

CHAPTER ELEVEN
Academic Practices

CHAPTER TWELVE
Students with Disabilities

TABLE OF CONTENTS

CHAPTER THIRTEEN
Private Schools

CHAPTER FOURTEEN
Interscholastic Athletics

TABLE OF CONTENTS

REFERENCE SECTION

INTRODUCTION

The *2002 Deskbook Encyclopedia of American School Law* is a completely updated encyclopedic compilation of state and federal appellate court decisions that affect education. These decisions have been selected and edited by the editorial staff of Oakstone Legal & Business Publishing, Inc., publishers of *Legal Notes for Education*. Topical classifications have been revised and edited to reflect rapid changes in education law, and many cases reported in previous editions have been re-edited or reclassified.

This edition contains a brief introductory note on the American judicial system and an updated appendix of recent U.S. Supreme Court cases. Also included are portions of the U.S. Constitution that are most frequently cited in education cases. This publication is intended to provide educators and lawyers with access to the most current available cases in education. We believe that you will find this edition even more readable and easier to use than previous editions.

Patricia Grzywacz
Editorial Director
Oakstone Legal & Business Publishing

ABOUT THE EDITORS

Steve McEllistrem is the editorial director of Oakstone Legal & Business Publishing, Inc. He co-authored the deskbook *Private School Law in America* and is a former editor of *Legal Notes for Education*. He graduated *cum laude* from William Mitchell College of Law and received his undergraduate degree from the University of Minnesota. Mr. McEllistrem is admitted to the Minnesota Bar.

Patricia Grzywacz is the managing editor of Oakstone's education and employment newsletters. She is the co-author of the deskbook *Students with Disabilities and Special Education*. Ms. Grzywacz graduated from Widener University School of Law and received her undergraduate degree from Villanova University. Prior to joining Oakstone, she was the managing editor of the *Individuals with Disabilities Education Law Report*® and authored the *1999 Special Educator Deskbook*, both published by LRP Publications. She is admitted to the Pennsylvania and New Jersey bars.

James A. Roth is the editor of *Special Education Law Update* and *Legal Notes for Education*. He is a graduate of the University of Minnesota and William Mitchell College of Law. Mr. Roth is admitted to the Minnesota Bar.

How to Use Your Deskbook

We have designed the *Deskbook Encyclopedia of American School Law* in an accessible format for both attorneys and non-attorneys to use as a research and reference tool toward prevention of legal problems.

Research Tool

As a research tool, our deskbook allows you to conduct your research on two different levels — by topics or cases.

Topic Research

♦ If you have a general interest in a particular **topic** area, our **table of contents** provides descriptive chapter headings containing detailed subheadings from each chapter.

➢ For your convenience, we also include the chapter table of contents at the beginning of each chapter.

> **Example:**
> For more information on charter schools, the table of contents indicates that a discussion of this topic takes place in Chapter Eleven on page 463:
>
> CHAPTER ELEVEN
> Academic Practices
>

How to Use Your Deskbook

♦ If you have a specific interest in a particular **issue**, our comprehensive **index** collects all of the relevant page references to particular issues.

> **Example:**
> For more information on student civil rights, the index provides references to all of the cases dealing with student rights instead of only those cases dealing with civil rights:
>
> Student rights
>   admissions and attendance, 146-154
> → civil rights, 216-225
>   compulsory attendance, 154-159
>   corporal punishment, 159-162
>   expulsions and suspensions, 162-194
>   generally, 146-229
>   searches and seizures, 194-215
>   sex discrimination, 225-229

Case Research

♦ If you know the **name** of a particular case, our **table of cases** will allow you to quickly reference the location of the case.

> **Example:**
> If someone mentioned a case named *Santa Fe Independent School District v. Doe,* looking in the table of cases, which has been arranged alphabetically, the case would be located under the "S" section.
>
> **S**
>
>   Sanchez v. Denver Pub. Schs., 285
> → Santa Fe Independent School District v. Doe, 66
>   Sargi v. Kent City Bd. of Educ., 57

✓ Each of the cases summarized in the deskbook also contains the case citation, which will allow you to access the full text of the case if you would like to learn more about it. *See, How to Read a Case Citation, p. 643.*

♦ If your interest lies in cases from a **particular state**, our **table of cases by state** will identify the cases from your state and direct you to their page numbers.

> **Example:**
> If cases from Illinois were of interest, the table of cases by state, arranged alphabetically, would list all of the case summaries contained in the deskbook from "Illinois."

ILLINOIS

→ Ahern v. Bd. of Educ. of City of Chicago, 278
Appenheimer v. School Bd. of Washington
    Community High School, Dist. 308, 76
Babcock v. Illinois State Bd. of Educ., 239
Batson v. Pinckneyville Elementary School
    Dist. No. 50, 25

✓ Remember, the judicial system has two court systems—state and federal court—which generally function independently from each other. *See, The Judicial System, p. 639.* We have included the federal court cases in the table of cases by state according to the state in which the court resides. However, federal court decisions often impact other federal courts within that particular circuit. Therefore, it may be helpful to review cases from all of the states contained in a particular circuit.

Reference Tool

As a reference tool, we have highlighted important resources that provide the framework for many legal issues.

♦ If you would like to see specific wording of the **U.S. Constitution**, refer to **Appendix A**, which includes relevant provisions of the U.S. Constitution such as the First Amendment (freedom of speech and religion).

♦ If you would like to review **U.S. Supreme Court decisions** in a particular subject matter area, our topical list of U.S. Supreme Court case citations located in **Appendix B** will be helpful.

How to Use Your Deskbook

We hope you benefit from the use of the *2002 Deskbook Encyclopedia of American School Law.* If you have any questions about how to use the deskbook, please contact Patricia Grzywacz at 610-225-0510 or Steve McEllistrem at 612-808-0550.

TABLE OF CASES

TABLE OF CASES

xi

TABLE OF CASES

TABLE OF CASES

TABLE OF CASES

TABLE OF CASES

TABLE OF CASES BY STATE

TABLE OF CASES BY STATE

MINNESOTA

MISSISSIPPI

MISSOURI

TABLE OF CASES BY STATE

TABLE OF CASES BY STATE

OKLAHOMA

OREGON

UTAH

VERMONT

VIRGINIA

CHAPTER ONE

Accidents, Injuries and Deaths

I.   NEGLIGENCE

Negligence refers to acts or omissions demonstrating a failure to use reasonable or ordinary care. Negligence may refer to inadvertence, carelessness, or the failure to foresee potential harm. There is some overlap in the cases between negligence and intentional misconduct. A pattern of negligence by school districts which shows a conscious disregard for safety may be deemed "wilful misconduct," a form of intentional conduct discussed in Section V of this chapter.

A. Elements

The essential elements of a negligence lawsuit are: 1) the existence of a legal duty to conform conduct to a specific standard in order to protect others from unreasonable risks of injury, 2) the breach of that duty that is, 3) the direct cause of the injury, and 4) damages. In short, negligence consists of a duty of care, followed by a breach of that duty which causes injury and damages.

◆   An all-state varsity basketball player who was highly recruited by Division I universities became dissatisfied with an class that was on the NCAA's list of approved core English courses. A guidance counselor suggested that he take a course called "Technical Communications" instead. The counselor advised the student that the class would be approved by the NCAA as a core course. However, the district failed to include the course on a list of classes submitted to the NCAA for approval. The student received a full scholarship from a Division I university. After he enrolled, the NCAA Clearinghouse notified him that Technical Communications did not satisfy its core course requirement. The student was unable to compete in the basketball program and lost his scholarship. **He sued the NCAA and school district in an Iowa court for claims including negligent misrepresentation**. The claim against the NCAA was voluntarily dismissed and the court awarded summary judgment to the school district.

The student appealed to the Iowa Supreme Court, which noted that courts must refrain from rejecting "all claims that arise out of a school environment under the umbrella of educational malpractice." The case instead arose under the tort cause of action for negligent misrepresentation. **Guidance counselors** assumed an advisory role and were aware that students would rely on the information they provided. They **owed students a duty of reasonable care when supplying information** and the district was not entitled to summary judgment on the claim for negligent misrepresentation. However, the trial court had properly awarded summary judgment to the district on the claim that the school had negligently failed to submit the Technical Communications course to the NCAA for approval. The district had no duty to submit this information, and the court remanded the case to the trial court. *Sain v. Cedar Rapids Community School District*, 626 N.W.2d 115 (Iowa 2001).

◆   An Idaho student enrolled in a weightlifting class. The instructor decided to cancel weightlifting one day and to hold a softball game instead. When the student slid into first base, he broke his ankle. He claimed that the instructor was negligent in requiring the class to play softball, failing to properly supervise students, failing to instruct students on how to play softball and not inspecting their footwear. He filed a lawsuit against the school district and instructor in an Idaho trial court, which granted summary judgment motions by the district and instructor. The student appealed to the Court of Appeals of Idaho, which determined that **the student had failed to show a sufficient causal connection between the alleged negligence and his injury**. There was no evidence that inspecting the student's shoes would have made any difference and no evidence that the use of running shoes, as opposed to baseball shoes, made a difference. The student could not show that there was a duty to inspect shoes or to instruct students in how to play softball. Thus, the trial court had properly granted summary judgment to the district and instructor. *Sanders v. Kuna Joint School Dist.*, 876 P.2d 154 (Idaho App.1994).

◆   A New York student was shot to death near his junior high school during lunch hour. The student's mother sued New York City and other defendants in a New York trial court alleging that the school had failed to adequately supervise lunch recess. The trial court set aside a jury verdict for the mother and dismissed the complaint. The New York Supreme Court, Appellate Division, First Department, affirmed the trial court's order, agreeing that the evidence was insufficient to support a finding of lack of supervision. **Although New York schools owed a special duty of care to their students, they could not be held liable for injuries not proximately related to the absence of supervision**. *Maness v. City of New York*, 607 N.Y.S.2d 325 (A.D.1st Dep't 1994).

B. Defenses

There are several defenses that may shield school districts and employees from liability in a negligence lawsuit. Traditionally, the doctrine of governmental (or sovereign) immunity protected any state agency, such as a school district, from liability. In states where the doctrine is retained, immunity is typically waived up to the amount of any liability insurance purchased by the defendant school district. In some states where the doctrine has been abolished, *in loco parentis* or *"save harmless"* laws have been implemented to shield school employees from some types of personal liability for injuries.

◆   While in a hallway during a class change, **a high school student was shot and killed by another student**. The deceased student's estate sued the school district in a state court for wrongful death. The court held a summary judgment hearing and took evidence in the form of affidavits by school employees, including a campus security monitor who formerly worked at the school. The affidavit stated that the employee had received absolutely no training from the district, was not properly equipped to conduct his duties and lacked authority to perform personal or locker searches of students. It also alleged that the high school's atmosphere was very volatile and that serious misconduct by students was often overlooked. The court granted the school district's summary judgment motion, finding insufficient evidence that the district had acted in a grossly negligent manner. The state court of appeals reversed and remanded the case, and the district appealed.

The South Carolina Supreme Court noted that under state law, **a governmental entity is not liable for a loss resulting from the responsibility or duty to take custody of a student or to confine, supervise, protect or control a student, except where the supervision is grossly negligent**. Gross negligence is defined as the intentional, conscious failure to do something that is incumbent upon one to do, or the intentional doing of a thing that one ought not do. In this case, there was no link between the deficiencies identified by the former security employee and the incident leading to the student's death. The district had no direct knowledge or notice of any problems between the two students and at the very least exercised "slight care" to ensure student safety by maintaining hallway supervisors and an intervention system to help resolve student conflicts. The fact that the district might have taken stronger security measures did not negate the efforts that it actually took. The court reinstated the trial court decision. *Etheredge v. Richland School District One*, 341 S.C. 307, 534 S.E.2d 275 (S.C. 2000).

◆   When a student reached grade nine, a school nurse detected scoliosis and she was referred to an orthopedic doctor. The doctor found that the scoliosis had progressed to the point that surgery was required. The student and her parents filed a state supreme court action against the school district for negligence and violation of New York Education Law Sec. 905(1), which requires scoliosis examination by schools for all students between the ages of eight and 16 in each school year. **According to the family, the student should have been tested for scoliosis during the seventh grade, and was not**. The court granted the district's summary judgment motion, and the decision was affirmed by a state appellate division court. The family appealed to the court of appeals, which considered whether the law created a private right of action.

The appeals court conducted a three-part analysis to determine whether a private right of action was available for violation of a statutory duty. The inquiry sought to resolve whether the plaintiff was a member of the class for whose benefit the statute was enacted, whether recognition of a private right of action would promote the law's purpose, and whether the right would be consistent with the legislative scheme. In this case, the student and her family satisfied the first two prongs of the analysis; since the legislation was undoubtedly enacted to benefit students and a private right of action would promote this legislative purpose. However, **the court held that the legislature clearly intended to immunize school districts from any liability arising out of the scoliosis screening program**. The legislature had amended the statute as recently as 1994 without providing for a private right of action. The appeals court rejected the family's claim under Education Law Sec. 905(1), and affirmed the lower court orders dismissing the common law negligence claim. *Uhr v. East Greenbush Central School Dist.*, 94 N.Y.S.2d 32, 720 N.E.2d 886 (N.Y. 1999).

◆   A New Mexico school district hired an architect to design and construct an addition to a middle school building. As part of the expansion, an exterior window became part of an interior wall and was fitted with non-safety glass without protective guards. Several years later, a student became involved in a fight and was pushed through the glass, severely lacerating his wrist. His family filed a state court action against the school district for negligence. The school district was granted summary judgment on the basis of immunity under the state Tort Claims Act, and the family appealed to the Court of Appeals of New Mexico.

The court rejected the district's claim that the act exempted the statutory waiver of governmental immunity for claims based on the negligent design of a building. The court held that the act contained no exception for negligence in design. **The state had a duty to exercise reasonable care to prevent or correct dangerous conditions on public property, which included a non-delegable duty to be accountable for the work of independent contractors where a special danger is created to the public**. Even where a private architect is hired to design a public building, the government entity retains the responsibility to maintain safe physical premises and inspect conditions after the work by contractors is completed. The court reversed and remanded the case. *Williams v. Central Consol. School Dist.*, 952 P.2d 978 (N.M.App.1997).

Traditional common law principles held that if a plaintiff's own negligence contributed to his or her injuries, the plaintiff could not hold the defendant liable. Any amount of negligence on the plaintiff's part would completely bar his or her recovery of money damages. The defense of contributory negligence is retained in a minority of states regardless of whether the plaintiff's negligence was slight or the defendant's negligence extreme. Most states have replaced this defense with the doctrine of comparative negligence.

In comparative negligence states, a plaintiff whose negligence contributes to the injury is not barred from recovering damages. Rather, the negligence causing the plaintiff's injury is apportioned by the court between the plaintiff and defendant on the basis of their degrees of fault. For example, in a student injury case, a jury may find that a student who slipped on a bar of soap while running down the stairs was 40 percent negligent, and that the school district whose agent left the bar of soap on the stairs was 60 percent negligent. Assuming the student's damages amount to $10,000, the student would be entitled to recover $6,000 from the district. In some comparative negligence states, the plaintiff may not recover if his or her negligence is the same as or greater than the defendant's negligence.

◆   An 18-year-old Louisiana special education student allegedly raped a 13-year-old special education student in a storage shed behind their school. He later pleaded guilty to juvenile court charges and was given a probationary sentence. The victim's parents removed their daughter from school and began teaching her at home. **They alleged that she suffered psychological injuries because of the incident and filed a lawsuit against the perpetrator and the school district in a Louisiana trial court**. Amongst the conflicted trial testimony, the court found that the victim had consented to having sex and had instigated the incident. However, it determined that the victim's consent was meaningless because of her status as a minor. The court ruled that the school board had not breached any duty to supervise its students and had not negligently maintained the shed in which the rape had occurred. The parties appealed to the Court of Appeal of Louisiana, Third Circuit. **The court of appeal affirmed the trial court's factual finding that the board had not failed to supervise its students.** It also affirmed the finding that the board's maintenance of the storage shed had not been a contributing cause of any of the victim's damages. The school board was not liable for any of the damages. **Although the trial court had apparently ruled correctly given the conflicting testimony, it should have applied principles of comparative fault instead of ruling that the victim's age alone invalidated consent**. Applying principles of comparative fault, the court of appeal reduced the $25,000 damage award against the perpetrator by 5 percent. *L.K. v. Reed*, 631 So.2d 604 (La.App.3d Cir.1994).

II. SCHOOL ATHLETICS

Generally, courts hold that student athletes assume the risks incidental to participation and, absent a showing of negligence by the coach, league or school, may not recover damages for their injuries. For more cases on athletics, please see Chapter 14.

A. Participants

1. Duty of Care

The cases indicate that where a participant is injured, but through ordinary care and common sense could have avoided the injury, the school and its agents will not be held liable. Further, some states require a showing that the school or its agents acted recklessly or wilfully as a prerequisite to overcoming the defense of governmental immunity.

◆   **A high school football player fell while attempting a tackle during a game and struck his head on the ground. He felt dizzy and disoriented**, but stayed in the game for a few plays, and then took himself out. Coaches observed that he was short of breath, but attributed his dizziness to hyperventilation, not a head injury. Because the student made normal eye contact with an assistant coach and had normal speech and movement, no medical attention was sought. When the student asked to return to the game during the next quarter, coaches allowed him to do so, observing that he seemed normal and did not complain of a headache. Although family members reported that the student suffered a headache the entire weekend, there was conflicting evidence that he shared this information with the coaching staff the following week. He was allowed to practice with the team and suffered a closed-head traumatic brain injury.

He sued the school district in a Nebraska trial court for personal injuries. The suit was dismissed on grounds that the school was not negligent. The student appealed to the state supreme court, which stated that the trial court should not have discredited testimony by the student's expert witnesses, who were certified athletic trainers. The trainers, who taught state-required courses for obtaining coaching endorsements, testified that Nebraska high school coaches should be aware that headache, dizziness and disorientation are symptomatic of a concussion. Instead of relying on this testimony, the trial court improperly relied on testimony by a high school coach, believing that local community standards governed the conduct of coaches. The Nebraska Supreme Court held that **the standard of care applicable to high school coaches did not vary among districts, but was instead that of a "reasonably prudent person holding a Nebraska teaching certificate with a coaching endorsement."** Because the trainers instructed the courses taken by coaches seeking endorsement, they were competent to testify about this standard. The court remanded the case to the trial court. *Cerny v. Cedar Bluffs Junior/Senior Pub. Sch.*, 262 Neb. 66, 628 N.E. 2d 697 (Neb. 2001).

◆   During softball tryouts, a ninth grader who was trying out for catcher used only a glove, not a facemask. The student signaled the pitcher to throw a straight fastball, but the pitcher threw a curve ball, which tipped the edge of the catcher's mitt and struck her in the face. As a result, the catcher suffered a concussion and a broken nose. The catcher sued the coaches and school officials, claiming she should have been provided with a facemask. At trial, a jury found the catcher 40 percent liable for her injuries and the district defendants 60 percent liable.

The defendants appealed, arguing that "customary practice" did not require catchers to wear a mask and helmet during warm-ups and practice sessions when no batter is present. The appeals court noted that the catcher's expert witness opined at trial that the association that governs softball requires players engaged in pitcher warm-ups to wear a mask and helmet. In addition, he testified that **it was a "customary practice" in most New York schools to require a catcher to wear protective equipment during warm-ups and practice sessions when no batter is present**. In reviewing the arguments, the appeals court cited case law, which supported the notion that the defendants' failure "constituted a breach of sound coaching practice, which enhanced the risk of injury normally associated with the activity." Accordingly, the court upheld the jury's verdict. *Zmitrowitz v. Roman Catholic Diocese of Syracuse*, 710 N.Y.S.2d 453 (N.Y. App. Div. 2000).

◆   A New York City high school senior was a member of the school volleyball team. **He attempted a gymnastic dive over a volleyball net** while other team members were raising the net prior to a team practice. He did so despite being warned by the coach and team captain against horseplay, **and became paralyzed when he landed on his head**. He claimed that the city school board should be held liable for his injuries since the coach had been absent for 20 minutes when the incident occurred. He filed a lawsuit against the board of education in a New York trial court, which awarded him $15 million after reducing a jury verdict by 20 percent for his own negligence. The school board appealed to the New York Supreme Court, Appellate Division.

The court recited the general rule that schools are under a duty to adequately supervise students and may be held liable for foreseeable student injuries related to the absence of adequate supervision. **A lesser standard of care applies to school-sponsored extracurricular activities, requiring only ordinary, reasonable care to protect student athletes from unassumed, concealed or unreasonably increased risks**. School boards are not required to protect students from the inherent risks of sports activities or from the consequences of unexpected acts of bad judgment by students. In this case, there was no evidence that the school board had been aware of an unassumed, concealed or increased risk or that it could have foreseen the injury. The student's action had been unreasonable and contrary to warnings by the coach and team captain. The court reversed and dismissed the complaint. *Barretto v. City of New York*, 655 N.Y.S.2d 484 (A.D.1st Dep't 1997).

◆   A Louisiana high school football player wore a neck roll during games and practices after having received minor neck injuries in practices. He established himself as a star player by his senior year and was recruited to play football by many colleges. However, **he was injured and temporarily paralyzed during a game when he was grabbed by his facemask and hit by two opponents while on the ground**. The neck roll had been torn from him earlier in the game and there was no replacement equipment available. Although the student recuperated, he was advised by physicians of the risk of permanent injury if he continued playing football and decided not to pursue a college football career. He filed a lawsuit for damages against the coach and school district in a Louisiana trial court. The court conducted a trial and awarded the student over $215,000 in damages for pain and suffering, medical costs and the loss of the opportunity to play college football. The coach and school district appealed to the Court of Appeal of Louisiana, Second Circuit.

     The court found sufficient evidence in the record to support the finding of liability by the coach, who had a legal duty to protect students from injury. There was evidence in the record that he belittled requests by students to wear necessary protective gear and failed to keep it available. There was no merit to the school board's argument that the pain and suffering damages were excessive, but the court agreed with the board that a $35,000 award for deprivation of the opportunity to play college football had been duplicated in the trial court judgment. The court affirmed the trial court judgment as amended. *Harvey v. Ouachita Parish School Bd.*, 674 So.2d 372 (La.App.2d Cir.1996).

◆   A Maryland high school junior was the first female football player in her county's history. She participated in weightlifting, strength training exercises and contact drills. However, in the first scrimmage with another team, **the student was tackled while carrying the football and suffered multiple internal injuries** including a ruptured spleen. She was hospitalized and her spleen and part of her pancreas were removed. Three years later, the student and her mother sued the school board claiming that the board had a duty to warn them of the risk of serious, disabling and catastrophic injuries. A Maryland trial court granted the board's motion for summary judgment, finding no such duty to warn of the risk of varsity football participation. The student and her mother appealed to the Court of Special Appeals of Maryland. On appeal, the student and her mother claimed that the lower court had erroneously ruled that the board had no duty to warn of catastrophic risks and that the student had assumed the risk of injury by participating. The court found no case from any jurisdiction holding that a school board had a duty to warn varsity high school participants that severe injuries might result. **The dangers of varsity football participation were self-evident and there was no duty to warn of such an obvious danger.** The court affirmed the order for summary judgment. *Hammond v. Bd. of Educ. of Carroll County*, 100 Md.App. 60, 639 A.2d 223 (1994).

2. Governmental Immunity

The doctrine of governmental immunity applies when the school district or its employees act within the scope of their employment. However, some states have abolished or limited the immunity defense.

◆   An Illinois student underwent spine fusion surgery and was advised by his doctor to permanently refrain from contact sports such as wrestling and football. The school was furnished with a copy of the doctor's letter concerning his physical restrictions. However, **a school employee required the student to participate in a water basketball game** during a physical education class. The student was severely and permanently injured by another student while participating in the game and filed a state court lawsuit against the school district and the other student for negligence. He asserted that the other student was known to be a rough player and that the district had knowledge of this and was aware of his medical restrictions. The other student filed a counterclaim against the school district, seeking contribution for any damage award he might be forced to pay. The court granted motions to dismiss the claims against the school district and the counterclaim, and both students appealed to the Appellate Court of Illinois.

The court agreed with the school district that it was entitled to immunity for negligent or improper supervision of students by a teacher and for wanton misconduct related to supervision. The state Tort Immunity Act protected public entities from liability for failing to supervise activities on public property, and the student was not entitled to avoid the immunity issue under a separate but analogous section of the state school code. The court held that the counterclaim had properly been dismissed since an action for contribution may not be maintained against a public entity that is entitled to immunity from suit. The court affirmed the trial court judgment. *Henrich v. Libertyville High School*, 683 N.E.2d 135 (Ill.App.2d Dist.1997).

◆   An Illinois school district modified a student's football helmet by removing a safety feature and replacing it with a static face guard. When the student suffered severe and permanent head injuries during a football game, his mother filed a negligence lawsuit against the school district in a state court. The court denied the district's dismissal motion under the state Local Governmental and Governmental Employees Tort Immunity Act, and the district appealed to the Appellate Court of Illinois, Third District. The court agreed with the school district that **the tort immunity act immunized state high school districts from liability for providing athletic equipment to students.** An exception to the statutory grant of immunity for wilful and wanton conduct did not extend to contact sports such as football. *McGurk v. Lincolnway Community School Dist. No. 210*, 679 N.E.2d 71 (Ill.App.3d Dist.1997).

◆   A North Carolina high school varsity softball coach decided to hit ground balls to players on a field that was rough and filled with rocks. She wanted them to have a game advantage against other teams by being familiar with balls taking bad hops. The property was owned by the city and no other school or city personnel were aware that the team was practicing on the field. **One player was hit in the face by a ground ball, losing a tooth and requiring dental treatment**. She filed a lawsuit against the school board, coach and city in a North Carolina trial court for negligence. The court granted summary judgment against the student on all claims, and she appealed to the Court of Appeals of North Carolina.

The court stated that under North Carolina law, **a government entity such as a school board or city was entitled to sovereign immunity for negligence unless waived by the purchase of liability insurance**. Although the school board had purchased a general liability policy, it excluded coverage for injuries to athletic participants. Because there was no coverage under the policy, the school district and board retained immunity. The trial court had properly granted summary judgment to the board. Although the coach had negligently conducted the practice on the rough field, the student's claim against her was barred by the student's own negligence in agreeing to practice on a field that she knew was potentially dangerous. Summary judgment for the coach was therefore appropriate, and the court affirmed the trial court judgment. *Daniel v. City of Morganton*, 479 S.E.2d 263 (N.C.App.1997).

◆   After a Montana teacher instructed an elementary student to mark the spots where shot puts would be landing, the teacher threw a shot and struck the girl. The child was injured and sued the school district and the teacher for negligence in a state trial court. The trial court granted summary judgment to the school district and teacher, and the child appealed to the Supreme Court of Montana. **On appeal, the child contended that the teacher was not immune from suit and that the school district had waived immunity by purchasing liability insurance**. The court noted that the school district was immune from suit for any act of its agent and that the teacher was its agent. Therefore, the teacher was also immune from suit. The court next turned to the question of whether immunity was waived to the extent of insurance coverage. The Montana Supreme Court had previously reached the conclusion that a school district's purchase of insurance in many cases may waive immunity to the extent of the insurance coverage. The school district in this case fell within the waiver because the school would have no need of liability insurance if it were immune. Therefore, **the school waived immunity by purchasing such insurance**. The court remanded the case to determine the extent of the coverage.

The day after that decision was published, Montana passed a new law amending the governmental immunity law. The amended statute was retroactively applied to the student's case. The trial court stated that the new law changed nothing and once again dismissed the case. The student again appealed to the Montana Supreme Court. **The supreme court noted that Montana's new immunity law provided immunity for "legislative acts" or duties associated with "legislative acts."** The court had previously interpreted this to mean that a teacher performing official duties was immune from suit since those duties were associated with the legislative acts of the school board. However, the "purpose" section of the new act stated that "legislative immunity extends only to legislative bodies of governmental entities and only to legislative actions taken by those bodies... governmental entities are not immune... for nonlegislative actions." **The throwing of the shot was not an official duty** associated with legislative acts. Therefore, the teacher and school district were not immune. The court remanded the case for further proceedings. *Hedges v. Swan Lake & Salmon Prairie School Dist.*, 832 P.2d 775 (Mont.1992).

3.   Assumption of Risk

Many courts have determined that when a participant has assumed the risks of playing sports, the school district should not be held liable for injuries suffered as a result.

◆   A California high school cheerleading team practiced a gymnastic stunt called "the cradle," in which two cheerleaders tossed a third cheerleader into the air, then caught her as she fell toward the ground. Their coach told them that they had bad technique and that they needed to keep practicing. A cheerleader suffered a knee injury while practicing the stunt. She filed a California superior court action against the school district for negligence. The court awarded summary judgment to the district, ruling that **the cheerleader had assumed any risk of injury** because certain risks are inherent in cheerleading activities and because the coach had not increased the risk of injury in any way. The cheerleader appealed to the California Court of Appeal, Second District.

The court agreed with the superior court's determination that **the cheerleading coach had not taken the team beyond its level of experience or increased the risk of an injury. The cheerleader had assumed the risks** inherent in cheerleading activities, including those arising from complicated gymnastic stunts such as the cradle. The release form signed by the cheerleader's parent was also a sufficient ground for granting summary judgment to the school district, and the court affirmed the judgment. *Aaris v. Las Virgenes Unified School Dist.*, 75 Cal.Rptr.2d 801 (Cal.App.2d Dist.1998).

◆   A New York student participated on his high school wrestling team and was instructed before a match to wrestle an opponent in the next higher weight class. The student agreed to do so and was injured when the opponent hit his jaw during a take-down maneuver. The student voluntarily continued participating in the match after a medical time-out. However, he later filed a personal injury lawsuit against the school district in a New York trial court, which denied the school district's motion to dismiss the suit. On appeal, the New York Supreme Court, Appellate Division, stated that **the student had assumed the risk of incurring a blow to the jaw and that the injury was reasonably foreseeable in a wrestling match**. There was evidence that the size of the opponent had not caused the injury and that the student was aware of the risks involved in participating on the wrestling team. The district's duty of care was limited to protecting the student from unassumed, concealed or unreasonable risks and the trial court judgment was reversed. *Edelson v. Uniondale Union Free School Dist.*, 631 N.Y.S.2d 391 (A.D.2d Dep't 1995).

B.   Spectators, Employees and Parents

A four-year-old girl accompanied her family to a public school gymnasium to watch her older brother play basketball in a department of education league game. The department used the gymnasium under a school board policy promulgated under

Maryland education laws that encouraged school boards to use their facilities for community purposes. The girl was severely injured when she either fell from or ran into a piece of damaged equipment. The Court of Special Appeals of Maryland reversed and remanded a trial court decision for the girl's parents. It determined that **while the board's policy encouraged public use of the gym, and the girl was entitled to the legal status of invitee, there was evidence in the record that the girl had exceeded the scope of her invitation**. *Howard County Bd. of Educ. v. Cheyene*, 99 Md.App. 150, 636 A.2d 22 (1994).

◆   An Illinois man and his son were watching a tennis match standing inside the fence encompassing the tennis court because the spectator bleachers were full. The man's son was hit in the eye with a tennis ball and was injured. The man and his son sued the school district for allowing them to watch the match in an unsafe area. The trial court ruled in favor of the school because the danger of being injured was open and obvious. The student appealed to the Appellate Court of Illinois, which affirmed the trial court's decision. It stated that **the plaintiffs had voluntarily placed themselves in a position of danger and thus would be unable to establish that they were placed in that area by the school**. Under most circumstances, when a danger is obvious, the student cannot recover for his injuries. *Chaveas v. Township High School Dist.*, 553 N.E.2d 23 (Ill.App.1st Dist.1990).

◆   **A spectator was struck by a football during pregame warm-ups**. She sued the school district for damages. The district moved for summary judgment claiming that governmental immunity barred the spectator's suit. The trial court granted the district's motion. The injured spectator appealed to the Commonwealth Court of Pennsylvania. Under the real property exception, a governmental entity may lose its immunity if the injury is due to its negligence in the care, custody or control of its real property. The spectator argued that the district was negligent when it failed to erect a barrier to prevent footballs from striking spectators. **The court held that the real property exception applies only when an artificial condition or defect in the land causes an injury. In this case, the spectator's injury was caused by the acts of a third person so the real property exception did not apply**. *Johnson v. Woodland Hills School Dist.*, 582 A.2d 395 (Pa.Commw. 1990).

III. OTHER SCHOOL ACTIVITIES

Courts have generally held schools or their agents liable for injuries sustained during the course of regular school events which resulted from the failure to provide a reasonably safe environment, failure to warn participants of known hazards (or to remove known dangers where possible), failure to properly instruct participants in the activity, or failure to provide supervision adequate for the type of activity and the ages of the participants involved.

A. Physical Education Class Accidents

1. Duty of Care

Courts have ruled that schools and those employees in charge of group activities cannot be held liable for injuries that occur during activities which are well supervised but are the result of conditions of which the school has no prior knowledge or are the result of actions taken by children contrary to instructions. The fact that each student is not personally supervised at all times does not in and of itself constitute grounds for liability.

◆   A New York student was injured in gym class when he was struck in the eye with a tennis ball. His parents filed a personal injury lawsuit against the school district and **a jury awarded him $56,000 for past pain and suffering, $10,000 for future pain and suffering and $20,000 for future medical expenses**. The parents moved to set aside the verdict as inadequate and when the trial court refused, the parents appealed to the New York Supreme Court, Appellate Division, Third Department. The appellate court affirmed the trial court verdict, reasoning that the award was sufficient to cover future expenses, pain and suffering. There was evidence that recovery was nearly complete, although there was a slightly greater risk for glaucoma in the injured eye. The award was reasonable because the student would continue to need an eye examination every six months. *Levine v. East Ramapo Central School Dist.*, 597 N.Y.S.2d 239 (A.D.3d Dep't 1993).

◆   A 14-year-old high school student was injured in a motorcycle accident and was required to undergo surgery to repair damage to his left knee. The doctor instructed the student that he was not to participate in any physical or strenuous activities that could result in further injury to his knee. After the student returned to school, he was instructed by his physical education teacher to go out to the high school football field with his class. The student did not engage in a game of touch football that was being played but stood on the sidelines. While the student was standing on the sidelines a player ran into him, reinjuring his knee. He sued the physical education teacher in an Alabama trial court alleging negligent supervision. The trial court entered summary judgment in favor of the teacher and dismissed the complaint. The student appealed to the Alabama Supreme Court, which stated that the student was not ordered to play in the game but only to go to the sidelines. Further, the student stated that he felt he was a safe distance away from the action. **The teacher had a duty of reasonable supervision but could not possibly be expected to personally supervise each student in his charge at every moment of the school day**. The court further stated that the student was a reasonable age and had a duty to maintain a certain vigilance over his own safety and well being. Thus, the court affirmed the trial court's decision and dismissed the complaint. *Stevens v. Chesteen*, 561 So.2d 1100 (Ala.1990).

2. Governmental Immunity

◆   A Kentucky appeals court affirmed a lower court's finding that a municipal board of education and a gym teacher employed by the board were entitled to sovereign immunity in a personal injury case arising from a student's injury that occurred during gym class. On appeal, the student's parents argued they were not allowed to make a record and discover whether or not the school board maintained liability insurance before the trial court granted the board's motion for summary judgment. Citing case law, the appeals court found that it didn't matter whether the parents were able to discover this information prior to an evaluation by the court of the defendants' summary judgment motion. The appeals court also rejected the parents' assertion that immunity did not apply because sovereign immunity does not extend to the employees of immune agencies. The court found this argument lacking, as recent court cases have found that **as long as the employee was acting within "the traditional role of government," then he is entitled to immunity**. The appeals court determined that the evidence did not indicate the gym teachers caused the student's injury, nor was the injury the type of injury that would not have occurred unless the gym teacher was negligent. *Turner v. Newport Board of Education et al.*, No. 1999-CA-001766-MR, 2000 WL 1364429 (Ky.Ct.App. 2000)

◆   A Kansas student asked his instructor if he and others could use a wooden springboard as a catapult for dunking a basketball during a required physical education class. When the student tried to perform the act, he lost control of himself and fell to the floor, suffering compound bone fractures in his right arm. The student sued the school district in state court for negligence. The court granted the district's motion for summary judgment, agreeing with the district's argument that **the Kansas Tort Claims Act (KTCA) provided qualified immunity in negligence cases**, in the absence of gross or wanton conduct. The state court of appeals affirmed the decision and the student appealed to the Supreme Court of Kansas.

The court recited that KTCA provided for governmental immunity for claims resulting from the use of any public property intended or permitted to be used as a park, playground or open area for recreational purposes in the absence of gross and wanton negligence. It rejected the student's assertion that a gymnasium was not "public property" as defined in the KTCA, as well as his alternative argument that the gymnasium was not a park, playground or open area. The student further argued that immunity should not apply because the injury occurred during a required class and the gymnasium was not property used for recreational purposes. The court held that the location must be intended or permitted to be used for recreational purposes, and need not be the result of recreation. **"The type of activity performed on the property when the injury occurs is not significant. Immunity depends on the character of the property in question, i.e., whether the property was 'intended or permitted to be used for recreational purposes,'"** according to the court. That determination required consideration of past usage of the property for recreational purposes. KTCA was intended to provide immunity to governmental entities for ordinary negligence for important public policy reasons, including control of the high cost of litigation. It was insignificant that planned class activities were completed at the time of the student's injury, but it was significant that the class was required. Because the gymnasium had more than one use, remand for development of the record was appropriate. The court reversed the lower court decisions and remanded the case for a factual determination of whether the gymnasium was intended or permitted for recreational use. *Jackson v. Unified School Dist. 259, Sedgwick County, Kansas*, 268 Kan. 319, 995 P.2d 844 (Kan. 2000).

◆   A Michigan ninth grader dove into a pool near an area marked five feet deep. He struck his head on the bottom of the pool, climbed out and informed a student assistant. He was then told to change into his clothes and lie down in the office. However, when the physical education department head arrived, **the student could not move and he eventually underwent corrective surgery for a fractured spine**. The student and his father filed a Michigan circuit court action against the school district, asserting that it had maintained a dangerous and defective pool. The court dismissed the action, and the judgment was affirmed by the Michigan Court of Appeals. The student appealed to the Supreme Court of Michigan.

The state supreme court stated that under Michigan law, a government agency is immune from tort liability when performing a governmental function. An exception exists in the case of a building that is open to the public and has a dangerous or defective condition of which the agency has knowledge yet fails to remedy after a reasonable time. In this case, the student had alleged that the pool depth markers falsely indicated a depth of five feet, and that the floor was uneven. Both of the lower courts had failed to properly evaluate this evidence and had mischaracterized the case as one for improper supervision. **Because the student had alleged that a dangerous or defective condition existed in the pool due to faulty construction or design, the court reversed the judgment and remanded the case** for further consideration. *Sewell v. Southfield Pub. Schools*, 576 N.W.2d 153 (Mich.1998).

◆   A Georgia physical education instructor made his class complete an obstacle course including a set of monkey bars. One student told the instructor that she could not cross the bars, but he told her to try. The student fell from the bars, breaking her arm, and her mother sued the teacher for negligent supervision and the school system and board of education for failing to publish rules governing the supervision of students with physical and mental disabilities. A Georgia trial court denied the teacher and district's summary judgment motion, and they appealed to the Court of Appeals of Georgia. The court stated the general rule that Georgia political subdivisions, including school systems, are protected by sovereign immunity unless specifically waived. Although the purchase of motor vehicle insurance by a political subdivision effects a waiver of sovereign immunity, the purchase of liability insurance does not automatically waive sovereign immunity under state law. **The school system, board and school employees, including the teacher, were entitled to immunity, which could not be defeated without a demonstration of actual malice that had not been proven here.** The court reversed the trial court judgment for the student. *Crisp County School System v. Brown*, 487 S.E.2d 512 (Ga.App.1997).

◆   An overweight teenager attended a Missouri middle school, and sustained injuries when she attempted to jump a hurdle in gym class. The hurdle was apparently placed on a concrete floor which was covered by linoleum. The student brought suit against the school district in a Missouri trial court, alleging that the gym teacher had created a dangerous condition by setting hurdles on a concrete floor and by urging students such as herself to jump over them. The court granted summary judgment to the school district, and the student appealed to the Missouri Court of Appeals, Western District. On appeal, the student conceded that the school district was protected by the doctrine of sovereign immunity. However, she maintained that her injury was caused by a dangerous condition of property (which would allow a lawsuit against the school district as an exception to immunity). The court of appeals determined that the injury did not result from a condition of school property, but from the inability of the student to physically jump over the hurdle. **If there was fault, it was simply negligence on the part of the teacher in urging an overweight girl to jump a hurdle.** Because **sovereign immunity protected the school district from claims based on negligence**, the court of appeals affirmed the trial court's decision. *Goben v. School District of St. Joseph,* 848 S.W.2d 20 (Mo.App.W.D.1992).

B. Shop Class Injuries

1. Duty of Care

Schools are generally held to a standard of care of providing students with a safe environment. Known shop class dangers must be minimized and manufacturers' safety devices should be in place and working. Failure to supervise, to warn students of the dangers, or to keep safety devices installed and in proper working order can result in a finding of school negligence.

◆   A Wisconsin high school shop teacher asked a student to help him remove a bearing from some farm equipment. He did not give the student safety glasses and the student was injured by flying metal fragments when the bearing exploded. The student sued the school district and its insurer in a Wisconsin circuit court for personal injury, claiming breach of contract damages on the theory that he was a third party beneficiary of school district contracts with the insurer and the shop class teacher. The court held that the $50,000 state law limit on damages against state agencies applied to the tort claim but not to the breach of contract claim. The student could therefore recover up to the $1 million policy limit on his breach of contract claims. The school district appealed the decision to the Court of Appeals of Wisconsin.

The court held that a party claiming to be the beneficiary of a contract between two other parties must demonstrate that the contract directly and primarily exists for his benefit. **Students were only incidental beneficiaries of teacher employment contracts and the student failed to show that he directly benefited from the employment of the shop teacher** by the school board. Student handbook provisions on supervision and liability benefited the school district and were not intended to confer contractual benefits on students. Because the student was not a third-party beneficiary of any school district contract, the court reversed the trial court decision concerning the contract claim. However, it affirmed the trial court's ruling that the $50,000 statutory limit applied to the student's tort claim. *Schilling v. Employers Mut. Cas. Co.*, 569 N.W.2d 776 (Wis.App.1997).

◆   An Illinois high school offered an automotive repair shop class at which some students furnished their own cars for repairs. Students who furnished vehicles were responsible for bringing them to the shop area, but other students were not allowed to leave the shop during class. One student who had not furnished a car jumped on the hood of another student's car and held onto it as it went through the parking lot at a high speed. The driver then hit his brakes abruptly, and the student was thrown onto the pavement. The student died four days later from his injuries, and his parents filed a lawsuit against the driver and school district in an Illinois trial court. The court dismissed the case against the school district, and the student's estate appealed to the Appellate Court of Illinois, First District. The complaint included a claim based on the legal theory of *respondeat superior* or vicarious liability (holding the employer liable for an employee's negligent acts). This involved considering the level of control exhibited by the employer over the employee. **Although the shop teacher** exerted control over his students, this authority was related to the educational process and did not resemble the employer-employee relationship. **Accordingly, the vicarious liability claim failed**. Illinois school districts are protected from liability in civil actions unless the conduct of their employees is found to be wilful or wanton. Because the claim against the district alleged only incompetence or failure to act, the trial court had properly dismissed it. The court also dismissed the driver's countersuit for contribution from the school district. *Knapp v. Hill*, 657 N.E.2d 1068 (Ill.App.1st Dist.1995).

◆ A Nebraska student's finger was severed in a shop accident. In his personal injury lawsuit against the school district, the evidence indicated that the shop teacher was negligent in failing to properly instruct the student in the proper use of a power tool. It was also shown that the power tool was unreasonably dangerous and that the student was contributorily negligent. The court awarded the student over $32,000, even though his medical expenses were only $2,300. It then granted the student's motion for a new trial, stating that the award of damages was inadequate "as a result of a mistake by the court." The school district appealed to the Court of Appeals of Nebraska, which reversed the order for a new trial and reinstated the verdict. **There were no grounds for granting a new trial in this case because there had been no showing that the verdict was contrary to law or that the evidence of damages had been insufficient**. It appeared that the trial court had merely changed its mind. *Cotton v. Gering Pub. Schools*, 511 N.W.2d 549 (Neb.App.1993).

2. Governmental Immunity

◆ **A North Carolina high school student left a school assembly without the permission of his instructor and went to a shop class where he gained entry from another student who was working there unsupervised**. He failed to position a safety guard on the table saw he was using and amputated the fingers and thumb of his left hand. He underwent reattachment surgery, but suffered permanent partial disabilities and sued the school board and shop teacher in a North Carolina superior court for negligence. The school board moved for judgment on the basis of governmental immunity and was granted judgment for all claims determined to be $1 million or less, for which there was no insurance coverage. The court also granted summary judgment to the teacher on grounds that he was a public officer who was immune from suit.

The state court of appeals held that the board was entitled to sovereign immunity but ruled that the trial court had erroneously awarded summary judgment to the teacher. He appealed to the Supreme Court of North Carolina, arguing that he was entitled to governmental immunity to the same extent as the school board, since he had been sued in his official capacity. The supreme court observed that the student had failed to specify whether the teacher was being sued in an official or personal capacity. However, by evaluating the nature of the relief sought by a complaint, a school employee's status may be determined. In this case, the complaint referred to liability insurance maintained by the school board, and named the teacher only as an agent who was acting on behalf of the board. **Since official capacity suits are simply another way of stating a claim against a government entity, the teacher was entitled to immunity to the same extent as the school board**. The court reversed and remanded the judgment. *Mullis v. Sechrest*, 495 S.E.2d 721 (N.C.1998).

◆   A Georgia high school student was injured when a former student at the school hit him with a rubber mallet in shop class. The shop teacher told the former student to leave and reported the incident to the school principal. Although the student was hospitalized, he did not suffer permanent injuries. He filed a lawsuit against the shop teacher, principal, school district and its education board in a Georgia trial court. The court dismissed the lawsuit and the student appealed to the Court of Appeals of Georgia. The court recited the general rule that official immunity protects public employees from personal liability for discretionary acts within the scope of their duties, if the duties are performed without malice. **Because the school officials in this case had not been engaged in ministerial actions but were instead performing discretionary duties, they were entitled to official immunity**. There was no showing of malice by the injured student. The school district was also immune from liability under the doctrine of sovereign immunity. The Georgia Constitution had been amended in 1991 to provide for sovereign immunity to all state departments and agencies including county school districts. The trial court had properly dismissed the lawsuit. *Teston v. Collins*, 459 S.E.2d 452 (Ga.App.1995).

C. Other Supervised Activities

1. Duty of Care

School districts have a duty to use reasonable care to supervise and protect students against hazards on school property that create an unreasonable risk of harm. Liability may also exist where no supervision is provided or where supervision is negligently performed.

◆   **After contracting a drug-resistant strain of tuberculosis from another student at her high school, a student sued the school district and county** in a California Superior Court, **claiming the district breached its duty to warn her of a dangerous condition** present on school property. Both the district and county were aware of an "index case" at the student's school for at least a year. Although state law requires cooperation among school districts and local health departments to eradicate tuberculosis from schools, and mandates reporting of tuberculosis cases to the health department, the county's policy was not to notify and test individuals coming into contact with the disease unless a case was deemed "communicable." Because the index case was noncommunicable when first reported to the county, other students at the high school were not informed of the risk for potential exposure or any need for testing. The district eventually identified a dozen cases of tuberculosis at the student's high school that were directly traceable to the index case. The court granted summary judgment to the district, ruling that it had no duty to warn students about tuberculosis. The county was also awarded summary judgment due to the lack of evidence that it had caused any damage to the student.

On appeal, the California Court of Appeal, Fourth District, affirmed the order for summary judgment on the student's 42 U.S.C. § 1983 claim against the county. However, after analyzing the duty to warn claim against the school district, the court held that the superior court should not have granted its summary judgment motion. Despite the label "premises liability," the student's duty to warn cause of action was not limited to dangerous conditions on property, as the district had argued. Instead, the claim extended to dangerous conditions of persons on the property. Previous California appellate decisions had found such liability in cases of physically violent students. The Court of Appeal held that the trial court should have analyzed California cases imposing a special duty on school districts to provide students with a safe school environment and to warn them of dangers of which the district has reason to know. It further held that **the district was not entitled to state law immunity**, which is available to public entities and employees making discretionary decisions related to communicable diseases. This **immunity was available only for policy decisions, and did not extend to ministerial decisions such as failure to warn students of a known danger**, and the summary judgment order was reversed. *French v. Garden Grove Unified School Dist.*, No. S082505 (Cal.App.4th Dist.1999).

♦   A Nebraska music teacher taught her class to play and sing "London Bridge," a game in which two students link arms and "swing" a third student back and forth. After demonstrating the game and warning them not to swing their arms too much, she allowed them to play on their own. While she was attending to other students in the class, **a student who was playing the game was thrown into a bookcase and cut above his right eyebrow**. He required 50 stitches and suffered headaches and blurred vision. His family sued the school district in a Nebraska district court for negligence under the Nebraska Political Subdivisions Tort Claims Act. The court held that the teacher's failure to directly supervise at least the early portion of the students' first game of London Bridge constituted negligent supervision. It awarded the student over $21,000 in damages. The school district appealed to the Supreme Court of Nebraska.

On appeal, the school district argued that the trial court had held the teacher to a higher standard of legal care than was appropriate, incorporating a standard that would in effect require the teacher to provide continuous and direct supervision of her students. The supreme court observed that the trial court had only stated that the teacher had been negligent for failing to supervise at least the early portion of the students' first game. The trial court had applied an appropriate standard of care and had reasonably found that **the teacher was negligent for failing to stop the aggressive swinging of the other students involved in the accident**. It had also reasonably held that this negligence caused the student's injury. The trial court judgment for the student was affirmed. *Johnson v. School Dist. of Millard*, 253 Neb. 634, 573 N.W.2d 116 (1998).

♦   A ninth grade New York student was injured in a drawing class when another student shot a pencil at him with a ruler, striking him in the eye. The injured student's family sued the school district and the other student in a state court for personal injury. The family claimed that the school district and board had failed to maintain a safe environment and to provide adequate supervision and discipline in the classroom. Evidence of disruptive and unruly behavior in the drawing class, including previous instances of propelled pencils, eraser-throwing and other daily disruptions, was presented to the court. The court denied a summary judgment motion by the school board and district, and the board appealed to the New York Supreme Court, Appellate Division. **The court found that the school board and district were on notice of the other student's dangerous conduct and a pattern of undisciplined, disruptive and unruly behavior** in the drawing class. The court had therefore appropriately denied the summary judgment motion. *Maynard v. Bd. of Educ. of Massena Central School Dist.*, 663 N.Y.S.2d 717 (A.D.3d Dep't 1997).

◆   A New York school district sponsored a school ethnic day which included a buffet lunch in the school cafeteria that was attended by over 80 third graders and ten senior citizens invited from the community. A third grader pushed a senior citizen during the event, causing her to fall and sustain injuries. The injured citizen and her husband filed a state court action against the school district for negligent supervision. The court denied the district's summary judgment motion, and it appealed to the New York Supreme Court, Appellate Division. The court found that **while schools are under a duty to adequately supervise their students and may be held liable for foreseeable injuries proximately related to the absence of adequate supervision, schools are not insurers of safety**. The pushing incident had been spontaneous and unanticipated, and did not create liability for the school district. The court reversed the trial court and granted the district's motion for summary judgment. *Borelli v. Blind Brook Unified Sch. Dist.*, 663 N.Y.S.2d 669 (A.D.2d Dep't 1997).

◆   Under California law, a school district is not responsible or liable for student safety any time the student is not on school property unless the district has undertaken to provide transportation to and from school premises, has undertaken a school-sponsored activity or has otherwise assumed responsibility or liability for a student. **A more specific statute authorizes school districts to conduct field trips and broadly immunizes districts by deeming field trip participants to have waived all claims against the district**. A California elementary school organized a field trip to a family farm during school hours. To save money, the school recruited teachers and parents to provide transportation in their own cars for individual students. One student was injured in a traffic accident while being driven home by a parent and he filed a lawsuit in a state court against the parent and school district.
    The court granted summary judgment to the school district, and the student appealed to the Court of Appeal of California, where he argued that the general statute created liability for the district since it had undertaken to provide transportation in a school-sponsored activity in which the district had failed to exercise reasonable care. The court disagreed, finding no reason to apply the general statute when the more specific statute pertaining to field trips applied. **The field trip was not a required activity,** even though participating students received attendance credit. **The student's interpretation of state law would discourage field trips and other supervised activities** and the court affirmed the summary judgment order. *Wolfe v. Dublin Unified Sch. Dist.*, 65 Cal.Rptr.2d 280 (Cal.App.1st Dist.1997).

◆   A Florida school district conducted an extended day program where students could remain at school supervised by teachers until their parents picked them up. A fourth grade student who was not an extended day program participant approached a teacher who was supervising the extended day program and joined the class in viewing a solar eclipse. Although the class was instructed on how to observe the eclipse indirectly, the student instead looked directly at the sun causing permanent eye damage. His mother filed a lawsuit on his behalf against the school board in a Florida trial court. After a verdict for the school board, the student's mother appealed to the

District Court of Appeal of Florida, Fifth District. The student and his mother argued that the trial court had improperly instructed the jury on whether the teacher had given permission to the student to participate in extended day program activities. The court of appeal held that the issue of supervision was critical in this case and that the trial court's instruction did not adequately explain Florida law. **The school board's policy and state law required school personnel to supervise students as long as they were on school premises, regardless of whether they had permission or whether they were engaged in school-sponsored activity**. Because of that policy and state law, the case was reversed and remanded for a new trial. *Versprill v. School Bd. of Orange County, Florida*, 641 So.2d 883 (Fla.App.5th Dist.1994).

2. Governmental Immunity

◆   A New Jersey education board cooperated with county health officials by organizing and operating a free immunization clinic at a high school during a 1975 measles and rubella outbreak. **Students were screened prior to vaccination and advised of vaccination risks for pregnant or sexually active females. One student who received the vaccine later gave birth to a child with congenital rubella syndrome** who required continuing medical treatment for birth defects. The student filed a negligence lawsuit against the high school, school board, county and state of New Jersey in a New Jersey superior court. The school board and other government entities moved the court for summary judgment on grounds of immunity. The court denied summary judgment to the board and agencies, but the New Jersey Superior Court, Appellate Division, reversed the judgment. The student appealed to the Supreme Court of New Jersey, which considered two state laws under which the state and local agencies claimed immunity. Under the state Tort Claims Act, the general rule is immunity, with certain exceptions, including one for medical examinations for the purpose of treatment. The court stated that treatment included the administration of a vaccine and that the vaccination in this case was subject to the exception. **The other statute under which the entities claimed immunity was in conflict with the Tort Claims Act, and immunity under that statute was thus inapplicable**. The supreme court held that the trial court had correctly denied summary judgment to the school board and government agencies under both statutes, and it reversed the appellate division's judgment. *Kemp by Wright v. State of New Jersey*, 147 N.J. 294, 687 A.2d 715 (1997).

◆   **A five-year-old Georgia student fell while playing in the school gymnasium during recess**, causing a severe elbow fracture. He filed a lawsuit against the district, teacher, and a teacher's aide in a Georgia trial court, which denied a motion for summary judgment by the district and employees. They appealed to the Court of Appeals of Georgia. The court observed that there was no evidence in the record of any purchase of liability insurance that might constitute a waiver of immunity. The district was therefore entitled to summary judgment. The employees were not liable in their personal capacities for actions taken within the scope of their employment. **The state constitution extended official immunity to state officers and employees who negligently failed to perform ministerial functions when they acted without actual malice or intent to cause injury**. Because there was no evidence of actual malice or intent to cause injury by either of the employees, they were entitled to immunity and the trial court decision was reversed. *Coffee County School Dist. v. Snipes*, 454 S.E.2d 149 (Ga.App.1995).

3. Assumption of Risk

◆   A 19-year-old New York student was injured while participating in a work study program. The student was learning disabled and his mother persuaded him to join a work study program so that he would have enough credits to graduate. He worked with lumber under the direct supervision of a company. **During his work study, the student severed two of his fingers and injured a third** when using a saw he was familiar with. Alleging negligent supervision, the student sued the school in a New York trial court. The school asserted that it had no duty to exercise control over the student because he was of majority age and because his mother encouraged him to participate in the program. **The New York state court held that schools were not insurers for the safety of students**. Further, the court stated that a less demanding standard of reasonable care was warranted when a student was 19 years old. The court also stated that there was no evidence that any of the machinery was unfit. Thus, the trial court ruled in favor of the school. *Kennedy v. Waterville Cent. School Dist.*, 555 N.Y.S.2d 224 (Sup.1990).

◆   A seventh grader at a Louisiana junior high school broke his right leg while engaged in a makeshift football game. **Although the students knew that they were not permitted to play such rough games, neither the teacher nor the teacher's aide were aware of their activities**. On this particular day, the teacher's aide was supervising a class so the teacher could attend a conference with the principal. The student's mother filed suit against the teacher, the teacher's aide, the school board and its insurer alleging negligence and failure to properly supervise the class. A trial court found the school board negligent and awarded the student $200,000 in damages but ruled that neither the teacher nor the teacher's aide were at fault. Both sides appealed. The Louisiana Court of Appeal observed that the teacher had already returned from her meeting with the principal when the student's injury took place. Although the teacher claimed that she would have stopped any "roughhousing" had she seen it, the court stated that she should have noticed what was going on. For this reason, the court ruled that she and her employer, the school board, were equally at fault. On the other hand, **the court stated that the students were old enough to understand that tackling each other could cause injury**. Moreover, it had not been shown that their parents would not have allowed the game at home. In light of these factors, the court reduced the percentage of fault attributable to the teacher and the school board to 5 percent. The student's mother would only be allowed to recover $10,000 rather than the $200,000 awarded by the trial court. *Marcantel v. Allen Parish School Bd.*, 490 So.2d 1162 (La.App.3d Cir.1986).

IV. UNSUPERVISED ACCIDENTS

In addition to the duty to supervise students in their daily activities, schools are required to exercise care in maintaining safe grounds and facilities. Schools can be found liable for maintaining or tolerating hazardous structures, fixtures or grounds.

A. On School Grounds

1. Duty of Care

◆   A Montana parent accompanied her son to school to explain his tardiness for that day. **She slipped and fell on a snow-covered path in front of the school** while returning to her car. She sued the school district for negligence, asserting that it had a duty to warn her that the path was over grass instead of pavement. The court granted summary judgment to the school district and the parent appealed to the Supreme Court of Montana. She argued that the school had altered the normal condition of the area where she had fallen and had affirmatively allowed the appearance of a walkway over uneven natural ground, creating a new or increased hazard. The school had thus created a hidden dangerous condition and had an obligation to warn pedestrians by providing a sign or by blocking off the area. The court held that property owners have a duty to use ordinary care in maintaining their property in a reasonably safe condition and to warn property users of hidden dangers. While a property owner's conduct is normally a fact inquiry which is appropriate for a jury, summary judgment may be appropriate where no material issues of fact exist. In this case, there were no material questions of fact, since the school had not created a hidden dangerous condition even by allowing the appearance of a paved area where none actually existed. **Injuries to parents crossing the path could not have been foreseen by the school district**, and the trial court had properly granted the summary judgment motion. *Richardson v. Corvallis Pub. School. Dist. No. 1*, 950 P.2d 748 (Mont.1997).

◆   **A 14-year-old South Carolina high school student reported being sexually assaulted by a 16-year-old special education student** who had a previous history of disciplinary violations, including improper touching of female students. The special education student and several others had been cleaning a school gymnasium under the supervision of a coach who had left them alone for at least 15 minutes before the assault. The special education student pleaded guilty to criminal sexual conduct in a state juvenile court action. The assaulted student filed a negligent supervision action against the school in a state trial court, which conducted a trial and awarded the student $20,000. The school district appealed to the Court of Appeals of South Carolina, where it argued that it could only be held liable for breaching its duty to supervise students if it had acted in a grossly negligent manner. **The court held that the abandonment of the special education student by the coach in this case created a fact question concerning the district's level of negligence**. A reasonable jury could have found that its actions had been grossly negligent, and the court affirmed this part of the judgment. However, the trial court had improperly excluded evidence of the victim's possible willing participation in sexual activity. Although this evidence would be inadmissible in a criminal action, it was relevant to the district's liability for damages in the negligent supervision case. The appeals court reversed and remanded the case for a new trial on that ground. On appeal to the Supreme Court of South Carolina, the appeals court decision was affirmed with one modification. The issue of the victim's possible consent to the sexual activity was admissible when determining damages, but not when determining liability, according to the state supreme court. *Doe v. Orangeburg County School Dist. No. 2*, 335 S.C. 556, 518 S.E.2d 259 (S.C. 1999).

♦   A New York student was injured on an elementary school playground when another child threw a screwdriver that struck her in the eye. The student's parents sued the school district in a New York trial court claiming that the school had negligently inspected and maintained the playground. No evidence was presented to the trial court concerning how long the screwdriver had been on the playground. The court refused to grant the school district's summary judgment motion. The Supreme Court, Appellate Division, Fourth Department, ruled that the trial court should have granted the district's motion because the district did not create or have constructive or actual notice of the condition causing the injury. **The other child's intervening intentional act of throwing the screwdriver relieved the school district of any liability**. *Mix v. South Seneca Cent. School Dist.*, 602 N.Y.S.2d 467 (A.D.4th Dep't 1993).

♦   A Georgia elementary school had two manually-operated merry-go-rounds on its playground. During nonschool hours, **the playground was open for public use**. A parent took his five-year-old kindergartner and two other children to the playground. The children played on one of the merry-go-rounds until another child was injured on it because a board was missing. The father told them to get off but did not instruct them not to use the other merry-go-round. He thought the children would recognize its obvious state of disrepair and not go on it. He believed it would not even turn. The children, however, got the merry-go-round to turn, and the kindergartner was injured when she stuck her foot between the framework and the ground where there was no flooring. The kindergartner's parents sued the county board of education for the injury sustained by their daughter. A Georgia trial court granted summary judgment to the school board, and the parents appealed to the Court of Appeals of Georgia.

The court of appeals stated that **where recreational property open to public use was involved, Georgia law provided that the school board was only liable for wilful or malicious failure to guard or warn against dangerous conditions**. In order to show that the school board's failure to guard was wilful or malicious, the parents needed to show that the school board had actual knowledge that: the property was being used for recreational purposes; a condition existed involving an unreasonable risk of death or serious bodily harm; the condition was not apparent to those using the property; and the owner having this knowledge chose not to guard or warn. The court stated that the parents could not meet this burden because the father admitted that the danger was apparent both to him and to his daughter. Therefore, the school board was not liable for the kindergartner's injuries. *Edmondson v. Brooks County Bd. of Educ.*, 423 S.E.2d 413 (Ga.App.1992).

2. Governmental Immunity

♦   A custodian, a clerical worker and a part-time swimming instructor at a Minnesota high school observed a non-student at the school at various times one school day. Although the school district had a policy requiring teachers to refer visitors to a school office, it had no policy for non-teaching employees. None of the employees referred the non-student to the school office, even though the custodian observed him coming out of the girls' locker room. The non-student was later convicted of sexually assaulting a student in the locker room. The student's family filed a negligence lawsuit against the school district and several district employees in a Minnesota trial court, which denied motions by the district and employees for summary judgment. On appeal, the Court of Appeals of Minnesota considered whether the district and employees were entitled to statutory or vicarious official immunity. It observed that governmental subdivisions are immune from claims based upon the exercise of a discretionary function or duty. **The school district** had no policy and therefore **had exercised no discretion, making statutory immunity inappropriate.** The district and employees were also not entitled to official immunity since imposing liability on the employees would encourage them to exercise greater care in the future. The court affirmed the judgment for the student and her parents.

The school district appealed to the Supreme Court of Minnesota, which held that **the district's failure to enact a security policy had occurred at the operational level, not the public policy-making level. Accordingly, the district was not entitled to statutory immunity**. However, the question of the employees' claim to official immunity was remanded for a determination of whether they had a common law duty to protect students and whether the duty was implicated in this case. The Supreme Court of Minnesota amended the decision in July of 1999, granting the parties' petitions for further review. *S. W. and J. W. v. Spring Lake Park School Dist. No. 16*, 580 N.W.2d 19 (Minn. 1998).

◆   **A craft fair patron who slipped on a sidewalk adjoining a junior high school gymnasium filed a negligence action against the school district**. The circuit court granted summary judgment to the school district, finding the district was entitled to immunity under the Illinois Tort Immunity Act's recreational purposes exclusion. The circuit court also refused to allow the patron's motion to amend her claim to incorporate wilful and wanton conduct as the cause of her injuries.

The appellate court discussed whether the sidewalk was public property intended or permitted to be used for recreational purposes within the meaning of the exclusion. A case-by-case analysis was appropriate to determine whether property was used for recreational purposes and thus subject to exclusion from liability under the act. **The court rejected the school's claim that use of the sidewalk for gymnasium access and occasional student recreation precluded a factual inquiry by a jury** in this case. It reversed and remanded the circuit court decision. *Batson v. Pinckneyville Elementary School Dist. No. 50*, 690 N.E.2d 1077 (Ill.App.5th Dist.1998).

◆   A Connecticut elementary school maintained a policy under which hallways were not monitored, but teachers kept their doors open to see and hear hallway activity. An eight-year-old second grader who had been dismissed for recess ran down a hallway and fell through a wire mesh window when another student tripped him. The injured student filed a personal injury lawsuit against the school district in a Connecticut trial court for negligence and nuisance, asserting that lack of supervision had caused an unreasonable risk of injury. The court conducted a trial and determined that the district had been negligent, but held that the damage award should be reduced in part because of the student's own negligence. The court granted the school district's motion for judgment on the basis of qualified governmental immunity, and the student appealed to the Appellate Court of Connecticut. The court held that **the lack of supervision alone did not create an unreasonable risk of injury**, and observed that in the 22 years prior to the student's injury, no such unsupervised accident had occurred at the school. The foreseeable risk of a student running in the hallway did not rise to the level necessary to overcome governmental immunity, and the court affirmed the judgment.

The **Supreme Court of Connecticut reversed, finding the imminent harm-identifiable person exception to the doctrine of governmental immunity applied** in this case. Because the evidence demonstrated a risk to students who were travelling down the hallway unsupervised after being dismissed from lunch, the district was not entitled to immunity. The jury verdict was reinstated. *Purzycki v. Town of Fairfield*, 244 Conn. 101, 708 A.2d 937 (1998).

♦   A Chicago high school student was injured while trying to break up a fight between a classmate and a student from another high school. The incident took place in front of a high school after school hours. Immediately prior to the incident, a school security guard had dispersed a large crowd of students and had twice instructed the student to go back inside the building. After he was injured, the student was offered medical assistance by a teacher, but chose to go to a hospital with other students instead. The student filed a lawsuit against the Chicago Board of Education, claiming that the board and its employees had wilfully and wantonly failed to supervise activities on school grounds. An Illinois circuit court granted dismissal motions by the school board and officials, and the student appealed to the Appellate Court of Illinois, First District. The court stated that the state Local Governmental and Governmental Employees Tort Immunity Act protected local government units and their employees from liability for failing to supervise an activity or use of public property. **Liability could result only if employees showed utter indifference or conscious disregard for public safety**. In this case, the student had been instructed at least twice by the security guard to stay inside the building. There was no evidence that school employees had acted wilfully or wantonly or delayed medical treatment. The court awarded summary judgment to the school board and officials. *Towner by Towner v. Bd. of Educ. of the City of Chicago*, 657 N.E.2d 28 (Ill.App.1st Dist.1995).

3.   Insurance Coverage

♦   A five-year-old girl fell from a slide on the grounds of an Oklahoma elementary school during the summer recess and sustained head injuries. She and her parents sued the school district for damages, but the trial court granted summary judgment against them. After the court of appeals affirmed, the girl and her parents appealed to the Supreme Court of Oklahoma. They first claimed that the school district had waived its governmental immunity under the Oklahoma Governmental Tort Claims Act by obtaining liability insurance coverage. The court, however, determined that **the school district had not waived its immunity by acquiring the policy because the policy specifically limited coverage to any liability "imposed by law."** The supreme court held that the girl and her parents could not recover from the school district under any exceptions to the governmental tort claims act. Because the only claims brought were under the exemptions, the school district could not be liable for the girl's injuries, and insurance coverage was not available. The risk of falling from a slide is one that children regularly encounter and appreciate on a playground. Since there were no hidden dangers of which the school district had to warn the girl, summary judgment had been properly awarded to the school district. *Brewer v. Independent School District Number 1*, 848 P.2d 566 (Okla.1993).

◆   A North Carolina teacher attended an evening fundraiser conducted by an honorary teacher's sorority. The event was held in the school building. While attending the event, the teacher slipped on the waxed floor of a restroom and was seriously injured. North Carolina law provides immunity for local boards of education for bodily injury from negligence, except to the extent that the board is covered by insurance. The teacher sued, seeking coverage of her injuries to the extent of the board's insurance, but the Court of Appeals of North Carolina denied coverage. **The court stated that North Carolina law also provided absolute immunity to school boards for personal injury suffered during nonschool use of school property. The waiver of immunity to the extent of insurance did not apply in this instance.** *Lindler v. Duplin County Bd. of Educ.*, 425 S.E.2d 465 (N.C.App.1993).

B. Off School Grounds

1. Duty of Care

◆   Two Arizona students were involved in a confrontation at school. One of the students was known to be a gang member. A school assistant principal brought the students to his office and believed that the situation had been defused. No disciplinary action was taken against either student and both returned to class. After school, a group of students gathered near school in anticipation of a fight between the two students. Several carloads of students left the scene and **the student who was believed to have a gang affiliation shot the other student to death**. The deceased student's family commenced an Arizona superior court action against the school district for wrongful death, also naming a teacher as a party to the suit. The court awarded summary judgment to the district and teacher, and the family appealed to the Court of Appeals of Arizona.

The court stated that Arizona teachers and school administrators have statutory and common law duties not to subject students to a foreseeable and unreasonable risk of harm through their acts, omissions or policies. It agreed with the trial court that **the only way to have prevented the death would have been to incarcerate the other student, which was outside the school's power**. The court rejected the family's claim that school officials knew or should have realized that the death was foreseeable or predictable. There was no evidence that any student had brought a weapon to school or that school officials had failed to follow appropriate guidelines or procedures, or their statutory or common law duties. The court affirmed the judgment. *Hill v. Safford Unified Sch. Dist.*, 952 P.2d 754 (Ariz.App.Div.2 1997).

◆   An Arizona high school maintained a closed campus policy requiring students to remain on campus from the time of their arrival until their dismissal. However, the policy was not strictly enforced, and a group of students left campus in a vehicle shortly after arriving at school one morning. Their car collided with a tractor-trailer, resulting in death and serious injury to some of the students. Parents of the victims sued the school district in a state superior court on the theory that the school had negligently supervised the students. The court granted the district's summary judgment motion and the parents appealed to the Court of Appeals of Arizona. **The court found that the school's failure to enforce its closed campus policy did not expose the students to any risk of vehicular collision beyond the risk that was already present to the public at large**. There was no unreasonable exposure to a foreseeable risk that was sufficient to create liability. The court rejected the parents' alternative argument that the school had negligently failed to perform a voluntary undertaking or had created legally-enforceable rights by failing to enforce the closed campus policy. The court affirmed the summary judgment order for the school district. *Tollenaar v. Chino Valley School Dist.*, 945 P.2d 1310 (Ariz.App.Div.1 1997).

♦   A spectator who attended a basketball game at a Missouri school gymnasium was unable to find a place to park in the school lot and parked her vehicle on an adjoining street where others had parked. Upon returning to her car after the game, she slipped and fell on snow or ice as she unlocked her door. She filed a state court negligence action against the school district, asserting that it exercised control over the street by knowingly using it as an overflow parking lot and that it negligently allowed the street to become unsafe. A Missouri circuit court granted the school district's summary judgment motion, and the spectator appealed to the Missouri Court of Appeals, Southern District. **The court found no evidence that the district had attempted to exercise control over the street, since the city maintained it and there was no evidence that the district knew that many spectators parked there**. Property owners generally have no duty to keep an adjoining public street clear of snow and ice. There was no evidence that any district employee required spectators to park on the street. The court affirmed the judgment for the district. *Lahr v. Lamar R-1 School Dist.*, 951 S.W.2d 754 (Mo.App.S.D.1997).

♦   **A 13-year-old Florida student twice attempted suicide on school grounds**. The school district had no suicide intervention policy. During the student's first attempt, another student entered a school lavatory in which he was attempting to hang himself. The other student called his own mother, who telephoned the school's dean of students. The dean failed to notify the suicidal student's mother of the attempt, instead bringing the student to his office to read and discuss Bible verses. Some time later, a school custodian observed a coat hanger and cord hanging in a lavatory after she apparently interrupted another suicide attempt by the student, who made a comment about suicide to her as he left the lavatory. The custodian told the school's vice principal that a student had talked about suicide but he took no action. **The student later committed suicide at his home before his family was notified of the attempts at school**. His estate sued the school board and school officials in a federal district court for constitutional violations and wrongful death. The court dismissed the officials from the lawsuit and granted the board judgment on the constitutional claims. It conducted a jury trial on the wrongful death claim and awarded the estate $500,000, but found certain family members partly responsible for the damages and reduced the award by two-thirds. It apportioned no liability to the student.

The parties appealed unfavorable aspects of the decision to the U.S. Court of Appeals, Eleventh Circuit. The court held that **the estate had failed to establish any constitutional violations, and rejected its arguments that the school board's failure to properly train employees in suicide intervention amounted to deliberate indifference that violated substantive due process rights.** However, **the court upheld the wrongful death claim** since Florida schools have a duty to supervise students within their care. Because the Florida Supreme Court has never ruled on whether an intentionally wrongdoing party may be subject to apportionment of a damage award, the court certified a question to the state supreme court to resolve the issue of whether the student should have been apportioned a share of the liability. *Wyke v. Polk County School Bd.*, 129 F.3d 560 (11th Cir.1997).

◆   A 15-year-old Georgia student was killed in a car accident after he and a friend left their voluntary summer school session in violation of school rules. The student's mother filed a lawsuit against the board of education, school superintendent, school district and other officials in the U.S. District Court for the Northern District of Georgia, claiming constitutional violations. The court granted summary judgment to the school board and officials, and the student's mother appealed to the U.S. Court of Appeals, Eleventh Circuit. **The court observed that the U.S. Constitution does not require the states to guarantee protection of individuals against the threat of third-party violence. Compulsory attendance laws did not impose a constitutional duty** on schools, and the student's voluntary school attendance during summer session did not create a custodial relationship between himself and the school. The death had resulted from the student's choice to leave school in violation of school policy. The district court had properly granted summary judgment to the school district and officials. *Wright v. Lovin*, 32 F.3d 538 (11th Cir.1994).

2. Governmental Immunity

◆   An Idaho English teacher required her composition class to maintain a daily journal. One student complained that he would not be able to fully express himself if she read his journal. The teacher assured the student that she would only check his entries for length and not read them. **The student later committed suicide and his parents alleged that the journal contained passages alluding to death and depression**, which indicated that he was contemplating suicide. They filed a state court action against the teacher and school district, asserting that the defendants had a duty to take affirmative action to detect and assist students who were suffering from depression or suicidal ideation and a duty to help students displaying suicidal tendencies at school. The court granted summary judgment motions filed by the teacher and district on the basis of immunity, and the family appealed to the Supreme Court of Idaho.

The supreme court held that the district was entitled to immunity, but determined that the teacher was not entitled to immunity for failure to warn the parents or school authorities. On remand, the district court held that **a teacher is not under a duty to ascertain potential suicidal activities by students and found no evidence that the teacher in this case had any actual knowledge of the student's emotional state or suicidal intentions**. The family appealed again to the supreme court, which found that schools only have a duty to exercise reasonable care in supervising students while attending school. Under this standard, the teacher and district were entitled to immunity. The court affirmed the judgment in their favor. *Brooks v. Logan*, 944 P.2d 709 (Idaho 1997).

◆   A delivery person slipped and fell on a driveway outside a Colorado high school cafeteria after delivering pizzas. The delivery person and her workers' compensation carrier sued the school district, claiming negligence by district employees for failing to remove gravel, water and mud from the driveway. A Colorado district court refused to grant the district's dismissal motion under the Colorado Governmental Immunity Act, and the district appealed to the Colorado Court of Appeals. The court found that **the driveway was not an area for which the legislature had waived immunity since it did not involve a dangerous condition of a public building, highway, road, street or sidewalk**. The immunity act waived immunity only in specific circumstances, none of which included the use of a driveway. The court reversed and remanded the case. *Stanley v. Adams County School Dist. 27J*, 942 P.2d 1322 (Colo.App.1997).

◆   An Illinois high school senior wrote suicide notes and told other students that he was going to kill himself. The students reported his intentions to a school counselor. After the student took a drug overdose at school, the counselor notified the student's mother and advised her to take the student to a hospital. Nothing was said about the suicide threats. Later that day, the student killed himself by jumping from a highway overpass. The student's estate filed a lawsuit against the school board in a state circuit court for negligently failing to inform the student's mother of the suicide threats and failing to implement a suicide prevention program. The court dismissed the lawsuit, and the estate appealed to the Appellate Court of Illinois, Third District. The court observed that **the student had left the control of school administrators at the time of the suicide, removing any basis for a negligence claim based on breach of a special duty to protect** the student. While the Illinois School Code empowers school boards to establish inservice training programs for suicide intervention, this is not mandatory and **a district's failure to develop an adequate suicide intervention program does not create the legal basis for a negligence claim**. The school board and its employees were entitled to immunity under state law since they had refrained from wilful and wanton conduct despite the absence of an intervention plan and the failure to inform the mother of the suicide threats. The court affirmed the dismissal of the case. *Grant v. Bd. of Trustees of Valley View School Dist. No. 365-U*, 676 N.E.2d 705 (Ill.App.3d Dist.1997).

◆   A Georgia student attended summer school and failed the first session after skipping class several times. The student's parent was aware of this and grounded him when she learned of the absences. The student attended the second session and left school one day during a break in violation of school policies. He was killed in a traffic accident while riding in a vehicle driven by a fellow student who was later convicted of vehicular homicide. The student's estate filed a lawsuit against school officials in a Georgia superior court, claiming that they had acted negligently in failing to enforce school attendance rules. The court granted summary judgment to the school officials, and the estate appealed to the Court of Appeals of Georgia. The court rejected the estate's argument that the implementation of attendance policies by school employees was not protected from governmental immunity. **The court stated that the supervision of students is a protected discretionary activity for which the employees could not be held liable**. The court also observed that **the student's death had been caused by the criminal act of the fellow student and would have been an unforeseeable circumstance even if the school employees had been negligent**. The court affirmed the trial court judgment for the school officials. *Wright v. Ashe*, 220 Ga.App. 91, 469 S.E.2d 268 (1996).

3. Comparative Negligence/Assumption of Risk

◆   A high school student was harassed and threatened by three classmates after he came to the defense of a new student the three classmates were harassing while on their school bus. He disembarked at a bus stop where he believed that he would be safer than if he disembarked at his regular stop, but was followed by the three classmates. Some other students also got off the bus in anticipation of a fight. While attempting to intervene, the student was thrown to the ground and beaten by the three students. He suffered personal injuries including tremors, loss of memory and post-traumatic stress disorder. His mother commenced a personal injury action against the students, their parents, the school board and four school officials, including the bus driver, in a Louisiana trial court. The assaulting students, their parents and insurers were voluntarily dismissed. **The court determined that the school board alone was liable for a general damage award of $75,000 for the student and $5,000 for his mother**. It also awarded special damages to the student in excess of $6,000.

A court of appeal determined the trial court had erroneously failed to compare the fault of the various parties in this case, as required by Louisiana law. While the school board was responsible for the reasonable supervision of students, it was not the insurer of student safety. Moreover, it was not possible for school employees to constantly supervise all students. In a personal injury case involving negligent supervision, it is necessary to show that an unreasonable risk of injury is foreseeable to the school board that is known and preventable in the exercise of proper supervision. The evidence in this case indicated that school administrators failed to follow board policies regarding the prevention of fights among students where they had received advance notice of the potential fight. In particular, the school disciplinarian had failed to inform the bus driver about the harassment of the new student, which had been reported to him shortly before the fight. The driver had in turn failed to take note of several unauthorized bus riders or to detect other problems on the bus, despite testimony by one student that "everyone on the bus knew there was going to be a fight." **The court found that the board was 20 percent at fault for causing the student's injuries. It further held that each of the assaulting students was 25 percent at fault, and the student was 5 percent at fault** for failing to report the strong possibility of a fight to the bus driver. The court reduced the award to the mother by 50 percent as an abuse of discretion by the trial court. Because the board was solely liable for 50 percent of the entire award, it was responsible for damages of almost $40,000, instead of the full amount of damages. *Frazer v. St. Tammany Parish School Board*, 774 So.2d 1227 (La.App.1stCir. 2000).

◆   A New York high school student, who stole an oxidizing agent from his science class, sued his school for personal injury damages when the chemical later ignited in his home. The student alleged that the school was negligent in not providing adequate supervision and allowing access to dangerous chemicals without appropriate warnings or precautions. The school filed a motion for summary judgment denying the student's allegations and raising contributory negligence as a defense. The trial court denied the motion, and the school appealed to the New York Supreme Court, Appellate Division, which relied on the student's own testimony in finding that the school was not negligent. Although the student claimed that the chemical had spontaneously ignited, the police later found matches in the room where the fire had occurred. Additionally, the student admitted that his teacher had gone over the safety procedures and specifically told the class never to remove chemicals from the classroom. The court further stated that **even if the school had been negligent, the student's act of intentionally stealing the chemical constituted a superseding force. The court stressed that the student's actions were unforeseeable and went beyond mere contributory negligence**. Because of the intentional nature of the student's actions, the school was absolved from any liability. The court thus reversed the trial court's decision and granted summary judgment to the school. *Brazell v. Bd. of Educ. of Niskayuna Public Schools*, 557 N.Y.S.2d 645 (A.D.3d Dep't 1990).

V.   LIABILITY FOR INTENTIONAL CONDUCT

The previous cases have involved school negligence. School districts may also be found liable for the intentional acts or omissions of school personnel. Courts often refer to intentional conduct as "wilful or wanton misconduct." Courts have also found school districts liable for intentional acts of third parties on or near school grounds. In those cases, courts may hold that the school district should have foreseen the potential for misconduct. In some cases, a finding of wilful or wanton misconduct will defeat the defense of sovereign immunity.

A.   Teacher Misconduct

1.   Types of Misconduct

◆   Three students attended a special education classroom and claimed that the teacher improperly touched them. **The students' homeroom teacher was aware of the alleged misconduct, but did not report the allegations for two weeks.** When she did, the city civil rights officer who received the report failed to contact the state Department of Social Services, despite a Massachusetts law requiring immediate reporting of such incidents. According to the students, the abuse did not stop until it was finally reported to the DSS by a doctor who examined one of them near the end of the school year. The DSS took immediate action to separate the students from the teacher upon receiving the report. A special education supervisor and school principal also failed to make such reports, and the students sued the city and a number of school employees in a federal district court for civil rights violations under Title IX, 42 U.S.C. § 1983 and state law.

    The city moved for summary judgment, asserting the students had failed to demonstrate deliberate indifference to the abuse. The court stated that in order to establish municipal liability under Section 1983 or Title IX, the complaining party must identify a municipal custom or policy that causes a deprivation of federal rights. The U.S. Supreme Court has held that even where a municipal policy is constitutionally valid on its face, the municipality may still be liable under Section 1983 if the policy is implemented with deliberate indifference. The failure to provide proper training to employees, where the failure causes injury, is a "policy" for which a municipality may be held liable. The city argued that it was not on "actual notice" of the abuse, since no employee with the authority to take action against the teacher knew of his misconduct. **The court agreed with the students that there was evidence of deliberate indifference by school employees. All four school employees who were notified of the abuse had the power to stop it** simply by notifying DSS. The court awarded summary judgment to the city on a number of state law claims, but the Title IX and Section 1983 claims against it could not be dismissed prior to trial. *Booker v. City of Boston et al.*, Nos. CIV.A.97-CV-12534MEL, CIV.A.97-CV-12675MEL and CIV.A.97-CV-12691MEL, 2000 WL 1868180 (D. Mass. 2000).

◆   During a lesson on drugs and alcohol, students identified "boo" as a street name for marijuana. **The instructor asked a student whose nickname was "Boo," to use her full name** on all assignments. He also advised classmates not to use the nickname, as did another teacher. The student claimed that classmates teased her by calling her "pot" and "marijuana." The teachers then changed their minds and allowed students to call her "Boo." The student's mother sued the district in an Oregon state court for psychic injury, intentional infliction of emotional distress and defamation. The court awarded summary judgment to the district and the family appealed to the Court of Appeals of Oregon, which found no basis for her claim for psychic injury. **The tort of psychic injury requires proof of a legally protected interest beyond general negligence and there was no basis in common law or the Constitution establishing a right to be referred to by a nickname**. The defamation claims also failed because the teachers did not falsely suggest that the student used or condoned the use of marijuana, or act with reckless disregard of that possibility. The complaint failed to meet the high legal standard required to prevail on a claim for intentional infliction of emotional distress. Apart from rhetoric, the student's complaint alleged only that two teachers required her to use her given name in class, and the appeals court affirmed the judgment for the school district. *Phillips v. Lincoln County School Dist.*, 984 P.2d 947 (Or.App.1999).

◆   **A Washington school district sought to dismiss a middle school teacher after his students found sexually explicit drawings in a class storage room and alleged that he sexually harassed them**. A local newspaper publicized the district's investigation, using information that a state court had ordered released. The teacher then initiated an action against the district for a number of personal injury claims. The court granted summary judgment to the teacher.

He appealed to the court of appeals, which first held that **the state does not recognize a claim for negligent investigation**. A contrary rule might have a chilling effect on investigations and was not authorized by state law. **There was no merit to the teacher's defamation claim**. The teacher was considered a public official because he was performing his duties pursuant to a public contract. Under the public official standard, the teacher needed to show that the release of information was made maliciously. There was no such showing in this case. The officials had made only general statements about the case, and had refrained from personal attacks on the teacher. There was no evidence of bad faith or ill will. The court affirmed summary judgment on the defamation and negligent investigation claims, but reversed the judgment on his common law privacy claim for further consideration. *Corbally v. Kennewick School Dist.*, 94 Wash.App. 736, 973 P.2d 1074 (Wash.App.3d Dist.1999).

◆   **A Maryland special education teacher beat a nine-year-old student with Down syndrome** because the student had urinated in his pants. The student was taken to an emergency room by his parents and criminal charges were later filed against the teacher for child abuse, assault and battery. The teacher pleaded guilty to assault and was forbidden from teaching or supervising individuals under the age of 21. **The student's family then initiated a Maryland circuit court action against the teacher and school board for negligence, assault, battery, intentional infliction of emotional distress and other claims**. The court granted the board's dismissal motion on the basis of the teacher's malicious and intentional acts, which fell outside the scope of his employment and were not in furtherance of school board business. The family appealed to the Court of Special Appeals of Maryland.

The court observed that corporal punishment was prohibited both by the Maryland Education Article and the school board's rules. In order to hold a school board vicariously liable for an employee's conduct, the conduct must occur in furtherance of the employer's business and must be authorized by it. Although it was conceivable that some intentional acts could result in school board liability, **the acts of corporal punishment** in this case **were specifically prohibited by state law and local rules and had resulted in the teacher's assault conviction. Because of the egregiousness of the teacher's misconduct, it was impossible to find his actions within the scope of his employment**. The board was awarded judgment in its favor. *Tall v. Bd. of School Commissioners of Baltimore City*, 120 Md.App. 236, 706 A.2d 659 (1998).

For additional cases involving corporal punishment, please see Chapter Four, Section III.

◆   A South Carolina middle school teacher was assigned to a summer school class. Several teachers and students observed a lax atmosphere in the classroom, and some witnesses observed students smoking, talking, playing the radio and massaging the teacher's shoulders. **The teacher offered to tutor one 15-year-old student at her home after he missed a day of school and required makeup work. He went to her home and she allegedly forced him to have sex with her**. The student reported the incident after the teacher was charged with a sex offense involving another student. The family sued the school district, teacher and other school employees in a South Carolina trial court for claims including negligent hiring and supervision, intentional infliction of emotional distress, false imprisonment, assault and battery and invasion of privacy. The court granted summary judgment to the school district concerning the negligent hiring and supervision claims, and the student appealed to the Court of Appeals of South Carolina. The court stated that **the South Carolina Tort Claims Act prohibits a governmental entity from being held liable for employee conduct that arises outside the scope of official duties and for crimes**

involving moral turpitude. There was no evidence in this case that other school employees were aware of inappropriate contact between the teacher and other students prior to the incident. The lax atmosphere in the classroom had not been reported to school administrators and it could not have been reasonably anticipated that the teacher would sexually assault the student in her home. The court affirmed the summary judgment order of the trial court. *Moore v. Berkeley County School Dist.*, 486 S.E.2d 9 (S.C.App.1997).

◆   **Two California school administrators gave favorable employment references to a teacher formerly employed by the school district without revealing his history of sexual misconduct with students.** A middle school hired the teacher to serve as a vice principal, in part based upon the references provided by the administrators. As vice principal, he sexually assaulted a 13-year-old student, who filed a lawsuit against him in a state court. She also named his former employing school district and the administrators for negligently or fraudulently giving favorable employment references. The court dismissed the claims against the former school district and administrators, but the Court of Appeal of California reversed the decision concerning negligent misrepresentation and fraud. The district and administrators appealed to the Supreme Court of California.

The supreme court agreed with the court of appeal that the former district and administrators could have reasonably foreseen that their positive references would lead to the hiring and create an opportunity for the sexual assault. Employers who write recommendation letters have a duty to prospective employers and third parties not to misrepresent facts in describing the qualifications and character of a former employee where that misrepresentation would present a foreseeable risk of physical injury. **Because the reference letters in this case contained unreserved praise for the vice principal despite the administrators' knowledge of his repeated sexual improprieties, the referring district and administrators could be held liable for misrepresentation and fraud.** The supreme court affirmed the court of appeal's judgment in part, reinstating the negligent misrepresentation and fraud claims. *Randi W. v. Muroc Joint Unified School Dist.*, 60 Cal.Rptr.2d 263, 929 P.2d 582 (1997).

◆   A New York student spent summer vacations with her aunt and uncle in New Jersey. She told two friends that she had been sexually abused by her uncle. They encouraged her to tell an adult and she decided to tell her social studies teacher. The student told the teacher what had happened, but the teacher stated that there was nothing she could do since the uncle was in New Jersey. The teacher did not report the abuse and the student continued to visit her aunt and uncle. A year later, she told a school counselor about the abuse and a report was filed. **The parents sued the school in a New York trial court, seeking to recover damages for the student's psychological trauma resulting from the teacher's failure to make a report.** The court granted the school's dismissal motion, ruling that the teacher had no common law duty to report abuse and did not breach her statutory duty as a mandatory reporter of child abuse. The court found that the student's uncle was not a "person legally responsible" for her care under the statute, and that the teacher had no duty to report his actions. The parents appealed to the New York Supreme Court, Appellate Division.

The court observed that whether a teacher is required to report suspected abuse is determined by the facts known to the teacher at the time. **Considering that the** teacher knew the student visited her relatives regularly, it would have been reasonable to believe that the uncle was a "person legally responsible" for the student. It is not the duty of a mandatory reporter to determine whether the abuser meets the technical definition of the statute. That is the duty of the investigating agency. The reporter must simply report immediately any suspected child abuse. The court held that the reporter can be held liable for a breach of duty even if it is eventually found that the abuse did not occur. The trial court's decision was reversed. *Kimberly S.M. v. Bradford Central School*, 649 N.Y.S.2d 588 (A.D.4th Dep't 1996).

2. Governmental Immunity

♦   **A New Mexico teacher called a 12-year-old student a prostitute in front of the class**. During the next six weeks, he continued to call her a prostitute and also encouraged students to do so. The student eventually left the school and filed a lawsuit against the school district and teacher in the U.S. District Court for the District of New Mexico, asserting constitutional rights violations under 42 U.S.C. § 1983. The court denied the teacher's summary judgment motion on the basis of qualified immunity finding that he had violated the student's protected liberty interest to be free from unjustified intrusions against her personal security. It also ruled that the teacher was not entitled to qualified immunity because the right to be free from unjustified intrusions upon emotional well-being was well established. The teacher appealed to the U.S. Court of Appeals, Tenth Circuit. **The court observed that other courts had found that a constitutional violation exists where a teacher sexually assaults a student. However, there was no authority for a recovery based on psychological abuse.** The court rejected the student's assertion that the standard of conduct governing Title VII sexual harassment should be applied to her constitutional claims. The court reversed and remanded the district court decision, noting that the student would have to obtain relief under state statutory or tort law. *Abeyta by Martinez v. Chama Valley Indep. School Dist. No. 19*, 77 F.3d 1253 (10th Cir.1996).

♦   A Texas high school teacher removed a disruptive student from his class by holding on to his hair and arm. The student had thrown an object at another student and used profanity in the classroom. The teacher took the student to the vice principal's office for discipline, which in this case was assignment to the opportunity center for students for the rest of the semester. The student was later suspended from school for the rest of the year for drawing obscene pictures at the opportunity center. The decision to discipline the student rested with the vice principal and school administrator; the teacher did not participate in the decision to place the student in the opportunity center. **The student's parents filed a lawsuit against the teacher in a Texas trial court claiming that the student had suffered injuries in being removed from the classroom**. The court granted summary judgment to the teacher, and the parents appealed to the Court of Appeals of Texas. The court of appeals observed that Texas teachers were protected by absolute immunity from personal liability for any act involving the exercise of discretion with only limited exceptions, including excessive force or negligence during student discipline. The parents argued that the act of removing the student from the classroom constituted discipline under the state education code. The court disagreed, stating that **the teacher had not** been engaged in disciplinary action but was merely transporting the student to the vice principal's office for the imposition of discipline. Accordingly, the teacher was entitled to absolute immunity from personal liability and the trial court had properly granted summary judgment in his favor. *Doria v. Stulting*, 888 S.W.2d 563 (Tex.App.—Corpus Christi 1994).

B. Coach and Other School Employee Misconduct

◆   Two brothers who were small in stature played on the school basketball teams, and endured name-calling, taunting and repeated verbal harassment throughout their high school careers. The brothers claimed that students were not disciplined for the harassing conduct directed towards then. The older brother stated that when he complained to the school principal, the response was that name-calling was part of growing up, "which he should accept and move on." **The older brother alleged that team coaches ignored harassment by other players, and even joined it. When he complained to an assistant principal about a specific incident, the peer harassment increased** and escalated into physical abuse. The brothers' parents met with the superintendent, who issued a memorandum for action that included assurances that the basketball coaches would not return the next year. The memorandum also stated that meetings would be held with administrators to ensure that they knew about the district's harassment policy. However, the harassment continued, and the brothers commenced a federal district court lawsuit against the district and school officials. The complaint included claims arising under Title IX of the Education Amendments of 1972 and 42 U.S.C. § 1983, and state law claims for negligence, assault and related torts.

The court considered a summary judgment motion by the district and school officials, and first observed that school officials cannot be sued under Title IX. Such claims are only possible against federal funding recipients. The officials were entitled to summary judgment on the Title IX and Section 1983 claims for due process and equal protection violations. The Title IX claim against the school district required analysis under *Davis v. Monroe County Board of Education*, 526 U.S. 529 (1999), in which the U.S. Supreme Court found that peer harassment may constitute discrimination under Title IX when a federal funding recipient directly harasses a student or shows deliberate indifference to harassment. **The court found evidence of widespread harassment of the brothers by students and some by coaches. Because it was possible that a jury would find that this went beyond mere teasing, the district was not entitled to summary judgment on the Title IX claims.** There was evidence that the principal did nothing to investigate the complaints. This was clearly unreasonable and, if proven, demonstrated deliberate indifference by a school official. There was no evidence that staff took action or responded to the superintendent's memorandum, leaving open the possibility that a jury would also find the superintendent's conduct deliberately indifferent and unreasonable. The court denied summary judgment to the district on the Title IX claims. *Snelling v. Fall Mountain Regional School District*, No. CIV. 99-448-JD, 2001 WL 276975 (D.N.H. 2001).

◆   An investigation revealed that **a high school track coach had been secretly taping team members in various stages of undress for three to four years**. A group of team members sued the school board, superintendent, athletic director, principal and the coach in a federal district court for depriving them of constitutional civil rights in violation of 42 U.S.C. § 1983. They presented evidence that a few years before the coach began secretly taping them, his conduct had come into question. At the conclusion of the school's investigation of the previous incident, the coach was directed to restrict his videotaping activities, refrain from driving students home, and bring a female chaperone to meets. The district court awarded summary judgment to the school board, superintendent, athletic director and principal. While the case against the coach proceeded to trial, the students appealed to the U.S. Court of Appeals, Fourth Circuit, on the issue of the board's liability.

The Fourth Circuit recited the rule that Section 1983 liability for civil rights violations applies to a school board or municipality only if the alleged injury was caused by an identifiable policy or custom. Section 1983 does not impose liability on a school board or municipality based on *respondeat superior* principles. Municipal or school board liability results only where decision-makers possess final policymaking authority over the conduct giving rise to liability. In this case, the students were required to show that the board had final policymaking authority over the alleged policy of acquiescence to the coach's conduct. The question of final authority is a matter of state law and custom. The Virginia Constitution vests control of public schools with local boards, which may retain final authority over discipline of school employees. However, the board in this case had not delegated final authority to investigate complaints against teachers and implement discipline. All employment decisions were subject to final review by the board. The court held that when official action is subject to review by authorized policymakers, the policymakers retain authority to measure official conduct for conformity with their policy. **Because the board retained final policymaking authority over personnel matters, the district court had properly held that it could not be held liable for the decisions of the superintendent and principal.** Even if this were not true, there would be no liability in this case because there was no link between the previous incident and the present action that would put the board on notice of dangerous propensities by the coach. He had been exonerated of wrongdoing after the prior investigation and the failure to foresee his misconduct did not amount to deliberate indifference. The court affirmed the judgment for the school board. *Riddick v. School Board of City of Portsmouth*, 238 F.3d 518 (4th Cir. 2000).

◆   Suspecting a member of the high school swim team was pregnant, the coach allegedly repeatedly asked the student if she was pregnant. The student consistently denied being pregnant, but eventually agreed to take a pregnancy test. The result was positive and the coach asked an orthopedist whether it was permissible for a pregnant swimmer to compete. After learning that there was no medical reason to prevent the student from swimming competitively, the coach let her remain on the team. However, she continued to deny her pregnancy, until a doctor determined she was six months pregnant. The student alleged that after her baby was born, the coach attempted to alienate her from her peers, refused to speak with her and retaliated against her by removing her from competition. She sued him in a federal district court for civil rights violations under 42 U.S.C. § 1983 and state law. **The court held that the coach was entitled to qualified immunity from suit because he had not violated any clearly established constitutional rights**, or because the claims did not give rise to constitutional violations.

The student appealed to the U.S. Court of Appeals, Third Circuit, which first explained that Section 1983 creates no substantive rights, but instead provides individuals with a means to vindicate federal rights under the Constitution or described in Section 1983. To prevail in a Section 1983 action, the complaining party must show that official conduct has caused a deprivation of federal rights "under color of state law." The district court in this case had improperly held that the absence of a U.S. Supreme Court decision on the subject of pregnancy test administration to students meant that the student had no clearly established right to be free of such testing. The specific official conduct need not have been previously deemed unlawful. Instead, **a review of current federal cases revealed that requiring a student to submit to a pregnancy test, if proven, would be an unlawful search and seizure under the Fourth Amendment**. The court found that a reasonable swim coach would not have forced a student to take a pregnancy test and recognized that the subject was unsuitable for public speculation. Because the coach failed to "justify his failure to respect the boundaries of reasonableness," he was not entitled to qualified immunity on the student's Fourth Amendment claim. This aspect of the district court's judgment was reversed and remanded. The court also reversed and remanded the student's claims based on violations of her constitutional privacy rights and state law. Her pregnancy was entitled to privacy protection under the Due Process Clause. The coach was not entitled to qualified immunity since current law put him on notice that the compelled disclosure of personal information was not objectively reasonable. Because the student's claim based on right to familial integrity and her parents' right to raise their children without undue state interference was not clearly established, the coach was entitled to immunity from this claim. The circuit court further affirmed the judgment in the coach's favor on the student's First Amendment claim based on freedom of association, since the student asserted an unrecognized claim based only on her association with the swim team. *Gruenke v. Seip*, 225 F.3d 290 (3d Cir. 2000).

◆   A high school student was involved in a fight with another player and complained to his football coach. The coach allegedly told him "you need to learn how to handle your own business." The student returned to the other player and hit him in the head with a weight lock. **The coach then allegedly asked the student, "What did you hit him with; if you hit him with it, I am going to hit you with it," then struck him with the weight lock**. The blow caused severe and permanent injury to the student's eye, and he sued the coach, principal, school board and district superintendent in a federal district court for civil rights violations. The court granted motions by the board, district, superintendent and principal for failure to state a claim under 42 U.S.C. § 1983 based on improper training, instruction and supervision by the coach. The district court held that while the coach's spontaneous action could have been an assault under state law, it was not corporal punishment.

The student appealed to the U.S. Court of Appeals, Eleventh Circuit, which held that corporal punishment in schools may be defined as the application of physical force by a teacher to punish a student for some kind of school-related misconduct. In this case, the coach was responding to an incident of misconduct on school grounds. The coach had not attempted to break up the fight between the students, but had instead used force against the student for the purpose of disciplining him. After ruling that the coach's action constituted corporal punishment, the court examined the leading U.S. Supreme Court case on corporal punishment, *Ingraham v. Wright*,

430 U.S. 651 (1977), and the Fifth Circuit decision in the same case. The *Ingraham* decisions did not foreclose the claim for substantive due process violations alleged by the student. *Ingraham* was distinguishable because the corporal punishment administered in that case came under a school policy with sufficient constraints and restrictions to prevent arbitrary action by school employees. **In this case, the coach's action was not expressly authorized by the school board and he had arbitrarily punished the student through the use of intentional and obviously excessive force that presented a reasonably foreseeable risk of serious injury.** The student alleged that the corporal punishment was so brutal, demeaning and harmful as to shock the conscience, implicating his substantive due process rights. The court reversed and remanded the judgment, ruling that excessive corporal punishment that is not administered in conformity with a valid school policy is actionable when arbitrary, egregious and conscience-shocking. *Neal v. Fulton County Board of Education*, 229 F.3d 1069 (11th Cir. 2000).

◆   A Utah high school student was assaulted by some of his varsity football teammates in a school locker room. He was bound to a towel rack and displayed to a female student. **His report of the incident to school administrators was met with hostility and he was dismissed from the football team for refusing to apologize to teammates** for reporting the incident. The five teammates who assaulted the student were allowed to play in the next football game, but the school district canceled the final game of the season in response to the student's complaint. He then transferred to another school in a different county. He filed a lawsuit against the football coach, school principal, high school and school district in the U.S. District Court for the District of Utah, claiming violations of Title IX and the U.S. Constitution. The court dismissed the lawsuit, and the student appealed to the U.S. Court of Appeals, Tenth Circuit.

The court agreed with school officials that the Title IX complaint had been properly dismissed since the student had failed to show that school officials discriminated against him on the basis of sex. **The constitutional claims had also been properly dismissed since the student failed to state that school officials took deliberate steps to dismiss him from school so as to deprive him of a liberty or property interest.** The U.S. Supreme Court has held that government entities have no duty to protect students from assaults by other students. However, **the district court had inappropriately dismissed the student's claim that the school officials had violated his free speech rights by dismissing him from the football team.** The case was remanded to the district court for further consideration of the officials' claim that they were entitled to immunity on the free speech claims. *Seamons v. Snow*, 84 F.3d 1226 (10th Cir. 1996).

On remand, the district court granted the defendant's motion for summary judgment on the student's free speech claims, finding no indication the student's speech rights were impinged upon by the defendants. On a second appeal to the Tenth Circuit, the panel first analyzed the unorthodox procedure employed by the district court in conducting an evidentiary hearing on a motion for summary judgment. There was a disputed issue of fact about whether the coach had asked the student to apologize to his teammates as a condition of rejoining the team. Given this dispute, the court rejected the district court's decision to award summary judgment. **There were genuine issues of material fact regarding whether the coach required the**

student to apologize to his teammates for reporting the assault as a condition of remaining on the team, and evidence existed supporting the First Amendment violation claim against the coach. Because the coach was vested with the authority to make final decisions about the team, the school district could also be held liable for his actions. However, there was no evidence that the principal took any action to suspend or remove the student from the team or that he had prior knowledge or control over any of the coach's actions. He had thus been properly dismissed from the lawsuit. The court reversed the district court judgment with respect to the coach and school district, affirmed it with respect to the principal, and remanded the case for further proceedings. *Seamons v. Snow*, 206 F.3d 1021 (10th Cir. 2000).

◆   A former student of an Iowa school district claimed that a district employee had abused him at school and at a boy scout camp in the late 1970s, and that he first discovered this in counseling years later. He sued the school district and employee in an Iowa district court for negligence. He admitted that he never told any other school employee about the abuse. The court granted the district's motion for a directed verdict based on insufficient evidence that any employee knew of the alleged abuse and the fact that the employee was not acting within the scope of his job duties during the alleged incidents.

On appeal, the Supreme Court of Iowa held that the alleged abuse by the employee was not within the scope of employment. For this reason, the district could not be held liable under the respondeat superior doctrine, in which an employer may be held liable for employee negligence while the employee is acting within the scope of employment. **There was no evidence that the abuse was expected, foreseeable, or sanctioned by the district. The court held that a school district's duty to supervise student safety is limited to reasonably foreseeable risks.** While it recognized legal causes of action for negligent hiring, negligent retention and negligent supervision, the court held that the standard of liability under these theories was not met in this case, because the district had no actual knowledge of any abusive acts. The court affirmed the judgment and remanded the claims against the employee for further proceedings. *Godar v. Edwards*, 588 N.W.2d 701 (Iowa 1999).

◆   A Texas high school coach engaged in sexual relations with a 15-year-old student. The student did not complain for several months. When she finally confided in a junior high school teacher employed by the district at another school, **the teacher failed to report the incident to appropriate authorities within 48 hours as required by the state family code.** When the student's parents learned of the sexual abuse, they filed a lawsuit against the coach, teacher, principal, athletic director and school district in the U.S. District Court for the Eastern District of Texas. The court granted summary judgment to the teacher in her official capacity, but denied the motion with regard to liability in her individual capacity. The U.S. Court of Appeals, Fifth Circuit, reversed the order denying summary judgment and remanded the case. The district court then denied motions for summary judgment by the principal and athletic director based on state law immunity. The principal and director appealed to the court of appeals, which found no basis for denying the director's immunity claim. The principal also was not liable for failing to report suspected child abuse to authorities within 48 hours. As the U.S. Supreme Court has noted in several cases, **a complaining party in a sexual abuse case must establish** knowledge by school officials of a pattern of inappropriate sexual behavior, deliberate indifference toward student constitutional rights and failure to take action that causes injury to the student. The court reversed the lower court's judgment and ruled in favor of the school employees. *Doe v. Rains County Indep. School Dist.*, 76 F.3d 666 (5th Cir.1996).

◆   A Louisiana physical education coach removed three kindergarten boys from a film presentation because they were being disruptive. He allegedly told the boys that if they did not stop annoying him he would kill them. The coach then enlisted two of the boys in a prank in which they were to pretend to lay dead in view of the third kindergartner. The coach told the third kindergartner that he had hung one of the boys with a jump rope. He showed the kindergartner one of the boys, who was lying on the floor pretending to be dead. The kindergartner became very upset and began crying. He later developed symptoms of anxiety and exhibited infantile behavior such as refusing to go to the bathroom alone and refusing to sleep in his own room. **The student's parents filed a lawsuit against the school board, which resulted in a judgment for the student and parents of over $117,000**, including loss of consortium damages of $5,000 for each parent. The school board appealed the damage award to the Court of Appeal of Louisiana, Fifth Circuit. On appeal, the school board argued that the damage award was excessive, that the award of loss of consortium damages was incorrect and that the parents had failed to mitigate their damages. **The court of appeal disagreed, finding no abuse of discretion by the trial court in awarding damages to the student and parents**. The court rejected the district's argument that the parents were overprotective and that they had made the injury worse by overreacting. The parents had made good faith efforts to seek professional counseling and abide by the recommendations of therapists. Accordingly, the court of appeal affirmed the district court's judgment. *Spears v. Jefferson Parish School Bd.*, 646 So.2d 1104 (La.App.5th Cir.1994).

C. Student Misconduct

1. Types of Misconduct

◆   **Two black brothers claimed in a lawsuit that they were disciplined for fighting back against white students who harassed them, and that the white students went unpunished**. One of the brothers said several students wore army fatigues, shaved their heads and pretended to be a militia group of "skin heads." These and other students repeatedly called the brothers racist names and used racial slurs. The brothers alleged they were forced to hide from the "skin heads" in the school library or classrooms. They stated that in some cases, the harassing students were not disciplined, and that in at least two cases, references to the use of racial epithets were omitted from disciplinary records. The brothers sued the school district and officials in a federal court for civil rights violations. The court considered summary judgment motions by the district and officials on the brothers' claims for equal protection and due process violations, retaliation, and emotional distress.

According to the court, the race discrimination claim relied on the assertion that the brothers were disciplined more harshly than white students for the same conduct. The court found evidence that racial comments by the harassing students were not officially recorded and sometimes went unpunished. Although only two of the eight incidents indicated disparate discipline, the court refused to dismiss the claim that racial harassment went virtually unreported and unpunished. The court found the school's failure to record the use of racial epithets as particularly telling evidence of an equal protection violation. Because the brothers presented evidence that school officials were deliberately indifferent to their reports of harassment, the court denied summary judgment to the school board. **The brothers demonstrated a clear and consistent pattern of abuse by other students, and a corresponding failure by school officials to discipline harassing students. According to the court, inaction by the officials created an atmosphere that allowed harassment.** Because the board had a custom and practice of failing to discipline racial harassment, liability could be imposed on it for racial harassment under the Equal Protection Clause of the Fourteenth Amendment. The court denied summary judgment to the principal and district superintendent, based on their acquiescence and failure to discipline reported harassment. The district and officials were, however, entitled to judgment on the claims by the brothers for violation of their due process rights and retaliation. Because a reasonable jury might find that it was outrageous to allow two children to undergo racial harassment while at school, the court retained the question for a jury to determine. The court found that any claim the brothers might have for punitive damages for violation of their federal civil rights was not barred by Ohio law. *Payne v. Worthington Schools*, No. C2-99-830, 2001 WL 506509 (S.D. Ohio 2001).

◆ **A Minnesota student alleged that he was tormented by classmates as early as kindergarten about his perceived sexual orientation and failure to meet masculine stereotypes.** Among the student's many allegations of abusive behavior was that students asked to see him naked and to participate in various sex acts with him. According to the student's complaint, the harassment deprived him of educational opportunities. The student claimed that over the years, no substantial discipline was ever applied to harassing students, discipline was inconsistent and unhelpful, and that his complaints often led to retaliatory conduct by his tormentors. It was only after the filing of a formal complaint that any student received more than a verbal reprimand. The student's parents filed an internal complaint and the district's human resources department investigated the charge. One of the harassing students was suspended for five days and another for one day. Although two students had their bus privileges revoked, they were reinstated after their father complained. The student's mother then filed a complaint against the district with the state department of human rights. During high school, the student transferred to another school system and then sued the district in a federal district court for violations of Title IX of the Education Amendments of 1972, the state human rights act and the U.S. Constitution.

The court noted that, unlike Title IX and other federal laws, the state human rights act prohibits discrimination and harassment on the basis of sexual orientation. The complaint stated facts that met statutory definitions of sexual harassment. State and federal courts have held that same-sex harassment may be grounds for a violation of anti-discrimination laws. It was not necessary for the student to allege that the harassment affected one gender differently than the other, or that the harasser was a homosexual. The harassing conduct came within statutory definitions even if it was motivated by the desire to humiliate the student as opposed to a true interest in sexual favors, and the district was denied summary judgment. The student's Constitutional rights violations claims under the Due Process and Equal Protection clauses also survived pre-trial dismissal. **The district could not articulate a legitimate reason for responding to harassment claims by boys differently than it responded to harassment claims by girls. The student made out a sufficient claim that the continuing harassment created an intimidating, hostile or offensive educational environment** that substantially interfered with his education. There was evidence that he had made hundreds of complaints to school officials, who did little more than administer ineffective verbal reprimands until the filing of a formal complaint. This raised the possibility that they were deliberately indifferent to his complaints, and the district was not entitled to summary judgment. The court held that actual knowledge of harassment by teachers could be sufficient to trigger school liability under Title IX. *Montgomery v. Independent School District No. 709*, 109 F.Supp.2d 1081 (D. Minn. 2000).

♦   **An Alabama student told the assistant principal of his school that he had twice been threatened by a classmate. The assistant principal responded by calling the classmate and another student to the office, where he warned them** that the punishment for fighting at school would be a two-day suspension. The classmate later assaulted and seriously injured the student. The student sued the school board and assistant principal in state court, asserting negligent supervision and a claim under 42 U.S.C. § 1983. A state trial court entered summary judgment for the board and assistant principal, and the student appealed to the Alabama Supreme Court on the sole issue of the assistant principal's entitlement to discretionary-function immunity.

On appeal, the student argued that the assistant principal was required by state law to notify law enforcement officers of the threats and to suspend the classmate when he learned of them. Under this rationale, the defense of discretionary-function immunity was unavailable, since the reporting was a ministerial function that required reporting without the exercise of discretion. The state supreme court disagreed, holding that the assistant principal's actions were not guided by any education board policy, but by his many years of experience and training. He was performing a discretionary function when evaluating the student's report and had exercised his judgment during the incident. **The mandatory reporting requirement called for the exercise of personal judgment in determining whether a rules violation had occurred** in the first instance. No evidence indicated that the assistant principal violated board policy or acted in bad faith, and the trial court had correctly entered summary judgment for him. *Carroll v. Hammett*, 744 So.2d 906 (Ala. 1999).

♦   Two Kansas students arranged to meet after school to fight. After school, they fought in a rural area. One of the students had an extensive disciplinary record that did not involve fighting. He caused serious injury to the other student, who filed a state court lawsuit against the student and his parents as well as the school district, alleging negligent supervision. The court granted the district's summary judgment motion, and the victim appealed to the Supreme Court of Kansas. He argued that certain school district officials had knowledge of the other student's disruptive nature but failed to take action to protect him. He asserted that a special relationship existed between himself and the district giving rise to a duty to protect him from harm and claimed that his injury was foreseeable. The supreme court observed that **the students had taken great care to avoid any detection by school authorities when they planned the off-campus fight. The school district owed the student no legal duty to prevent an off-campus injury,** even though the fight had been arranged at school. The district had no special relationship that created a duty to protect students from unknown off-campus fights and the injuries were not foreseeable. The district was not required to expel or otherwise discipline the other student and had the discretion to refrain from doing so. The court affirmed the summary judgment order for the district. *Beshears v. Unified School Dist. No. 305,* 930 P.2d 1376 (Kan. 1997).

◆   **Three Tennessee high school students alleged that their school board and several school employees were responsible and liable for sexual assaults they suffered in the office of a high school coach** during a two-year period. The coach had installed his own locks on the office, one of which locked the office from the inside. The students claimed that this violated school policy, and that a further violation was created by the failure of the school to maintain a duplicate key for the office in the school vault. The students filed a lawsuit against the school board and various school officials in a state trial court for negligent hiring, negligent supervision, failure to report the assaults and false imprisonment. The court granted judgment to the school board and employees, and the students appealed to the Court of Appeals of Tennessee, Western Section. **The court agreed with the trial court findings that the alleged negligence by the school board and its employees was not a substantial factor in the reported assaults**. The failure to keep a duplicate key did not cause the students' injuries, and the students failed to prove that a school policy forbade locking the coach's door from the inside. Since the actions of the school board were not a substantial factor in bringing about the injuries, the trial court decision was affirmed. *Doe A v. Coffey County Bd. of Educ.,* 925 S.W.2d 534 (Tenn. App. 1996).

◆   **Two Indiana high school girls enrolled in a lifeguarding class conducted by the Red Cross. The pool used for the class was loaned by a public high school,** but the school district had no other involvement and students earned no course credit. A group of high school boys planted a video camera in the locker room and obtained a tape of the girls dressing and undressing. The school principal learned about the taping and expelled one of the boys from school. The two girls sued the school district, Red Cross and a teacher in an Indiana trial court for negligence. The court granted summary judgment against the girls and they appealed to the Indiana Court of Appeals, Second District. **The court of appeals held that the school district was under no legal duty to protect students enrolled in the lifeguarding class. There could be no liability and the videotaping had been entirely unforeseeable**. The lifeguarding class took place after school hours and there was no merit to the girls' argument that the school district had assumed a duty to protect them by periodically checking the locker room as part of its normal maintenance routine. The court of appeals affirmed the award of summary judgment. *Roe v. North Adams Community School Corp.,* 647 N.E.2d 655 (Ind. App. 2d Dist. 1995).

◆   California high school students published a multiple-choice test as a humorous feature in the entertainment section of their high school newspaper. The test was readily identifiable as a parody including questions concerning Michael Jackson's sexual preference, condom use by students and other school and media issues. One of the questions concerned "the new narc" at the school, and the answers included possible choices that he had committed murder and sold drugs. An African-American school security officer was shown the question and believed it referred to him. Although he obtained a written apology, which was read over the school's public address system, **the officer submitted his resignation and filed a lawsuit against the school district in a California trial court for invasion of privacy, emotional distress and libel**. The court rejected the invasion of privacy and emotional distress claims as cumulative and then granted the district's summary judgment motion concerning libel. The officer appealed to the California Court of Appeal, Third District. On appeal, he argued that the trial court had erroneously refused to consider evidence that the local media had republished parts of the high school publication and that the wider, adult audience could not have reasonably construed the item as a parody. The court disagreed, finding that **the multiple-choice test was easily recognizable as a parody and not defamatory** as a matter of law. **The trial court had properly disallowed the invasion of privacy and emotional distress claims as cumulative and had properly granted summary judgment on the libel claim**. *Couch v. San Juan Unified School Dist.*, 39 Cal.Rptr.2d 848 (Cal.App.3d Dist.1995).

2. Governmental Immunity

◆   The Appeals Court of Massachusetts reversed a trial court order in favor of the city of Boston in a case involving the knifing death of a student at school. The trial court had awarded summary judgment to the city on the basis of public employer immunity, but in support of its summary judgment motion, the city had presented the court with little more than a copy of a school disciplinary code condemning weapons possession on school grounds. **The appeals court commented that a pre-trial judgment for the city would have required evidence that its actions involved the weighing of alternatives and the making of choices with respect to public policy and planning**. It should have presented evidence concerning its consideration of the perpetrating student's placement (given his history of weapons possession), school safety measures and other actions which demonstrated that it had been engaged in discretionary functions. *Allen v. City of Boston*, 44 Mass.App.Ct. 679, 693 N.E.2d 699 (1998).

◆   Two Texas high school students became involved in a confrontation that had to be broken up by a school security guard. One of the students threatened to kill the other, and a student allegedly told a teacher that the threatening student had a knife in her purse. The threatening student used the knife later in the day to fatally stab the other student. The deceased student's estate filed a lawsuit against the school district in a Texas district court for wrongful death and civil rights violations. The court granted summary judgment to the school district, and the estate appealed to the Court of Appeals of Texas, Corpus Christi. **The court rejected the estate's argument that the district could be held liable for negligently failing to discipline the** threatening student. **Texas law shields school officials from negligence actions with a narrow exception that applies only to cases of excessive discipline.** Because this exception was not implicated, the negligence claims failed. The court also dismissed the civil rights claims since they depended upon the finding of a special relationship between the student and the school district that did not exist. *Johnson v. Calhoun County Indep. School Dist.*, 943 S.W.2d 496 (Tex.App.—Corpus Christi 1997).

♦　An Oklahoma high school student was hit in the face by another student while he was standing in a school activity room. **The incident occurred during a lunch break in an area that was unsupervised** by any school employee. The student brought an action against the school district in an Oklahoma district court for negligent supervision. After the court granted the district's summary judgment motion, the student appealed to the Supreme Court of Oklahoma. The court observed that the Oklahoma Governmental Tort Claims Act adopted the doctrine of sovereign immunity and waived immunity only as expressly stated by law. Immunity protects school entities from liability when their employees are performing discretionary functions. This includes injuries resulting from the performance of a discretionary act or the failure to exercise discretion by a school official in policymaking and planning decisions, but not where the negligent performance of school policies is alleged. In this case, **the school had properly exercised its discretionary functions in deciding what type of supervision was required during a school lunch period.** Accordingly, the court affirmed the district court judgment for the school district. *Franks v. Union City Pub. Schools*, 1997 OK 105, 943 P.2d 611 (Okla.1997).

♦　A Texas first grader was hit or pushed down by another student during recess. When he informed his teacher, he was told to hold a wet paper towel against his cheek. The teacher did not take him to the school nurse. When the student later complained of pain in his arm, another teacher also decided not to take him to the school nurse. The next day, **the student's parents took him to a doctor who diagnosed him with a fractured collarbone.** The parents filed a lawsuit against the teachers and school principal for negligence in denying him access to the school nurse and failing to take disciplinary action against the other student. The employees claimed immunity under the Texas Education Code and a Texas trial court granted their summary judgment motion. On appeal, the Texas Court of Appeals, Corpus Christi, observed that **each of the elements for immunity had been satisfied in this case, since the named employees were acting in the scope of their employment and were involved in the exercise of discretion. They were not involved in disciplining the student by use of excessive force or negligence—the only exception to immunity** under the Texas School Code. The court affirmed summary judgment for the officials. *Davis v. Gonzales*, 931 S.W.2d 15 (Tex.App.—Corpus Christi 1996).

♦　**A Utah student pushed another student into a window in a middle school lavatory, causing nerve and tendon damage when the victim's hand was forced through the glass.** The student was charged with assault and a juvenile court ordered him to pay a fine and restitution. However, the victim filed a lawsuit against the school district in a Utah trial court, asserting negligence for failure to install safety glass in the school lavatory or to take some other safety measure to prevent injury. The district moved for summary judgment on the basis of government immunity. The court held that the district was immune from liability because the injuries arose out of an assault and because the decision not to place safety glass in the lavatory was protected by discretionary immunity. The student appealed to the Supreme Court of Utah, where he asserted that immunity was waived because the assault was not caused by a government employee. The court disagreed, ruling that immunity must be broadly construed. **Because there was a causal link between the assault and the injury, the school district was entitled to immunity** and the court did not have to consider the discretionary immunity argument. *Taylor v. Ogden City School Dist.*, 927 P.2d 159 (Utah 1996).

D. Parent Misconduct

✦   A student's parent was accused of yelling at two teachers when he came to school to ask why his son was not enrolled in computer classes. The school principal wrote him a letter responding to his questions, directing him to control his anger, refrain from yelling at her staff and to sign in at the school office when he visited campus. The parent responded with a threatening letter to the principal. Later in the school year, the parent came to school and became angry when he learned that a class in which he was attempting to enroll his son was unavailable. According to the principal, he shouted that he was going to leave his son at school all day, then left the premises saying he would return in five minutes "with witnesses." The principal called 911 as a precaution, but the parent did not return to the school. **The school district petitioned a Minnesota court for an anti-harassment restraining order**. The court issued a temporary order and held a hearing for a permanent order. After a hearing, the court found that the parent's letter and yelling incidents constituted harassment. It issued a permanent restraining order against the parent, and he appealed to the Minnesota Court of Appeals.

The court of appeals applied an abuse of discretion standard to the trial court findings. Under that standard, only findings that are clearly erroneous may be set aside, and due regard is given to the trial court's opportunity to judge the credibility of witnesses. There was sufficient evidence to support a finding of harassment under the harassment restraining order statute. The statutory term "harassment" included a single incident of physical or sexual assault, or repeated incidents of intrusive or unwanted acts, words or gestures that had a substantial adverse effect on the safety, security or privacy of another. It was unnecessary to show that the harassing conduct is obscene or vulgar. **The record showed that the parent had yelled at staff members and wrote a threatening letter to the principal. Based on this evidence, the trial court did not abuse its discretion in permanently restraining him from harassing school staff**. The court rejected the parent's arguments concerning a number of other claimed errors by the trial court, and affirmed the trial court judgment. *Independent School District No. 381 v. Olson*, No. C9-00-888, 2001 WL 32807 (Minn. App. 2001).

✦   The non-custodial parent of a high school student complained repeatedly to school employees that his son was not selected for the varsity basketball team. The student's mother had previously requested notice from the school so that she could be present for discussions involving her children. The school principal notified the father that such meetings had to be scheduled in advance to accommodate the mother's request, and that he should otherwise limit his presence on school property to public events. The father asserted that the limitations regarding his attendance at meetings violated his constitutional rights, and that school officials were misusing public funds by paying the litigation costs of board members and school officials. He contacted district personnel about official "corruption." Shortly thereafter, **the school superintendent sent the father a letter barring him from school property due to what he described as a continuing pattern of inappropriate behavior toward school officials, staff, and board members.** The father claimed that school officials conspired with local law enforcement officers. After his next series of demands went unfulfilled, he filed a federal district court action for constitutional rights violations. He included a claim against the superintendent for monetary damages under 42 U.S.C. § 1983. A federal district court denied the father's request for preliminary relief, and dismissed the case.

The father appealed to the U.S. Court of Appeals, Fourth Circuit, which held that "school officials have the authority and responsibility for assuring that parents and third parties conduct themselves appropriately while on school property." While the specific contours of this authority and responsibility were defined by state law, "officials should never be intimidated into compromising the safety of those who utilize school property." In this case, the school district gave the father ample opportunity to complain about the conduct of school board members and officials before the superintendent sent the notice. **The superintendent concluded that the father's conduct was a threat and appropriately requested that he not enter school property**, according to the court. The right to communicate is not limitless and the letter banning the father from school property did not implicate the father's constitutional rights. The court characterized the father's claims against the superintendent for money damages as frivolous. *Lovern v. Edwards*, 190 F.3d 648 (4th Cir. 1999).

♦   A Florida statute makes school teachers and school officials mandatory reporters of child abuse or neglect. A Florida student was subjected to repeated abuse by his stepmother. His teacher reported a series of incidents to the school principal, which led to an investigation by a state agency. The investigation concluded that the abuse reports were unfounded. **The abuse continued, and the student's teacher continued to report her observations to school personnel; however, no further reports were made** to the state agency. The stepmother then broke the student's femur, permanently injuring him. Child abuse charges were renewed, resulting in a change of custody to the student's mother. She sued the school board in a Florida trial court, stating that the child abuse statute created a private cause of action for abuse victims. The trial court granted the school board summary judgment, and the student's mother appealed to the District Court of Appeal of Florida, Fifth District. The court of appeal affirmed the trial court's summary judgment for the school board. **Although the statute made the knowing and wilful failure to report child abuse a second degree misdemeanor, there was no authority to indicate that the reporting statute created a private cause of action** for personal injury damages. *Freehauf v. School Bd. of Seminole County*, 623 So.2d 761 (Fla.App.5th Dist.1993).

◆   When an 11-year-old Tennessee student complained of illness, the school was unable to reach her parents. A co-worker of the father asked the girl's uncle to take the child home. The uncle went to the school and obtained her custody by signing a sign-out sheet in the school office. He then took her to a secluded place and brutally raped her. The parents sued the uncle, school board and school officials in a Tennessee trial court, which dismissed the claims brought against the school officials and board. The Court of Appeals of Tennessee affirmed the dismissal as to the school board and officials. **There was no merit to the parents' argument that they had specifically instructed the school not to release the child into anyone else's custody, and the school officials had no notice that the uncle presented a threat to children**. Because the injury was entirely unforeseeable to school officials, they had not breached their duty to exercise ordinary care for the child's safety. *Snider v. Snider*, 855 S.W.2d 588 (Tenn.App.1993).

◆   A referee officiated several matches during a wrestling tournament held at a New York county high school. After watching a match that his son lost, **a spectator physically assaulted the referee**. The referee sued the board of education, the school district, the high school's principal and athletic director, and the spectator. The board of education and the district brought a motion for summary judgment dismissing them. The trial court held for the referee, and the district and school board appealed to the New York Supreme Court, Appellate Division. The appellate court stated that public entities in New York are immune from tort claims arising out of the performance of their governmental functions, including the provision of security against physical attack, unless the injured party establishes a special relationship with the entity. **Although the public high school athletic association handbook delineated several preparations and guidelines made in order to improve safety and control of students and spectators, the handbook did not support a finding that the referee was to be treated any differently from students, or members of the general public**. *Perry v. Bd. of Educ.*, 592 N.Y.S.2d 493 (A.D.3d Dep't 1993).

E. Unknown Assailant

◆   **A 14-year-old Florida high school student was shot and killed by nonstu-dent assailants who were attempting to rob him while he awaited a ride in his school parking lot**. The student had attended a school-sponsored function, was denied a request to telephone his father from the school administrative office and told to use a pay phone outside. The student's estate filed a lawsuit against the school board and school officials claiming that its policies had deprived the student of certain constitutional rights. A federal district court granted the board's dismissal motion. The estate appealed to the U.S. Court of Appeals, Eleventh Circuit, which recited the general rule that a government entity has no duty to protect individuals from the criminal acts of third parties. The court therefore rejected the estate's assertion that the school had violated a constitutional duty owed to the student. It also rejected the estate's claim that the board was under a duty to protect the student from a danger created by the district. **There was no merit to the assertion that the school's policy of disallowing student use of the administrative office for emergency telephone calls placed the student in an inherently dangerous**

situation, and there was no evidence that the parking lot area was a dangerous location. There were other places for students to wait for rides, including inside the building. The court affirmed the dismissal of the lawsuit. *Mitchell v. Duval County School Bd.*, 107 F.3d 837 (11th Cir.1997).

◆   **The New York Supreme Court, Appellate Division, reversed a jury award of $350,000 in favor of a student who was stabbed in his classroom by nonstudent intruders**. The incident arose in a special education classroom in which a mathematics teacher was preparing for class. A student seated in the classroom was approached by three teenagers, who were not recognized as students at the school. The intruders disregarded the teacher's request to identify themselves and quickly stabbed the student. The teacher left the classroom briefly to obtain help after the stabbing. The student filed a personal injury action against the school board in a New York trial court, and it awarded judgment to him on the basis of past pain and suffering. On appeal, **the appellate division court found no reasonable basis for concluding that the teacher had acted inappropriately or that the school's safety guidelines were a cause of the attack**. *Transon v. Bd. of Educ. of City of New York*, 659 N.Y.S.2d 102 (A.D.2d Dep't 1997).

◆   A Huntsville, Ala., middle school was the site of 42 police reports, 19 of which involved assaults on school employees. An instructor was assaulted on school grounds by four students and a nonstudent. He filed a lawsuit against the school board and its individual members, alleging that the incidents gave the board sufficient notice that teachers could come to harm, and that the board's safety policy created an enforceable contract under which the board had assumed a duty to protect faculty members. An Alabama trial court granted the board's summary judgment motion on the grounds that the state teacher tenure act barred any contractual claim. On appeal to the Supreme Court of Alabama, the court ruled that the tenure act did not bar a contractual claim that was unrelated to the employment contract between a teacher and school board. However, **the trial court had correctly granted summary judgment to the school board, because the board's safety policy did not constitute a contract, and because there was no tort liability against the board**. Despite the widespread violence at the middle school, the board was not liable for the teacher's personal injuries. *Steiger v. Huntsville City Bd. of Educ.*, 653 So.2d 975 (Ala.1995).

◆   A Louisiana high school security employee observed a small group of youths near a student's car. **The employee told the student that his alarm had sounded twice, and when the student observed the youths near his car, he asked the employee to accompany him**. The employee responded that she was not responsible for providing security beyond school grounds. The student went to his car alone and was shot twice by one of the youths. He filed a lawsuit in a Louisiana trial court against the school board, security company and employee claiming negligence. The court found the assailant 80 percent liable and the school board 20 percent liable for the damage award of over $15,000. The school board appealed to the Louisiana Court of Appeal, Fourth Circuit.

On appeal, the school board argued that the incident had been unforeseeable and that the trial court had improperly failed to apportion part of the liability to the student. The court applied ordinary negligence principles in analyzing the case, and found that **the school board had assumed a duty to protect students from third party criminal actions by hiring the security employee. The school board's affirmative duty to protect its students extended to adjacent areas**. The school security employee had been aware of the presence of the assailant prior to the incident and the trial court had not committed error by finding the board partly responsible for the student's injury due to her inaction. However, the trial court had erroneously failed to assign any liability to the student. The court found him five percent negligent for not simply waiting for the youths to leave the area. Accordingly, it reduced the damage award and affirmed the trial court judgment as amended. *Peterson v. Doe*, 647 So.2d 1288 (La.App.4th Cir.1994).

VI. SCHOOL BUS ACCIDENTS

Courts have often found school bus operators negligent and their employers liable for injuries received by passengers when the injuries are the result of a failure by the operator to follow generally accepted standards of good judgment in the operation of the vehicle.

A. Duty of Care

◆   A Georgia statute requires school boards to purchase accident and collision insurance to cover liability for bodily injury to students riding school buses. **A student** who **was attacked and cut with a knife by another student during a bus ride home** sued her school district, principal and bus driver in the U.S. District Court for the Middle District of Georgia, alleging negligence and constitutional rights violations. She later amended her claim to include the school district's insurer. The district, principal and driver moved for summary judgment, which the court granted. After the insurer's motion was unsuccessful, it appealed to the U.S. Court of Appeals, Eleventh Circuit. The court certified a question to the Supreme Court of Georgia to determine whether the Georgia statute requiring school boards to purchase school bus insurance for student riders allowed a direct cause of action against school bus insurers where one student is injured by another student on a school bus.

   The court held that the board was not required by the statute to insure against the risk of harm to students from an attack by another student. There was no causal connection between the student's injuries and the use of a school bus. The court rejected the student's alternate argument that she was an intended beneficiary of the insurance policy. Because the district was not obligated by state law to maintain insurance for student attacks on school buses, the court answered the certified question in the negative. *Payne v. Twiggs County School Dist.*, 496 S.E.2d 690 (Ga.1998).

◆   Two New York school boards contracted with private transportation companies to provide public school bus service. **Both of the companies were accused of negligence when one student in each district was injured**. In the first case, a student disembarked from the bus and was run over when she attempted to pass in front of it. In the other case, the student was injured when she crossed the street to reach an undesignated bus stop because she had missed the bus at her designated stop.

The school district in that case had provided for stops on both sides of the highway, but the contractor tolerated the practice of crossing the street to catch the bus at undesignated stops. A New York trial court found the school district in the first case liable for the driver and transportation company's actions, but the New York Supreme Court, Appellate Division, reversed the judgment. In the second case, the appellate division affirmed a summary judgment order for the school district. The families of both students appealed to the New York Court of Appeals.

The families argued that the school boards in both cases were responsible for the injuries because the students were in school district custody at the time of injury. **The court determined that the school boards had contracted out their transportation responsibilities to the private carriers and could not be held vicariously liable.** State traffic laws did not impose an affirmative obligation on school districts to protect students, but rather imposed this duty on school bus drivers. There was no evidence in the second case that the school board had any knowledge of the contractor's policy of picking up students at undesignated stops. The decisions imposing potential liability only on the drivers and transportation companies had been correct, and the appellate division court decisions were affirmed. *Chainani v. Bd. of Educ. of City of New York*, 87 N.Y.2d 370, 639 N.Y.S.2d 971, 663 N.E.2d 283 (1995).

◆   A Texas sixth grade teacher was also employed as a bus driver by the county transportation department. **The department was a separate agency from the teacher's employing school district, and served 12 other school districts in the county**. The teacher's bus struck a car, causing a pregnant passenger to go into premature labor. She gave birth to a child with multiple injuries. The couple claimed that the teacher caused the accident by failing to obey a stop sign and filed a lawsuit against her, the school district and the county transportation department. After the teacher and transportation department reached a settlement with the couple, the district obtained a summary judgment order from a Texas trial court which determined that the district was not the teacher's employer at the time of the accident. The Court of Appeals of Texas, Texarkana, remanded the case, finding that it was possible for an employee to be under the control of two employers at the same time and instructing the trial court to determine whether the teacher was under the district's control at the time of the accident.

The court conducted a trial as ordered by the court of appeals, and **a jury determined that the teacher was not acting as a school district employee at the time of the accident**. The couple appealed again to the court of appeals, arguing that the court had given the jury inappropriate instructions. The court found that two of the contested jury instructions were taken verbatim from Texas law and were not erroneous. Another instruction concerning dual employment was a misstatement of law but was not reversible error as it could not have created prejudice. The court also rejected the couple's argument that there was insufficient evidence to support the judgment. There was evidence that the teacher was under the control of the transportation department and not the school district at the time of the accident. *White v. Liberty Eylau Indep. School Dist.*, 920 S.W.2d 809 (Tex. App.–Texarkana 1996).

◆   A 15-year-old New York student usually rode a school bus, but decided to ride home with a friend one day. After leaving school grounds, the friend's car was involved in an accident, causing the student severe injuries. The student's parents filed a lawsuit against the school district and driver. A New York trial court granted summary judgment to the school district, and the family appealed to the New York Supreme Court, Appellate Division, Third Department. The court stated that in general, a school district has no duty to compel students to ride a school bus home. However, the student's parents alleged that they had specifically advised a school district employee to ensure that the student took the bus home at the end of each day. This allegation, if proven, would create a special duty to the student that was distinguishable from that typically owed to students. **Because the parents had presented evidence that the school district had assumed a special duty beyond the general duty to protect students, the court modified the trial court judgment**. *Wenger v. Goodell*, 632 N.Y.S.2d 865 (A.D.3d Dep't 1995).

◆   An Ohio student with a heart condition known as Q.T. syndrome collapsed on her school bus while being driven home. The driver was unable to contact the garage because of a radio malfunction. She believed that the student was having a seizure that did not require medical attention. **She continued the bus route and by the time the bus reached the student's home, the student had stopped breathing**. She fell into a coma and died three days later. The student's estate filed a lawsuit against the school board and some of its employees in the U.S. District Court for the Northern District of Ohio asserting violations of the U.S. Constitution and Ohio law. The court granted summary judgment to the school district and employees, and the estate appealed to the U.S. Court of Appeals, Sixth Circuit. The court observed that in order to find a government entity liable for constitutional violations under 42 U.S.C. § 1983 the complaining party must have a special relationship with the government entity. To date, courts have found a special relationship only where the government entity deprives the complaining party of freedom. **Because compulsory attendance laws did not create a special relationship, the district had no constitutional duty to protect the student from the consequences of a seizure while on the school bus**. The court also affirmed the district court's dismissal of the state law claims. *Sargi v. Kent City Bd. of Educ.*, 70 F.3d 907 (6th Cir.1995).

B. Governmental Immunity

◆   After an accident between a school bus and a car, the driver of the car commenced a personal injury suit against the board and school bus driver based on the bus driver's negligence in a Virginia trial court. The driver moved for judgment against the bus driver and the board, and they asserted the defense of sovereign immunity. **The court granted their request and dismissed the driver's motion for judgment, ruling that the bus driver was entitled to sovereign immunity** for simple negligence and the board's liability was entirely dependent upon and derived from the bus driver's negligence. Because the driver did not allege gross negligence against the bus driver and the board, the court held that the board was entitled to judgment.

The driver appealed to the state supreme court, which observed that state law abrogated the immunity of a school board for acts of simple negligence to a limited degree. When the conditions of the statute are met, sovereign immunity will not bar an action for recovery in an amount up to the limits of a board's insurance policy. The court held that the common-law principle of coterminous liability among principles and agents was inapplicable when altered by statute. In this case, the legislature had subjected school boards to limited liability under Section 22.1-194 of the Virginia Code for injuries caused by the acts of employees and did not require that boards and employees be jointly sued. The legislature had created an exception to the common law and imposed liability on school boards for simple negligence, even where their employees were liable only for gross negligence. The court reversed the trial court judgment dismissing the driver's motion for judgment against the board. Section 22.1-194 included language preserving the immunity of governmental employees for acts of simple negligence. The limited abrogation of immunity, which allowed the driver to pursue his claims against the board, did not preclude the bus driver's immunity. The court held that the transportation of students on school buses constituted a governmental function over which the government exercised significant control. **The transportation of students involved discretion and judgment by bus drivers, and the court rejected the driver's argument that the bus driver was not entitled to immunity.** *Linhart v. Lawson*, 540 S.E.2d 875 (Va. 2001).

◆   **A student was permanently injured when the bus she was riding in collided with an automobile and another school bus.** She sued each of the drivers and her school board in an Alabama trial court for personal injury. The court granted a dismissal motion filed by the board and employees, and the student appealed to the state civil court of appeals, where she noted that the Alabama Supreme Court had recently redefined its test for determining whether a state agent acting in his or her individual capacity is immune from civil liability. The court agreed the state's high court had rejected the traditional test based on whether the agent was performing a discretionary function or a ministerial task. The state supreme court found it more relevant to determine whether the agent is involved in the formulation or application of governmental policy. Under this approach, a state agent is immune from civil liability in his or her personal capacity when the conduct upon which the claim is based involves formulating plans, policies or designs or the exercise of judgment in the administration of a government department or agency that makes administrative adjudications, allocates resources, negotiates contracts or makes hiring, firing or similar personnel decisions. An agent may also qualify for immunity when discharging duties imposed on a department or agency in the manner prescribed by a statute, rule or regulation and when carrying out certain law enforcement, criminal detention, counseling and education duties. **The drivers were not entitled to immunity because they did not apply judgment or discretion to formulate or apply governmental policy.** The state supreme court reversed and remanded the case. *Horton v. Briley et al.*, No. 2991218, 2001 WL 29327 (Ala. Civ. App. 2001).

◆   A Georgia school district permitted its bus drivers to drop students off at unapproved bus stops where requested by parents. **A five-year-old kindergartner was struck and killed by a van shortly after being dropped off at an unapproved stop on a heavily-traveled highway with no sidewalk.** His parents sued the school district in a Georgia trial court for wrongful death, seeking the $1 million policy limit under the district's comprehensive liability insurance policy. The court held that because the incident had occurred after the student exited the school bus, the injury was not excluded from coverage under the board's comprehensive liability policy because it did not arise from the use of a school bus under the district's liability policy. Because sovereign immunity was waived to the extent of insurance coverage, the parents were entitled to receive the policy limit. Coverage did not exist under the board's motor vehicle policy. The school district appealed to the Court of Appeals of Georgia, which dismissed the case, finding that any causal connection or relationship between the death and the use of a school bus arose out of the use of the bus, defeating the parents' claim that sovereign immunity had been waived. The parents appealed to the Supreme Court of Georgia, which determined that the analysis used by the court of appeals strained the meaning of "use" of the school bus as contemplated by the policy and improperly disturbed the trial court findings. **Because the trial court had correctly determined that the death could not have arisen from the use of the bus within the meaning of the liability policy, the court reversed and remanded the case.** *Roberts v. Burke County School Dist.*, 482 S.E.2d 283 (Ga.1997).

◆   An Arizona elementary school bus route included a stop on a heavily traveled road where traffic typically moved at speeds over 45 miles per hour. **A student was seriously injured when he was hit by a car after disembarking at the stop.** He filed a lawsuit against the school district in an Arizona trial court, which held that the district was entitled to absolute immunity, and granted its summary judgment motion. The student appealed to the Court of Appeals of Arizona, Division One, which commented that the Arizona legislature has restricted the application of sovereign immunity to cases involving the exercise of fundamental governmental policy decisions, including budget and personnel decisions. In this case, **bus stop placement was the responsibility of the district transportation supervisor and reflected the district's day-to-day operations. Because the placement decision was an operational function that did not involve a fundamental governmental policy, the district was not entitled to absolute immunity.** The court distinguished Arizona law from the majority of states in which immunity remains the rule except where specifically abrogated. The case was reversed and remanded for further proceedings to determine whether the district had been negligent. *Warrington v. Tempe Elementary School Dist. No. 3*, 928 P.2d 673 (Ariz.App.Div.1 1996).

◆   A Michigan kindergartner was dropped off at the wrong bus stop on the first day of school and was severely injured in a traffic accident a few minutes later. The district's general liability insurer denied coverage under the policy's motor vehicle use exclusion, and the district's automobile carrier denied coverage under the argument that the accident had not occurred through the use of a school bus. **The Supreme Court of Michigan agreed with the liability carrier that the dropping off of a student at the wrong stop arose out of the use of the school bus and was reasonably foreseeable. Therefore, the automobile carrier was required to provide coverage.** *Pacific Employers Ins. Co. v. Michigan Mut. Ins. Co.*, 549 N.W.2d 872 (Mich.1996).

VII. WORKERS' COMPENSATION

Employees of school districts are covered by workers' compensation benefits when their injuries result from accidents in the course of employment. Workers' compensation cases are delegated to individual state workers' compensation courts or appeal boards, subject to judicial review.

◆   After being diagnosed with tonsil cancer, a teacher underwent surgery that included the partial removal of his jaw and mouth, which were later reconstructed. He utilized his available sick time and submitted a workers' compensation claim that was denied by his employing school board, which asserted that the cancer was not work related. The teacher claimed his cancer was work related because he shared an office for 26 years with a chain smoking co-worker. The teacher appealed to the state department of labor, which held a hearing before a workers' compensation judge. The judge agreed with the teacher's witness, who testified that secondhand smoke contains the same toxins as inhaled cigarette smoke, but at greater levels. The teacher's small office was poorly ventilated and no other known cancer cause was identified. **The judge found that the teacher's cancer probably arose out of and in the course of employment and was peculiar to his place of employment**, and awarded benefits, along with other relief.

The board appealed to the Superior Court of New Jersey, Appellate Division, denying a causal relationship between the teacher's cancer and his employment. The court held that the teacher had met the state workers' compensation act requirement for claimants to demonstrate the link between employment and disease by a material degree. The smoke exposure had been constant, consistent and pervasive. **While there was no definitive data on the subject of secondary smoke and head and neck cancer, the teacher's expert had presented testimony that was not "a subjective guess or a mere possibility."** The court affirmed the compensation judge's finding of a nexus between the teacher's disease and his place of employment. However, state law vested the commissioner of education with the authority to determine the proper interpretation of teacher sick leave law. The compensation judge had exceeded his powers by ordering the board to reinstate the teacher's sick time, and that part of the decision was reversed and vacated for consideration by the school board. *Magaw v. Middletown Bd. of Educ.*, 323 N.J. Super. 1, 731 A.2d 1196 (1999).

◆   A Hawaii teacher was accused of violating school rules which prohibited the use of rewards to motivate students. The school principal met with her to warn against rewarding students and the teacher claimed that she began suffering from flu-like symptoms as the result of stress. She continued to reward students with free time, treats and video game use. **Three months after being called into the principal's office, the teacher was accused of striking a student**. The Hawaii Department of Education prohibits the use of corporal punishment by teachers upon students. The principal recommended a five-day suspension for violating the prohibition and the teacher's stress-related symptoms increased. She stopped going to work and filed a claim for workers' compensation benefits arising from the initial meeting with the principal and from the suspension recommendation. The state labor and industrial relations department found the injuries to be outside the scope of employment and denied benefits. An appellate board agreed with the teacher that the stress-related symptoms from the meeting with the principal were compensable, but that the claimed stress-related injury on her final day of work was not compensable.

Following a number of subsequent appeals and partial settlement agreements by the parties, appeal reached the Supreme Court of Hawaii on the issue of the injury arising from the suspension. **The supreme court found that while the discipline imposed on the teacher had arisen from her own misconduct, she had sustained a compensable injury because she was acting within the course of her employment at the time of the misconduct.** Unlike several other states including New York, Alaska, Maine and Montana, Hawaii's workers' compensation law contains no exclusion for mental injuries resulting from disciplinary action. The court vacated the board's decision denying benefits. *Mitchell v. State of Hawaii, Dep't of Educ.*, 942 P.2d 514 (Haw. 1997).

◆   A Kansas employee worked for a school district for 25 years as a bus driver and supply clerk. She was treated for intermittent medical problems but did not miss significant time from work until she injured her back while moving a file cabinet. She applied for and received an award of workers' compensation benefits. **Because the district was unable to accommodate her work restrictions as a supply clerk, she opted for early retirement,** in the process rejecting alternate work as a study hall monitor or assistant for students with disabilities. Her workers' compensation benefits were initially reduced by the amount of her early retirement benefits funded by the school district, but this reduction was later overturned by the state Workers' Compensation Board. The board also found that the district failed to show that the employee was handicapped within the meaning of state law so as to avoid liability and assess the award against the state workers' compensation fund.

The parties appealed to the Court of Appeals of Kansas, which held that **the employee was not precluded from receiving permanent partial disability compensation benefits because the district had never offered her a comparable job.** The award was reasonable, and there was no error in the finding that she was not handicapped for purposes of assessing liability against the fund since the district had failed to notify the workers' compensation director that it knew of a handicap. The court rejected the employee's claim that the setoff of her award violated the Constitution since the statutory setoff provision was consistent with the primary purpose of compensating injured workers for wage losses. The board had properly excluded vacation and sick leave in computing the employee's average weekly wage, and the court affirmed its order. *Bohanan v. USD No. 260*, 947 P.2d 440 (Kan.App.1997).

◆   A Maryland speech pathologist worked part-time for a county school board for 20 years. She divided her time between two schools and designed her own schedule. The school board reimbursed her for her mileage between schools, but not between her home and the base school. **She was killed in a traffic accident on the way to work one morning, and her estate filed a claim on her behalf with the state Workers' Compensation Commission.** The commission held that the pathologist had been injured in an accident that arose out of and in the course of her employment, and awarded the estate partial dependent benefits. A Maryland county court reversed the commission's decision, and the Court of Appeals of Maryland agreed to review the case. It stated that a work-related injury must both arise out of and in the course of employment to be compensable. **Injuries suffered in transit are typically not compensable because transportation is the employee's responsibility and**

does not further the interest of the employer. The speech pathologist's estate argued that the board's failure to provide transportation to its speech pathologists while assigning them to more than one location implicitly required them to furnish their own vehicles, which excused the application of the in transit rule. The court disagreed, finding that the pathologist was not required to furnish her own vehicle as a condition to employment. The board did not control her transportation decisions and driving a car was not an integral feature of fulfilling her job duties. The court affirmed the county court's judgment. *Morris v. Bd. of Educ. of Prince George's County*, 339 Md. 374, 663 A.2d 578 (1995).

◆   A Missouri teacher claimed that he was unable to return to his classroom after experiencing hyperventilation that a psychiatrist later linked to panic disorder and a passive-dependent personality structure. **The teacher never returned to work and filed a claim for workers' compensation, alleging that he became disabled by a job-related injury**. The state industrial relations commission denied his claim for benefits and he appealed to the Missouri Court of Appeals, Southern District. The court considered testimony produced at the commission hearing indicating that the teacher had a depressive illness and a generalized anxiety disorder. The parties presented conflicting evidence from psychiatrists that the teacher's work environment had affected his mental condition. The teacher argued that his claim was similar to that of a worker with a degenerative back condition that is exacerbated by physical exertion. **The court disagreed with this analysis, stating that the teacher had failed to prove a causal connection between his mental disorder and alleged harassment by his supervisor**. The court affirmed the denial of benefits. *Duncan v. Springfield R-12 School Dist.*, 897 S.W.2d 108 (Mo.App.S.D.1995).

CHAPTER TWO

Freedom of Religion

I. ESTABLISHMENT OF RELIGION IN PUBLIC SCHOOLS

The Establishment Clause of the First Amendment to the U.S. Constitution prohibits Congress from making any law respecting the establishment of a religion. Because public schools and administrators are subject to this mandate by operation of the Fourteenth Amendment, the courts have struck down state and local education practices that improperly entangle public school employees and administrators with religion. The U.S. Supreme Court has set forth different tests over the years which lend some guidance to school administrators seeking to avoid Establishment Clause violations. In Engel v. Vitale, *370 U.S. 421, 82 S.Ct. 1261, 8 L.Ed.2d 601 (1962), and* Abington School District v. Schempp, *374 U.S. 203, 83 S.Ct. 1560, 10 L.Ed.2d 844 (1963), below, the Court first held that public school students could not be coerced to pray at the instruction of their teachers.*

A. Religious Activities

1. Prayers and Bible Readings

◆   **A New York board of education directed a principal to have a prayer read aloud by each class in the presence of a teacher at the beginning of the school day**. This procedure was adopted on the recommendation of the state board of regents. State officials had composed the prayer and published it as part of their "Statement on Moral and Spiritual Training in the Schools." The parents of ten students sued the board in a New York state court, insisting that use of this official prayer in public schools violated the Establishment Clause of the First Amendment. The New York Court of Appeals upheld the use of the prayer as long as the schools did not compel any pupil to join in the prayer over the parents' objections. On appeal, the U.S. Supreme Court held that the practice was wholly inconsistent with the Establishment Clause. **The Court stated that there could be no doubt that the classroom invocation was a religious activity**. Neither the fact that the prayer was denominationally neutral nor that its observance was voluntary served to free it from the limitations of the Establishment Clause. *Engel v. Vitale*, 370 U.S. 421, 82 S.Ct. 1261, 8 L.Ed.2d 601 (1962).

◆   Following the decision in *Engel v. Vitale*, the Supreme Court struck down two Pennsylvania laws which required scripture reading and prayer at the opening of the school day. In doing so, it formulated the "primary purpose and effects" test, which would later become the first two prongs of the *Lemon* test. **Pennsylvania law required that "[a]t least ten verses from the Holy Bible shall be read, without comment, at the opening of each public school on each school day. Any child shall be excused from such Bible reading, or attending such Bible reading, upon written request** of his parents or guardian." A family sued school officials to enjoin enforcement of the laws as violative of the First Amendment. A three-judge district court panel held that the statutes violated the Establishment Clause and granted injunctive relief. **The school commissioner of Baltimore** had also **adopted a rule which mandated at the opening of the school day a chapter of the Bible or the Lord's Prayer be read without comment**. The rule was challenged in the Maryland state court system which eventually reached the conclusion that the rule did not violate the First Amendment.

On appeal, the Supreme Court consolidated the cases and held that both rules violated the Establishment Clause. The Court reiterated the premise of *Engel v. Vitale*, above, that **neither the state nor the federal government can constitutionally force a person to profess a belief or disbelief in any religion. Nor can it pass laws which aid all religions as against nonbelievers**. The Court stated that the primary purpose of the statutes and rule was religious. The Court also noted that it was intended by school officials to be a religious ceremony. The compulsory nature of the ceremonies was not mitigated by the fact that students could absent themselves. *Abington School District v. Schempp*, 374 U.S. 203, 83 S.Ct. 1560, 10 L.Ed.2d 844 (1963).

◆   The U.S. Supreme Court invalidated an Alabama statute allowing meditation or voluntary prayer in public school classrooms. The case was initiated in 1982 by the father of three grade school children who filed a lawsuit in a U.S. district court challenging the validity of two Alabama statutes: a 1981 statute that allowed a period of silence for "meditation or voluntary prayer"; and a 1982 statute authorizing teachers to lead "willing students" in a nonsectarian prayer composed by the state legislature. **The district court declared that the First Amendment to the U.S. Constitution did not prohibit the state of Alabama from establishing a state religion**. The father appealed to the U.S. Court of Appeals, Fifth Circuit, which reversed the district court's ruling and held that both statutes were unconstitutional. The state of Alabama then appealed to the U.S. Supreme Court, which agreed to review only that portion of the court of appeals' decision which invalidated the 1981 statute allowing "meditation or voluntary prayer." The Supreme Court reviewed the legislative history of the 1981 statute and concluded that the intent of the Alabama legislature was to affirmatively re-establish prayer in the public schools. **The inclusion of the words "or voluntary prayer" in the statute indicated that it had been enacted to convey state approval of a religious activity and violated the first prong of the *Lemon* test and the First Amendment Establishment Clause**. *Wallace v. Jaffree*, 472 U.S. 38, 105 S.Ct. 2479, 96 L.Ed.2d 29 (1985).

◆   Two students who attended schools within the Santa Fe Independent School District filed an Establishment Clause challenge against the district aimed at a number of district practices, including the district's policy regarding **overtly Christian prayers at graduation ceremonies and football games**. The district also permitted nondenominational prayers at graduation ceremonies, read by students selected by vote of the graduating class without review or approval. In response to the complaint, the district revised its policies for prayer at school functions, subjecting pregame invocations to the same controls applying to graduation prayers, requiring that they be "nonsectarian" and "nonproselytizing." Shortly thereafter, the district enacted new policies deleting the nonsectarian, nonproselytizing requirements for pregame invocations and graduation prayers. A federal district court issued an order precluding enforcement of the open-ended policy under *Lee v. Weisman*, 505 U.S. 577 (1992), finding that the graduation prayers and pregame invocations coerced student participation in religious events. The parties appealed to the U.S. Court of Appeals for the Fifth Circuit, which upheld the validity of the district policy allowing nonsectarian and nonproselytizing high school graduation prayers. **The circuit court further held that the district could not extend the graduation policy to athletic events** and reversed that part of the district court's decision. The school district appealed to the U.S. Supreme Court, which agreed to decide whether the policy of allowing student-led and initiated prayers at school football games violated the Establishment Clause.

The Supreme Court rejected arguments by the school district that the student invocations could be characterized as private speech that was not subject to scrutiny under a public forum analysis. Although the district asserted that students determined the content of the pregame message without review by school officials and with approval by the student body, the Court found that school officials regulated the forum. The majoritarian process for selecting speakers guaranteed that minority candidates would never prevail and that their views would be effectively silenced.

Fundamental rights such as freedom of religion cannot be subjected to a vote, and the voting mechanism encouraged divisiveness along religious lines. **The degree of school involvement in the pregame prayers created the perception and actual endorsement of religion by school officials**, according to the Court. The Court examined the context of student pregame messages delivered over a public address system under control of school officials during a ceremony featuring school colors and insignia, and held that an objective viewer would find that it was delivered with the approval of school administrators. The text of the policy and the history of school prayer in the district also supported the view that the policy encouraged religion. There was no requirement that students forfeit their constitutional rights as the price for objecting. Finding that the district policy had an unquestionable purpose that created the perception of official encouragement of religion, the Supreme Court affirmed the Fifth Circuit decision. *Santa Fe Independent School District v. Doe*, 530 U.S. 290, 120 S.Ct. 2266, 147 L.Ed.2d 295 (2000).

◆   A 1993 Alabama law permitted non-sectarian, non-proselytizing student-initiated voluntary prayers, invocations and benedictions during school-related events, assemblies, sporting events and graduation ceremonies. A county school administrator and his son asserted that the law violated their constitutional rights and sued state and local officials in a federal district court for declaratory and injunctive relief. The district court held the law unconstitutional, ordered local school officials to refrain from assisting students in religious activity, and appointed a monitor to ensure that schools obeyed its order. State and local officials appealed to the U.S. Court of Appeals, Eleventh Circuit, asserting that the First Amendment prohibition on the official establishment of religion is inapplicable to the states. The circuit court summarily rejected the appeal by state officials concerning the constitutionality of the law, and considered the appeal by DeKalb County officials regarding the part of the order prohibiting them from allowing student-led prayers and appointing a monitor. It rejected arguments that students acted on behalf of the school when saying prayers in school settings and that student-led prayers created peer pressure that unconstitutionally coerced others. The circuit court held that **student-initiated religious speech must be permitted, subject to the same reasonable time, place and manner restrictions that apply to all student speech in schools**. *Chandler v. James,* 180 F.3d 1254 (11th Cir. 1999).

The complaining parties then appealed to the U.S. Supreme Court, which remanded the case to the Eleventh Circuit for reconsideration in light of *Santa Fe, above*. **The Eleventh Circuit again held that the district court opinion was overbroad, requiring school officials to censor all student public religious expression**. After discussing the *Santa Fe* decision, the circuit court noted that the district court had "assumed that virtually any religious speech in schools is attributable to the State," and had enjoined the school district from permitting any prayer in a public context at any school function. According to the circuit court, the Constitution does not require or permit all religious speech by students in public places while at school. The court distinguished the facts of the case from those of *Santa Fe* and found that entanglement with the state, not the public context of school speech, created the constitutional violation in *Santa Fe*. Nothing prevented public school students from voluntarily praying at any time before, during or after the school day, including prayers said "aloud or in front of others, as in the case of an audience assembled for some other purpose." **So long as the student prayer was genuinely student-initiated and not the product of a school policy, the speech was protected**. The circuit court reaffirmed its prior opinion, and again reversed and remanded the district court judgment on the grounds that it was overbroad because it equated all student religious speech in any public context at school with state speech. *Chandler v. Siegelman*, 230 F.3d 1313 (11th Cir. 2000).

◆   **A Louisiana law formerly permitted school authorities to allow a brief** silent **prayer or meditation period at the start of each school day**. However, the legislature amended the law in 1999 by deleting the word "silent." Parties objecting to the amendment sued the Ouachita Parish School Board in a federal district court, seeking a declaration that the amended law violated the Establishment Clause. The court considered the objectors' summary judgment motion and examined the law under the three-part test from *Lemon v. Kurtzman*, 403 U.S. 602 (1971), which evaluates whether a statute has a secular purpose, has the primary effect of neither advancing nor inhibiting religion, and does not excessively entangle government with religion.

The court found the case strikingly similar to *Wallace v. Jaffree*, above, in which the Supreme Court found that an Alabama law was changed for the sole purpose of expressing the state's endorsement of prayer at the start of the school day. Similarly, the Louisiana legislature had enacted the amendment to endorse or promote school prayer and had violated the first part of the *Lemon* test. Language disavowing any religious purpose did not save it from violating the secular purpose part of the test. The law also had the primary effect of advancing religion by allowing verbal prayer that encouraged the observance of a religious ritual in classrooms. Since school attendance is compulsory and prayers were to take place on school property, school officials and employees would necessarily become involved in implementing the law, causing excessive entanglement with religion in violation of the third *Lemon* factor. The law created a level of coercion by forcing students to attend school, then forcing them to listen to prayers in violation of the test described in *Lee v. Weisman*, 505 U.S. 577 (1992). School supervision and control of classes placed public and peer pressure on students to stand or at least remain silent during prayers. Finally, the court held that the law violated the endorsement test found in *County of Allegheny v. ACLU*, 492 U.S. 573 (1989), because **the law could not help but create the appearance that the state of Louisiana endorsed religion by creating a venue for public prayer in public facilities under the supervision of public school teachers and officials**. The court found that the law violated each of the relevant tests and granted summary judgment to the complaining parties. *Doe v. Ouachita Parish School Board*, No. 99-2203 (W.D. La. 2000).

◆   A student who attended two school board meetings and one teacher who was frequently in attendance at meetings objected to **the board's practice of having prayers said at board meetings**. They commenced a federal district court action against the board for Establishment Clause violations. **The court upheld the practice, finding that the meetings resembled legislative sessions, rather than school events, and that they were attended primarily by adults**. The student and teacher appealed to the Sixth Circuit.

The circuit court emphasized that the board meetings occurred on school property, were regularly attended by students and did not resemble legislative sessions. **Board meetings had a function that was uniquely directed toward school business and students actively participated in them**, often as a matter of necessity. The court held that the prayers violated the Establishment Clause under a line of Supreme Court cases on the subject of government sponsoring of religion in school settings. It held that **a prayer said at a school board meeting was potentially coercive to students in attendance, and might be more coercive than a graduation prayer**. The court reversed and remanded the case, finding questions about the true motivation behind the practice, and holding that the prayers tended to endorse Christianity while excessively entangling the board in religious matters. *Coles v. Cleveland Bd. of Educ.*, 171 F.3d 369 (6th Cir.1999).

◆   The District of Columbia Board of Elections and Ethics accepted a proposed prayer initiative as the proper subject of a voter-initiated measure. **The initiative allowed for nonsectarian, nonproselytizing, student-initiated voluntary prayer, invocations or benedictions during compulsory or noncompulsory, school-related student assemblies, sporting events, graduation ceremonies and other school events**. The initiative contained two sections disclaiming approval by the District of Columbia or its political subdivisions of the content of any prayer and reciting that student rights were not diminished in any way. A group opposed to the initiative sued the board in a District of Columbia superior court, which granted summary judgment in the group's favor. After the board failed to appeal, a group supporting voluntary prayer intervened and appealed to the District of Columbia Court of Appeals.

The court stated that while the constitutionality of a voter initiative is generally improper for courts to consider prior to a vote, an exception exists in extreme cases where the initiative is patently unconstitutional. **The court found that the initiative had the clear purpose of encouraging prayer in public schools. It would place public school teachers and principals in the position of endorsing student prayer and would violate the principles of neutrality contained in the Establishment Clause** of the U.S. Constitution. The saying of nonsectarian, nonproselytizing, student-initiated voluntary prayer at graduation ceremonies and other school functions carried the particular risk of indirect coercion of students not sharing the religious beliefs of those initiating the prayers. The court affirmed the judgment, finding that the initiative violated the Establishment Clause. *Committee for Voluntary Prayer v. Wimberley*, 704 A.2d 1199 (D.C.1997).

◆   **The Georgia Moment of Quiet Reflection in Schools Act requires each public school teacher to conduct a period of quiet reflection for not more than 60 seconds at the opening of each school day**. The statute recites that the moment of quiet reflection is not intended to be a religious service or exercise, but is considered an opportunity for silent reflection on the anticipated activities of the day. Another section of the act states that it shall not prevent student-initiated, voluntary school prayers of a nonsectarian, nonproselytizing nature. A Georgia high school teacher refused to comply with the moment of quiet reflection law. He was instructed to comply with the statute, but instead left the school and was subsequently fired. He then filed a lawsuit against the district and state officials in a federal district court, asserting that the statute violated the Establishment Clause of the First Amendment. The court upheld the statute, and the teacher appealed to the U.S. Court of Appeals, Eleventh Circuit.

The court observed that the statute sanctioned only a moment of quiet reflection, not silent prayers. **The legislation had a secular purpose—to provide an opportunity for students to reflect on the day's anticipated activities. The act also expressly disclaimed any religious purpose and did not affirmatively authorize any religious activity.** The act did not have the primary effect of advancing or inhibiting religion since objecting students were not forced to pray or listen to others pray. The case did not involve impermissible government coercion of religious activity and did not excessively entangle school employees with religion. The court affirmed the judgment for the school district and officials. *Bown v. Gwinnett County School Dist.*, 112 F.3d 1464 (11th Cir.1997).

◆   **A high school principal allowed students to read a prayer over the school's intercom system at the beginning of the school day** for three consecutive days, after which he was disciplined for demonstrating a lack of professional judgment. Following the public outcry resulting from the suspension and threatened termination of the principal, the Mississippi legislature passed a statute allowing student-led prayer in schools. **The statute permitted "nonproselytizing student-initiated voluntary prayer" at all assemblies, sporting events, commencement ceremonies and other school-related events.** The American Civil Liberties Union joined students and parents opposed to school prayer in a lawsuit seeking an order to prevent enforcement of the statute. The U.S. District Court for the District of Mississippi considered the ACLU's motion for a preliminary injunction and a motion to dismiss the lawsuit by the state attorney general.

The court allowed the injunction, and the attorney general appealed to the U.S. Court of Appeals, Fifth Circuit, which observed that the statute required school officials to determine which prayers were allowable under the statute and to make other decisions that entangled the state with religion. The statute allowed school officials to lead students in prayer and to punish students who left classes or assemblies to avoid praying. **The statute had no secular purpose, advanced religion through school employees, coerced students into prayer participation and unconstitutionally endorsed religion.** There was no merit to the argument that the requested injunction would have a chilling effect on school prayer. Students continued to have a right to pray in a silent, nondisruptive manner in the absence of the statute. The court affirmed the district court injunction. *Ingebretsen v. Jackson Pub. School Dist.*, 88 F.3d 274 (5th Cir.1996).

2. Religious Choral Music

◆   A Utah high school sophomore was chosen for her school choir. The choir's director selected religious songs for the choir and scheduled performances at religious sites. **The student claimed that the director ostracized her for dissenting from the religious content of the choir's music, and she further claimed that he scheduled two Christian devotional songs for the school's graduation ceremony.** Although the director offered to exempt her from singing religious songs without penalty, she filed a federal district court action against the school district and officials including the director in which she asserted constitutional rights violations. The court denied her request for a temporary restraining order and preliminary injunction prohibiting the performance of the religious songs at the graduation ceremony. The U.S. Court of Appeals, Tenth Circuit, consolidated the student's appeal with another appeal of an order dismissing her complaint and denying her further motions.

The court of appeals observed that the student had transferred to a private school and had now graduated, rendering her appeals on the injunctive relief issues moot. The Establishment Clause complaint required the court to view the school district's actions according to an objective standard, and not the student's subjective feelings. **It accepted the district's reasons for performing religious music at religious sites, observing that a substantial amount of choral music is religious in nature and that many religious sites had superior facilities. The district's actions therefore had a secular purpose**. The student's other claims did not rise to the level of constitutional violations. The court affirmed the district court orders but remanded certain state law issues. *Bauchman v. West High School*, 132 F.3d 542 (10th Cir. 1997).

◆   A Texas student who played on her school basketball team disagreed with the team's policy of praying before and after games, at practices and at pep rallies with encouragement from school employees. When her father complained about the prayers to the assistant school superintendent, the practice of praying at pep rallies was discontinued, but no action was taken to stop post-game prayers. **The student also participated in the school's choir, which sang religious songs, including a theme song based on Christian text**. The student filed a lawsuit against the district in the U.S. District Court for the Northern District of Texas, seeking an order to enjoin school-sponsored religious practices. The court agreed with the student and issued an order in her favor. On appeal to the U.S. Court of Appeals, Fifth Circuit, the district argued that it could not prohibit its employees from participating in student prayers without violating their free speech and free exercise of religion rights. The court disagreed, noting that employee free expression rights were subordinate to the Establishment Clause prohibition on school-endorsed religious activities. The district court had appropriately prohibited school employees from participating in or supervising student prayers. However, it had improperly ordered the school district to discontinue its use of religious songs by the school choir. **Evidence indicated that most choral music is based on sacred themes and that forbidding religious songs would disqualify appropriate choral music. The use of religious songs did not constitute endorsement of religion** and the court reversed that portion of the district court judgment. *Doe v. Duncanville Indep. School Dist.*, 70 F.3d 402 (5th Cir. 1995).

B. Instruction of Students

1. Curriculum

◆   In 1981, the Louisiana legislature passed an Act called "Balanced Treatment for Creation-Science and Evolution-Science in Public School Instruction." **The Act provided that any school offering instruction in evolution must provide equal**

time to instruction in creation science. The Act required that curriculum guides be developed and research services supplied for creation science but not for evolution. The stated purpose of the Act was to protect academic freedom. A group of parents, teachers, and religious leaders challenged the law's constitutionality. After a U.S. district court and the U.S. Court of Appeals, Fifth Circuit, both held that the Act was an unconstitutional establishment of religion, Louisiana state officials appealed. The U.S. Supreme Court addressed the issue of whether the Creationism Act was enacted for a clear secular purpose. It noted that **because the Act provided for sanctions against teachers who chose not to teach creation science it did not promote its avowed purpose of furthering academic freedom**. The Court ruled that "[b]ecause the primary purpose of the Creationism Act is to advance a particular religious belief, the Act endorses religion in violation of the First Amendment." The Creationism Act was therefore declared unconstitutional. *Edwards v. Aguillard*, 482 U.S. 578, 107 S.Ct. 2573, 96 L.Ed.2d 510 (1987).

◆   A teacher worked for a Minnesota school district for 13 years as a high school science and math teacher before being assigned to teach a 10th grade biology class, including the subject of evolution. The curriculum was governed by a "Biology Program Curriculum Proposal" and course syllabus. When the teacher arrived at the course's evolution component, he spent only one day on the topic, and told the science department co-chair that he could not teach in accordance with the curriculum. The co-chair complained to the principal, prompting a meeting at which the teacher stated that he did not regard evolution as a viable scientific concept. School administrators met to discuss the teacher's instruction methods and the principal asked him to write a "position paper" on how he proposed to teach evolution. **The principal reassigned the teacher to a ninth grade natural science class the following year, based on concerns that he would dilute the theory of evolution in his present assignment**. The district superintendent reaffirmed the decision, stating that the teacher's insistence on teaching the inconsistencies of evolution was not an appropriate method of teaching the approved curriculum. The teacher sued the district, principal, superintendent, and curriculum director in a state trial court for violation of his religious free exercise, free speech and due process rights. The court awarded summary judgment to the district and officials, and the teacher appealed.

The Court of Appeals of Minnesota observed that the teacher had based his lawsuit on First Amendment protections, and not on laws prohibiting religious discrimination. **He failed to explain how the reassignment equated to a violation of his right to freely exercise religion**. The district had an important pedagogical interest in establishing a curriculum and a legitimate concern for ensuring that its schools were religiously neutral. The teacher's position paper revealed that he did not find evolution theory credible and that his proposed manner of teaching it directly conflicted with curricular requirements. The district had well-founded concerns about his inability to teach the curriculum and there was no merit to his speech rights claims. The due process claim failed because a school board may regulate a teacher's classroom speech if teachers are provided specific notice of what conduct is prohibited. The teacher understood that the curriculum included the teaching of evolution, undercutting his assertion that he received insufficient notice about what could be taught in the class. His employment contract specified that he would faithfully perform the teaching prescribed by the school board. The teacher admitted that he told the science co-chair that he could not teach evolution, and his position paper emphasized his belief that it was an incredible theory. Because he failed to show that his reassignment violated any constitutional rights, the court affirmed the judgment for the district and school officials. *LeVake v. Indep. School Dist. No. 656*, 625 N.W.2d 502 (Minn. Ct. App. 2001).

♦   **The families of several students who attended schools in a New York school district asserted that specific aspects of the district's curriculum were offensive to their Catholic beliefs.** The court rejected the families' claim that the disputed practices could be considered part of the district's general curriculum. Instead, each contested item was a separate controversy, to be evaluated under the relevant tests set forth by the U.S. Supreme Court in Establishment Clause cases. The court agreed with the parents that one teacher's assignment that students construct images of a Hindu deity, impermissibly endorsing the Hindu religion. An Earth Day celebration at one district school was held to violate the Establishment Clause, because a school employee instructed students to recite a liturgy in which the earth was worshipped, and one teacher made statements that were a clear attempt to teach an Earth-based religion. Schools were prohibited from requiring students to make likenesses of a god or any religious symbol. **The court directed the school district to adopt a published policy clearly instructing employees** to implement the standards set forth by the U.S. Supreme Court and **to remain neutral toward all religions. The district was required to neither sponsor nor disparage any religious belief, and forbidden from coercing any student to participate in religion.** Allowing students to participate in role-playing as a part of a DARE program presented by law officers did not violate any constitutional rights. The district did not violate the constitution by allowing a self-proclaimed psychic to visit one school, or by allowing peer facilitator and meditation programs. The court entered an order awarding partial relief to the parents.

The district and school officials appealed to the Second Circuit, where they argued that the district court no longer had jurisdiction over the case, as two of the families had moved out of the district and the child of the third had advanced to high school and was no longer being exposed to the challenged practices The appeals court agreed, noting that under the mootness doctrine of constitutional law, an actual controversy must exist at all times during a dispute, not simply at the time an action is initiated. Because there was no longer a live controversy among the parties, the district court should have dismissed the claims involving the families who were now nonresidents. The appeals court rejected the argument that the family that remained in the district was still entitled to sue the district based on their status as taxpayers. The Second Circuit disagreed with the district court's ruling that a high school Earth Day celebration violated the Constitution. **The Establishment Clause does not prohibit schools from teaching about religion, but only prohibits the preference for a religious doctrine.** The district court did not find that the school district intended to establish a religion by sponsoring the Earth Day celebration, and there was no coercion of students to attend. **Earth Day attendance was not compulsory and while some aspects of it might be offensive to student religious beliefs, there was no interference with their rights.** The court reversed the district court judgment to the extent that it was not moot, observing that the injunction was impermissibly vague. It was so general as to provide no guidance to the district and it ran the risk of foreclosing activities without religious significance. *Altman et al. v. Bedford Central School District et al.*, 245 F.3d 49 (2d Cir. 2001).

♦   The Beaumont, Texas, school district solicited clergy volunteers to counsel groups of students on secular topics. The program's stated goals were to provide a dialogue between students and clergy concerning civic values and morality, as well as to encourage a safe school atmosphere and furnish volunteer opportunities. The program required participating clergy to wear non-clerical clothing, avoid mentioning their religious affiliation and avoid religious discussions, prayers or Biblical references. A parent objected to the program after learning that non-clerical counselors could not participate. **The district denied the parent's request to integrate secular professional counselors into the program, and she then sued the district**, asserting that the program violated the Establishment Clause and the Texas Constitution. The district court held that the parent and other parents and students who joined the action did not have standing to challenge the program and that it did not violate the Establishment Clause. The challengers appealed to the U.S. Court of Appeals, Fifth Circuit, where a three-judge panel reversed the district court's decision.

A sufficient number of Fifth Circuit judges voted to review the panel decision, and the full circuit court issued a new decision. The judges filed four separate opinions, including a plurality opinion reflecting the view of three of the 15 judges. The plurality opinion, which controlled the result of the case, held that the challengers had standing to bring the action. However, it refused to hold that the program violated the Establishment Clause without a trial, and allowed the case to return to district court. The plurality opinion found that while the challengers had standing to bring the action, their evidence of unconstitutionality was insufficient to earn summary judgment. It found that **the ultimate question of whether the district had preferred religion over non-religion required examination by the district court of all district volunteer programs**. The plurality found that **an interfaith group of clergy was not pervasively sectarian**, and presumed that the volunteers would comply with the program's secular guidelines. There was no violation of the test developed by courts to test for religious coercion under the Establishment Clause, as the presence of ministers did not coerce students in any way. The court chose to view "the District's entire menu of volunteer mentoring and counseling programs," and found that there were other opportunities for both religious and secular figures. The court held that because the district monitored all of its volunteer programs, it had no unique supervisory burdens under the clergy program sufficient to create a religious entanglement issue. *Doe v. Beaumont Independent School District*, 240 F.3d 462 (5th Cir. 2001).

♦   **A Louisiana school board adopted a resolution requiring** elementary and high school **teachers to read a** two-paragraph **disclaimer whenever the theory of evolution was to be presented** stating that presentation of the scientific theory of evolution was not intended to dissuade students from the Biblical version of creation. The resolution was passed even though Louisiana law requires public school curriculums to include the theory of evolution. A group of parents representing public school students residing in the district filed a federal district court action against the board and individual board members, challenging the constitutionality of the resolution and seeking injunctive and declaratory relief. **The court** examined minutes of the board meeting at which the resolution was adopted and **determined that the resolution had been passed for religious reasons**. The resolution failed to confer any new rights upon students to maintain dissenting views, since they already held the right to use and apply their own critical thinking skills. Teachers at district schools already had the right to discuss alternative theories. Because the disclaimer had no secular purpose, it violated the Establishment Clause of the Constitution. The court granted judgment to the parents and ordered the school board to refrain from implementing the resolution so that no teacher could read the disclaimer.

On appeal to the U.S Court of Appeals, Fifth Circuit, the court held that the disclaimer had the effect of advising students to disregard their school lessons in evolutionary theory in favor of knowledge that they may have already acquired from their parents or learned at their churches. In applying prevailing Establishment Clause law to the case, the court noted **the resolution did not further the articulated purpose of encouraging students to use critical thinking** because it advised students that the teaching of evolution was not intended to challenge or dissuade them from the Biblical version of creation "or any other concept." **The disclaimer also conveyed a message of government approval of religion**, as it urged students to think about a religious theory as an alternative to the state mandated curriculum. *Freiler v. Tangipahoa Parish Bd. of Educ.*, 185 F.3d 337 (5th Cir. 1999).

◆   Prior to developing courses in the Old and New Testaments of the Bible, a Florida school district held meetings and established a citizens advisory committee to discuss the proposed courses. It considered this input, and that of its attorneys, for over one year before including the classes in its curriculum. **A group of taxpayers and parents of students attending district schools filed a court challenge, seeking a preliminary order prohibiting the district from offering either class**.

A district court held that the Old Testament class had the secular purpose of teaching history, not religion. It stated that **the complaining parties had failed to meet the necessary standard of proof to receive the injunction barring the Old Testament class**. However, the New Testament offering contained some religious interpretations, such as the discussion of miracles, that had no secular purpose and threatened the constitutional rights of the complaining parties. Even the school district attorney had advised against the New Testament curriculum, and the court urged the complaining parties to bring further evidence to identify specific violations. **It declared the New Testament class offering in its present form unconstitutional, noting that a new curriculum was already being formulated**. *Gibson v. Lee County School Bd.*, 1 F.Supp.2d 1426 (M.D.Fla.1998).

◆   A New Jersey school board policy called for sensitivity to different religions in a manner consistent with the U.S. Constitution. The stated purpose of the policy was to teach about religion and its role in the social and historical development of civilization. **The policy called for the maintenance of calendars in classrooms and in one central location which displayed cultural, ethnic and religious** customs and traditions of various cultures for no more than 10 days "during the appropriate season." A group of parents and taxpayers filed a lawsuit against the school board in the U.S. District Court for the District of New Jersey, claiming violations of the First and Fourteenth Amendments to the U.S. Constitution. The parties filed cross-motions for summary judgment.

In considering the summary judgment motions, the court applied the three-part test of *Lemon v. Kurtzman*. It also considered factors such as the age of the children involved, the context in which the government practice appeared, the permanence of the display, whether the symbol was displayed actively or passively, whether the religious holiday has obtained a secular meaning, whether the government practice endorses a particular religion, and whether it is hostile toward religion. **The school board's policy passed the *Lemon* test because it had a genuine purpose that did not impermissibly promote religion and did not entangle the government in church-state relationships.** Because of the policy's emphasis on religious diversity, it could not be said to favor any particular religion or to favor religion over nonreligion. The use of religious symbols had a genuine secular purpose that emphasized both tolerance and diversity. The court granted the board's cross-motion for summary judgment. *Clever v. Cherry Hill Township Bd. of Educ.*, 838 F.Supp. 929 (D.N.J.1993).

◆ In 1987, the New York State Commissioner of Education promulgated regulations requiring all elementary and secondary schools to provide AIDS instruction to students. In public schools, advisory councils had to be established to make recommendations regarding the content, implementation and evaluation of the instruction. **The regulations mandated that representatives from religious organizations sit on the councils**. No other segment of the community at large was given this preference. The New York State Boards Association sued the education commissioner in a state court, claiming that the regulations violated the Establishment Clause. The trial court upheld the regulations and the state appellate division affirmed. The association appealed to the New York Court of Appeals. The court applied the three-part test of *Lemon v. Kurtzman*, and upheld the regulations. First, the court stated that **the regulations had the secular purpose of requiring broad community input into AIDS instruction**. Second, **the regulations did not impermissibly endorse religion** because the councils were merely advisory and would not be perceived as providing an endorsement of religious beliefs. Third, the regulations did not impermissibly entangle government with religion since government was not monitoring religious activity and religious institutions were not exercising discretionary governmental functions. *New York State School Bds. Ass'n v. Sobol*, 582 N.Y.S.2d 960 (N.Y.1992).

2. Content of Textbooks

◆ A California school district language arts task force searched for a new set of elementary school textbooks. It publicly displayed the six sets of books under consideration for over three months, published a notice in the local newspaper, addressed a school parents' association and held open houses to review textbooks. **The board obtained approval from the state board of education to purchase a set of textbooks. The selected textbook series was the unanimous choice of**

grade-level representatives. Halfway through the following school year, two sets of parents filed complaints resulting in the appointment of a review committee comprised of teachers and parents. When one parent was refused appointment to the committee, she filed a lawsuit against the school district in a California trial court, seeking an order that the school board actions had violated her constitutional rights and California state open meetings laws.

The California Court of Appeal, First District, affirmed the trial court's decision that the school board had not violated any constitutional rights of the parents. **Evidence indicated that the school board had provided parents with appropriate notice and time to evaluate the textbooks.** However, the school board had violated a state open meetings law by privately viewing a videotape on the subject of censorship entitled "Holy Wars in Education." The state law defined meetings broadly to include even informal gatherings that included a quorum of public officials. The court remanded a portion of the complaint for a determination of whether the board's violation of the open meetings act required reconsideration of the board's adoption of the textbook series. *Frazer v. Dixon Unified School Dist.*, 22 Cal.Rptr.2d 641 (Cal.App.1st Dist.1993).

◆   The U.S. Court of Appeals, Sixth Circuit, ruled that a group of fundamentalist Christian students in Tennessee had to participate in classroom use of the Holt, Rinehart and Winston basic reading series. **The court held that the Free Exercise Clause does not require public school textbooks to be free of conflict with student religious beliefs.** Although the Holt series exposed student readers to a multitude of competing ideas and philosophies, some of which were contrary to the students' religious beliefs, requiring the students to read the series did not place an unconstitutional burden on their free exercise of religion. The court of appeals ruled in favor of the school district. *Mozert v. Hawkins County Bd. of Educ.*, 827 F.2d 1058 (6th Cir.1987).

C.   Commencement Ceremonies

◆   **A student and her father filed suit in a Rhode Island federal court against their school district, seeking to prevent prayer at graduation ceremonies for city public schools.** A federal district court held that prayer at public school commencement ceremonies violated the Establishment Clause of the First Amendment. The defendants appealed to the U.S. Court of Appeals, First Circuit, which determined that prayers at a public school violated the Establishment Clause of the First Amendment, and it affirmed the district court's decision.

On appeal to the U.S. Supreme Court, **the Court held that including clergy members who offer prayers as part of an official public school graduation ceremony is forbidden by the First Amendment's Establishment Clause.** The government may not coerce anyone to support or participate in religion or its exercise, or otherwise act in any way which establishes a state religion or religious faith, or tends to do so. In this case, state officials directed the performance of a formal religious exercise. The principal decided that a prayer should be given, he selected the religious participant, and through a pamphlet which provided guidelines, directed and controlled the prayer's content. The school district's supervision and control of a high school graduation ceremony placed subtle and indirect public and peer pressure on attending students to stand as a group or maintain respectful silence during the invocation and benediction. The state may not force a student dissenter to participate or protest. The argument that the ceremony was voluntary was unpersuasive. The Court affirmed the lower court decision. *Lee v. Weisman*, 505 U.S. 577, 112 S.Ct. 2649, 120 L.Ed.2d 467 (1992).

◆   **A Florida school district permitted a brief opening and/or closing message by a student volunteer at graduation, if the graduating senior class voted for a message**. If the class chose to have a message, the policy mandated that "the content of that message shall be prepared by the student volunteer and shall not be monitored or otherwise reviewed by Duval County School Board, its officers or employees." After students at 10 of the district's 17 high schools voted for a graduation prayer, a group of objecting students sued the board and school officials. A federal district court upheld the policy and dismissed the case. On appeal, the U.S. Court of Appeals, 11th Circuit, held that the case was mooted by the graduation of the complaining students, but the action was renewed a year later by new student objectors. The district court again held for the school district and the 11th Circuit reversed, finding that the school system exerted overwhelming control over graduation ceremonies. Less than a month after invalidating the policy, the 11th Circuit vacated its decision and reheard the case. A three-judge panel held that the policy coerced students into participating in prayer. **A majority of the 11th Circuit judges** then vacated the panel decision and **held that the absence of state involvement in the decisions of having a graduation message, nominating the student speaker, and determining the content of the speech insulated the policy from any finding of facial unconstitutionality**. On appeal to the U.S. Supreme Court, the Court remanded the case to the 11th Circuit for further consideration in light of *Santa Fe Indep. School Dist. v. Doe, above.*

The Eleventh Circuit reviewed its pre-*Santa Fe* decision and reiterated its finding that **the policy explicitly divorced school officials from the graduation message decision-making process.** Control over this aspect of the graduation ceremony rested with students, and schools did not adopt or endorse private religious speech by failing to censor messages. The court refused to assume that Duval County seniors would interpret the failure to censor student messages as an endorsement of religion, rejecting the view that the state's role in providing the means for a student graduation message itself transformed student speech into state-sponsored speech. The court pointed to numerous factual distinctions between the Duval County case and the Texas school district policy at issue in *Santa Fe*. The Santa Fe Independent School District allowed students to read overtly religious prayers at graduation ceremonies and football games under a policy characterizing the speech as invocations and benedictions. The Duval County policy referred only to graduation "messages," and did not encourage prayers, affirmatively forbidding school officials from reviewing the contents of the messages. By contrast, the Santa Fe policy subjected student messages to regulation by the high school principal, and therefore, the state. The Duval County policy, unlike Santa Fe's, did not declare a purpose of "solemnizing the event," but instead declared a purpose of student autonomy to direct graduation messages. **The policy did not pre-ordain that a prayer would be delivered** as the Supreme Court had found in *Santa Fe*. The court reinstated its decision for the county. *Adler v. Duval County School Bd.*, 250 F.3d 1330 (11th Cir. 2001).

◆   After the U.S. Supreme Court's decision in *Lee v. Weisman*, 505 U.S. 577 (1992), an Illinois high school with an 80-year tradition of graduation prayers substituted student speakers for clergy members in an effort to avoid constitutional violations. Each year, **the superintendent asked senior class officers to determine a volunteer to give the invocation or benediction**. The school English department chair read the volunteer's planned presentation and reserved the authority to change inappropriate speech. Although the superintendent stated that class officers had the opportunity to reject a benediction or invocation, no class ever did so. As the 2001 commencement approached, the superintendent invited officers to make changes to the traditional format, and they voted in favor of an invocation or benediction. However, three officers objected to the planned graduation prayer and sued the school district in a federal district court.

The court held that forcing a school-sponsored graduation prayer upon an unwilling student constituted state sponsorship of religion. The Constitution prohibits the government from coercing anyone to support or participate in religious exercises. The *Lee* court found that state control of graduation ceremonies could be found in the form of subtle and indirect pressure to participate. Under *Santa Fe* and earlier Supreme Court cases, state action must have a secular purpose that neither advances nor inhibits religion and does not excessively entangle the government with religion. Even when students were allowed to select and deliver a message, the hand of the government was present when a government policy encouraged an inherently religious message, such as an invocation. The ceremony took place on school property and was a school-sponsored event. **The court characterized the student election process as "a circuit breaker" that unsuccessfully attempted to disentangle school officials from a student-led religious method**. As in *Santa Fe*, the student election system ensured that only messages deemed "appropriate" by the district would be delivered, silencing minority viewpoints and serving as a government endorsement of religion. This degree of school involvement prevented the finding that a student invocation was "private speech." The audience "would inevitably perceive the graduation prayer as stamped with the [school's] seal of approval," and the ability of school officials to exercise final authority amounted to an impermissible content restriction on speech. The court held that **the district policy encouraged students to deliver religious messages and placed religious minorities at the mercy of the officially approved majority**. The policy was unconstitutional and easily distinguished from the Florida policy upheld in *Adler, above*. The court granted the students' motion for a temporary restraining order. *Appenheimer v. School Bd. of Washington Community High School, Dist. 308*, No. 01-1226 (C.D. Ill. 2001).

◆   A California high school's annual graduation ceremony included a "spiritual invocation" delivered by a student chosen by student election, and graduation speeches by the valedictorian, salutatorian and others. The school principal reviewed all graduation speeches and invocations for content, including inspection for offensive or denominational content. Faculty advisors also had input, but the policy did not specify what content was prohibited. Two speakers scheduled to speak at the 1998 ceremony submitted drafts indicating that they would deliver proselytizing and sectarian messages. **When the students refused to delete the religious aspects from their speeches, they were prevented from delivering their**

unedited speeches at the ceremony, although they were allowed to attend. The court granted the school district's motion to dismiss the students' court action for injunctive relief, including the individual claims against school officials. The court dismissed the students' claims for monetary damages based on speech rights violations and held that the claims for monetary relief against the district and officials were barred by the Eleventh Amendment. It also held that the claims against the officials in their individual capacities were protected by qualified immunity. Over six months after they graduated, the students filed an amended complaint against the district and officials to include a new group of plaintiffs who were still enrolled in the school, including a student who planned to deliver a sectarian valedictory speech for the 1999 graduation ceremony. The court held that the current valedictorian had standing to pursue claims for injunctive relief against the district, but denied permission for the others to join the action. It again denied the request for an order prohibiting school officials from interfering with graduation speeches and granted summary judgment to the district and officials on all claims.

The students appealed to the U.S. Court of Appeals, Ninth Circuit, which held that the claims for injunctive relief were moot, since there was no longer a live controversy between the district defendants and the graduated students. The addition of students who currently attended the school did not create a live controversy. It was highly speculative that any of them would be chosen as valedictorian, salutatorian or a speaker nominated by classmates to deliver the invocation, and the district court properly dismissed the claims for injunctive relief. It correctly held that the school officials were entitled to qualified immunity from monetary damage claims. **The district's refusal to allow sectarian speeches and prayers was necessary to avoid an Establishment Clause violation under constitutional law principles. Compliance with the Establishment Clause is a compelling state interest that justified content-based speech restrictions**. Invocations and valedictory speeches were not private speech, as the students argued. The nomination of a student by classmates to give an invocation reflected an impermissible state purpose to encourage a religious message that was prohibited by the *Santa Fe* decision. The district's control over graduation ceremonies resulted in the creation of official approval of student valedictory speeches. If a student gave a sectarian or proselytizing message, it would constitute government-endorsed speech under both *Santa Fe* and *Lee* that would have sent the message to dissenting members of the audience that they were outsiders and not full members of the community. The sectarian, proselytizing speech proposed by the valedictorian of the 1998 class would have constituted district coercion of dissenting students and government sponsorship of a particular religious practice if the speech had been delivered. The court affirmed the district court judgment for the school district and officials. *Cole v. Oroville Union High School District*, 228 F.3d 1092 (9th Cir. 2000).

◆   **Under an Idaho school district policy, the four highest ranked students could individually determine the content of an address, poem, reading, song, prayer or presentation to deliver at graduation**. The policy forbade school administrators from censoring any presentation and from requiring the inclusion of any particular content. A student's family sued the school district, challenging the policy under the Establishment Clause. A district court granted summary judgment to the school district, and the family appealed.

The U.S. Court of Appeals, Ninth Circuit, upheld the policy under the coercion test of *Lee v. Weisman,* 505 U.S. 577 (1992), finding the students, not school officials, determined the content of their speech. The policy also passed the three part test established in *Lemon v. Kurtzman,* 403 U.S. 602 (1971). The students were selected by neutral and secular criteria, academic performance, and their speeches did not bear any official imprimatur. **The policy had the secular purpose of giving the district's top students an opportunity to deliver uncensored graduation speeches**. There was no requirement that speakers either say or refrain from saying a prayer. A policy that prohibited prayers was more likely to entangle the school district with religion. The district court decision was affirmed. *Doe v. Madison School Dist. No. 321,* 147 F.3d 832 (9th Cir. 1998).

Two days after the issuance of the Ninth Circuit decision, the objecting student graduated from high school. A Ninth Circuit judge sought to have the decision heard en banc and be vacated as moot. The court agreed. Taxpayers residing in the school district attempted to persuade the court that the case still presented a live controversy. The court rejected this suggestion, finding that the taxpayers lacked standing to pursue the case. The taxpayers failed to allege the school district policy involved the expenditure of public funds. **Since the student had graduated and was no longer threatened by the policy, the case was moot**. The district court decision was vacated. *Doe v. Madison School Dist. No. 321,* 177 F.3d 789 (9th Cir. 1999).

♦   A New Jersey school board traditionally allowed a nonsectarian invocation and benediction at high school graduation ceremonies. It allowed graduating seniors to select from three options including a prayer, a moment of reflection or no prayer. After the senior class voted for a prayer, a student requested that a member of the American Civil Liberties Union also be allowed to address the ceremony, but his request was denied. **The ACLU and the student filed a** lawsuit against the school board in the U.S. District Court for the District of New Jersey, **seeking an order that would prohibit any student-led prayer at graduation**. The court denied the request, and the ACLU obtained an emergency order from the U.S. Court of Appeals, Third Circuit. The school board's motion to vacate the order was denied, and the district court entered a permanent order prohibiting any school-sponsored graduation prayers. The board appealed to the court of appeals.

The court observed that high school graduation ceremonies are not public forums. **It rejected the school board's argument that because the students had voted for the graduation prayer, there was no state involvement**. The court stated that **the school board maintained control over the graduation ceremony and could not delegate this control to students**. Students were compelled to attend the ceremony in a practical sense, and because many students would have to listen to the prayer against their will, there was an element of official coercion which has been disapproved of by the U.S. Supreme Court. The permanent order prohibiting graduation prayers was affirmed. *American Civil Liberties Union of New Jersey v. Black Horse Pike Regional Bd. of Educ.,* 84 F.3d 1471 (3d Cir.1996).

♦   In a case involving graduation prayers at Indiana University, the U.S. Court of Appeals, Seventh Circuit, distinguished the ceremonies from public school ceremonies involving younger students. **There was no element of coercion** requiring students to participate in the large, impersonal university commencement exercises, and many students and family members remained in their seats during the prayer. **Adult students were unlikely to succumb to peer pressure and could choose not to attend the ceremony without suffering any severe consequences.** The court agreed with the university that the prayers solemnized the ceremony, did not endorse any particular religion and allowed the university to continue a 155-year-old tradition. *Tanford v. Brand*, 104 F.3d 982 (7th Cir.1997).

D. School Policies

◆   Maryland law establishes a public school holiday from the Friday before Easter through the Monday after Easter. **A Maryland teacher asserted that the statute violated both the Establishment and the Equal Protection Clauses of the U.S. Constitution because she was required to use personal leave or leave without pay to observe Jewish holidays.** She filed a federal district court action against state education officials, seeking a declaration that the school holiday was unconstitutional. The court considered the parties' cross-motions for summary judgment and observed that Easter is a highly secularized holiday. The statutory vacation period surrounds Easter and does not mention Good Friday. Further, the vacation day on the Monday after Easter has no religious significance. The school officials advanced a secular purpose for the statute since many students and teachers would be absent on the Friday and Monday surrounding Easter, which might disrupt effective instruction and cause monetary outlays for substitute teachers. Because secular effects predominated, and the statute did not create excessive state entanglement with religion, and because the law did not have a principal or primary effect of advancing or inhibiting religion, it did not violate the Establishment Clause. There was also no merit to the teacher's equal protection claim since individuals of all religions were granted a holiday on the specified days. The court granted the summary judgment motion of the school officials and denied the teacher's motion.

On appeal by the teacher, the Fourth Circuit initially stated that **the statute was not facially unconstitutional, as it provided an annual holiday to all students and teachers, regardless of religious affiliation**. The law passed the *Lemon* test, due to its legitimate secular purpose of economizing scarce educational resources that would otherwise be wasted on days when many students and teachers would be absent. The holiday did not advance or endorse Christianity over other religions. Entanglement between the state and religion also did not occur. The district court decision was upheld. *Koenick v. Felton,* 190 F.3d 259 (4th Cir. 1999).

◆   A Florida student's parent wrote a letter to the state department of health stating that she objected on religious grounds to the statutorily mandated immunization requirements for school children. **The department responded that the letter was legally insufficient to grant a religious exemption, effectively excluding the student from school**. The parent initiated a state trial court action against the department for a declaration and order entitling her daughter to an exemption. The court granted the relief requested and the department appealed to the District Court of Appeal of Florida, First District.

The court resolved the two implicated conflicting public policies, one protecting public health, the other guarding fundamental parental rights, in the favor of the parent. The legislature intended this result and had acted to protect public health by including an emergency provision in the law allowing the department to declare a communicable disease emergency and exclude non-immunized students in such cases. **The legislature could have required parents to attest to their religious beliefs, but had not done so**. The court also rejected the department's claim that the parent was required to exhaust her administrative remedies prior to filing legal action. Since the suit was based on a claim that the department had exceeded its statutory authority, the parent was relieved of this requirement. *Dep't of Health v. Curry*, 722 So.2d 874 (Fla.App.1st Dist.1998).

II. USE OF SCHOOL FACILITIES

School districts may allow the use of public facilities by religious groups. Over the years, state and federal courts have developed a substantial body of case law to help resolve the conflict that arises between the competing constitutional goals of free speech and government neutrality toward religion. A school district must allow the use of facilities on a religiously-neutral basis where an open forum exists as defined by the federal Equal Access Act (EAA), 20 U.S.C. §§ 4071-4074, which makes it unlawful for a public secondary school to deny equal access to facilities on grounds including religion. An open forum exists where student groups have been accorded the right to meet in noncurricular groups on school grounds during noninstructional time. A large body of case law also prohibits public schools from denying access to school facilities for students based upon the content of their speech. In Lamb's Chapel v. Center Moriches Union Free School Dist.*, 508 U.S. 384, 113 S.Ct. 2141, 124 L.Ed.2d 352 (1993), the U.S. Supreme Court reaffirmed a long-standing rule of the federal courts that school officials must refrain from appearing to endorse any particular religion.*

A. Student Groups

◆   A Nebraska high school student wanted permission to begin a Christian Club. The high school permitted its students to join, on a voluntary basis, a number of groups and clubs that met after school. The school required that each of these clubs have faculty sponsors. However, the student who wished to start the Christian Club did not have a faculty sponsor. **The principal and superintendent both denied the student's request because she did not have a sponsor and because they believed a religious club at the school would violate the Establishment Clause**. After the board of education affirmed their decision, the student sued the school board, the superintendent, and the principal in a federal district court. She alleged a violation of the Equal Access Act, which prohibits public secondary schools that receive federal funding and that maintain a "limited open forum" from denying equal access to students who wish to meet. The district court ruled in favor of the school, holding that the other clubs at the school related to the school's curriculum and thus, the school was not under the Equal Access Act because it did not have an open forum. The student appealed to the U.S. Court of Appeals, Eighth Circuit, which ruled in her favor. The school appealed to the U.S. Supreme Court, asserting that the Act violated the Establishment Clause.

The Supreme Court stated that the other clubs did not relate to any of the school's curriculum. Thus, **the school had to provide a limited open forum to all students wishing to participate in groups**. The Act provided that the school could limit activities that substantially interfered with the orderly conduct of the school. The Court also stated that **the Act did not violate the Establishment Clause because the Act had a secular purpose and because it limited the role of teachers working with religious clubs**. The Supreme Court affirmed the court of appeals' decision, holding that the school violated the Equal Access Act. *Bd. of Educ. of Westside Community School v. Mergens*, 496 U.S. 226, 110 S.Ct. 2356, 110 L.Ed.2d 191 (1990).

◆   Under a California school district's "closed forum" policy, on-campus facilities were only available to groups that were curriculum-related. The school board also adopted a policy incorporating community service as a component of the high school curriculum. Students could satisfy the requirement in a "qualified community service organization." A student requested official recognition of the Fellowship of Christian Athletes by the high school. The school principal denied the application, finding that school sponsorship of the FCA would violate the state and U.S. constitutions. The student sued the district in a California superior court, asserting that the application denial violated the federal Equal Access Act, arguing that the recognition of the Key Club and Girls League had created a "limited open forum" on the high school campus. The court awarded summary judgment to the district, accepting its argument that the campus remained a closed forum. It found that the Key Club and Girls League were curriculum-related because students could satisfy their community service graduation requirement through membership. According to the superior court, **the high school maintained a closed forum to which the EAA was inapplicable**. Moreover, **the Fellowship of Christian Athletes was not a student-initiated group, and its use of school facilities was unconstitutional**. The superior court also found that a district coach and teacher maintained authority over FCA officer selection, which created unconstitutional state sponsorship of religion.

The student appealed to the California Fourth District Court of Appeal, which explained that the EAA applies only where a school creates a limited open forum. In such cases, the EAA prohibits discrimination against students based on religious, political or philosophical speech. **Under the EAA, a school creates a limited open forum whenever it permits at least one "noncurriculum related" group to meet on school grounds during non-instructional times**. The act does not define "noncurriculum related," but the Supreme Court explained in *Mergens, above,* that the term is to be interpreted broadly. A curriculum-related student group is one having more than just an attenuated relationship to courses offered by the school. Any student group "that does not directly relate to the body of courses offered by the school" is a "noncurriculum related student group." In making the determination of curriculum relatedness, courts are to look at actual school practices rather than school policies. The court held that the school district did not establish that the Key Club and Girls League were curriculum-related by virtue of the community service graduation requirement. It held that community service clubs were "at best, only marginally related to the usual high school curriculum." Otherwise, the school could evade the EAA by simply making participation in selected groups a graduation prerequisite. The appeals court remanded the case to the superior court, since it had summarily found that the district had not created a limited open forum. The court would have to determine whether the Key Club and Girls League were curriculum-related in order to determine whether the EAA applied. *Van Schoick v. Saddleback Valley Unified School District*, 104 Cal.Rptr.2d 562 (Cal.App.4th Dist. 2001).

◆   Students at a New York high school applied for official recognition of their Christian club and permission to meet at school during noninstructional time. The school principal and district superintendent noted that school district policy prohibited discrimination on the basis of race, national origin, religion and other conditions. **The school board recognized the student club on condition that it remove an exclusionary policy limiting three club officer positions to professed Christians**. The students stated that this amounted to non-recognition, and they filed a lawsuit against the school district in the U.S. District Court for the Eastern District of New York, seeking an order that district officials had violated the federal Equal Access Act and the Constitution. The court denied the application for a temporary order, and the students appealed to the U.S. Court of Appeals, Second Circuit.

The court commented that the Equal Access Act guarantees public school students the right to form extracurricular groups engaging in religious, philosophical or political discussion. **A school district which opens its facilities to student groups may not deny access to certain groups for discriminatory reasons**. The court rejected the school district's argument that it was required by the act to prohibit the club from religious discrimination in the selection of its officers. In this case, the act required the school district to allow the club to maintain its own internal policies. The students were likely to prevail on their Equal Access Act claim, and the district court had erroneously granted judgment to the school district. The court also found that the Establishment Clause did not prohibit school recognition of the religious club. Nor was the Equal Protection Clause implicated by official recognition. Holding that the school district had to respect the club's officer selection policy, the court ruled that the students were entitled to injunctive relief. *Hsu v. Roslyn Union Free School Dist. No. 3*, 85 F.3d 839 (2d Cir.1996).

◆   A Wyoming school district opened its facilities to the public, so long as the public use did not interfere with school activities. **A group of graduating senior class officers arranged for a baccalaureate ceremony that was "sponsored by the community."** The ceremony was scheduled to take place in the school gymnasium and the student officers contacted a printer to publish announcements. More than one month after the officers obtained verbal authorization for use of the gym, the school board adopted a new policy which prohibited them from using the gymnasium for the service, because of its fear that the ceremony might violate the Establishment Clause of the U.S. Constitution. The seniors sought declaratory and injunctive relief in a lawsuit filed in the U.S. District Court for the District of Wyoming. The court observed that there was little danger of the appearance of state sponsorship of this privately sponsored ceremony. **The board had changed its constitutionally permissible open access policy for one that was applied to the student group in a discriminatory manner and that violated their First Amendment free speech rights**. The alteration of the free access policy based on a particular point of view was a constitutional violation. Accordingly, the court granted the injunction and restrained the school district from enforcing its revised policy. *Shumway v. Albany County School Dist. No. 1 Bd. of Educ.*, 826 F.Supp. 1320 (E.Wyo.1993).

B. Nonstudent Use

◆   **A New York school district issued regulations allowing social, civic, or recreational uses of its property as well as limited use by political organizations, but provided that the school not be used for religious purposes.** An evangelical church sought permission to use school facilities to show a film series on traditional Christian family values. The district denied permission to use its facilities because the film was religious. The church filed a lawsuit in a federal court alleging that the district's decision violated its rights under the First Amendment. The district court determined that the school district's action was "viewpoint neutral" and held for the district. The U.S. Court of Appeals, Second Circuit, affirmed, holding that public school facilities were a "limited public forum" and that the district could exclude certain groups provided that the exclusion was "reasonable and viewpoint neutral." The church appealed to the U.S. Supreme Court.

   The Court determined that exclusion of the subject matter because of its religious content would impermissibly favor some viewpoints or ideas at the expense of others. Therefore, the regulation discriminated on the basis of viewpoint. The exclusion of this particular church from using school property was not viewpoint neutral. Next, the Court determined that since the film series was not to be shown during school hours and was to be open to those outside the church, the public would not perceive the district to be endorsing religion. Since use of school facilities by the church did not violate the test articulated by the Court in *Lemon v. Kurtzman*, permission by the school district would not violate the Establishment Clause. The film had a secular purpose, its primary effect did not advance religion and the showing of the film would not "foster excessive state entanglement with religion." Thus, speech about "family and child related issues" from a religious perspective could permissibly be aired on public school grounds. The Court reversed the lower court decisions. *Lamb's Chapel v. Center Moriches Union Free School Dist.,* 508 U.S. 384, 113 S.Ct. 2141, 124 L.Ed.2d 352 (1993).

◆   A student submitted a request to use school facilities for meetings of the Good News Club, a private religious club, after school hours. The superintendent denied the request, stating that the club's use of facilities amounted to school support of religious worship. After receiving further information on the content of club meetings, the school board adopted a resolution denying the request. The club commenced a federal district court action against the school under 42 U.S.C. § 1983 for violation of student speech rights, equal protection and other federal rights. The district court entered a preliminary order enjoining the school from prohibiting the club's use of school facilities, but later awarded judgment to the school. The club appealed to the U.S. Court of Appeals, Second Circuit, which rejected its argument that it sought only to teach morals and values, like the Boy Scouts, Girl Scouts, 4-H Club and other groups that used school facilities. According to the Second Circuit, religious instruction was integral to the club's meetings, distinguishing it from other groups. **The school's decision to deny the club access to its facilities was based on content, rather than viewpoint, and was permissible.**

The club appealed to the U.S. Supreme Court, which observed that the nature of the forum determines the limits that a school may place on speech taking place in the forum. The school had established a limited public forum in which it could reasonably seek to avoid identification with a particular religion. **While the school was not required to allow all speech, limits on speech could not be based upon viewpoint and had to be reasonable in light of the purpose of the forum.** The court relied on two of its recent decisions interpreting government time, place and manner restrictions, *Lamb's Chapel v. Center Moriches Union Free School District*, 508 U.S. 384 (1993), and *Rosenberger v. Rector and Visitors of Univ. of Va.*, 515 U.S. 819 (1995). In this case, the school's policy broadly permitted speech about the moral and character development of children. **The school had excluded the club from school facilities solely because of its religious viewpoint. This resulted in unconstitutional viewpoint discrimination** under both *Lamb's Chapel* and *Rosenberger*. The court found no difference between the Good News Club and other student organizations that were not excluded, and held that "speech discussing otherwise permissible subjects cannot be excluded from a limited public forum on the ground that the subject is discussed from a religious viewpoint." It rejected the school's argument that it was required to prohibit the club's speech to avoid an Establishment Clause violation. Club meetings took place after school hours and were not sponsored by the school. No risk of coercion was present, because students had to obtain permission from their parents before attending meetings. Allowing the club access to school facilities for its meetings furthered the important Establishment Clause purpose of religious neutrality, ensuring that all groups could speak about the same topics. The district failed to show any risk of school endorsement and the court reversed and remanded the case. *Good News Club v. Milford Central School*, 121 S.Ct. 2093, 150 L.Ed.2d 151 (2001).

◆   **A West Virginia school board allowed community members to make Bibles available to students in public schools by placing them on unattended tables with a sign stating "please feel free to take one."** A group of individuals opposed to the policy filed a lawsuit against the board in the U.S. District Court for the Northern District of West Virginia, seeking a preliminary order against implementation of the policy. The court granted a preliminary order in the group's favor and later considered its request for a permanent order. The court ruled that the board's policy did not create a public forum that opened the schools to all forms of communication. In creating a particular manner of access to Bibles, the board had not shown favoritism toward religion and the placement of Bibles was performed by nonschool individuals. Applying tests in use by the U.S. Supreme Court to assess the religious neutrality of a school practice, the court ruled that allowing citizens to place Bibles on tables in public schools was neutral since the board's policy was not limited to the distribution of Christian materials. The court found that the policy did not endorse religion since no student was forced to take a Bible. Because the policy was consistent with a limited public forum and survived the neutrality and endorsement tests, it did not violate the Establishment Clause. The court denied the request for a permanent order and vacated the preliminary order. The court then considered the group's motion to reinstate the preliminary order pending appeal to the U.S. Court of Appeals, Fourth Circuit. The court held that the preservation of the *status quo* as set forth in the preliminary order was unnecessary to prevent school disruption and would compel the board to engage in a continuing violation of the constitutional rights of certain students. Accordingly, it denied the request for an order pending appeal, but ordered the board to place a sign on Bible tables that disclaimed any board involvement in Bible distribution.

Bible distribution opponents appealed to the U.S. Court of Appeals, Fourth Circuit, which held that the board's policy was neutral and did not create the impression of official sponsorship of religious speech. Students were not coerced to accept a Bible. Prior to adopting the challenged policy, the board had unconstitutionally denied private religious speech on the same basis as that afforded to private non-religious speech. **Withholding access to the Bible group would have created the impression that religious speech was disfavored. However, the policy was invalid at the elementary school level in view of the greater potential for coercing younger students and the difficulty they might have distinguishing between official and private speech.** The court otherwise affirmed the district court judgment. *Peck v. Upshur County Bd. of Educ.*, 155 F.3d 274 (4th Cir.1998).

♦ **A religious congregation submitted an application to a New York school district, requesting the use of a public school to conduct religious worship services. The district rejected the request**, citing a New York education law and a school board policy that prohibited the use of school facilities for religious services. The church and its pastor initiated a federal district court action against the school district and certain officials for constitutional violations. The school district admitted that it had previously allowed religious worship services on school grounds in two instances. However, it submitted evidence that it had erroneously approved the applications by the groups and had remedied its review process since that time. The court held that the education law created a limited public forum at district schools which specifically excluded religious worship services. **Since the school district had not opened the forum for religious worship services, and had taken corrective measures to address previous policy violations, the exclusion of the religious group from school facilities was constitutional.** The court upheld the denial of the group's application and granted the district's summary judgment motion. *Full Gospel Tabernacle v. Community School Dist. 27*, 979 F.Supp. 214 (S.D.N.Y.1997). On appeal, the U.S. Court of Appeals, Second Circuit, affirmed the district court opinion for the same reasons.

♦ An evangelical church sought to use a New York public middle school auditorium for weekly religious services during non-school hours. A New York statute permits local school districts to adopt regulations governing the use of their property for various educational, social, civic and recreational purposes, provided that they are nonexclusive and open to the public. **The New York City Board of Education established a written policy governing building use which allowed religious groups to discuss religious material or viewpoints, but which prohibited the use of public school facilities for worship services.** The church challenged the city board's standard operating procedure in court. The case reached the U.S. Court of Appeals, Second Circuit, which disagreed with the argument by the church that use of public school grounds under the standard operating procedure involved an open public forum. **The school was a limited forum, and the board had reasonably applied state legislation in denying permission to use school grounds for regular religious services**. The regulation was viewpoint neutral, clear and reasonable and did not violate the Establishment or Free Exercise Clauses of the Constitution. *Bronx Household of Faith v. Community School Dist. No. 10*, 127 F.3d 207 (2d Cir.1997).

C. Teacher Proselytizing

◆   **A California high school biology teacher** claimed that the theory of "evolutionism" was in reality a government-backed religion. He **sought the right to teach creationism in his classes and to discuss religious matters with students outside class**. He claimed that the school district and certain individuals had conspired to destroy his career and reputation in violation of his constitutional rights. The school district reprimanded the teacher in writing for proselytizing to students and teaching religion in his classes. He filed a lawsuit against the district in the U.S. District Court for the Central District of California under 42 U.S.C. §§ 1983 and 1985(3). The court dismissed the lawsuit and awarded the school district attorney's fees, stating that the claims were frivolous. The teacher appealed to the U.S. Court of Appeals, Ninth Circuit.

The court of appeals found no error in the district court's treatment of the constitutional claims. There was no merit to the teacher's argument that the district violated the Establishment Clause by including evolution in the curriculum as a valid scientific theory. While the U.S. Supreme Court has never held that "evolutionism" or "secular humanism" were religions under the Establishment Clause, the Court has held that belief in a divine creator is a religious belief and not a scientific theory. See *Edwards v. Aguillard*, 482 U.S. 578, 107 S.Ct. 2573, 96 L.Ed.2d 510 (1987), above. **The restriction on religious speech during nonclass time served an important state interest in avoiding Establishment Clause violations**. The district court had properly dismissed the claim of injury to the teacher's reputation, and the district had not deprived him of any constitutional rights. However, the complaint was not entirely frivolous and the court reversed the award of attorney's fees. *Peloza v. Capistrano Unified School Dist.*, 37 F.3d 517 (9th Cir.1994).

◆   A physiology professor at the University of Alabama occasionally mentioned his religious beliefs during classes. He also scheduled an after class discussion group entitled "Evidence of God in Human Physiology," which several of his students attended. Although he stated that his remarks were his own personal bias, a group of his students complained to the head of the physiology department. **The department head**, after meeting with the dean and the school's attorney, **drafted a memo directing the professor to stop interjecting his personal religious beliefs in class and not to hold the optional classes**. The professor petitioned the president of the university for a rescission of the order, but the president affirmed the restrictions. The professor filed suit in federal court under 42 U.S.C. § 1983 seeking an injunction lifting the restrictions placed on his speech. The professor moved for summary judgment. The trial court determined that the university had created a public forum for the exchange of ideas, and that the university's interests were not sufficient to justify restricting the professor's freedom of speech. The court granted summary judgment in favor of the professor. The university appealed to the U.S. Court of Appeals, Eleventh Circuit.

The appeals court rejected the district court's determination that a classroom constituted a public forum. It relied on the U.S. Supreme Court's decision in *Hazelwood School Dist. v. Kuhlmeier*, Chapter Three, § I.B.1., below, in which the Court stated that "school facilities may be deemed to be public forums only if school authorities have ... opened those facilities for indiscriminate use by the general public." If the facilities, as in this case, have been reserved for other intended purposes, no public forum has been created. **Where no public forum exists, school officials may impose reasonable restrictions on the speech rights of students and teachers. Accordingly, the appeals court held that the professor's classroom was not a public forum and the university could reasonably regulate his speech**. In addition, the university could prohibit the professor from promoting and scheduling optional classes. The court reversed the district court's judgment. *Bishop v. Aronov*, 926 F.2d 1066 (11th Cir.1991).

D. Religious Literature and Symbols

◆   **A Kentucky statute required the posting of the Ten Commandments, purchased with private contributions, on the wall of each public classroom in the state**. A group of citizens sought an injunction against the statute's enforcement claiming that it violated the First Amendment's Establishment and Free Exercise Clauses. The Kentucky state courts upheld the statute, finding that its purpose was secular, not religious, and that the statute would neither advance nor inhibit any religion, nor involve the state excessively in religious matters. Utilizing the three-part test first announced in *Lemon v. Kurtzman*, above, the U.S. Supreme Court struck down the statute. **The Court concluded that the posting of the Ten Commandments had no secular purpose**. Kentucky state education officials insisted that the statute in question served the secular purpose of teaching students the foundation of western civilization and the common law. The Court stated, however, that the pre-eminent purpose was plainly religious in nature. **The Ten Commandments undeniably came from a religious text** despite the legislative recitation of a secular purpose. The Court stated that the text here was not integrated into a course or study of history, civilization, ethics, or comparative religion, but simply posted to induce children to read, meditate upon, and perhaps, to venerate and obey them. The Court also stated that it made no difference that the cost of posting the commandments was paid for through private funds and that they were not read aloud. *Stone v. Graham*, 449 U.S. 39, 101 S.Ct. 192, 66 L.Ed.2d 199 (1981).

◆   **The Harlan County (Kentucky) School Board resolved to post the Ten Commandments in district classrooms**. Three students sued over the posting, and **the board added documents of historic or religious significance to the displays**. These documents included excerpts from the Declaration of Independence, the Kentucky Constitution, the Mayflower Compact and proclamations by Presidents Lincoln and Reagan. A federal district court granted the students' motion for an order prohibiting the display, finding that all of the documents were religious in nature. *Doe v. Harlan County School District,* 96 F.Supp.2d 667 (E.D.Ky. 2000).

The court then consolidated the case with two others involving Kentucky counties that erected similar displays on government property. The counties and school district created new displays, including the text of the Magna Carta, the Declaration of Independence, the Bill of Rights, the Star Spangled Banner, the Ten Commandments and the Mayflower Compact, with explanations of their historical and legal significance. After the plaintiffs again moved the court to order removal of the displays, the counties eliminated scriptural references. The school district implemented a procedure for posting historical documents. The plaintiffs then moved the court to expand its previous orders to include the current displays.

The court considered the motion under the Establishment Clause test described in *Lemon v. Kurtzman*, 403 U.S. 602 (1971), as refined by later U.S. Supreme Court cases. In order to satisfy this inquiry, the government action must have a secular purpose, and a principal or primary effect that does not create religious endorsement. The court held that each of the purposes advanced by the government entities in this case was religious. The Supreme Court declared in *Stone v. Graham, above,* that a state's desire to proclaim the value of the Ten Commandments in American law and government was itself a religious purpose. The history of litigation among the parties undercut the argument that there was no religious purpose to the displays, and the court noted that the selection of the second set of displays accentuated the religious purpose. **The purpose of posting the Ten Commandments by each of the government entities was improper and violated the Establishment Clause because it sent non-adherents the message that they were outsiders and not favored members of the community**. The displays had no secular purpose, which by itself violated the *Lemon* analysis. The court found that the displays caused government endorsement of religion, and the fact that the displays were placed in important public places heightened the effect of religious advancement. The Supreme Court has given clear guidance for the use of the Ten Commandments, and each of the government entities in this case had stepped outside the bounds of permissible uses. The students and other plaintiffs were entitled to a preliminary order requiring the immediate removal of the displays from the courthouses and Harlan County schools. *American Civil Liberties Union of Kentucky v. McCreary County*, 145 F.Supp.2d 845 (E.D. Ky. 2001).

◆   Two Indiana high school students were suspended from a cadet teaching program for wearing Wiccan pentagram necklaces. The students assisted teachers at an elementary school through the program. **The principal of the school the students were assigned to instructed them to either hide or remove necklaces bearing a Wiccan pentagram** in order to remain on school premises. The students walked out of the elementary school and were later found truant for the incident. The principal later met with the students and informed them that their decision to leave the elementary school was considered an abandonment of the cadet teaching program. One student sued the school district in a federal district court, seeking a declaration that the district's actions violated her religious exercise rights under the First Amendment and an order preventing the district from prohibiting the wearing of pentagram necklaces at the elementary school.

The court entered a temporary restraining order in the student's favor and added the other student as a party to the action. The court then conducted a preliminary injunction hearing. The district argued that the students should be considered employees in this case and that no constitutional scrutiny should be applied to its actions. The court disagreed, finding that even if they were considered teachers, their First Amendment claims had merit. The students testified that they were adherents of the Wiccan religion and that the district violated their religious expression rights when they were told to hide the pentagram symbols. **The court found no evidence the students had disrupted the elementary school by wearing the pentagrams, or that anyone had even noticed them until the day they were excluded from the school.** The evidence indicated that the students had been excluded from the cadet program solely for declining the principal's ultimatum. Their early departure that day had been justified in view of the ultimatum, and the incident did not support the decision to permanently remove them from the elementary school. The students had been irreparably harmed, since they were no longer exposed to an elementary teaching environment that could assist them in making career choices. The court rejected the school district's assertion that there was a risk that elementary school students would be exposed to inappropriate Wiccan material if the students were allowed to remain on elementary school grounds, finding the assertion was based on speculation. The court issued a preliminary injunction permitting the students to return to the elementary school to participate in the cadet program with permission to wear pentagram necklaces. *Lehman v. Elwood Community School Corp.*, No. IE-00-0529-C-D/F (S.D. Ind. 2000).

◆ A high school baseball booster club sold space on signs to be displayed on the fence surrounding a high school baseball field. After a potential advertiser had two proposed ads rejected for length and religious content, the district decided to end the fundraiser and remove all signs from the field. The advertiser commenced a state superior court action against the superintendent and board members. The school district removed the case to the U.S. District Court for the Central District of California, which remanded the California constitutional claims to the state superior court. The superior court granted summary judgment to the board and school officials, and **rejection of the advertisement was reasonable and that acceptance of the advertisement would have violated the Establishment Clause**.

The federal district court granted summary judgment to the school officials on the federal claims and the advertiser appealed to the U.S. Court of Appeals, Ninth Circuit, which analyzed the case under the nature of the forum established by the district when it began selling advertising space on the ballpark fence. This requires consideration of the nature of the property and its compatibility with expressive activity, as well as the policy and practices of the government. Government policies that historically allow commercial advertising, but exclude political and religious expression, do not create an open public forum for all expression. The school's decision to reserve space for commercial speech indicated a goal of making money, not encouraging political or religious speech. **The Ninth Circuit held that when schools act in a proprietary capacity, they operate nonpublic forums, subject only to the requirements of reasonableness and viewpoint neutrality**. In this case, the school district did not designate the fence as a public forum for expressive activity. It sold advertising space to defray athletic program expenses, and had excluded not only the advertiser's submission, but others from controversial sources such as Planned Parenthood and local taverns. By excluding certain subjects, the school defined the forum as a non-public one that was open only for limited purposes. The stated reasons for excluding the advertisement were disruption and the possibility of violating the Establishment Clause and risking the attribution of the advertisement to the district. The court agreed with the district court that these concerns were reasonable and did not amount to impermissible viewpoint discrimination. Closing the forum was a constitutionally permissible solution to the problem of providing equal access while avoiding the appearance of religious endorsement, and the court affirmed the judgment. *DiLoreto v. Downey Unified School Dist. Bd. of Educ.*, 196 F.3d 958 (9th Cir. 1999).

◆   A West Virginia school board historically allowed non-student groups to distribute literature in schools through an informal, unwritten policy under which the superintendent reviewed materials before they were actually distributed to students. It then adopted a formal policy declaring neutrality in religious and political matters and restricting the distribution of religious and political materials to students. **The board allowed a group to distribute Bibles to students from tables located in school hallways after obtaining a legal opinion that refusing to do so might violate the Establishment Clause**. A group opposed to the distribution of Bibles sought an order from a federal district court to prohibit the action. After temporarily prohibiting any Bible distribution, the court held a trial and denied the group's application for a permanent order. However, it required the board to disclaim any association with the distribution.

Bible distribution opponents appealed to the U.S. Court of Appeals, Fourth Circuit, which held that the board's policy was neutral and did not create the impression of official sponsorship of religious speech. Students were not coerced to accept a Bible. Prior to adopting the challenged policy, the board had unconstitutionally denied private religious speech on the same basis as that afforded to private non-religious speech. **Withholding access to the Bible group would have created the impression that religious speech was disfavored. However, the policy was invalid at the elementary school level in view of the greater potential for coercing younger students and the difficulty they might have distinguishing between official and private speech**. The court otherwise affirmed the district court judgment. *Peck v. Upshur County Bd. of Educ.*, 155 F.3d 274 (4th Cir. 1998).

◆   Three Ohio public school students objected to their school district's use of the blue devil mascot also used by other schools, including Duke University. The school board sent a newsletter survey to all households in the district and also surveyed its students concerning retention of the mascot. The public response was overwhelmingly in favor of retaining the mascot, and the board refused to make any change. **The students and their parents filed a lawsuit against the school district** in the U.S. District Court for the Northern District of Ohio, **claiming that use of the mascot violated the Establishment Clause** of the First Amendment, based on their belief that the mascot was satanic. The court granted summary judgment to the school district, and the family appealed to the U.S. Court of Appeals, Sixth Circuit. The court observed that the blue devil mascot was adopted by many schools following World War II and was named after an elite corps of French alpine soldiers who wore blue berets and were known as the French Blue Devils. **The symbol was secular and no reasonable person would believe that its display would have the primary effect of advancing or inhibiting religion** in violation of the Establishment Clause. Accordingly, the use of the symbol did not violate the Constitution, and the district court had properly granted summary judgment to the school district. *Kunselman v. Western Reserve Local School Dist.*, 70 F.3d 931 (6th Cir.1995).

◆   A Florida public elementary school celebrated Halloween by decorating the school with pictures of witches, pumpkins and other typical holiday symbols. Some teachers dressed as witches and other characters. **The parent of a student attending the school claimed that the depiction of witches constituted the establishment of a religion** by the school. The parent kept his children home on Halloween, and filed a lawsuit in a Florida district court, seeking an order to permanently bar the school from portraying witches in Halloween celebrations. He claimed that Halloween was a religious holiday. The school board argued that it had permitted Halloween activities in a secular manner with no attempt to promote witchcraft. School officials argued that they simply sought to make Halloween a fun day for students and to promote educational purposes by enriching the educational and cultural awareness of students. The court ruled that the use of Halloween symbols did not constitute the establishment of religion. The parent appealed to the District Court of Appeal of Florida, First District.

The court of appeal stated that the public school celebration of Halloween did not violate the Establishment Clause of the First Amendment. **Although witches and cauldrons might convey a religious message to some, the context in which the symbols were displayed determined whether a constitutional violation existed**. In this case, **the symbols were not displayed in a manner that endorsed or promoted religion** and there was no danger of any public perception of school endorsement. The district court had properly granted summary judgment to the board. *Guyer v. School Bd. of Alachua County*, 634 So.2d 806 (Fla.App.1st Dist.1994).

III. LIMITATIONS ON THE FREE EXERCISE OF RELIGION

The Free Exercise Clause of the First Amendment provides that Congress shall make no law prohibiting the free exercise of religion. The Free Exercise Clause, like the Establishment Clause, applies to state governmental entities such as school districts and universities through the Fourteenth Amendment. Courts have imposed restrictions on the free exercise of religion where such restrictions serve an overriding public interest.

A. Students

◆   The University of Missouri at Kansas City, a state university, made its facilities available for the general use of registered student groups. **A registered student religious group that had previously received permission to conduct its** meetings in university facilities was informed that it could no longer do so because of a university regulation that prohibited use of its facilities for the purposes of religious worship or teaching. Members of the group brought suit against the district in federal court, alleging that the regulation violated their First Amendment rights to free exercise of religion and freedom of speech. The court upheld the school's regulation, but the U.S. Court of Appeals, Eighth Circuit, reversed, stating that the regulation was discriminatory against religious speech and that the Establishment Clause does not bar a policy of equal access in which facilities are open to groups and speakers of all kinds.

The Supreme Court agreed with the court of appeals' assessment, stating that **the university policy violated the fundamental principle that a state regulation of speech must be content-neutral**. It is obligatory upon the state to show that the regulation is necessary to serve a compelling state interest and that it is narrowly drawn to achieve that end. The state was unable to do that here. The state's interest in achieving greater separation of church and state than is already ensured under the Establishment Clause was not sufficiently "compelling" to justify content-based discrimination against religious speech of the student group in question. *Widmar v. Vincent*, 454 U.S. 263, 102 S.Ct. 269, 70 L.Ed.2d 400 (1981).

◆   The federal Religious Freedom Restoration Act of 1993 (RFRA) was enacted to prohibit government actors, including public school administrators, from substantially burdening the free exercise of religion, even if the burden results from a rule of general applicability. An exception existed where the government could demonstrate that the burden furthered a compelling governmental interest in the least restrictive way. **A Texas municipality denied a building permit application filed by a Catholic archbishop to enlarge a church located in a historical district. The archbishop sued the city in a federal district court, asserting that the application denial violated the RFRA**. The court held that the RFRA was unconstitutional, but the U.S. Court of Appeals, Fifth Circuit, reversed, and the U.S. Supreme Court agreed to review the case.

The Supreme Court held the RFRA unconstitutional, noting that it attempted to grant individuals greater religious protection than the U.S. Constitution itself provided. The RFRA's sweeping coverage ensured its intrusion at every level of government. **The law was not simply remedial or preventive of unconstitutional behavior, but proscribed state conduct that the Fourteenth Amendment did not reach**. The Court stated that when the exercise of religion has been burdened by a law of general applicability, it does not follow that the persons affected have been burdened any more than other citizens or that they have been burdened because of their religious beliefs. **Since the RFRA contradicted vital principles necessary to maintain the separation of powers and the federal-state balance of power, the Court held that it was unconstitutional**. *City of Boerne, Texas v. Flores*, 117 S.Ct. 2157, 521 U.S. 507, 138 L.Ed.2d 624 (1997). *Editor's Note: However, it is not certain whether this ruling means that the RFRA is unconstitutional in all respects, or whether it is still valid as applied to the federal government and federal laws.*

◆   A New Jersey kindergarten teacher instructed his students to make posters depicting things for which they were thankful. One student made a poster expressing thanks for Jesus. The posters were displayed in a school hallway, but the student's poster was removed. It was later returned to the display. When the student reached first grade, a teacher chose him to read a story to the rest of the class. The student selected an adaptation of a Biblical story. **The teacher did not allow the student to read the story to the class, but instead had him read it to her privately**. The student's mother demanded permission to allow him to read the story to the entire class. When school officials refused, she filed a federal district court action against the teacher, school board, state education department, school commissioner and other officials. State and local officials then petitioned the court for summary judgment. The court rejected arguments by the state officials that the suit was barred by the Eleventh Amendment or the separation of powers and political question doctrines. It held that there was no evidence that a classroom constituted a public forum where speech rights were at their maximum level of protection. **Because the activities had taken place in the classroom, it was permissible for teachers to exercise viewpoint-neutral regulations that were reasonably related to legitimate educational purposes**. The teachers' actions were reasonably related to educational concerns and not based on a particular viewpoint. Allowing the student to read a Biblical story might create the impression among students that the teacher endorsed the story, and she had appropriately accommodated his speech rights by allowing him to read it only to her. The accommodation did not affect his ability to practice his religion, and the school officials were entitled to judgment. *C.H. v. Oliva*, 990 F.Supp. 341 (D.N.J.1997).

The full Third Circuit heard the case, and voted evenly on whether the district court had properly entered judgment for the school officials with respect to the Bible reading incident, resulting in an affirmation of the judgment. The court agreed with the district court that the education department was entitled to Eleventh Amendment immunity in the case, and vacated that portion of the judgment with instructions to dismiss for lack of jurisdiction. **The remaining allegations of constitutional rights violations arising from the poster incident failed to state a claim against the school officials**. However, the court remanded the case to the district court with instructions to grant the parent an opportunity to amend the complaint to allege the personal involvement of school officials in the poster removal incident. *C.H. v. Oliva*, 226 F.3d 198 (3d Cir. 2000).

◆   An Indiana first grade student distributed religious leaflets to his classmates. The school principal instructed the student's classroom teacher to return them to the student. The student later made a second unsuccessful attempt to distribute religious literature at school and several months later he distributed religious information to students on the school bus. The principal did not discipline the student, but asked him not to pass out any more literature. **The school district then adopted an official policy requiring students to notify the school principal in advance of distributing more than ten copies of a writing, and to provide a copy to the superintendent**. The student's parents filed a lawsuit on his behalf against the school district, teacher, school, principal and superintendent in the U.S. District Court for the Southern District of Indiana, asserting violations of the state and federal constitutions, the Religious Freedom Restoration Act (RFRA) and other state and federal laws.

The parties filed cross-motions for summary judgment. The court deferred any ruling on the new official policy and the state and federal civil rights act questions until the parties submitted further information. However, it agreed with the teacher, principal and superintendent that each of them were entitled to immunity for prohibiting the distribution of religious material prior to adoption of the official policy, since none had final policymaking authority under Indiana law. Indiana school boards have final policymaking power and because the board had not participated in efforts to prohibit any distribution prior to the development of an official policy, the district was also entitled to immunity. *Harless by Harless v. Darr*, 937 F.Supp. 1339 (S.D.Ind.1996).

The parties submitted additional materials requested by the court concerning the new official policy and state law questions. The court observed that **the policy did not provide for suppression of speech by any school official, but only required the submission of a copy to the superintendent and advance notice to the principal of any distribution of written material by a student**. These restrictions did not constitute an impermissible prior restraint on speech, and the student had failed to allege that the policy curtailed his freedom of speech. The court dismissed the remaining federal civil rights claims and refused to assert jurisdiction over the state law claims. *Harless by Harless v. Darr*, 937 F.Supp. 1351 (S.D.Ind.1996).

◆ **A Florida school district policy vested the superintendent of schools with broad discretion to restrain the distribution at public schools of any material that was not related to school courses. The policy also described appropriate places for distribution of material** that was not course-related. An elementary student in the district brought religious pamphlets to distribute to her classmates. When she asked her homeroom teacher for permission to distribute the brochures, her teacher confiscated them and brought them to the principal. The principal destroyed the brochures, stating that he could not permit the distribution of religious material at school. The student and her mother filed a lawsuit in the U.S. District Court for the Middle District of Florida, seeking a preliminary injunction against enforcement of the policy. The court held that the motion was premature, and that the school had never actually applied the policy. The U.S. Court of Appeals, Eleventh Circuit, affirmed the district court's decision.

The district court then conducted a trial on the student's request for a permanent injunction against enforcement of the policy. The court observed that the policy was a content-based prior restraint on speech that could only be justified by showing that the speech or literature would materially and substantially interfere with school operations or the rights of other students. In this case, the broad powers accorded to the district superintendent could not be supported under law. The Establishment Clause of the First Amendment to the U.S. Constitution prohibited the government from inhibiting the free exercise of religion. **The district could not show that religious speech by students would materially and substantially interfere with school operations or the rights of other students. Accordingly, the student was entitled to a permanent injunction** against enforcement of the policy. The court also awarded nominal damages and attorneys' fees. *Johnston-Loehner v. O'Brien*, 859 F.Supp. 575 (M.D.Fla.1994).

B. Employees

◆   A Connecticut high school teacher belonged to a church that required its members to refrain from secular employment during designated holy days. This practice caused the teacher to miss approximately six school days each year for religious purposes. The teacher worked under terms of a bargaining agreement between the school board and his teachers' union that allowed only three days of leave for religious observation. **The agreement** also **allowed leave for "necessary personal business," which could not be used for religious purposes**. He repeatedly asked permission to use three days of his "necessary personal business" leave for religious purposes. He also offered to pay for a substitute teacher if the school board would pay him for the extra days that he missed. These alternatives were turned down by the school board. When all administrative alternatives were exhausted, he filed a lawsuit alleging that the school board's policy constituted religious discrimination. A U.S. district court dismissed the teacher's lawsuit and he appealed.

The U.S. Court of Appeals, Second Circuit, said that the school board was bound to accept one of the teacher's proposed solutions unless that accommodation caused undue hardship. The school board appealed. **The U.S. Supreme Court decided that the school district was not required to accept the teacher's proposals even if acceptance would not result in "undue hardship."** The school board was only bound to offer a fair and reasonable accommodation of the teacher's religious needs. The bargaining agreement policy of allowing three days off for religious purposes was found to be reasonable. Because none of the lower courts had decided whether this policy had been administered fairly, the case was remanded for a determination of that question. *Ansonia Bd. of Educ. v. Philbrook*, 479 U.S. 60, 107 S.Ct. 367, 93 L.Ed.2d 305 (1986).

After several evidentiary hearings, **the district court found that providing the teacher with unpaid leave for religious observance beyond the three-day limit constituted a reasonable accommodation** of the teacher's religious needs unless paid leave was provided for all purposes except religious ones. The teacher again appealed to the U.S. Court of Appeals, Second Circuit. The court of appeals held that the findings of fact made by the trial court were not clearly erroneous. Therefore, it affirmed the district court's decision. *Philbrook v. Ansonia Bd. of Educ.*, 925 F.2d 47 (2d Cir.1991).

◆   A teacher with over 12 years of experience teaching socially and emotionally disturbed high school students converted to Christianity. **He did not abide by a cease and desist memorandum from the special education director that instructed him not to incorporate noncurricular religious references into his classes.** The director suspended the teacher indefinitely for violating the directive. The teacher then signed an affirmation indicating that he would adhere to the directive. He wrote to the director asking if the directive prevented him from having private prayers with students. The director then reassigned the teacher to a class attended by students with autism and other disabilities who had little or no communication skills. After a student's parent sent a tape of religious songs to calm his son at school, the teacher sent him a thank you note containing religious references. The teacher's supervisor advised him that the letter violated the directive, and the teacher responded by filing a federal district court action against the BOCES, asserting violations of his speech rights and claiming that the directive was unconstitutionally vague. The court granted summary judgment to the BOCES and the teacher appealed.

The U.S. Court of Appeals, Second Circuit, found that **schools have the ability to restrain teacher speech in view of legitimate government interests such as avoiding litigation for Establishment Clause violations**. In this case, the teacher's letter introduced religious content into a curricular matter. The agency could not risk giving the impression that it endorsed religion, and the directive did not infringe on the teacher's speech rights. There was no merit to the teacher's claim that the directive was unconstitutionally vague since its basic meaning gave him fair notice of what he was not supposed to do. The agency was not required to explain the term "instructional program" or describe every possible example of prohibited speech. The court affirmed the judgment for the education agency. *Marchi v. Bd. of Cooperative Educ. Services of Albany*, 173 F.3d 469 (2d Cir.1999).

◆   An Idaho elementary school principal enjoyed favorable performance evaluations for 15 years. He told an assistant school superintendent that he was considering, for religious reasons, home schooling his own children, who at that time were enrolled in public schools. The assistant superintendent advised the principal that he must submit information to the board to determine whether the home instruction would conform with Idaho law. Although the principal's annual performance evaluation was again satisfactory, **the superintendent advised him that he would be demoted to an elementary teaching position if he decided to home school his children**. The principal failed to respond to the ultimatum and rejected the teaching assignment. He then filed a federal district court action against the school district, school board members, superintendent and other school employees, claiming that their decisions violated his religious and due process rights and breached his employment contract. The court conducted a jury trial and awarded him $300,000 in damages. The school district and officials appealed to the U.S. Court of Appeals, Ninth Circuit.

On appeal, the district argued that its actions did not violate the principal's constitutional rights, since his membership in the Church of Jesus Christ of Latter-Day Saints did not require home schooling. The court of appeals held that **the Constitution protects acts that are rooted in religious belief, without regard to the requirements of a particular church. The school district had no compelling interest in restricting the principal's exercise of religious freedom**. It had succumbed to public pressure and deprived him of his due process rights by demoting him without allowing him to gain approval of his home school program and by violating its own antidiscrimination policies. The court affirmed the award of damages and remanded the case for an award of attorneys' fees. *Peterson v. Minidoka County School Dist. No. 331*, 118 F.3d 1351 (9th Cir.1997).

◆   A Pennsylvania teacher, who was a devout Muslim, was prevented from wearing traditional Muslim dress by a state statute that barred teachers from wearing religious garb in the classroom. The teacher filed discrimination charges with the EEOC. **The EEOC conducted an investigation and determined that there was reasonable cause to believe that both the school board and the**

Commonwealth of Pennsylvania had violated Title VII. The U.S. Justice Department then filed a complaint against the school board and the commonwealth in a federal district court. The Justice Department sought a declaration that the garb statute was in conflict with Title VII and an injunction preventing the school board from enforcing the statute. The trial court entered judgment against the school board and enjoined it from enforcing the statute. However, the court found that the statute was sporadically enforced and therefore did not constitute a pattern or practice of discrimination. Both the board of education and the U.S. Justice Department appealed. On appeal to the U.S. Court of Appeals, Third Circuit, the school board argued that although the restriction on religious attire placed a burden on the teacher's free exercise of religion, the state had a compelling interest in maintaining the appearance of religious neutrality in the public schools. In reviewing the lower court's finding that the garb statute did not conflict with Title VII, **the court held that maintaining religious neutrality in the classroom was a compelling state interest and therefore the statute was not unconstitutional**. *United States v. Bd. of Educ. for the School Dist. of Philadelphia*, 911 F.2d 882 (3d Cir.1990).

IV. FINANCIAL ASSISTANCE AND VOUCHER PROGRAMS

◆   The Ohio General Assembly adopted the Cleveland School Voucher Program as part of the state's biennial appropriations bill for 1996-97. **The program allowed students in the Cleveland City School District to attend a public school in an adjacent school district, or receive a scholarship to attend a registered private school**. Scholarships were awarded for up to 90 percent of the private school tuition for families below a specified income level. Private school vouchers were payable to parents, but were sent directly to schools for restrictive endorsement by parents to the schools. Parties who objected to the voucher program sued Ohio and Ohio officials in separate state court actions, asserting state and federal constitutional violations. The cases were consolidated and the court granted summary judgment to the state and officials. The Court of Appeals of Ohio declared the program unconstitutional, ruling that it violated the Establishment Clause of the U.S. Constitution and various sections of the Ohio Constitution.

The state appealed to the Supreme Court of Ohio, which invalidated the program because it violated the state constitution's prohibition on bills containing more than one subject. The voucher program had become law as part of an appropriations bill, and there was a resulting disunity between it and other portions of the legislation of which it was a part. **The court held that this violated the one-subject rule of the Ohio Constitution, and therefore, the program was invalid under the Ohio constitution**. *Simmons-Harris v. Goff*, 711 N.E.2d 203 (Ohio 1999).

In response to the decision, the general assembly reauthorized the program in time for the 1999–2000 school year, and a new lawsuit was initiated challenging the program. The court enjoined operation of the program on a preliminary basis days before the start of the 1999–2000 school year. State officials appealed to the Sixth Circuit, which did not immediately enter an order. The U.S. Supreme Court granted the state's motion to allow program participants to attend their participating schools that year, pending final disposition by the Sixth Circuit. The district court then permanently enjoined the state from administering the program under *Committee for Public Education and Religious Liberty v. Nyquist*, 413 U.S. 756 (1973). In

Nyquist, the U.S. Supreme Court held that direct aid from states to sectarian schools "in whatever form is invalid." It found the Cleveland school voucher program indistinguishable from the program struck down in *Nyquist*, because only private schools received funds and the vast majority of schools were sectarian.

State officials appealed again to the Sixth Circuit, which found the *Nyquist* decision similar to the Cleveland case. Under both the New York and Cleveland programs, parents received government funds to pay for private schools, the great majority of which were sectarian. The Cleveland program placed no restrictions on the use of funds and had no means of guaranteeing that they would be used for secular, neutral, and non-ideological purposes. The Sixth Circuit found no evidence that the use of vouchers was a neutral form of state assistance that excused direct state funding of religious institutions. Instead, the program discouraged participation by non-religious schools and limited the schools to which parents could apply for funding. No public school participated in the program, nor were places available in suburban public schools for students seeking transfers. The circuit court rejected the state's argument that the government-religious nexus was broken by the idea of parental choice. Their choice was limited to the overwhelmingly sectarian private schools that could afford the tuition restrictions placed on them by the program. The circuit court held that **the program was calculated to attract religious institutions and chose its beneficiaries by non-neutral criteria. It had the primary effect of advancing religion, constituted an endorsement of religion and was a direct monetary subsidy to religious institutions** that was prohibited by the Establishment Clause. *Simmons-Harris v. Zelman*, 234 F.3d 945 (6th Cir. 2000).

◆   Maine law provides that students who live in districts that do not maintain their own schools may attend public schools in other districts or obtain direct state funding to attend qualified private schools. About half the districts in the state do not maintain school facilities. The law excludes sectarian schools from participating in the tuition program. A group of Maine parents sued the state education department and education commissioner in a federal district court, asserting that the exclusion of sectarian schools from the program violated their constitutional rights. **The district court held that while the parents were entitled to send their children to sectarian schools, they were not entitled to require taxpayers to subsidize that choice**.

The parents appealed to the First Circuit. Relying on the U.S. Supreme Court's decision in *Committee for Public Education and Religious Liberty v. Nyquist*, 413 U.S. 756 (1973), the court found that direct tuition payments by a state to sectarian schools violate the Establishment Clause. The First Circuit agreed with the Supreme Court of Maine, which upheld the exclusion of religious school students from the program in *Bagley v. Raymond School Dept.*, below. The state had a paramount interest in avoiding Establishment Clause violations. The First Circuit refused to apply a line of recent Supreme Court cases allowing government funding in the context of target grants available to limited populations for specific purposes, such as the provision of supplemental special education instruction on sectarian school grounds by government employees. The court also rejected claims by the parents that the exclusion of sectarian schools violated their rights under the Equal Protection, Free Exercise, Speech and Due Process Clauses of the Constitution. **The court found that there was no restriction on the use of tuition funds once**

received by the schools, and that the exclusion of religious schools from the program did not prevent any student from attending a religious school. The state was not required to directly pay for sectarian education in order to protect individual rights, and the court affirmed the judgment. *Strout v. Albanese*, 178 F.3d 57 (1st Cir.1999).

◆   Maine's education tuition law provides that local school districts that do not maintain their own schools must pay the tuition of resident students so that they may attend private schools or public schools located in other districts. Only half of the districts in the state maintain their own schools. Districts may contract with one public school to take all of their students, or pay tuition to public and private schools that will accept them. District payments under the second option go directly to the school at which a resident student is accepted. In 1981, the state legislature excluded religious schools from the tuition program, finding that their inclusion would violate the Establishment Clause. **A town which did not maintain its own schools denied tuition requests by five families with children enrolled at a Catholic high school.** The parents sued the town, state education board and commissioner of education in a state superior court, asserting that the exclusion of religious schools from the tuition program violated their constitutional rights. The court granted summary judgment to the town and officials.

The families appealed to the Maine Supreme Judicial Court, which observed that unlike recent state supreme court decisions allowing private schools to benefit from public funding legislation in other states, the Maine tuition program excluded religious schools from participating in the state's existing program. **Exclusion of religious schools from the program did not violate the families' rights under the Free Exercise Clause, since failure to receive state funding did not impair their ability to obtain religious instruction for their children.** The exclusion did not violate the Establishment Clause, and to the contrary, the legislature had enacted the exclusion to prevent violation of the Establishment Clause. Otherwise, the program would require direct government payments to religious schools, with no safeguards to ensure that state funding was used only for secular purposes. According to the court, although the U.S. Supreme Court now applies a different analysis to Establishment Clause cases than the one which prompted the 1981 legislative change, it has never approved of direct state payments to religious schools. There was no merit to the argument of the families that the exclusion of religious schools from the program created an equal protection violation. While the law treated religious schools differently than non-religious schools, the state justified the exclusion in order to comply with the Establishment Clause. The court affirmed the judgment for the town and state officials. *Bagley v. Raymond School Dep't,* 728 A.2d 127 (Me.1999).

◆   Vermont law requires school districts that do not maintain schools to pay the tuition for resident students to attend approved public schools in other districts or an approved independent school selected by parents. Until 1997, one district without a high school authorized tuition payments only for nonsectarian schools. It then adopted a policy allowing tuition reimbursement for the costs of sectarian schools. The parents of 15 students residing in the district selected a parochial school that required instruction in theology prior to graduation and attendance at mass on some occasions. **The state education commissioner terminated state assistance to the district when it voted to reimburse the parents**. The district sued the commissioner and state education department in a state superior court, which held that the payments violated the federal Establishment Clause and the Compelled Support Clause of the Vermont Constitution.

The district appealed to the Supreme Court of Vermont, which declined to evaluate the case under the U.S. Constitution, instead focusing on the Compelled Support Clause of the Vermont Constitution. The court observed that no state law or department rule discussed payment for sectarian education, and that **the method for tuition payment selected by the district in this case would result in the impermissible commingling of public and private funds and the expenditure of public funds for religious education**. It stated that the Compelled Support Clause prohibits compelled worship, church attendance or support of any place of worship contrary to the dictates of a person's conscience. The district argued that the sectarian school was not a place of worship and that the state constitutional provision did not pertain to religious education. The court stated that the Compelled Support Clause also pertained to "any place of worship," which could include a school. The Vermont Supreme Court criticized the Supreme Court of Wisconsin's 1998 opinion upholding the constitutionality of the Milwaukee School Choice Program, and refused to apply it to the present case. The court held that **allowing the district to pay tuition for parochial school students would result in a direct state payment for religious instruction that violated the state constitution**. This was primarily because of the lack of any restriction on the schools' expenditure of public funds once they were received. The court rejected the argument that parental choice in the selection of the sectarian school precluded a finding that the payments to sectarian schools made them constitutional. It affirmed the superior court judgment for the education commissioner and state education department. *Chittenden Town School Dist. v. Vermont Dep't of Educ.*, 169 Vt. 310, 738 A.2d 539 (Vt.1999).

CHAPTER THREE

Freedom of Speech and Association

I. STUDENTS

Although students retain considerable speech rights under the First Amendment, these rights must be balanced by the strong school interest in maintaining an appropriate educational environment. School administrators have a legitimate interest in restricting obscene or disruptive student speech. As a result, they have considerable discretion in determining what constitutes such speech.

A. Protected Speech

◆   A male high school student in Bethel, Washington, delivered a speech nominating a fellow student for elective office before an assembly of over 600 peers. All students were required to attend the assembly as part of the school's self-government program. **In his nominating speech, the student referred to his candidate in terms of an elaborate, explicit sexual metaphor, despite having been warned in advance by two teachers not to deliver it**. Students' reactions during the speech included laughter, graphic sexual gestures, hooting, bewilderment and embarrassment. When the student admitted that he had deliberately used sexual innuendo in his speech, he was informed that he would be suspended for three days and that his name would be removed from the list of candidates for student speaker at graduation.

The student brought suit against the school district in U.S. district court, claiming that his First Amendment right to freedom of speech had been violated. The district court agreed and awarded him damages and attorney's fees. The court also ordered the school district to allow the student to speak at graduation. The U.S. Supreme Court, however, ruled that **while public school students have the right to advocate unpopular and controversial views in school, that right must be balanced against the schools' interest in teaching socially appropriate behavior**. The Constitution does not protect obscene language and a public school, as an instrument of the state, may legitimately establish standards of civil and mature conduct. *Bethel School Dist. No. 403 v. Fraser*, 478 U.S. 675, 106 S.Ct 3159, 92 L.Ed.2d 549 (1986).

◆   In December 1965, a group of adults and high school students, determined to publicize their objections to the hostilities in Vietnam and their support for a truce, wore black armbands during the holiday season and fasted on December 16 and New Year's Eve. Three students and their parents had previously engaged in similar activities and they decided to participate in this program. The principals of the Des Moines schools became aware of the plan and adopted a policy that **any student wearing an armband to school would be asked to remove it, and if he refused he would be suspended until he returned without the armband.** The three students wore their armbands and were all suspended until they agreed to come back without the armbands. They did not return to school until the planned protest period had ended.

The students sued the school district under 42 U.S.C. § 1983 for an injunction restraining school officials from disciplining the students and for nominal damages. A federal district court dismissed the complaint and the Eighth Circuit Court of Appeals summarily affirmed. On appeal to the U.S. Supreme Court, the decision was reversed and remanded. The Court stated that neither students nor teachers shed their constitutional rights to freedom of speech or expression at the schoolhouse gate. **In order for the state to justify prohibition of a particular expression of opinion, it must be able to show something more than a mere desire to avoid the discomfort and unpleasantness that always accompany an unpopular viewpoint**. Where there was no evidence that an expression would materially interfere with the requirements of appropriate discipline in the operation of the school, the prohibition was improper. The expressive act of wearing black armbands did not interrupt school activities, nor intrude in school affairs. The expression had to be allowed. *Tinker v. Des Moines Community School Dist.*, 393 U.S. 503, 89 S.Ct. 733, 21 L.Ed.2d 733 (1969).

◆   A Pennsylvania school district adopted a harassment policy with the goal of providing all students with a safe, secure and nurturing environment, noting that disrespect was unacceptable behavior that threatened the school environment. It defined harassment as verbal or physical conduct based on race, gender, sexual orientation, disability "or other personal characteristics" which substantially interfered with a student's educational performance or created "an intimidating, hostile or offensive environment." The policy cited examples of harassment, including derogatory or demeaning comments, mimicking, name-calling, graffiti, gestures, stalking, threatening, bullying and physical contact. **The definitional section of harassment included comments based on characteristics such as clothing, physical appearance, social skills, peer group, intellect, educational program, hobbies or values**. A state board education member, who was also the guardian of two district students, asserted that the policy was unconstitutional. He filed a federal district court action against the district on behalf of two students, seeking a declaration that the policy violated their First Amendment speech rights. The court granted the district's dismissal motion, finding that the policy was valid.

The parent appealed to the Third Circuit, which reversed the district court decision. **While there was no question that physically harassing conduct is unprotected by the First Amendment, content- or viewpoint-based restrictions on speech are subject to the highest scrutiny by the courts**. Harassing or discriminatory speech, while offensive, might still be used to communicate ideas or emotions that implicate the First Amendment. The district court incorrectly assumed that harassment was never protected. The circuit court held that the district policy swept in personal characteristics that were unprotected by federal anti-discrimination law, such as clothing, appearance, hobbies, values and social skills. It deemed the district's attempt to banish negative comments about appearance, clothing and social skills to be "brave, futile or merely silly." The Third Circuit found that the policy struck at the heart of moral and political discourse and thus the core concern of the First Amendment. The policy was unconstitutionally overbroad under the major U.S. Supreme Court cases concerning student speech, according to the circuit court. It contained several separate passages attempting to define key terms and prohibited a substantial amount of non-vulgar student speech, including private speech that happened to occur on school grounds. It punished speech that actually caused disruption, as well as that which only intended to do so, in violation of the "material disruption" standard established in *Tinker,* above. *Saxe et al. v. State College Area Sch. Dist. et al.*, 240 F.3d 200 (3d Cir. 2001).

◆   A South Dakota school district published an anti-profanity policy in student handbooks distributed at the start of the school year. **Violation of the policy resulted in an in-school suspension and a 2 percent grade reduction for each class missed**. A student who cursed to herself while in the principal's office received a two-and-a-half-day in-school suspension and a 2 percent reduction in her nine-week grade report for each class missed. The sanctions had no impact on the student's semester grades.

The student challenged the discipline through a federal district court action brought against the district for alleged constitutional rights violations. The court held that the student had suffered no injury of any legal consequence and therefore lacked standing to challenge certain generalized grievances alleged in her complaint. While the student's speech had no political or social message of any kind, it was not disruptive to the educational environment or to others at school. The school board had the right to establish the anti-profanity rule and to enforce it against students while they participated in school-sponsored activities. School officials can constitutionally regulate indecent language because it undermines their responsibility to promulgate standards of decency and civility in school. The First Amendment does not prevent reasonable efforts to maintain these standards on campus. **Lewd, obscene, profane, libelous or insulting words are of such slight value to society that any benefit derived from them is outweighed by societal interests in order and morality**. The school district was entitled to summary judgment. *Anderson et al. v. Milbank School District 25-4*, No. CIV 00-1008 (D.S.D. 2000).

♦   After being sent to the hallway for disruptiveness, **a student turned in a writing assignment that was a story describing a student sent out of his class who returns the next day to behead his teacher with a machete**. The teacher believed that the student intended to harm her if she disciplined him again, and reported him to an assistant principal. The police filed a delinquency petition against the student for submitting a death threat to his teacher that constituted abusive conduct in violation of the state disorderly conduct statute. The juvenile court found **that the student** engaged in abusive conduct under circumstances that tended to cause a disturbance, and **made a direct threat that was unprotected by the First Amendment**. The student was found guilty of disorderly conduct and placed on formal supervision for one year.

A state court of appeals affirmed the delinquency adjudication and the student appealed. The Wisconsin Supreme Court stated that in order to support a delinquency petition based on disorderly conduct, the state would have to show violent, abusive, indecent or similar disorderly conduct. The court rejected the student's claim that he could not be convicted solely on the basis of speech. **Speech that constitutes a "true threat" is unprotected because it is not considered an expression of ideas**. "True threats" are a narrow category of unprotected speech that states may regulate without violating the First Amendment. Under some circumstances, the disorderly conduct statute could apply to speech alone and the state was not barred from prosecuting the student because his speech was in writing. According to the court, the student's writing tended to cause or provoke a disturbance. The fact that it may not have caused an actual disturbance was irrelevant. The lower courts had failed to consider the student's First Amendment rights. His writing was not a "true threat" because it did not express an unequivocal, unconditional and specific expression of an immediate intent to inflict injury. There was no evidence that he had threatened the teacher in the past or had a propensity toward violence. **In the context of a creative writing class, the student's story was not a true threat.** Under the specific circumstances of the case, **the story was protected by the First Amendment**. The court cautioned that its decision should not be interpreted as undermining school disciplinary authority. The school had appropriately suspended the student for crude and repugnant writing. As shown by this case, there are circumstances when school authorities may discipline for conduct that law officers may not. The court reversed the judgment. *In the Interest of Douglas D.*, 243 Wis.2d 204, 626 N.W.2d 725 (2001).

♦   A Kansas school board responded to racial incidents in its schools by adopting a harassment policy that in part, prohibited certain clothing and materials, including Confederate flags. A student was disciplined numerous times during the school year and accused of using racial slurs on several occasions. Later that year, **the student drew a Confederate flag during class, which resulted in a three-day suspension for intentionally violating the anti-harassment policy**. The student's father filed a federal district court action against the district. The court dismissed the action. The court stated that the case involved no fundamental speech rights, but was rather a question of appropriate discipline for wilful violation of a school policy. The policy had been adopted to prevent further racial disturbances at district schools, and the district had acted reasonably and within its constitutional authority in doing so. The suspension was upheld because it was clear to the court that the student had intentionally violated the policy. The fact that his conduct did not cause actual disruption did not deprive the school of the authority to enforce the policy.

On appeal to the U.S. Court of Appeals, Tenth Circuit, the circuit court rejected the student's assertion that the district denied him due process before suspending him. The student was provided with notice of the charges against him, the evidence against him and an opportunity to explain his position, in accordance with the applicable requirements. The court also rejected the student's assertion that the district was required to demonstrate he intentionally violated the harassment policy before taking disciplinary action against him. Schools do not have to prove intent, and the court found no reason to mandate a finding of intent before school districts can impose disciplinary sanctions. Second, the circuit court determined no Equal Protection violation occurred. Students are not a protected group, therefore, only a rational basis for the harassment policy was needed. Because of the district's history of racial tension, the policy was an acceptable way to protect the district's legitimate interest in avoiding disruptions to the educational process. Third, the circuit court stated that **the district did not violate the student's First Amendment rights, finding the district's interest in avoiding additional racial disputes was enough to trump the student's free speech rights**. Lastly, the circuit court rejected the student's facial challenge to the harassment and intimidation policy, concluding that the policy was neither unconstitutionally vague nor overbroad. The district court decision was upheld. *West v. Derby Unified School District No. 260*, 206 F.3d 1358 (10th Cir. 2000).

♦   **A Florida high school student displayed a Confederate flag to other students during a school lunch break**. An administrator allegedly preempted any explanation by the student and advised him that the flag was a racist symbol that he had no First Amendment right to display on school grounds. Upon reaching the school office, the student encountered another student who had been detained for wearing a T-shirt depicting a Confederate flag and indicated his approval of the shirt. **The school suspended him for nine days and recommended expulsion for attempting to incite a riot, insubordination and disruption**. School officials filed a criminal complaint against the student for disturbing the school in violation of state law. He sued the school district and officials for constitutional rights violations. The district court considered summary judgment motions by the district and officials and agreed with the student that the school maintained an unwritten ban on Confederate symbols. This policy had to be considered at a trial and the claim against the district could not be dismissed. However, the claims against the officials failed to allege any clearly-established constitutional rights violation and were properly dismissed.

The circuit court then vacated and withdrew its previous opinion and issued a new opinion, reaffirming the initial decision in favor of the school board. However, the circuit court agreed with the assistant principals that the *Bethel Sch. Dist. v. Fraser* decision, *above*, had cast sufficient uncertainty on the area of student expression to create doubt in the mind of a reasonable school administrator attempting to respond to a student's display of a controversial symbol. The court found that a reasonable school official would be charged with knowledge of both *Tinker* and *Fraser*, the two most relevant decisions in the area of student expression. It further acknowledged the tension between the two cases. Under *Tinker*, school officials may halt student expression only where the display would likely lead to a material and substantial disruption of school. However, *Fraser* states, "schools must teach by example the shared values of a civilized social order." Because a reasonable school official might understand that *Fraser* represented an alteration of the legal landscape created by *Tinker*, and because the display of a Confederate flag is offensive to many people, the court could not conclude that prohibiting the display demonstrated incompetence by the assistant principals. **The student's display tested the boundaries of acceptable school conduct, and the discipline did not violate his clearly established constitutional rights** under the *Fraser* standard, according to the circuit court. The court was therefore not required to decide the underlying issue of whether the display of the Confederate flag was unconstitutional. Instead, it ruled that the assistant principals were entitled to immunity and affirmed the district court judgment. *Denno v. School Board of Volusia County, Florida,* 218 F.3d 1267 (11th Cir. 2000), *cert. denied,* 121 S.Ct. 382, 148 L.Ed.2d 295 (2000).

◆   A rule adopted by a Missouri school board required students to obtain prior approval by the principal or assistant principal whenever they intended to distribute materials at school. A student candidate for office met with a faculty advisor and signed a contract agreeing to obey all rules. He also received notice from a student council member that all campaign flyers and posters required approval by the school administration. The administration approved his campaign slogan, and on the day of the election, the student handed out condoms with stickers bearing this slogan, without first notifying the administration. Another student complained to the student council advisor about the student's tactic as the votes were being counted, and the principal disqualified him from the election for violating the rule against distributing materials without prior approval. The student sued the school district, principal and assistant principal in a federal district court for violation of his speech rights. **The court held that the school election rules did not violate the Constitution and that the election was a school-sponsored activity taking place in a non-public forum.** It upheld the principal's decision to disqualify the student for failing to comply with school rules as reasonably related to the school's legitimate pedagogical goals. The student appealed the court's order for summary judgment to the U.S. Court of Appeals, Eighth Circuit.

The circuit court noted that under *Hazelwood School Dist. v. Kuhlmeier*, 484 U.S. 260 (1988), schools have great authority to control student speech content in the context of a school-sponsored activity that is not also a public forum. **In the absence of a public forum, school officials may limit student speech in school-sponsored activities if it is reasonably related to legitimate pedagogical concerns**. In this case, the school district did not open the election to the public and intended to control speech that was related to the election. Accordingly, the election took place in the context of a non-public forum that was part of the school curriculum. The student asserted that the district allowed other students to distribute candy and gum to classmates during previous elections and that it violated his First Amendment rights by prohibiting the distribution of condoms. The court disagreed, noting that the condom distribution might lead to the mistaken impression that school officials approved of the tactic. Unlike the distribution of candy or gum, the distribution of condoms carried with it the implication that the school was making a statement, and the district had a legitimate interest in disassociating its extracurricular programs from controversy. The court affirmed the judgment for the school district. *Henerey v. City of St. Charles School Dist.*, 200 F.3d 1128 (8th Cir. 1999).

◆   A high school band instructor selected the song *White Rabbit* for inclusion in the marching band's program, which featured music from the 1960s and 1970s as its theme. Students who participated in marching band received academic credit and letter grades. **The superintendent decided to remove the song from the program after a parent noted that the song was considered a part of the 1960s drug culture**. After reviewing the song's lyrics (which were not a part of the band's presentation), the superintendent agreed that the song could be considered as promoting the illegal use of drugs.

Some of the students sued the school district in a federal district court for First Amendment speech violations. **The court found that while students have certain speech rights in school, their rights are not as strong as those of adults in other settings**. In this case, the speech was a part of a school-sponsored event and could be considered as having the school's imprimatur. As a matter of law, school officials had the authority to regulate school-sponsored expressive activities, so long as the regulation was reasonably related to legitimate pedagogical concerns. The court expressed its unwillingness to second guess the superintendent's judgment, finding that he acted reasonably when contacted by the parent. He conducted an investigation that revealed the song's history of association with the 1960s drug culture and reasonably concluded that inclusion of it in the band program would send the wrong message that the school tolerated drug use. The court awarded summary judgment to the school district and officials. *McCann v. Ft. Zumwalt School Dist.*, 50 F.Supp.2d 918 (E.D.Mo.1999).

◆   A tenth grade California student experienced difficulties changing her class schedule. After spending several hours attempting to obtain class reassignments, a guidance counselor advised her that some of the courses she requested were already full. Although the student's response was later disputed, **the guidance counselor claimed that she stated, "if you don't give me this schedule change, I'm going to shoot you!"** The counselor complained to an assistant principal later in the day and the school suspended the student for three days. The student filed a lawsuit against the school district in the U.S. District Court for the Southern District of California, claiming that the suspension violated her free speech rights under the California and U.S. Constitutions and the California Education Code. The court held that the student's statement was protected by the First Amendment. The school district appealed to the U.S. Court of Appeals, Ninth Circuit.

The court held that the district court had improperly expanded upon the student's First Amendment free speech guarantees by incorporating a standard contained in the state education code. The U.S. Supreme Court has permitted school officials to restrict student free speech rights due to educational and disciplinary concerns. **Threats of physical violence are not protected by the First Amendment or by state law, and the student's statement was not protected**. The court determined that a reasonable person would have interpreted the student's statement as a threat. Because the guidance counselor felt threatened during the confrontation, the student's speech was not protected, and the district court judgment was reversed. *Lovell v. Poway Unified School Dist.*, 90 F.3d 367 (9th Cir.1996).

B. Student Publications

1. Elementary and High Schools

High school or elementary school administrators may exercise prior restraint over student publications if a reasonable basis exists for the belief that a publication would materially disrupt class work, involve substantial disorder or invade the rights of others.

◆   **A Missouri high school principal objected to two articles that had been prepared for publication in the school newspaper**. Because the principal believed that there was no time to edit the articles before the end of the school year, **he deleted the two pages on which the articles appeared**. Former high school students who were members of the newspaper staff filed a lawsuit against the school district and school officials alleging that their First Amendment rights were violated when the pages were removed from the newspaper before publication.

A U.S. district court ruled in favor of the school district. The U.S. Court of Appeals, Eighth Circuit, reversed, holding that the newspaper was a public forum "intended to be and operated as a conduit for student viewpoint." The school district filed for review by the U.S. Supreme Court, which agreed to hear the case. The U.S. Supreme Court noted that school facilities, including school sponsored newspapers, become public forums only if school authorities have intentionally opened those facilities for indiscriminate use by either the general public "or by some segment of the public, such as student organizations." The Court determined that since the school district allowed a large amount of control by the journalism teacher and the principal, it had not intentionally opened the newspaper as a public forum for indiscriminate student speech. **The Court determined that school officials can exercise "editorial control over the style and content of student speech in**

school-sponsored expressive activities so long as their actions are reasonably related to legitimate [educational] concerns." Because the decision to delete two pages from the newspaper was reasonable under the circumstances, no violation of the First Amendment occurred. The Supreme Court ruled in favor of the school district and its officials. *Hazelwood School Dist. v. Kuhlmeier*, 484 U.S. 261, 108 S.Ct. 562, 98 L.Ed.2d 592 (1988).

◆   A publication titled *OUTSIDE!* was distributed to students at a Washington high school. The publication included criticism of the school administration and an article containing a list of "the top ten things I would like to see happen at school," which included suggestions that students "feed snake bite antidote or Visine to someone" in order to make them sick. The newsletter suggested throwing explosives in school toilets; making bomb threats in order to leave school early; accessing the school public address system; and using teacher names and addresses to place or answer homosexual personal advertisements. Also included were teacher addresses and telephone numbers, which were supplied with the suggestion that students make harassing calls to their homes. **A student who was identified as a contributor to the publication was suspended from school and then expelled** for the remaining four weeks of school and the first semester of the following school year. The penalty included a provision that allowed the student to re-enter the school system at the beginning of the next school year.

The student's family commenced a state court action against the school district for a declaratory judgment and a writ of review. The court dismissed both actions, and the family appealed to the state appeals court, adding claims for civil rights violations under 42 U.S.C. § 1983. The court held that both the petition for writ of review and declaratory judgment actions were properly dismissed. Even though the underlying appeals from adverse disciplinary decisions were dismissed, the civil rights claims under Section 1983 could go forward. The student asserted violation of his First Amendment rights, claiming that school discipline cannot be based on the use of threatening and vulgar language and the failure to obtain prior approval for distribution of the publication on campus. In addressing these arguments, the court synthesized a trio of U.S. Supreme Court cases that, together, define the rights of student expression in schools: *Tinker v. Des Moines Community School Dist.*, 393 U.S. 503 (1969); *Bethel School Dist. No. 403 v. Fraser*, 478 U.S. 675 (1986); and *Hazelwood School Dist. v. Kuhlmeier*, 484 U.S. 260 (1988). Based on these cases, the court found that the school was not required to tolerate student speech that was inconsistent with its educational mission. It could not be legitimately argued that the use of vulgar or threatening language that did not result in actual disruption was exempt from discipline. The student advocated methods for causing personal injury, property damage and disruption of schools. He also identified the source of necessary materials to carry out the disruption. School officials could reasonably believe that the publication would substantially interfere with the school environment and the rights of others. **Unlike the situation in *Tinker*, this case did not involve the suppression of an unpopular viewpoint. The advocacy of bomb threats, interfering with a school public address system, poisoning and harassing school employees and other violence was not simple protest** and was distinguishable from *Tinker*. The court dismissed the state-law declaratory judgment claim and otherwise affirmed the trial court judgment in favor of the school district.

Pangle v. Bend-LaPine School District, 169 Or.App. 376, 10 P.3d 275 (Or.App. 2000).

✦   A Massachusetts school district decided to make condoms available to students through a school distribution policy. A parent who was a leading opponent of the policy submitted advertisements to the school yearbook and newspaper containing a brief endorsement of abstinence. **The student editors of the newspaper and yearbook rejected the advertisements, stating that neither publication accepted political statements under an unwritten policy**. Although the school superintendent and other officials and administrators recommended publishing the advertisements, the students rejected them, and invited the parent to submit a letter to the editor. The parent instead filed a federal district court action against the town, school officials and committee members, asserting constitutional rights violations. The court denied the parent's request for a temporary order and awarded summary judgment to the town and officials.

The parent appealed to the U.S. Court of Appeals, First Circuit, which reversed the district court judgment. However, the court later reheard the case, and issued a new opinion in favor of the town and officials. It held that there was no state action by the town or officials which created constitutional liability. The court rejected the parent's claim that the decisions of the students could be attributed to school officials. Evidence indicated that the students had acted independently and contrary to the advice of school officials. **State law did not impose a duty upon the officials to intervene in the editorial process and supported the independence of student editors**. The students were not state actors by virtue of their public school attendance, and the court affirmed the district court judgment. *Yeo v. Town of Lexington*, 131 F.3d 241 (1st Cir.1997).

✦   A Wisconsin school district policy allowed school principals to review non-school publications prior to distribution by students 24 hours in advance. **The policy allowed a principal to halt the distribution of a publication containing libelous or obscene language, or containing insults to particular groups of individuals or that would otherwise disrupt or interfere with school procedures**. An elementary school principal relied on the policy in denying permission to a fourth grader who sought to hand out invitations at school for a church group meeting. After several months of unsuccessfully negotiating with district officials to distribute the invitations, the student filed a lawsuit against the district in a federal court, seeking declaratory and injunctive relief that the policy was unconstitutional. The court upheld the policy except for its requirement that all handouts disclaim school involvement, but held that the principal had violated the First Amendment by prohibiting distribution of the invitations based on religion. The student appealed to the U.S. Court of Appeals, Seventh Circuit, and the district cross-appealed the disclaimer issue.

The court of appeals rejected the argument that the elementary school was a traditional public forum where free speech rights were at a maximum level of protection. **Elementary schools are not open for unrestricted communication and school administrators may reasonably restrict student expression where it is required to preserve a proper educational environment and prevent younger students from exposure to obscenity, insults and other disruptive**

speech. Because schools are free to screen student handouts, and reasonable regulation of speech is permissible in the school environment, the policy did not violate the Constitution. The court reversed the district court judgment concerning the disclaimer, finding it reasonable. *Muller by Muller v. Jefferson Lighthouse School*, 98 F.3d 1530 (7th Cir.1996).

◆   **The principal of a New Jersey junior high school censored two film reviews from the school's official student-written newspaper.** The films, *Mississippi Burning* and *Rain Man*, were both R-rated and the principal took the action without notice. A student's mother filed a lawsuit against the school board, superintendent and principal in a New Jersey trial court, claiming violations of the student's constitutional right to free expression. The court held that the principal's action was reasonably related to the school's legitimate educational concerns under the U.S. Constitution. However, the action violated the student's rights under the state constitution, which afforded broad protection to free speech rights. The Superior Court of New Jersey, Appellate Division, substantially affirmed the trial court's judgment, ruling instead that the censorship violated the First Amendment, but not the state constitution. The school board and officials appealed to the Supreme Court of New Jersey.

The supreme court agreed with the appellate division court's decision, and cited portions of it in its opinion. It agreed that the school newspaper was not a public forum and that school officials could exercise editorial control over style and content in a manner that was reasonably related to legitimate educational concerns. In this case, however, the school board's policy was vaguely defined and had no specific rule concerning R-rated films. There was also evidence that the policy was often ignored or inconsistently applied. **The school board and officials failed to establish a legitimate educational policy to govern school publications, and the result was a violation of the student's rights under the First Amendment**. *Desilets v. Clearview Regional Bd. of Educ.*, 137 N.J. 585, 647 A.2d 150 (1994).

2. Colleges and Universities

◆   A student newspaper at a Virginia university published an article describing the success of a student placement program. The article quoted a university official who facilitated student participation in the program and referred to her as "Director of Butt Licking." **The official filed a Virginia circuit court action against the student newspaper for defamation and use of insulting words** in violation of state law. The court held that the newspaper reference was void of any literal meaning and not reasonably susceptible to interpretation as containing factual information. The official appealed.

The Supreme Court of Virginia observed that **statements which cannot reasonably be interpreted as stating facts about a person cannot form the basis of a defamation action**. The court rejected the official's claim that she was entitled to present her case to a jury on grounds that literal interpretation of the offensive phrase imputed to her a criminal violation of the state sodomy statute and was defamatory. It also rejected her assertion that the statement injured her reputation and held her up to ridicule by implying that she lacked integrity. The court affirmed the judgment for the newspaper. *Yeagle v. Collegiate Times*, 497 S.E.2d 136 (Va.1998).

◆   **The Board of Regents of Oklahoma State University (OSU) temporarily suspended the showing by the university Student Union Activities Board (SUAB) of** *The Last Temptation of Christ*, a film depicting Jesus descending from the cross to marry, father children and return to the cross. An association of students and faculty members advocating free speech rights filed a lawsuit in the U.S. District Court for the Northern District of Oklahoma, seeking declaratory relief. The regents lifted the suspension, and the film was shown as originally scheduled. The district court held that school officials could not be held liable for damages under 42 U.S.C. § 1983 and the association appealed to the U.S. Court of Appeals, Tenth Circuit. The court remanded the case to determine whether the association was entitled to nominal damages and whether the regents had qualified immunity from liability. The court determined that the association was not entitled to nominal damages and that the board enjoyed qualified immunity. The association filed a second appeal with the Tenth Circuit.

The court rejected the association's argument that the regents had violated the constitutional rights of its members by imposing content-based censorship. The regents had merely imposed a temporary suspension while obtaining a legal opinion concerning OSU's potential liability if it chose to allow the showing of the film. The regents could not be held liable for violating any clearly-established constitutional rights and the regents' action did not violate constitutional restraints on censorship. Because the SUAB and OSU were closely related in funding and staffing, the regents had merely displayed caution in their decisionmaking process. The association was entitled to an award of attorney's fees for work done before the district court's initial order. *Cummins v. Campbell*, 44 F.3d 847 (10th Cir. 1994).

◆   A group of student journalists and an organization that promoted the rights of the student press brought a lawsuit against the U.S. Department of Education and the Secretary of Education. **They sought to enjoin the government from enforcing a provision of the Family Educational Rights and Privacy Act (FERPA), which allows the complete withdrawal of federal funding from any university which discloses personally identifiable student records**. The journalists alleged that this prohibition, as applied to campus security arrest reports, violated their First Amendment right to receive information. The journalists moved for an injunction in a federal district court to immediately halt enforcement of FERPA's prohibition. After resolving numerous procedural matters, the court examined the burdens imposed by FERPA and balanced them against the corresponding governmental interest. The journalists argued that the general arrest reports, which are provided by local law enforcement officials, do not distinguish which arrestees are students. Further, any attempt at matching those lists to student records is difficult and makes the effort to report campus crime ineffectual. The government maintained that the burden was trivial. **The court held that the government's position was "untenable," and that its interests were outweighed by the rights of the journalists**. A temporary injunction was issued which prevented the withdrawal of federal funding from any campus which disclosed its arrest reports. *Student Press Law Center v. Alexander*, 778 F.Supp. 1227 (D.D.C.1991).

C. Nonschool Publications

◆   A New York high school senior produced a publication advocating the destruction of school property and other acts of insubordination. Copies were found in classrooms and the school cafeteria. **The school's assistant principal suspended the student for five days after he obtained the student's admission that he had produced the publication and distributed copies at school.** School district officials notified the student of a hearing to further consider the suspension. A hearing officer held that the student had participated in the publication and distribution on school grounds of an unauthorized publication containing vulgar language and calling for the destruction of school property. He recommended that five days be added to the previously-imposed suspension. The district superintendent adopted the recommendation, and the school board upheld it. The student and his parents appealed to the state commissioner of education who determined, first, that the student had been denied due process because the disciplinary notice failed to advise him that distribution of the publication on school grounds would be examined at the hearing and, second, that the determination of guilt was unsupported by the evidence.

The New York Supreme Court, Appellate Division, annulled the commissioner's decision, finding that the notice adequately advised the student of the subject matter of the hearing and that proof of the student's guilt was overwhelming. The family appealed to the Court of Appeals of New York, which held that the notice to the student satisfied due process requirements. **While school officials need not specify every single charge against a student, the notice must be sufficiently specific to advise the student and his or her counsel of the incidents giving rise to discipline.** If students are given a fair opportunity to tell their side of the story and present evidence, due process is served. The district had complied with this requirement and **the court held that the commissioner had abused his discretion by reversing the suspension.** *Bd. of Educ. of Monticello Central School Dist. v. Comm'r of Educ.,* 91 N.Y.2d 133, 667 N.Y.S.2d 671, 690 N.E.2d 480 (1997).

◆   A Washington school district adopted a policy requiring its high school students to submit all student-written material to school officials before that material could be distributed on school premises or at school functions. The policy was aimed at student writing that was not contained in official school publications. **A group of students published and distributed a newspaper at a school barbecue without submitting it for review. As a result, the students received reprimands** on their permanent records. The students sued the school district in a federal district court under 42 U.S.C. § 1983, claiming that the district's predistribution review policy violated their free speech rights. The district court held that the policy did not violate the students' rights. The students then appealed to the U.S. Court of Appeals, Ninth Circuit. The court of appeals contrasted the case to *Hazelwood School Dist. v. Kuhlmeier,* above, wherein the U.S. Supreme Court held that a policy of prior review and censorship of student writing is justified when it is a part of educators' reasonable exercise of authority over school-sponsored publications. In this case, **the policy was aimed at curtailing communications among students which were unassociated with school sponsorship or endorsement. Therefore, the court held that the policy violated the students'**

free speech rights guaranteed by the First Amendment. *Burch v. Barker*, 861 F.2d 1149 (9th Cir.1988).

D. Personal Appearance and Dress Codes

1. Dress Codes

◆   **Two students** who **wore T-shirts displaying Confederate flags on the back with the phrase "Southern Thunder" to school** were told the shirts violated the school's dress code, which prohibits clothing or emblems that contain "slogans, words or in any way depicts alcohol, tobacco or any illegal, immoral or racist implication." The students were directed to turn the shirts inside out or go home and change. The students refused and received three-day suspensions. They returned to school wearing the T-shirts after serving the initial suspensions, only to receive another three-day suspension. The students' families sued the school board, superintendent and principal in a federal district court for First Amendment rights violations. The court held that wearing the T-shirts did not qualify as "speech" under the Constitution and awarded summary judgment to the district and school officials.

The families appealed to the U.S. Court of Appeals, Sixth Circuit, which held that the students intended to express themselves by wearing the shirts. This was particularly evident because the students chose to wear them upon their return to school after serving the first suspensions. **There was evidence that the dress code had been selectively enforced, in violation of the requirement** established in *Tinker v. Des Moines Community School District*, 393 U.S. 503 (1969), **that school speech regulations that discriminate according to viewpoint violate core principles of the Constitution**. The students testified that other students were allowed to wear clothing venerating Malcolm X and that the wearing of their shirts did not disrupt any school activities. The court found that there was no way that the personal choice to wear clothing could be construed as "school-sponsored." Under *Tinker*, undifferentiated fear or apprehension of a disturbance is insufficient to overcome personal speech rights. The district court would have to reconsider evidence that the district's facially neutral policy was enforced against the students in a content-specific manner. *Castorina et al. v. Madison County School Board et al.*, 246 F.3d 536 (6th Cir. 2001).

◆   **A Minnesota student who was told by school administrators that he could not wear a sweatshirt bearing the message "Straight Pride" obtained a temporary order from a federal district court allowing him to wear it in the absence of substantial disruption of the school or material interference with school activities**. The court held that the student demonstrated a strong likelihood of success on the merits of his constitutional claim. There was no evidence linking a previous racial incident at the school with a threat of disruption caused by issues of sexuality that might occur as the result of his selection of clothing, nor did the district not present any evidence of disruption. Under the U.S. Supreme Court's decision in *Tinker v. Des Moines Community School District*, 393 U.S. 503 (1969), school officials must have a reasonable belief that student expression will materially and substantially interfere with school activities or infringe on student rights before they take action to stifle it. The court only reinstated the existing status quo before the sweatshirt ban, leaving open the possibility that school officials could act to protect the school environment where they had a reasonable belief that student expression could lead to substantial disruption of the school environment or to material interference with school activities. While the school had made "a conscious and commendable effort at creating an environment of tolerance and respect for diversity," the student's sweatshirt message itself had to be tolerated, absent evidence of disruption. *Chambers v. Babbitt*, 145 F.Supp.2d 1068 (D. Minn. 2001).

◆   An Ohio school district's dress and grooming policy forbade students from wearing clothing with offensive illustrations and slogans. A student came to school wearing a T-shirt depicting a three-faced Jesus with the words "See No Truth. Hear no truth. Speak No Truth." It also displayed the name "Marilyn Manson" and the word "believe" in capital letters, with the letters "LIE" highlighted. A school administrator told the student that the shirt was offensive and instructed him to turn it inside out, go home to change, or leave school and be considered truant. The student elected to leave school and returned on each of the next four school days wearing a different Marilyn Manson T-shirt. He then stayed home for four school days and commenced a federal district court action against the school board and three school administrators for civil rights violations. The district court denied the student's request for preliminary relief and then granted the board and administrators' motion for summary judgment, determining that **the administrators were entitled to prohibit a student from wearing an offensive but not obscene T-shirt to school** under *Bethel School Dist No. 403. v. Fraser,* 478 U.S. 675 (1986), even in the absence of the substantial disruption requirement standard from *Tinker v. Des Moines Indep. School Dist.*, 393 U.S. 503 (1969).

The student appealed to the U.S. Court of Appeals, Sixth Circuit. Along with the *Tinker* and *Fraser* decisions, the Supreme Court's decision in *Hazelwood School Dist. v. Kuhlmeier*, 484 U.S. 260 (1988), established the proper framework for analyzing the case. The circuit court determined that the school administrators had banned the T-shirts because the Marilyn Manson band promoted destructive conduct and demoralizing values that were contrary to the educational mission of the school. The mocking of a religious figure was contrary to the school's educational mission and disrespectful to the beliefs of others. Lyrics from Marilyn Manson songs were also contrary to the school's mission and goal of establishing a common core of values. **Since the T-shirts were counterproductive and against the educational mission of the school and community, the district court had correctly found that the school was not unreasonable in prohibiting the T-shirts** under its dress code. The *Fraser* decision held that schools maintain the authority to prohibit student speech that is inconsistent with the basic educational mission of a school, even though such speech might not be censored outside the school environment. The student's arguments that the administrators had demonstrated viewpoint discrimination and violated his due process rights were without merit, and the court affirmed the district court judgment for the school board. *Boroff v. Van Wert City Bd. of Educ.*, 220 F.3d 465 (6th Cir. 2000).

◆   A group of parents of students attending Bossier Parish schools sued the board in a federal district court for an order preventing implementation of the recently enacted, mandatory dress code policy. The district court awarded summary judgment to the school board, and the parents appealed to the U.S. Court of Appeals, Fifth Circuit. Although the district court had concluded that students' choice of clothing was not protected under the First Amendment, the Fifth Circuit ruled that in circumstances where attire intends to communicate a message, it may be entitled to constitutional protection. The court presumed that the First Amendment applied to the case, but held that **the board's interest in regulating the school environment permitted it to institute a student dress code**. In doing so, the court applied the same standard of review used to evaluate time, place and manner regulations. Under that analysis, a school board regulation satisfies constitutional requirements if it furthers an important or substantial government interest, if the interest is unrelated to the suppression of student expression and if incidental restrictions on speech are no more than necessary to promote the government interest. In this case, **the dress code furthered the school interest in increasing test scores and reducing disciplinary problems, and did so in a manner that was not related to suppressing student speech**. The circuit court rejected the parents' Fourteenth Amendment claim that requiring parents to buy uniforms created a financial burden and denied some students the right to a free education. There was evidence that the uniforms were inexpensive and were available through a donation program where necessary, undercutting the assertion that it created a financial burden on poor students. The court affirmed the judgment for the school board. *Canady v. Bossier Parish School Board*, 240 F.3d 437 (5th Cir. 2001).

◆   A Texas school district approved a new dress code that limited student apparel and forbade the wearing of denim, leather or suede clothing except as outerwear, along with any clothing suggesting gang affiliation. The dress code contained an opt-out provision through which parents could apply for an exemption on behalf of their children based on philosophical or religious objections or medical necessity. Those seeking to opt out were required to submit a questionnaire designed to elicit information about the sincerity of their beliefs. A three-step grievance procedure was included for review of decisions rejecting opt-out requests. The parents of 72 children sought to opt out of the uniform requirement, and the district granted 12 of the requests. **Some of the families who failed to obtain relief through the grievance procedure commenced a federal district court action against the school district for alleged constitutional rights violations**.

The court considered the district's motion for summary judgment and determined that the students were entitled to advance the action, even though none of them had been suspended or expelled yet as a consequence of failing to abide by the uniform policy. Because assignment to an alternative school and expulsion were available sanctions for failure to comply with the policy, the complaining parties had established a particularized, imminent injury and had legal standing to assert their claims. **The court observed that expressive conduct in school may be constitutionally limited where the conduct is inconsistent with the school's educational mission**. The state had a compelling interest in promoting education, while the intrusion on student rights created by the policy was minimal. The court rejected the students' assertion that the wearing of the clothing of their choice had symbolic meaning that conveyed a message. **The students did not have the requisite intent to convey a message that warranted First Amendment protection**. The court rejected the students' due process claims, as the policy caused only a minimal intrusion on their rights, while serving a legitimate educational purpose. The court rejected the students' arguments based on violation of their religious rights, because the policy was not enacted for the purpose of inhibiting any religious practice or belief. Although some of the religious exemption requests had been denied, this had occurred not on the basis of religion but because the students had worn other types of uniforms in the past without objection and did not indicate why they objected to the current school uniform. In some cases, parents simply did not bother to explain their objections. The court rejected the students' remaining arguments and awarded summary judgment to the district. *Littlefield v. Forney Indep. School Dist.*, 108 F.Supp.2d 681 (N.D. Tex. 2000).

◆   A Connecticut city school board adopted a dress code prohibiting students from wearing jeans and specifying that they wear conventionally styled clothing within a narrow range of colors. Students could wear solid color pants that were to be belted or worn at the waist, and solid color tops and sweaters without emblems and logos. The policy prohibited: jeans, torn clothing, tank tops, halter tops, bare midriffs, transparent clothing, plunging necklines, hoods and undershirts worn as outerwear. It expressly prohibited clothing or items indicating gang affiliation. Students were also precluded from wearing jewelry or chains that could be dangerous, beepers and other electronic devices, noisy footwear and skirts or shorts shorter than knee length. The policy did not regulate clothing required by religious practices and provided options for students who could not afford to buy specified clothing. The policy initially contained an opt-out provision, but the board later modified it so that it was mandatory. **Students who were subjected to or threatened with discipline for failure to comply with the dress code sued the city in a state trial court, asserting that its enforcement would violate their rights to privacy and liberty.** They were joined in the action by parents who asserted that enforcement of the policy interfered with their asserted rights of parental autonomy.

In considering the school board's motion for summary judgment, the court observed that the policy limited students to conventionally styled clothing with a narrow choice of colors and fabrics. There was no definitive standard for analyzing student dress code cases, but three federal circuit courts had required proof that school district restrictions on hair styles had an effect upon school health, discipline or decorum. While school codes involving hair length also regulate appearance outside school, those which concern clothing do not, and **clothing regulations thus needed only to have a rational relation to achievement of a legitimate state purpose, such as removing disruption from schools.** Even though the court determined that this relatively low standard should apply, the school board in this case failed to meet the standard. **The only evidence of disruption presented by the board was that the wearing of very large, baggy jeans impeded student movements on stairs.** Although there was also some evidence of brand competition among students, the school board had failed to show that it was entitled to summary judgment on any other aspect of the dress code. The board would have the burden of showing in later proceedings that it could justify a policy that could subject the students to the risk of discipline. The parents' claims were also entitled to judgment unless the board could sufficiently justify the policy. The court granted the board's motion for summary judgment solely on the baggy pants portion of the policy. *Byars et al. v. City of Waterbury*, No. X01-CV-990152489S, 2000 Conn. Super. Lexis 1888 (Conn. Super. Ct. 2000).

◆   The New York City Education Board adopted a mandatory citywide uniform policy for all students in grades pre-kindergarten through eight who attended "elementary schools." Students at schools designated as middle schools, intermediate schools, junior high and high schools were not covered by the policy. The board found that a uniform policy would promote a more effective learning climate, foster school unity and pride, improve student performance and self-esteem, reduce parental expenses, eliminate label competition and improve student conduct and discipline. The policy required approval at individual schools with the consultation of parent and parent-teacher associations, and individual families could chose to opt out of a program after implementation by the individual school. **A fifth grader and her father objected to the implementation of the policy and sued the school board** in a federal district court. The board moved for summary judgment.

The court ordered the student to obtain counsel, since non-attorney parents are not permitted to represent their children in the courts. The court then considered the father's argument that the program violated his right to direct his child's upbringing, and that this right would be infringed even if she opted out of it because she would "stick out" by not wearing a uniform. According to the court, parents do not have an unencumbered right to bring up their children without reasonable government regulation. The policy rationally furthered the board's interest in educating students. **The opt-out provision addressed the perceived intrusion on parental rights, and courts have upheld far more intrusive public school programs,** including curricular requirements to perform community service prior to graduation. The court awarded summary judgment to the board with respect to the father's claims. *Lipsman v. New York City Bd. of Educ.*, 1999 U.S. Dist. LEXIS 10591 (S.D.N.Y.1999).

◆   A Louisiana elementary school maintained a dress code that prohibited boys from wearing earrings at school. A second grader came to school numerous times wearing an earring and was eventually suspended for habitual violation of the dress code. His mother asked a state district court for a temporary order allowing him to wear the earring to school. The court rejected the mother's claim that the gender-based rule violated the student's Fourteenth Amendment right to equal protection of the laws. **There was evidence that a male student wearing an earring could disrupt an elementary classroom and that implementation of the dress code was reasonable to avoid disruption**. The school's dress code had a valid educational objective and was a reasonable reflection of prevailing community values. The court affirmed the trial court judgment for the school board. *Jones v. W.T. Henning Elementary School*, 721 So.2d 530 (La.App.3d Cir.1998).

2.   Hair Length and Appearance

◆   **A Texas school board adopted a student grooming policy that prohibited boys from wearing their hair below the shirt collar.** An elementary school principal observed a third grade boy with a ponytail and advised him and his mother that he was in violation of the grooming policy. **The school board suspended the**

student for three days for refusing to comply with the policy, and placed him on in-school suspension. The student's mother removed him from school and filed a Texas district court action against the board for violation of the Texas Constitution and state law. The court granted summary judgment to the board, but the Court of Appeals of Texas reversed the decision in part. On remand, the district court held a jury trial resulting in a decision for the board. The court later modified its judgment, ruling that the board had violated the Texas Equal Rights Amendment and state law. **It permanently enjoined the board from enforcing the policy**, and its judgment was affirmed by the court of appeals.

The board appealed to the Supreme Court of Texas, which held that school grooming policies do not implicate constitutional issues, and should not be reviewed by the courts. Therefore, there was no violation of the Texas Constitution. The Texas statute relied upon by the trial court was similar to Title VII of the Civil Rights Act of 1964, since both prohibited certain types of discrimination on the basis of sex. However, neither was intended to address hair-length regulations in schools. The court noted that seven federal courts of appeals have held that employer grooming regulations do not violate Title VII. **The grooming policy did not deprive male students of equal educational opportunities or impose other improper barriers. The regulation of hair length and other grooming or dress requirements was not discriminatory on the basis of sex**, and the court reversed the trial court's judgment. *Bd. of Trustees of Bastrop Indep. School Dist. v. Toungate*, 958 S.W.2d 365 (Tex.1997).

◆   A fourth grade Indiana student wore a gold stud earring to school. The elementary school had no written dress code, but the district's junior and senior high schools prohibited male students from wearing earrings. The school principal met with the student and his parents and advised them that he would enforce the policy against elementary students. **The student continued to wear an earring, even after the school board revised its school handbook to include a prohibition on the wearing of jewelry by male students** if inconsistent with community standards or if they presented a health or safety hazard. Following a five-day suspension for noncompliance with the dress code, the parents sought an administrative hearing. The hearing examiner recommended transfer of the student to another school in the district that did not have similar policies. The school board adopted the hearing examiner's recommendations, but the student refused to transfer. The family filed a lawsuit against the school district in an Indiana trial court, seeking a declaration and order prohibiting enforcement of the policy. The court held for the school district, and the family appealed to the Court of Appeals of Indiana.

The court rejected the student's argument that the policy denied him equal protection of the law because girls were permitted to wear earrings. Although the court expressly rejected some of the reasons advanced by the school district in justification for the policy, it found evidence that the enforcement of a strict dress code was a factor in improving student attitudes toward school. There was evidence that the local community associated earrings with female attire and that the policy discouraged rebelliousness. **The policy served a valid educational purpose to instill discipline and create a positive educational environment**. Because the dress code was a reasonable exercise of school board authority, and did not violate constitutional rights, the trial court decision was affirmed. *Hines v. Caston School Corp.*, 651 N.E.2d 330 (Ind.App.1995).

3. Gang Affiliation

◆   The School Based Decision Making Council (SBDM council) of a Kentucky school devised a student dress code through a parent/teacher subcommittee. The subcommittee heard evidence of student conflicts over clothing, including gang symbols. There was also evidence of other gang activity. The SBDM council adopted the subcommittee's recommendation for a new dress code. **The council based the recommendation on the need to address the gang problem, promote student safety, prevent violence, end disputes over clothing and enable the identification of non-students and intruders**. The dress code limited the clothing available to students as well as the manner of wearing it. It prohibited logos, shorts, cargo pants, jeans, the wearing of jewelry outside uniforms and other specified items. Discipline for violations of the dress code included detention and school suspension. A number of students who were disciplined for dress code violations sued the school board, challenging the code.

The court considered the board's motion for summary judgment and noted that the students did not seek to communicate a particular message by wearing clothing. The SBDM council and subcommittee believed that the dress code would help reduce gang activity, ease tension among students over attire, and otherwise support student safety goals. The students were entitled to constitutional speech protection, even though they did not seek to convey a particular message. Accordingly, the court applied a standard of review that sought to determine whether school officials had an important and substantial interest in creating an appropriate learning environment by preventing the gang presence and limiting fights in its schools. Under this standard, the regulation of expressive conduct was upheld since it furthered an important or substantial government interest without suppressing free speech. The code regulated student dress in a manner that was unrelated to student expression. **Students do not have the same rights as adults do in non-school settings, and school officials may control student speech or expression that is inconsistent with the educational mission of a public school**. In this case, the school board had an important and substantial interest in creating an appropriate learning atmosphere by preventing the presence of gang activity and limiting fights in schools. The dress code did not prohibit alternative student expression, such as the wearing of buttons or badges. The school board's goal of maintaining a safe and focused educational atmosphere was viewpoint neutral and did not offend the First Amendment. The SBDM council adopted the dress code after careful deliberation, and it was unnecessary to show that the code was required to stop actual disruption. **The school board struck a reasonable balance between the need to anticipate problems at school before they arise and the sometimes conflicting personal rights of students**. The court awarded judgment to the school board, also rejecting the students' assertion that any suspensions meted out under the policy violated their due process rights. *Long v. Board of Education of Jefferson County, Kentucky*, 121 F.Supp.2d 621 (W.D. Ky. 2000).

◆   A Texas school district adopted a student dress code prohibiting students from wearing "gang-related apparel," specifically mentioning baggy pants, baseball caps, hair nets and bandannas. The handbook policy stated that a list of specific items identified by law enforcement agencies as gang-related was available in the high school principal's office, but the school failed to maintain such a list. Two high school students began wearing white plastic rosaries outside their shirts to display their religious faith. Although no other students or school administrators commented about the rosaries, **two school district police officers advised the students that they should discontinue wearing the rosaries outside their shirts. The officers told the students that rosaries were gang-related apparel**. The students filed a federal district court action against the school district seeking injunctive relief and damages for violating their First Amendment speech and religious rights.

The court conducted a trial and **agreed with the students that the rosaries were well-recognized religious symbols, and that wearing them was a form of religious expression protected by the First Amendment**. The court rejected the district's argument that wearing rosaries caused actual disruption that justified infringement on this protected right. The policy was also void for vagueness since it failed to adequately define "gang-related apparel" and was ambiguous. Rosaries were not included on any list of gang-related apparel and the policy vested law enforcement officers with complete discretion to ban any symbol or speech by students. The students were not entitled to an award of damages, but the court enjoined the district from enforcing the prohibition on wearing rosaries. *Chalifoux v. New Caney Indep. School Dist.*, 976 F.Supp. 659 (S.D.Tex.1997).

II. EMPLOYEES

The extent to which school employees may exercise freedom of speech depends on whether the subject matter concerns the public interest. Speech that concerns purely private matters is not protected by the Constitution. In Pickering v. Board of Education, *below, the U.S. Supreme Court announced that an employee may not be disciplined for speaking as a citizen upon matters of public concern unless the employee's interest in such speech is outweighed by a reasonable belief on the part of the school district that the speech would disrupt the school, undermine school authority, or destroy close working relationships. The content, form and context of a given statement determine whether an employee's speech addresses a matter of public concern.*

A. Protected Speech

◆   An Illinois school district fired a teacher for sending a letter to the editor of the local newspaper. The letter criticized the board and district superintendent for their handling of school funding methods. Voters in the district had voted down a tax rate increase to fund a bond issue for two new schools. The teacher also charged the superintendent with attempting to stifle opposing views on the subject. **The board then held a hearing at which it charged the teacher with publishing a defamatory letter. After deeming the teacher's statements to be false, the board fired the teacher**. An Illinois court affirmed the board's action, finding substantial evidence that publication of the letter was detrimental to the district's interest. The Illinois Supreme Court affirmed the dismissal, ruling that the teacher was unprotected by the First Amendment because he had accepted a position that required him to refrain from statements about school operations.

The U.S. Supreme Court reversed and remanded the case, finding no support for the state supreme court's view that public employment subjected the teacher to deprivation of his constitutional rights. The state interest in regulating employee speech was to be balanced with individual rights. The Court outlined a general analysis for evaluating public employee speech, ruling that **employees were entitled to constitutional protection to comment on matters of public concern. The public interest in free speech and debate on matters of public concern was so great that it barred public officials from recovering damages for defamatory statements unless they were made with reckless disregard for their truth**. Because there was no evidence presented that the letter damaged any board member's professional reputation, the teacher's comments were not detrimental to the school system, but only constituted a difference of opinion. Since there was no proof of reckless disregard for the truth by the teacher and the matter concerned the public interest, the board could not constitutionally terminate his employment. The Court reversed and remanded the state court decision. *Pickering v. Board of Education*, 391 U.S. 563, 88 S.Ct. 1731, 20 L.Ed.2d 811 (1968).

◆   Three California school administrators assisted a Sacramento City deputy superintendent who served as the city's acting superintendent on two occasions. Each of the administrators complained to three city school board members that they believed their employment evaluations violated district policy. They also charged the deputy superintendent with violating Title I spending guidelines. Two of the administrators formed a city school management association, which hired an attorney to complain about the evaluation practices. **Two of the administrators who complained about the deputy superintendent were demoted to school-level positions, and all three sued the school district and deputy superintendent in a federal district court for retaliation and violation of their speech and equal protection rights** under the U.S. Constitution through 42 U.S.C. § 1983. The district court granted summary judgment to the deputy superintendent, accepting his claim that he could not have retaliated against the administrators for joining the association because he did not know they were members. He was entitled to qualified immunity because it was not clearly established that it was illegal to retaliate against administrators for bringing charges for misuse of public funds.

The administrators appealed to the Ninth Circuit, which rejected the district court's conclusion that the law establishing the public interest in identifying misuse of public funds was not clearly established. **A series of federal cases has established that the public interest in learning about illegal conduct by public officials outweighs an employer's interest in avoiding workplace disruption**. In order to overcome qualified immunity in a First Amendment retaliation case, an employee must show that the speech involved a matter of public concern and that the interest in expression outweighs the employer's interest in avoiding workplace disruption. While the district court had improperly found that the deputy superintendent was entitled to qualified immunity, he was still entitled to summary judgment because there was no evidence of improper motive in the decision to reassign the administrators. The administrators claimed that the deputy superintendent's actions also constituted racial discrimination because the organization they formed was comprised largely of minority members. However, they could not show any direct evidence of discriminatory intent, thus summary judgment was appropriate on this claim. The Ninth Circuit affirmed the district court's judgment. *Keyser et al. v. Sacramento City Unified School District*, 283 F.3d 1132 (9th Cir. 2001).

◆ A Chicago school district teacher alleged that the principal of her school lowered her evaluations and reassigned her in retaliation for her complaints regarding the administration of special education at the school. A second teacher who also criticized the principal for improper implementation of special education programs was cited for chronic tardiness and conduct unbecoming a teacher. A third teacher complained to the principal about academic issues, including the treatment of special education teachers by regular education teachers. The principal reprimanded him for tardiness and suspended him for one day. **The teachers filed a federal district court action against the principal and city education board for First Amendment and other civil rights violations**, seeking monetary damages under 42 U.S.C. § 1983. A jury returned a verdict for the principal and board.

The employees appealed to the U.S. Court of Appeals, Seventh Circuit, arguing that there was insufficient evidence in support of the verdict. The court stated that a party seeking an award of damages under Section 1983 based on First Amendment violations must show that his or her conduct is entitled to constitutional protection and that this conduct is the motivating factor in the adverse employment action. The court found that **there was ample evidence in support of the jury's verdict that the principal's actions had nothing to do with free speech**. The principal had continued to evaluate the first teacher "superior" even after she had complained about him, and only lowered her evaluation for the year in which she violated state law concerning IEP documents. She was one of several teachers who were moved to different classrooms due to vacancies in the school. The principal and board had acted with restraint when disciplining the second teacher, in view of her tardiness and insubordination. **Employee insubordination toward supervisors and co-workers may justify adverse employment action, even in the context of protected speech**. The third teacher was disciplined in response to severe tardiness and other substantive violations that were not a pretext for retaliation. The panel found no error by the district court and affirmed the judgment. *Love v. City of Chicago Board of Education*, 241 F.3d 564 (7th Cir. 2001).

◆ The U.S. Court of Appeals, Sixth Circuit, held that even though two Kentucky special education teachers who were transferred as a part of a school improvement plan had constitutionally protected interests in speaking out on school issues, their school district was entitled to transfer them to another school. The teachers received the due process described in their collective bargaining agreement and the school had a strong interest in implementing an improvement plan. The court observed that the teachers had clearly spoken on matters of public concern, including student discipline. One teacher had suggested that proposed school changes might violate the law, a statement that was of the highest possible concern to the public. Her speech had to be balanced against the school district's strong interest in efficient performance of its functions. The school was in a state of near-crisis and required radical and decisive action. There was evidence that the teachers were often disruptive to the efficient functioning of the school. The district court had undertaken an appropriate balancing of these interests and its decision that the teachers' speech was protected was affirmed. However, **the teachers had failed to make a sufficient showing that their transfers were motivated primarily because of their protected speech**.. *Leary v. Daeschner*, 228 F.3d 729 (6th Cir. 2000).

♦   As part of the Los Angeles Unified School District's designation of June as "Gay and Lesbian Awareness Month," gay and lesbian awareness posters and information appeared on school bulletin boards. In response, **a high school teacher created his own bulletin board titled "Testing Tolerance."** The following year, he devised a board titled "Redefining the Family," which included information tending to portray homosexuality in an unfavorable light. After other faculty members complained, **the school principal instructed the teacher to take down the material**. The teacher received warnings from the principal and district legal counsel that he was obligated as a district employee not to make discriminatory speech and to maintain the separation of church and state in his statements. The principal noted that the teacher's communications had "nothing to do with school work, student work or District approved information" and were divisive and disrespectful. The teacher sued LAUSD in a federal district for First Amendment violations. The court denied the district's first motion for summary judgment, but ruled in its favor some months later. It held that the district goal of promoting tolerance was a legitimate pedagogical goal.

The teacher appealed to the U.S. Court of Appeals, Ninth Circuit, which observed that **materials posted on high school bulletin boards were the equivalent of speech by the district, board or the high school**. Any speech appearing on a board was directly attributable to LAUSD through the principal and school board policy. The case was distinguishable from cases involving student speech and newspapers because of the direct school oversight of the content of all school bulletin boards. When a public high school is the speaker, control over its own speech is not subject to the constitutional safeguards and forum analysis of other First Amendment cases. Instead, the speech is measured by the same practical considerations applying to any person's choice of communication. **The First Amendment does not preclude government entities from exercising editorial control over its own methods of communication**. The district was permitted to talk about gay and lesbian awareness and tolerance in general if it so decided, and to restrict the contrary speech of a representative, such as the teacher. Because the teacher had no right to dictate or contribute to the content of district speech, LAUSD did not act unconstitutionally by requiring him to remove his materials. *Downs v. Los Angeles Unified School District*, 228 F.3d 1003 (9th Cir. 2000).

♦   **Six employees of Virginia public higher education institutions sued various state officials in a federal district court, challenging the constitutionality of a state statute barring public employees from using agency owned or leased computers to access, download, print or store sexually explicit material** without the written approval of the agency head. The employees claimed that the restrictions on their use of state-owned or leased equipment violated their right of free expression under the First Amendment. The court agreed, and the state officials appealed to the Fourth Circuit. The circuit court observed that the law provided an avenue for employees to obtain permission from agency heads when access was required for a legitimate research project and did not prohibit all access by state employees to sexually explicit materials. The Virginia law only regulated the speech of public employees while they acted within their capacity as employees. **Because the state retained the ability to control the manner in which employees performed their work and to direct employee activities, the court reversed the district court judgment and upheld the law.** *Urofsky v. Gilmore*, 167 F.3d 191 (4th Cir.1999).

A majority of the Fourth Circuit then voted to rehear the panel decision as a full court. The full court noted that the law did not prohibit all access to explicit material by state employees, since they could still view such material on computers not owned or leased by the state. None of the professors had actually requested access to explicit material and no request had been denied. The court stated that public employee speech is protected when it involves matters of public concern, as opposed to private matters. **Speech involves public concern when it involves issues of social, political or other interest to a community; and in making the determination of whether First Amendment protections apply, the court must evaluate whether the speech is primarily made in the employee's role as a citizen or as an employee.** The court held that access to materials through the use of state-owned or leased computers involved a professor's role as employee, not as private citizen. Since the law did not regulate speech that was of public concern, it did not violate the professors' First Amendment speech rights. The court considered and rejected the professors' alternative argument that the law violated their right to academic freedom. Since the law did not infringe on any constitutional right, the court reversed the district court decision. *Urofsky v. Gilmore*, 216 F.3d 401 (4th Cir. 2000).

♦ A teacher with a K-9 certificate was hired for the freshman dean position at a Chicago school with a history of problems despite her lack of certification for high school students, with the understanding that she not teach any grade above freshman level. She asserted that various school officials who represented the "old guard" harassed her because of her association with the school committee president and the school principal, who had arranged for her employment. She also asserted that the "old guard" resisted her interest in promoting educational improvements at the school. The school was declared as being in "educational crisis" under state law, allowing officials to take widespread remedies, including employee transfers. The principal was removed from her position and **the teacher was reassigned to an elementary school where her hourly pay rate remained the same, but her work hours were substantially reduced**. She sued the school board and school officials in a federal district court, alleging defamation and constitutional rights violations. The court dismissed the action and the teacher appealed to the U.S. Court of Appeals, Seventh Circuit.

The court stated that the First Amendment protects public employee speech only where the speech relates to matters of public concern. While the teacher asserted that her association with the principal and committee president concerned the public because it expressed a desire for educational improvements and fiscal responsibility, the district court had properly found that **the claimed association was "more devoted to petty office politics than to matters of public concern."**

In the context of the tremendous conflict among staff at the school, the teacher's association concerned the public only in the abstract and was thus not protected. The claim based on freedom of association had been properly dismissed, as was the claim for deprivation of a constitutional liberty interest in the freshman dean position. No person has a protected interest in a particular job assignment. Moreover, the teacher had been transferred, not discharged. The teacher's defamation claim also failed because statements made by school officials about the teacher were not demonstrably false and the officials were protected by immunity. The court affirmed the judgment for the school board and officials. *Klug v. Chicago School Reform Bd. of Trustees, Dist. No. 299 Trustees*, 197 F.3d 853 (7th Cir. 1999).

◆   A California teacher engaged in a course of conduct that included false claims and threats against co-workers, surreptitious tape recording of conversations among coworkers and the filing of a fraudulent workers' compensation claim. Without the authority to do so, the teacher ordered a counselor to transfer a student to another counselor's caseload, despite the opposition of the student's parent. After an alleged incident in which the teacher accused a smaller, female employee of assault in order to prosecute a workers' compensation claim, co-workers noted his increasingly bizarre behavior. He continued making misrepresentations to parents and co-workers, and threatened some co-workers. He presented an ultimatum to a co-worker over whom he had no supervisory powers concerning events in her personal life. **The district placed the teacher on administrative leave, then discharged him for dishonesty and unprofessional conduct**. He responded by suing the district for wrongful discharge.

A federal court declined to consider the teacher's state law claims against the district and ultimately dismissed the case. The state Commission on Professional Competence upheld the discharge and a California trial court affirmed. The California Court of Appeal then considered the wrongful discharge claims. The court of appeal found **that while the employee had incidentally exercised his speech rights in the process of his longstanding feud with the district and his co-workers, he was not actually fired until the district received evidence of his multiple acts of dishonesty and false claims**. The district's motive was not retaliatory and discharge would have occurred in any event, even if he had not exercised First Amendment rights. The court rejected the teacher's assertion that certain evidence should have been considered and noted that he had pursued personal vendettas against district employees for years that had culminated in the acts of dishonesty for which he was fired. This justified the commission's finding of unprofessional conduct, warranting discharge. *Clemes v. Comm. on Professional Competence*, No. A084356 (Cal.App.1st Dist.1999).

◆   **A Texas school superintendent believed that an elementary school principal spoke improperly to community members concerning the possible placement of an alternative education program at her school**. The principal denied making the statements, but the superintendent, who had previously awarded her outstanding evaluations, rated her unsatisfactory in many categories on her performance evaluation the following school year. He then recommended that the school district not renew her contract and she was reassigned to an assistant principal position at another school. She sued the district and superintendent in a federal district court, asserting denial of due process and retaliation for exercising her First Amendment rights. The court awarded summary judgment to the district and superintendent on most of the claims, but refused to grant the superintendent qualified immunity.

The superintendent appealed to the U.S. Court of Appeals, Fifth Circuit, which recited the general rule that **public employees are protected from retaliation for speech if their expression relates to a matter of public concern for which the employee's interest in fair comment outweighs the public employer's interest in promoting efficient public service**. The principal had denied making any public comment about the prospective placement of the alternative education program at her school, instead claiming that she had been retaliated against based upon a false perception. The court held that the First Amendment protects speech, not the perception of actual expression. Since the principal had engaged in no constitutionally protected conduct, she did not establish a First Amendment violation, and the superintendent was entitled to qualified immunity. The court vacated and remanded the case. *Jones v. Collins*, 132 F.3d 1048 (5th Cir.1998).

◆   An untenured kindergarten teacher worked at an Illinois early childhood education center serving students with learning disabilities and behavior problems. Because she found that her time was consumed with student disciplinary problems, she requested assistance more frequently than other teachers at the school. She also asked that certain students be removed from her classroom. **When the school principal denied her request to remove a student from her class, she took a medical leave and wrote a lengthy memorandum asserting that the school's lack of disciplinary procedures led to the deterioration of her health**. The principal failed to respond to the memorandum but circulated a copy of it to the school superintendent and assigned the teacher a poor performance evaluation. Her contract was not renewed for the following year.

The teacher demanded and received arbitration at which the arbitrator sustained the discharge action. She then filed a federal district court action against the school board for violation of her speech rights. The court granted summary judgment to the school board, and the teacher appealed to the U.S. Court of Appeals, Seventh Circuit, where she asserted that she had been fired for engaging in constitutionally-protected speech. The court stated that while a public school teacher's speech can address both public and private matters, **an employee's decision to deliver a message in private supports an inference that it is a private employment matter, not a matter of public concern**. The school board was entitled to insist that its staff carry out the school's educational philosophy, and the court affirmed the district court judgment. *Wales v. Bd. of Educ. of Community Unit School Dist. 300*, 120 F.3d 82 (7th Cir.1997).

◆   A Pennsylvania high school English teacher held a number of paid extracurricular supervisory positions including chairman of the English department, business manager for the school play and yearbook faculty advisor. The school principal annually determined who would receive the assignments. A local newspaper published unfavorable news articles about dust and fumes from a construction project at the school which had caused minor illnesses to students and teachers. The principal believed that the teacher contacted the newspaper reporter who had written the articles and called the teacher to his office. **The teacher denied contacting the reporter, but within three months, the principal reassigned the teacher's extracurricular job duties**. The teacher sued the principal in the U.S. District Court for the Eastern District of Pennsylvania, which granted the principal's summary judgment motion. The teacher appealed to the U.S. Court of Appeals, Third Circuit.

The court stated that the First Amendment protects public employees from retaliation by their employers where they speak on a matter of public concern and their interest in the speech outweighs the government employer's interest in efficiency. In this case, **the teacher could not claim any kind of protection under the First Amendment because he denied reporting the environmental conditions to the newspaper reporter in the first place, resulting in an absence of any speech**. The absence of any speech was fatal to the teacher's constitutional claim. The court affirmed the district court judgment for the principal. *Fogarty v. Boles*, 121 F.3d 886 (3d Cir. 1997).

◆   A Massachusetts special needs teacher supervised a small therapy session attended by seventh grade male students. **During a discussion of words with multiple meanings, one student interrupted the discussion with an obscenity. The teacher allowed the discussion to continue as the word had multiple meanings. The last ten minutes of the class were devoted to a discussion of similar words** and their literal definitions. At the end of class, the teacher admonished students not to use these words and to consult an adult or dictionary if they had further questions. When a parent complained about the discussion, the school superintendent suspended the teacher for two days and refused to recommend her for reappointment. The teacher was not reappointed and did not gain tenure. She filed a lawsuit against the school committee in a Massachusetts trial court, asserting a constitutional right to academic freedom. The court granted summary judgment to the school committee and the teacher appealed to the Supreme Judicial Court of Massachusetts. The court stated that **a teacher may not be punished for exercising speech rights protected by the First Amendment and that constitutionally protected conduct must not be a motivating factor in an unfavorable employment decision**. The teacher had demonstrated that she was not rehired because of the classroom discussion. The district's resource room discipline guidelines required her to respond to difficult situations in creative ways without sending students to the principal's office for discipline. The evidence indicated that she had responded to the situation appropriately. The court ruled that the teacher was entitled to be reinstated for one year of untenured service and economic damages. The court reversed and remanded the trial court decision. *Hosford v. School Comm. of Sandwich*, 421 Mass. 708, 659 N.E.2d 1178 (1996).

B. Personal Appearance and Dress Codes

◆   The history department of a Minnesota university maintained a display case in a university building hallway. Two student members of the university history club proposed that professors pose in photographs depicting their areas of historical interest for a display in the case. Eleven professors posed in period costumes and their pictures were displayed with their written comments. **The university's** affirmative action officer observed that two of the photographs showed professors posed with weapons and declared them insensitive and inappropriate. The university chancellor agreed to remove the pictures, and the students and professors filed a federal district court action against the chancellor and university, asserting constitutional violations. The court granted the university's summary judgment motion. However, the court denied summary judgment to the chancellor on the issue of qualified immunity, finding that his actions violated the clearly established First Amendment rights of the professors and students.

The chancellor appealed to the U.S. Court of Appeals, Eighth Circuit, which reversed the district court decision, but later granted a petition to review the matter. On review, **the court found that the history display was an appropriate use of the display case** and that once the university recognized the use of the case by the history department, it could not discriminate against different types of speech being expressed there. The chancellor's decision to discriminate against the viewpoint expressed by the professors and students violated clearly established First Amendment rights. Because there was no valid reason for curtailing this expression, the district court had correctly denied the chancellor's summary judgment motion for qualified immunity. *Burnham v. Ianni*, 119 F.3d 668 (8th Cir.1997).

◆   A California school district advised its employees that public school districts were prohibited by state law from sponsoring or subsidizing the distribution of partisan election campaign materials on school grounds. Employees were also forbidden from engaging in political campaigning during work hours. The collective bargaining representative of San Diego teachers objected to the policy and demanded its immediate rescission so that teachers could wear buttons expressing their opposition to an education finance initiative then before California voters. The San Diego County Superior Court found that the policy violated the First Amendment speech rights of teachers. The school district appealed to the Court of Appeal of California, Fourth District.

The court stated that California law allows school districts to restrict the political speech of teachers during work hours. **Because public school teachers have considerable power and influence in classroom situations and their speech may be reasonably interpreted as being official views of their employing school districts, it was reasonable to prohibit them from wearing political buttons in classrooms**. This restriction did not violate the First Amendment or the California Constitution because school authorities must have the power to disassociate themselves from political controversy and the appearance of approval of political messages. However, it was unreasonable for the school district to restrict political speech by teachers outside their classrooms. Accordingly, the court modified the superior court order so that teachers were prohibited from wearing political buttons only in the classroom. *California Teachers Ass'n v. Governing Bd. of San Diego Unified School Dist.*, 53 Cal.Rptr.2d 474 (Cal.App.4th Dist.1996).

◆   A Mississippi woman was a member of the African Hebrew Israelites and at times wore a head-wrap as an expression of her religious and cultural heritage. A local school district hired her as a teacher and she wore the head-wrap from time to time without incident. Eventually, she sought and received a transfer to another school closer to her home. However, that school's principal disapproved of the teacher's head-wrap and instructed her not to wear it anymore. Because she was afraid of losing her job, **the teacher acquiesced until she attended a district-wide multi-cultural workshop where she discovered that the school district supported multi-cultural diversity. She then resumed wearing the head-wrap**. Following a memorandum and discussion with other school officials, the school administration terminated the teacher's employment. The teacher followed the district's grievance procedure, and claimed that she wore her head coverings in compliance with her religious beliefs. The district denied her grievance and she appealed to the U.S. District Court for the Southern District of Mississippi.

The court found that although the teacher held sincere religious beliefs, she had failed to communicate them to the school administration at any time until the final stage of her grievance. **Because she had failed to timely communicate her religious beliefs to the school district, it was not required to accommodate her beliefs under the First Amendment or Title VII**. The district had offered the teacher an opportunity for reemployment following the denial of her grievance if she would agree to remove her head coverings. However, the teacher rejected this offer and the court granted the school district's motion to dismiss the lawsuit. *McGlothin v. Jackson Municipal Separate School Dist.*, 829 F.Supp. 853 (S.D.Miss.1993).

C. Association Rights

◆   An untenured Massachusetts elementary school teacher received a superlative written performance evaluation during her first year. Three months later, an assistant district attorney and two Massachusetts state troopers attempted to serve a subpoena on her on school grounds to secure her testimony in felony child abuse charges against her live-in fiancé. The following month, the teacher received a negative performance evaluation and learned that she would not be recommended for reappointment for the following academic year. **After the school board voted unanimously not to rehire her, she filed a federal district court action against the town and school officials for violation of her constitutional right to intimate association**. The town and officials moved to dismiss the action on the basis of qualified immunity.

The court stated that government officials are generally shielded from liability in their official capacities by qualified immunity unless the complaining party demonstrates that their conduct violates a clearly established statutory or constitutional right of which a reasonable person would have knowledge. Because the associational rights implicated in the teacher's complaint were not clearly established in the eyes of a reasonable person at the time of the action, the claims against the officials in their individual capacities were properly dismissed. However, **the town, acting through its officials, could be held liable for constitutional violations if the teacher could show that town officials made a deliberate choice not to rehire her because of her intimate association**. Because privacy rights including the right to raise a family, cohabitate and marry are fundamental rights implicating personal liberty, the court refused to dismiss the action against the town. *LaSota v. Town of Topsfield*, 979 F.Supp. 45 (D.Mass.1997).

◆   **An Ohio secondary vocational education system maintained an unwritten anti-nepotism policy** for over 20 years. Although the policy prohibited teachers who were married to each other from working at the same facility, the policy was not applied to employees who were cohabiting or dating. Two instructors, each employed by the system for over nine years, got married without telling system officials. When a human resources officer learned of the marriage, she arranged for the transfer of the wife to a different campus. The transferred teacher was required to commute an extra hour each day and began to suffer psychiatric problems. The couple filed a complaint against the school system in a federal district court, asserting that the anti-nepotism policy violated their First Amendment associational rights. The court granted summary judgment to the school system, and the couple appealed to the U.S. Court of Appeals, Sixth Circuit.

The court of appeals agreed with the couple that marriage is a constitutionally protected association and a fundamental right, but held that the anti-nepotism policy did not directly and substantially burden that right. The policy only prohibited employees who were married to each other from teaching at the same facility, and did not require the couple to end their marriage. The stated reasons for maintaining the policy represented legitimate educational concerns of avoiding workplace friction in the event of a marital breakdown and minimizing other identified employment problems. The teachers failed to meet the system's evidence that allowing married teachers to work together may lead to problems, and the court affirmed the district court judgment. *Montgomery v. Carr*, 101 F.3d 1117 (6th Cir. 1996).

III. ACADEMIC FREEDOM

School administrators have broad discretion in curricular matters and courts are unwilling to closely scrutinize the reasonable exercise of their discretion. However, First Amendment prior restraint protections apply to decisions involving school library books. Classroom assignments made by teachers that do not conform to school standards are also subject to close judicial review.

A. Library Materials

◆   The U.S. Supreme Court determined that the right to receive information and ideas is "an inherent corollary of the rights of free speech and press" embodied in the First Amendment. **A decision to remove books from a school library is unconstitutional if it is motivated by school officials' intent to deny students access to ideas with which the school officials disagree.** The U.S. Supreme Court upheld a U.S. Court of Appeals decision regarding the removal of books from high school and junior high school libraries. The case arose when a board of education, rejecting recommendations of a committee of parents and school staff that it had appointed, ordered that certain books, which the board characterized as "anti-American, anti-Christian, anti-Semitic, and just plain filthy," be removed from high school and junior high school libraries. Students in those schools then brought an action for declaratory and injunctive relief against the board and its individual members, alleging that the board's actions violated their rights under the First Amendment. The U.S. Supreme Court noted that while local boards have broad discretion in the management of curriculum, they do not have absolute discretion to censor libraries and are required to comply with the First Amendment. *Bd. of Educ. v. Pico*, 457 U.S. 853, 102 S.Ct. 2799, 73 L.Ed.2d 435 (1982).

❖   The Livermore, Calif., Public Library maintained computer terminals that were open for public use. Its Internet access policy supported "free and equal access to the entire range of library resources, regardless of content," and applied to adults and minors. The policy stated, "parents are expected to monitor and supervise" their children's usage of library materials, and that "the Livermore Public Library does not provide this monitoring or supervision." A 12-year-old boy downloaded porno-graphic images from Internet sources accessed on library computers, then printed some pictures on a relative's computer. His mother filed suit in California Superior Court, alleging that the boy showed these pictures to other minors. **The parent sought an award of monetary damages or a court order enjoining the library from acquiring or maintaining computers upon which minors could access harmful material.**

The trial court dismissed the case and the parent appealed. The California Court of Appeal, First District, held that the parent's state law claims were barred by 47 U.S.C. § 230(c)(1), which provides immunity to "interactive computer services" for any information provided by another information content provider. **The section created federal immunity for any cause of action attempting to hold service providers liable for information originating with a third-party user of an Internet service.** The court held that the library was an "interactive computer service" as defined in the statute because it enabled multiple users to access the Internet. The term also applied to "educational institutions." According to the court, federal law immunity under 47 U.S.C. § 230 served the purpose of minimizing state regulation of Internet speech by prohibiting lawsuits of the kind advanced by the parent. The parent had failed to allege that librarians helped minors locate obscene material on library computers. In any event, this was contrary to the library policy prohibiting use for illegal purposes. Librarians could not be prosecuted for simply instructing users on electronic research skills. The court found a crucial distinction between providing minors with harmful material and maintaining computers where such material could be obtained, in view of the federal law immunity for interactive computer service providers. The parent's claim for damages under 42 U.S.C. § 1983 failed because of the general rule that a state has no duty to prevent harm inflicted by a private actor. The complaint did not satisfy the requirements for any exception to the general rule of government non-liability in Section 1983 actions. **The library's endorsement of individual rights to constitutionally protected materials did not amount to an endorsement of access to obscenity.** The court affirmed the judgment for the library. *Kathleen R. v. City of Livermore*, 87 Cal.App.4th, 104 Cal.Rptr.2d 772 (2001).

❖   A gay and lesbian organization donated two books with homosexual themes to a Kansas school district. The district conducted a review for their acceptability. One of the books was already on the library shelves of several district schools, but no one had ever checked out a copy. However, the media publicized the donation and individuals opposed to it burned copies of the book on district property. **The district superintendent recommended removing existing copies from the libraries and rejecting the donation**. The school board voted to remove the books and refuse the donation, and a teacher and some present and former students filed a lawsuit against the district in the U.S. District Court for the District of Kansas, claiming that the action violated their constitutional rights. The court granted a temporary order to the complaining parties.

The court then considered a motion to make the order permanent and observed that the book contained no vulgarity or explicit sexual language and had won numerous literary awards. The district had failed to abide by its own rules in rejecting the donation and removing existing copies from its shelves. Testimony of board members indicated that they disapproved of the book's subject matter and had voted to remove it because of their disagreement with it. The failure of the school board to follow its own procedures for library procurement affirmed the court's belief that **board members had been motivated to remove the book based on their personal disagreement with ideas expressed in the book**. Removal of the book violated the constitutional rights of students presently attending district schools. The court issued an order requiring school officials to return copies of the book to district libraries. *Case v. Unified School Dist. No. 233, Johnson County, Kansas*, 908 F.Supp. 864 (D.Kan.1995).

◆   The parent of a Louisiana seventh grader discovered a copy of a school library book entitled *Voodoo & Hoodoo* in the student's possession. The book described African religions and included instructions on casting spells. **The parent claimed that the book might incite students to attempt the spells contained in the book and filed a complaint with the school principal**. After the principal and other local authorities refused to remove the book from the library, the parent appealed to the school board, which voted to remove the book from all school libraries in the district. Parents of other students enrolled in district schools then filed a lawsuit against the school board in the U.S. District Court for the Eastern District of Louisiana, seeking an order declaring that the action violated the First Amendment.

The court granted summary judgment to the parents. The school district appealed to the U.S. Court of Appeals, Fifth Circuit, which determined that it had been improper for the district court to determine without a trial the motivation of school board members who had voted to remove the book. **There had been insufficient evidence presented to the district court for it to have made the critical determination of the board's motivation for the decision to remove the book**. In order to determine whether the board's action violated the First Amendment, the district court would have to conduct a trial. A decision concerning the removal of a library book was not a curricular matter and was subject to court review of whether the board members sought to deny students access to ideas with which they disagreed. The court reversed and remanded the case. *Campbell v. St. Tammany Parish School Bd.*, 64 F.3d 184 (5th Cir.1995).

B. Textbook Selection

◆   A teacher in a Michigan public school district taught a life science course using a textbook approved by the school board. He showed movies to his class regarding human reproduction ("From Boy to Man" and "From Girl to Woman") after obtaining approval from his principal. The movies were shown to his seventh grade classes with girls and boys in separate rooms, and only students with parental permission slips were allowed to attend. Both movies had traditionally been shown to seventh grade students in the school. However, **after a school board meeting at which community residents demanded that the teacher be tarred and feathered for showing the movies, the superintendent of schools suspended the teacher with pay pending "administrative evaluation."** The school board approved this action. The teacher then sued the school district in U.S. district court for violation of his First Amendment freedoms as well as his civil rights. The jury awarded the teacher $321,000 in compensatory and punitive damages. The U.S. Supreme Court reversed the court of appeals' decision and remanded the case to the district court. According to the Supreme Court, an award of money damages may be made only to compensate a person for actual injuries that are caused by the deprivation of a constitutional right. **The Court held that damages for abstract violations of the U.S. Constitution were not allowed.** *Memphis Community School Dist. v. Stachura,* 477 U.S. 299, 106 S.Ct. 2537, 91 L.Ed.2d 249 (1986).

◆   A group of parents whose children attended grade school in an Illinois school district filed a lawsuit in the U.S. District Court for the Northern District of Illinois, seeking an order to prevent use of the Impressions Reading Series as the main supplemental reading program for grades kindergarten through five. **The parents alleged that the series "foster[ed] a religious belief in the existence of superior beings exercising power over human beings," and focused on "supernatural beings"** including "wizards, sorcerers, giants and unspecified creatures with supernatural powers." The court granted a motion to dismiss the lawsuit. The parents appealed to the U.S. Court of Appeals, Seventh Circuit. The court stated that the parents' argument that use of the textbook series established a religion was speculative. Although the series contained some stories involving fantasy and make-believe, their presence in the series did not establish a coherent religion. The intent of the series was to stimulate imagination and improve reading skills by using the works of C.S. Lewis, A.A. Milne, Dr. Suess and other fiction writers. **The primary effect of using the series was not to endorse any religion, but to improve reading skills.** Use of the series did not impermissibly endorse religion under the Establishment Clause or the Free Exercise Clause. The parents failed to show that use of the series had a coercive effect that prevented the parents from exercising their religion. The school directors were entitled to judgment as a matter of law. *Fleischfresser v. Directors of School Dist. 200,* 15 F.3d 680 (7th Cir.1994).

◆   A California school district used the *Impressions* reading series for grades one through six. The series contains 59 books with over 10,000 passages from North American literature and folklore. **The parents of two students formerly enrolled in the district claimed that 32 passages from the series promoted the practice of witchcraft and that witchcraft was a religion.** They claimed that the selections called for students to role play characters including witches and sorcerers in a manner which violated their constitutional rights. The U.S. District Court for the Eastern District of California granted the school district's motion for summary judgment and the parents appealed to the U.S. Court of Appeals, Ninth Circuit. On appeal, the parents argued that it was appropriate for courts to analyze Establishment Clause cases according to the subjective beliefs of school-aged children. The court of appeals disagreed, ruling that **the appropriate analysis was whether an objective observer in the position of a student would perceive a message of endorsement of religion by the school district**. The contested passages were a very small part of a clearly nonreligious program. It was unlikely that an objective observer would perceive the use of the series as governmental endorsement of religion. The court held that use of the series did not violate either the U.S. or California Constitutions. *Brown v. Woodland Joint Unified School Dist.*, 27 F.3d 1373 (9th Cir.1994).

C. Curriculum

◆   A Colorado language arts teacher with 25 years of experience received occasional disciplinary notices for tardiness, failing to complete paperwork and other misconduct. However, no formal disciplinary proceedings were ever brought against him until he showed the film *1900* to his logic and debate class. The R-rated film depicts nudity, sexual conduct, drug use and violence. After a parent complained about the showing, the principal placed the teacher on administrative leave. **The district superintendent recommended dismissal for** insubordination, neglect of duty and other good cause for **violation of a district policy requiring teachers to provide their principals with 20 days' prior written notice before using a controversial learning resource**. However, a hearing officer recommended retaining the teacher since the district had failed to publish its policy to teachers and the other charges would not warrant dismissal. The school board unanimously resolved to dismiss the teacher. He appealed to the Colorado Court of Appeals, which reversed, finding the teacher lacked formal notice of the policy and that the other alleged misconduct was insufficient to justify dismissal. The board appealed to the Supreme Court of Colorado.

The supreme court reversed, stating that the teacher violated the controversial learning resources policy, and that no First Amendment violation occurred. Schools can regulate the curriculum, as long as the regulation is "reasonably related to a legitimate pedagogical concern," without violating the First Amendment. **The policy established a reasonable method of regulating possibly inappropriate materials, therefore, it did not violate the First Amendment**. The supreme court rejected the teacher's assertion that the policy was overbroad and vague, finding no evidence to support this assertion. Although the teacher may have lacked formal notice of the policy, he had reasonable notice, given his knowledge that prior approval was required before using controversial materials in his classroom. Accordingly, no due process violation occurred. The dismissal of the teacher was upheld. *Board of Educ. of Jefferson County Sch. Dist. R-1 v. Wilder,* 960 P.2d 695 (Colo. 1998).

◆   A tenured Pittsburgh high school teacher worked at an alternative learning center where she instructed at-risk students. From 1976 to 1988, she used a classroom management technique called Learnball, which utilized a sports format including teams of students and in-class competitions. Students who performed well and conformed to class rules were allowed to play a radio in class and shoot baskets. **The school principal advised the teacher that she could no longer employ the Learnball motivational technique in her classes as he felt that it did not benefit students**. The teacher filed a lawsuit and a grievance against the school board, both of which were resolved against her. Six years later, the teacher resumed use of the Learnball technique without permission and was again instructed to discontinue its use by the school principal. The teacher filed another lawsuit against the board of education, principal, and other education officials in the U.S. District Court for the Western District of Pennsylvania, seeking a declaratory order that they violated her constitutional rights.

The court considered evidence that Learnball was not curricular in nature and was disapproved of by the principal and school board for taking up class time, which should have been devoted to instruction. **The teacher's argument that she was entitled to constitutional protections failed because she could not demonstrate that her classroom was a traditional public forum**. The U.S. Supreme Court has specifically held that a public high school classroom is not a public forum where First Amendment rights must be protected. There was also no constitutional violation in the board's refusal to sanction an after-school event promoted by the teacher that featured the technique. Because the board did not violate the teacher's constitutional rights, the court denied the relief she requested. *Murray v. Pittsburgh Bd. of Public Educ.*, 919 F.Supp. 838 (W.D.Pa.1996).

◆   A Tennessee junior high school teacher assigned a research paper to her ninth grade class. Students were required to select a topic subject to her prior approval. The subject matter requirement was only that it be "interesting, researchable and decent." Each student was further required to use four sources and could not merely develop their own ideas. **One student submitted an outline entitled "The Life of Jesus Christ" without obtaining prior approval. The teacher rejected the proposal**, and the student's father protested to school officials. He then filed a lawsuit on his daughter's behalf against the school board in the U.S. District Court for the Middle District of Tennessee, claiming violation of the student's free speech rights. The court granted summary judgment to the school board, and appeal was taken to the U.S. Court of Appeals, Sixth Circuit.

The court of appeals observed that **the free speech rights of public school students must be subject to some limitations in order to maintain classroom control and to focus the class on assignments**. Teachers had broad authority to base their grades on the merits of a student's work. They were to be given broad discretion to assign grades and to conduct appropriate classroom discussions. Because learning was more important than free speech rights, the court was unwilling to overrule the teacher's decision that the student should not write a research paper on a topic about which she felt the student already had substantial knowledge and strong feelings and could therefore not write an effective research paper. The court affirmed the district court's judgment. *Settle v. Dickson County School Bd.*, 53 F.3d 152 (6th Cir.1995).

The concept of freedom of speech also includes the right to refrain from speaking. The U.S. Supreme Court has held that a student may not be disciplined for refusing to recite the Pledge of Allegiance.

◆   In 1979, **the Illinois legislature enacted a statute that required the Pledge of Allegiance "be recited each school day by pupils in elementary educational institutions supported or maintained in whole or in part by public funds."** A student who attended an elementary school in Illinois and his father challenged the statute in federal court, claiming that the words "under God" violate the Establishment and Free Exercise Clauses of the First Amendment. They also claimed that the mandatory language of the statute violated *West Virginia State Bd. of Educ. v. Barnette*, 319 U.S. 624, 63 S.Ct. 1178, 87 L.Ed. 1628 (1943). *Barnette* held that students could not be compelled to participate in the recitation of the Pledge of Allegiance. A federal district court granted summary judgment to the school district, and the student and his father appealed to the U.S. Court of Appeals, Seventh Circuit. The court of appeals upheld the statute. The court stated that any statute that compelled student participation in the recitation of the Pledge of Allegiance was flagrantly unconstitutional. In this case, however, **the language of the statute was not necessarily mandatory**. The statute could be interpreted to simply mean that the pledge was to be recited by all willing students. In fact, **the student in this case had suffered no penalty in refusing to participate in the pledge**. The court continued by noting that **the pledge could only be banned if the "under God" phrase made the pledge a prayer whose recitation violated the Establishment Clause**. The court stated that the phrase was simply ceremonial deism without any true religious significance. The court affirmed the ruling for the school district. *Sherman v. Community Consol. Dist. 21*, 980 F.2d 437 (7th Cir.1992).

D. School Productions

◆   A North Carolina high school English and drama instructor won numerous awards for directing and producing student plays. She selected a play for a state competition that depicted a divorced mother with a lesbian daughter and a daughter who was pregnant with an illegitimate child. Her advanced acting class won 17 of 21 possible awards at a regional competition for performing the play. However, when a scene from the play was performed before an English class, a parent objected and the principal forbade students from performing the play at the state finals. He later allowed the performance with the deletion of certain scenes, and the students won second place in the finals. When **the principal sought to transfer the teacher to a middle school for violating the school district's controversial materials policy,** the superintendent approved the transfer. The school board upheld the transfer and the teacher filed a state court retaliatory discharge action against the board and school officials. The case was removed to a federal district court, which dismissed the action. The teacher appealed to the U.S. Court of Appeals, Fourth Circuit.

A panel of the court rejected the board's argument that the First Amendment protects only original expression and not the selection of a play by a teacher. The court held that because of the important role that teachers play in society, the First Amendment extended to the selection of plays for high school drama classes. The court of appeals then agreed to rehear the case and vacated its prior decision. **The full court held that the selection of a school play is part of a public school curriculum, and does not constitute a matter of public concern for which a teacher might enjoy constitutional protection**. The court vacated the panel decision and upheld the transfer. *Boring v. Buncombe County Bd. of Educ.*, 136 F.3d 364 (4th Cir.1998).

◆   An Illinois high school banned a student from participating in a lip sync contest at a school homecoming assembly due to his disruption of the previous year's contest. However, **the student and some classmates interrupted a scheduled group during the contest and simulated a chainsaw attack on a woman with a child. The student also simulated sexual action and pretended to throw a boa constrictor into the audience**. The school principal met with the student and his mother to discuss a three-day suspension for the disruption, showing them a videotape of the contest, interviewing a witness, and giving the student and mother an opportunity to present their case. The principal then suspended the student for three days for insubordinate conduct which was upheld by the school board for the additional reasons of possession of a weapon (the chainsaw), disorderly conduct and gang activity. A federal district court affirmed the suspension and the student appealed to the U.S. Court of Appeals, Seventh Circuit.

On appeal, the student claimed that the suspension violated his due process rights, arguing that he had received no opportunity to explain his side of the story and that the additional grounds of weapons possession, disorderly conduct and gang activity were never brought up at the meeting. The court disagreed, stating that the totality of the principal's actions informed the student that his suspension was based on insubordinate conduct. The lack of actual notice of the grounds for suspension added by the school board did not implicate constitutional rights. **Due process is satisfied where a student and parent are given a pre-suspension notice of appropriate charges and the conduct supports the charges. The court found no due process or equal rights violations** and commented that the lawsuit was a frivolous action that trivialized the Constitution and wasted judicial resources. *Smith on Behalf of Smith v. Severn*, 129 F.3d 419 (7th Cir.1997).

IV. USE OF SCHOOL FACILITIES

Schools may establish reasonable rules governing the time, place and manner of speech on school property. The reasonableness of restrictions depends upon the type of forum. A public forum exists on property that is generally available for use by the public. Time, manner and place regulations regarding a public forum must be content neutral and narrowly tailored to serve a significant governmental interest. They must also provide for ample alternative channels of communication. A limited public forum exists when a school opens part of its campus to expressive activities on the part of groups of certain character. A regulation regarding a limited public forum must allow equal access to all groups that have a similar character. The U.S. Congress has declared it unlawful for a public secondary school which receives federal funds to deny students the opportunity to hold meetings in a limited public forum on the basis of the religious, political, philosophical, or other content of speech at the meetings. Equal Access Act, 20 U.S.C. § 4071 et seq. For Equal Access Act cases involving religious speech, see Chapter Two, Section II of this volume.

A. Time, Place or Manner Regulations

◆ A student submitted a request to use school facilities for meetings of the Good News Club, a private religious club, after school hours. The superintendent denied the request, stating that the club's use of facilities amounted to school support of religious worship. After receiving further information on the content of club meetings, the school board adopted a resolution denying the request. The club commenced a federal district court action against the school under 42 U.S.C. § 1983 for violation of student speech rights, equal protection and other federal rights. The district court entered a preliminary order enjoining the school from prohibiting the club's use of school facilities, but later awarded judgment to the school. The club appealed to the U.S. Court of Appeals, Second Circuit, which rejected its argument that it sought only to teach morals and values, like the Boy Scouts, Girl Scouts, 4-H Club and other groups that used school facilities. According to the Second Circuit, religious instruction was integral to the club's meetings, distinguishing it from other groups. **The school's decision to deny the club access to its facilities was based on content, rather than viewpoint, and was permissible.**

The club appealed to the U.S. Supreme Court, which observed that the nature of the forum determines the limits that a school may place on speech taking place in the forum. The school had established a limited public forum in which it could reasonably seek to avoid identification with a particular religion. While the school was not required to allow all speech, limits on speech could not be based upon viewpoint and had to be reasonable in light of the purpose of the forum. The court relied on two of its recent decisions interpreting government time, place and manner restrictions, *Lamb's Chapel v. Center Moriches Union Free School District*, 508 U.S. 384 (1993), and *Rosenberger v. Rector and Visitors of Univ. of Va.*, 515 U.S. 819 (1995). In this case, the school's policy broadly permitted speech about the moral and character development of children. **The school had excluded the club from school facilities solely because of its religious viewpoint. This resulted in unconstitutional viewpoint discrimination** under both *Lamb's Chapel* and *Rosenberger*. The court found no difference between the Good News Club and other student organizations that were not excluded, and held that "speech discussing otherwise permissible subjects cannot be excluded from a limited public forum on the ground that the subject is discussed from a religious viewpoint." It rejected the school's argument that it was required to prohibit the club's speech to avoid an Establishment Clause violation. Club meetings took place after school hours and were not sponsored by the school. No risk of coercion was present, because students had to obtain permission from their parents before attending meetings. Allowing the club access to school facilities for its meetings furthered the important Establishment Clause purpose of religious neutrality, ensuring that all groups could speak about the same topics. The district failed to show any risk of school endorsement and the court reversed and remanded the case. *Good News Club v. Milford Central School*, 121 S.Ct. 2093, 150 L.Ed.2d 151 (U.S. 2001).

◆ A 1993 Alabama law permitted non-sectarian, non-proselytizing student-initiated voluntary prayers, invocations and benedictions during school-related events, assemblies, sporting events and graduation ceremonies. A county school administrator and his son asserted that the law violated their constitutional rights and sued state and local officials in a federal district court for declaratory and injunctive relief. The district court held the law unconstitutional, ordered local school officials to refrain from assisting students in religious activity, and appointed a monitor to ensure that schools obeyed its order. State and local officials appealed to the 11th Circuit, asserting that the First Amendment prohibition on the official establishment of religion is inapplicable to the states. The circuit court summarily rejected the appeal by state officials concerning the constitutionality of the law, and considered the appeal by DeKalb County officials regarding the part of the order prohibiting them from allowing student-led prayers and appointing a monitor. It rejected arguments that students acted on behalf of the school when saying prayers in school settings and that student-led prayers created peer pressure that unconstitutionally coerced others. The circuit court held that **student-initiated religious speech must be permitted, subject to the same reasonable time, place and manner restrictions that apply to all student speech in schools**. *Chandler v. James,* 180 F.3d 1254 (11th Cir. 1999).

The complaining parties then appealed to the U.S. Supreme Court, which remanded the case to the Eleventh Circuit for reconsideration in light of *Santa Fe Indep. Sch. Dist. v. Doe, see Chapter 2*. **The Eleventh Circuit again held that the district court opinion was overbroad, requiring school officials to censor all student public religious expression**. After discussing the *Santa Fe* decision, the circuit court noted that the district court in this case had "assumed that virtually any religious speech in schools is attributable to the State," and had enjoined the school district from permitting any prayer in a public context at any school function. According to the circuit court, the Constitution does not require or permit all religious speech by students in public places while at school. The court distinguished the facts of the case from those of *Santa Fe* and found that entanglement with the state, not the public context of school speech, created the constitutional violation in *Santa Fe*. Nothing prevented public school students from voluntarily praying at any time before, during or after the school day, including prayers said "aloud or in front of others, as in the case of an audience assembled for some other purpose." **So long as the student prayer was genuinely student-initiated and not the product of a school policy, the speech was protected**. The circuit court reaffirmed it prior opinion, and again reversed and remanded the district court judgment on the grounds that it was overbroad because it equated all student religious speech in any public context at school with state speech. *Chandler v. Siegelman,* 230 F.3d 1313 (11th Cir. 2000).

◆   A Rhode Island high school art teacher with over 20 years of experience began to develop skin rashes, headaches and breathing difficulties. Her physician linked these symptoms to her working conditions, and the teacher filed a grievance through her teachers' association, claiming that the school had failed to provide her with a clean, safe working environment. Although a private service determined that the school's air quality was acceptable, it offered nine recommendations for improving environmental conditions. When the district failed to implement the recommendations, the teacher videotaped her classroom, the kiln room, and some storage areas to document potential health and safety violations. The Rhode Island Department of Labor, Division of Occupational Safety (DOS), determined that the kiln room should not be used pending installation of an adequate ventilator. The school installed a new ventilation system, but the DOS returned and found numerous health and safety code violations. **The principal ordered the teacher to stop all videotaping and to refrain from releasing videotapes without permission**.

The teacher filed a lawsuit against the school district in the U.S. District Court for the District of Rhode Island, claiming that the principal's order violated her First Amendment rights. The district argued that the teacher's complaints were of private concern only, and that it could not tolerate further disruptions from the teacher. The court stated that the teacher's complaints concerned the public because taxpayers and parents were concerned about building conditions and potential safety hazards. **The teacher had a protected right to make the videotapes, and the court enjoined school officials from prohibiting their release** to the public. The court limited the teacher's right of access to the school grounds to times when she was normally on the premises. At other times, she would have to apply to school officials for admittance on the same basis as other members of the public. *Cirelli v. Town of Johnston School Dist.*, 897 F.Supp. 663 (D.R.I.1995).

B. Student Organizations and Demonstrations

◆   The Supreme Court upheld an activity fee assessed to all students of a university, finding that the university assessed the fee to facilitate the free and open exchange of ideas among students. Objecting students could insist upon certain safeguards to mitigate the compelled support of expressive activities. Even though the student activities fund was not a traditional public forum, the case was controlled by the standard from public forum cases including *Widmar v. Vincent*, 454 U.S. 263 (1981), and *Lamb's Chapel v. Center Moriches Union Free School Dist.*, 508 U.S. 384 (1993). The standard of germane speech from *Abood* and *Keller* gave insufficient protection to objecting students and the university program. To insist upon germaneness to the university's mission would contravene the program's purpose of encouraging a wide range of speech. The court held that although the fees would subsidize speech that some students would find objectionable, the Constitution did not compel a requirement that the university refund student fees. Viewpoint neutrality was the proper standard for the protection of the rights of the objecting students, as set forth in *Rosenberger v. Rector and Visitors of Univ. of Virginia*, 515 U.S. 819 (1995). The court held that **the university could require students to support the extracurricular speech of other students in a viewpoint-neutral manner, and observed that the parties had stipulated, in this case, that the program was viewpoint neutral**. The university had wide latitude to adjust its extracurricular speech programs to accommodate students. The court reversed the judgment of the Seventh Circuit, and remanded the case for further proceedings on the issue of the student referendum. The record required further development on whether a referendum by students undermined constitutional protection for viewpoint neutrality. *Board of Regents of Univ. of Wisconsin System v. Southworth*, 529 U.S. 217, 120 S.Ct. 1346, 146 L.Ed.2d 193 (2000).

◆   The Broward County School Board had a longstanding practice of permitting many organizations to use its facilities under leases or partnership agreements. The Boy Scouts used its facilities for many years. In 1998, the parties agreed to a five-year "partnership agreement" authorizing the use of school facilities and buses by the scouts. The partnership agreement required school administrators to assist in the promotion of the club's events by making school announcements and distributing promotional materials. Board members took note of the U.S. Supreme Court's decision in *Boy Scouts of America v. Dale*, 530 U.S. 640 (2000), in which the organization was allowed to bar an avowed homosexual from serving as a scout leader. **The board voted to terminate the partnership agreement with the Boy Scouts, declaring the organization ineligible to lease school facilities because it discriminated on the basis of sexual orientation.**

The Boy Scouts of America sued the school board and superintendent in a federal district court for First Amendment and equal protection violations, and moved the court for a preliminary order declaring the board's actions unconstitutional. The parties agreed that the board had created a limited public forum in which many organizations and groups could use district facilities after school. The board argued that it had a compelling government interest in enforcing its anti-discrimination policy so that students learned respect and tolerance. The court found that the board was entitled to disapprove of intolerance and did not have to assist the Boy Scouts in solicitation efforts under the partnership agreement. It was not required to embrace or endorse the organization's message and could fashion its own contrary message. However, **the board was not allowed to punish any group for its message. The government must abstain from regulating speech based on a group's specific motivating ideology or opinion.** Once the board had created a limited public forum in its facilities, it could not exclude groups from access to the forum based on unreasonable distinctions. The board allowed many other student groups to use its facilities, and some of them restricted their memberships in a way that could be viewed as discriminatory, without interference by the board. The speech that the board had found objectionable did not take place during school hours, and its attempt to regulate the Boy Scouts' speech was not narrowly tailored in the least restrictive manner available. The court held that the board could not prevent the Boy Scouts from using school facilities and buses during non-school hours by reason of its membership policy, pending further consideration of the case. *Boys Scouts of America et al. v. Till,* 136 F.Supp.2d 1295 (S.D. Fla. 2001).

♦   **Two students who wished to promote acceptance among gay and straight students decided to start an on-campus Gay-Straight Alliance Club.** An application was submitted to the principal and the students obtained a faculty advisor. The application was denied under the school's procedures, but was referred instead to the school board. The board unanimously rejected the application, on the grounds that the club had a subject matter related to sexual conduct and that the district offered courses addressing sex, abstinence and disease prevention. The students rejected an offer by the principal to edit the name of the group and to declare that sex would not be discussed at meetings. They sued the school district and board in a federal district court for constitutional rights violations and violation of the Equal Access Act, moving the court for a preliminary order that would prevent school officials from blocking the club.

The court held that **the school board had established a limited open forum at the high school by allowing non-curriculum related student groups to meet on school grounds during non-instructional time. The board was precluded**

from discriminating against groups seeking access to the open forum on the basis of content. There was no merit to the board's assertion that the Gay-Straight Alliance was unprotected by the Equal Access Act on grounds that it was "related to the curriculum." The club did not intend to discuss human sexuality, its behavior or consequences, but intended to discuss tolerance, issues related to sexual orientation and homophobia, and the need to treat persons with respect. The court found that even if there was some overlap between the curriculum and club discussions, the Gay-Straight Alliance, like other clubs, was unrelated to the curriculum in the absence of a direct relationship to courses offered by the school. No other group was required to submit to a name change or declare that group meetings would include no discussion of sex. The students were entitled to a preliminary order in their favor, and granting the order would conform with recent California legislation declaring it a state policy to prevent discrimination on the basis of sexual orientation. *Colin v. Orange Unified School Dist.*, 83 F.Supp.2d 1135 (C.D. Cal. 2000).

Generally, students enjoy the same First Amendment protections as other citizens. This extends to their right to peacefully gather, to demonstrate and to form groups and associations. Balanced against their rights as individuals, however, are the rights of others. Thus, disruptive demonstrations on school grounds may be enjoined if the demonstrations materially disrupt the normal class routine and invade the rights of other students.

◆   A group of 100 to 150 African-American students attending a Denver high school staged a two-day political walkout from school. One parent allegedly encouraged students to walk out of school and denounced school officials. **When some of the students submitted a request to the Denver public school board for permission to hold a rally at the high school, the board denied access under its policy for reviewing applications,** which allowed the board to deny approval for the use of facilities when "necessary for the best interests of the school district." The students filed a lawsuit against the board in the U.S. District Court for the District of Colorado, asserting violations of their free speech rights under the U.S. Constitution.

The court considered the students' motion for a preliminary injunction to allow the rally on school grounds. The students contended that the board's policy constituted an unlawful prior restraint on their speech. The court stated that the policy placed unlimited discretion in the board to determine what speech was in the best interests of the community. This was an unconstitutional prior restraint on speech. **The denial of the application for the rally had been based on the anticipated content of student speech. Potential controversy was not a constitutional basis for denying access to a limited public forum** and there was no evidence that the planned rally would encourage any immediate unlawful action. Because the denial of permission to hold the rally was an unconstitutional prior restraint on student speech, the students were entitled to an order allowing them to hold the rally. *Local Organizing Committee, Denver Chapter, Million Man March v. Cook*, 922 F.Supp. 1494 (D.Colo.1996).

CHAPTER FOUR

Student Rights

I.   ADMISSIONS AND ATTENDANCE

The U.S. Constitution does not make a free public education a fundamental right. However, the states have enacted legislation for the establishment and enforcement of education laws. The Equal Protection Clause of the Fourteenth Amendment requires that once a program of free public education has been established, the law must be applied equally to any person within the jurisdiction of the state. Thus, children of illegal aliens, children with disabilities, and minority students are all entitled to equal protection of the laws. A school district may, within certain limits, establish health regulations, make minimum age requirements for all students beginning school, require immunization, adopt a curriculum and require that all students meet certain graduation requirements. Students with contagious diseases may not be excluded from class unless they present a medically demonstrable threat to health and safety.

A.   Age and Residency Requirements

◆   In May 1975, **the Texas legislature revised its education laws to withhold from local school districts any state funds for the education of children who were not legally admitted into the United States**. It also authorized local school districts to deny enrollment to children not legally admitted into the country. One group filed a class action on behalf of school-age children of Mexican origin who could not establish that they had been legally admitted into the United States. The action complained of the exclusion of the children from public school. A federal district court enjoined the school district from denying a free education to the children, and the U.S. Court of Appeals, Fifth Circuit, upheld the decision. The legislation was also challenged by numerous other plaintiffs whose cases were consolidated and heard as a single action before a federal district court. The district court held that the law violated the Equal Protection Clause of the Fourteenth Amendment, and the Fifth Circuit summarily affirmed the decision. The Supreme Court consolidated the two cases and granted review.

The state claimed that undocumented aliens were not persons within the jurisdiction of Texas, and were not entitled to equal protection of its laws. The Court rejected this argument, stating that whatever an alien's status under the immigration laws, an alien is a person in any sense of the term. The term "within its jurisdiction" was meant as a term of geographic location and the Equal Protection Clause extends its protection to all persons within a state, whether citizen or stranger. **The statute could not be upheld because it did not advance any substantial state interest**. The Court stated that **the Texas statute imposed a lifetime hardship on a discrete class of children not accountable for their disabling status**. There was no evidence to show that exclusion of the children would improve the overall quality of education in the state. *Plyler v. Doe*, 457 U.S. 202, 102 S.Ct. 2382, 72 L.Ed.2d 786 (1982).

◆   The Texas Education Code also permitted school districts to deny free admission to public schools for minors who lived apart from a "parent, guardian, or the person having lawful control of him" if the minor's primary purpose in being in the district was to attend the local public schools. A minor left his parent's home in Mexico to live with his sister in a Texas town for the purpose of attending school there. When the school district denied his application for tuition-free admission, his sister sued the state in federal court, alleging that the law was unconstitutional. The district court held for the state, and the Court of Appeals affirmed. The U.S. Supreme Court upheld the residency requirement. **The Court noted that a bona fide residence requirement, appropriately defined and uniformly applied, furthered a substantial state interest in assuring that services provided for its residents were enjoyed only by residents.** Such a requirement with respect to attendance in public free schools did not violate the Equal Protection Clause of the Fourteenth Amendment. Residence generally requires both physical presence and intention to remain. The statute stated that as long as the child was not living in the district for the sole purpose of attending school, he satisfied the statutory test. The Court held that this was a bona fide residency requirement and that the Constitution permits a state to restrict eligibility for tuition-free education to its bona fide residents. *Martinez v. Bynum*, 461 U.S. 321, 103 S.Ct. 1838, 75 L.Ed.2d 879 (1983).

◆   Under Maine law, school districts without high schools can provide a tuition subsidy for high school students to attend private schools or public schools located in other districts. The Whiting district, which did not have a high school, declined to pay the subsidy for a student to attend a private school in Bangor. When the student's mother sued the district, the parties reached a settlement agreement, under which the district paid a tuition subsidy contingent on the mother's "continuing status as both a legal resident of Whiting and legal custodian" of the student. A few months later, the mother entered law school and purchased a house in Cape Elizabeth. **The district** then **determined she no longer resided in Whiting and discontinued the subsidy.** The mother sued the district in a state trial court for a determination of her rights under the settlement agreement. The court found that the mother no longer resided in the district and was not entitled to the subsidy.

On appeal to the Supreme Judicial Court of Maine, the court observed that the district was not allowed to expand upon the statutory term "reside" when it required that the mother remain a "legal resident" of the district in order to obtain the subsidy. The law required that a district provide the subsidy to those parents who reside in the district. **Applying dictionary definitions of "reside," the court held that the term meant more than simply owning a house located in the district. "Residence" indicated a degree of permanency and actual residence with the student.** The legislation creating the tuition subsidy was not intended to encourage attendance at a student's school of choice, but was limited to the provision of funding for parents who resided in districts without the funds to operate schools. The student and his siblings were eligible for free public education in Cape Elizabeth and would not be deprived of educational opportunities there. It was evident that the mother was not residing in Whiting while attending law school, and her decision to move did not require her to move from place to place for the purposes of her employment. Since she was not a legal resident of Whiting, the court affirmed the judgment for the school district. *Hallissey v. School Administrative Dist. No. 77*, 755 A.2d 1068 (Me. 2000).

◆   The Ohio Court of Appeals held that a school district was entitled to consideration of its claim against a non-resident family for tuition. **The family had previously obtained a favorable ruling from the state commissioner of public instruction that it resided in the district, but the mother later admitted moving to another district while her children continued to attend district schools** for eight months. The school board commenced a state court action against the family for fraud, seeking a declaration that the family owed tuition for the children's educational costs. The court dismissed the complaint for lack of subject matter jurisdiction. The Shaker Heights School Board appealed to the state court of appeals, which observed that the action was one for fraud and the collection of tuition, not for a determination of residence. Although the superintendent had made a determination about the family's residence prior to its move to the Cleveland district, the Shaker Heights district was claiming reimbursement for the eight-month period subsequent to the move. Since the children's mother admitted that the family now lived in Cleveland, the trial court had jurisdiction to determine the issue of whether tuition should be paid to the Shaker Heights district. The court reversed and remanded the case for further proceedings. *Shaker Heights City School District Board of Education v. Cloud*, 137 Ohio App.3d 284, 738 N.E.2d 473 (Ohio App., 8th Dist. 2000).

◆   A student attended school in the district from kindergarten through middle school, when his family moved out of the district. After attending school in another district for two years, he sought to return under **Wisconsin's open enrollment law, which provides students with the opportunity to attend any public school of their choice, even if the student resides in another district**. The district denied the application on the basis of a priority assignment for three students transferring under another program. The student appealed the decision to the state superintendent of public instruction, who affirmed the district's decision despite the impermissible preference. The superintendent ruled that the district action was still valid because of the lack of class space in the district, and the student appealed to a Wisconsin circuit court. The court found the district's action arbitrary, because it accepted the other three students.

The superintendent appealed to the Wisconsin Court of Appeals, which held that the superintendent's decision was entitled to due weight and was not subject to substitution of judgment. The court agreed with the student and circuit court that the district's decision had been arbitrary and could not be upheld. The district had permitted three other non-resident students to enroll in its schools, despite the fact that no space was available in two core courses. The preference cited by the district and superintendent in favor of particular classes of students, such as siblings, had no application where no class space was available. The court agreed with the circuit court that the district's decision had been based on priority, not class space. **There was no rational explanation for admitting three students who would push average class sizes over the acceptable limit, while excluding one whose presence would increase class size by less than one percentage point**. The court affirmed the judgment for the student. *McMorrow v. Benson*, 238 Wis.2d 329, 617 N.W.2d 247 (Wis. App. 2000).

◆   The mother of an elementary school student maintained an apartment outside of the school district where the student attended school. The student attended school in the district where his grandfather resided. **At the start of the student's third year in the district, the district notified the mother of its intent to deny him admission to school, based on the lack of appropriate residency documents.** The grandfather responded by letter to the state commissioner of education. The letter was construed as an appeal of the school board's decision. At a hearing, the board presented evidence indicating that the student and his mother actually resided in their apartment outside the district, and not at the grandfather's residence, as contended by the mother. An administrative law judge agreed, and held that they were not residents. The grandfather appealed to the education commissioner, who held that the student did not reside in the district and was not entitled to a free public education there. The school board commenced a state court action against the grandfather seeking $18,000, the cost of three years tuition. The court awarded judgment to the board, and the grandfather appealed.

The Superior Court of New Jersey, Appellate Division, noted that the commissioner's residency determination became final when the grandfather failed to timely appeal the education commissioner's decision. Prior to the third year in which residency was at issue, the school board had not contacted the grandfather for the collection of tuition, and he had made no assertion on behalf of the student's residency in the district until the third year. **There was a valid basis for charging one year of tuition to the grandfather, since he had actively pursued the residency contest** that had been initiated against the student's mother. However, there was no such basis for a tuition award for the first two years of contested residency. The commissioner's order did not clearly indicate an intent to charge the grandfather for these two years, when the mother alone had communicated with the board and superintendent. Because he was not a party to these communications, the court reduced his liability to $6,190, the tuition for one year. *Woodbury Heights Bd. of Educ. v. Starr*, 319 N.J.Super. 528, 725 A.2d 1180 (App.Div.1999).

◆   When a student's mother became unable to care for her, she moved into her aunt's home. The aunt petitioned the district within which she resided for the student's admittance without responsibility to pay tuition. **The school board stated that the aunt had submitted insufficient documentation and denied the petition.** The commissioner reversed the board, ruling that its decision had been arbitrary and capricious but did not violate the family's constitutional rights. The state education board agreed, finding that school districts were not allowed to "mechanically deny" admissions that were not accompanied by certain documentation.

The local board appealed to the Superior Court of New Jersey, Appellate Division, asserting that the administrative orders were unsupported by competent evidence. The court found ample evidence that the family had provided appropriate residency documents to the district, including tax forms, residential closing documents and sworn statements of residency. **The family did not withhold any material documentation that was requested by the district, and the application satisfied state law requirements.** The court affirmed the administrative orders in favor of the family and held that failing to inform the student of the grounds for its decision violated her due process rights. *J.A. v. Bd. of Educ. for Dist. of South Orange and Maplewood*, 318 N.J.Super. 512, 723 A.2d 1270 (App.Div.1999).

❖   A 16-year-old Florida student with special needs lived with his mother until she became unable to care for him. The student then went to live with his grandmother in North Carolina and applied to the county school board for enrollment as a student with special needs. **School administrators denied the application, stating that he was neither a resident nor a domiciliary of the district**. The student appealed to the state office of administrative hearings, which found that he was a resident of the county and was entitled to a free appropriate education. This decision was affirmed in later administrative proceedings, and by a North Carolina superior court. The school board appealed to the Court of Appeals of North Carolina. The court observed that residence and domicile are distinct legal concepts. A student may reside in one district and be domiciled in another. Because an unemancipated minor may not establish a domicile separate from his parents or guardian, the student remained domiciled in Florida. However, his actual place of residence was in North Carolina. Although North Carolina law generally provides for the education of students domiciled in a school administrative unit, **the statute pertaining to students with special needs specified that each local education agency had to provide free appropriate special education services to all students with special needs residing in the district**. The specific requirement of special education law superseded the generally applicable statute. Compliance with the statute was also necessary for the state to receive federal funds under the Individuals with Disabilities Education Act. Accordingly, the trial court decision was affirmed. *Craven County Bd. of Educ. v. Willoughby*, 466 S.E.2d 334 (N.C.App.1996).

❖   A Connecticut parent sought to enroll his daughter in a public school located in the city of New Canaan. His property was on the boundary line of that city and the city of Norwalk and part of the house was located in New Canaan. The New Canaan board and superintendent refused to grant the request because only five percent of the family's property taxes went to New Canaan, while the balance went to Norwalk. The family had previously lived in New Canaan and continued to use a New Canaan mailing address. The family also voted in New Canaan, obtained public library cards there and participated in social and community activities there. The state board of education affirmed the school board's decision, and a Connecticut trial court affirmed. The family appealed to the Appellate Court of Connecticut. On appeal, the family argued that **the proper analysis to employ in boundary line cases was not the amount of property tax paid but the family's complete community of interests, including affiliations developed by the student and the family's participation in the community**. The court agreed, finding that the lack of definition of the term "residing in" as used in the applicable statute supported taking into account multiple factors, rather than the rigid and arbitrary application of the property tax issue. The court reversed and remanded the trial court's decision. *Baerst v. State Bd. of Educ.*, 34 Conn.App. 567, 642 A.2d 76 (1994).

❖   **The revised Texas Education Code required students to be at least six years old for admission to first grade. The code also granted school boards the authority to make exceptions** for students over or under the normal school age. The mother of a student who was five years and 10 months old on September 1 of the coming school year lived in a school district in which the board had adopted a policy excluding from first grade all students who were not six by September 1.

Because the student had completed kindergarten at a private school, her mother petitioned the school board to consider allowing her to enroll the student as a first grader. The board denied the petition. The mother sued the school district, superintendent and board in a Texas trial court alleging due process and civil rights violations. She also claimed that the state Gifted and Talented Act, which made no reference to age, created an exception to the requirement that students be at least six for admission to first grade. The court granted the board and superintendent summary judgment, and the mother appealed to the Court of Appeals of Texas, El Paso.

The court of appeals determined that the legislature had vested school boards with wide discretion concerning public school admissions. **The school board had discretion to adopt the policy excluding students from first grade who had not attained their sixth birthday prior to September 1.** The trial court had not abused its discretion by granting summary judgment to the school, school board and superintendent. There was no evidence that the Gifted and Talented Act applied in this case. The court affirmed the trial court's decision. *Wright v. Ector County Indep. School Dist.*, 867 S.W.2d 863 (Tex.App. —El Paso 1993).

◆   The parents of a New York girl presented an altered birth certificate to a school district in order to enroll their daughter in kindergarten the year before she was eligible for a free education. Near the end of the school year, the school discovered the deception, and the district sought to be reimbursed for the cost of the girl's schooling. When the parents refused to pay, the district sued. The trial court held for the school district, and the New York Supreme Court, Appellate Division, affirmed. **The district could recover from the ineligible resident just as it could recover from a nonresident who enrolled under false pretenses.** Further, the parents were not entitled to offset the amount of school taxes they paid to the district. *Bd. of Educ. v. Marsiglia*, 582 N.Y.S.2d 256 (A.D.2d Dep't 1992).

B. Immunization

Generally, a school district or a state educational agency has a compelling state interest in requiring immunization of all incoming students in an effort to prevent and control communicable diseases.

◆   A school secretary asked the parents of two children to provide immunization requirements for the eldest of their two children. **The parents presented the school with a letter claiming exemption from immunization of their son against six diseases under a statutory exemption governing objection on grounds of genuine and sincere religious beliefs.** The district superintendent found the letter insufficient and requested additional documentation supporting the family's beliefs. The student was allowed to attend school for over two years, but the school advised the family that he would not be allowed to attend school without immunization or a religious exemption. The parents contacted an attorney who wrote the district a letter including references to verses from the Book of Corinthians and stating that the parents believed immunization to be a violation of supreme authority. School officials rejected the letter as not substantiating a religious exemption, and excluded the student and his brother from school.

The family commenced a federal district court action against the district, and sought a preliminary injunction to allow the students to enroll in district schools. They presented the court with testimony concerning their religious beliefs. According to the court, the testimony of the parents was often evasive and inconsistent. It appeared that some of the documentation prepared by the parents and their attorney was not original and contained identical expressions of sentiments written on behalf of other parents seeking religious exemption from vaccinations. This undermined any contention that the parents' objections were based on personally held, genuine, sincere, religious beliefs. The verbatim repetition of boilerplate religious sentiments and biblical quotations did not by itself render the parents' testimony incredible. However, they insisted that the views expressed were their own, tending to cast doubt on their sincerity. The parents also waffled on questions concerning the nature of their beliefs. **Their testimony indicated that their objections to vaccination were not based on religion but on fear of perceived health risks**. The court held that, based on its observation of the parents' testimony, their objections were not based on genuine and sincerely held religious beliefs. It denied their motion for a preliminary injunction. *Farina v. Board of Education of City of New York*, 116 F.Supp.2d 503 (S.D.N.Y. 2000).

♦   A Nebraska school district suffered its first outbreak of measles in nearly a decade. As a result, the school district determined that all unimmunized children should be excluded from the high school at which the confirmed case had arisen for a period of two weeks or until no further cases were reported. Alternately, the students could reenter school upon proof of immunization. **Two sisters whose parents had decided not to immunize them based on personal preference, and not for religious or medical reasons, were excluded**. The parents sued, stating that the district's decision lacked statutory authority and violated the students' equal protection rights. The Nebraska trial court upheld the district's decision, and the parents appealed to the Supreme Court of Nebraska. The supreme court stated that **Nebraska law allowed school districts to exclude students whenever the students' conduct presented a clear threat to the physical safety of the students or others. This "emergency" situation statute took precedence over the general statute which allowed children who were not immunized to attend school**. The high communicability of measles justified the exclusion under this section. The court also stated that the parents' equal protection arguments failed. Where a suspect classification is not involved, the statute must merely rationally further a legitimate interest. Here, the state had a legitimate basis for excluding the students. The court affirmed the trial court's ruling. *Maack v. School Dist. of Lincoln,* 491 N.W.2d 341 (Neb. 1992).

♦   A New York couple requested a religious exemption from their school district's mandatory immunization requirements for their daughter. They filled out a questionnaire, which was in the form of an affidavit, and denied that they were seeking a medical exemption from immunization. The district denied the petition. The couple then sought to obtain a medical exemption by presenting a note from a doctor. That request was denied. The couple later submitted a second claim for a religious exemption stating that they were now members of the Congregation of Universal Wisdom. The school district again denied the request. The student in question was a six-year-old child who had been diagnosed with Rett Syndrome, which results in severe multiple disabilities in affected children. She had received one dose of oral polio vaccine at approximately three months of age, and was shortly thereafter hospitalized with a viral syndrome. She had not received any other immunizations. Her parents attributed the onset of her condition to the administration of the oral polio vaccine. The student received home instruction provided by the school district, although evaluations had shown she would benefit from a structured special education environment. **The school district, however, refused to admit the student to its special education school because of the parents' refusal to comply with the mandatory immunization requirements**. The parents sued, seeking an injunction and enforcement of their right to free exercise of religion. A federal court denied the religious exemption and refused to hear the parents' claim for a medical exemption. The parents then took that claim before a New York state court.

The New York Supreme Court held for the school district. The court stated that the district had not acted in an arbitrary or capricious manner. **Based on the school district's chief medical officer's own investigation into Rett Syndrome, the school district was able to legitimately determine that there was no medical reason not to immunize a child with the syndrome**. The school district was not bound to follow the opinion of the doctor who had given the parents their certificate. Expert testimony at the trial also failed to indicate that there should be no immunization. Since no medically recognized reason existed not to immunize the student, the court upheld the school district's decision. *Lynch v. Clarkstown Cent. School Dist.*, 590 N.Y.S.2d 687 (Sup.Ct.–Rockland County 1992).

C. Gifted Student and Honor Programs

◆   The Wisconsin Open Records Law requires public authorities to allow public access to all documents and records in their possession, subject to certain exceptions, such as student records. **A Wisconsin student asked her school district for interim grade averages for herself and another student**, believing that she should have an opportunity to determine whether she was entitled to certain student honors. The district denied the request, stating that the records were incomplete, would have no impact on the naming of class valedictorian and were immaterial in its decision to award the school board's academic excellence scholarship to the other student. The student filed a lawsuit against the board in a Wisconsin trial court, seeking release of the requested information. The court determined that the interim grade records were not public records maintained by a public authority and were exempt from the disclosure provisions of state law.

The student appealed to the Court of Appeals of Wisconsin, which rejected the board's claim that the records were not in its possession simply because they were in the immediate possession of teachers. A public agency may not avoid the open records law by delegating the possession of its records to agents and employees. However, **the trial court had properly exempted the records from disclosure as student records**, even though the student had intentionally refrained from identifying the other student. The board's failure to specify a statutory reason for denying access to the records did not entitle the student to disclosure, and the court affirmed the judgment. *State of Wisconsin ex rel. Blum v. Bd. of Educ., School Dist. of Johnson Creek*, 565 N.W.2d 140 (Wis.App.1997).

♦   An 11th-grade Pennsylvania student was an "exceptional student" entitled to an individualized education program (IEP) under state law. During an IEP meeting, his mother proposed that he take college courses in science and computers. **She unilaterally enrolled the student in two college courses and sought reimbursement** from the school district for his tuition and transportation expenses. The district refused to reimburse the parents for these expenses, and they requested a due process hearing. The hearing officer determined that a new IEP should be developed, but held that the family was not entitled to reimbursement for their college expenses. A special education appeals review panel reversed the hearing officer's decision and ordered the district to reimburse the family for the science and computer courses.

The school district appealed to the Commonwealth Court of Pennsylvania, which observed that the state supreme court had already resolved the question of a school district's obligation to serve exceptional students. While state law requires the creation of an IEP and a general education plan for each exceptional student, **there is no statutory obligation to provide an exceptional or mentally gifted student with an IEP that is outside the scope of a school district's existing special education curriculum**. A school district is not required to maximize the abilities of an exceptional student and the district in this case was not obligated to provide the student with tuition and transportation reimbursement for college courses. The court reversed the review panel's decision since the college courses and transportation were beyond the school district's current curriculum. *New Brighton Area School Dist. v. Matthew Z.*, 697 A.2d 1056 (Pa.Commw. 1997).

♦   A Connecticut special education statute defined "gifted children" as being "exceptional children" who did not progress effectively without special education. Although this definition coincided with the state law definition of children with disabilities, **the statute did not mandate special education for gifted students, as it did for students with disabilities**. The parents of a Connecticut student identified as gifted demanded that the school board provide him with special education individually designed to meet his needs. The board refused to provide an individualized education program for the student and the parents filed a lawsuit in a Connecticut trial court for a declaration that he was entitled to special education. The court granted summary judgment motions by the state and local education boards, and the Supreme Court of Connecticut observed that although the legislature had categorized gifted children within the definition of exceptional children, **the statute did not create a right to special education for gifted children**. Because students with disabilities had different needs than gifted children, there was a rational basis for treating the two groups differently, and there was no violation of the state constitution on equal protection grounds. The court affirmed the trial court's order for summary judgment. *Broadley v. Bd. of Educ. of the City of Meriden*, 229 Conn. 1, 639 A.2d 502 (1994).

II. COMPULSORY ATTENDANCE

The states have a compelling interest in seeing that their citizens receive at least a minimal education and they may establish and enforce reasonable school attendance laws to that end. For compulsory education cases involving private schools, see Chapter Thirteen, Section II of this volume.

A. Compulsory Attendance Laws

◆   A New York school's attendance policy required students to attend 90 percent of all classes in each course to receive credit, and dropped students from any course from which they were deliberately absent. **A group of students brought suit** in a state trial court **challenging the constitutionality of the attendance policy**. The students argued that the denial of credit for a class is equivalent to dropping a student from enrollment, which is contrary to New York law. The school district's motion for summary judgment was granted. The students appealed to the New York Supreme Court, Appellate Division. **The court** rejected the students' arguments and **held that the denial of credit was not equivalent to dropping a student from enrollment since it did not bar a student from attending classes or make-up classes**. The court upheld the lower court's entry of summary judgment on behalf of the school. *Bitting v. Lee*, 564 N.Y.S.2d 791 (A.D.3d Dep't 1990).

B. Home Study Programs

◆   Two children were not enrolled in school and lacked the required approved home-schooling plans. The parents contended that school committee approval of their home-schooling activities would conflict with their learner-led approach to education, and that the Massachusetts constitution prohibited infringement on their privacy and family rights. The school committee initiated a state district court proceeding for care and protection of the children. The court found that the parents had failed over a two-year period to show that the children's educational needs were being met, effectively preventing any evaluation of their educational level and instructional methods. **The parents failed to comply with a court order to file educational plans**, resulting in adjudication of the children as in need of care and protection. The court transferred legal custody of the children to the social services department, although they remained in the physical custody of the parents.

The Appeals Court of Massachusetts noted on appeal that the trial court order had required the parents to submit a detailed home-schooling plan to the school committee in order to allow assessment of the program and the children's progress. **This was a legitimate educational condition that a school committee could impose on a home-school proposal without infringing on the constitutional rights of a family**. The record indicated that the parents had been unwilling to permit any verification of their children's educational progress. The U.S. Supreme Court has recognized a degree of parental autonomy to direct the education of children, but state laws effectively incorporated this requirement by allowing for flexibility in the evaluation of private instruction in homes and private schools. The parents had rejected accommodations proposed by the school committee, and the custody order was entered only after they had received a final opportunity to comply with the committee's requests. The court affirmed the order for temporary care and protection of the children. *Care and Protection of Ivan*, 717 N.E.2d 1020 (Mass. App. 1999).

◆   The parents of an Oklahoma student educated her at home for religious reasons. They enrolled her as a part-time seventh grade student in public school classes on foreign language, music and science to better prepare her for college. However, their registration for two eighth-grade classes was rejected by the district's new superintendent, and **the school board** then **voted to prohibit part-time enrollment in district schools except for fifth-year seniors and special education students**. The board stated that its decision was based on the exclusion of part-time students from state financial aid computations. The family sued the school district in a federal district court for constitutional rights violations. The court granted summary judgment to the district and officials, and the family appealed to the U.S. Court of Appeals, Tenth Circuit.

The court rejected the family's claim that the attendance policy burdened the free exercise of their religious beliefs or interfered with parental rights. The policy did not prohibit home schooling and did not force them to do anything contrary to their beliefs. The policy was neutral, of general application and based on the district's inability to receive state financial aid for part-time students. Parents have no unlimited right to control each phase of public education, and education officials have the authority to allocate scarce resources and devise curriculums. Contrary to the family's argument, they had not been denied part-time public school access, because they were actually seeking special treatment not accorded to other students. Because there is no parental right to control education in a manner that would dictate local attendance policies, the court affirmed the judgment. *Swanson By and Through Swanson v. Guthrie Indep. School Dist. No. I-L*, 135 F.3d 694 (10th Cir. 1998).

◆   **A New York school district refused to allow a home schooled student residing within the district to play on any of its interscholastic sports teams**. Her mother filed a lawsuit against the state commissioner of education, challenging the state education department regulation under which the board had denied her participation. The court granted summary judgment to the commissioner, and the parent appealed to the New York Supreme Court, Appellate Division, Third Department. The appellate court stated that the regulation required a student to be regularly enrolled in the school during a semester of sports competition and take a specified number of academic subjects. Because the regulation called for public school enrollment in the district, and the student was not enrolled, she was excluded under the regulation.

The court rejected the parent's claim that the student should be considered enrolled in a public school because of the authority exercised by the local school superintendent over home school instruction. There was no merit to her constitutional claims as there is no constitutional right to interscholastic sports participation. There was no equal protection violation because the classification created by the regulation was not based upon home schooled status. The regulation also applied to private school students. **Because there was a legitimate and rational purpose to the regulation, it did not violate the Constitution and the student was properly excluded from sports participation.** *Bradstreet v. Sobol*, 650 N.Y.S.2d 402 (A.D.3d Dep't 1996).

◆   Maryland education law permits parents to educate their children at home but requires them to maintain a portfolio of instructional materials with examples of coursework. The law also requires observation of teaching methods and up to three annual portfolio reviews. Parents must sign a consent form indicating their intent to comply with state regulations. One Maryland parent who selected home schooling for her child for religious reasons came under scrutiny by local authorities for possible child neglect. She alleged that this suspicion arose from her disagreement with her compliance obligations under the home schooling regulations. The neglect charges were not substantiated, but the parent's name remained on a county registry of potential child neglecters. **The parent** then **filed a lawsuit** against the county education board in the U.S. District Court for the District of Maryland, **seeking a declaration that her right to free exercise of religion required exemption from state home schooling laws**. She also claimed that the county's retention of her name on a list of possible child neglecters justified a permanent order and monetary damages. The district filed a motion to dismiss the lawsuit.

The parent argued that public schools indoctrinated children in atheism and sought to suppress their religious upbringing. The court found no support for this argument under the First Amendment to the U.S. Constitution, or the Religious Freedom Restoration Act. **The home schooling regulations did not substantially burden her exercise of religion. The parent and her child were not compelled to affirm beliefs they did not hold, and the state law and regulations did not discriminate against them**. The court observed that Maryland was not required to subsidize the family's religious beliefs by eliminating items from the state's required curriculum. The court also denied the parent's demand to remove her name from the list of potential child neglecters as the information was confidential and already shielded from public release. *Battles v. Anne Arundel County Bd. of Educ.*, 904 F.Supp. 471 (D.Md.1995).

C. Truancy

♦ According to a school's unexcused absence policy, upon a student's third unexcused absence, the school was obligated to provide the parents with written notification of the laws of compulsory education. After the fifth day, the school was required to hold an informal conference with the parents, student and a probation officer, and upon the 10th day of unexcused absence, a formal hearing was required. **A student was absent without excuse approximately 20 days during a four-month period**. On some occasions the parents called the school and typically explained that there was a medical problem. The school accepted these explanations until the parents applied to the county educational service center for permission to home school their daughter. Although the county service center advised the parents orally that their daughter should continue attending school while the home school application was pending, they kept her home during this period. However, they did not tell the school about the pending home school application, and the school did not send them any notices concerning truancy proceedings. The service center advised the school principal that the student's home school application was being denied, and he filed a complaint against the parents in an Ohio county court on charges of contributing to the delinquency of a minor.

The trial court conducted a jury trial and sentenced the parents to seven days in jail and fines of $250. They appealed to the Ohio Court of Appeals, Seventh Appellate District. The appeals court found that in order to uphold the conviction, the state was required to prove that the student was actually delinquent or unruly. The definition of an unruly child included one who was habitually truant from home or school. Reference to the school board policy on absence was a crucial factor in determining whether habitual truancy occurred. The state presented the school's policy on unexcused absences as contained in its parent/student handbook and was required to show under local standards that the student was habitually truant. It failed to make this showing. **Because truancy involved more than absenteeism, the state was required to show a lack of excuse or permission as established by school policy**. It was therefore required to show evidence that it sent the parents written notices that their daughter was absent without an excuse for three or more days. Without this proof, the state could not satisfy the essential element of habitual truancy under state law. Oral statements to parents were insufficient to satisfy mandatory written notice requirements and the opportunity for a hearing. The school was bound to follow its own policies and was accountable to abide by them. The state failed to show that the student was habitually truant, and the court reversed the judgment. *State of Ohio v. Smrekar*, No. 99 CO 35, 2000 Ohio App. Lexis 5381 (Ohio App. 7th Dist. 2000).

◆   An 18-year-old West Virginia student missed five days of school without an excuse. He was warned that continued absences could result in criminal prosecution. **After continuing unexcused absences, the county prosecutor's office filed a criminal complaint against the student in a West Virginia trial court**. The student was convicted of violating a state compulsory attendance statute. He then petitioned the Supreme Court of Appeals of West Virginia for a writ of prohibition. The court of appeals observed that the compulsory attendance statute under which the student was prosecuted mandated school attendance for children between the ages of six and 16 and provided enforcement sanctions against parents, guardians or custodians, and not against individual students. **There was no possibility of liability under the statute for a nonattending student regardless of age**. A different statute applied to cases involving students who were 18 or older, and school boards were allowed to suspend students for improper conduct. For students under the age of 18, the possibility of a delinquency adjudication also existed. The court granted the writ as requested. *State of West Virginia ex rel. Estes v. Egnor*, 443 S.E.2d 193 (W.Va.1994).

◆   **Wisconsin's compulsory school attendance statute requires any person having control of a school-aged child to "cause the child to attend school regularly...."** The statute cross-references other Wisconsin statutes detailing state procedures for truancy, including a statute which requires each school board to establish written attendance policies. The parent of a student who was absent without excuse eight times during a three-month period failed to respond to repeated notices from the school to meet with officials to resolve the problem. **The local district attorney's office brought charges against the student's parent, resulting in a misdemeanor conviction**. The parent appealed to the Court of Appeals of Wisconsin. On appeal, the parent argued that the compulsory attendance statute was unconstitutionally vague because it failed to describe the word "regularly." **The court determined that the statute was sufficiently definite and understandable to a person of average intelligence to preclude a finding of unconstitutional vagueness**. The dictionary definition of "regularly" was not technical and had a common and approved meaning. The compulsory attendance statute sufficiently cross-referenced other statutes so that the full statutory scheme of mandatory attendance was clear. The court also rejected the parent's defense that the student was uncontrollable, because evidence in the record indicated that she had a consistent pattern of unexcused absences dating from her kindergarten year. The court affirmed the conviction and found the statute constitutional. *State of Wisconsin v. White*, 509 N.W.2d 434 (Wis.App.1993).

III. CORPORAL PUNISHMENT

Many states specifically allow the use of reasonable physical force by school authorities to restrain unruly students, to correct unacceptable behavior and to maintain the order necessary to conduct an educational program. Some states, however, specifically prohibit corporal punishment. Where state law permits, courts generally uphold the reasonable application of punishment and have been reluctant to find that such punishment violates student due process rights.

◆   The U.S. Supreme Court upheld the beating of two Florida students by school administrators in which one student was beaten so severely as to miss 11 days of school. Another student suffered a hematoma and lost use of his arm for one week. The parents sued school authorities on the ground that the beatings constituted cruel and unusual punishment. **The Supreme Court** upheld the beatings and **ruled that the Eighth Amendment prohibition against cruel and unusual punishment did not apply to corporal punishment against students**. The Court's reasoning for this decision lay in the relative openness of the school system and its surveillance by the community. The protections of the Eighth Amendment were intended to protect the rights of incarcerated persons. Such surveillance is not so readily apparent in the prison system, and thus the Eighth Amendment safeguards are necessary for convicted criminals but not for students, who have the ability to file civil lawsuits against school districts and employees to vindicate their rights. *Ingraham v. Wright*, 430 U.S. 651, 97 S.Ct. 1401, 51 L.Ed.2d 711 (1977).

◆   **A middle school student was** singled out for talking to a classmate during roll call and **required to do 100 squat-thrusts before participating in a 20- to 25-minute weightlifting class. Within days, he was diagnosed with a degenerative skeletal-muscular disease, renal failure and esophagitis/gastritis**. The student was hospitalized and missed three weeks of school. After his return, he was unable to participate in school athletics and physical education classes. His mother claimed that the teacher told her that squat-thrusts were a necessary form of punishment. The family sued the teacher and district in a federal district court for constitutional rights violations under 42 U.S.C. § 1983, also alleging a claim under Title IX of the Education Amendments of 1972, and state claims for negligence and intentional infliction of emotional distress. The court awarded summary judgment to the teacher and district, and the family appealed to the U.S. Court of Appeals, Fifth Circuit.

To state a claim under Section 1983, the complaining party must allege violation of a right secured by the Constitution or laws of the United States and demonstrate that the violation was "committed by a person acting under color of state law." The family failed to meet the threshold requirement of demonstrating a constitutional violation. **The Fifth Circuit has consistently held that if a state remedy is present to redress the denial of substantive due process through excessive corporal punishment, there can be no federal claim based on denial of due process rights against a school system, administrator or school employee**. Corporal punishment violates due process only where it is arbitrary, capricious or wholly unrelated to educational goals. Excessive corporal punishment intended for disciplining a student does not implicate due process, irrespective of the severity, if state-law civil or criminal remedies are available to a student. There were adequate common-law remedies in Texas available for the vindication of the student's claim, such as criminal conviction for assault or injury to a child. There was also the possibility of a civil recovery in a personal injury suit. The federal claim had been properly dismissed on this basis, but the district court should have simply declined to exercise jurisdiction over the state-law cases instead of awarding summary judgment. This would allow the family to prosecute the state law claims in the state court system. *Moore et al. v. Willis Independent School District et al.*, 248 F.3d 1145 (5th Cir. 2000).

◆   Two students engaged in horseplay in the school cafeteria. When a teacher instructed them to leave, one of the students refused. The teacher again instructed the student to leave, but he stated that he was going to get his books. The teacher placed his hands on the student, who retaliated by slamming him into a table. During the course of a struggle, **the teacher allegedly dragged the student across the floor and banged his head on a metal pole**. When the teacher brought the student to the principal's office, the student struck the principal's arms, and the police were called. The principal called the student's mother and advised her that he would commence expulsion proceedings. He sent her a letter stating that the student was suspended for 10 days pending expulsion. The superintendent of schools agreed with the principal's expulsion decision. The mother requested a hearing before the school board. The board voted to expel the student for the rest of the school year, and the family initiated a federal district court action against the board, superintendent, teacher, and principal, asserting constitutional rights violations. The court conducted a trial and granted judgment to the school board and employees.

The family appealed to the Eighth Circuit, arguing that the suspension, expulsion, and use of corporal punishment violated the student's due process rights. The court evaluated the use of corporal punishment under the four-factor test described in *Wise v. Pea Ridge Sch. Dist.*, 855 F.2d 560 (8th Cir.1988). According to the court, **the teacher and principal did not violate the student's substantive due process rights because they had used corporal punishment in good faith as a response to his disobedience, in a manner that was not excessive under the circumstances**. The court also rejected the student's assertion that the suspension and expulsion proceedings violated his procedural due process rights. The court found that the student was advised of the charges against him and received an adequate opportunity to respond to them. Although the school district had violated its own rules by failing to supply the family's attorney with the statements of two witnesses prior to the hearing, this did not amount to a constitutional violation, since the attorney did not indicate that he would have acted differently if they had been timely provided. The court rejected an additional claim by the family that the district staffed its schools in a discriminatory manner. *London v. Directors of DeWitt Pub. Schs.*, 194 F.3d 873 (8th Cir.1999).

◆   A Louisiana teacher told a student to stop bothering a female classmate. The student refused to stop misbehaving and **the teacher grabbed his jacket collar and pulled him away from other students. The student either tripped on a desk and fell to the floor, or was forced to the floor by the teacher**. The student went to an emergency room for treatment and underwent chiropractic treatment for the rest of the year. The student's family filed a criminal complaint against the teacher for battery. After an investigation, local authorities declined to institute charges. The family sued the school board, its insurer, and the teacher in a state trial court for personal injuries. At the conclusion of a trial, the court dismissed the case.

The family appealed to the Court of Appeal of Louisiana, which noted that school officials and teachers had to establish discipline and maintain an orderly learning environment to achieve their educational objectives. The trial court decision was justified without regard to the teacher's commission of a battery, because state law authorizes every teacher to hold every student strictly accountable for disorderly conduct in school or on school property. Moreover, **school boards are allowed the discretion of using reasonable corporal punishment. The evidence indicated that the teacher was taking reasonable protective disciplinary action**. There was no error in the trial court finding that the teacher's attempt to restore order was not unreasonable. Teachers are authorized by law to use reasonable force to maintain order in classes and on school property, and the court affirmed the judgment for the school board, insurer and teacher. *Young v. St. Landry Parish School Bd.*, 759 So.2d 800 (La.App.3d Cir. 1999).

◆   A middle school teacher hit or slapped a student who he had detained after class for disruptive behavior. A number of witnesses disagreed on how to characterize the contact, but **the school board chose to suspend the teacher without pay for 30 days, in part based on his own admission that the contact with the student was out of frustration**. The board found that the teacher was insubordinate and engaged in unprofessional conduct. The teacher appealed his suspension and an order requiring him to obtain counseling to a Nebraska district court, which found insufficient evidence for the discipline. It held that the teacher's actions did not constitute corporal punishment, insubordination or unprofessional conduct.

The board appealed to the Supreme Court of Nebraska, which observed that state law prohibited corporal punishment in schools, but did not define corporal punishment. The court discussed decisions from other states that have attempted to define corporal punishment, and found that **"corporal punishment is reasonably understood to be the infliction of bodily pain as a penalty for disapproved behavior."** The Nebraska Student Discipline Act, while not permitting corporal punishment, provided authority to "teachers and administrators to use physical contact short of corporal punishment to the degree necessary to preserve order and control" in schools. The law also allowed for incidental physical contact, which could not include the infliction of pain or physical punishment for disapproved behavior. The court dismissed the teacher's argument that the state law was unconstitutionally vague in failing to define corporal punishment. It held that the district court had impermissibly substituted its judgment for that of the board. The teacher had admitted acting out of frustration. However, **the act of restraining the student was permissible since it was intended to preserve order**. State law also failed to define "unprofessional conduct," and the court reasoned that it was "conduct which breaches the rules or ethical code of a profession, or conduct which is unbecoming a member in good standing of a profession." The teacher's use of corporal punishment in violation of state law was directly related to his fitness to act in a professional capacity, and the court upheld the board's findings. *Daily v. Bd. of Educ. of Morrill County School Dist. No. 62-0063*, 256 Neb. 73, 588 N.W.2d 813 (1999).

◆   A Kentucky school district maintained a policy allowing corporal punishment. Parents who objected to the practice could notify school officials upon a student's enrollment. **The parents of an eighth grade student in the district advised the school's assistant principal that corporal punishment should not be used**. However, **when the student experienced behavior problems, the father allegedly gave a teacher permission to paddle the student**. The teacher administered a paddling which caused bruising and swelling. A grand jury indicted the teacher on assault charges. Although the indictment was quashed, the parents sued the school board, assistant principal, teacher and principal in a federal district court for constitutional violations. The court denied summary judgment motions by the school officials based on immunity, and they appealed to the U.S. Court of Appeals, Sixth Circuit.

The court found no evidence that the teacher and assistant principal lacked a good faith belief that the parents had withdrawn their instructions not to paddle the student. **The punishment had been administered with the consent of the student for a disciplinary purpose and was not so severe or disproportionate to the violation to be considered an abuse of official power**. In order to establish a constitutional violation, an official's action must violate a clearly established constitutional right, and there was substantial uncertainty concerning whether corporal punishment in violation of a parent's instructions could be deemed a violation of a clearly established right. The district court had erroneously denied qualified immunity to the officials, and the court reversed and remanded its decision. *Saylor v. Bd. of Educ. of Harlan County, Kentucky*, 118 F.3d 507 (6th Cir.1997).

IV. EXPULSIONS AND SUSPENSIONS

School districts and colleges have the power to control student behavior through the use of disciplinary suspensions and expulsions. This power is limited by student constitutional rights to due process. Failure to follow due process requirements can lead to orders reversing suspensions or expulsions, expunging of records of proceedings from student files, and damages against school districts and board members.

A. Academic Expulsions or Suspensions

◆   A student enrolled in the University of Michigan's "Inteflex" program—which was a special six-year course of study leading to both an undergraduate and medical degree—struggled with the curriculum and barely achieved minimal competence. He failed the NBME Part I, receiving the lowest score ever in the brief history of the Inteflex program. **The university's medical school executive board reviewed the student's academic career and decided to drop him from**

registration in the program, and further denied his request that he be allowed to retake the NBME Part I. The student then sued the university in U.S. district court claiming a violation of his due process rights under the U.S. Constitution. At trial the evidence showed that the university had established a practice of allowing students who had failed the NBME Part I to retake the test up to four times. The student was the only person ever refused permission to retake the test. The district court held that his dismissal was not violative of the Due Process Clause. The U.S. Supreme Court upheld the district court's ruling against the student. **The Due Process Clause was not offended because "the University's liberal retesting custom gave rise to no state law entitlement to retake NBME Part I."** *Regents v. Ewing*, 474 U.S. 214, 106 S.Ct. 507, 88 L.Ed.2d 523 (1985).

◆   **Four students submitted work for a history project that included significant portions that were copied verbatim from reference sources.** Each of the students received a zero grade, but the parents of one of the students believed he was treated unfairly, claiming that the teacher's instructions had been unclear. The parents argued their cause twice before the school principal, who refused to change the grade. The superintendent of schools affirmed the grade after he conducted a hearing and determined that the teacher had clearly explained plagiarism.

The parents appealed a final decision of the school board affirming the zero grade to the Court of Appeals of Minnesota, which rejected their argument that the student handbook, which contained a plagiarism provision, formed a contract between the school and its students. It also rejected the claim that the district had violated the student's property and liberty rights when charging him with plagiarism. In this case, there was no protected property or liberty interest of which the student could claim to have been deprived of. The court stated that the judiciary must use restraint when considering academic matters. The U.S. Supreme Court has declined to enlarge the role of the courts when academic discipline is being considered. The student was not entitled to a hearing before an impartial hearing officer, and the informal meetings held by the principal and superintendent had been sufficient to protect any due process interest. **The court found that the process afforded the student had been fair and reasonable and that the grade was fair and supported by the record.** *Zellman v. Indep. School Dist. No. 2758*, 594 N.W.2d 216 (Minn. App.1999).

◆   Three Ohio high school students stole copies of an algebra test from their teacher's file cabinet. They distributed copies to two other students. After they took the test, the teacher noted their identical answers. The school held a disciplinary hearing at which witnesses testified that one of the students acted as a lookout while the other two stole copies. **The five students who had cheated on the test were given Fs for the class. The three students who participated in the theft were suspended for 10 days in addition to receiving Fs.** One of the students who was suspended sued the school district in an Ohio trial court, which abated the suspension, finding it unreasonable. The Court of Appeals of Ohio, Erie County, reinstated the suspension, finding that it was both rational and reasonable. **The school had appropriately imposed separate penalties for the separate offenses of cheating and theft.** *Reed v. Vermilion Local School Dist.*, 614 N.E.2d 1101 (Ohio App.6th Dist.1992).

◆   A senior at an Indiana high school left school to go to her medical biology class located at a medical center. On the way, she stopped and drank some beer. After admitting this to school officials, **she was suspended for five days, and her grades were reduced by 20 percent in each class for the semester**. The student handbook provided for a grade reduction of four percent for each class missed each day during the suspension. The student then brought suit against the school in a federal district court, asserting that the grade reduction was violative of her constitutional right to substantive due process. Both the student and the school moved for summary judgment. The school asserted that a rational relationship existed between the grade reduction and the use of alcohol because the use of alcohol during school hours adversely affected the academic accomplishment of the student user. The student, on the other hand, argued that the use of academic sanctions for nonacademic misconduct constituted arbitrary and capricious action because the penalty was not rationally related to the misconduct and not rationally related to the disciplinary purpose. The court noted that a student's grade or credit should reflect the student's academic performance or achievement, and that reducing grades for misconduct unrelated to academic conduct results in a skewed and inaccurate reflection of the student's academic performance. Here, the court found that the rule was unreasonable and arbitrary on its face. The grade reduction was not imposed for lack of effort in academics, but was imposed as part of a disciplinary action to discourage the consumption of alcohol during school hours. **Because the student's misconduct was not directly related to her academic performance, an academic sanction was not warranted**. The court granted summary judgment to the student. *Smith v. School City of Hobart,* 811 F.Supp. 391 (N.D.Ind.1993).

B. Drug and Alcohol Use and Possession

◆   Within weeks of a student's graduation from high school, police conducted a sweep search of her high school and the school grounds for drugs. They noticed a beer carton in her vehicle and after obtaining her permission to conduct a search, found a box containing 45 pills of Ecstasy. She acknowledged that the pills were hers, was arrested and taken into custody. **The school immediately placed her on probation pending an expulsion hearing**. While she awaited the hearing, the district provided her with a home tutoring program and allowed her to take and pass her final examinations. An expulsion hearing was held after she completed her coursework and she was admitted to a state university, contingent on receipt of her diploma. The district voted to expel the student and deny her a diploma. She earned a graduate equivalency degree and was admitted to the university.

A state common pleas court ordered the school district to issue her a diploma because of her completion of graduation requirements. The school district appealed to the Pennsylvania Commonwealth Court, which held that **a student cannot be denied a high school diploma after completing all coursework required for graduation, despite being expelled thereafter**. Since the student had completed all her coursework and had taken her final examinations pending the expulsion, she could not be denied a diploma. This ruling did not undermine school authority to discipline students for disobedience, as the district had itself provided her with tutoring and the opportunity to sit for her final examinations. The court affirmed the judgment in the student's favor. *Ream v. Centennial School District,* 765 A.2d 1195 (Pa. Commw. 2001).

◆   An Oregon school district adopted a policy with extensive provisions governing the impermissible use of drugs, alcohol and tobacco by students. Students committing a first offense for possession of an illegal substance were subject to a five-day suspension from school and a four-week suspension from extracurricular activities. The policy created a separate category for co-curricular activities, but did not state whether student government constituted an extracurricular, co-curricular or curricular activity. **The student** came to school in possession of marijuana near the end of the school year, after he **had been elected president of the student body for the following school year**. **The school stripped him of the title for violating the drug, alcohol and tobacco policy**. The student sued the district in an Oregon trial court, which granted his request for an order preventing the disciplinary sanction.

The district appealed, arguing that every school district in the state had inherent powers to discipline students under Or. Rev. Stat. § 339.250, a state law authorizing student discipline, suspension or expulsion "of any refractory student." It further asserted that while its policy provided for a four-week suspension from extracurricular activities as part of the permitted discipline for rules violations, the policy also distinguished between extracurricular and co-curricular activities. According to the district, participation in student government was a curricular activity The appeals court held that state law provided general authority for school officials to make and enforce rules that have some reasonable connection with school functions where students faced the possibility of suspension or expulsion. In this case, the right to attend school was not at stake. The district was permitted to exercise residual disciplinary authority, subject to constitutional and statutory restraints of consistency and fairness, even where rules were not drawn to cover every possible circumstance. In this case, **the rules emphasized the importance of controlling student drug use, and the discipline selected by the school was not unlawful**. The appeals court reversed the district court judgment, finding that the lack of specific sanctions for student government participants did not preclude barring an offending student from taking student office. *Ferguson et al. v. Phoenix-Talent School District No. 4, Jackson County, Oregon*, 172 Or.App. 389, 19 P.3d 943 (2001).

◆   Two students admitted leaving school to smoke marijuana. They expressed regret, and evidence indicated that they were not disruptive students. The students' families received notices that the students were being suspended pending expulsion hearings for use/possession of controlled substances. The parents of both students urged school officials to give them a second chance, contending that the expulsions were unsupported by evidence. Even after the board assigned the students to alternative schools instead of expelling them, **the families challenged the actions, noting that the students were never actually found in possession of** drugs but had only skipped classes and returned smelling of marijuana. The parents obtained a court order requiring the district to readmit the students to their school, but the court later dissolved the order and denied their requests for relief.

The students appealed to a Louisiana Court of Appeal, which observed that state law permits the discipline of students for certain enumerated offenses but requires expulsion for possession of controlled substances in school buildings, grounds or buses. The trial court had found that because the students returned to school under the influence of drugs, there was clear and convincing evidence of drug possession. The court of appeal rejected the trial court's reasoning that the intent of the statute covered the conduct of the students. The placement of a student in an alternative school, while not considered expulsion, involved student due process rights, since it had the potential for harming a student's reputation. Schools had to comply with minimal requirements of due process when considering such placements. **The appeals court agreed with the students that drug "possession," as defined in the statute, did not occur because the students did not bring drugs to their school campus**. Instead, they had only violated school rules by leaving campus without permission in order to commit a serious offense. According to the court, the school board's technical error of charging the students with possession of drugs in violation of the statute did not result in a due process violation. However, the proceedings themselves were tainted by confusion about the mandatory expulsion provision of state law for drug possession on campus. It appeared that the disciplinary action against the students was taken with the understanding that expulsion was mandatory. Because the students were deprived of the opportunity to seek lesser punishment, the appeals court vacated and remanded the case to the school board for further proceedings. *McCall et al. v. Bossier Parish School Board*, Nos. 34983-CA and 34984-CA, 2001 WL 259180 (La. App., 2d Cir. 2001).

◆   An assistant principal and local police officers conducted a canine search in a high school parking lot. Two dogs alerted on a student's vehicle, and she was summoned from her classroom. She opened the vehicle and the **officers discovered fragments of what was later confirmed to be small amounts of marijuana**. The officials brought the student to the school office and summoned her parents. The assistant principal met with the parents and explained what had happened. He suspended the student for 10 days. The school principal sent the parents a letter confirming the suspension and notifying them of an expulsion hearing. The principal and assistant principal held the hearing, which was attended by the student with her parents and counsel. **The principal then notified the parents of his intention to expel the student and place her in an alternative school**. The student appealed to the superintendent of schools, who conducted another hearing at which the student presented evidence and was represented by counsel. The superintendent affirmed the expulsion order. The student rejected placement in the alternative school and sought a preliminary injunction from a federal district court to set aside the order.

The court considered the due process claims arising from both the suspension and expulsion proceedings. Under *Goss v. Lopez*, 419 U.S. 565 (1975), due process requires only that a student receive oral or written notice of the charges and an opportunity to explain her side of the story for discipline resulting in a suspension of 10 days or less. The student had received two hearings to challenge her expulsion with the opportunity to present evidence and be represented by counsel. In finding that this satisfied her due process rights, the court found that **there was strong evidence that she had been in possession of marijuana and that "[d]ue process demands only that Plaintiff be permitted to present her side of the story, not that school administrators accept it."** The failure of the assistant principal to testify at the hearings did not violate the constitution. The court rejected the student's assertion that the school violated her substantive due process rights by transferring her to an alternative school. According to the court, schools have a compelling interest in remaining drug-free. Disciplining students found in possession of drugs is rationally related to this interest. The district's disciplinary regulations and code of student conduct were not unconstitutionally vague or imprecise in vesting school officials with discretion to issue discipline. The court rejected the student's assertion that she would be irreparably harmed by attending the alternative school. The student could graduate on time by attending the alternative school, and the court refused to issue the requested injunction. *Hammock v. Keys*, 93 F.Supp.2d 1222 (S.D. Ala. 2000).

◆   **A high school student was caught with alcohol** in the parking lot of the off-campus facility where the senior prom was held and charged with underage purchase, consumption or transportation of alcohol under state law. **The school suspended the student for 10 days and excluded him from participating in graduation ceremonies** under its "Five Day Rule." Under the Five Day Rule, any senior suspended during the last five days of each semester could be excluded from graduation exercises. The student filed a lawsuit in state court, seeking an order compelling the district to allow him to participate in graduation. A Pennsylvania trial court found the district's attempt to exclude the student from graduation inequitable in view of his academic record, post high-school plans and family support.

The school district appealed to the commonwealth court, which observed that the case was technically moot, since the student had now graduated. However, it found the case capable of repetition, yet likely to evade review and that it involved an important public question that would otherwise never reach an appellate court. The commonwealth court held that the school district was empowered by state law to adopt and enforce reasonable rules and regulations for managing schools and the conduct of students. **School boards have broad discretion in determining student disciplinary policies and challenges to this discretion will only succeed if the board action is arbitrary, capricious and prejudicial** to the public interest. State law permitted school principals to suspend students for no more than 10 days, and these determinations were not subject to review as adjudications under local agency law. In this case, the trial court admitted substituting its judgment for that of the school administration. The trial court failed to find that the district's action was arbitrary, capricious or prejudicial to the public interest, instead finding that when the student was held accountable for his actions, the result was unfair. Because the trial court had improperly substituted its judgment for that of the school district, the commonwealth court reversed its order. *Flynn-Scarcella v. Pocono Mountain School Dist.*, 745 A.2d 117 (Pa.Commw. 2000).

◆   **A Pennsylvania high school teacher noticed that two students entering the school late smelling of marijuana.** He referred them to the school office, where **an assistant principal notified one student that he was suspended for three days**. That student complained that he had only been standing next to some other students who were smoking marijuana. The student's mother complained about the three-day suspension, and obtained a private drug test indicating that the student was drug free. She also noted that the other student apprehended by the teacher was not disciplined. The school claimed that it did not suspend the other student because he was a foreign exchange student who was not officially enrolled at the school. The family sued the district, the principal, the assistant principal and the teacher in a federal district court for constitutional rights violations including equal protection, due process and Fourth Amendment claims.

The court rejected the assertion that failure to discipline the foreign exchange student violated the student's equal protection rights, since the exchange student was not similarly situated to the complaining student. There was no merit to the due process claim based on lack of medical evidence of marijuana ingestion, because the student received notice of the suspension and an opportunity to present his side of the story. School employees had reason to suspect that the student had used marijuana because they detected its odor on his person, he arrived late, and admitted standing with others who were smoking marijuana. The assistant principal and teacher had conducted a search of the student's pockets, shoes, book bag and locker that was supported by reasonable suspicion. The search was reasonable under the circumstances and furthered the school's legitimate interest in maintaining a drug free environment. The district and school officials were entitled to summary judgment. *Bartram v. Pennsbury School Dist.*, 1999 U.S. Dist. LEXIS 7916 (E.D.Pa.1999).

◆   A middle school student was suspended twice for 10-day periods during the same school semester. The first suspension resulted from selling stolen property at school, and the second from possession of marijuana and smoking paraphernalia. The school board's disciplinary committee held an expulsion hearing and **the board voted to permanently expel the student. He appealed to a state trial court, which affirmed the expulsion**. However, the Commonwealth Court of Pennsylvania observed that the school's code failed to specify guidelines or define specific offenses which could result in expulsion. The district's code, which did contain guidelines and specify offenses, was held inapplicable and the court reversed the expulsion order.

The state supreme court agreed to review the case and ruled that state court rules permitted the middle school and district codes to be read together, as the district had argued. The pertinent sections of the codes were complementary and **the exclusion of specific expulsion guidelines in the middle school code did not prohibit the expulsion**. Under Pennsylvania law, the school board, and not school administrators, wielded the power to expel students, making it appropriate to enumerate expulsion guidelines only at the district level. The court reversed the commonwealth court decision and reinstated the expulsion. *Hamilton v. Unionville-Chadds Ford School Dist.*, 714 A.2d 1012 (Pa.1998).

◆   Maryland school officials questioned a high school student enrolled in a regular education course of study about her possible possession of controlled substances on school grounds. **After signing a written admission that she had brought LSD onto school grounds, she was expelled** by the school superintendent. A school board panel voted to affirm the decision following a hearing and the student appealed to the state board of education. The state board summarily affirmed the local board's decision, and the student appealed to a Maryland circuit court, arguing that the admission had been coerced and that the school district had failed to first assess her special education needs before taking disciplinary action. The court affirmed the expulsion order, and the student appealed to the Court of Special Appeals of Maryland.

The court of special appeals rejected the student's assertion that the district was required to perform a special education evaluation prior to taking disciplinary action against her, despite evidence that she had attention deficit hyperactivity disorder. The procedural safeguards of state special education law applied only to students who were unable to achieve their educational potential in general education programs. **A parental request for a special education evaluation did not bring regular disciplinary proceedings to a halt.** The court also rejected the student's claim that her oral admission had been coerced since she had ratified the admission in writing and again at the hearing where she was represented by an attorney. The court affirmed the expulsion order. *Miller v. Bd. of Educ. of Caroline County*, 114 Md.App. 462, 690 A.2d 557 (1997).

For other cases involving the suspension of students with disabilities, see Chapter 12, § II.C.

◆   **A Massachusetts principal suspended a student for three days and excluded him from competing on the school soccer team for the rest of the year for coming to a school dance under the influence of alcohol.** A few days after returning to school, the student was issued another three-day suspension for skipping study hall and threatening a teacher who confronted him in the school hallway. The student's parents withdrew him from school and enrolled him in a private school. They then filed a lawsuit against the school district in the U.S. District Court for the District of Massachusetts, asserting constitutional rights violations. The parties moved for summary judgment. The student and parents claimed that the school had deprived the student of his constitutional rights to due process by failing to give him appropriate notice and opportunities to respond in both suspensions. They also claimed that the school had deprived him of due process in excluding him from the soccer team and for revoking his parking privileges following a previous incident during the same school year. The court found these arguments meritless, observing that in each case, school administrators had explained the charges against him, given him an opportunity to respond and provided adequate notice of disciplinary action. **The loss of parking and athletic team privileges did not rise to the level of constitutional violations** and the school officials had not violated student handbook rules. The court granted the school district's summary judgment motion. *Zehner v. Central Berkshire Regional School Dist.*, 921 F.Supp. 850 (D.Mass.1996).

◆   A South Carolina associate high school principal detected alcohol on a student's breath at a football game and school administrators issued him a 10-day suspension. An assistant principal contacted the student's parents and held a meeting to discuss the matter. **The student admitted drinking alcohol before coming to the football game, and the suspension was upheld.** The student's parents appealed the decision to the school principal, who was vested with the final decision making authority under the school district appeals procedure. The principal upheld the suspension, and the student filed a lawsuit against the district in a South Carolina circuit court. The court dismissed the action, and the student appealed to the Supreme Court of South Carolina.

The court agreed with the district that state courts lacked jurisdiction over short term suspensions. A statute describing student disciplinary procedures specified that appeals from expulsion orders could be brought before an appropriate court.

However, **the statute did not confer a right of appeal for suspensions and the court was unwilling to imply one. A general statute providing circuit court jurisdiction in school board matters did not apply to short-term suspensions.** School officials had provided adequate due process procedures by allowing the student to present his side of the story and advising him of the reasons for discipline. The student was not entitled to any further due process protections, and the court affirmed the circuit court decision. *Byrd v. Irmo High School*, 468 S.E.2d 861 (S.C.1996).

◆   An Alabama junior high school student showed some marijuana to other students in a classroom. The other students reported the incident, and the teacher searched the desk at which he had been sitting. She discovered a plastic bag containing marijuana and reported it to the sheriff on duty at the school. **The principal notified the student of an immediate 10-day suspension** and advised his parents by letter that an indefinite expulsion would be recommended at a hearing. The hearing was postponed twice to allow other students to testify; however, their parents refused to allow them to do so. The school board considered some written statements by the students who did not testify in deciding to expel the student. The student appealed to the state board of education, which affirmed the expulsion. The student filed a lawsuit against the school board and state education officials in the U.S. District Court for the Middle District of Alabama, asserting constitutional and state law violations. The court considered the school officials' summary judgment motion.

The court first determined that **the 10-day suspension did not violate minimal constitutional notice standards as there was evidence that the student had been told of the reason for suspension.** There was no evidence that the notice of the expulsion hearing was deficient because it adequately advised the student and his family of the reasons for the expulsion. Students do not have a constitutional right to cross-examine witnesses at a full adversarial hearing. Because the student had received two hearings, there was no constitutional violation. The school officials were entitled to summary judgment. *L.Q.A., by and through Arrington v. Eberhart*, 920 F.Supp. 1208 (M.D.Ala.1996).

C. Weapons

◆   A student left a pellet gun in a car parked on school grounds. Another student took the gun from the car and fired it in a school parking lot, superficially wounding a third student. The first two students admitted possessing the pellet gun on school grounds and the principal suspended them. The school board discussed the incident the same day, but delayed voting on it. The next day, the superintendent and principal met with the involved students and their parents to discuss the suspension and inform them of the hearing at the next board meeting. A letter from the school principal dated five days after the incident further informed the students and parents of the hearing, as did a letter from the superintendent dated seven days after the incident. The delay in conducting the hearing resulted in a 13-day suspension from school for both students, in violation of a district policy limiting suspensions to eight school days. When the board finally considered the matter, it voted to expel both students for more than three months. **The district sent the students notices that they had**

been expelled for violating the Gun Free Schools Act and Idaho law. The students sought reconsideration and the board scheduled a second hearing. The board again voted for expulsion, and the students petitioned a state trial court for an order prohibiting the discipline. The court found that the board acted arbitrarily, unjustly and in abuse of its discretion, and issued the requested order plus an award of attorneys' fees.

The board appealed to the Idaho Supreme Court, which noted that it became involved in school cases only when the actions of a school system directly implicate basic constitutional values. While procedural errors during a suspension may justify some forms of judicial relief, the trial court had no grounds for issuing the specific order entered in this case. There was no finding that procedural errors affected the determination that the students should be expelled. By the time the students had requested the order from the court, their suspension had been over for two months and they had received two hearings before the board. Since the procedural errors pertained only to the suspension, it was error for the trial court to issue relief on that basis. State procedures for student discipline are not as strict as those in the criminal or juvenile systems. The court held that in school disciplinary proceedings, notice of the incidents or activities giving rise to a disciplinary hearing is generally sufficient. **The board had properly invoked Section 33-205 of the Idaho Code as authority for expelling the students for carrying a weapon or firearm on school property**. The students understood that they had harmed another student and the board could find that their presence was detrimental to others at school. The state supreme court reversed the trial court's decision. *Gooding Public Joint School District No. 231, In re Expulsion of Rogers et al.*, 20 P.3d 16 (Idaho 2001).

◆   Tennessee Code Annotated § 49-6-4216 encourages county and local education boards to include zero tolerance policies for student misconduct. The Knox County Board of Education adopted a zero tolerance policy in conformity with the state legislature's direction to "impose swift, certain and severe disciplinary sanctions on any student" bringing a dangerous weapon onto school property. School administrators discovered a knife while searching a student's car during a school function, based on reports that he had consumed alcohol before attempting to enter the building. The student explained in a written statement that a friend had placed the knife there without his knowledge. School **administrators suspended the student and recommended his expulsion, despite testimony that he had no idea that the knife was in the car**. The student appealed to the school board, which unanimously voted for expulsion. He then sued the superintendent, board and other school officials in a federal district court for constitutional rights violations. The court dismissed the principal, individual board members and disciplinary hearing officer from the action, but denied the superintendent and board's motion for summary judgment. The court made a dispositive ruling in the student's favor, and the superintendent and board appealed to the Sixth Circuit.

On appeal, the student argued that the board's decision was irrational and violated his substantive due process rights in view of evidence that he lacked knowledge that the knife was in his car, and therefore had no intent to carry a weapon onto school grounds. The board asserted that the zero tolerance policy uniformly required expulsion for weapons violations because it contained no knowledge or intent requirement. The court observed that in school discipline cases, a substantive due process claim would succeed only where there is no rational relationship between the punishment and the offense. However, the concept of possession of a contraband item ordinarily implied knowing or conscious possession and was not a mere technicality. **The circuit court found a zero tolerance policy would be irrational if it subjected to punishment students who did not knowingly or consciously possess a weapon**. The district court awarded summary judgment to the board despite any evidence about the student's knowledge of the knife. Because it was not clear whether the board had made a rational decision to expel the student, summary judgment was improper. The court reversed this part of the judgment and remanded the case for further proceedings. The Sixth Circuit also held that qualified immunity protects school officials from civil liability for performing discretionary functions where their conduct does not violate clearly established rights, which a reasonable person would have known. A reasonable school superintendent at the time of the student's suspension would not be on notice that a zero tolerance policy without a conscious-possession requirement could violate student rights. Therefore, the superintendent was entitled to qualified immunity. *Seal v. Morgan,* 229 F.3d 567 (6th Cir. 2000).

◆   A Texas school district transferred a student from his high school to an alternative school for bringing a shotgun to school. The principal made the decision to transfer the student after holding a hearing at which the student appeared with his parents and an attorney. **The principal expelled the student from campus and from participation in extracurricular activities, but allowed him to attend alternative classes on the school's campus the following semester**. The superintendent of schools modified the principal's decision by allowing the student to attend on-campus alternative classes in the evening. The school board heard a presentation by the student's attorney at its next meeting, but refused to take action, effectively upholding the superintendent's decision. However, a state trial court held that the board violated the student's due process rights by failing to provide him a full hearing before the board, as required by the state education code in cases involving felony offenses by students.

The school board appealed to the state appeals court, which observed that the student had not been disciplined for conduct that was punishable as a felony. The trial court had improperly applied the education code, and the student was not entitled to the due process rights created by that section of the law. The appeals court instead applied the law applicable to placement in alternative education. It rejected the student's assertion that he had been expelled. **According to the court, the Texas Legislature did not intend that assignment to alternative programs be construed as an expulsion**. The student had not been entirely excluded from campus as he was allowed to attend evening alternative classes five nights a week. He had received the appropriate procedural protections to which he was entitled, since the board considered the superintendent's decision. The trial court was without jurisdiction to overturn the board's decision and the court reversed the judgment. *Aledo Indep. School Dist. v. Reese,* 987 S.W.2d 953 (Tex.App.1999).

◆   **A Minnesota student was expelled for a limited time period for possession of a BB gun. The district also prohibited the student from participating in extracurricular activities** for several months. The student appealed the expulsion order to the state education department, asserting constitutional due process violations and failure to comply with the state Pupil Fair Dismissal Act. The department reversed the expulsion and ordered related disciplinary records expunged on grounds of insufficient notice. However, the department found no violation of the dismissal act. The student then filed a lawsuit against the school district, alleging that school officials violated his constitutional rights by expelling him and curtailing his participation in extracurricular activities without substantial evidence of misconduct and without a fair hearing.

A federal district court held that the state education department's decision was entitled to the same deference as a state court order and could not be reheard by a federal district court. It also held that even if the complaint was not barred, the student had received far more than adequate due process by the school's principal and the school board. **He had received an opportunity to explain the incident in the principal's office, proper notice to appear at an expulsion hearing based on his admission to the principal, a statement of the reasons for expulsion and the opportunity to testify and cross-examine witnesses**. No violation of state law had occurred. The court rejected the student's claim that the board had retaliated against him by barring him from extracurricular activities. There is no constitutional right of students to participate in such activities. The court also held that the principal was entitled to qualified immunity, since his conduct did not violate any of the student's clearly established rights and he had acted reasonably in construing the school's dangerous weapons policy. The court granted summary judgment to the school district and officials. *Peterson v. Indep. School Dist. No. 811*, 999 F.Supp. 665 (D.Minn.1998).

◆ A Florida middle school maintained a student disciplinary policy which prohibited students from disrupting classes, distracting others, defacing school property or endangering the safety of self or others. The only items that were expressly prohibited by the policy were telephone pagers, weapons and firearms. Students were prohibited from carrying knives, weapons or any item which could be used as a weapon, and the policy declared that use or possession of a weapon on school property or while attending a school function constituted grounds for expulsion and referral to law enforcement agencies. **The school board expelled a student for possessing eight bullets on a school bus**. At a hearing to consider the expulsion, the school's assistant principal acknowledged that the student had not been disruptive on the bus, while the school's principal testified that the incident had constituted a major disruption on the school campus.

The board voted to expel the student, and he appealed to the District Court of Appeal of Florida, Fifth District. He argued on appeal that he could not be found guilty of violating the disciplinary policy because bullets are not weapons. He also argued that any item could be dangerous under the policy and denied that any person had been placed at risk by his conduct. The court agreed, finding that the policy did not prohibit possession of any item except paging devices and items which could be used as weapons. **The policy forbidding dangerous and disruptive items could not be relied upon in this case because there was no evidence that the bullets had been used by the student in any way**. The court reversed and remanded the expulsion order. *M.K. v. School Bd. of Brevard County*, 708 So.2d 340 (Fla.App.5th Dist.1998).

◆   A Kansas high school student brought to school a pellet pistol which resembled a real gun. He displayed the gun to friends during the school day and no student who observed the gun believed it was a threat to their safety. However, a parent who saw the gun reported the student to school security officials. **The principal imposed an extended suspension on the student for possession of a look-alike handgun** in violation of a student handbook code section prohibiting unruly conduct that disrupts school and another code section broadly extending to other matters covered by Kansas law. The suspension was affirmed by the school board and a Kansas district court. The student appealed to the Court of Appeals of Kansas, which found that **the board and principal had not exceeded their authority by issuing the suspension despite the lack of specific language in the student code prohibiting possession of look-alike handguns**. The U.S. Supreme Court has recognized that the need for school discipline requires the ability to impose discipline for a wide range of conduct. The court held that the suspension was supported by substantial evidence and affirmed the district court decision. *Spencer v. Unif. School Dist. No. 501*, 935 P.2d 242 (Kan.App.1997).

◆   After a West Virginia student was expelled for weapons possession, the student's mother petitioned a West Virginia circuit court for an order requiring the school board to readmit the student to regular classes or provide state-funded alternative educational services. The school board agreed to provide the student with home instruction for four hours weekly, but on condition that his parents reimburse the board for the teacher's time. The case reached the Supreme Court of Appeals of West Virginia, which rejected the board's assertion that it need not provide any state-funded educational opportunities to the student during his expulsion. Where the state could safely provide basic educational opportunities to an expelled student, there was no state interest in compelling parents to reimburse a local agency for costs. Students have constitutional, fundamental rights to education under the state constitution. However, **the strong state interest in safe and secure schools left open the possibility of the complete deprivation of all educational services**, including an alternative placement in an extreme case, and **the court held that a case-by-case analysis was appropriate for determining the level of services to which a student may be entitled**. *Cathe A. v. Doddridge County Bd. of Educ.*, 490 S.E.2d 340 (W.Va.1997).

◆   A Michigan school district adopted a dangerous weapons in school policy which called for the permanent expulsion of students for weapons possession in a weapon-free school zone. **The policy's definition of prohibited weapons included BB guns**, and it defined school property as the area up to 1,000 feet around school property. However, the policy made reference to Michigan laws, including the state weapon-free school zones act, which did not include BB guns within the definition of dangerous weapons. Michigan middle school administrators learned that three students were in possession of a BB gun on school grounds. After an investigation and disciplinary hearing, the school district expelled two of them, who both appealed to a Michigan trial court. The court noted the discrepancy between the school policy and the state law excluding BB guns from the definition of dangerous weapons and issued a permanent injunction forbidding the district from enforcing the expulsions.

The school district appealed to the Michigan Court of Appeals, which observed that **the district had the authority to prohibit BB guns on school property, and the state legislature had not prohibited school boards from doing so by enacting the weapon-free school zones act**. Because the statute did not expressly prohibit the expulsion of a student for BB gun possession on school property, and the school board maintained its inherent disciplinary powers, the trial court had erroneously enjoined the permanent expulsions. The court reversed and remanded the trial court judgments. *Davis v. Hillsdale Community School Dist.*, 573 N.W.2d 77 (Mich.App.1997).

◆   A Virginia high school student admitted carrying a pocketknife on a school field trip, prompting the school's assistant principal to suspend him for 10 days for violation of the school's code of student conduct. The school board conducted a hearing, finding that the student had violated the student code and Virginia laws prohibiting the possession of firearms on school property. **A Virginia trial court held that the student's pocketknife was not a firearm under the state criminal code, but let stand the board's finding that the student had violated the student conduct code**. After the board voted to expel the student for a full year, he appealed to the Supreme Court of Virginia. The court affirmed the trial court judgment. *Wood v. Henry County Pub. Schools*, 495 S.E.2d 255 (Va.1998).

◆   **A California high school used a hand-held metal detector to conduct daily random weapons searches of students based on neutral criteria**. It notified parents and students before implementing the practice. A student brought a knife to school on a day when the assistant principal decided to search all students who were late for school and those without hall passes. The student was one of eight to ten students who met the criteria, and her knife was discovered. A California juvenile court denied the student's motion to suppress the knife as unlawfully seized evidence and placed her on probation. She appealed to the California Court of Appeal, Second District, asserting that student searches without individualized suspicion violate the Fourth Amendment. The court held that schools have a substantial interest in keeping weapons off school campuses. **The metal detector search had been minimally intrusive, and no less intrusive means existed to detect weapons**. The court noted that courts in other states including Florida, Pennsylvania, Illinois and New York have upheld random searches of students without individualized suspicion, and held that the search did not violate the Fourth Amendment. *People v. Latasha W.*, 70 Cal.Rptr.2d 886 (Cal.App.2d Dist.1998).

◆   Alabama law requires all education boards in the state to implement policies requiring the expulsion of students who have brought a firearm to school buildings, school-sponsored functions, school grounds or school buses. Although the law specifies a one-year expulsion, education boards are allowed to modify the time of an expulsion on a case-by-case basis. Police officers discovered a gun under the front seat of a vehicle parked in a high school lot. **The vehicle had been driven by a student to school. She stated that her mother had left the gun in the car the previous night and that she was not aware that it was in the car when she drove it to school**. The board held a hearing and expelled the student for eight weeks. She petitioned a juvenile court for an order preventing the board from expelling her. The court found that the eight-week expulsion was shockingly disparate to the offense. The school board appealed to the Court of Civil Appeals of Alabama, which noted that the school board had taken into account mitigating factors when it decided not to expel the student for a full year. **The board had not acted arbitrarily in reaching its decision and because of the compelling public interest in preventing students from bringing guns to school, there was no shocking disparity between the offense and the punishment imposed by the board**. The court reversed the juvenile court decision and remanded the case. *Enterprise City Bd. of Educ. v. C.P., By and Through J.P. and M.P.*, 698 So.2d 131 (Ala.Civ.App.1996).

◆   A 12-year-old Georgia student brandished a knife on school property and stabbed another student with it during a fight. The school administration expelled the student permanently from all district schools, and the decision was affirmed at a county education board review hearing. The state board of education affirmed the permanent expulsion, and this result was affirmed by a state superior court. **The student appealed** to the Court of Appeals of Georgia, **arguing that the Georgia Constitution required the state to provide a free public education to each student and thus prohibited permanent expulsion. The court disagreed, finding that permanent expulsion was permissible**. The court affirmed the expulsion order. *D.B. v. Clarke County Bd. of Educ.*, 220 Ga.App. 330, 469 S.E.2d 438 (1996).

◆   An Indiana fourth grader with diabetes attended school as a regular education student. While on a field trip, **she used a small nail file instrument containing a knife to threaten two students who had been harassing her** during the bus ride. The student was expelled for six weeks for violating a state law prohibition on the knowing possession or handling of a weapon at school. The student's parents appealed to the school board, and presented evidence that her actions had been caused by her diabetic condition. The board upheld the expulsion. The parents filed a lawsuit against the school district, asserting that the school district had violated the Individuals with Disabilities Education Act (IDEA) by failing to identify the student as requiring special education services. The court held that the IDEA and related § 504 claims were barred by the family's failure to first request an administrative hearing. Participation in the expulsion hearing did not meet the IDEA's administrative exhaustion requirement. **The board had not acted arbitrarily or capriciously by expelling the student without finding that her behavior was causally related to her disability**. The court granted the district's dismissal motion. *Brown v. Metropolitan School Dist. of Lawrence Township*, 945 F.Supp. 1202 (S.D.Ind.1996).

D. Misconduct

◆   **An Illinois school board's anti-gang rule specifically prohibited students from representing gang affiliation, recruiting others for gang membership and threatening or intimidating others to act against their will to further gang purposes**. The school board voted to expel six black students for two years each because of their involvement in a bleacher-clearing fight. The board reviewed a videotape of the incident and found that the students were members of rival street gangs. The videotape revealed that each of the students actively participated in the fight and that seven bystanders were injured. After twice voting to expel each student for two years, the board met with representatives of Reverend Jesse Jackson's organization, the Rainbow/PUSH Coalition, and Illinois Governor George Ryan. One student withdrew from school, but the board agreed to reduce the expulsions to one year and allow the others to immediately attend alternative education programs. Despite the board's concessions, the students sued the board in a federal district court for civil rights violations, alleging that the anti-gang provision violated the Constitution. The court awarded judgment to the board.

The students appealed to the U.S. Court of Appeals, Seventh Circuit, arguing that the anti-gang rule was unconstitutionally vague due to the lack of clear definitions. The board asserted that the case was moot because the expulsions had been served and two of the students had graduated. The court disagreed, noting that expulsions of the severity undergone by these students could have serious consequences and because relief such as expunging their records was available. According to the court, **the anti-gang rule clearly defined what conduct it prohibited and was not unconstitutionally vague. The rule did not involve speech rights and fighting by the students in support of their gang was clearly within its definitions**. It was reasonable for school officials to see the fight as gang-like activity, and the rule was sufficiently definite to avoid the constitutional challenge. The court affirmed the judgment for the school board. *Fuller v. Decatur Public Sch. Bd. of Educ. Sch. Dist. 61*, 251 F.3d 662 (7th Cir. 2001).

◆   An eighth grader repeatedly disrupted his art class and was required to sign a disciplinary contract. One day, his teacher placed him in the hallway for misconduct. The student and a classmate twice interrupted the classroom by pushing open the door, making sound effects, holding their hands as if they held guns and pretending to shoot individuals. Earlier in the day, school administrators had warned students against making references to guns or bombs, in view of the then-recent Columbine incident. **Administrators expelled the student on an emergency basis to determine whether he posed a legitimate threat of school violence**. After deciding he did not, they converted his emergency expulsion into a short-term suspension, awarding him credit for the school days he missed.

The student appealed to an administrative hearing officer, arguing that he had only made playful gestures with no intent to threaten others. The hearing officer upheld the discipline, and a Washington trial court affirmed the decision. The student appealed to the Washington Court of Appeals, arguing that pretending to shoot at a class from a doorway with his hands in the position of a gun was not "disruptive conduct" as defined by the school district's disciplinary policy. **The appeals court rejected the student's assertion that the district had no authority to expel him for simulated gunplay**. Even though no written rule specifically made this conduct punishable by emergency expulsion, a school rule against disruptive conduct gave students notice that such conduct was grounds for expulsion. The appeals court affirmed the superior court judgment. *Hanna v. Kent Sch. Dist.*, No. 46306-3-I (Wash. App. Div. 1 2001).

◆   During one school year, a 12-year-old student received 41 write-ups, most of them for minor incidents. His band teacher employed a no-tolerance rule prohibiting students from criticizing or laughing at a classmate's instrumental ability. The student violated the rule and the teacher escorted the student to the principal's office. The student escaped from the teacher while in the hallway and twice eluded her. After she caught him and grabbed his backpack, he pushed and hit her several times. He then attempted to hit the teacher with a clenched fist. When another teacher restrained the student, he threatened to kill him. The school suspended the student for 10 days for being disrespectful to teachers, refusing to go to the office and attempting to leave school grounds. **The school board unanimously adopted the principal's recommendation to expel the student for the rest of the school year for threats and violence**.

The student's mother disputed the board's decision and challenged the expulsion order in an Arkansas trial court, which issued an order finding the student would not have responded with inappropriate words if he had not been tackled and thrown to the ground by a faculty member. The court credited the parents for placing the student in counseling to deal with his behavior and ruled that the expulsion was a gross abuse of discretion. The school district appealed to the Arkansas Court of Appeals, which noted that a reviewing court does not have the power to interfere with a school board's decision in the absence of a clear abuse of discretion. Although courts do not typically approve of expulsion as a remedy to enforce a student's nonconformity to rules, they do so where the misconduct is of such a grave nature that it disrupts the school. State law vested school boards with the discretion to direct school operations without judicial interference. Although the infraction leading to the student's assignment to the office was trivial, this did not form the basis for expulsion. Instead, **the principal had based the recommendation for expulsion on his threats and violent conduct**. The court agreed with the board that the trial court had interfered with its discretion based on evidence that the student hit one teacher several times and threatened the faculty member upon being restrained. The board did not abuse its discretion by expelling the student, and the court reversed the judgment. *Wynne Public Schools v. Lockhart*, 72 Ark.App. 24, 32 S.W.3d 47 (Ark. App. 2000).

♦   A Nebraska seventh-grader who accidentally struck and injured an assistant principal who was trying to break up a fight failed to convince the state's highest court that the district violated its statutory authority by expelling her for a semester. **The use of violence or force against a school employee constituted substantial interference with school purposes under state law**. The Nebraska Supreme Court explained that while the state legislature set broad school disciplinary policies, local boards were charged with publishing rules to maintain order and foster a safe and appropriate learning environment. The state Student Discipline Act ensured that students' constitutional rights were protected "within the context of an orderly and effective educational process." The school district had patterned its student code after the disciplinary act, which permitted long-term suspension, expulsion or reassignment based on the use of violence, force, coercion, threats, intimidation and conduct that "constitutes a substantial interference with school purposes." The same section of the act permitted discipline for causing personal injury to a school employee, volunteer or student, and there was no merit to the student's assertion that the district had exceeded its statutory authority when it crafted a student code incorporating similar language. There was no legal requirement that a student have the actual intent to cause personal injury in order to violate the section. The school rule was clear and put the student on notice of the conduct it prohibited. *Busch v. Omaha Public School District et al.*, 261 Neb. 484, 623 N.W.2d 672 (2001).

◆ **An Ohio appeals court affirmed the 10-day suspension of a student accused of paying a student to beat up another child on his behalf**. The court observed that state law permits school principals to order suspensions of up to 10 days without approval by a school board. The principal issued a notice of suspension for 10 days, pursuant to Ohio Rev. Code § 3313.66, for violating a school policy prohibiting student threats, assault, and defiance of school rules. The court held that the school policy stated with specificity the type of prohibited conduct that could result in discipline. The student was not denied due process, and his claims about the truth of the evidence had no bearing on whether he had received due process. *Kipp v. Lorain Board of Education*, No. 99CA007517, 2001 WL 324405 (Ohio App. 9th Dist. 2001).

◆ **A federal district court dismissed a suit brought against a Pennsylvania school district by a student who was expelled after a transcript of his home Internet conversation with another student was seized at a school-sponsored event**. The district suspended, and later expelled the student who had sent the message, based on its allegedly anti-Semitic and racist content. The district did not perform any act that created liability under state and federal wiretap statutes. Because the receiving student did not violate the federal wiretap law by saving the conversation, there was no violation by school officials, and the complaint failed. The use by school officials of the saved message was lawful. Moreover, even if the reception of the message by the receiving student had been unlawful, the complaint failed to allege that school officials had anything to do with his action. The court granted the school officials' motion, dismissing the action in its entirety. *S.L. by and through P.L. and V.L. v. Friends Central School*, Civil Action No. 00-472, U.S. Dist. Lexis 4276 (E.D. Pa. 2000).

◆ A Pennsylvania student created a Web site at home called "Teacher Sux." The Web site accused the school principal of having an extramarital affair with another district principal, included an image of his algebra teacher changing into an image of Adolph Hitler and a diagram of her with her head cut off and blood dripping from her neck. The site also declared: "Why Should She Die?" Another page from the site directed profanities at the same teacher 136 times. An instructor learned of the web site and reported it to the principal, who contacted authorities. Law enforcement agencies identified the student as the creator of the Web site and he voluntarily removed it. The district suspended the student and scheduled an expulsion hearing prior to the start of the upcoming school year. The district determined **the Web site had seriously affected the algebra teacher, had a negative impact on school morale, and disrupted the educational process**. The district had been forced to use substitute teachers as the result of the algebra teacher's leave. The statement "Why Should She Die? ... Give me $20.00 to help pay for the hitman" constituted a threat, and this and other statements were harassing and disrespectful to the teacher and principal, resulting in actual harm. Based on these findings, the district voted to permanently expel the student.

A state trial court upheld the expulsion, and the student appealed to the Pennsylvania Commonwealth Court, where he advanced a constitutional rights violation challenge. **The court observed that even though the creation of the Web site had occurred off school grounds, the student was still subject to discipline for the disruption he had created at school**. The Web site had hindered the academic process by forcing the algebra teacher to take a medical leave of absence for an entire school year. The teacher continued to suffer emotional distress from the student's actions. School officials were justified in taking student threats seriously. There was no merit to the student's constitutional claims. His family had received adequate notice of the expulsion hearing and he was not entitled to additional opportunities for pre-hearing discovery. The district had attempted to accommodate the family's unavailability for the hearing by rescheduling it, and was not required to continue it for three months. Since lewd, obscene, profane, libelous and insulting content is not entitled to constitutional protection, the student's Web site was not protected speech. The school district policy furthered a legitimate government interest in avoiding school disruption. The student had no privacy right in information contained on the Web site, since entry to the site was not controlled and a disclaimer he utilized had no legal effect. The trial court had properly affirmed the decision to permanently expel the student and the court affirmed the judgment. *J.S. v. Bethlehem Area School Dist.*, 757 A.2d 412 (Pa. Commw. 2000).

♦   A Kansas school board responded to racial incidents in its schools by adopting a harassment policy stating in part that "student(s) shall not racially harass or intimidate another student(s) by name calling, using racial or derogatory slurs, wearing or possessing items depicting or implying racial hatred or prejudice." It listed examples of prohibited clothing and materials, including Confederate flags. A student was disciplined numerous times during the school year and accused of using racial slurs on several occasions. Later that year, **the student drew a Confederate flag during class, which resulted in a three-day suspension for intentionally violating the anti-harassment policy**. The student's father filed a federal district court action against the district, asserting constitutional violations. The court denied the family's petition for a temporary order, then permanently denied relief and dismissed the action. **The case involved no fundamental speech rights, but was rather a question of appropriate discipline for willful violation of a school policy**. The policy had been adopted to prevent further racial disturbances at district schools, and the district had acted reasonably and within its constitutional authority in doing so. The suspension was upheld, even though there was no evidence that the student intended to harass anyone, because it was clear to the court that he had intentionally violated the policy. The fact that his conduct did not cause actual disruption did not deprive the school of the authority to enforce the policy.

The student appealed to the 10th Circuit, which reiterated the principle that public education is generally committed to the control of state and local authorities. Students facing suspension from public schools were entitled only to the minimal due process protections established by *Goss v. Lopez*, 419 U.S. 565 (1975), including only some kind of notice and an opportunity to explain the incident giving rise to the discipline. The student had received notice and an opportunity to explain his side of the story prior to the assistant principal's decision. The suspension was based on the determination that there had been a willful violation of the school's harassment and intimidation policy. The student's First Amendment claim failed because the district could maintain a policy prohibiting students from possessing a Confederate flag unrelated to school materials as long as the policy was rationally related to a legitimate government interest. The legitimate interest in this case was to prevent potentially disruptive student conduct from interfering with the educational process. The suspension also did not violate student speech rights. While the possession of a Confederate flag outside the school context could be considered political speech, students do not enjoy similar rights in the school setting. Based on the course of events in district schools, school officials legitimately believed that a student's display of the flag might cause disruption and interfere with the rights of other students. **Because it was reasonable for school officials to believe that a student's display of the flag, unconnected from any legitimate educational purpose, might disrupt the educational setting, the district was not restricted from prohibiting and punishing student violations of the policy.** The court rejected the student's facial challenge to the harassment and intimidation policy, since the policy was not unconstitutionally vague or overbroad. *West v. Derby Unified School Dist. No. 260*, 206 F.3d 1358 (10th Cir. 2000).

The U.S. Supreme Court subsequently denied the student's petition for *certiorari,* thereby refusing to disturb the 10th Circuit's decision.

◆   Missouri's Safe Schools Act did not permit a school board to exclude a former parochial school student from enrollment in a public school system, according to a state appellate court. The act permits school districts to apply an expulsion or suspension from another school district where the underlying offense would be grounds for excluding the student from the district where enrollment is sought. A student committed burglary, theft and property damage at his parochial school. After being expelled, he sought enrollment in the school district in which he resided. The school board held a hearing under the Safe Schools Act and denied the student's application on grounds that if he had committed the same acts on district property, he would have been expelled from district schools. A state trial court affirmed the board's decision making the parochial school expulsion effective in the school district. The Missouri Court of Appeals held that the statute applied only to school districts, and not parochial schools. While the statute did not define "school district," the term was defined in state law and connoted a public school system. Accordingly, **a school district in which a student is attempting to enroll may make an expulsion effective from another school district, but not a non-public school**. Because the school board and trial court had erroneously applied state law, the court reversed the judgment. *Hamrick by Hamrick v. Affton School Dist. Bd. of Educ.*, 13 S.W.3d 678 (Mo. Ct. App. 2000).

◆   **An 18-year-old high school senior created a Web site from his home computer titled the "Unofficial Kentlake High Home Page."** The site included a disclaimer informing viewers that the site was not created or sponsored by the school and was not intended to offend anybody. The site contained mock obituaries of two of the student's friends, prepared with their consent. One indicated that a student had died from a social disease, and the other stated that a student died in gym class attempting "to bench press with 2 – 45s on each side." The student also created a message board for the posting of comments. After the site was in operation for three days, a local television news crew interviewed the student at school. According to the student, the newscast misleadingly indicated that his Web site included a "hit list" threatening to injure people. **He removed the site from the Internet, but was called to the principal's office the next day and suspended for five days based on "intimidation, harassment, disruption to the educational process, and violation of Kent School District copyright."** He was also suspended from participating on the basketball team. The student sought a temporary restraining order from a federal district court to set aside the suspension.

The court relied on *Tinker v. Des Moines Comm. School Dist.*, 393 U.S. 503 (1969), and *Bethel School Dist. No. 403 v. Fraser*, 478 U.S. 675 (1986), to conclude that the student was entitled to the requested order setting aside the suspension. The court distinguished the student's case from that of the student in *Bethel*, who made sexually oriented comments at a school assembly, noting that the student had not produced the Web site in connection with any school class or project. The site was entirely outside the school's supervision and control. **Even though the court credited the district's argument that schools must be alert to threats of school violence, there was no evidence that the mock obituaries manifested any violent intent** by the student. The court found it likely that the student would prevail on the merits of his claim. The court further found that if the suspension was enforced, the student would miss four additional days of school and a basketball game. Because this constituted irreparable injury, the court enjoined the school district from suspending the student, ordered the student to post a $100 bond, and scheduled a hearing on a preliminary injunction. The hearing was later avoided when the parties agreed to continue it for two weeks, pending discussion of a nominal damage award for the student and possible limits on his school-related communications. *Emmett v. Kent School Dist. No. 415,* 92 F.Supp.2d 1088 (W.D. Wash. 2000).

◆   An administrative hearing officer determined that two students battered the same school employee, but found that they were unaware of her official position at the time of the offenses, therefore, they should not be punished under the section of the school code that applied when students harmed a school employee. The district superintendent accepted the hearing officer's findings in part, rejecting the conclusion that the students should not suffer enhanced penalties under a section of the student code pertaining to cases of student assault or violent confrontation involving a school board employee. **The school board concluded that the section imposed strict liability on any student involved in a confrontation with a school employee and that lack of knowledge of official status was immaterial.** It held both students in violation of the student code and expelled them for the remainder of the current school year and the entirety of the following school year.

The students appealed to the Second District Florida Court of Appeal, which stated that a student must know or have reason to know the identity or position of employment of a victim in order to be convicted under a state law pertaining to offenses against school employees. School boards are required to adopt rules providing that violators be expelled or placed in alternative settings as appropriate, with immediate removal from the classroom. The court rejected the board and superintendent's position that they had an inherent right to issue student disciplinary rules. While they had significant authority in this respect, school officials were powerless to issue rules at variance with state legislation. **The board's strict liability interpretation of the student code was inconsistent with the state law requirement that a student have knowledge of a victim's official status in order to suffer increased penalties applying to crimes against school board employees.** Accordingly, the court held that the students should have been disciplined under the school code section governing intentional harm against another person, rather than the section governing harm against a school employee. *W.E.R. v. School Bd. of Polk County*, 749 So.2d 540 (Fla. App. 2d Dist. 2000).

◆   A Texas school suspended a 12-year-old student for three days after he admitted repeatedly touching female students on the breast or bottom. The principal determined that this violated the student code of conduct, warranting an alternative school placement. The student received in-school suspension pending the placement, and the parents requested and received two separate hearings before the school board. **The alternative school placement was upheld and the parents sued the district in a state court, seeking an order that would set aside the placement.** The court issued a temporary order forbidding the alternative placement and the district appealed to the state court of appeals.

The appeals court reviewed the Texas Education Code, which provides only for an administrative hearing in the case of an alternative school placement that extended beyond the end of the next grading period. Unlike expulsion cases, the code made final and nonappealable any decision concerning an alternative school placement by a school board or designated school official. The court commented that **the state school code specifically required school districts to establish student conduct standards and to specify circumstances under which students may be removed from regular classes and placed in alternative schools.** The school board in this case had specified in its handbook for parents and students that alternative placements were permitted in cases of inappropriate physical or sexual contact or sexual harassment. Since the district court lacked jurisdiction to review an alternative school placement under state law, the court of appeals dissolved the temporary order and awarded judgment to the school district. *Hankins v. P.H.*, 1 S.W.3d 352 (Tex. App 1999).

◆   A Wisconsin high school student contributed an article to a student-produced underground newspaper which advocated student hacking of the school computer system and gave students general instructions on computer hacking. **The school suspended the student just prior to the end of his junior year and recommended his expulsion** for endangering school property. The school board conducted an expulsion hearing and voted to expel the student until the summer after his class would graduate. He responded with a lawsuit against the school board, asserting violations of his speech rights under the state and federal constitutions. **A federal district court granted the student's request for a preliminary order, preventing enforcement of the expulsion.** The board appealed to the U.S. Court of Appeals, Seventh Circuit.

On appeal, the student argued that he had not actually violated any Wisconsin computer crimes laws or made an unauthorized entry into the school's computer system. He alleged that he would suffer irreparable harm by losing the opportunity to graduate with his class. **The court found that the distribution of the article on school property could be reasonably characterized as a threat to school property or activities**. The district court had failed to consider the public interest in its analysis of the preliminary order and had failed to properly give credit to the board's argument that the preliminary order would undermine its authority to take disciplinary action for a serious threat to school property. **Because the district court improperly found that the student would be likely to prevail on the merits of the case, the court vacated the preliminary order**. *Boucher v. School Bd. of School Dist. of Greenfield*, 134 F.3d 821 (7th Cir.1998).

◆   A Tennessee school board implemented a student isolation policy as an alternative in-school suspension method. The policy did not specify particular means of isolating students, and one high school decided to isolate suspended students in textbook storage closets adjacent to a coach's office and a library room. **Two students who were forced to spend at least one day in isolation alleged that they received no advance notice that they were being disciplined**. One had left the school for a medical emergency two weeks earlier and was not notified of any pending disciplinary action. The other claimed that she had left school for a dental appointment and that upon being told she would be punished, the principal denied her request to have her mother come to school. The students filed a lawsuit against the county, board of education, superintendent, principal and other school employees in a federal district court for constitutional rights violations.

The court considered summary judgment motions by the county, education board and education officials. It commented that the isolation of convicted criminals violated the Eighth Amendment where basic necessities including food or lavatory access were denied. **The placement of students in isolation for an entire school day without food or use of facilities similarly shocked the conscience, and if proven, would be unconstitutional**. A reasonable teacher in the position of the school officials should have known that this treatment was unconstitutional, and summary judgment for the school employees was denied. Because the isolation of students in the closets had originated with school board action, the board's summary judgment motion was also denied. *Orange v. County of Grundy*, 950 F.Supp. 1365 (E.D.Tenn.1996).

◆   The assistant principal of an Alabama middle school suspended a student for two days because of unexcused absences. Although school district procedures required telephone notification and prompt written notice by mail to parents, the school only sent a notice with the student. He threw away the notice and said nothing to his parents. The student was then accidentally shot and wounded while visiting a friend's house during the second day of the suspension. His parents filed a lawsuit in the U.S. District Court for the Northern District of Alabama, claiming constitutional violations by school officials, including the assistant principal. **The court held that there was no duty of school officials to protect students from other students while off school grounds**, for any reason. **There was no reason to believe that the suspension created imminent danger for the student and there was no constitutional violation** by the school officials. The court granted the school officials' motion for summary judgment. *Thrower v. Barney*, 849 F.Supp. 1445 (N.D.Ala.1994).

E. Due Process

At the very heart of the American system of criminal law is the concept that due process protections will be enforced and that all people subject to the law will be given fair play. Due process is accorded an individual when the governmental body undertaking the proceeding against that individual adequately informs the accused of the charges, gives the accused enough notice to prepare a proper defense, allows the accused the opportunity to confront witnesses and challenge the testimony given, and permits the presentation of evidence on his or her own behalf.

❖   In *Goss v. Lopez*, the U.S. Supreme Court affirmed the constitutional rights of suspended students to due process protection through notice and hearing. In this case, the students had been suspended from school for up to 50 days for misconduct. Their suspensions were handed down without benefit of a hearing either before or after the school board's ruling. The Supreme Court held that students facing temporary suspensions from a public school have property and liberty interests and are protected by the Due Process Clause of the Fourteenth Amendment. **Students faced with suspension or expulsion must be given oral or written notices of the charges against them along with the opportunity at a hearing to present their version of what happened.** Recognizing that situations often do not allow time to follow adequate procedures prior to the suspensions, such as in cases where there is a danger to students or property, the court stated that, at the very least, **proper notice and hearing should be given as soon after the suspension as is practicable.** The Court also stated that if a student is threatened with a suspension longer than ten days, more elaborate procedural safeguards are necessary. *Goss v. Lopez*, 419 U.S. 565, 95 S.Ct. 729, 42 L.Ed.2d 725 (1975).

❖   The U.S. Supreme Court has addressed the question of whether federal courts may construe school regulations differently than a school board has construed them. **A 10th grade Arkansas student left school grounds, consumed alcohol and returned to school intoxicated. He was immediately suspended from school pending a board hearing at which he was expelled.** His parents sued for injunctive relief, which was granted by a district court and later upheld by the U.S. Court of Appeals, Eighth Circuit. School regulations provided for suspension or expulsion of any student for "good cause" which was defined as including use or possession of alcoholic beverages or drugs. A subsequent section mandated expulsion for students using or under the influence of drugs or controlled substances. The district court and the court of appeals held that the school board had acted under a section mandating expulsion but held the expulsion violative of substantive due process since the student had not used drugs but alcohol and, in any event, had used the alcohol off campus. For these reasons the lower courts held the student had been unfairly suspended. On appeal to the U.S. Supreme Court, however, the school board's decision was upheld. **The high court ruled that it was not within the purview of the district court or the court of appeals to substitute their own view of the facts for that of the school board. The school board clearly had the authority to suspend and later expel the student** for consuming alcohol off campus and returning to school. *Bd. of Educ. v. McCluskey*, 458 U.S. 966, 102 S.Ct. 3469, 73 L.Ed.2d 1273 (1982).

◆   A student moved to Pennsylvania from New Jersey, where he had been placed on probation for blowing up a shed on school property. **During the 10th grade, the student wrote a note stating, "there's a bomb in this school Bang Bang!!"** in a class. An assistant principal and a police lieutenant questioned the student. The student admitted to the lieutenant that he was on probation in New Jersey and confessed to leaving the note. The assistant principal met with the student's father and notified him that his son would be suspended for 10 days for making terroristic threats. The school district's attorney sent the parents a letter advising them that the district was recommending expulsion and noting that at the time of his enrollment, the father had falsely indicated that his son had never been suspended. The school district held an expulsion hearing that was not attended by the student, his parents or their attorney. **The district permanently expelled the student** and he filed a civil rights action against the district in a federal district court.

The school district moved for summary judgment, arguing that it complied with due process requirements by providing the family with adequate notice and an opportunity to respond to the charges. The court agreed, finding that the district satisfied all due process requirements of *Goss v. Lopez*, 419 U.S. 565 (1975). **The assistant principal and police lieutenant explained to the student that his handwriting sample matched the note, giving him notice of the charges and an opportunity to present his side of the story.** They performed all that was required of them to satisfy due process. The student received adequate notice of the expulsion hearing and the district did not deny him due process by failing to reschedule the hearing upon request. The parents received at least five days of warning and were aware of the pending expulsion long before the hearing was scheduled. There was a rational relationship between the expulsion and the writing of a note threatening to bomb a school building. The note caused an evacuation of a school building and disrupted school operations. The lack of a reference to terroristic threats in the school handbook did not mean that school officials could not issue discipline when such threats occurred. The handbook warned students that illegal conduct at school could result in suspension or expulsion. It put students on notice that writing a threatening note was a serious violation of school policy. School disciplinary codes do not have to be as detailed as criminal codes. The court held that the assistant principal was not required to read the student his *Miranda* warnings, since students facing discipline in school are not entitled to be advised of their Fifth Amendment right to be free of compelled self-incrimination. The court awarded summary judgment to the district. *Brian A. v. Stroudsburg Area Sch. Dist.*, 141 F.Supp.2d 502 (M.D. Pa. 2001).

◆   **A 10th grader and four others plotted to bring guns to school and shoot administrators and students. Police stopped the planned attack and the school began expulsion proceedings** against the student. The school district sought a state court order preventing him from coming within 200 yards of school property during a suspension or expulsion. The parties agreed that the student should remain off school grounds pending a court hearing. Police learned that before their intervention, the student had advised the group's leader that he would not participate. Neither the student nor his attorney attended the hearing. The principal presented evidence that the student was involved in the plot, but did not tell the board that the county had dropped any criminal charges against him. The board voted to expel the student until the year 2003, when he would turn 21 years old, and to bar him from entering school property during this period. The parties settled the state court action by agreeing to exclude him from school property until he turned 21.

The student filed a federal district court action against the district, asserting that it violated his due process rights and that the principal and district superintendent conspired to deprive him of his liberty interest in a public education. The court dismissed the action on the basis of the state court stipulation, but the U.S. Court of Appeals, Seventh Circuit, reversed and remanded the decision. On remand, the district court held that the student had a claim of entitlement to a public education that was protected by due process. **To satisfy due process, school expulsion procedures had to be fundamentally fair by providing an opportunity to be heard in a meaningful manner**. The Seventh Circuit has held that due process is satisfied where a student is informed of the charges, receives notice of a hearing and an evidentiary hearing. The student received notice of the charges, a hearing and an opportunity to present evidence, fully satisfying his procedural due process rights. There was no evidence board members were biased. It was not necessary that the student actually attend the expulsion deliberations. Students who do not to present their cases when given the opportunity waive this right. The court rejected the student's argument that an expulsion through the year 2003 violated his substantive due process rights as irrational and punitive. While the punishment was harsh, the court refused to second-guess the board's decision. The district was entitled to summary judgment. *Remer v. Burlington Area School District,* No. 99-C-209 (E.D. Wis. 2001).

◆   A Mississippi school board adopted a zero tolerance policy, forbidding alcohol and other substances on school grounds. Acting on a tip, a principal and a school security officer found empty beer cans in the back of a student's truck. The student was summoned and he agreed to unlock a toolbox in the truck where unopened beer bottles were found. He admitted that he had purchased the beer. The principal advised the student's mother about the incident and suspended the student for five days. **Although the school district's student handbook required that the board's attorney provide notice of an expulsion within 24 hours of an incident, the superintendent notified the family by letter of the expulsion hearing**. The board voted to expel the student for the rest of the school year. The student obtained a state chancery court order permitting his return to school until a hearing could be conducted in compliance with the handbook. The board then re-mailed notices to the student and his parents and scheduled a second hearing, at which it again voted to expel the student. The court issued a temporary restraining order preventing the board from expelling the student and later held that the board had violated the handbook and was precluded from expelling the student. The board appealed to the Mississippi Supreme Court.

The state supreme court found that while the student had a property interest in continued school attendance and was entitled to certain protections under the Due Process Clause of the Fourteenth Amendment, his own admission negated the possibility that he had been deprived of due process. **The superintendent's notice of the expulsion hearing did not create substantial prejudice**, as it notified the family of the hearing date, explained the basis for the proposed action, stated that expulsion was to be considered, and advised the family that it was entitled to be represented by counsel. While the board's notice for the first hearing had been deficient, these deficiencies had been remedied by the second hearing. Although the notice should have been hand delivered, instead of delivered by certified mail, the fact that the parents attended the first hearing indicated that they had received adequate notice. The board had the discretion to enforce a zero tolerance policy and did not violate the student's due process rights. There was no merit to the student's claim that the search of his vehicle violated the Fourth Amendment. School officials were not required to obtain a search warrant under the circumstances of this case. **The student enjoyed no higher expectation of privacy in a vehicle parked on school property than he might have in property placed in a school locker**. His mother had signed a vehicle registration form, which acknowledged "vehicles will be routinely checked/searched." There was reasonable suspicion the student had been drinking beer before class, and reasonable school officials should have regarded their information as sufficient to take action. The board did not deprive the student of any constitutional rights, and the court affirmed its decision. *Covington County School Dist. v. G.W.*, 767 So.2d 187 (Miss. 2000).

♦   A California student was suspended by his school principal for possession of a pipe bomb, which violated the California Education Code's prohibition on explosives or other dangerous objects on school grounds. The school board granted his parents' request to postpone an expulsion hearing for 15 days. An administrative panel met and recommended expulsion, but before the recommendation could be adopted by the board, it adjourned for the summer. Upon its return, the board voted to expel the student, 51 days after it received the recommendation. The student appealed to the county board of education, which reversed the school board's decision on grounds that the summer recess did not extend the 40-day period for such decisions specified in the Education Code. The school board appealed to **a California trial court**, which **affirmed the county board's finding that the untimely decision deprived the school board of jurisdiction over the case**.

The board appealed to the California Court of Appeal, Third District, arguing that the summer recess should not be included in the 40-day calculation and that any delay did not deprive it of the power to discipline the student. The court observed that while the Education Code states that a school governing board "shall decide whether to expel the pupil within 40 school days after the date of the pupil's removal from his or her school," it contained no penalty for failing to meet the deadline. Unless the legislature declares otherwise, statutory time limits are directory, rather than mandatory. The absence of a statutory penalty for failing to comply with the deadline indicated only that the remedy against a noncomplying school board was a court order requiring it to make a decision. The court refused to construe the 40-day requirement in a manner that would defeat the purpose of the statute. The overall purpose of the Education Code indicated that the time limit did not impose an absolute jurisdictional deadline. Otherwise, proceedings that had already occurred would be nullified and a student who had made serious rules violations would be reinstated. **Because the court found it unlikely that the legislature intended to allow a dangerous student back into school due to a technicality, it reversed the trial court decision**. *Board of Education of Sacramento City Unified School District v. Sacramento County Board of Education*, 85 Cal.App.4th 1321, 102 Cal.Rptr.2d 872 (2001).

◆   A school board sought to expel a student for violating its dangerous weapons policy. The principal suspended the student and gave him a notice of expulsion, but no hearing was held for two weeks. Ohio law states that a student whose expulsion is being proposed must be provided with written notice of the intention to expel. The notice must be provided to the student's parents and explain the right to appear in person before the superintendent. The time for such a hearing "shall not be earlier than three nor later than five school days after the notice is given, unless the student's parents request an extension." The student appealed the board's decision to expel him to an Ohio trial court.

The court reversed the decision, finding that the expulsion hearing was untimely and that the dangerous weapons policy was ambiguous.

The board appealed to the Ohio Court of Appeals, Sixth District, where it argued that it had "substantially complied" with state law and that the trial court had improperly substituted its own interpretation of the school weapons policy for the board's judgment. The court of appeals observed that public school disciplinary proceedings implicate student property and liberty interests, and are protected by the Due Process Clause of the Fourteenth Amendment. The "substantial compliance" test suggested by the board was inapplicable in this case because the statute provided for time extensions only where requested by the parents of a student for whom expulsion is proposed. **The statute required a hearing in the specified time frame and the board's delay was not excused.** The court affirmed the judgment. *Kresser v. Sandusky Board of Education*, 140 Ohio App.3d 634 (2001).

◆   An Indiana school's tardiness policy called for a teacher-student conference following the second incident, and referral to the assistant principal following the third, with notice to the parent. In the event of a fourth incident, the policy called for a conference among the assistant principal, student, parent and teacher to resolve the problem, with withdrawal from class specified as the remedy for failure to reach a resolution. The policy vested the assistant principal with final decision-making authority. A student was referred to the assistant principal after being late for geometry class three times. No conference was held with the teacher, as required after the second incident. The assistant principal assigned the student to detention and wrote a notice to the parent, which the student failed to deliver. After two more tardiness incidents, a conference was held with the student and parent, and the assistant principal advised that the student would be withdrawn from geometry if he was tardy again. **The student was** soon **late for geometry again and was withdrawn from the class.** He appealed to the school board, which affirmed the action.

A state superior court affirmed the school's decision, and the student appealed to the state court of appeals, which considered his claim that the school tardiness policy violated state law. The court agreed with the student that state law limited the length of a suspension issued by a teacher to five days, but observed that the disputed action was taken by an assistant principal. As the principal's designee for disciplinary action, the assistant principal could take any action reasonably necessary for education functions. The student argued that his removal from the class under the school policy violated a state law prescribing a minimum of six instructional hours. However, the court found that an exception from the minimum requirement applied when a school "removes a student from an educational function, as well as when a student is suspended or expelled." The school's policy thus did not conflict with the state student discipline act. **There was no merit to the student's claim that the school violated his due process rights by failing to follow its own policy**. Even though he had not received the specified teacher conference after his second tardiness, and the teacher had failed to attend the conference with his parent and the assistant principal, he received adequate notice and the opportunity to speak. He also failed to show how the teacher's attendance harmed him or would have added any procedural protection. The court affirmed the superior court judgment. *M.S. by P.S. v. Eagle-Union Community School Corp.*, 717 N.E.2d 1255 (Ind.App.1999).

◆   A school district suspended a student six times in a two-year period for threats, fighting, harassment and intimidation. An assistant principal notified the student of an emergency expulsion hearing, including a statutory explanation of his rights to be represented by counsel and question witnesses. **At the hearing, witnesses to the incident leading to the proposed expulsion did not testify**. Instead, the assistant principal summarized their evidence. The superintendent expelled the student, and the decision was affirmed by the school board.

   A Washington superior court affirmed the expulsion, and the student appealed to the Court of Appeals of Washington, where he argued that the school district had violated his due process rights by depriving him of the opportunity to confront and cross examine adverse witnesses. **The school district asserted that it had no power to compel witnesses to appear by subpoena, and that the summarization of testimony preserved student anonymity**. The court rejected that argument, because the district had failed to explain why it was not possible for any witnesses to appear. The court noted that due process must be provided whenever a school threatens a student with expulsion. Because the student had a substantial interest in attending school and the district had not explained why witnesses could not testify at the hearing, the court reversed and remanded the case. *Stone v. Prosser Consol. School Dist. No. 116*, 971 P.2d 125 (Wash.App.Div.3 1999).

◆   A group of students arrived at school wearing clothing that certain other students and school administrators described as indicating a gang affiliation. **The principal and a vice principal questioned the students about their clothing** in a school courtyard. After some argument, the students' parents were called to school and some of them continued to argue with the principal on behalf of their children. **He then imposed three-day suspensions on the students**, which each student served. When they returned to school, another conference was held with each student. The families filed a federal district court action against the school district and principal, asserting constitutional rights violations. The court denied the defendants' motion for qualified immunity, they appealed to the Fifth Circuit.

   The circuit court observed that under *Goss v. Lopez*, above, students are entitled to explain their actions when threatened with discipline. The *Goss* case does not, however, discuss whether meetings between school officials and parents are appropriate. **The court held that, in some circumstances, a parent may serve as an appropriate surrogate for a student**. *Goss* is satisfied as long as the student's story is told, either directly or through a reliable person standing in the role of a parent. According to the court, the principal violated student due process rights because he did not allow the students to present their version of the facts prior to the suspensions. Therefore, the district court had properly denied the motion for summary judgment. *Meyer v. Austin Indep. School Dist.*, 161 F.3d 271 (5th Cir.1998).

✦   A North Carolina student became involved in a fight on his school bus which required the bus driver to summon the police. **He was one of nine students identified by others as being involved in the disruption and was suspended from school for 10 days and from riding the bus for the rest of the school year**. The school principal notified the student's father of the suspension and informed him of the school's appeal process. The school district's assistant superintendent affirmed the suspension, as did the county education board after hearings on the matter. The student's father petitioned a North Carolina superior court for judicial review of the suspension. The court dismissed the father's petition for lack of jurisdiction. The father appealed to a state court of appeals.

The appeals court stated that North Carolina law confers authority upon school principals to suspend students for ten days or less for willful violations of school policies, as long as the student is afforded the opportunity to make up any missed examinations. **The statute provided for judicial review of suspensions in excess of 10 days, but does not provide for the review of suspensions of 10 days or less**. The court rejected the parent's argument that the student's receipt of a failing grade during the grading period and his loss of bus riding privileges converted the suspension into one for more than 10 days. The court noted that the student had a statutory right to make up missed examinations at the conclusion of a suspension and that judicial review of the question of grade reinstatement was premature. The court affirmed the judgment for the school board. *Stewart v. Johnston County Bd. of Educ.*, 498 S.E.2d 382 (N.C.App.1998).

✦   **The Texas Education Code prohibits any appeal of a school board order transferring a student to an alternative education program for three or more consecutive school days, or five or more school days within a semester**. A high school student was found in possession of marijuana in a student parking lot, and the school district notified his parents that it would take disciplinary action against him for violation of its zero tolerance drug policy. The district conducted two hearings and recommended transferring him to an alternative education program instead of expulsion. Although the student received a GED and later attended college, the family brought a declaratory judgment action against the school district in a state court, seeking an order that the Education Code section making unappealable decisions to transfer students to alternative education programs violated the open courts provision of the Texas Constitution.

The court granted summary judgment to the school district, and the family appealed to the Court of Appeals of Texas, Houston. The court of appeals observed that the Texas Supreme Court has held that the open courts provision protects only the right to bring well-established common law claims. **There is no common law cause of action for judicial review of an administrative agency action**, and the trial court had correctly refused to hold that the statutory prohibition against appeal violated the open courts provision. *Sutton v. Katy Indep. School Dist.*, 961 S.W.2d 216 (Tex.App.–Houston 1997).

✦   A Georgia student was suspended for five days and ordered to apologize to her class for using inappropriate language. She refused to apologize to the class after serving the suspension, and the principal summoned the police to escort her from school when she tried to return. **The student sat out the entire academic year rather than apologize,** but was readmitted to school the following year when a new administrator dropped the apology requirement. During her time away from school, the student failed to challenge the suspension through the school's appeal process. She dropped out of school after only six weeks, claiming that others were talking about her and pointing at her. She filed a federal district court action against the school district and individual employees under 42 U.S.C. § 1983, asserting that the entire sequence of events was linked to her pregnancy by an African-American.

The court found no constitutional right to attend a public school. Because any such right is created by state law, the district and officials were entitled to pretrial judgment on the substantive due process issue. **There had also been no procedural due process violation since the student had failed to follow the district's suspension appeals process.** There was no merit to the student's argument that the district had no authority to compel her apology, since this requirement was within the school's authority. The court found an absence of any linkage between the discipline and the student's pregnancy, and granted pretrial judgment to the school district. The court dismissed the complaint in its entirety. *Kicklighter v. Evans County School Dist.*, 968 F.Supp. 712 (S.D.Ga.1997).

✦   An Ohio school principal suspended a student for egging a teacher's house. The decision was based upon a police report and interviews with four students who were allegedly involved in the incident. The student denied the charge and his mother sought an appeal to the board of education on the first day of the suspension. Although the board was to meet that night and it agreed to place the appeal on the agenda, **the family obtained a temporary restraining order** from a state trial court **prohibiting the board from imposing the second day of the suspension.** The family did not attend the board meeting. The school board moved to dismiss the trial court action because the student had failed to exhaust his administrative remedy before the board. The court issued a permanent injunction prohibiting the school from suspending the student for the incident, finding that he had been deprived of minimal due process protections including specific charges of the conduct for which he was suspended, the names of the adverse witnesses and the opportunity to call his own witnesses. The school board appealed to **the Court of Appeals of Ohio,** which **agreed with the board that the trial court possessed no jurisdiction to hear the matter because the student had failed to exhaust his administrative remedy before the board.** The court reversed and remanded the case to allow the student to pursue his administrative remedy. *Webb v. Ironton City Schools*, 115 Ohio App.3d 699, 686 N.E.2d 285 (Ohio App.4th Dist.1996).

✦   A Tennessee junior high school assistant principal observed students throwing rocks at his car. He telephoned the police, who arrived at the school and took an African-American student into custody. At the police station, an officer determined that he should be released to his parents and not placed in juvenile detention. However, the parents were unavailable to pick up the student, and the officer instructed him to wash police vehicles until they arrived. The student washed police vehicles for four hours until his mother arrived. **The assistant principal later decided to let the student and his mother choose between a 10-day at-home suspension or 10 days at an alternative school**. The mother selected the alternative school placement. She then filed a lawsuit on behalf of her son in a federal district court against the municipality, county, board of education, superintendent, and city and school officials, asserting violations of Title VI of the Civil Rights Act of 1964 and the Thirteenth Amendment prohibition on involuntary servitude. The court dismissed the case, and the mother appealed to the U.S. Court of Appeals, Sixth Circuit.

The court affirmed the dismissal of the Title VI claim because it failed to state the threshold requirement that the school and police department received federal financial assistance. The police officers were entitled to summary judgment because there was no showing that their actions had been motivated by race. The involuntary servitude claim had been properly dismissed because there was no evidence that the police had threatened physical restraint or injury. The city, county and officers were entitled to governmental immunity because there was no clearly established right to be free from washing police vehicles. The equal protection complaint failed because there was no evidence that similarly situated Caucasian students had been treated differently. However, **the district court had improperly dismissed the due process complaint against school officials concerning the suspension. There was no evidence that the student had received an opportunity to present his side of the story prior to the imposition of punishment**. Remand of this issue for proper consideration was necessary. *Buchanan v. City of Bolivar, Tennessee*, 99 F.3d 1352 (6th Cir.1996).

◆   The U.S. Court of Appeals, Eleventh Circuit, upheld two suspensions involving Georgia students. In the first case, the principal satisfied due process by giving the student (who had been involved in a fight) an opportunity to explain her side of the story via a telephone conference with the student's parent. The second student had received two opportunities to contest drug possession charges (after a search uncovered a substance resembling marijuana) and had been represented by an attorney. **Because both students had received hearings that satisfied due process, and reasonable suspicion supported the search of the second student, the suspensions were affirmed**. *C.B. by and through Breeding v. Driscoll*, 82 F.3d 383 (11th Cir.1996).

◆   An Ohio high school principal responded to an anonymous tip that a student was smoking. He called the student to his office, where the student admitted smoking in the past but stated that he was not presently smoking. The principal went to the student's locker and found two cigarettes inside the student's coat pocket. He suspended the student for five days for possession of tobacco. **The student argued that the suspension was improper because possession of tobacco was not included in the list of offenses for five-day suspensions in the school's student handbook**. He appealed the suspension to an Ohio court, which affirmed the school board decision. The student appealed to the Court of Appeals of Ohio, Sixth District. The court reviewed an Ohio statute which requires education boards in the state to adopt suspension and expulsion policies that specify the type of misconduct for which a student may be disciplined. The law requires suspension and expulsion policies to be posted in schools where they are available to all students. **The court agreed with the student that the board** in this case **had failed to specify that possession of tobacco was misconduct for which a student could be suspended**. The court rejected the school board's assertion that tobacco possession could still fall within the category of "very serious offenses" and justify a suspension. Possession of cigarettes did not reasonably parallel serious offenses such as possession of guns and knives and selling drugs, and the court reversed and remanded the case. *Wilson v. South Central Local School Dist.*, 107 Ohio App.3d 610, 669 N.E.2d 277 (1995).

V.   STUDENT SEARCH AND SEIZURE

The U.S. Supreme Court has ruled that under the Fourth Amendment to the U.S. Constitution, searches of students by school officials need not adhere to the strict standard of "probable cause" imposed upon law enforcement officers. Rather, the legality of searches will depend upon the "reasonableness" of the search in light of all the circumstances. There must be reasonable grounds to believe that the search will reveal a violation of school rules or produce evidence of unlawful activity. The states remain free to provide greater protection for students, as Louisiana and California have done. See Chapter Fourteen of this volume for cases concerning student searches in interscholastic athletics.

A.   Fourth Amendment 'Reasonable Suspicion'

1.   *New Jersey v. T.L.O.*

◆   A teacher at a New Jersey high school found two girls smoking in a school lavatory in violation of school rules. She brought them to the assistant vice principal's office where one of the girls admitted to smoking in the lavatory. However, the other girl denied even being a smoker. The assistant vice principal then asked the latter girl to come to his private office where he opened her purse and found a pack of cigarettes. As he reached for them he noticed rolling papers and decided to thoroughly search the entire purse. **He found marijuana, a pipe, empty plastic bags, a substantial number of one dollar bills and a list of "people who owe me money."** The matter was then turned over to the police. A juvenile court hearing was held and the girl was adjudged delinquent. She appealed the juvenile court's determination, contending that her constitutional rights had been violated by the search of her purse. She argued that the evidence against her should have been excluded from the juvenile court proceeding.

The U.S. Supreme Court held that the search did not violate the Fourth Amendment prohibition against unreasonable search and seizure. Stated the Court: "The legality of a search of a student should depend simply on the reasonableness, under all the circumstances, of the search." Two considerations are relevant in determining the reasonableness of a search. First, **the search must be justified initially by a reasonable suspicion**. Second, **the scope and conduct of the search must be reasonably related to the circumstances which gave rise to the search, and school officials must take into account the student's age, sex and the nature of the offense**. The Court upheld the search of the student in this case because the initial search for cigarettes was supported by reasonable suspicion. The discovery of rolling papers then justified the further searching of the purse since such papers are commonly used to roll marijuana cigarettes. The court affirmed the delinquency adjudication, ruling that the "reasonableness" standard was met by school officials in these circumstances and the evidence against the girl had been properly obtained. *New Jersey v. T.L.O.*, 469 U.S. 325, 105 S.Ct. 733, 83 L.Ed.2d 720 (1985).

2. Drug Searches

◆   **A school district adopted a policy requiring all students who wished to participate in extracurricular activities to submit to drug testing**. The policy required random testing in any year in which a student participated in an activity, and reasonable suspicion testing for extracurricular participants. A student who participated in a school show choir, marching band and academic team filed a federal district court action against the school board and district, challenging the policy. The court awarded summary judgment to the district, ruling that the policy did not violate the Fourth Amendment's prohibition on unreasonable searches and seizures. The student appealed to the U.S. Court of Appeals, 10th Circuit.

The circuit court examined recent school and non-school drug-testing cases involving the "special needs" exception to the Fourth Amendment. The U.S. Supreme Court developed the "special needs" exception allowing drug testing in the absence of reasonable suspicion of drug use when the government identifies a special need that makes adherence to the normal warrant and probable cause requirements of the Fourth Amendment improper. In the school context, the existence of a "drug culture" led by student-athletes was held to justify a random testing program of student-athletes in *Vernonia School District v. Acton*, 515 U.S. 646 (1995). The Tenth Circuit noted that special needs cases require the courts to balance the competing interests of the school in controlling student drug use against student privacy interests. Applying the *Vernonia* test, the circuit court found that student drug use in the Oklahoma district was far from epidemic or an immediate crisis. Because the evidence indicated that drug use among extracurricular activities participants was negligible, the district failed to show that there was a need to test all prospective participants for drug use through a random testing policy. The district policy tested too many students who were apparently at little risk of drug abuse by selecting only extracurricular activities participants. Concern for safety and degree of school supervision over these students also did not justify random testing. **Without a demonstrated drug-abuse problem in the group being tested, the policy violated the *Vernonia* balancing test and the U.S. Constitution**. The Tenth Circuit reversed and remanded the district court judgment. *Earls et al. v. Board of Education of Tecumseh Public School District*, 242 F.3d 1264 (10th Cir. 2001).

◆   All middle and high school students or their parents were required by their school district to sign a contract consenting to drug and alcohol testing by breath, urine and blood tests throughout the school year as a prerequisite for participation in extracurricular activities and school driving/parking privileges. There was no provision for reporting unlawful activity for law enforcement or school disciplinary purposes. Parents or students could elect to opt out of activities or participate in mandatory drug/alcohol assistance programs in order to continue the activity. Repeat offenders could be barred from extracurricular activities and school parking/driving privileges. **Students and parents who objected to the policy sued** the school district in a Pennsylvania trial court, **asserting violations of the search and seizure provisions of the U.S. and Pennsylvania constitutions**. The court upheld the policy and the students and parents appealed to the Pennsylvania Commonwealth Court.

The court observed that Article I, Section 8 of the Pennsylvania Constitution requires that a search be based on a compelling government interest and that the state interest be justified by the purpose of the search in order to avoid a gratuitous invasion of personal privacy. Students do not have unlimited privacy rights while at school and the school has an interest in protecting the health of all students. This case could be distinguished from other school search cases because it singled out a select group of students. It also did not call for criminal prosecution and possible surrender of extracurricular or school parking/driving privileges. The U.S. Supreme Court has held that schools must show a special need for selective testing of students without individualized suspicion. The court disagreed with the school district's assertion that just by exercising a privilege, a student's privacy expectation in school was reduced. The district could not condition participation in an activity just because the activities were optional. **The school district was required to state a special need to test only those students who sought to engage in optional activities when compared with the general student population. The district's sweeping policy without stating a reason for singling out this group infringed student privacy rights**. This part of the trial court decision was vacated and remanded for further proceedings. *Theodore et al. v. Delaware Valley School District*, 761 A.2d 652 (Pa. Commw. 2000).

◆   After holding meetings to consider evidence from community members about school drug problems, a Texas school board resolved to implement a policy that called for **mandatory testing of all students in the district attending grades six through 12 for drugs, alcohol and tobacco**. The resolution was passed in spite of evidence that student drug use in district schools was lower than statewide rates in Texas and a letter from the board's attorney recommending against the resolution. The policy declared that certain school officials had the discretion to order mandatory testing of all students at any time. Refusal to consent to testing was deemed the equivalent of a positive test result. A sixth-grade student sued the district and school officials in a federal district court, asserting that the policy violated the Fourth Amendment's prohibition on unreasonable searches and seizures.

In this case, the court found that no special need for the policy existed under the standard set forth in *Vernonia School District 47J v. Acton*, 515 U.S. 646 (1995). Unlike in *Vernonia*, there was very little evidence of students' drug or alcohol abuse. The district attempted to subject the entire school population to drug testing, in contrast to a limited group of athletes with lower privacy expectations. The court found that compulsory attendance at school was much different than voluntary participation in extracurricular activities, and that the students in this case had higher privacy expectations than student-athletes. There was no drug epidemic in this case, in contrast to *Vernonia*. Courts have found that special needs do not encompass the commitment of the government to fighting drug abuse. The court found that there are two methods of establishing special needs. This includes situations in which an individual performs highly regulated functions concerning public safety or special governmental roles, such as a railway engineer or airline pilot. The special-needs exception also applies where there is a showing of exigent circumstances and continued government failure to alleviate the problem, as in *Vernonia*. **Because general concerns about maintaining drug-free schools or the desire to detect illegal conduct are insufficient as a matter of law to demonstrate special needs, the policy was held unconstitutional under the Fourth Amendment.** *Tannahill v. Lockney Independent School District*, 133 F.Supp.2d 919 (N.D. Tex. 2001).

◆ **A school board policy** deemed the use of tobacco, alcohol and illegal drugs to be a threat to the safety, health and welfare of students and employees, and **subjected five groups of students to random drug, alcohol and nicotine testing**. The groups included extracurricular activities participants, students who drove to school, students under reasonable suspicion of being under the influence of drugs or alcohol, and student and staff member volunteers. Students who refused to take a required drug test were deemed to have admitted being under the influence of drugs or alcohol in violation of school rules and thus subject to discipline as described in the student handbook. The handbook prohibited the sale, use, possession and other handling of drugs, paraphernalia and alcohol on school grounds, and prohibited smoking or possession of tobacco products on school property at any time. A group of students filed a federal district court action against the school board and its officials, asserting violations of the Fourth Amendment. The court upheld the policy in all respects and awarded summary judgment to the defendants, agreeing that the safety issues related to student driving justified the testing.

The students appealed to the Seventh Circuit, which found that students participating in extracurricular activities and those who drove to school had reduced privacy interests than those enjoyed by the general public. The intrusion on their privacy was minimal and the test results were disclosed only to school personnel who had a need to know the information. Test results were not provided to law enforcement officers or used for school discipline. **The school board had a legitimate and pressing need for drug and alcohol testing of students who drove to school in view of the risk of serious injury. However, there was no apparent correlation between tobacco use and serious risks associated with driving**. The panel thus reversed the district court judgment with respect to the testing of student drivers for nicotine. The court held that the education agency was required to show a correlation between drug use and student participation in extracurricular activities, or other evidence of a particularized special need, before implementing the suspicionless drug testing policy for extracurricular participants. The panel affirmed the district court decision on this part of the policy, admonishing against a broad reading of *Todd v. Rush County Schools*, 133 F.3d 984 (7th Cir. 1998), which allowed suspicionless drug testing of all students participating in extracurricular activities. It urged that the special needs exceptions to the probable cause requirement of the Fourth Amendment must be justified according to the methodology employed by the Supreme Court in *Vernonia School District 47J v.*

Acton, 515 U.S. 646 (1995). The court stated that the decision could not become the basis for the suspicionless testing of an entire student population. *Joy et al. v. Penn-Harris-Madison School Corp.*, 212 F.3d 1052 (7th Cir. 2000).

♦   A teacher observed that a high school student was acting strangely and that her face was flushed, her eyes were red and her pupils dilated. The teacher reported the student's conduct to a school administrator, stating that he suspected she was high. In accordance with school policy, the student was escorted to the nurse for examination. The nurse found that the student "looked high," had red, glassy eyes, and appeared "just out of it." A school security guard searched the student's locker and book bag under a school policy allowing searches based on reasonable suspicion, and found two kinds of pills, in apparent violation of a policy prohibiting any kind of medication at school. **The principal advised the student's father that before the student could return to school, she would have to undergo a physical examination**. The results of a blood test were negative for drugs and alcohol. The school promptly re-admitted the student upon learning of the test results, but the student asserted that other students overheard the school nurse expressing disbelief about the test results, the result of which was her loss of friends and employment opportunities. She sued the school principal, school board and other officials in a federal district court for civil rights violations arising under 42 U.S.C. § 1983 for the allegedly intrusive search without reasonable suspicion. The suit asserted violation of privacy rights for unlawful disclosure of the test results, and state law claims for assault and battery. The district court awarded summary judgment for the defending parties and the family appealed to the U.S. Court of Appeals, Third Circuit.

The circuit court rejected the district court's basis for granting summary judgment to the school board and clinic defendants based on a state law immunity provision for suits arising from administration of drug and alcohol abuse laws. However, the district court decision was affirmed on the alternative ground that **the testing was supported by reasonable suspicion that the student was under the influence of illegal substances at school**. The actions against the teacher and school nurse were properly dismissed, as the searches performed by the school nurse were not excessively intrusive, given the student's age and sex and the nature of the suspected violation. Her possession of pills was a violation of school policy, and her explanation for having them was contradicted by her father. **The principal acted reasonably in requiring the student to undergo testing before returning to school, because observations by the teacher and school nurse created reasonable suspicion** of drug or alcohol use. Requiring the student to submit to testing administered by professionals in a medical clinic was reasonable under the circumstances, and summary judgment for the school officials was appropriate. The Third Circuit rejected the student's assertion that school officials violated her privacy rights by inadvertently disclosing the results of the drug tests to other students. The Third Circuit found no connection between the injury claimed by the student and the nurse's inadvertent release of the test results. Because there was no link between the release of information about the negative test results by the nurse, the court affirmed the district court's judgment. *Hedges v. Musco*, 204 F.3d 109 (3d Cir. 2000).

◆   **A sheriff's drug sniffing dog sniffed high school students as they left a classroom. A sheriff's deputy then accompanied the dog while it sniffed student belongings left in the classroom**. The search yielded no drugs. One student asserted that the incident was an unlawful search and seizure, and he sued the school district, sheriff's department, and several of their employees and officers in a federal district court for injunctive relief and monetary damages. The court agreed with the student that the search was unreasonable, but dismissed his request for a preliminary injunction as moot, since he was by then no longer a student in the district. It denied his request for class certification, and ruled in favor of school and sheriff's department officials in their official and individual capacities on the 42 U.S.C. § 1983 claims.

The student appealed to the Ninth Circuit, which affirmed the mootness issue on the alternate ground that he lacked standing to seek injunctive relief. The court also affirmed the judgment for school officials as barred by the 11th Amendment, and for the sheriff's department officials, because department policy allowed dog sniff searches of objects, not persons. The Ninth Circuit stated that in this case, school officials admitted the lack of individualized suspicion of wrongdoing by any student. It agreed with the district court that the dog sniff search of the students as they left the room was highly intrusive and potentially distressing. Even though there is an important government interest in deterring drug use, **the random, suspicionless search of students by dog sniffing was unreasonable under the circumstances, especially since there was no countervailing evidence of a drug problem in the school**. The officials were entitled to immunity because there was no clearly established law that the use of a dog sniff search of students in a school setting constituted a search. There was no merit to the student's suggestion that his removal from the classroom was a seizure of his person, since school officials retain a degree of supervision and control over students. The court affirmed the judgment. *B.C. through Powers v. Plumas Unified School Dist.*, 192 F.3d 1260 (9th Cir. 1999).

◆   Prior to leaving for a school sponsored trip, students were informed that drugs and alcohol were banned and that participants would be subject to room searches. Each student who came on the trip signed a pledge to avoid alcohol and drugs and reciting that a violation would result in disqualification from senior activities and graduation ceremonies. **The principal** smelled marijuana where many of the students had congregated in the hallway of their motel. He then **obtained a hotel security pass key and searched most of the student rooms. He found marijuana** in the safe of one of the rooms. The principal sent two students home early and suspended them from school for three days. The suspended students sued the principal and school district for violation of their Fourth Amendment rights.

The court held that students who are under supervision in school activities, including field trips, are subject to the reasonable cause standard for student searches first announced by the U.S. Supreme Court in *New Jersey v. T.L.O.*, 469 U.S. 325 (1985). The more stringent probable cause standard applicable to police searches was inapplicable. **The court held that the students had no legitimate reason to expect complete privacy in their rooms. It was reasonable for the principal to search the rooms** based on the detection of marijuana smoke and the gathering of students. This was true even though he was without individualized suspicion that any one student possessed drugs. The court upheld the search, noting the existence of specific evidence that students were using drugs. Even if the principal had committed a constitutional violation, he would still be entitled to immunity, since there was no clearly established law on the subject at the time of the alleged violation. The court granted summary judgment to the principal and school district. *Rhodes v. Guarricino*, 54 F.Supp.2d 186 (S.D.N.Y.1999).

◆   **An Indiana school district adopted a student drug testing policy which called for drug tests when individualized suspicion of drug use existed, along with when a student was suspended for fighting, was habitually truant, possessed tobacco products or violated other school rules resulting in a three-day suspension.** Sanctions for failing a drug test included expulsion from school if the student failed to participate in a drug education program. One student who was suspended for fighting refused to provide a urine sample. The school issued another suspension for refusing the test and advised him that continued refusal to submit to testing would lead to expulsion proceedings. The student responded by filing a federal district court action against the school district in which he asserted that the policy violated the Fourth and Fourteenth Amendments to the U.S. Constitution. The court entered judgment for the school district and the student appealed to the U.S. Court of Appeals, Seventh Circuit.

The circuit court reiterated the general rule that school officials need not have probable cause to justify the search of a student, and may conduct a search that is justified at its inception and reasonably related in scope to the circumstances of the case. This means that a student's conduct must indicate that a particular rule has been violated. In this case, the student had been subjected to drug testing solely because of his suspension for fighting, as required by the policy. A school administrator had admitted under oath that he had no reasonable suspicion that the student had used drugs. **The policy calling for testing without a causal nexus between the offense and suspicion of drug use violated the constitution.** The conclusive presumption in favor of drug use was not reasonable because individualized suspicion can only be determined on a case-by-case basis. The court observed that a suspicion-based approach would achieve the same means as the existing policy, and it reversed the judgment. *Willis v. Anderson Community School Corp.*, 158 F.3d 415 (7th Cir.1998).

◆   **A Colorado school board published a policy calling for school officials to test any extracurricular activities participant who was suspected of using illegal drugs or alcohol.** A student who violated the policy was subject to discipline, with increasingly severe consequences based on successive violations, leading to suspension from activities in current and future years. Students were required to submit to urinalysis testing and if a positive result was obtained, the student was further required to participate in a drug assistance program with further testing. **A student who participated in marching band objected to the testing program** and filed a state court action against the school district, asserting state and federal constitutional violations.

The court upheld the testing program and appeal reached the Supreme Court of Colorado, which observed important distinctions between the program and the one approved by the U.S. Supreme Court in *Vernonia School Dist. 47J v. Acton*, 515

U.S. 646 (1995). In this case, marching band participants were also required to take a class for credit. In contrast, the *Vernonia* program had been upheld in part because it applied only to voluntary participants in extracurricular activities. **The school district failed to justify the program on the basis of safety concerns, since it produced no evidence of drug-related injuries to band participants**. Band participants did not consent to the communal undressing and showering in a locker room, which was another reason for upholding the program in *Vernonia*, and the court held the policy unconstitutional. *Trinidad School Dist. No. 1 v. Lopez*, 963 P.2d 1095 (Colo.1998).

◆   A Louisiana school board maintained a written policy that allowed drug detection teams to use dogs for periodic random drug searches of public schools. The principal of one high school followed the policy by selecting six classes for random searches by drug detection teams. As the teams went through the classrooms, students emptied their pockets and left the room. A dog became alert when sniffing one student's wallet, and the principal found $400 inside it. The principal then searched the student's book bag and a drug detection officer obtained the student's permission to search his car. Marijuana was discovered in the car. The state filed criminal charges against the student, who moved to suppress the evidence seized by the principal and officer as illegally obtained. The court denied the motion, and he appealed to the Court of Appeal of Louisiana, First Circuit. The court held that while the action of a dog sniffing personal effects does not constitute a search, examination of the contents of a student's pockets is a search. There had been no probable cause to suspect that the student's wallet contained drugs until the dog sniffed it, but the U.S. Supreme Court has upheld random searches of students in school. **There was probable cause to search the wallet and book bag because of the dog's response. The student was not in the custody of a law officer when asked to open the car for a search, and his permission had not been illegally obtained**. The court affirmed the denial of the motion to suppress the evidence. *State of Louisiana v. Barrett*, 683 So.2d 331 (La.App.1st Cir.1996).

◆   A New Hampshire school administrator received an anonymous phone call advising him that a particular student would be carrying drugs to school that day. The student had previously been suspected as a drug distributor. **The principal called the student into his office and told him to empty his pockets, which contained drug paraphernalia. He then asked him to open his book bag and discovered several bags of marijuana**. After calling the police, the student was taken into custody and additional drugs and a semiautomatic pistol were discovered in his bag. A state trial court convicted him of two drug possession counts and one felony charge for firearm use. The student's motion to suppress the evidence discovered by the principal was denied and he appealed to the Supreme Court of New Hampshire. On appeal, the student argued that the search violated the probable cause and warrant requirements of the Fourth Amendment to the U.S. Constitution. The supreme court disagreed, stating that Fourth Amendment warrant and probable cause requirements were particularly unsuited for public school officials in view of their need to protect other students and maintain school discipline and order. **Public school administrators were not bound by the same requirements as law enforcement officers because of their greater responsibility to students than law enforcement**

officers had to the general public. Accordingly, the actions of school officials in this case had been reasonable. The court affirmed the denial of the motion to suppress evidence. *State of New Hampshire v. Drake*, 662 A.2d 265 (N.H.1995).

3. Weapon Searches

◆   A Maryland student attended a school for students with significant emotional, learning and behavioral difficulties. The county school system's search and seizure policy permitted school administrators to search students or their lockers if there was probable cause to believe that the student had items whose possession would constitute a criminal offense under Maryland law, including weapons, drugs and drug paraphernalia, alcohol or pagers. The school principal followed through on an anonymous tip that there were drugs or weapons at the middle school and authorized a search of all middle school lockers. **The school security officer opened the student's locker in the student's absence and found a book bag containing a folding knife and pager**. The student was detained and admitted that the items belonged to him. In juvenile court proceedings, the student admitted possessing the items, but moved to suppress them as evidence, claiming that the local policy created a reasonable expectation of privacy in his locker. The juvenile court disagreed, and its decision was affirmed by the Maryland Court of Special Appeals.

The appeals court reviewed the case under *Vernonia School Dist. v. Acton*, 515 U.S. 646 (1995), and *New Jersey v. T.L.O.*, 469 U.S. 325 (1985). According to the student, school officials require some individualized suspicion as a predicate to a locker search under *T.L.O.*, in which the Supreme Court found the Fourth Amendment's probable cause standard inapplicable in the school environment. The court disagreed, finding that the *T.L.O.* court held only that school searches need to be justified at their inception and reasonably related in scope to the circumstances that justified the search in the first place. *Acton*, on the other hand, involved the appropriateness of urinalysis testing among student-athletes in the context of school-sponsored athletics. The court held that both cases provided the analytical process for determining whether a student's legitimate privacy interests were violated by a locker search. This is a factual inquiry, and the only evidence indicating that the student had a legitimate privacy expectation in his locker was the school policy statement. While the policy statement purported to limit searches to cases in which school authorities had probable cause of contraband items that gave rise to violations of state criminal laws, Maryland law, not the local policy, defined and controlled the authority of school officials to conduct public school locker searches. **Section 7-308 of the Maryland Education Article permitted reasonable searches of students based on a reasonable belief that a student possessed an item whose possession would create a criminal offense**. The court held that county school boards were powerless to adopt or enforce school policies that were inconsistent with state law or with the bylaws of the state board of education. School lockers were designated school property and subject to search by school officials in the same manner as other school property. Accordingly, the policy in this case was invalid and could not serve as the basis for a student's reasonable expectation of privacy in a school locker. Since the student had no reasonable expectation of privacy in the school locker temporarily assigned to him, the court affirmed the judgment of the lower courts. *In re Patrick Y.*, 358 Md. 50, 746 A.2d 405 (Md. 2000).

◆   A student reported to the assistant principal of a middle school that "Murray had something in his book bag that he should not have at school." The assistant principal confronted the suspected student, and the student denied having a book bag, even though he was an arm's length away from one. He then admitted that the bag was his, but refused to allow the assistant principal to search the book bag She summoned the school's dean of students and a resource officer. The resource officer physically restrained the student with handcuffs after a brief scuffle. **The assistant principal then found a pellet gun in the bag. The state of North Carolina prosecuted the student for possessing a weapon on school property**. A juvenile court denied the student's motion to suppress the pellet gun as evidence of a criminal violation, and adjudicated him delinquent.

The student appealed to the North Carolina Court of Appeals, which evaluated the case under the reasonable cause standard for school officials, since the assistant principal, not the resource officer, had conducted the search. Applying the standard from *New Jersey v. T.L.O.*, 469 U.S. 325 (1985), the court found that **the unsolicited tip, along with the student's lie, provided the assistant principal with sufficient grounds to decide that searching the book bag would yield evidence of a school rules violation**. The court rejected the student's claim that the handcuffing had been improper and excessive and failed the second part of the *New Jersey v. T.L.O.* test. The officer acted reasonably under the circumstances, inasmuch as the assistant principal had the right to search the book bag and the student physically protected it instead of turning it over. The handcuffing insured that the assistant principal could search the bag without interference and avoided a potentially dangerous situation. The officer released the student as soon as the assistant principal found the pellet gun and the danger of disruption had dissipated. The court affirmed the trial court order denying the student's motion to suppress the evidence as unlawfully seized, and affirmed the denial of a motion to dismiss the case for insufficiency of evidence. *In the Matter of Patrick Jason Murray*, 525 S.E.2d 496 (N.C. App. 2000).

◆   A Kansas school police resource officer received an anonymous telephone call from a parent stating that a student had brought a handgun to school in a vehicle. The officer informed the school's associate principal of the tip, and they detained the student. The student was allowed to telephone his father and consented to a search of his vehicle after the father gave his consent. **During the search of the vehicle, the officer discovered a loaded handgun, and arrested the student for unlawful use of a weapon** in violation of state law. The student was then advised of his Fifth Amendment rights to obtain a legal representative and to refrain from making any statement. The school district voted to suspend the student through the following semester. He sued the district and officials in a federal district court under 42 U.S.C. § 1983, asserting constitutional violations. The court denied the student's motion for a temporary restraining order requiring him to be readmitted to school.

The court considered motions for pretrial judgment filed by the officials. **It agreed with the school superintendent and police chief that there was no evidence that they had actual knowledge of any violation that might allow for their personal liability** since supervisors cannot be held strictly liable for constitutional rights violations. The court also granted pretrial judgment to the police officer and associate principal concerning the decision to expel the student. Finally, the court stated that there is no civil rights remedy under § 1983 for failure to timely advise a suspect of his criminal procedural rights under the Fifth Amendment. The officials were entitled to immunity. *James by and through James v. Unified School Dist. No. 512*, 959 F.Supp. 1407 (D.Kan.1997).

◆   A Florida school board maintained an open campus policy for its high schools. **It responded to an increase in weapons confiscation from students and reports of on campus homicides and aggravated batteries by instituting a random search policy**. The policy authorized random searches of students in their classrooms with a handheld metal detector. Students could not refuse to be searched without being subject to discipline. A search team entered a high school classroom and observed students passing a jacket to the back of the room. A security employee discovered a gun in the jacket and turned its owner over to police officers. The state filed a delinquency petition against the student for carrying a concealed weapon on school property. He filed a motion in a state court to suppress evidence of the firearm on grounds that there had been no probable cause for the search. The court agreed with the student that the search was a police search that was subject to the Fourth Amendment probable cause standard, not an administrative search as characterized by the state which was subject to a lower standard of scrutiny.

The state appealed to the Court of Appeal of Florida, Third District, which determined that the circuit court had improperly characterized the search as a police search. The U.S. Supreme Court has approved of random searches in the school setting where the search furthers a valid administrative purpose. **The board's policy involved a minimal intrusion into student privacy and was justified by the legitimate need to deter and curtail the presence of weapons in schools to promote a safe learning environment**. The search was constitutional and the lower court had improperly granted the motion to suppress the evidence. *State of Florida v. J.A.*, 679 So.2d 316 (Fla.App.3d Dist.1996).

◆   A rural Arkansas school district maintained one school for all grades with a total enrollment of 225 students. **The school's principal responded to reports that a school bus had been vandalized by ordering a search of all male students in grades six through 12**. The boys were brought to a classroom and searched for concealed weapons. They were required to remove their jackets, shoes and socks and in some cases they were patted down. The search did not reveal any weapons, but **a ninth grader was found in possession of crack cocaine**. He was expelled for the rest of the school year, and his family responded by filing a lawsuit against the school district, superintendent, principal and other officials in the U.S. District Court for the Eastern District of Arkansas, claiming constitutional rights violations. The court held for the student and awarded him $10,000 in compensatory damages. The district and officials appealed to the U.S. Court of Appeals, Eighth Circuit. **The court held that allowing the Fourth Amendment exclusionary rule of criminal law cases to be applied in school disciplinary proceedings would frustrate the purpose of educating and protecting public school students**. School officials are not law enforcement officers and there is little need for the deterrent effect of the rule. The court also rejected the student's argument that the search violated his constitutional rights because there was no individualized suspicion that he possessed a weapon. The U.S. Supreme Court has upheld more intrusive random drug testing despite the absence of individualized suspicion. The district court judgment was reversed and remanded. *Thompson v. Carthage School Dist.*, 87 F.3d 979 (8th Cir.1996).

4. Other Searches

◆   A school district policy authorized the search of student automobiles even in the absence of reasonable suspicion of a rules violation. Students had to consent to the policy as a condition of obtaining a parking permit. One of the district's high schools had a policy requiring students to obtain a pass in order to go to their cars during the school day. A school security officer noticed a student walking through the lot and questioned him after he returned to the building. The student admitted he did not have a pass and a search of his car yielded a pack of cigarettes, two lighters and two pocket knives. The school expelled the student for tobacco possession, but later modified the punishment to allow probationary school attendance. **The student sued the district in a federal district court for monetary relief and a declaration prohibiting the district from searching student vehicles without reasonable suspicion or consent to be searched**.

The court considered the parties' motions for summary judgment and scrutinized the testimony of the security officer. He testified that the student first ignored his shouts, then claimed that he was going to his car to retrieve an art project. He did not have a pass, and the art project was not found in the car. The student had violated the rule requiring a pass, and the officer had reasonable suspicion to believe that the student was also smoking and possibly skipping class. Under the standard announced by the U.S. Supreme Court in *New Jersey v. T.L.O.*, 469 U.S. 325 (1985), a search of a student will be upheld where it is justified at its inception and reasonably related in scope to the circumstances giving rise to suspicion. In this case, the officer had reasonable cause to believe that the student was violating school rules. Upon confronting the student, the officer learned that he had violated the rule requiring a pass to leave school during the day. Therefore, **the officer had a reasonable basis for believing that the student could also be violating other school rules**. The court found that the officer was entitled to draw on circumstances existing at the school in the weeks immediately prior to the student's apprehension. There had been a number of complaints about students smoking in the parking lot, and **the decision to question the student was based on the officer's sound professional judgment and experience**. The circumstances exceeded the minimum standard for reasonable suspicion described by the Supreme Court in *T.L.O.*, and the search was reasonable under the U.S. Constitution. Because the court held that the search was constitutional, it did not reach the question of the constitutionality of the district's implied consent policy. The court awarded summary judgment to the district. *Anders v. Ft. Wayne Community Schools*, 124 F.Supp.2d 618 (N.D. Ind. 2000).

◆   Two Indiana junior high school students reported $4.50 missing from the locker room during their physical education class. The school principal ordered a search of each student in the class and all their lockers. **The principal, a teacher and substitute food service worker conducted partial strip searches** of each student, asking some students to remove their shirts and undergarments and patting down their pants pockets. In some cases, the school employees also checked the waistlines of pants by going around them with fingers or thumbs. The students were allowed to leave when the search failed to recover the missing money. Three of the students who had been searched filed a lawsuit against the principal, school board, superintendent and other school employees in the U.S. District Court for the Northern District of Indiana, asserting violations of their constitutional rights under 42 U.S.C. § 1983 and Indiana law. The parties moved for summary judgment.

The court found no liability of the school board or superintendent under § 1983 as there was no indication that a custom or practice of unconstitutional searches had been established. The principal was not a final policy maker and the single act of ordering the search was insufficient to establish the existence of a governmental policy or custom. However, **the principal, teacher and food service worker were not entitled to immunity** because the strip search, instituted to recover a small amount of money, was a clear violation of constitutional rights. The court denied these employees qualified immunity and also denied their request to dismiss the state law claims for battery and negligent infliction of emotional distress. *Oliver by Hines v. McClung*, 919 F.Supp. 1206 (N.D.Ind.1995).

♦   A Kansas woman accused a 13-year-old middle school student of stealing $150 from the front seat of her car. **The school's assistant principal removed the student from a gym class and took him to school offices, where he searched the student in the presence of the school principal**. The assistant principal removed several items of clothing from the student, and patted down his crotch area, but did not remove his underwear. The principal and two assistant principals also searched the student's locker, but discovered no money. The student filed a lawsuit against the school board, principal and assistant principals in a Kansas trial court, alleging constitutional and state law violations. The school board removed the action to the U.S. District Court for the District of Kansas, then filed a motion for summary judgment on the basis of qualified immunity. The court stated that a complaining party seeking to overcome qualified immunity must show that official conduct violates a right that is clearly established at the time of the alleged violation. The constitutionality of student searches has been clearly established by the U.S. Supreme Court's decision in *New Jersey v. T.L.O.*, above. In that case, the Court ruled that a student search need only be reasonable under all the circumstances by being justified at its inception and reasonably related to the circumstances giving rise to the search. **Because information supplied by an informant may serve as the basis for reasonable suspicion, the search was justified at its inception. The search was reasonable in view of the student's age and sex and the nature of the suspected wrongdoing**. The court granted summary judgment to the school board and officials, and declined jurisdiction over any state law claims. *Singleton v. Bd. of Educ. USD 500*, 894 F.Supp. 386 (D.Kan.1995).

♦   **A New Jersey school district policy required parents of students who wished to go on field trips to sign permission slips containing a statement that hand luggage taken on the trip could be searched**. A seventh grader planned to attend a field trip. He was subjected to a search of his gym bag and cooler prior to boarding the bus, and no contraband was discovered. The hand luggage of all other students boarding the bus was also searched. The seventh grader's parents sued the school board, school superintendent, and principal, claiming that the search violated the student's Fourth Amendment rights against unreasonable search and seizure. A

New Jersey trial court ruled for the school board and employees, and the parents appealed to the Superior Court of New Jersey, Appellate Division. **The appellate division court held that the school's policy could be justified by the deterrent factor of announcing the hand luggage search**. Chaperones on field trips were less able to deal with emergencies, and students had more opportunities to violate school rules while on field trips. Any intrusiveness created by the search was eliminated by the advance notice given and the fact that it was performed in the open. The appellate division court affirmed the trial court's decision for the school board and officials. *Desilets v. Clearview Regional Bd. of Educ.*, 627 A.2d 667 (N.J.Super.A.D.1993).

B. Police Involvement

Most courts have taken the position that where police are involved in a student search, the Fourth Amendment standard of probable cause must exist and students must be advised of their rights.

◆ **A 14-year-old student brought a gun to school**, claiming that a group of bullies had been harassing him. **School administrators and a school police officer escorted him to a school office for questioning**. The officer left the office during the questioning and the student asked to speak to his mother and his lawyer. He first denied, then admitted bringing the gun to school. A Texas district court adjudicated the student delinquent, and placed him in a treatment facility for 14 months. The student appealed to the Texas Court of Appeals in Austin, arguing that his confession and the seized gun evidence should have been suppressed because he had not received his *Miranda* warnings.

The court stated that minors have the same constitutional privilege against self-incrimination that adults enjoy. Minors taken into custody for questioning must be informed that anything said may be used in court, that they enjoy the right to remain silent and have an attorney present during questioning. The questioning of a minor who is "in custody" must stop upon a request to speak to an attorney. However, the student in this case was not considered to be in police custody, even if school officials were serving as agents of the state. The court agreed with cases from Rhode Island, New Jersey, Massachusetts, Florida and California holding that **school officials are not required to meet the strict requirements of probable cause and need not issue *Miranda* warnings when questioning students about school rules violations**. School officials do not act as agents of the police when asking students about violations of school rules. The court affirmed the district court judgment. *In the Matter of V.P.*, No. 03-00-00422-CV, 2001 WL 578518 (Tex. App.–Austin 2001).

◆ In contrast, the Minnesota Court of Appeals held that the questioning of a seventh grade student in a middle school principal's office with the participation of a police officer was a custodial interrogation requiring the reading of the student's criminal rights. The presence of the officer made necessary the so-called "Miranda warning," and as a result, the student's admissions could not be used in juvenile court proceedings. According to the court's decision, juveniles are entitled to receive Miranda warnings. The warnings are required when a law enforcement officer initiates questioning after a person has been taken into custody, or has been deprived of freedom in any significant way. The student was told that he had no choice but to answer the questions. While he was not told that he was under arrest or that he was free to leave, the presence and participation of a uniformed officer suggested a formal arrest. The student was repeatedly asked whether he had something inappropriate in his backpack. He was then told that he would have to deal with law enforcement and asked questions that were reasonably likely to elicit criminally incriminating responses. Although school officials had the right to reasonably inquire about the student's conduct on school grounds, *Miranda* warnings were required in this case. The court reversed and remanded the case, holding that **where a peace officer interrogates a student in custody in a manner likely to elicit criminally incriminating responses, the student must be afforded Fifth Amendment protection.** *In the Matter of the Welfare of G.S.P.*, 610 N.W.2d 651 (Minn. App. 2000).

♦   Five high school students who were suspected of arranging a potential after school fight with students from another school were summoned to the office of the vice principal of the other school. The students met with their football coach and several football team members and admitted that a fight with baseball bats was being planned for later that day. **The police interviewed the students in a school office** for 10 to 15 minutes, warning them that their parents would be called if a fight actually occurred. The action succeeded in diffusing the fight, but the five students who were interviewed by the police sued the city police department and police officers in a federal district court for constitutional rights violations. **The trial court** held a trial and dismissed the claim against the city. However, it **ruled that the officers were not entitled to qualified immunity and had violated the Fourth Amendment prohibition on unreasonable searches**. The court awarded the students nominal damages, but refused to award them compensatory damages or attorneys' fees.

The parties both appealed unfavorable parts of the decision to the Fifth Circuit, which stated the general rule that qualified immunity shields public officials from damage actions unless their conduct is unreasonable under clearly established law. The district court had improperly evaluated the case under criminal law precedents and had failed to consider that the police were acting in the context of the school environment at the time of the questioning. Because the questioning took place in a school office and was intended to protect students from the threat of violence, there was a compelling government interest in summoning the students to the office. The court rejected their argument that they had a privacy interest in remaining in their classes during the school day without police interrogation. The Fourth Amendment does not protect all subjective expectations of privacy. **Students generally have a lesser expectation of privacy than that enjoyed by the general population, as their movements are controlled by teachers and administrators from the moment they arrive at school**. They are not free to simply walk out of a class or leave a school office during a conference. The actions of the officers in this case were reasonable and intended only to discourage the fight. The district court had improperly found that they violated the Constitution and the Fifth Circuit reversed that part of its judgment. *Milligan v. City of Slidell*, 226 F.3d 652 (5th Cir. 2000).

◆   A middle school student assaulted a classmate and told others on their school bus that if questioned about the incident, they were to tell authorities that the classmate had "touched his butt." The next day, a police officer informed the school principal about the assault and sought to speak to those involved. After interviewing the classmate and his parents, the principal called the student to the office, where he admitted hitting the classmate. The principal also obtained a written admission of the conduct, which was furnished to police in accordance with longstanding policy. In later juvenile court proceedings, **the student moved to suppress the statement under the theory that the principal had acted as an agent of the police in obtaining the statement,** and had violated his constitutional rights in the process by failing to advise him of available Fourth Amendment protections.

The court denied the motion and the student appealed to the state supreme court, where he argued that the questioning in the principal's office amounted to custodial police interrogation in a coercive environment. The court noted that the police officer had left school before any interrogation occurred. **When an interrogation is performed without police participation and for a school-related purpose,** such as potential disciplinary sanctions, **there is no need to advise a student of Fourth Amendment protections,** commonly known as "*Miranda* warnings." In this case, the principal supplied information to police in accordance with school policy and there was no evidence that he had acted as an agent for the police. The court found no element of coercion in the principal's interrogation. It agreed with courts from Massachusetts and New Jersey, which have held that *Miranda* warnings apply only to questioning by the police. School administrators are afforded leeway to investigate rules violations and do not act on behalf of the police even though they may share information obtained from students in the course of questioning. The court rejected the student's asserted reason for attacking the classmate and affirmed the juvenile court's decision. *In re Harold S.*, 731 A.2d 265 (R.I. 1999).

◆   A Wisconsin high school student informed a school assistant principal that he had seen a knife in a female student's backpack at school. He also claimed that she might have access to a gun. **The assistant principal contacted a police school liaison officer with the information and the officer searched her jacket and pants. After she denied carrying a weapon, he found a knife in her waistband.** The state filed a juvenile delinquency petition against the student for carrying a concealed weapon and the student filed a suppression motion, claiming that the search was highly intrusive and lacked the required probable cause. The court granted the suppression motion and the state appealed to the Court of Appeals of Wisconsin. The court of appeals certified the case for review by the Supreme Court of Wisconsin.

The student argued that the search of a student by a school liaison officer required evaluation under the probable cause standard of the Fourth Amendment and not the reduced reasonable cause standard established by the U.S. Supreme Court for searches by school officials. However, **the court determined that police officers who work with or at the direction of school officials should be subject to the reasonable cause standard due to the need to protect student safety, since school officials are responsible for the safety, welfare and education of all students.** Police liaison officers who perform student searches at the request of a school official are similarly advancing the cause of student welfare and safety.

The search in this case had been reasonably related to the suspected offense and no more intrusive than necessary. Therefore, the court reversed the motion to suppress the knife as evidence. *In the Interest of Angelia D.B.*, 564 N.W.2d 682 (Wis.1997).

◆   The Chicago Police Department maintains a unit that conducts random metal detector searches inside Chicago public high schools to deter and prevent the bringing of weapons into schools. The unit set up two detectors at a high school and posted notices that any person on the premises would be subject to search. **A 16-year-old student entered the school, observed the detectors, and turned around to leave. An officer stopped the student**, identified himself as a police officer **and instructed him to go through the detector**. The student responded by raising his shirt to display a gun. The officer arrested him, and the state filed criminal proceedings against him. The student moved to suppress evidence of the gun as illegally obtained. The trial court determined that the student could have turned around for any number of innocent reasons unrelated to the metal detectors and granted the motion. The state appealed to the Appellate Court of Illinois, First District.

On appeal, the state argued that there had been no unlawful search because the student had put the gun in plain view by raising his shirt. The court stated that the issue was whether the stop had been constitutional, since the officer had instructed the student to walk through the metal detector, even though the student had already turned around and was leaving the building. The court determined that the officer had no reasonable suspicion that the student had a weapon, and agreed with the trial court that the student had a right to turn away if he wanted to and might have done so for any number of reasons. **Because the apprehension of the student had not been reasonable, the state was not permitted to use the evidence seized when the officer stopped him**, and the trial court order was affirmed. *People v. Parker*, 672 N.E.2d 813 (Ill.App.1st Dist.1996).

◆   However, the Supreme Court of Illinois held that **the reasonable suspicion standard should be applied in a case involving a full-time police officer at a school**. The court reasoned that even though the officer was a police employee, the school environment required application of a lesser legal standard than that used to review police conduct. *People v. Dilworth*, 169 Ill.2d 195, 661 N.E.2d 310 (1996).

◆   A Texas student was suspected by a school administrator of carrying a pistol. A police officer assigned to the school district confronted the student the following day when she observed the student skipping class. The officer took the student to the administrator's office. **The administrator asked the student to empty his pockets. The contents included a pager, cigarette lighter, two small bags of marijuana and over $1,100.** The city police department arrived, searched him, and found another bag of marijuana. In criminal proceedings that followed, the student's attorney filed a motion to suppress the evidence obtained in the search, arguing that the U.S. Constitution provided the officer with grounds only to investigate the student for being out of class and not to conduct a search of his pockets. The trial court denied the motion and the student pleaded guilty. On appeal, the Court of Appeals of Texas, El Paso, affirmed the trial court's judgment. **The officer had acted appropriately upon receiving information that the student was carrying a weapon and this was her primary reason for detaining the student.** The student's truancy developed during the investigation and was reasonably related to the investigation for a weapon. Because the search was reasonably related in scope to the circumstances justifying detention, it did not violate the Constitution. *Wilcher v. State of Texas*, 876 S.W.2d 466 (Tex.App.–El Paso 1994).

C. Anti-Crime Statutes and Ordinances

1. Weapons

◆   When the father of a student who had been disciplined 10 times during one school year learned that the student had been suspended again, he became enraged and attempted to remove him from school. The student feared that his father would become violent, hid a gun and ammunition in his clothing and attempted to run away. His father found him and brought him back to the school, where the student surrendered the gun and ammunition. **The principal suspended the student for 10 days, pending expulsion, pursuant to the terms of the West Virginia Safe Schools Act,** which called for a 12-month expulsion from school for weapons violations. The school board considered the expulsion at a hearing and voted to suspend the student for one calendar year and to place him in an alternative education program. A state circuit court upheld the suspension, and the supreme court of appeals agreed to review the case.

The court noted that the state had a compelling interest in providing a safe and secure school environment. **Because a 12-month exclusion from school was a reasonably necessary and narrowly tailored method of maintaining school safety, the mandatory suspension period described in the state Safe Schools Act was constitutional.** The court observed that the act provided for expulsion in certain circumstances and required a principal to suspend a student from school, pending an informal hearing. A county school board would then hold a hearing to determine whether the student should be reinstated or be expelled for up to one school year. There was no question that the student had a gun in his possession while on school grounds. Although he claimed that he was brought to school against his will and thus lacked the necessary intent to be guilty of a violating the act, the principal had afforded him the opportunity to explain his side of the story. The court explained that the act requires a principal to ask a student to admit or deny the charges and permit the student to offer an explanation. If a principal does not find the charge credible, the proceeding ends. The student had received appropriate notice and an opportunity to respond to the charges, as contemplated by the act. Even if a board makes a determination of a violation of law, the superintendent of schools still has the opportunity to reduce the punishment if warranted. When a superintendent reduces the discipline, there must be a written statement describing the reasons for the action, which is submitted to the board, principal, school staff and others. The court concluded that the Safe Schools Act provides a student found with a weapon "several opportunities for exoneration." Ruling that it would be inappropriate to undermine the authority of school officials, the court affirmed the judgment for the school board. *J.M., L.M. and P.M. v. Webster County Bd. of Educ.*, 207 W.Va. 496, 534 S.E.2d 50 (2000).

◆   A student admitted possessing a starter pistol on school grounds in violation of a Washington state law prohibiting dangerous weapons on school grounds and waived his right to receive *Miranda* warnings. A county juvenile court convicted him of violating the law and sentenced him to community service. The student appealed to the Court of Appeals of Washington, which agreed with his assertion that a starter pistol is not dangerous according to the statutory definition. **While state law made it unlawful to carry onto school grounds or to possess a firearm or other dangerous weapon, a starter pistol was not a deadly or dangerous weapon**. The court noted that starter pistols can only fire blank cartridges. The pistol in this case had only rested in the student's pocket and there was no evidence that it was dangerous. The court dismissed the case. *State of Washington v. C.Q.*, 96 Wash.App. 273, 979 P.2d 473 (1999).

♦ A Pennsylvania student stated in the presence of a teacher and two other students that he would bring spray paint to school and destroy the school communications system. **He also talked about bringing a gun to school**. The teacher interpreted the statement as a direct threat and informed school officials, who contacted the police. The student was then adjudicated delinquent for making terroristic threats. After the court placed him on informal school probation and ordered him into ongoing counseling, he appealed his conviction to the Superior Court of Pennsylvania.

On appeal, the student argued that the students had been "chit-chatting amongst themselves" and that he had no intent to terrorize or carry out any threats. The court disagreed, ruling that **the misdemeanor offense of terroristic threats required only a threat to commit a crime of violence, communicated with the intent to terrorize another or with reckless disregard for the risk of causing terror**. The crime did not require a demonstration of the ability to carry out a threat and the harm sought to be prevented was psychological distress resulting from such threats. The court found that even a single threat can support the inference of intent to create terror. In this case, the student had made unequivocal statements that he would destroy school property and commit a violent crime, and the teacher who heard the threat was within the group whose safety was threatened. The court found it significant that the threats occurred only two days after a widely publicized incident of school violence in Edinboro, Pennsylvania. It affirmed the juvenile court adjudication. *In the Interest of B.R.*, 1999 PA Super 126, 732 A.2d 633 (Pa.Super.1999).

♦ A Georgia high school principal searched a student on suspicion of drug possession. He found three single-edged razor blades in a small plastic container in her possession. A Georgia superior court adjudicated her delinquent for possession of weapons within a school safety zone. The student appealed her delinquency adjudication to the Court of Appeals of Georgia, where she argued that a single-edged razor blade is not a weapon within the meaning of the Georgia School Safety Zone Act. The court found that the statute contained an extensive list of prohibited weapons, including pistols, revolvers, specified types of knives, clubs, chains and blades designed to be thrown. The list was specific enough to include four definitions for a nunchahka, yet failed to list a common razor blade as a prohibited object. **Given the specificity of prohibited objects in the statutory weapons list and the more appropriate categorization of a single-edged razor as a tool, the court found that the razor blades in this case were not weapons within the**

meaning of the statute. Because the juvenile court's judgment was erroneous, the court reversed the adjudication of delinquency, noting that the student's actions might nonetheless support a charge for violation of school rules or probation. *In the Interest of RFT*, 492 S.E.2d 590 (Ga.App.1997).

♦   The South Carolina Code prohibits any person from carrying onto school property a knife with a blade over two inches long, blackjack, metal pipe, firearm or any other type of weapon which may be used to inflict bodily injury or death. A seventh grader carried a box cutter onto the grounds of a South Carolina middle school and was later convicted under the statute. A county family court sentenced him to indefinite probation, and he appealed the conviction to the Court of Appeals of South Carolina. He argued that the family court had erroneously failed to acquit him in view of evidence that the box cutter had a blade of two inches or less and should not be considered a weapon within the meaning of the statute. The court disagreed, ruling that **the family court retained the discretion to determine whether the box cutter was a weapon that could be used to inflict bodily injury or death**. Other courts have held that a BB gun and even a fist could be considered deadly weapons for purposes of the statute. The court affirmed the conviction. *In the Interest of Dave G.*, 477 S.E.2d 470 (S.C.App.1996).

2. Drugs

♦   A middle school dean received a report from police that a student had brought marijuana to school. The student voluntarily produced it when asked. In subsequent criminal proceedings, the student moved to suppress any statement he had made to the dean on the grounds that she had subjected him to a custodial interrogation without advising him of his constitutional rights. The court denied the motion and the student appealed. **The state court of appeals disagreed with the student's assertion that he had been interrogated in a custodial setting that required the reading of *Miranda* warnings**. These warnings are required to safeguard the rights of criminal defendants against compulsory self-incrimination only in police custodial interrogations. There was also no merit to the student's claim that he was improperly denied the right to consult with his parents before the dean's questioning. Although Indiana law states that children have the right to have their parents present during police custodial interrogations, the police were not present, therefore, this statute did not apply. The evidence obtained by the dean was not the product of an illegal search or seizure. A search for criminal law purposes involved prying into hidden places where an unlawful substance might be concealed. The court affirmed the judgment for the state. *G.J. v. State of Indiana*, 716 N.E.2d 475 (Ind.App.1999).

♦   A Mississippi school district maintained a policy imposing a ten-day suspension on students for the consumption or possession of intoxicants on school grounds. During any suspension or expulsion, the student would receive no credit for classes missed. The district's student handbook stated that a student automatically failed a class for accumulating seven unexcused absences in a semester. The school board voted to suspend a student accused of violating the alcohol policy and he appealed to a Mississippi youth court, which granted his request for an order reinstating him to school. The board refused to place the student in an alternative setting in which he could avoid unexcused absences from class. **The youth court later held that the board's alcohol and absence policies violated the student's constitutional rights. It enjoined the board from further disciplinary action** concerning the incident, and the board appealed to the Supreme Court of Mississippi.

The court observed that recent amendments to the Mississippi Code made attendance in an alternative placement mandatory in the case of a suspension or expulsion. The state Compulsory School Attendance Law limited the power of school boards to deny students placement in an alternative setting while serving a suspension or expulsion. In this case, the school board had an alternative program in which it could have placed the student, but refused to do so in violation of state law. **Because the policy violated the compulsory attendance law and was arbitrary and capricious, it was set aside on statutory grounds**. The court affirmed the trial court order with modifications to allow the school board to deny the student class credit during only the final five days of his suspension. *In the Interest of T.H., III,* 681 So.2d 110 (Miss.1996).

◆   A Michigan federal grand jury indicted four suspects on nine drug trafficking counts. **Three of the suspects were found guilty of charges including conspiracy, illegal drug possession and possession with intent to distribute crack cocaine within 1,000 feet of an elementary school**. The Comprehensive Drug Abuse Prevention and Control Act of 1970, 21 U.S.C. § 860(a), doubles the maximum penalty for possession with intent to distribute controlled substances when the offense occurs within 1,000 feet of a school. The three convicts appealed their convictions on grounds that the act violated the Commerce Clause of the U.S. Constitution. The U.S. District Court for the Western District of Michigan upheld the act, and the convicts appealed to the U.S. Court of Appeals, Sixth Circuit. The court distinguished the drug abuse prevention and control act from the Gun-Free School Zones Act of 1990, which was declared unconstitutional by the U.S. Supreme Court in 1995 on Commerce Clause grounds. Although the Court held in that case that Congress lacked the power to regulate gun possession on school grounds, **drug trafficking was an area of interstate commerce that was within the power of Congress to regulate. Each individual transaction involving illegal drugs affected interstate commerce and the act did not violate the Commerce Clause**. The court upheld the act, but remanded two of the convictions partly because of concerns over the amount of illegal drugs involved. *U.S. v. Tucker,* 90 F.3d 1135 (6th Cir.1996).

3.   Bodily and Emotional Harm

◆   A teacher intervened in an argument among three students. One of the students pushed the teacher out of the way to pursue a third student. A second teacher arrived, and grabbed and restrained the student who had pushed the other. The teachers brought the pushing student to the superintendent's office and one telephoned for assistance while the other stood by the door. The student charged the teacher at the door with a football-style dive. The other teacher dropped the phone and tackled the student and both teachers subdued him. They called the sheriff's department and **the state brought delinquency complaints against the student for two counts of assault on a teacher**. The school also imposed discipline on the student for the incident. In juvenile delinquency proceedings, **a juvenile magistrate consolidated the charges and held that both counts of assault on a teacher had been proven**. He determined that the student caused one of the teachers to be shaken and upset and that the teacher who had tackled the student had been injured as a direct result of trying to restrain an out-of-control student. The court overruled the student's objection to the magistrate's report and fined him $50 for each count, placing him on indefinite probation.

The student appealed to the Ohio Court of Appeals, where he argued that the trial court had erroneously held that he was guilty of assault, since no physical injury had resulted and the only injury claimed by one of the teachers was emotional upset. Moreover, the student asserted that any injury to the other teacher had resulted from the teacher's actions in restraining him. The court held that the student's football-style dive into the first teacher manifested a clear intent by the student to move him without regard to whether the physical contact would cause harm. It was clear that such an attack might cause physical harm, and the elements of assault were proven. The court affirmed the trial court's judgment with respect to the first charge of assault. However, it agreed with the student that the struggle with the other teacher was qualitatively different. The teacher who tackled the student was the initiator of the physical contact between them. **Even though the teacher was justified in taking the action of tackling the student, his initiation of physical contact did not create the necessary mental culpability in the student to establish assault**. While the student may have been guilty of a lesser offense, he was not guilty of assault, and the court reversed the judgment on the second count. *In the Matter of Mark M.*, 2000 Ohio App. LEXIS 311 (Ohio App. 2000).

◆   An Arizona student attended an alternative middle school for those who were unsuccessful in regular school settings. The student came to school without his required uniform, explained to the teacher that his uniform was not clean, then laughed while she attempted to go over the day's schedule. The teacher confronted the student, and he refused to respond to her before finally uttering an obscenity and kicking a chair. The teacher escorted the student to the school office, and the state of Arizona eventually pursued a disorderly conduct charge against him in juvenile court. The court found that the student's behavior was seriously disruptive and adjudicated him delinquent. On appeal, the delinquency adjudication was upheld by an Arizona appeals court.

The Supreme Court of Arizona reversed, finding no evidence the student's behavior was seriously disruptive. **The court characterized the student's behavior as rude and offensive, but not disruptive**. There was no evidence that the principal was threatened by the student's behavior, the principal did not physically retaliate against the student as a result of his behavior, and the student never threatened or harmed anyone. The court noted the student's behavior had no impact on the school, and was fairly normal for students assigned to the alternative school. The previous decisions were reversed. *In re Julio L.*, 3 P.2d 383 (Ariz. 2000).

VI. STUDENT CIVIL RIGHTS

Although many lawsuits are filed each year against school districts and school officials for constitutional rights violations, the legal standard applied by courts limits recovery to those infrequent cases in which the student demonstrates deliberate indifference to well-established constitutional rights. This occurs only where an institutional pattern or practice of civil rights violations is proven to exist that is attributable to policy-making employees.

◆   The Department of Education at the University of Texas considered the race of applicants during the admission process for a Ph.D. program in counseling psychology. The program received 223 applications for the 1996-97 academic year and offered admission to 20 candidates. The school rejected an African immigrant's application while offering admission to at least one minority applicant. He sued the university system and officials in a federal district court for monetary damages and injunctive relief. **The court awarded summary judgment to the university and officials, finding that race took no part in the decision** not to admit the immigrant, since he was eliminated from consideration prior to the stage at which race was taken into account. The immigrant appealed to the Fifth Circuit, which found that fact issues existed concerning whether the university admissions committee had considered race in the early stages of screening. The award of summary judgment on the damage claim was inappropriate because he might still be entitled to some relief, and the court remanded the case for a trial.

State officials appealed to the U.S. Supreme Court, which found the Fifth Circuit decision inconsistent with its decision in *Mt. Healthy City Bd. of Educ. v. Doyle*, 429 U.S. 274 (1977). Under *Mt. Healthy*, an employment case involving the discharge of an untenured Ohio teacher, **even if a government entity has considered impermissible criteria in making a decision, it can defeat liability by demonstrating that it would have made the same decision even in the absence of the forbidden consideration**. The court observed, "Our previous decisions on this point have typically involved alleged retaliation for protected First Amendment activity rather than racial discrimination, but that distinction is immaterial. The underlying principle is the same: The government can avoid liability by proving that it would have made the same decision without the impermissible motive."

Because the immigrant suffered no cognizable injury warranting relief under 42 U.S.C. § 1983, the Fifth Circuit decision contradicted *Mt. Healthy*, and the Supreme Court reversed that part of the circuit court's judgment holding that state officials were not entitled to summary judgment. The other matters raised in the complaint were remanded for further proceedings. *Texas v. Lesage*, 528 U.S. 18, 120 S.Ct. 467, 145 L.Ed.2d 347 (1999).

◆   Pennsylvania law provided that persons under the age of 21 who were confined to adult county correctional facilities and were otherwise eligible for educational services, were entitled to services to the same extent as expelled students. This translated into about five hours of services per week. **The law differentiated between juveniles who were convicted as adults based on their place of incarceration, since those placed in state facilities received full-education programs, while those over the age of 17 incarcerated in county facilities**

received no educational services. Generally, juveniles who were sentenced to two years or less were confined in county facilities, while those sentenced to terms of five years or more were confined in state facilities. Sentences of between two and five years could be served at either type of facility at the sentencing judge's discretion. A group representing juveniles incarcerated in adult county facilities sued the commonwealth of Pennsylvania and numerous state officials in a federal district court, asserting violation of their constitutional right to equal protection under the laws. The parties agreed that all students who were confined as pre-trial detainees should receive full-educational programs. Students with disabilities who required special education services were also entitled to receive full-educational programs.

The court then held that the remaining students were not entitled to a preliminary order, and they appealed to the Third Circuit, which observed that **education is not a fundamental right**. Accordingly, equal protection claims based on deprivation of educational services do not warrant a heightened degree of constitutional scrutiny. The state was required only to show that the disproportionate allocation of state educational resources had some rational relationship to a legitimate end. The circuit court found that the state had met this showing by providing four justifications for the distinction between county and state adult corrections facilities. Space limitations existed in county correctional institutions that were not present in state facilities. State facilities also had higher youth populations, reducing the cost of providing education there. The state argued convincingly that the discontinuation of full educational services at state institutions would result in security concerns. There was a greater need for educational services at state facilities where longer terms were served. **The legislature was entitled to allocate state resources on these grounds, and its judgment was not subject to judicial second-guessing**. The court affirmed the district court decision denying relief to the students. *Brian B. v. Commonwealth of Pennsylvania Department of Education*, 230 F.3d 582 (3d Cir. 2000).

◆   **Section 159.051 of the Kentucky Revised Statutes allows the revocation of student driver's licenses upon a school superintendent's report that a student has either dropped out of school or been declared academically deficient**. The law requires school boards to adopt standards for academic deficiency for students in alternative, special education or part-time programs. Students who are subject to license revocation receive opportunities for hearings to seek reinstatement, and reinstatement can also be made for undue hardship. A group of students sued state officials in a Kentucky circuit court, seeking to invalidate the law on seven grounds. The court agreed with the students on five of their claims, and the parties appealed to the Court of Appeals of Kentucky.

The appeals court held that Section 159.051 did not deny students meaningful judicial review in violation of the state and U.S. Constitutions. Students received notices if they were found in violation of the statute and received a timely hearing at which they received the opportunity to demonstrate undue hardship and correct clerical errors. They enjoyed rights to appeal. It was unnecessary to allow pre-suspension hearings in order to satisfy student due process rights, since driving is a privilege, not a fundamental right. There was no merit to the argument that the law violated the rights of students with disabilities. These students were not required to meet unattainable standards based on their natural abilities. The court rejected the argument that the law created unconstitutional age-based classifications. Drivers under the age of 18 did not constitute a "suspect class" that was entitled to heightened constitutional protection. **The law was reasonably related to its purpose of encouraging students to stay in school. The court found that the law did not infringe upon student educational rights**, and reversed that part of the circuit court decision. However, the court agreed with the students that application of state regulations by the transportation cabinet violated the Family Educational Rights and Privacy Act. This ruling did not require striking the law from the books. It meant that the state had to apply the law in a manner that did not violate federal law. Because FERPA prohibited non-consensual disclosure of student information, it was only necessary to get parental consent in order to avoid losing federal funds. *Codell v. D.F.*, Nos. 1998-CA-002895-MR, 1998-CA-003176-MR, 1998-CA-002897-MR, 1998-CA-03177-MR, 1998-CA-003069-MR, and 1998-CA-003178-MR, 2001 WL 705635 (Ky. App. 2001).

◆   Two students claimed that school officials detained and questioned them at school in connection with the theft or pirating of school computer software and programs. According to the students, they were coerced into giving statements implicating themselves and others in the thefts. **They also claimed that the school security guard accompanied them to their homes and conducted warrantless searches**. The school principal initially suspended the students for five days, and then suspended them for an additional five days. The students claimed that during the time they were suspended, school officials posted their pictures at the entrance of their school with the statement "they are not allowed in the building." They also claimed that a teacher threatened and assaulted them when investigating the incident. The students sued the district and various school officials in a federal district court for monetary damages. They asserted federal civil rights violations and state law defamation and assault claims.

   The court dismissed the claims for monetary damages against the high school and individual officials in their official capacities. The students had failed to show that their civil rights had been violated by an express policy or widespread district custom. The court also dismissed the state law defamation claims based on the posting of the pictures at the school entrance. The statement "they are not allowed in the building" was true at the time of the posting and the students failed to show any special damages they might have suffered, destroying two necessary elements of a defamation claim. The court refused to dismiss the remaining parts of the complaint, including claims that the security officer violated the Fourth Amendment by conducting the warrantless search of the students' homes. Although the U.S. Supreme Court has applied a lower threshold of suspicion to school cases than that employed in criminal cases, the standard it announced in *New Jersey v. T.L.O.*, 469 U.S. 325 (1985), related to the diminished privacy expectations students have in school, and had never been applied to the search of a student's home. The court observed that the "Fourth Amendment has drawn a firm line at the entrance to the house," and denied the motion to dismiss the claim against the security guard. There was evidence that school officials had improperly failed to afford the students with appropriate notice concerning their suspensions, therefore, the court refused to grant the school officials' motion to dismiss the due process claim. The court also refused to dismiss the state law claim for assault brought against one of the teachers. Because assault involves an intentional act, the teacher was unprotected by the Illinois Local Governmental and Governmental Employees Tort Immunity Act. *Ianson v. Zion-Benton Township High School*, No. 00 C 2133, 2001 WL 185021 (N.D. Ill. 2001).

◆ The Seattle School District's schools were racially imbalanced due to city housing patterns. **The school board eventually chose to assign students to its 10 regular high schools according to an "open choice" policy** by which students listed their preferred schools. Students were assigned to their first choices if possible, but **because five schools were oversubscribed, the district allocated available spaces in them by using tie-breakers**. The first tie-breaker considered whether the student had a sibling in attendance at the desired school. The second, used only where a school was racially imbalanced, considered whether the student's race would mitigate the imbalance. The integration tie-breaker became inapplicable if an entering class was racially balanced. In that case, the district employed other tie-breakers to determine remaining spots. In 1998, voters passed Initiative 200, which became the Washington Civil Rights Act. The act declared that state government, including school districts, could not discriminate against or grant preferential treatment to any group or individual on the basis of race, sex, color, ethnicity or national origin in the operation of public education. A group of parents sued the school district in a federal court, asserting the use of racial criteria in the student assignment plan violated the Civil Rights Act and the Equal Protection Clause.

The court observed that Article IX, Section One of the Washington Constitution prohibits segregated schools. The state constitution imposed a duty on school boards to operate racially integrated schools and recognized that in some cases, race had to be taken into account. **The court found that Washington courts have consistently held that a school board's race-conscious assignment policy does not constitute a "preference" or "discrimination" when instituted to integrate schools.** Case law dictated that the Seattle policy did not constitute a preference or discrimination under the Washington Civil Rights Act. In general, school boards have authority to adopt policies to mitigate *de facto* forms of segregation that courts themselves may not. The policy in this case was a "reshuffling program" in which no government benefits were at issue, as opposed to a "stacked deck" program in which minority members were favored for government benefits. In a case involving California's Proposition 209, which is identically worded to Washington's Initiative 200, the U.S. Court of Appeals, Ninth Circuit, held that school desegregation reshuffling programs are distinct from other affirmative action programs because they do not work wholly to benefit one group at the expense of another. The Seattle policy fell indiscriminately on students of different races, ensuring a racially integrated system. The policy served the compelling government interest of mitigating the historical effects of residential segregation and allowing students to benefit from racially diverse educations. The U.S. Supreme Court has recognized the authority of school boards to take measures to desegregate schools beyond minimal constitutional requirements. The policy was narrowly tailored to promote its goals, maximizing the effect of student choices, in stark contrast to mandatory busing plans of earlier decades. The policy did not specify racial quotas and the racial tie-breaker was abandoned for racially balanced schools. The policy did not violate the Washington Civil Rights Act or the Equal Protection Clause, and the court awarded summary judgment to the school district. *Parents Involved in Community Schools v. Seattle School District No. 1*, 137 F.Supp.2d 1224 (W.D. Wash. 2001).

♦   The Arlington County, Va., school system used a weighted lottery admission system to promote racial and ethnic diversity in the student body of an oversub- scribed alternative school. A federal district court held previously in another case that diversity could never constitute a compelling state interest that would justify racial balancing. The board responded by approving a new policy that employed three weighted factors, including family income, English usage and race/ethnicity. **The formula was intended to obtain a student body that was proportionate to the distribution of students from those groups in the district's overall popula- tion**. Admission to the school was offered first to applicants who were siblings of students who already attended the school. The district then conducted a sequential, weighted, random lottery among non-sibling applicants to determine remaining admissions. Applicants from under-represented groups had an increased probability of selection. Two students who were excluded from the school by the lottery sued the school board in a federal district court to enjoin the weighted admission process. The district court reiterated its decision that diversity was not a compelling government interest and entered an order requiring the use of a lottery without the use of any preferences.

The board appealed to the Fourth Circuit, which observed that all racial classifications are subject to strict scrutiny by a reviewing court. Accordingly, a policy must serve a compelling interest and be narrowly tailored to achieve that interest in order to survive. The school system had achieved unitary status as the result of desegregation litigation that ended in 1972, and the purpose of the admissions policy was to promote diversity, not to address past discrimination. The court found it unnecessary to decide whether diversity was a compelling govern- ment interest, leaving the question unanswered. Instead, the court held that the policy was not narrowly tailored to because it relied upon racial balancing. **Nonremedial racial balancing is unconstitutional, and the board had one or more race-neutral alternatives to promote diversity**. The court held that the applicants were entitled to an order, but not a permanent injunction ordering the school board to adopt a particular admissions policy. It vacated that part of the district court order and remanded the case for an evidentiary hearing to allow the board to present alternative admissions policies. *Tuttle v. Arlington County School Bd.*, 195 F.3d 698 (4th Cir.1999).

♦   Montgomery County, Md., schools were never subject to a desegregation order and voluntarily dismantled the formerly segregated school system. The district used magnet schools to promote student diversity, and considered race as a factor in processing student transfer requests. Transfers that negatively affected diversity were usually denied because they would contribute to the racial isolation of a school. **The county refused to transfer a white student to a math and science magnet program because of the impact on diversity**. His parents sued the county in a federal district court, which denied their motion for a preliminary order. It held that the county had a sufficient interest in promoting diversity and avoiding segregative enrollment patterns to survive strict review under the Equal Protection Clause.

The family appealed to the Fourth Circuit, which followed *Tuttle*, above. The county policy used race as the sole determining factor for student transfers, unless a unique personal hardship existed. As in the *Tuttle* case, the transfer policy was not designed to remedy past constitutional abuses by the county. Without determining whether diversity may ever be a compelling government interest, the court found that the use of racial classifications was not narrowly tailored to serve the interest of diversity. The transfer policy was impermissible racial balancing that violated the Constitution. **Potential racial imbalance did not justify the use of race as an eligibility factor for student transfers**, and the court reversed and remanded the district court decision. *Eisenberg v. Montgomery County Public Schools*, 197 F.3d 123 (4th Cir.1999).

◆   The University of California Los Angeles graduate program operated an elementary school as a research laboratory to identify "issues relevant to the education and social development of children in multicultural, urban communities," and to conduct research and develop teaching innovations based on laboratory research. **UCLA admitted 460 students annually, with consideration of gender, income, race and ethnicity, dominant language, permanence of residence, and parental involvement**. The parent of an applicant who was not selected for admission sued university regents in a federal district court for alleged violations of Title VII of the Civil Rights Act of 1964, and violations of the U.S. Constitution through 42 U.S.C. § 1983. The court held that the state had a compelling interest in operating a research-oriented elementary school dedicated to improving the quality of public education in urban schools. The use of race and ethnicity was narrowly tailored to further this purpose

The parent appealed to the U.S. Court of Appeals, Ninth Circuit, which applied strict judicial scrutiny to the race classification, requiring the state to demonstrate a compelling interest for using racial and ethnic admissions criteria. The court agreed with university regents that the state had a compelling interest in performing the school's research. The district court had received extensive testimony on the current problems in urban schools, including an increasingly diverse student population. Cultural, economic, and linguistic differences among children of different racial and ethnic backgrounds created problems for educators that required innovative teaching strategies and research to promote more effective education. Without an ethnically diverse student population, the school's research and innovations would be lost. **Because the school was a valuable resource to the state public education system, the district court had correctly found that the use of racial and ethnic criteria in the admissions policy was narrowly tailored to serve a compelling state interest**, and the Ninth Circuit affirmed the decision. *Hunter v. Regents of the Univ. of California*, 190 F.3d 1061 (9th Cir. 1999).

◆   A New York student's family moved frequently and he attended four different schools during a 16-month period. After a kindergarten year marked by frequent absences, his teacher recommended that he attend a transitional class instead of advancing to first grade. However, the family moved and he was placed in a first grade class. In February, the student's teacher and mother agreed to refer him to a child study team for assessment, but the family moved before the end of the month. After the move, the student began attending a school with a very low minority enrollment rate. He was the only African-American student in his class and soon heard racial epithets from classmates and even a parent at his bus stop. After two weeks, **he was reassigned to a kindergarten class because he was "academically overplaced" and struggled with reading assignments**. The family commenced a federal district court action against school officials, alleging race discrimination. The court dismissed the case, finding that it failed to make out a case for race discrimination but on appeal, the Second Circuit reversed the decision. It held that there was evidence that the transfer was improperly motivated by a desire to relieve racial tension in the first grade class. On remand, the district court again entered judgment for the school board and the family appealed to the Second Circuit.

The court stated that in order to succeed in their claims based on the racial epithets, the family had to demonstrate deliberate indifference by school officials to the student's complaints. The student's teacher explained her inaction when others allegedly called him a "black spot" or "chocolate drop" as the result of her uncertainty that the remarks had been heard by the student, and her belief that the speakers did not have a malicious intent. She was also afraid that further reporting might do more harm than good. The court accepted this explanation as reasonable, and noted that school officials had no responsibility for disciplining the parent accused of insulting the student at the bus stop. Their conduct did not meet the relatively high standard of deliberate indifference and summary judgment was affirmed on the claim arising from the racial epithets. There was ample evidence that the transfer of the student from first grade to kindergarten only three months before the end of the school year was based on the fact that he was several months behind his classmates in reading. **Although no other students had been subject to a similar transfer, there was no evidence of intentional discrimination on the basis of race**, and the court affirmed the order for summary judgment on the transfer issue. *Gant v. Wallingford Bd. of Educ.*, 195 F.3d 134 (2d Cir. 1999).

◆   The U.S. Court of Appeals, Eleventh Circuit, determined that a Florida school board was entitled to summary judgment on some claims that it used impermissible race-conscious policies in order to comply with a consent decree arising from earlier discrimination lawsuits. However, the court found that **two African-American students could proceed with their claims for damages arising from the remedial policies regarding busing and admission to magnet programs because there was no evidence that the policies were sufficiently narrowly tailored** to achieve the interest of compliance with the consent decree. *Citizens Concerned About Our Children v. School Bd. of Broward County, Fla.*, 193 F.3d 1285 (11th Cir. 1999).

◆   The Boston Latin School, one of three public examination schools within the Boston school district adopted a new admissions policy for the examination schools following a 1995 lawsuit. Under the policy, applicants were ranked by their composite scores, with the top half being designated as qualified applicants. **Half of the seats were awarded by composite score rank alone, with the other half being awarded based on score rank and flexible racial and ethnic guidelines**.

The flexible guidelines allocated the remaining seats in proportion to the racial and ethnic composition of the remaining qualified applicants. A white applicant who was not selected for admission for the 1996-97 school year sued the school committee and individual members in federal court, claiming she would have been admitted if not for the racial and ethnic considerations of the selection policy. The court applied the strict scrutiny constitutional standard and upheld the admissions policy. The student appealed.

The U.S. Court of Appeals, First Circuit, reversed, finding the admissions policy unconstitutional under the strict scrutiny test. The circuit court stated that the policy was not necessary to achieve diversity within the class of students admitted to the examination schools, and that **diversity was not a compelling enough interest to justify the policy** under the circumstances of this case. Further, the policy was not necessary to remedy past discrimination, the other ground asserted by the district as justification for upholding the policy. Because the policy was unconstitutional, the district court decision was reversed. *Wessmann v. Gittens,* 160 F.3d 790 (1st Cir. 1998).

◆ A Michigan family had an ongoing dispute with their school district concerning the education and discipline of their five children. The parents eventually removed the children from public school and attempted to home school them. However, **their teaching methods did not conform to state law, and they were convicted of violating state truancy laws**. They filed a federal district court action against the school district based upon asserted constitutional rights violations. The court considered the district's motion to dismiss the case. **The court first found no evidence of racial discrimination by the district against the family, a common theme in each of the claims**. There was no legal support for the family's assertion that one of the students was entitled to appeal a suspension of ten days or less since no Michigan statute provides for the appeal of a short-term suspension. The court also found no legal authority for the asserted right to a hearing concerning the repeating of grades. There is no constitutional interest in promotion to a grade, and this claim was properly dismissed. The court granted the district's dismissal motion in its entirety. *Hartfield v. East Grand Rapids Pub. Schools*, 960 F.Supp. 1259 (W.D.Mich.1997).

◆ A teacher and a speech therapist employed by a New York school district utilized facilitated communication to communicate with a student with disabilities. Based on the student's responses to them as solicited through facilitated communication, they began to suspect that she was a possible victim of child abuse. They reported their suspicions to the school principal, who determined that reasonable cause existed to make a report to the New York State Child Abuse Central Registry, and **the student was temporarily removed from the custody of her parents**. The family then filed a federal district court action against state and county education, social services and sheriff's department employees, alleging that the action violated an asserted constitutional right to remain together as a family. The court dismissed the social services and sheriff's department employees from the lawsuit, and considered a motion for pretrial judgment by the school district employees.

The court considered specific allegations by the family that facilitated communication is an experimental and unreliable method which had yielded false information and that its use had violated their constitutional rights. **The court**

found no evidence that the teacher, speech therapist and principal had reason to believe that facilitated communication would yield false results. They were therefore entitled to pretrial judgment. The school district and super-intendent were also entitled to judgment since there was no evidence that the district had failed to train personnel in proper child abuse reporting procedures or that there had been previous problems with facilitated communication which could have put them on notice of the need to further train district personnel. *Zappala v. Albicelli*, 980 F.Supp. 635 (N.D.N.Y.1997).

◆ New York education law requires that a public school student showing symptoms of any contagious or infectious disease be excluded from school and immediately sent home. A student who returned to school after a one-day absence was inspected by the school nurse. She found evidence of nits and sent the student home in conformance with state law. The student reported to school the next day and was again sent to the school nurse to be re-checked before returning to class. The student became upset and refused to report to the nurse, and school officials called her parents. **The student's father** appeared at school with a deputy sheriff and **demanded that the inspection be performed by a school physician**. School officials refused to authorize an inspection by a school physician and sent the student home. The parents filed a federal district court action against the school officials, asserting constitutional rights violations. The court observed that the action of the school officials did not concern fundamental constitutional rights. **The dispute over whom would perform an inspection of the student concerned no right to educational choice** as asserted by the parents and the court lacked jurisdiction over the case. It granted the school officials' motion for dismissal. *Kampfer v. Gokey*, 955 F.Supp. 167 (N.D.N.Y.1997).

◆ A Texas student of African-American descent was disciplined repeatedly by his junior high school. **His parents claimed that several nonminority students were not disciplined in the same manner** and that the school refused to change his schedule as it had done for several nonminority students. They began complaining to school officials that their son was being subjected to retaliatory discipline and that the school principal ordered teachers to monitor him. The family filed a lawsuit against the school district, principal and other school officials in the U.S. District Court for the Southern District of Texas, asserting violations of Title VI of the Civil Rights Act of 1964, the U.S. Constitution and Texas law. The court considered motions by the district and officials for summary judgment.

The court found that the Title VI claim was unavailable to the parents and could only be considered as an action on behalf of the student. However, **the complaint on the student's behalf did not demonstrate discriminatory intent**, an essential requirement of a Title VI claim. The only claimed departure from the school's normal disciplinary procedures was the monitoring of the student, which was explained by the district as an effort to prepare for a meeting with the parents to review disciplinary issues. **The district and officials had legitimate, nondiscriminatory reasons for disciplining the student, and the discipline it issued had been routine**. The court granted summary judgment to the district and officials on the Title VI, constitutional and state law claims. *Jackson v. Katy Indep. School Dist.*, 951 F.Supp. 1293 (S.D.Tex.1996).

◆   A New York high school student was a member of his school marching band. He learned of a conflict between the band's performance schedule and an ethnic cultural event he hoped to attend. He asked his band instructor for permission to miss two performances. The instructor allowed the student to miss an exhibition but not a competition. The student instead attended the exhibition and skipped the competition to attend the ethnic festival. Upon returning to school, **a guidance counselor stated that the student was no longer a marching band member and was ineligible to participate in the all-state band**. The U.S. District Court for the Western District of New York held that although the student had a property interest in education that was protected by the Due Process Clause and state education law, this interest concerned entitlement to the educational process as a whole. **There is no right to individual components of an education, such as band membership**. *Mazevski v. Horseheads Central School Dist.*, 950 F.Supp. 69 (W.D.N.Y.1997).

VII. SEX DISCRIMINATION

Sex discrimination is prohibited by Title IX of the Education Amendments of 1972. There has been an increasing amount of litigation by students under Title IX, in addition to claims of discrimination based on violations of the Equal Protection Clause of the U.S. Constitution.

◆   A Georgia fifth grader complained to her teacher of sexual harassment by a male student. The teacher did not immediately notify the principal of the harassment. **Although the harasser was eventually charged with sexual battery, school officials took no action against him**. The student sued the school board in federal district court under Title IX. The district court dismissed the case and the student appealed to the U.S. Court of Appeals, Eleventh Circuit. The circuit court reversed the judgment but granted the board's petition for rehearing. On rehearing, the circuit court observed that if it adopted the student's argument, a school board must immediately isolate an alleged harasser to avoid a Title IX lawsuit. Because Congress did not discuss student-on-student harassment during consideration of the Title IX amendments, there was no merit to this assertion. The circuit court affirmed the dismissal of the student's clams.

The Supreme Court reversed, holding that **school districts may be liable for deliberate indifference to known acts of peer sexual harassment under Title IX, in cases where the response of school administrators is clearly unreasonable under the circumstances**. A recipient of federal funds may be liable for student-on-student sexual harassment where the funding recipient is deliberately indifferent to known students sexual harassment and the harasser is under the recipient's disciplinary authority. In order to create Title IX liability, the harassment must be so severe, pervasive and objectively offensive that it deprives the victim of access to the funding recipient's educational opportunities or benefits. The Supreme Court stated that the harassment alleged by the student was sufficiently severe enough avoid pretrial dismissal, thus reversing and remanding the case. *Davis v. Monroe County Board of Educ.*, 526 U.S. 629, 119 S.Ct. 1661, 143 L.Ed.2d 839 (1999).

◆   In 1998, the U.S. Supreme Court examined the potential liability of a Texas school district in a case involving a student who had a sexual relationship with a teacher. The Court rejected the liability standard advocated by the student and by the U.S. government, which resembled *respondeat superior* liability under Title VII. Title IX contains an administrative enforcement mechanism that assumes actual notice has been provided to officials prior to the imposition of enforcement remedies. **An award of damages would be inappropriate in a Title IX case unless an official with the authority to address the discrimination failed to act despite actual knowledge of it, in a manner amounting to deliberate indifference to discrimination.** Here, there was insufficient evidence that a school official should have known about the relationship. Accordingly, the school district could not be held liable for the teacher's misconduct. *Gebser v. Lago Vista Indep. School Dist.*, 524 U.S. 274, 118 S.Ct. 1989, 141 L.Ed.2d 277 (1998).

◆   The U.S. attorney general's office filed a complaint against the Commonwealth of Virginia and Virginia Military Institute (VMI) on behalf of a female high school student seeking admission to the male-only college. The U.S. District Court for the Western District of Virginia found that because single gender education conferred substantial benefits on students and preserved the unique military training offered at VMI, the exclusion of women did not violate the Equal Protection Clause. The U.S. Court of Appeals, Fourth Circuit, vacated the district court judgment, ruling that Virginia had failed to justify the men-only program. On remand, **the district court found that the institution of coeducational methods at VMI would materially affect its program.** It approved the commonwealth plan for instituting a parallel program for women even though the program differed substantially from VMI in its academic offerings, educational methods and financial resources. The court of appeals affirmed the district court decision, and the attorney general's office appealed to the U.S. Supreme Court.

The Court stated that Virginia had failed to show an exceedingly persuasive justification for excluding women from VMI. There was evidence that some women would be able to participate at VMI, and the court of appeals had improperly relied on the district court judgment that most women would not gain from the adversative method employed by VMI. The remedy proposed by Virginia left its exclusionary policy intact and afforded women no opportunity to experience the rigorous military training offered at VMI. The parallel women's program was substantially limited in its course offerings and participants would not gain the benefits of association with VMI's faculty, stature, funding, prestige and alumni support. The Court reversed and remanded the case. *U.S. v. Virginia*, 518 U.S. 515, 116 S.Ct. 2264, 135 L.Ed.2d 735 (1996).

◆   A student experienced taunts and was called "that German gay girl" by classmates after enrolling in a school district for sixth grade. **The harassment continued for almost three years and included vulgar comments, sexual propositions and physical violence. The school district did not take disciplinary action against the harassers** or offer to remove them from her classes. Perpetrators were not disciplined, even where physical violence was involved. Although the student's mother reported one incident, no action was taken. The harassment increased so that propositioning and inappropriate touching occurred in virtually every class, but the student's reports led only to escalated harassment. She filed a complaint with the school under Title IX of the Education Amendments of 1972, but the school's Title IX coordinator took no action addressing the harassment. Although the district implemented a new sexual harassment policy the following school year, boys continued to ask the student for sexual favors, touch her inappropriately, hit her with books and threaten violence. The student was diagnosed with depression and withdrew from school. Her family sued the school board in a federal district court for Title IX violations, including a hostile environment created by peers. The court denied summary judgment motions by the school board and held a trial. It let stand a jury award of $220,000 for the student, and the board appealed.

The Sixth Circuit observed that while the board's appeal was pending, the U.S. Supreme Court decided *Davis v. Monroe County Bd. of Educ.*, above. The student met each of the Supreme Court's requirements for holding an education institution liable for peer harassment. First, she demonstrated that the harassment was severe and pervasive, with evidence of verbal and physical sexual harassment so frequent and severe that she was diagnosed with depression. Second, the school had actual knowledge of the harassment because both the student and her mother made frequent verbal and written reports to teachers and principals at the school, culminating in a Title IX complaint. The circuit court also found that the district had been deliberatively indifferent to the student's complaints, satisfying the third *Davis* requirement. According to the circuit court, schools are not required to expel every student accused of misconduct, but are only required to respond to known harassment in a manner that is not clearly unreasonable. The court held that **when a district has knowledge that its efforts to remediate harassment are ineffective but offers only to continue using those methods, it has failed to act reasonably. The district did not discipline any of the harassers, separate any of them from the student or establish a sexual harassment policy** at a relevant time. It did not perform any investigation of sexual harassment against the student even after two boys attempted to rip her clothes off, and there was no evidence that it attempted to discipline the perpetrators. These incidents were evidence of deliberate indifference by the district. Once it received information about the harassment, it was required to take reasonable action to avoid liability. Since it had not, the court affirmed the district court's decision to deny the school board's post-trial motion. *Vance v. Spencer County Public School Dist.*, 231 F.3d 253 (6th Cir. 2000).

◆   A Nebraska student alleged that she had attempted suicide for reasons including a teacher's attempts to convince her that she was gay. **The teacher had engaged her in sexual relations over a four-year period, which resulted in an investigation of their relationship by the school district**. After confirmation that they had had ongoing sexual relations, the teacher was fired for violating a district policy prohibiting such relationships for up to two years after a student's graduation. She also had her license revoked. The former student sued the teacher, school district, an assistant school superintendent and school principal in a federal district court for claims including violations of Title IX. The court approved a jury verdict against the school officials in their official capacities, and they appealed to the Eighth Circuit. The court held that under Title IX, a school district may be held liable for sexual harassment of a student if its officials knew or should have known of harassing behavior.

In 1998, the U.S. Supreme Court held in *Gebser,* above, that a school district may not be held liable for Title IX violations unless the complaining party shows that a school official with authority to remedy the violation had actual notice of harassing conduct, yet failed to adequately respond. The Eighth Circuit then reconsidered the Nebraska student's case and reversed its judgment, observing that **school officials had investigated her complaint and fired the teacher upon proof of the sexual relationship**. The school district and officials were entitled to judgment. However, the student was entitled to a default judgment against her former teacher, who had failed to appear at any stage of the proceedings. Although Title IX did not permit individual liability, there were other grounds for finding the former teacher liable for violating the student's rights, and the court remanded this claim for further consideration by the district court. *Kinman v. Omaha Pub. School Dist.*, 171 F.3d 607 (8th Cir.1999).

◆   **A former student filed suit against a Texas school district and elementary school principal, alleging that his third grade teacher had sexually molested him**. He stated that the principal and district were liable to him under 42 U.S.C. § 1983, and that the district had discriminated against him in violation of Title IX. The district court dismissed the action in its entirety, and the student appealed.

The U.S. Court of Appeals, Fifth Circuit, affirmed the dismissal of the § 1983 claim against the principal, because while her failure to reprimand or transfer the teacher when advised of the abuse represented a tragic error in judgment, it did not demonstrate deliberate indifference to the student's constitutional rights. Under § 1983, a school district may only be held liable for constitutional rights violations where an official policy or custom actually causes the violations. The board's alleged failure to adopt a formal policy was not an intentional choice, and did not manifest deliberate indifference under § 1983. The district court judgment was therefore correct. Although the court dismissed the § 1983 claims, it reversed and remanded the dismissal of the Title IX claim against the district, which had been dismissed because the teacher and student were of the same sex. Under a recent U.S. Supreme Court decision arising under Title VII of the Civil Rights Act of 1964, the Court found that **discrimination claims arising from same-sex perpetrators are not necessarily barred for that reason alone**. *Doe v. Dallas Indep. School Dist.*, 153 F.3d 211 (5th Cir.1998).

◆   An Indiana high school teacher initiated a sexual relationship with a 17-year-old high school senior. The student kept the relationship secret until the summer after she graduated. As soon as she revealed the relationship to her parents, they reported it to school officials, who suspended the teacher and forced him to resign. The officials also recommended that his teaching license be revoked. The student and her parents filed a federal district court action against the school district and officials, alleging sex discrimination in violation of Title IX and 42 U.S.C. § 1983. **The U.S. Court of Appeals, Seventh Circuit, held that it was improper to create Title IX liability under agency principles since employees and agents are not programs or activities and a contrary interpretation might create strict liability for school districts in Title IX cases**. *Smith v. Metropolitan School Dist. Perry Township*, 128 F.3d 1014 (7th Cir.1997).

◆   A Minnesota resident who was over the age of 30 alleged that he had been sexually abused by a school counselor when he was a seventh grader. He never revealed the abuse until 22 years later. He then filed a lawsuit against the counselor and school district in a Minnesota trial court, claiming that the abuse caused him to suffer from alcoholism, anger, memory loss, juvenile delinquency and other symptoms. **The court rejected evidence that the former student did not fully understand that he had been sexually abused and dismissed the lawsuit as time-barred** by the state's six-year statute of limitations for personal injury cases. The Court of Appeals of Minnesota reversed this decision, applying the delayed discovery rule for sexual abuse cases under a 1989 amendment to state law. The school district appealed to the Supreme Court of Minnesota, which ruled that there was overwhelming evidence in the record that the former student was fully aware of the abusive situation 10 years prior to filing the lawsuit. Because there was sufficient evidence that a reasonable person would have known of an injury more than six years earlier than the filing of the lawsuit, the delayed discovery rule did not apply and the trial court judgment was reinstated. *Blackowiak v. Kemp*, 546 N.W.2d 1 (Minn.1996).

◆   **A Wisconsin high school student who did not attempt to hide his homosexuality from classmates was subjected to repeated and violent harassment** that escalated from name calling to a mock rape and physical beatings, including one that caused internal bleeding. Although school officials at times expressed sympathy and made attempts to intervene, the student twice attempted suicide and was forced to leave the school system. He alleged that on two occasions, school officials stated that he should expect abusive treatment because of his sexual orientation. He filed a lawsuit against school officials in the U.S. District Court for the Western District of Wisconsin, seeking damages for violation of his constitutional rights. The court dismissed the lawsuit and the student appealed to the U.S. Court of Appeals, Seventh Circuit.

The court of appeals disagreed with the district court's dismissal action, finding sufficient evidence that school officials had discriminated against the student on the basis of his gender and sexual orientation. There was evidence that he had been treated differently from other students and that school administrators had failed to enforce their own anti-harassment policies and allowed classmates to batter and harass him for a period of years. Because a reasonable person would have understood that school officials violated the student's clearly-established constitutional rights, they were not entitled to qualified immunity from the student's equal protection complaint. That part of the district court decision was reversed and remanded. However, the court agreed with the district court's dismissal of the due process claim because there was no evidence that school officials had acted with deliberate indifference by maintaining a policy that encouraged the harassment. Their actions did not place the student in danger or increase the threat of harm to him. *Nabozny v. Podlesny*, 92 F.3d 446 (7th Cir.1996).

CHAPTER FIVE

Employment Practices

I. PERSONNEL RECORDS

State data privacy acts protect the confidentiality of public employee personnel files. Common law rules of defamation may also provide a basis for legal action against a school district or its officers for wrongful disclosure of private facts or erroneous factual statements. Cases involving open meetings acts may be found in Chapter 10, Section IV.C., of this volume.

A. Media Access

◆ **An Arizona broadcasting company** learned that a school district employed a substitute teacher who was a registered sex offender. The company **sought the names, addresses, places of employment and birthdates of all teachers in the county in order to conduct criminal background checks**. The school districts released teacher names, places of employment and business addresses but refused to disclose their home addresses and birthdates based on confidentiality and privacy concerns. The broadcasting company continued to seek the release of teacher birthdates, and the school districts filed an Arizona superior court motion, seeking an order that the state Public Records Law did not require disclosure of the birthdates. The court held that the birthdates constituted private information that was available through other public sources and that disclosure invaded the teachers' personal privacy interests. The Court of Appeals of Arizona held that the birthdates were neither private nor confidential because of their availability though other public records.

The school districts appealed to the Supreme Court of Arizona, which reversed the court of appeals' judgment, noting that the teachers' privacy interests in information was not eliminated simply because the information was available from other public sources. Birthdates were private information and, like social security numbers, they could be used to gather significant private data about individuals. **The broadcasting company did not provide any basis for believing that other teachers in the district posed a threat to public safety, and its speculative interest in disclosure did not overcome the significant interest of the teachers in personal privacy**. The court reinstated the superior court judgment. *Scottsdale Unified School Dist. No. 48 v. KPNX Broadcasting Co.*, 955 P.2d 534 (Ariz.1998).

◆   A Pennsylvania newspaper publisher requested access to the employment applications of candidates for teacher in a school district. **The district superintendent denied access to the application packets completed by prospective teachers**, which included home addresses, social security numbers, home telephone numbers, college transcripts, physical examination reports and child abuse clearances from public agencies. She also denied access to applicant summaries that were considered by school boards in reviewing employment applications.

A state trial court denied the publisher's request for access, and it appealed to the Commonwealth Court of Pennsylvania. The publisher argued that employment applications constituted public records under the state Right to Know Act because they were essential components of the district's hiring decisions. The district responded that the hiring entities never saw the completed applications and that they were not an essential component of the hiring decisions. **The court found that the requested applications were not public records** as defined by the act. The fact that the district required completed applications as a formal prerequisite for hiring did not convert them into public records. The confidential information contained in the applications was an additional reason for refusing to disclose the information, and the court affirmed the trial court judgment. *Cypress Media, Inc. v. Hazleton Area School Dist.*, 708 A.2d 866 (Pa.Commw. 1998).

◆   An Oregon school district believed that some of its employees had misused and stolen district property. It divulged an investigation report from their personnel files to the county district attorney, and an investigator disclosed most of the report at an unemployment compensation hearing for one of the affected employees. Also, **a newspaper publisher sought the employees' records** under the state public records inspection law. When the school district refused to disclose them, the publisher brought a state court action against the district to compel disclosure. The court ordered partial disclosure, and the parties appealed to the Court of Appeals of

Oregon. The court observed that the investigator's testimony at the unemployment hearing disclosed substantially all of the information in the report. The district therefore had disclosed the information, and waived its right to keep it from the public. The court rejected the district's argument that confidentiality may not be waived by a public agency under state law. **Because the district had waived its confidentiality rights in the records, the publisher was entitled to inspect them.** *Oregonian Publishing Co. v. Portland School Dist. No. 1J*, 152 Or.App. 135, 952 P.2d 66 (1998).

◆   A Wisconsin school district took disciplinary action against an administrator who soon resigned from his position. **Two newspaper companies sought records relating to the action, but the district agreed only to release the minutes of several closed meetings.** The newspapers filed a lawsuit against the school district in a Wisconsin circuit court, seeking disclosure of further information under the state open records law. The court held that public employee disciplinary records were protected from disclosure by an exception to the open records law, and the newspapers appealed to the Supreme Court of Wisconsin. **The court determined that the open records law required courts to engage in a balancing test to determine whether the public interest in being informed outweighed the potential harm to the employee's reputation resulting from public inspection.** Applying the balancing test, the court rejected the district's argument for refusing to release the records. The court held that the public has a strong interest in information about public officials who have been derelict in their duties. Prominent public officials have a low expectation of privacy concerning their employment records. The fact that the investigation had already been completed limited the possibility of creating false impressions and the public's interest in knowing about the investigation outweighed the risk of harm to the administrator. The court reversed the circuit court's decision concerning some of the records, but affirmed the circuit court order to protect information contained in a letter from the administrator's attorney as protected by the attorney-client privilege. *Wisconsin Newspress, Inc., v. School Dist. of Sheboygan Falls*, 546 N.W.2d 143 (Wis.1996).

◆   Rhode Island law requires school districts to serve notice on teachers prior to March 1 if they are to be laid off in the following school year. Because school committees typically did not know their budgetary status for the following fiscal year as of that date, a common practice was to send out layoff notices in order to protect the committee's right to lay off a number of teachers and then to rescind the notices prior to the end of the school year where possible. Teachers were deemed to be laid off as of the end of the school year if no rescission notice was sent by the end of the school year. **A newspaper publishing company sought the names of 28 teachers who were to receive layoff notices.** The school committee refused to release the names, claiming that the state Access to Public Records Act (APRA) did not require release of the records until actual employment termination. A Rhode Island trial court granted the committee's summary judgment motion and the publisher appealed to the Supreme Court of Rhode Island. The supreme court stated that the APRA limited public access to public employee information that personally identified individual employees with a number of exceptions. The publisher argued that the requested information should be disclosed because it pertained to policy-making functions of a public body that were exempt from the APRA. The court, however, agreed with the committee's interpretation of the statute. None of the teachers who had received a rescission notice had been terminated from employment. Under the APRA, **the employment records were not public records because they contained personally identifiable information and no exception applied**. There was no final government action under the APRA, and the court affirmed the summary judgment order of the trial court. *Edward A. Sherman Publishing Co. v. Carpender*, 659 A.2d 1117 (R.I.1995).

B. Third Party Access

✦   In response to a teacher's sending of an inappropriate message to two seventh grade students, the district superintendent compiled an investigative summary of the incident. The teacher was suspended for four weeks. **A member of the public requested information from the superintendent about the suspension**. The supervisor of public records concluded that disclosure was mandated by the state public records act, subject to redaction of the names and identifying writings of any students. The local teacher's association challenged the decision to release the report. A state superior court judge held that the report was a public record requiring disclosure with the exception of writings identifying students. He enjoined disclosure of the report pending appeal to the Massachusetts Court of Appeals, which remanded the case for in camera inspection of the report by the superior court judge. The judge again ordered disclosure of the report subject to redaction of student information, and the case again reached the appellate court.

The appellate court once again concluded the report could be released, and the association appealed to the Supreme Judicial Court of Massachusetts. **According to the state supreme court, personnel records were statutorily exempt from disclosure under any circumstances**. Since disciplinary reports are part of an individual's personnel records, the disputed report could not be released. The appeals court decision was reversed. *Wakefield Teachers Ass'n v. School Comm. of Wakefield*, 431 Mass. 792, 731 N.E.2d 63 (2000).

✦   **The collective bargaining organization representing teachers at an Illinois high school district requested the names and addresses of the parents of all students attending public schools within the district**. It sought to conduct mail surveys and communicate with students and parents concerning collective bargaining proposals. The district refused to release the information, and the organization filed a lawsuit against it in an Illinois circuit court under the state Freedom of Information Act. The court granted judgment to the school district, and the organization appealed to the Appellate Court of Illinois, First District. The court found that while the Freedom of Information Act was based upon a general policy favoring public disclosure of government records, a specific exemption in the statute protected personal information maintained with respect to students. **Names, addresses and telephone numbers constituted personal information under the act, thereby excluding the requested records from disclosure**. The court rejected the organization's claim that disclosure should be granted in the public interest, finding that the negotiation process of collective bargaining agreements does not rise to the level of a public concern. The court affirmed the trial court decision. *Local 1274, Illinois Fed'n of Teachers, AFT, AFL-CIO v. Niles Township High School, Dist. 219*, 678 N.E.2d 9 (Ill.App.1st Dist.1997).

✦   The South Carolina Freedom of Information Act (FOIA) guarantees public access to government records and requires that each public body hold open meetings and take formal actions in open session. The FOIA allows the discussion of employee appointments by school boards prior to an executive session but prohibits voting on these matters in executive sessions. **A citizen group filed a lawsuit against a county school board and the governor in a state trial court, seeking to set aside a board action ratifying an appointment** by the governor. The court granted the injunction requested by the citizens, and the governor and board members appealed to the Supreme Court of South Carolina. The supreme court considered the citizens' argument that the ratification of the governor's candidate had been accomplished by improperly circulating a sign-up sheet during an open meeting. The citizens contended that the use of the informal document violated FOIA requirements. **The court stated that the circulation of the document at a public meeting complied with the open meeting requirement and allowed the public to view the voting in public session.** The trial court had erroneously granted the requested injunction, and the state supreme court dissolved it. *Fowler v. Beasley*, 472 S.E.2d 630 (S.C.1996).

C. Employee Access

✦   A Maine school district employed a special education director under a series of one-year contracts approved by the district school committee. In her fifth year of service, the school superintendent recommended dismissing her, and at a public meeting the committee voted not to renew her contract. Two weeks after the vote, **the committee denied the director's request to inspect her personnel records.** She submitted a written request for inspection of public records and unsuccessfully sought a hearing on the nonrenewal of her contract. She then filed a state court complaint against the school committee asserting violation of the state teacher employment law, state freedom of access act and her due process rights. The court granted summary judgment to the school committee and the director appealed to the Supreme Judicial Court of Maine. The court rejected the director's assertion that the Maine teacher employment law extended to her. Although the law did not define "teacher" it was inapplicable to an administrator, such as herself, whose duties were managerial and supervisory and involved no classroom instruction. The director was unable to demonstrate that she had a property interest that was sufficient to invoke due process guaranties, and the trial court had properly granted summary judgment on these claims. However, **the state freedom of access act required a government entity to allow every person to inspect and copy any public record**, and the committee had failed to state any reason for denying her request for the records. *Cook v. Lisbon School Comm.*, 682 A.2d 672 (Me.1996).

✦   Voters in a Vermont school district rejected a local school district budget, which required a reduction in the district's allocation for sports activities. Three faculty members criticized the action and sent district voters a letter printed on official high school stationery. The school board condemned the faculty members in public at a special meeting to consider the budget cuts. The faculty members filed a grievance against the board, which denied the grievance in a closed executive session. **The board also denied access by one of the complaining parties to see grievance documents and the board's response**. These actions were then formally adopted by the school board at an open session. The complaining faculty members responded by filing a lawsuit against the school district in a Vermont trial court, seeking declaratory relief. The trial court ruled for the school board and the faculty members appealed to the Supreme Court of Vermont.

The Vermont supreme court held that the school board had inappropriately conducted the grievance before a closed executive session of the board. The Vermont open meetings law required such action to be open to the public. However, the complaining parties had not raised this issue at the time of the meeting and on remand the trial court was to determine whether they had standing to bring their open meetings violation claim. The supreme court also reversed the trial court's decision concerning access by the complaining parties to the grievance documents. **The documents in question did not fall within the exception to the Vermont public records act merely because they were personnel-related documents**. In order to invoke the protection of the act on the basis of protecting personal privacy, the information had to be personal in a limited sense, such as intimate details of a person's life. The court had erroneously granted the school district summary judgment and the case was reversed and remanded. *Trombley v. Bellows Falls Union High School Dist. No. 27*, 624 A.2d 857 (Vt.1993).

II. EMPLOYEE QUALIFICATIONS

In determining an employee's qualifications for a position, schools consider academic records, past experience and any certification required by state law.

A. Certification and Continuing Education

◆   **The U.S. Supreme Court has held that the nonrenewal of a tenured teacher's contract because of her failure to earn certain continuing education credits was constitutionally allowable and not a deprivation of her substantive due process and equal protection rights**. The teacher persistently refused to comply with her district's continuing education requirements and, in fact, forfeited several salary increases to which she would have been entitled. After several years, the Oklahoma Legislature mandated certain salary increases for teachers regardless of compliance with the continuing education requirements. Faced with this loss of sanction, the district threatened dismissal unless the requirements were fulfilled. They were not and she was fired. The Supreme Court held in favor of the school board, noting that the desire of the district to provide well-qualified teachers was not arbitrary, especially when it made every effort to give this specific teacher a chance to meet the requirements. There was no deprivation of equal protection since all teachers were equally obligated to obtain the credits, and the sanction of contract nonrenewal was rationally related to the district's objective of enforcing the continuing education obligation of its teachers. *Harrah Indep. School Dist. v. Martin*, 440 U.S. 194, 99 S.Ct. 1062, 59 L.Ed.2d 248 (1979).

◆   State law prohibited the California Commission for Teacher Preparation and Licensing from issuing credentials, permits or certificates to applicants who were unable to demonstrate reading, writing and mathematics skills in English. CTPL used a basic skills proficiency test, the California Basic Education Skills Test, to make this assessment. **Groups representing minority educators asserted that they had historically failed the test at a higher rate than Caucasians, and that the test had a disproportionately adverse impact on minorities** that violated Titles VI and VII. A federal district court awarded summary judgment to the state. The educators appealed to a three-judge panel of the Ninth Circuit, which held that Title VI was inapplicable to the state commission's administration of the test, since it received no federal funds. The Title VII claim had also been properly dismissed, according to the panel, since the test was a properly validated licensing exam. The panel withdrew its decision when the Ninth Circuit voted to rehear the case *en banc*. The full Ninth Circuit observed that Title VII may apply to an entity that is not the complaining party's "direct employer" if it interferes with the party's employment opportunities with another employer. The level of control exerted over local school districts by the state of California was particularly strong and extended to day-to-day local operations. Districts were considered state agencies in other legal contexts, so that the state was in a practical position to "interfere with" local employment decisions. This brought the state within the reach of Title VII, as determined by the district court. Because a decision on the Title VI question was unnecessary to resolve the case, the court did not determine whether it applied. Under a test first described by the U.S. Supreme Court in *Albemarle Paper Co. v. Moody*, 422 U.S. 405 (1975), discriminatory employment tests are held unlawful unless they are proven to be predictive or significantly correlated with important elements of work behavior that comprise or are relevant to the job for which applicants are being tested. The complaining parties successfully showed that the CBEST requirement had a disparate impact upon minority applicants. However, the circuit court concluded that the district court correctly held that **the test was properly validated in that it had a manifest relationship to school employment. It adequately identified specific job duties to which the CBEST could be correlated and established a minimum level of competence in three areas of basic education skills.** The skills measured by it were important elements of work behavior for employment in public schools, and the state did not set passing scores at an impermissible level. For these reasons, the circuit court concluded the CBEST requirement did not violate Title VII. *Association of Mexican-American Educators v. State of California*, 231 F.3d 572 (9th Cir. 2000).

◆   **A federal district court approved an interim Illinois State Board of Education rule deleting language that would prohibit holders of special education teaching certificates from serving only in classrooms of students with the specific disability for which the certificate holder is endorsed.** The ruling is part of a class action suit brought against the Chicago Board of Education and ISBE that alleges a systemic failure to comply with the IDEA's least restrictive educational environment requirement. As part of the case, the ISBE was ordered to ensure that teacher certification in Illinois complied with, rather than contradicted, the LRE requirement. A court-appointed monitor had recommended accepting the ISBE's proposed new certification framework, and directives had been issued requiring two administrative rules concerning state certification standards. The monitor recommended the elimination of language from an ISBE rule that prohibited special education certificate holders from serving only in classrooms composed of students with the particular disability for which the holder's certificate was endorsed. The court approved the rule recommended by the monitor, and ordered its implementation. It reserved a specific ruling on the ISBE's draft rules for the implementation of standards for certification in special education, in view of the ongoing settlement efforts. The court also approved an agreed-upon order of the parties requiring the ISBE to issue a public notification of its proposed rules governing the transition to the new certification structure and standards for certification in special education. **The transition rules would describe procedures for teachers to acquire and maintain the special education certification designations reflected in the new standards**. The ISBE was to hold public meetings for consideration of the proposed rules and submit a final certification proposal for transition rules at the end of the public comment period. *Corey H. et al. v. Board of Education of City of Chicago*, No. 92 C 3409 (N.D. Ill. 2001).

◆   Local police investigated a teacher accused of engaging in inappropriate conduct with a student at his house and arrested him for simple assault on a minor female. He was found guilty and received a conditional deferred sentence, was ordered to obtain a sex offender evaluation, and was prohibited from having unsupervised contact with minors in his house. His employing school district suspended the teacher upon learning of the proceedings, and the New Hampshire Education Department performed its own investigation. The department uncovered allegations of earlier claims against the teacher for sexual abuse of a former foster daughter. It held a four-day hearing before a hearing officer who found that the teacher had a "pattern of serious inappropriate conduct toward adolescent females, utilizing his positions of authority to overpower them." **The New Hampshire Board of Education then revoked his teaching certificate for conduct that violated the state Code of Ethics for the Teaching Profession**.

The teacher appealed to the state supreme court, which rejected his argument that activities outside the classroom should not have been considered in his revocation proceedings. **There was a sufficient nexus between the outside conduct and his fitness and ability as a teacher, since his conduct demonstrated a serious disregard for children under his supervision**. Parents and school administrators had reasonable grounds for concern and the resulting loss of trust affected his ability to perform as a teacher. There had been no deficiency in the notice of revocation, despite the teacher's claim that he had been unfairly required to respond to the allegations of sexual abuse involving his former foster daughter. There was no merit to his argument that the board could not revoke his certificate for lack of good moral character. The court rejected the teacher's argument that there had been religious discrimination in the revocation, since he was found guilty of assaulting a 13-year-old student, not for having particular religious views. *Appeal of Morrill (New Hampshire State Board of Education)*, 765 A.2d 699 (N.H. 2001).

◆   The Illinois School Code was amended in 1999 by a provision requiring certificated employees, including teachers, to meet certain continuing personal development requirements. The amended law provided that the state teacher certification board and Illinois State Board of Education "jointly promulgate" rules for certificate holders, including the establishment of professional development committees at local and regional levels to approve individual professional development plans. The ISBE published proposed amendments to the state Administrative Code in the Illinois Register that were adopted without the consent of the teacher certification board. The following day, the certification board moved the Cook County Circuit Court for a temporary restraining order prohibiting the unilateral action, claiming that publication of the rules would cause confusion among certificate holders and jeopardize their efforts to meet the new continuing professional development requirements. The circuit court agreed with the teacher certification board, ruling that the certificate holders would suffer irreparable harm due to "the likelihood that such certificate holders may believe themselves to be in compliance with the school code when they are merely in compliance with invalid rules." **The court enjoined the named defendants, including the ISBE and the Illinois secretary of state, from publishing the unilaterally proposed rules in the state register for a period of 30 days.** *Babcock v. Illinois State Bd. of Educ.,* No. 00 CH 2640 (Ill. Cir. 2000).

◆   **The New York City Board of Education denied an application for a teaching license allowing an individual to teach high school Spanish, finding the individual's previous felony conviction for selling cocaine was serious in nature**. The board further found that the individual was a risk to the safety and welfare of students and employees. The applicant appealed to a state trial court, noting that the conviction had taken place nine years earlier, and that the board's decision was arbitrary and capricious. The court agreed and ordered the board to award the individual a license. A state appellate division court affirmed the judgment and the board appealed.

The Court of Appeals of New York rejected the individual's argument that a state law prohibiting discrimination against ex-offenders required the board to issue a license. **The board had considered each of the factors required by the law to determine whether a direct relationship existed between the prior offense and the license or employment sought**. The board had properly balanced the statutory factors and was justified in assigning greater weight to certain factors than to more favorable factors. The lower courts were powerless to reverse the board's decision and the court reversed their judgments. *In the Matter of Arrocha,* 93 N.Y.2d 361, 712 N.E.2d 669 (N.Y. App. 1999).

◆   A West Virginia school board selected an assistant high school principal who was ranked ninth on a list of ten applicants according to the board's scoring system. He possessed no professional administrative certificate at the time of his selection and had only one year of experience as an assistant principal. Under the scoring system, applicants were rated on their responses to written and oral questions, with some points awarded for experience. The seventh-ranked applicant objected to the board's selection since he had twelve years of experience and possessed a professional administrative certificate, which was required for the position. **The selected applicant received his certificate prior to the commencement of the school year**. An administrative law judge denied the nonselected applicant's grievance. He appealed to a West Virginia circuit court, which affirmed the administrative decision. The nonselected applicant appealed to the Supreme Court of Appeals of West Virginia.

The court found that West Virginia law does not expressly state that an applicant must actually possess a certificate during the selection procedure. **Because the selected applicant satisfied the job requirement by obtaining a certificate before the school year began, this portion of the administrative decision was correct.** However, West Virginia law distinguishes between amount of experience and existence of experience, and the board's method of awarding a similar point value for applicants despite the disparity in experience was not reasonable. Despite this error, the selected applicant was still entitled to the position, since the difference in their scores was insignificant and higher ranked applicants had declined the position. The court affirmed the judgment for the school board. *Keatley v. Mercer County Bd. of Educ.*, 490 S.E.2d 306 (W.Va.1997).

◆   The Ohio administrative code was amended to require teachers to complete certain coursework before receiving "Early Education of Handicapped" certification. The code contained a grandfather clause allowing the certification of degreed individuals already employed to teach handicapped infants, toddlers or young children by a chartered school or school district as of the effective date of the amendment. **One teacher** who was employed by an Ohio school district to teach handicapped children in grades one through three **sought to obtain her early education certification under the grandfather clause,** asserting that young children as defined by the code could include students in first through third grade. The state board of education denied her application because she was not a teacher of handicapped infants, toddlers or young children as of the date of the amendment.

An Ohio county court denied her petition for review, and she appealed to the Court of Appeals of Ohio, where she renewed her argument that the term "young children" could encompass first through third graders and that the cognitive ages and abilities of her students were comparable to those of younger children. **The court found that the department's definition of the term "young children" reasonably applied only to prekindergarten special-needs children.** This interpretation was consistent with separate certification requirements for teachers in other grade classifications. The court rejected the teacher's claim that a student's cognitive or mental age should be considered. The court affirmed the decision for the state board. *State ex rel. DeMuth v. State Bd. of Educ.*, 113 Ohio App.3d 430, 680 N.E.2d 1314 (Ohio App.10th Dist.1996).

◆   The Georgia State Board of Education issued nonrenewable three-year teaching certificates to all new teachers. After the initial three years, teachers were required to pass a performance assessment test to receive renewable teaching certificates. The Supreme Court of Georgia determined in a 1989 case that the board of education had issued its regulations concerning the teaching certificates in violation of the state administrative procedure act. **A group of teachers who at one time held nonrenewable teaching certificates were later denied renewable teaching certificates because of their failure to pass the assessment test.** They sued the state board and its individual members, claiming a right to receive damages. A Georgia trial court dismissed the complaint against the board members in their individual capacities, but ruled that the teachers were entitled to monetary damages against the board under the theory that it had violated their constitutional property rights to engage in the teaching profession. Appeal reached the Supreme Court of Georgia. **The supreme court ruled that the teachers had no property interest in the nonrenewable teaching certificates, and that the certificates had not been taken from them.** The teachers were not entitled to monetary damages based upon the invalidly issued regulations because the teachers had no property interest in certificates that were never issued. The teachers failed to advance a viable complaint under 42 U.S.C. § 1983. The trial court had correctly ruled that the individual board members were not liable for damages and that portion of its decision was affirmed. The state board and its members prevailed on all issues that were appealed. *State Bd. of Educ. v. Drury*, 437 S.E.2d 290 (Ga.1993).

◆   **Several teachers and a teachers' union filed suit against the state of Louisiana seeking declaratory and injunctive relief to have teacher decertification provisions of the Children First Act (CFA) declared unconstitutional.** The CFA provided for the implementation of a teacher evaluation and remediation program and required the state Board of Elementary and Secondary Education (BESE) to issue teaching certificates to state teachers according to their evaluations. A teacher receiving a nonsatisfactory evaluation receives a provisional certificate for one year and must undertake a program of remediation of identified deficiencies and reevaluation. If the teacher does not receive a satisfactory evaluation at the end of the year, the evaluation team may elect to deny certification. Since teachers are required to maintain valid teaching certificates, the plaintiffs contended that by providing for revocation or expiration of teaching certificates, the CFA effectively allows the BESE to discharge a local school employee in violation of the Louisiana Constitution. A district court ruled that the provisions of the act were unconstitutional and the defendants appealed to the Supreme Court of Louisiana. The Louisiana Constitution provides that BESE may exercise supervision and control over the schools. **The power to certify was at the core of BESE's functions. Therefore, the court found that the decertification provisions of the CFA did not violate the constitution.** *Eiche v. Bd. of Elementary and Secondary Educ.*, 582 So.2d 186 (La.1991).

B. Academic Qualifications

◆   A substitute teacher with a master's degree in education administration applied for a fulltime teaching position at a West Virginia high school. The school board hired a teacher who had no master's degree but five years of elementary teaching experience. The substitute teacher filed a grievance with the State Employees Grievance Board, which affirmed the school board's decision. The Supreme Court of Appeals of West Virginia affirmed the trial court's decision, ruling that **the board could properly rely upon the greater teaching experience of the selected applicant despite her lack of a master's degree.** *Butcher v. Gilmer County Bd. of Educ.*, 429 S.E.2d 903 (W.Va.1993).

◆   A Colorado man was employed as a counselor by a school district. Among other qualifications, the school district required that its counselors have a master's degree. He made $36,590 per year. In addition to counselors, the district also employed school social workers who performed many similar duties. The district required that its social workers have a master's or higher degree in social work. Social workers made more money. The counselor sued the school district, contending that it breached his employment contract to pay him less for his work as a counselor than a person with a similar education and the same level of experience would receive for substantially similar work as a school social worker. The Colorado trial court held against the counselor, who appealed to the Colorado Court of Appeals. The court stated that classifications in salary schedule need only be reasonable and result in uniform treatment compared to those performing similar functions and having like training and experience. Differentiations among teachers on a salary schedule need only be based on differences germane to the education function. Here, **even if the duties of the counselors and social workers were identical, the different educational requirements provided a reasonable basis under the statute for the salary differential**. Moreover, the district's determination that a person with a master's degree in social work warranted a higher salary than one with a master's degree in another field was not unreasonable. *Osborn v. Harrison School Dist. No. 2*, 844 P.2d 1283 (Colo.App.1992).

◆   A West Virginia county board of education advertised for a teaching position for gifted students in grades five through eight and for learning disabled students in grade six. **After the board hired one applicant, another applicant claimed she was better qualified** and filed a petition for a writ of mandamus in a West Virginia trial court seeking appointment. The court denied the petition and the applicant appealed to the Supreme Court of Appeals of West Virginia. Courts have granted boards of education broad discretion in matters relating to the hiring of school personnel. However, this discretion must be exercised in a manner which "best promotes the interest of the schools." The court compared the qualifications of the applicants and noted that the rejected applicant had 14 years teaching experience, a master's degree, was certified to teach grades kindergarten through eight, and was in the process of receiving her certificate to teach gifted children. The applicant who was hired had only a bachelor's degree, was certified to teach grades kindergarten through six, and was not in the process of receiving a certificate to teach gifted children. **Since the position in the present case was to teach gifted and learning disabled students in grades kindergarten through eight, the court found the rejected applicant clearly had superior qualifications**. Accordingly, the court ordered the board to hire her, and awarded backpay and attorney's fees. *Egan v. Bd. of Educ. of Taylor County*, 406 S.E.2d 733 (W.Va.1991).

C. Residency

The U.S. Supreme Court addressed the issue of citizenship requirements for certification of non-U.S. citizens lacking a manifest intent to apply for citizenship. Two teachers who consistently refused to seek citizenship despite their eligibility to do so challenged the law under the Fourteenth Amendment to the U.S. Constitution. In upholding the state law, **the U.S. Supreme Court held that teaching in the public schools was a state function so bound up with the operation of the state as a governmental entity as to permit exclusion from that function of those who have not become part of the process of self-government**. The Constitution requires only that a citizenship requirement applicable to teaching in the public schools bear a rational relationship to a legitimate state interest. Here, a rational relationship existed between the educational goals of the state and its desire that citizenship be a qualification to teach the young of the state. *Ambach v. Norwick*, 441 U.S. 68, 99 S.Ct. 1589, 60 L.Ed.2d 49 (1979).

III. EMPLOYEE EXAMINATIONS

Physical and mental examinations of teachers and other school personnel may be required by school districts as a condition of employment, provided that the examinee's privacy is not unreasonably violated.

A. Psychological and Physical Examinations

◆   A personnel official at a Pennsylvania school district became concerned about an employee's fitness to teach. She decided to order a complete medical examination, including a psychiatric evaluation. The teacher missed the first exam and, on the eve of the rescheduled examination, she filed a motion for a restraining order in a federal district court. **She contended that a compelled psychiatric examination was an unconstitutional invasion of privacy and that the examination was retaliatory**. The teacher was granted a temporary restraining order to allow her time to prepare a motion for a preliminary injunction. In that motion, the teacher alleged that the ordering of the examinations was part of a plan of retaliation by the school district's personnel director aimed at driving her out of the school district.

Generally, a high expectation of privacy with regard to medical and psychological records exists; however, positions such as teaching often require such information in the employment application process. The court noted that while the gravity of potential harm from disclosure of the information was great, the school district established that the risk of such disclosure was slight. Moreover, the school district's need for the information outweighed the teacher's privacy interest given the important role teachers play in the lives of children. **The court also noted that the constitution did not require a finding of probable cause to compel the examination and concluded that the decision to order an examination of the teacher in this case was not made in an arbitrary and capricious manner**. There was evidence of frequent absenteeism, confrontations with other school employees, and reports from the teacher's supervisor about her ability to function in the classroom. Accordingly, the court dissolved the temporary restraining order. *Murray v. Pittsburgh Bd. of Educ.*, 759 F.Supp. 1178 (W.D.Pa.1991).

◆   A Minnesota teacher's mental health became the concern of her school district. In accordance with state law, **the district and the teacher assembled a three member panel of mental health professionals to complete an examination**. Based on the panel's determination, the teacher was suspended. The teacher then received treatment from the physician she had selected for the panel. She was eventually determined by that physician to be fit to return to teaching. The school refused to reinstate her and asserted that she must be reinstated by using the same "panel approach." The teacher refused to be reexamined, and the case was appealed to a state appellate court. **The statute which creates the system for suspension** provides that a teacher may be reinstated "upon evidence from such a physician" of recovery. The court held that the statute called for evidence of recovery from any physician on the earlier panel. It was held to be irrelevant that the teacher could control the selection of the physician. The teacher had also been fired for insubordination due to her refusal to be examined. Because no such duty existed, her termination was reversed. *In re Mary Silvestri's Teaching Contract*, 480 N.W.2d 117 (Minn.App.1992).

B. Drug Testing

◆   Police officers conducted a random drug search of a district high school, using a drug sniffing dog. The dog alerted on a teacher's unlocked vehicle, which was parked in a school lot. A campus officer opened the door and found marijuana in a closed ashtray in the vehicle. **The teacher refused to undergo urinalysis testing within two hours, as required by school policy**. The school had enacted a zero tolerance policy for drugs, alcohol and weapons providing for testing of employees based on reasonable suspicion of drug and alcohol use. Testing was to occur within two hours of the suspected violation. Refusal to consent to testing or a search of personal property was grounds for employment termination, as was a positive test for alcohol or illegal drugs. The teacher received a written notice of potential disciplinary action, and was recommended for employment termination. After a hearing, the school board accepted the superintendent's recommendation to termi- nate the teacher's employment for insubordination. The decision was affirmed by the state board of education and later by a federal district court.

On appeal to the Eleventh Circuit, the teacher argued that she could not be discharged for refusing to take a test because there was no reasonable suspicion of a violation of the board's policy. This argument depended upon the theory that the search of the teacher's vehicle had been illegal under both the board policy and the Fourth Amendment. The court rejected the teacher's assertion that the board's policy applied to the search of her vehicle, since it only applied to intra-school events involving school officials and employees. The policy did not apply to a drug sweep of the school parking lot by law enforcement officers. The presence of a campus police officer did not alter this fact, and the police were not bound by the board's policy. The teacher had no "expectation of privacy in the odors emanating from her car." Dog sniff searches of personal property located in public places are not protected by the Fourth Amendment. The Constitution permits the immediate, warrantless search of a vehicle when a dog alerts to the vehicle. **There was reasonable suspicion that the teacher was in violation of the board policy, and her refusal to undergo testing gave rise to a proper reason for termination of her employment**. The court affirmed the judgment for the school board. *Hearn v. Bd. of Public Educ.*, 191 F.3d 1329 (11th Cir. 1999). The U.S. Supreme Court subsequently denied a certiorari petition filed by the teacher involved in this case.

◆   **A school board adopted an employee drug testing policy that required employees in safety-sensitive positions to submit to random drug testing**. An elementary school custodian employed by the board submitted a urine sample that tested positive for marijuana use, and the board ordered him into a substance abuse program. The custodian denied drug use and obtained a federal district court order allowing him to attend individual, rather than group, therapy treatment with periodic drug testing. The court then granted summary judgment to the school board, holding that the drug testing was proper. The Fifth Circuit reversed and remanded, finding insufficient evidence concerning the board's interest in protecting students and the custodian's Fourth Amendment rights.

On remand, the district court again awarded summary judgment to the board and the custodian brought a second appeal to the Fifth Circuit. This time, the court found that the board had properly identified the custodian as a safety-sensitive employee, whose performance affected almost 900 students and could place them at significant risk. It agreed with the board that **the interest in protecting students was compelling, that the custodian had received adequate notice that he would be subject to testing, and that the intrusiveness of the testing was minimal.** Because the board's need to conduct suspicionless searches outweighed the custodian's privacy interests, the court affirmed the judgment for the school board. *Aubrey v. School Bd. of Lafayette Parish*, 148 F.3d 559 (5th Cir.1998).

◆   **Employee organizations sued two Louisiana school districts for maintaining policies under which failure to submit to drug testing after a workplace injury would result in discipline.** A federal district court denied the organization's application for a preliminary order and the organization appealed to the Fifth Circuit.

The circuit court held that there was an insufficient connection between suffering a workplace injury and engaging in drug use and that the boards had failed to show how their rules addressed any identified drug problem in their schools. The rules had been adopted under a Louisiana workers' compensation law that did not require the testing of urine samples for all employees injured at work without regard to the circumstances. The law only created a presumption against the award of benefits by employees who refused to take a drug test. **Because the boards failed to justify their rules allowing for the suspension of any employee who did not submit to testing,** the court reversed and remanded the district court order denying preliminary relief for the employees. *United Teachers of New Orleans v. Orleans Parish School Bd.*, 142 F.3d 853 (5th Cir.1998).

◆   A Pennsylvania woman called the transportation services department of her school district and complained that the driver of her son's bus could not stand up and smelled of marijuana. She had never complained before and the administrator of quality services therefore decided that the driver should be tested for drug use. A street supervisor was instructed to meet the bus driver and take him to a health service for a drug test. The bus driver refused to be tested because he felt it was in violation of his rights. The street supervisor reported the refusal to the supervisor who suspended the bus driver. A hearing was held before the personnel administrator and the driver was charged with insubordination. Based on the bus driver's entire work record and the charge of insubordination, the personnel administrator recommended that he be discharged. **The bus driver then brought a civil rights action in a federal district court claiming that he was discharged for refusing to submit to a urinalysis in violation of his constitutional rights.**

A school district may require an employee to submit to a drug test if there is reasonable suspicion of drug use. Factors that may affect the reasonableness of the suspicion are: 1) the nature of the tip or information; 2) the reliability of the informant; 3) the degree of corroboration; and 4) other facts contributing to the suspicion. The school district acknowledged that its decision to have the driver tested was based solely on the information taken from the parent's telephone complaint. **The court noted that this was not a strong case, but given the nature of the job and the reliability of the parent, there was reasonable suspicion of drug use.** Therefore, the school district's motion for summary judgment was granted. *Armington v. School Dist. of Philadelphia,* 767 F.Supp. 661 (E.D.Pa.1991).

IV. VOLUNTARY EMPLOYEE LEAVE

A. Family and Maternity Leave

The federal Pregnancy Discrimination Act, 42 U.S.C. § 2000e(k), prohibits any employer from discriminating against an employee on the basis of pregnancy, and further requires that pregnancy be treated the same as any other disabling illness for purposes of health benefits programs and all other employment-related purposes. The Family and Medical Leave Act of 1993, 29 U.S.C. §§ 2601–2654, allows eligible employees to take up to 12 weeks of unpaid leave per year under specified circumstances relating to family health care and childbirth. Many state legislatures have passed parallel statutes protecting the rights of employees to take family leave.

◆   **The U.S. Supreme Court has held that rules of school boards requiring that maternity leave be taken at mandatory and fixed time periods violate the Due Process Clause** of the Fourteenth Amendment to the U.S. Constitution. Two cases were involved in this appeal to the Supreme Court. In both cases school district rules required mandatory leaves at a fixed time early in pregnancy. The Court said that the rules were unconstitutional. The test in this case and other similar cases is that the maternity policy, in order to be valid, must bear a rational relationship to legitimate school interests. If there is a relationship the rules pass constitutional examination; if not, they are unconstitutional and cannot be enforced. *Cleveland Bd. of Educ. v. LaFleur,* 414 U.S. 632, 94 S.Ct. 791, 39 L.Ed.2d 52 (1974).

◆   Indiana statutes require school districts to grant their employees a leave of absence for the duration of a pregnancy, plus one year following the birth of the child. A teacher who had given birth to a child in March advised her employer that she intended to return to work in August. However, she changed her mind and requested an extension for one year following the birth of her child. The school board voted to reject her request for extension of the maternity leave, and hired another teacher to take her place. The teacher filed a lawsuit in an Indiana trial court, claiming violation of state law. The court granted the teacher's summary judgment motion and the school board appealed to the Court of Appeals of Indiana, Fifth District. The court stated that **the school board was required to grant a leave of absence as set forth in the statute, assuming the teacher had complied with statutory notice requirements**. Teachers were entitled to take leave for the entire gestational period plus one year following the birth of the child if sufficient notice was given. Here the teacher had given ample notice to the board. The board's contention that it was entitled to hold the teacher to her initial statement was in conflict with the statute, and the trial court's decision had been correct. *Bd. of School Trustees of Salem Community Schools v. Robertson*, 637 N.E.2d 181 (Ind.App.5th Dist.1994).

♦   A part-time medical assistance instructor at a Virginia private college suffered from an autoimmune system disorder. She frequently missed work because of her condition and also missed work to take care of her son, who suffered from gastroesophageal reflux disease. The college permitted the instructor to take sick leave and to take breaks whenever she felt ill. It granted her requests for accommodation and permitted her to keep flexible hours. The instructor was also permitted to take a leave of absence to be with her son while he was undergoing surgery. However, **her request for additional time off to take care of his postoperative problems was denied**. The instructor resigned, and signed a report prepared by the college stating that her separation was "mutual." She then filed a lawsuit against the college in a U.S. district court, alleging discrimination under the Americans with Disabilities Act (ADA). The ADA proscribes actions taken based on an employer's mere belief that an employee would have to miss work to take care of a disabled person. The court entered summary judgment for the college, and the instructor appealed to the U.S. Court of Appeals, Fourth Circuit.

   The court of appeals stated that an employee who cannot meet the attendance requirements of a job is not protected by the ADA. The instructor's absences had rendered her unable to function effectively as a teacher. Consequently, she was not a "qualified individual with a disability" under the ADA and was unable to avail herself of ADA protections. The court also rejected her claim that the discharge constituted discrimination based on her association with her disabled son. The ADA did not require the college to restructure the instructor's work schedule. The instructor was permissibly discharged based on her past absences and her statement that she would miss more work to take care of her son. This, coupled with the college's reasonable accommodations, established that disability was not a motivating factor in the dismissal. The district court decision was affirmed. *Tyndall v. National Education Centers*, 31 F.3d 209 (4th Cir.1994).

♦   A tenured New Jersey English teacher lost her job through a reduction in force. **The board of education placed her name on its preferred eligibility list for rehire, but failed to hire her as a long-term substitute for another tenured English teacher who took a one-year maternity leave**. The teacher who had been laid off claimed that the maternity leave had created a vacancy within the meaning of a New Jersey tenure statute and brought an administrative proceeding challenging the board's action. The state commissioner of education adopted an administrative law judge's decision, ruling that the board had violated the laid off teacher's tenure rights, but this decision was reversed by the state board of education. Appeal reached the Supreme Court of New Jersey. The supreme court upheld the education board's decision. In doing so, it adopted the reasoning of courts in Michigan, Pennsylvania, and New York which held that **where positions are temporarily unoccupied due to extended sick leave, no vacancy is created** because the incumbent teacher has a right to return to the position. The term vacancy applies only to unoccupied positions for which the incumbent has no intent to return. Because the teacher who took the maternity leave intended to return to her position in this case, there was no vacancy under the New Jersey tenure statute and, accordingly, the teacher who had been laid off was not entitled to it. *Lammers v. Bd. of Educ. of Borough of Point Pleasant*, 633 A.2d 526 (N.J.1993).

◆   A Wisconsin teacher was covered by a collective bargaining agreement, which provided that certificated employees would be granted ten days of paid leave each year up to a maximum of 120 days. The teacher had accumulated 18 days of reimbursable leave under the collective bargaining agreement when he learned that a child would be placed with his family for adoption. He requested five days leave to be used upon the child's arrival. The school district refused his request to substitute the accumulated reimbursable leave for the unpaid leave that was provided by the Wisconsin Family and Medical Leave Act. **The act stated that an employee could substitute, for portions of family or medical leave, "paid or unpaid leave of any other type provided by the employer."** However, the school district maintained that although the teacher had accumulated 18 days of reimbursable leave, he had not met any of the conditions for leave under the collective bargaining agreement. He had only met the *statutory* conditions for leave. The Department of Industry, Labor and Human Relations ruled in favor of the teacher, a state trial court affirmed this decision, and the court of appeals also affirmed.

On further appeal to the Supreme Court of Wisconsin, the school district maintained that because the teacher had not met any of the conditions for leave under the collective bargaining agreement, it had no obligation to provide him with a substitution for the unpaid leave to which he was entitled under the act. The court, however, disagreed. It stated that **the act was intended to make the employee eligible for paid leave if any was provided by the employer**. Accordingly, if an employer already provided other types of paid leave, employees could substitute that leave for unpaid leave available under the act. The supreme court also determined that the teacher was entitled to attorneys' fees. The decision of the court of appeals was affirmed. *Richland School Dist. v. Dep't of Industry, Labor and Human Relations,* 498 N.W.2d 826 (Wis.1993).

B. Compensatory, Vacation and Sick Leave

◆   Congress amended the Fair Labor Standards Act (FLSA) in 1985, by permitting states and their political subdivisions to compensate their employees for working overtime at one and one-half their rate of pay for every hour in excess of 40 per week. **Employers may agree with their employees either orally or in writing to provide compensatory time off work instead of cash compensation**. The act requires employers to honor requests to use compensatory time within a reasonable time period, so long as it does not disrupt the employer's operations. FLSA regulations limit the compensatory time that an employee may accrue. After the maximum is reached, the employer must pay the employee for additional hours worked. A group of Texas county deputy sheriffs agreed individually to accept compensatory time off in lieu of cash compensation for working overtime. The county implemented a budgetary protection policy under which supervisors set a maximum number of hours that could be accumulated by an employee. Employees were advised of the maximum and asked to take voluntary steps to reduce comp time accumulations. Supervisors could specify that employees take their compensatory time at scheduled times.

The deputies sued the county in a federal district court, alleging that the compelled use of comp time violated the FLSA. The court awarded summary judgment in their favor, but the county obtained reversal of the order on appeal to the U.S. Court of Appeals, Fifth Circuit. The deputies, with the support of the U.S. Department of Labor, appealed to the U.S. Supreme Court, contending that the FLSA implicitly prohibits public employers from compelling their employees to take accrued comp time. The court found that the FLSA establishes "a minimum guarantee that an employee will be able to make some use of compensatory time when he requests to use it." However, **the law does not expressly or implied limit a public employer from scheduling employees to take time off work with full pay**. Because the FLSA was silent on the matter of employer-compelled comp time usage, the court refused to find that the county policy violated the statute. It held that "under the FLSA an employer is free to require an employee to take time off work and an employer is also free to use the money it would have paid in wages to cash out accrued compensatory time." The Fifth Circuit's decision was affirmed. *Christensen v. Harris County et al.*, 529 U.S. 576, 120 S.Ct. 1655, 146 L.Ed.2d 621 (2000).

◆   A bus mechanic worked for an Ohio district for more than 10 years and routinely requested to use of part of his vacation time during hunting season. After generally approving these requests for a number of years, the school superintendent began denying them. On one occasion, she approved only three days of the mechanic's request for 17 nonconsecutive vacation day requests during a two-month period. **The superintendent relied on a district policy giving her the responsibility to see that vacations were scheduled to cause the least interference with school operations**. The mechanic then sued the school board in a state trial court for a declaration that he was entitled to vacation time under state law and that the board violated the law when the superintendent denied his requests. The court dismissed the action and the mechanic appealed to a court of appeals, which remanded the case. The trial court took testimony from the parties, then issued the requested declaratory relief.

The board appealed, arguing that the mechanic should not have the unfettered right to use his vacation time whenever he chose. The appeals court held that the trial court decision did not grant the mechanic unfettered rights to use his vacation time, but rather declared that the board policy was an abuse of discretion under Ohio Rev. Code § 3319.084. The trial court found that the board had acted arbitrarily by summarily rejecting the mechanic's requests for time off when school was in session. Moreover, the court had found that it was not convenient for the board if the mechanic took his vacation either during the summer or during the school year. This resulted in a situation in which the mechanic could not use his accrued vacation time as contemplated in § 3319.084. According to the appeals court, the trial court was entitled to reject the superintendent's testimony that no other district employee could perform the mechanic's duties. There was evidence that another school employee could perform his duties. The trial court had properly interpreted § 3319.084 as creating an employee right to accrue vacation time, while vesting school boards with the discretion to schedule use of the time. **The board had**

abused its discretion by applying its rules in a manner that deprived the mechanic of the use of vacation time, and the appeals court affirmed the trial court's decision. *Johnson v. North Union Local School District Board of Education*, 750 N.E.2d 1233 (Ohio App., 2001).

♦   A teacher worked for an Arkansas district for 20 years, then resigned to work in Missouri. **She sought payment for 90 days of accrued unused sick leave**, representing the maximum amount of leave that could accumulate under the state Teachers' Minimum Sick Leave Law. The district refused her request and she sued in a state trial court, asserting that the law and her collective bargaining agreement required payment for unused sick leave. The court dismissed the complaint and the teacher appealed to the Arkansas Court of Appeals, asserting that she had a vested right in her accumulated sick leave.

The appeals court found that the law allowed teachers to take unused sick leave as credit when employed by another Arkansas school district. Districts were permitted to provide more liberal benefits to their employees if they chose. There was no merit to the teacher's assertion that a 1979 amendment to the law required the district to pay her for unused sick leave. The amendment repealed the former law's prohibition against paying teachers for unused sick leave if they chose to do so. The law also required that if a district voluntarily agreed to make such payments, they must come from district salary funds. According to the appeals court, there was also no merit to the teacher's argument that the applicable collective bargaining agreement called for the requested payment. **The agreement only stated that a teacher could receive payment for unused sick leave upon retirement or be credited when the teacher went to work for another district in the state**. Since the teacher was not eligible for retirement and was not seeking credit from another Arkansas district, the court affirmed the judgment dismissing the complaint. *Turnbough v. Mammoth Spring Sch.*, 45 S.W.3d 430 (Ark. App. 2001).

♦   A tenured Louisiana teacher took maternity leave but exhausted her accumulated sick leave when she developed complications. The school board granted her first request for extended leave subject to a pay reduction for the amount paid to a substitute teacher as required by Louisiana law. **The board denied the teacher's second request for additional leave** and refused to pay her any amount for the remainder of the school year. It also adopted a policy prohibiting extended sick leave for teachers. The teacher filed a lawsuit against the school board in a Louisiana trial court, claiming a violation of state law. The court granted summary judgment to the teacher, and the state court of appeal affirmed. The teacher appealed to the Supreme Court of Louisiana. Louisiana's pay differential statute expressly allowed teachers a minimum of 10 days annual sick leave which could be accumulated from year to year without pay loss. The law encouraged school boards to grant sick leave. The board had no discretion to deny extended sick leave and discontinue payment of salary, except for amounts paid to a substitute. **If the teacher had exhausted her accumulated sick leave, all the board could do was subtract the amount paid to the substitute from the amount owed the teacher**. The court awarded the teacher pay differential with interest. *Dagenhardt v. Terrebonne Parish School Bd.*, 650 So.2d 1161 (La.1995).

◆   Missouri law prohibits public school teachers from striking. However, when St. Louis teachers and their school district reached a collective bargaining impasse, about 1,200 teachers, almost a third of the force, called in sick on the same day. **The superintendent of schools retroactively required the 1,200 teachers to furnish physician statements to document their absences and withheld their pay** for the day. The teachers' union filed a grievance that was denied, but a Missouri trial court determined that St. Louis school board regulations prohibited the compelled submission of physician statements, except for those employees who had been absent for five consecutive days or for 10 days during a school year. The Missouri Court of Appeals, Eastern District, affirmed the trial court's ruling that the superintendent was not authorized to order medical documentation for most of the absent employees. However, the trial court had inappropriately ordered the board to pay the absent employees. Although the superintendent was powerless to demand medical substantiation from most of the employees for taking leave, he still had the authority to seek nonmedical verification for the absences. A separate issue of fact existed for each employee who had missed work on that day, and **each employee had the burden to establish that the absence resulted from a legitimate reason**. The court reversed and remanded this aspect of the case to the trial court for further consideration. *Franklin v. St. Louis Board of Education*, 904 S.W.2d 433 (Mo.App.E.D.1995).

◆   A Colorado school district employed a superintendent of schools under a written contract which stated that he was entitled to take 20 days of vacation each year. The superintendent could accumulate up to 60 days from year to year. The contract did not specify whether the superintendent would be entitled to compensation for unused vacation upon the expiration of the contract. However, if the school board unilaterally terminated the employment contract without cause, the superintendent would not be entitled to compensation. After two contract extensions, the superintendent advised the school district that he would not renew the contract for a third year. **The school district refused to pay the superintendent for 33 days of accrued unused vacation time** and he sued it in a Colorado trial court for over $9,000, which was the value of the unused vacation time. The court granted the school district's summary judgment motion. The Colorado Court of Appeals reversed the judgment and held that the superintendent was entitled to compensation. The school district appealed to the Supreme Court of Colorado. The state supreme court observed that silence in a contract creates an ambiguity where the matter involved is naturally within the scope of the contract. **Because compensation for approved vacation time was naturally within the scope of the contract, an ambiguity existed that required remand of the case to the trial court**. The trial court would have to consider on remand whether the parties intended to compensate the superintendent upon expiration of the contract. Because this subject was missing from the contract, the parties were free to introduce additional evidence outside the contract in support of their arguments. The court refused to adopt a ruling by the court of appeals that public employees had an implied right of compensation for unused vacation time. *Cheyenne Mountain School Dist. No. 12 v. Thompson*, 861 P.2d 711 (Colo.1993).

V.   REASSIGNMENTS, TRANSFERS AND SUSPENSIONS

Subject to state laws and the terms of any applicable collective bargaining agreement, courts have evaluated reassignment, transfer and suspension cases on the basis of whether the action violates the law or contract, or is arbitrary and capricious or an abuse of discretion.

◆   A district employee was promoted to the position of assistant superintendent for curriculum and program accountability in 1997. By the fall of 1998, she was reassigned to an administrative assistant position. **She asserted that she was improperly reassigned for reporting misconduct by district employees associated with the Texas Assessment of Academic Skills.** The administrator claimed that teachers "paced" students on the untimed TAAS. She alleged that the district exempted a disproportionate number of recent immigrants, special education students and "second-year sophomores" from taking the TAAS and that some teachers had advance knowledge of a TAAS writing-test prompt. The administrator filed a federal district court action against the district, board and superintendent, asserting federal civil rights violations and a claim against the district under the Texas Whistleblower Act. The court awarded summary judgment to the district, board and superintendent, and the administrator moved for reconsideration.

The court stated that in order to hold a school district liable for civil rights violations for inaction under 42 U.S.C. § 1983, a complaining party must show a policy of inaction when a decision-maker is deliberately indifferent to the risk of clear constitutional violations. **The administrator could produce no evidence of deliberate indifference by the district in her reassignment.** There could be no district liability through the superintendent because the board did not delegate final decision-making authority to him. The superintendent was entitled to qualified immunity because the administrator's allegations of testing improprieties were not protected forms of speech, since they did not involve a public interest nor did they involve a public controversy." An employee may invoke the Texas Whistleblower Act only where there is a good faith report based on a subjective and objectively reasonable belief that the reported conduct violates the law. It was not clear that the practice of pacing, by itself, violated Texas law. She had no firsthand knowledge that pacing actually took place, and her report was therefore not in good faith. The administrator also did not make a good faith report of improper coding of special education students by the district. Although the court found that the administrator made a good faith report of the disclosure of a TAAS writing prompt, it rejected the possibility that there was evidence that her report was the reason for her reassignment. **There was evidence that the superintendent reassigned her for failing to follow his orders.** Finding no evidence to support the teacher's claims, the court denied her reconsideration motion. *Rodriguez v. Board of Trustees of Laredo Indep. Sch. Dist.*, 143 F.Supp.2d 727 (S.D. Tex. 2001).

◆   **A teacher who was only certified to teach art classes was placed on unrequested leave of absence for 65 minutes per** day after her employing school district eliminated an elementary art section due to declining enrollment and budget. The teacher requested a hearing, arguing that she had the right to bump less senior teachers from supervisory work during lunch and study hall periods. The hearing officer disagreed, noting that the teacher's schedule did not coincide with periods supervised by less senior teachers and would require students to go unsupervised for several minutes each day. The school board adopted the hearing officer's findings and the teacher appealed to the Court of Appeals of Minnesota, asserting that state law entitled her to bump less senior teachers whenever supervisory positions were available.

The court observed that the matter required interpretation of state education statutes, since the applicable collective bargaining agreement had no provision governing unrequested leave. State law prohibited a teacher with continuing contract rights from being placed on unrequested leave while probationary employees retained positions for which the continuing-contract teacher was licensed. However, **bumping rights did not require districts to make unlimited staffing changes, and teachers had no right to demand that a board create new positions**. The teacher had a right to bump into schedules for her area of certification, but the district had no other art classes available. Seniority rights normally do not apply to the supervision of study halls, but instead depend on the past practices of the school district. The district had allowed licensed teachers to take supervisory assignments from time to time, but the exercise of school management prerogatives was limited by student educational interests. The school board properly found that the teacher's seniority and bumping rights did not require scheduling that was adverse to student interests. There was evidence that the teacher's schedule and assignment to supervisory work performed by less senior employees would have resulted in several overlapping times during which students would be without supervision. There was no existing position for her to bump other employees and the district appropriately placed her on leave. The court affirmed the decision for the school district. *Moe v. Indep. School Dist. No. 696, Ely, Minn.*, 623 N.W.2d 899 (Minn. App. 2001).

◆   A 28-year employee of the Houston Independent School District was transferred to a new school at the same time her daughter was experiencing severe psychological problems. The employee advised the administration that she could not work at the new school because the increased commuting time would make her less able to cope with her daughter. School administrators warned her verbally and in writing to report to the new school, but she failed to do so, even after a letter from the district superintendent warned her of serious consequences if she did not report. The employee filed a grievance against the district. A hearing examiner affirmed the transfer, but did not recommend termination. The employee showed up for work three days after the hearing examiner's decision. **The school board modified the decision and notified her that she would be discharged for repeated failure to comply with official directives and board policy as well as continuing neglect of her duties**. The employee appealed to the state education commissioner.

The commissioner affirmed the discharge order and his decision was in turn affirmed by a Texas district court. The employee appealed to the Texas Court of Appeals, which outlined state employee discharge and review provisions. It noted that a reviewing court may not reverse a decision by the commissioner unless it is unsupported by substantial evidence or is legally erroneous. There was no merit to the employee's argument that the school board lacked the authority to change the hearing examiner's findings in favor of the conclusion that "for a period of approximately three months, she did not report to work during her grievance process." **The employee indisputably failed to report to work for almost three months**, and the board was entitled to incorporate this as a factual finding. Even though the hearing examiner had recommended against discharge and in favor of reinstatement without pay, the board was not prevented from rejecting the recommendation. The evidence conclusively established that the employee did not report to work despite receiving notice of the severity of her conduct. The commissioner's decision was not erroneous and the court affirmed the judgment for the school district. *Miller v. Houston Independent School District*, No. 01-99-01437-CV, 2001 WL 225698 (Tex.App.1st Dist.–Houston 2001).

◆   The Youngstown (Ohio) City School District laid off a teacher with seven years of experience as part of a reduction in force. The board employed her the following year as a substitute for another teacher on sick leave, and she continued working in the position for 180 days during the school year. The board compensated the teacher according to the minimum salary under its salary schedule for teachers with a bachelor's degree and zero years of teaching experience. The following school year, the board rehired the teacher for full-time work, crediting her with eight years of experience on the salary scale. **The teacher sued the board in a state court, seeking the salary and benefits that would reflect nine years of teaching experience**.

The trial court held for the school board, and the Court of Appeals of Ohio affirmed the decision. The teacher appealed to the Supreme Court of Ohio, which held that Ohio R.C. § 3319.10 confers certain "local privileges" upon long-term substitutes, including salary not less than the minimum on the current adopted salary schedule. **School boards were required only to pay the minimum amount to substitutes** under the plain language of the statute. The court agreed with the board and Ohio School Boards Association that the legislature would have stated in the law if it intended that long-term substitutes earn additional service credit or be entitled to additional amounts beyond the minimum. The court affirmed the judgment for the school board. *State ex rel. Antonucci v. Youngstown City School Dist. Bd. of Educ.*, 87 Ohio St.3d 564, 722 N.E.2d 69 (2000).

◆   For 13 years, a gym and driver's education teacher also served as the senior high school basketball coach and the varsity golf coach. The teacher had always received satisfactory work evaluations. However, the district superintendent sought to oust him from his coaching duties and notified him in writing about expected performance improvements. **The school board then voted not to renew the coach's contract and approved the superintendent's recommendation to reassign him** as alternative school director/teacher. The coach accepted reemployment by the district but protested the reassignment and petitioned an Arkansas circuit court for an order compelling the school board to renew the contract under the same terms and conditions as the previous school year. The court granted the requested order and the district appealed to the state supreme court.

On appeal, the district asserted that the coach had received a lateral "reassignment" rather than a contract nonrenewal. The court observed that while school boards may reassign and transfer teachers upon recommendation of a superintendent, the Teacher Fair Dismissal Act requires notice to the teacher by May 1 of the existing contract year if the superintendent will recommend that the contract not be renewed. In this case, **the circuit court had properly held that the assignment to the alternative school was not a reassignment of duties, but a nonrenewal of the coaching contract**. This was because the contract was not on the same terms and conditions as those of the previous year, which clearly indicated that the teacher would perform coaching duties. Reassignment to an administrative position constituted contract nonrenewal and required compliance with the Teacher Fair Dismissal Act. The coach was entitled to automatic renewal of his contract under the same terms and conditions as the previous year's contract, and the court affirmed the judgment in his favor. *Manila School Dist. No. 15 v. White*, 338 Ark. 195, 992 S.W.2d 125 (1999).

◆   Intermediate unit employees who provided services to disabled students requested suspension so they could be transferred to other duties under the state Transfer Between Entities Act. Even though each had more than seven years of experience with the intermediate unit, **the school district they were being transferred to allowed only seven years of service to be counted toward salary steps**, citing a limit of seven years that applied to newly appointed teachers under the parties' collective bargaining agreement. It also claimed that the agreement superseded contrary language contained in the transfer act. The employees filed a state court action seeking a declaration of their rights. The court agreed with the employees, and the district appealed to the Commonwealth Court of Pennsylvania. The commonwealth court reversed the trial court decision, and the state supreme court agreed to review the case. It agreed with the employees that the transfer act had been enacted with recognition for the unique situation present in the state special education system. **The transfer act contained the legislative intent to distinguish between employee transfers and new hire situations to ensure that intermediate unit employees retained their benefits** within the education system. The court reversed the commonwealth court judgment, holding that the employees were entitled to credit for all years of service. *Corbett v. Scranton School Dist.*, 557 Pa. 118, 731 A.2d 1287 (Pa.1999).

◆   Several St. Louis elementary school students reported that a physical education teacher made sexual comments, improperly touched and looked at them and cursed at them. The school's principal interviewed the students, then contacted parents, the police and a state agency to conduct further interviews. **The superintendent of schools reassigned the teacher to a non-teaching position and later suspended him without pay pending a hearing**. The state agency found no evidence of abuse and the police decided not to prosecute the case. At the hearing, some students repudiated their statements and the board discredited other student testimony. As a result, **the teacher was reinstated**. He sued the school board, the superintendent, and two of the superintendent's assistants in a Missouri circuit court for claims including malicious prosecution and tortious interference with contract. The court dismissed many of the claims and conducted a trial on the malicious prosecution claims which resulted in a $400,000 jury verdict for the teacher against the superintendent and assistants. The court granted post-trial motions for the superintendent and assistants, and the teacher appealed to the Missouri Court of Appeals.

The court held that the superintendent was protected from liability for malicious prosecution by official immunity, since there was no evidence of reckless or malicious conduct on his behalf. The assistants were entitled to judgment since they

had not initiated any prosecution but had simply reported the matter to the superintendent. **The interference with contract claims** also **failed because the school
board had voted not to remove the teacher, his suspension and reassignment
did not constitute removal within the meaning of state law and he had suffered
no loss of salary or benefits.** There could be no tortious interference with contract
where there was no breach of contract. The court affirmed the judgment. *Davis v.
Bd. of Educ. of City of St. Louis*, 963 S.W.2d 679 (Mo.App.E.D.1998).

◆   **A Kentucky special education administrator with 15 years of experience
was demoted to a teaching position.** The school superintendent notified him in
writing of the demotion, which was based on insubordination, conduct unbecoming
a professional and failure to work as an administrative team member. The letter
included notice that the administrator must respond within 10 days to request a
hearing. The administrator requested a hearing within the stated time frame but the
board failed to approve the demotion by the deadline established in state law. At his
hearing, he moved to dismiss the action since the school board had failed to timely
ratify the superintendent's decision. The board denied the motion, and the administrator appealed to a Kentucky circuit court. The court affirmed the demotion action,
and the Court of Appeals of Kentucky also affirmed it. **The administrator
appealed to the Supreme Court of Kentucky, which held that the board's
failure to timely ratify the superintendent's action did not violate Kentucky
law.** This was true even though Kentucky law stated that personnel actions by a
superintendent did not take effect until board ratification. The superintendent still
had the authority to take the action, which was effective because the administrator
had received proper written notice and an opportunity for a hearing. There was no
merit to the administrator's claim that the charges against him were not specific
enough under law. The court affirmed the judgment for the school board. *Estreicher v.
Bd. of Educ. of Kenton County, Kentucky*, 950 S.W.2d 839 (Ky.1997).

◆   A Texas school district announced a pay increase for its special education
supervisors but soon retracted the notice. Two years later, the district reported a
budget reduction of $20 million to be implemented in part through a reduction in
force. **A group of African-American special education supervisors were
reassigned to teaching positions when their jobs were eliminated by the
reduction in force.** They claimed that the job reassignment and previous pay
increase revocation violated their constitutional rights on several grounds. They
alleged that the actions came in retaliation because they had been outspoken
concerning the district's methods of special education funding and diagnosis of
special education students. They filed a lawsuit against the school district in the U.S.
District Court for the Southern District of Texas, which considered the district's
summary judgment motion. **The court dismissed the claim of entitlement to a
pay increase** on statute of limitations grounds. **It also held that the reduction in
force had been genuine and not a pretext for dismissal** based on the claimed First
Amendment violations. The Constitution does not create a protected property
interest in noneconomic benefits such as work assignments or supervisory status.
There was no merit to the argument that the district had not provided the supervisors
with adequate due process protections, and the court granted summary judgment to
the district. *Johnson v. Houston Indep. School Dist.*, 930 F.Supp. 276 (S.D.Tex.1996).

✦   **A California high school assistant principal received notice that he would be reassigned to a teaching position based on his arrest for an alcohol-related misdemeanor offense for which he was never convicted.** He responded by filing a lawsuit against the school district in a California superior court for violation of the state Labor Code. A jury awarded him actual damages of over $250,000. The court reduced the damage award to $213,000, then trebled it pursuant to the Labor Code and also awarded attorney's fees. The school district appealed to the California Court of Appeal, Fourth District. The court agreed with the school district that while the pertinent section of the Labor Code prohibited an employer from asking an employment applicant about any arrest that does not result in a conviction, the monetary remedies section of the code referred only to applicants, not to present employees. It had therefore been inappropriate for the superior court to treble the damage award under the code. However, **the lack of statutory remedies did not deprive the assistant principal of his remedies at law and he was entitled to the award of actual damages.** The court reversed the attorney's fee award because it had also arisen under the Labor Code. *Faria v. San Jacinto Unified School Dist.*, 59 Cal.Rptr.2d 72 (Cal.App.4th Dist.1996).

✦   A Tennessee school administrator held office as a state senator. He openly opposed a candidate for county school superintendent who was from a different political party. The candidate won the election, and formed an advisory committee to study reorganization of the school system. **The committee recommended eliminating the administrator's position** along with another supervisory position. The administrator was assigned to teach physical education at a district middle school. His former administrative job duties were performed by a secretary. He sued the school board and superintendent in a Tennessee trial court, claiming violation of the state tenure law, which prohibits the transfer of a teacher where motivated by political or other improper reasons. The court upheld the transfer, and the former administrator appealed to the Court of Appeals of Tennessee. **The court observed that the reorganization plan had been devised by the committee and not by the new superintendent.** The fact that the former administrator's duties could be performed by a secretary indicated that the reorganization had been appropriate. *Springer v. Williamson County Bd. of Educ.*, 906 S.W.2d 924 (Tenn.App.1995).

✦   **A Maryland teacher with 17 years of experience and good performance ratings was selected for transfer to another school** by the superintendent of schools. She alleged that the transfer was arbitrary, capricious and discriminatory, and appealed the decision to the school board. The board affirmed the superintendent's decision, and denied the teacher's request for a full evidentiary hearing. The state board of education determined that the superintendent's stated reason for the transfer was legitimate. Evidence indicated that the transfer of a good teacher tended to rejuvenate the teacher's career and benefit students. The teacher appealed to a county circuit court, which affirmed the administrative decision, and she appealed to the Court of Special Appeals of Maryland. The court of special appeals found that the state administrative agency had applied the correct legal standard to the case and had appropriately denied the teacher's request for an evidentiary hearing. A full evidentiary hearing was required only where the complaining party alleged that a transfer was in violation of state education law or constituted an abuse of discretion by the superintendent. The superintendent's action in this case had been justified by legitimate educational purposes. **Experienced teachers with good records were not immune from transfer, and could be transferred to take advantage of their abilities and experience by placing them where they were needed.** The court of special appeals affirmed the superintendent's action. *Hurl v. Bd. of Educ. of Howard County*, 107 Md.App. 286, 667 A.2d 970 (1995).

CHAPTER SIX

Employment Discrimination

I. OVERVIEW

Employment discrimination on the basis of race, sex, religion or national origin is expressly prohibited by Title VII of the Civil Rights Act, even if it is unintentional. Disparate treatment (intentional discrimination) on the basis of those characteristics violates the Equal Protection Clause of the U.S. Constitution.

The constitutional prohibition against employment discrimination is found in the Equal Protection Clause of the Fourteenth Amendment, which commands that no state shall "deny to any person within its jurisdiction the equal protection of the laws." The Equal Protection Clause is an important safeguard against discrimination by states and state agents, such as school boards. Its coverage, however, is limited both to government bodies and to situations involving *intentional* discrimination.

The latter requirement was imposed by the U.S. Supreme Court in *Washington v. Davis*, 426 U.S. 229 (1976), which involved a written verbal skills test that was a requirement for employment as a police officer. The test resulted in a disproportionately high percentage of black applicants being rejected for employment. **The Supreme Court held that an adverse impact or effect on racial minorities was not sufficient to show a violation of the Equal Protection Clause. Proof of intent to discriminate was required**. Because in most cases it is difficult to prove an intent to discriminate (except in affirmative action-"reverse discrimination" cases), federal civil rights statutes provide a much more common basis for claims of employment discrimination in the school context.

Title VII of the Civil Rights Act of 1964 prohibits discrimination in employment based upon race, color, sex, religion or national origin and applies to any employer with 15 or more employees. Discrimination based upon age, disability and alienage is covered by other federal statutes. In addition, every state has enacted anti-discrimination statutes. The prohibition against discrimination in employment extends to all "terms or conditions of employment" including hiring and firing decisions, promotions, salary, seniority, benefits, and work assignments. Reverse discrimination claims are also recognized under Title VII. The U.S. Equal Employment Opportunity Commission (EEOC) is empowered to enforce Title VII. Private individuals alleging discrimination must pursue administrative remedies within the EEOC before they are allowed to file suit against employers under Title VII. Plaintiffs who prevail in employment discrimination lawsuits are entitled, where appropriate, to backpay, front pay, accumulated seniority and other benefits, and attorney's fees. Punitive and compensatory damages are available in Title VII cases where the discrimination has been shown to be intentional.

Title VII lawsuits may be divided into two categories: disparate treatment and disparate impact. In a disparate treatment lawsuit, an individual usually claims that he or she was not hired, was fired, or was denied a promotion simply because of his or her race, color, sex, religion or national origin. Such lawsuits proceed in three stages. First, the plaintiff must set forth a *prima facie* case by showing: a) that he or she belongs to a protected class (male, female, black, white, Jewish, Catholic, etc.); b) that he or she was qualified for the position; c) that despite the plaintiff's qualifications, he or she was rejected; and d) that after rejection the position remained open. Second, the burden then shifts to the defendant to "articulate" a legitimate, nondiscriminatory reason (such as incompetence or lack of qualifications) for rejecting the plaintiff. Third, the plaintiff must show that the reason given by the employer in step two is a pretext for unlawful discrimination. As the Supreme Court noted in *St. Mary's Honor Center v. Hicks*, 509 U.S. 502, 113 S.Ct. 2742, 125 L.Ed.2d 407 (1993), **intentional discrimination *can* be inferred from a disbelief of the employer's proffered reason for the adverse employment action, coupled with the elements of a *prima facie* case**. No further proof of discrimination is required.

Title VII's bona fide occupational qualification (BFOQ) exception allows employers (especially religiously-affiliated private schools) to use sex, religion or national origin as a hiring criteria if one of those three characteristics is a "bona fide occupational qualification necessary to the normal operation of that particular business or enterprise." However, the BFOQ exception is narrowly construed by the courts. While being female can be a BFOQ for counseling high school girls, numerous cases have indicated that BFOQ defenses will fail unless the qualification at issue is a matter of "necessity," not merely employer convenience. In any case, successful assertion of a BFOQ defense will result in dismissal of a disparate treatment claim. It is important to note that race can never be a BFOQ.

Disparate impact lawsuits differ from disparate treatment claims because they do not allege overt discriminatory actions. Instead, disparate impact lawsuits claim that a facially neutral employer policy (*e.g.*, high school diplomas or I.Q. testing as a condition of employment) has an adverse or disparate impact on minorities. If such a policy does have an adverse impact, it will constitute a violation of Title VII unless the policy is "necessary" to the operation of the employer's business. Simply put, the policy must be related to job performance.

II. SEX DISCRIMINATION

A. Title VII of the Civil Rights Act

◆   A female teacher also coached high school boys' basketball teams for 12 years, including nine years as the high school boys' junior varsity coach, and eight years as an assistant varsity boys' coach. She coached at many clinics and basketball camps, managed and coordinated tournaments, served as the social studies department head and at the same time served as head coach of the girls' varsity basketball team. When the boys' varsity coach announced his resignation, **a selection committee interviewed the female coach for the position, but decided to hire a male applicant** who had served under the female coach for two years. He had a total of four years of experience as a junior high gym teacher.

The female coach sued the school district in a federal district court for sex discrimination under Title VII of the Civil Rights Act of 1964 and Michigan's Elliot-Larsen Civil Rights Act. She stated that the district deliberately excluded the high school athletic director from the selection committee because he favored her application. The athletic director testified that the normal coaching progression was to coach the freshman team, then junior varsity, then varsity. The coach also presented testimony from the school principal that certain board members and the superintendent opposed her application due to "community problems." The court rejected the district's argument that because no financial gain was involved, the coach had not suffered an "adverse employment action" when she was passed over for the boys' coaching position. The case involved the denial of a promotion, since the head boys' coach supervised junior varsity and freshman coaches and enjoyed higher visibility, a more distinguished title and higher pay. The court noted there was evidence that the district had failed to hire the coach in favor of a less qualified male applicant, which could lead a jury to believe discrimination occurred. **Because there was evidence that the district may have asserted pretextual reasons for not hiring the coach, the court denied the district's summary judgment motion.** *Fuhr v. School Dist. of City of Hazel*, 131 F.Supp.2d 947 (E.D. Mich. 2001).

◆   A Florida teacher who claimed to be qualified in special education, elementary education, music and psychology twice sought employment with a Florida school district. **He was not hired, and believed that the reason was his gender and his**

nonmarried status. He learned that almost 80 percent of the board's employees were females and that less than ten percent of its elementary school teachers were males. He filed a federal district court action against the school board, claiming violations of Title VII of the Civil Rights Act of 1964.

The court considered cross-motions for summary judgment by the parties and found the employment statistics offered as evidence by the teacher inadequate to demonstrate discriminatory intent by the board. There was evidence that the teacher was only certified for instruction in specific learning disabilities, and not for the special education positions for which he had sought statistical comparison. The school board presented evidence that **the teacher lacked necessary college coursework for working with emotionally handicapped students** and that the teachers ultimately hired for the disputed positions had significant teaching experience the applicant lacked. Because the board had permissibly found that he was not the most qualified candidate for the positions, and he was unable to present contrary evidence, the board was entitled to summary judgment. *Longariello v. School Bd. of Monroe County Florida*, 987 F.Supp. 1440 (S.D.Fla.1997).

◆   Louisiana State University opened the position of admissions counselor for applications. A female university employee with a poor job performance history decided not to apply because she was led to believe that the position required frequent travel when in fact it did not. Approximately six months later, the employee was notified that she would be fired in 90 days because of poor job performance unless her work skills improved. After a dispute with her supervisor, **the employee met with an Equal Opportunity Compliance officer and complained of alleged misrepresentations regarding the admissions counselor position as well as maternity leave harassment**. A few days later, she received notice that she would be fired, and she resigned. The employee sued the university in the U.S. District Court for the Middle District of Louisiana, asserting gender discrimination and retaliatory discharge under Title VII. The university moved for summary judgment.

Although the employee was a member of a protected class and was not hired for the admissions counselor job, she failed to establish that she was qualified for the position because of her previous performance problems. **Even if she had established a *prima facie* case of gender discrimination, the university offered a legitimate nondiscriminatory reason for why she wasn't hired—poor job performance**. The employee did not offer any evidence that the university's proffered reason was pretextual. The court also rejected the employee's claim of retaliatory discharge. Even though her meeting with the Equal Opportunity Compliance officer was a protected activity, she failed to establish a causal connection between the meeting and the adverse employment decision. The court granted the university's motion for summary judgment. *Keenan v. State of Louisiana*, 985 F.Supp. 658 (M.D.La.1997).

◆   A Virginia school board eliminated 299 full-time administrative positions due to declining revenues. A female employee who lost her job sued the school board in the U.S. District Court for the Eastern District of Virginia alleging sex discrimination and retaliatory and constructive discharge under Title VII, and denial of her constitutional due process and equal protection rights. The court granted the board's summary judgment motion, observing that the board had presented overwhelming evidence that the decision was not based on sex discrimination. **The board had eliminated an equal number of men and women from positions in the employee's division indicating a neutral decisionmaking process**. The board had also presented evidence that the employee had poor communication skills. *Green v. Fairfax County School Bd.*, 832 F.Supp. 1032 (E.D.Va.1993).

B. Pregnancy Discrimination Act of 1979

The Pregnancy Discrimination Act of 1979, 42 U.S.C. § 2000e(k), an amendment to Title VII, prohibits employers from discriminating on the basis of pregnancy. The courts have held that the Act requires employers to treat pregnancy the same as any other disabling illness for purposes of health benefits programs and all other employment-related purposes. For example, if an employer's policy is to allow two months unpaid leave to employees with disabling illnesses, a pregnant employee must be granted two months unpaid leave. The Act requires only that pregnancy be treated the same as other disabilities. Some states grant more protection to pregnant employees. For other cases involving employee maternity and family leave, please see Chapter Five, Section IV., A.

◆   An Illinois high school teachers' association entered into a collective bargaining agreement with the board of education. The agreement prohibited pregnant teachers from taking sick leave for pregnancy-related disability and then taking maternity leave at the expiration of the sick leave. The collective bargaining agreement excluded maternity benefits from the sick leave bank. The government brought suit in a federal district court against the board of education and the teachers' association for violation of the Pregnancy Discrimination Act. **The court determined that the collective bargaining agreement provision allowing teachers to take sick leave in conjunction with any other leave exclusive of maternity leave did not violate the Pregnancy Discrimination Act as maternity leave was a gratuitous extra option**. However, it did determine that the sick leave bank provisions that automatically excluded maternity benefits discriminated against pregnant teachers who elected to utilize accumulated sick leave for a pregnancy-related disability. This clearly violated the Pregnancy Discrimination Act of Title VII. *U.S. v. Bd. of Educ. of Consol. High School Dist. 230,* 761 F.Supp. 519 (N.D.Ill.1990).

◆   After an Illinois teacher became pregnant, she requested to use the sick leave she had accumulated during her employment for a period of disability caused by her pregnancy, followed by a maternity leave that would last for the remainder of the school year. The superintendent responded by informing the teacher that **the collective bargaining agreement between the union and the school district barred teachers from taking maternity leave immediately following a period of disability for which they used sick leave**. Therefore, the teacher had to choose between using sick leave or maternity leave. After obtaining a right to sue letter from the EEOC, the teacher brought this action in a federal district court. The district court found in favor of the school district, and the teacher appealed to the U.S. Court of Appeals, Seventh Circuit.

The teacher alleged that the school district's leave policy violated the Pregnancy Discrimination Act by preventing women from using their sick leave for pregnancy-related disability, leading them to forego the use of accumulated sick days for what was likely to be the longest period of disability they would experience during their careers. She pointed out that when a teacher retired, the school district compensated the teacher for unused sick days at a lower rate than the teacher's per diem pay. This, she argued, resulted in teachers accumulating sick days that were worth less at retirement than if they were used during the teacher's career. She claimed that the school district's leave policy resulted in women who choose to have children accumulating a greater number of sick days than men or women who choose to forego childbirth. A statistical basis for this argument might have been established by showing that women who have been disabled due to pregnancy accumulated sick days at a higher rate per year of service than their male coworkers or women who have not experienced a pregnancy-related disability. However, the teacher offered evidence only on the absolute number of sick days women accumulated over their teaching careers. **This evidence failed to establish that the school district's leave policy had a disproportionate and adverse impact on women teachers who experience a pregnancy-related disability**. The court found in favor of the school district and determined that the policy did not have a disparate impact on women. *Maganuco v. Leyden Cmty. High School Dist. 212*, 939 F.2d 440 (7th Cir.1991).

C. Equal Pay Act

Enacted by Congress in 1963, the Equal Pay Act requires that employers pay males and females the same wages for equal work. The Act applies only to sex discrimination in pay, and thus racially-based equal pay claims must be litigated under the more general provisions of Title VII. Because the Equal Pay Act is part of the Fair Labor Standards Act, employees are protected by the Act as long as the employer is engaged in an enterprise affecting interstate commerce. The employee's burden of proof under the Act has been interpreted by the courts to require only that the jobs under comparison be "substantially" equal. Strict equality of the jobs under comparison is not required. The Act requires equal pay for jobs involving "equal skill, effort, and responsibility, and which are performed under similar working conditions, except where such payment is made pursuant to (i) a seniority system; (ii) a merit system; (iii) a system which measures earnings by quantity or quality of production; or (iv) a differential based on any other factor other than sex."

♦   A public school administrator asserted in a lawsuit filed in a North Dakota court that the school board voted not to renew her contract in violation of state law. **She claimed that the board president stated that "a woman can't handle [the administrator's] job," and that she was "a woman in a man's job."** Although the administrator was paid $37,200 in her last year of employment, the board hired a male to replace her at a salary of $60,000. It hired another male employee to help the replacement and paid him $46,500. The trial court rejected her claims, but the Supreme Court of North Dakota reversed. The parties then reached a settlement that preserved the administrator's right to pursue claims with the Equal Employment Opportunity Commission for gender discrimination and unequal pay. The EEOC issued the administrator a right-to-sue letter and she commenced a federal district court action against the school district. The district court dismissed the claims, ruling that they were barred by the settlement in the state court action.

The administrator appealed to the Eighth Circuit, which held that while her claims would normally be barred by the settlement, she had explicitly reserved her right to bring the EEOC claims that formed the basis for her federal lawsuit. The board president's comments provided sufficient evidence of discrimination to allow the case to go to trial. While stray remarks in the workplace do not constitute evidence of discrimination, the president's comments were not stray remarks. Instead, they directly related to the decision-making process. The president was the head of the decision-making body that had voted not to renew the contract. Since the president's remarks constituted direct evidence of discrimination, the administrator was entitled to the inference that the president influenced other board members to vote against the contract. The district did not argue that the male employees hired to replace the administrator performed additional duties that might justify higher salaries. **Because it was permissible to infer that she was paid less than male employees for performing the same work, there was evidence of an equal pay violation** that had to be considered by a jury. The circuit court reversed the summary judgment order and remanded the case. *Simmons v. New Public Sch. Dist. No. Eight*, 251 F.3d 1210 (8th Cir. 2001).

◆   A Kentucky school board adopted a new salary policy in response to a management audit which identified higher than average salaries among its administrators. It reduced the compensation paid to administrators from a maximum of 260 days per year to 240 days for existing employees (with a 10 percent bonus), and 220 days for new hires, with no bonus. The district hired an administrator at the 220-day limit. **She asserted that the board discriminated against her because her male predecessor had been paid at a higher rate of pay,** and she filed a federal district court action against the school board under the Equal Pay Act, Title VII, Title IX and other state and federal laws. The court granted the board's motion for judgment as a matter of law and the administrator appealed to the U.S. Court of Appeals, Sixth Circuit.

The court stated that the Equal Pay Act prohibits employers from paying opposite sex employees at dissimilar rates for performing similar work. Equal Pay Act analysis requires the complaining party to show that different wages are being paid to employees of the opposite sex for performing work requiring equal skill, effort and responsibility under the same working conditions. In this case, the school board claimed that the 220-day wage limit was based on budgetary reasons and not sex discrimination. However, the administrator offered evidence that none of the male employees hired under the 220-day policy had replaced predecessors who were paid at the higher rate, as she had. The board had also failed to reduce the 220-day policy to writing, and **there was evidence that it had chosen to cap the administrator's salary because of her gender**. The court vacated the district court judgment. *Buntin v. Breathitt County Bd. of Educ.*, 134 F.3d 796 (6th Cir.1998).

◆   **An employee of a private college in Massachusetts sued the college and various officials alleging that they discriminated against her on the basis of**

sex in setting her rate of pay. She claimed violations of Title VII, the federal Equal Pay Act and the Massachusetts Equal Pay Act. She also asserted that the college and its officials violated the statutes by retaliating against her for pursuing rights guaranteed by the laws. The officials moved to dismiss the complaints against them for failure to state a claim upon which relief could be granted. The U.S. District Court for the District of Massachusetts noted that eight circuit courts had addressed the issue of individual liability under Title VII, and that seven had rejected the idea. It agreed with this majority of circuit courts in finding that although a literal reading of the statute allows the imposition of liability on individual employees, Congress likely did not intend to impose individual liability under Title VII. However, under both the federal and state Equal Pay Acts, **the individual defendants could qualify as employers by virtue of their involvement in decisions affecting the employee's employment terms, conditions and compensation, and their relative operational control in the workplace**. Accordingly the court denied the motions to dismiss the Equal Pay Act claims against the individual defendants. *Danio v. Emerson College*, 963 F.Supp. 61 (D.Mass.1997).

D.　Sexual Harassment

Sexual harassment constitutes a form of sex discrimination that violates Title VII. Harassment creating a hostile work environment entails discriminatory behavior to the extent a reasonable person would find it hostile, as well as the victim's subjective perspective. See *Harris v. Forklift Systems, Inc.*, 510 U.S. 17, 114 S.Ct. 367, 126 L.Ed.2d 295 (1993).

◆　In 1998, the Supreme Court decided three sexual harassment cases. In the first, *Oncale v. Sundowner Offshore Services, Inc.*, 523 U.S. 75, 118 S.Ct. 998, 140 L.Ed.2d 201, **the Court held that same-sex harassment was protected by Title VII**. Accordingly, where an employee is "exposed to disadvantageous terms or conditions of employment to which members of the other sex are not exposed[,]" Title VII is violated. In the other two cases, *Burlington Industries, Inc. v. Ellerth*, 524 U.S. 742, 118 S.Ct. 2257, 141 L.Ed.2d 633, and *Faragher v. City of Boca Raton*, 524 U.S. 775, 118 S.Ct. 2275, 141 L.Ed.2d 451, **the Court held that Title VII allows the imposition of vicarious liability on employers for sexual harassment committed by their supervisors**. However, where no adverse action is taken against the employee (such as discharge or demotion), an affirmative defense is available. In such cases, the employer may be able to avoid liability by showing that it exercised reasonable care to prevent and promptly correct any sexual harassment, and that the employee unreasonably failed to avail herself of any employer remedies or otherwise avoid harm.

◆　A school district employee met with two male co-workers to review psychological evaluation reports from job applicants seeking employment with the district. She alleged that during one meeting, her supervisor read from a report that one applicant had commented to a co-worker, "I hear making love to you is like making love to the Grand Canyon," and that the supervisor then said, "I don't know what that means." According to the complaining employee, the other employee responded, "Well, I'll tell you later," and then both male employees chuckled. **The employee** asserted that **when she complained that this incident constituted sexual harassment, she was transferred to another position in retaliation**. The transfer took place 20 months after the alleged harassment. The employee obtained a right-to-sue letter and commenced a federal district court action against the school district. The court awarded summary judgment to the district and the employee appealed. The Ninth Circuit reversed, observing that the employee had a reasonable belief that the harassing incident violated Title VII and that the EEOC had issued its right-to-sue letter within three months of the job transfer, making summary judgment improper.

The U.S. Supreme Court accepted the district's petition for review concerning the question of the employee's reasonable belief that a Title VII violation had occurred. It held that no reasonable person could have believed that the single incident giving rise to the lawsuit violated Title VII. Sexual harassment is actionable only if it is so severe or pervasive as to alter the conditions of the victim's employment and create an abusive working environment. According to the Supreme Court, **simple teasing, offhand comments and isolated incidents that are not extremely serious will not amount to discriminatory changes in the terms and conditions of employment**. In this case, the employee's job required that she review the offensive statement. She conceded that it did not upset her to read the written remark in the applicant's file. Significantly, the supervisor's comment and the male employee's response was at worst "an isolated incident" that could not remotely be considered serious under recent Supreme Court precedents. The high court found "no causality at all" between the job transfer proposed by the school district and the employee's complaint. It noted that there must be a very close proximity in time between an employer's knowledge of an employee's protected conduct and an adverse employment action if this is the employee's only evidence of retaliation. The court reversed the Ninth Circuit's judgment, in effect reinstating the district court's summary judgment order for the school district. *Clark County School District v. Breeden*, 121 S.Ct. 1508, 149 L.Ed.2d 509 (2001).

◆   Two Texas elementary school teachers filed grievances against their principal, stating that he made sexual comments about them and consistently made obscene, profane and offensive comments to others. **They claimed that the principal began a campaign of harassment after the filing of the grievances** and within several weeks, the school board advised the teachers that their contracts would not be renewed. They filed a federal district court action against the school district and principal, asserting violations of Title VII of the Civil Rights Act of 1964, the Texas Human Rights Act and the First Amendment. The school district and principal moved to dismiss the case.

The court agreed with the district and principal that the teachers had never been required to exchange sexual favors for job benefits, resulting in dismissal of the claim for *quid pro quo* sexual harassment. However, **there was substantial evidence that the principal's comments created a hostile work environment**, and that portion of the Title VII claim was retained. The teachers had successfully argued that their First Amendment rights were implicated when the board voted not to renew their contracts on the heels of their sexual harassment claims. The court held that even a single decision by a school board may constitute an act of official government policy for the purposes of a constitutional violation. Title VII protects employees from retaliation for asserting their rights under the statute, and the retaliation claims against the principal and district were retained. *Matthews v. High Island Indep. School Dist.*, 991 F.Supp. 840 (S.D.Tex.1998).

◆ A mentally disabled custodian with a mild personality disorder and epilepsy worked for a Pennsylvania school district for eight years without problems. He was then subjected to physical and sexual harassment by two male co-workers. **The custodian endured severe harassment for several months before mentioning the harassment to his supervisor and quitting**. He filed a sexual harassment complaint against the school district with the U.S. Equal Employment Opportunity Commission (EEOC) and the state Human Relations Commission. The EEOC issued a right-to-sue letter, and the custodian filed a complaint against the district in a federal district court, asserting violations of Title VII. The district moved for summary judgment. The court held that a same-sex sexual harassment claim was permissible under Title VII of the Civil Rights Act of 1964, but required a showing that the harassment was based on the complaining party's sex. The court agreed with the school district that the harassment in this case had resulted from the custodian's vulnerability, not because of his sex. Although there were sexual overtones to the harassment, there was no evidence that any of the parties were homosexual. **The custodian failed to complain to a supervisor until the day before he quit, and because an employer cannot be liable for harassment of which it has no knowledge, the district was entitled to summary judgment**. *Ward v. Ridley School Dist.*, 940 F.Supp. 810 (E.D.Pa.1996).

III. RACE AND NATIONAL ORIGIN DISCRIMINATION

A. Title VII of the Civil Rights Act

◆ A black district employee was arrested for battery of his wife and a lewd assault on his six-year-old stepdaughter in 1979. He was arrested twice in 1995 for battery of his wife and aggravated assault of his son with a machete. While criminal charges were pending for the machete incident, a television station reported his child molestation incident. It also reported a 1977 incident involving a white employee in which the employee exposed himself to a group of young boys in a locker room, engaged in a graphic sexual discussion with them, and made homosexual advances. **The school board voted to discharge the black employee, but did not take action against the white employee**, who retired within one year. The black employee sued the board in federal district court for race discrimination. The court conducted a trial and found that the board had violated Title VII of the Civil Rights Act of 1964. It awarded the employee over $137,000 in lost wages and denied post-trial motions by the parties concerning unfavorable aspects of the decision.

The parties appealed to the 11th Circuit, which observed that **the board had offered legitimate, nondiscriminatory reasons for discharging the black employee, whose arrests were more frequent, recent and violent than those of the white employee**. When an employer offers nondiscriminatory reasons for an adverse employment action, the employee must cast doubt on the reasons to show that they were not the actual motivating force for the action. The employee failed to contradict the board's evidence that it was bound by a 1977 agreement not to discharge the white employee. The employees were not "similarly situated" for the purposes of a Title VII action. Although they were both arrested in the 1970s for lewd assaults on children, the white employee had only committed one other offense since then, a 1994 drunk driving charge. In contrast, the black employee was arrested three times for violent assault or battery against family members. Because the black employee failed to contradict the board's nondiscriminatory explanation for firing him, the court reversed and remanded the district court's decision. *Silvera v. Orange County School Bd.*, 244 F.3d 1253 (11th Cir. 2001).

◆   During the school year, **a black male teacher was reprimanded for violating a school corporal punishment policy and for showing his class an R-rated film**. A written evaluation outlined his deficiencies and the board placed him on an intensive assistance plan. The superintendent recommended that his contract not be renewed, but the board did not vote on the recommendation. The superintendent then falsely notified the teacher that the board had voted against renewing his employment, and a white female was hired to take the teacher's place. The teacher sued the board in a federal district court for race discrimination under Title VII of the Civil Rights Act of 1964 and 42 U.S.C. § 1981.

The court awarded summary judgment to the board and the teacher appealed to the Fifth Circuit, which agreed that he had made a *prima facie* case of race discrimination. The board responded with a legitimate, nondiscriminatory reason for failing to renew his contract, and the teacher was then required to show that the reason was pretextual. To show pretext by an employer, the complaining party's evidence must be substantial. A subjective belief that discrimination has occurred is insufficient. **The board had given a legitimate, nondiscriminatory reason for not renewing the teacher's contract based on his poor employment evaluation and inappropriate conduct**. The teacher admitted that the incidents had occurred and they justified nonrenewal. The superintendent's unlawful conduct and the board's assumption that he had the unilateral authority to terminate the employment of a nontenured teacher had no bearing on whether the contract nonrenewal was pretextual. Without evidence that the superintendent would be more tolerant of similar conduct by a white teacher, his allegedly racial comments at the time the teacher was hired did not establish a discriminatory motive. The court affirmed the judgment for the school board. *Auguster v. Vermilion Parish Sch. Bd.*, 249 F.3d 400 (5th Cir. 2001).

◆   Despite a teacher's inability to speak, read or write Chinese, a California school district employed her as a long-term substitute teacher for a fifth grade Chinese bilingual class. The district then replaced her with a Chinese-speaking substitute. The teacher filed a federal district court action against the school district and a number of school officials, **asserting that she had been replaced because of her age and race**. She later asserted that the district retaliated against her for filing the lawsuit by refusing to hire her for other long-term assignments, denying her probationary status and the possibility of gaining tenure. The court awarded summary judgment to the district and the teacher appealed to the Ninth Circuit.

The circuit court observed that the federal discrimination laws under which the teacher sued required proof of intentional discrimination. She had failed to produce specific and substantial evidence, instead relying on

speculation that the district had been motivated by discriminatory intent when it selected the Chinese-speaking substitute. The court found that her affidavit stating her belief about the reason for her replacement was unfounded, because it was not based on her own knowledge, but rather speculation. The court refused to consider a statement from the voluminous district court record that a school board official had told the teacher she could not gain employment so long as she maintained legal proceedings against the district. The teacher's attorney had failed to mention this evidence in opposition to the district's summary judgment motion and it was unavailable on appeal. Courts were not required to scour the record for any evidence that might support a party's argument, and the circuit court affirmed the summary judgment order for the district and officials. *Carmen v. San Francisco Unified School District*, No. 98-16555, 2000 WL 1946726, 2001 WL 38422 (9th Cir. 2001).

◆   The Virginia State Education Board enacted a mandate designed to reduce time spent in non-core subjects, such as physical education, art and music. In response, a school principal had to reallocate three full-time physical education teacher positions among the school's two nontenured teachers and one tenured physical education teacher. After retaining the tenured teacher full-time, **the principal split the remaining time into two three-quarters-time positions for both non-tenured teachers**. A white, nontenured physical education teacher claimed the principal's decision violated the Age Discrimination in Employment Act and Title VII of the Civil Rights Act of 1964. She asserted that the principal should have retained her as a full-time employee and reduced the other nontenured teacher to a half-time position because she was the senior of the two. The white teacher filed a federal district court action against the school board, which the court assigned to a federal magistrate judge. The magistrate agreed with the teacher, and the school board filed objections with the court, arguing it was entitled to summary judgment.

The court observed that the ADEA and Title VII employ the same analysis under *McDonnell Douglas v. Green*, 411 U.S. 792 (1973). The board had properly retained the tenured teacher in a full-time position, leaving only one and a half positions to allocate between the two nontenured employees. The principal's failure to consider other alternatives besides dividing the remaining one and a half positions evenly was not evidence of discrimination. Seniority considerations, while permitted, were not required, and the board's policy was "in accord with the extensive managerial discretion generally afforded school principals under Virginia law." The court rejected the employee's assertion that the principal's friendship and association with the other nontenured employee was evidence of discrimination. Although the two men attended the same church and social functions and had a friendship "rooted in their common race," this did not create a presumption that the principal's employment decisions were biased. **It is well established that cronyism, while unfair, is not the same as race discrimination under Title VII** or age discrimination under the ADEA. There was additional support for the decision to retain the other nontenured teacher in a three-quarters-time position, since doing so would avoid leaving some students without a supervisor for over one hour each day. It also allowed the district to keep a male supervisor for the boys' locker room at another school where the male teacher performed part of his daily work. The court rejected the magistrate's report and recommendation, and awarded summary judgment to the school board. *Dugan v. Albemarle County School Board*, 148 F.Supp.2d 688 (W.D. Va. 2001).

◆   An African-American high school teacher taught physical science, chemistry and physics and coached varsity soccer. The principal received complaints by students that he talked down to them and was hostile to them. Students and parents complained that he employed an unrealistic grading policy. After a number of incidents, the principal reassigned the teacher to a school with a poor reputation, where he allegedly assaulted a student. **The principal recommended the teacher's dismissal, based on an assault, his prior record of classroom profanity, and prior threats of harm to students**. The teacher resigned and sued the district for disparate treatment race discrimination.

A federal district court awarded summary judgment to the district and the teacher appealed to the Third Circuit, which found that the district court had overlooked adverse employment actions during the course of his employment by focusing only on the alleged constructive discharge. The circuit court observed that an adverse employment action may be something less than discharge and that transfers and demotions may establish pretext by the employer. The district court had erroneously granted summary judgment on the constructive discharge claim, but there was insufficient evidence to support the claim of pretext. **Because the teacher's evidence was unsupported, the school district was entitled to summary judgment on the Title VII and state law claims for race discrimination**. The court also found no evidence supporting the claims brought under 42 U.S.C. § 1981, and it affirmed the order for summary judgment. There was no evidence that the district had acted to retaliate against the teacher, and while it had taken a series of adverse actions against him, they had been taken in response to his unacceptable conduct. *Jones v. School Dist. of Philadelphia*, 198 F.3d 403 (3d Cir. 1999).

◆   A clerical employee who worked for a Louisiana school board for 18 years assumed some of the duties of an office services manager upon the retirement of another employee. The retired services manager earned about $12,000 more than the clerical employee. **She sought reclassification based upon her assumption of a number of the retired manager's duties** from the district superintendent, who did not process her repeated requests. When he was replaced by an African-American superintendent, he recommended upgrading her, but not to the same the level of the retired manager. The school board's personnel director, a white female, recommended against any upgrade. The employee quit her job and filed a federal district court action against the African-American superintendent, school board and certain employees, alleging race and sex discrimination in violation of Title VII of the Civil Rights Act of 1964. The court conducted a jury trial, which resulted in a judgment for the employee of $200,000 against the board, and $125,000 against the superintendent. It denied post-trial motions by the board, which then appealed to the Fifth Circuit.

The court stated that the case concerned the employee's entitlement to additional compensation for performing duties that went beyond her job description, not discrimination. **She was unable to link her complaints about compensation and reclassification with any evidence of race or sex discrimination**, and did not perform all of the retired manager's duties. Many had been phased out or reassigned to other employees. Moreover, the board did not fill the employee's position after she quit, lending support to its claim that there was no discrimination. Because there was no evidence of race and/or sex discrimination, the court reversed the district court decision. *Baltazor v. Holmes*, 162 F.3d 368 (5th Cir.1998).

❖   The school district of East Haven, located in a town with an African-American population of less than one percent, is a suburb of New Haven, a city with an African-American population of over 36 percent. The district had no black teachers and was perceived as being an employer that discouraged minority applications, although it sometimes used minority media resources to advertise jobs. **The NAACP and other interested groups sued the town**, asserting violations of Title VII of the Civil Rights Act of 1964, and **seeking an order that would require the town to enhance its minority recruiting efforts**.

The court observed that under Title VII, a complaining party must show that the application of a specific employment practice has created a discriminatory impact on a protected class of persons. Even though the complaining parties in this case did not identify any discriminatory practices by the town or school board, the court accepted their argument that the town's facially-neutral hiring practices had a substantial, negative impact on black applicants. **The town's failure to hire a single black teacher in an area with a substantial minority population created an inference of discrimination**. The perception of the town as being unfriendly to blacks was a significant factor that required it to implement an outreach program to increase the number of qualified black applicants for future employment. *NAACP v. Town of East Haven*, 998 F.Supp. 176 (D.Conn.1998).

B.   Affirmative Action

Generally, an affirmative action in employment plan voluntarily adopted by a school district will not result in unlawful reverse discrimination under Title VII if: 1) there exists a statistical disparity between the races or sexes in a given job category, or if the institution was guilty of discrimination in the past; 2) the affirmative action plan does not "unnecessarily trammel" the rights of nonminority employees; 3) the plan does not stigmatize nonminority employees; and 4) the plan is temporary in nature and is scheduled to terminate upon the achievement of a racially or sexually integrated work force. See *United Steelworkers of America v. Weber*, 443 U.S. 193 (1979), and *Johnson v. Transportation Agency*, 480 U.S. 616 (1987). However, school districts need to comply with the Equal Protection Clause as well as Title VII when devising affirmative action programs. To that end the U.S. Supreme Court struck down a no-minority-layoff (or "affirmative retention") clause in a teacher collective bargaining agreement in *Wygant v. Jackson Bd. of Educ.,* below. While such clauses generally are acceptable under Title VII, the Court held that the clause ran afoul of the Constitution.

❖   An affirmative action (or "affirmative retention") plan implemented by the Jackson, Michigan, Board of Education, called for the layoff of nonminority teachers with greater seniority than some minority teachers. **The district court ruled that the importance of providing minority teachers as "role models" for minority students as a remedy for past "societal discrimination" justified**

the layoff provision. The U.S. Court of Appeals, Sixth Circuit, affirmed the district court's decision and the nonminority teachers appealed to the Supreme Court. The Supreme Court reversed the lower courts' decisions and held that the nonminority teachers had been unfairly discriminated against in violation of the Equal Protection Clause.

The Court held that **clear and convincing evidence must be presented that the government entity in question engaged in past racial discrimination**. Similarly, the Supreme Court rejected the "role model" justification for retaining minority teachers (*i.e.,* minority children benefit from having minority teachers) on the ground that such a theory would allow racially-based layoffs long after they were needed to cure the ills of past discrimination. The majority held that even if the Jackson school board had sufficient justification for engaging in remedial or "benign" racial discrimination, layoff of white teachers was too drastic and intrusive a remedy. **While hiring goals and promotion policies favorable to minorities are acceptable under the Equal Protection Clause, the actual laying off of a certain race of employees was held unconstitutional**. "Denial of future employment is not as intrusive as loss of an existing job," observed the Court. The lower court rulings were reversed. *Wygant v. Jackson Bd. of Educ.,* 476 U.S. 267, 106 S.Ct. 1842, 90 L.Ed.2d 260 (1986).

◆   The University of Nevada hired minority faculty members under an unwritten affirmative action policy to rectify an imbalance in the faculty's racial composition. **A white female applicant was hired at a rate of pay $5,000 less than that offered to an African-American male applicant for a similar position**. The pay gap increased due to merit increases and she filed a complaint against the state university system in a Nevada district court for violation of the Equal Pay Act and Title VII. The court granted summary judgment to the university system on a bad faith claim made by the female instructor, but conducted a trial on the equal pay and Title VII claims. After a jury ruled that the applicant was entitled to $40,000 in damages, the court denied a motion to set aside the award. The university system appealed to the Supreme Court of Nevada.

The supreme court observed the tension between affirmative action goals and Title VII's prohibition on discriminatory employment practices. It cited U.S. Supreme Court cases approving of voluntary affirmative action plans which further Title VII's purposes through temporary measures that do not unnecessarily harm the rights of white employees and that avoid racial quotas. **The university's affirmative action plan did not violate Title VII because it was not strictly based upon race but allowed the university to make employment decisions on criteria including educational background, publishing history, teaching experience and areas of specialization**. The plan did not violate the Equal Pay Act because the university demonstrated a legitimate business reason for the wage disparity between the two employees. The university had a legitimate business-related reason for seeking a culturally diverse faculty. The court reversed the district court judgment. *Univ. and Community College System of Nevada v. Farmer,* 930 P.2d 730 (Nev.1997).

◆   Illinois State University (ISU) required employment applicants to pass a civil service examination, and its employment policies were regulated by the state universities' civil service system. A veterans' preference program awarded veterans points that could be added to their civil service test scores. This resulted in many veterans reaching the top of the ISU hiring register with higher than perfect scores. Minority applicants composed only 4.3 percent of the local labor force, and most of the veterans on the hiring register were white males. **ISU adopted a "learner program" to diversify its workforce by hiring short-term apprentices as building service workers. White males were excluded from the learner program** even though ISU's minority hiring rate was two to three times the local minority population. The U.S. Equal Employment Opportunity Commission (EEOC) prosecuted a discrimination charge on behalf of a white male applicant excluded from the program, forcing ISU to accept the applicant and other white males. The EEOC also brought an action in a federal district court asserting Title VII violations.

The court held that ISU had adopted the learner program solely to defeat the effect of the veterans' preference program. This constituted a pattern or practice of discrimination on the basis of race in violation of Title VII. **Because an affirmative action policy that is inconsistent with Title VII is impermissible, and because ISU was not required to hire more minorities to achieve racial balance, the program violated Title VII.** Although women were underrepresented as employees of ISU, the learner program had not been adopted to eliminate the imbalance, but to circumvent a lawful veterans' preference program. The court granted an order enjoining the exclusion of white males from the learner program. *U.S. v. Bd. of Trustees of Illinois State Univ.*, 944 F.Supp. 714 (C.D.Ill.1996).

C.   42 U.S.C. §§ 1981 and 1983

Section 1983 of the federal Civil Rights Act prohibits any "person" (including school districts) from depriving any other person of rights protected by the U.S. Constitution or federal statutes. For example, it is a violation of § 1983 for a school district to deprive a person of his or her Fourteenth Amendment right to equal protection of the laws, or any other federally protected right. Accordingly, the vast majority of lawsuits claiming constitutional violations are litigated under § 1983. The remedies available to a § 1983 plaintiff are broader than those available under many other statutes. While Title VII allows chiefly for back pay, reinstatement and attorneys' fees, § 1983 allows compensatory and punitive damages to be awarded in appropriate cases.

Section 1981 of the federal Civil Rights Act provides, among other things, that all persons will enjoy the same right to make and enforce contracts as "white citizens." A post-Civil War measure, § 1981 has been held by the U.S. Supreme Court to apply in the employment context. It applies to claims of discrimination on the basis of race or ethnic origin where a contract is involved. Unlike § 1983, § 1981 does not require that the discriminatory action be attributed to the state or a state actor; it applies equally to claims against public or private persons or entities.

◆   A white male was employed by the Dallas Independent School District (DISD) as a teacher, athletic director and head football coach at a predominantly black high school. After numerous problems, the principal recommended that the teacher be relieved of his duties as athletic director and coach. **The district's superintendent reassigned the teacher to a teaching position in another school where he had no coaching duties.** The teacher sued the school district and the principal, claiming that they had discriminated against him on the basis of race in violation of 42 U.S.C. §§ 1981 and 1983. A federal district court held in the teacher's favor. The U.S. Court of Appeals, Fifth Circuit, reversed in part and remanded, finding that the district's § 1981 liability for the principal's actions could not be predicated on a vicarious liability theory and that municipalities could not be liable for their employees' acts. The court noted that Congress did not intend that municipalities be subject to vicarious liability under § 1983. The teacher appealed to the U.S. Supreme Court.

The Supreme Court stated that a municipality may not be held liable for its employees' violations of § 1981 under a vicarious liability theory. The express "action at law" provided by § 1983 for the deprivation of rights secured by the Constitution and laws of the United States is the exclusive federal remedy for the violation of rights guaranteed by § 1981 when the claim is pressed against a state actor. The Supreme Court affirmed part of the court of appeals' decision and remanded the case in order to determine if the superintendent possessed policy-making authority in the area of employee transfer, and if so, whether a new trial was required to determine the DISD's responsibility for the principal's actions in light of this determination. *Jett v. Dallas Indep. School Dist.*, 491 U.S. 701, 109 S.Ct. 2702, 105 L.Ed.2d 598 (1989).

On remand, **the court of appeals observed that there was no evidence in the record that the principal or the superintendent had policymaking authority that would create liability**. Because it was inappropriate for a court to base liability upon the actions of officials who lacked final policymaking authority, there could be no liability placed upon the school district. The court reversed the judgment and remanded the case to the district court. *Jett v. Dallas Indep. School Dist.*, 7 F.3d 1241 (5th Cir.1993).

◆   The U.S. Supreme Court unanimously ruled that persons of Arab descent are protected from racial discrimination under § 1981 of the federal Civil Rights Act of 1866. This Pennsylvania case involved a college professor, born in Iraq, who was a U.S. citizen and a member of the Muslim faith. **The professor sued St. Francis College in U.S. district court under Title VII and § 1981 of the Civil Rights Act after St. Francis denied his tenure request**. The district court ruled that § 1981, which forbids racial discrimination in the making and enforcement of any contract, did not reach claims of discrimination based on Arab ancestry. The professor appealed. The U.S. Court of Appeals, Third Circuit, reversed. St. Francis appealed to the U.S. Supreme Court.

Section 1981 states that "[a]ll persons ... shall have the same right to make and enforce contracts ... as is enjoyed by white citizens. . . ." In affirming the court of appeals' decision, the Supreme Court noted that although § 1981 does not use the word "race," the Court has construed the statute to forbid all racial discrimination in the making of private as well as public contracts. The Court cited several dictionary and encyclopedic sources to support its decision that for the purposes of § 1981, Arabs, Englishmen, Germans and certain other ethnic groups are not to be considered a single race. Based on the history of § 1981 it concluded that Congress "intended to protect from discrimination identifiable classes of persons who are subjected to intentional discrimination solely because of their ancestry or ethnic characteristics." **If the professor could prove that he was subjected to intentional discrimination because he was an Arab, rather than solely**

because of his place of origin or religion, the lawsuit could proceed under § 1981. The court of appeals' decision in favor of the professor was affirmed. *St. Francis College v. Al-Khazraji*, 481 U.S. 604, 107 S.Ct. 2022, 97 L.Ed.2d 749 (1987).

◆   A white applicant interviewed for an assistant principal position at a Texas school where the ability to speak Spanish was considered mandatory. The applicant represented that she was bilingual, and the school principal recommended her to the district superintendent. When the superintendent learned that the applicant's Spanish skills were insufficient for the job, he withheld making a permanent appointment for the position. The applicant sued the school district, principal, superintendent and other officials in a federal district court for civil rights violations. The court refused to grant a summary judgment motion filed by the principal, ruling that any discriminatory motive held by the superintendent could also be imputed to the principal. The principal appealed to the U.S. Court of Appeals, Fifth Circuit. **The court of appeals held that qualified immunity shields government officials exercising discretion from individual liability where their conduct does not violate clearly-established statutory or constitutional rights of which a reasonable person would have knowledge**. The applicant had failed to allege any constitutional rights violation by the principal. The court rejected the district court's ruling that the superintendent's allegedly discriminatory actions could be imputed to the principal, since a racial discrimination claim under the Equal Protection Clause and 42 U.S.C. § 1983 must be supported by proof of intentional discrimination. Intent cannot be imputed vicariously. The court reversed and remanded the case. *Coleman v. Houston Indep. School Dist.*, 113 F.3d 528 (5th Cir.1997).

◆   A 54-year-old African-American teacher sought to become an elementary school principal. Although two vacancies were posted in district schools, she was not selected for either one. **She asserted that the school superintendent had failed to promote her for discriminatory reasons**, based on his statements that more male principals were needed in the district and that the district's present ratio of black and white principals should be preserved. She filed a race and sex discrimination complaint against the school board and superintendent in an Alabama federal district court, asserting violations of the Equal Protection and Due Process Clauses of the U.S. Constitution under 42 U.S.C. § 1983. The court denied the superintendent's summary judgment motion, and he appealed to the U.S. Court of Appeals, Eleventh Circuit.

The court stated that a school official is entitled to qualified immunity in a lawsuit unless the conduct alleged by the complaining party violates clearly-established law in a manner that a reasonable person would know was unlawful. **A government official cannot be held liable for violating an individual's equal protection rights without proof of the intent to discriminate**. In this case, the teacher's exclusive evidence of intent to discriminate had been the superintendent's comments. These were insufficient to raise an inference of the necessary intent to prove a constitutional violation. Because no reasonable person in the superintendent's position could have known that his conduct violated the teacher's clearly-established constitutional rights, the court reversed the district court judgment. *Mencer v. Hammonds*, 134 F.3d 1066 (11th Cir.1998).

D. State Statutes

◆   An African-American guidance counselor alleged that a principal told her in a meeting that she needed to "become more teachable." She construed the comment as a racial epithet. The principal memorialized the meeting a few days later, and explained that the "teachable" comment referred to her "inability to receive directions or advice 'without giving a retort.'" The memo directed her to meet with a counseling administrator to address her performance problems. The counselor replied in writing to the principal, explaining her position and stating that she was offended by the comment. The guidance counselor was placed on a plan of assistance to address her performance and the school board voted not to renew her contract. She sued school officials in a state trial court alleging race discrimination and violation of the New Jersey Conscientious Employee Protection Act (CEPA). **School officials moved the court for summary judgment, asserting that she failed to establish a *prima facie* case of race discrimination because they had replaced her with an African-American employee**. The trial court awarded summary judgment to the district, and the counselor appealed to the Superior Court of New Jersey, Appellate Division.

The court observed that in race discrimination cases, a *prima facie* case varies according to factual situations. Federal courts have struggled with the proper formulation of the fourth element of a discrimination case, which considers the employer's actions after the complaining party suffers an adverse action such as discharge. The U.S. Supreme Court has not yet faced the question of whether replacement of an individual by someone outside the protected class of employees is a required element of a discrimination claim. However, the U.S. Supreme Court held in an age discrimination case that "the fact that a replacement is substantially younger than the plaintiff is a far more reliable indicator of age discrimination than is the fact that the plaintiff was replaced by someone outside the protected class." **The appellate division court found that it would be unwise to require a plaintiff in an employment discrimination lawsuit to always establish replacement by a person outside the protected class of employees in order to establish a *prima facie* case of discrimination**. Despite the ruling favorable to the counselor's *prima facie* case, the court held that the circumstances did not indicate unlawful discrimination. The principal's comment about being unteachable did not connote racial hostility and depended on the counselor's subjective interpretation of the statement. The trial court had properly awarded summary judgment to the district on the discrimination claim. There was also no merit to the counselor's CEPA claim, and the court affirmed the judgment. *Williams v. Pemberton Township Pub. Schools*, 323 N.J.Super. 490, 733 A.2d 571 (App.Div.1999).

◆   The Chicago Board of Education adopted a desegregation plan in 1977 in response to pressure from the federal government to comply with Title VI of the Civil Rights Act of 1964. **The plan included certain employment protections for principals employed by the board** including advance notice of possible adverse action, protection of compensation rights and other due process protections. In 1980, the board and the U.S. government entered into a consent decree. The decree was approved by a federal district court and included many of the terms of the 1977 desegregation plan for eliminating race discrimination from the school system, but did not include the protective language for principals. **Many district principals were dismissed after the state legislature passed the School Reform Act of 1989,** which established local school councils in an effort to comprehensively reform city schools.

A number of principals who were dismissed under the school reform act asserted that the protections granted them in the 1977 desegregation plan still existed since the school board continued to mention the plan in its hiring bulletins and policy statements. They filed a federal district court action against the school board, claiming that it had violated the plan. The U.S. District Court for the Northern District of Illinois granted summary judgment to the board, and the principals appealed to the U.S. Court of Appeals, Seventh Circuit. **The court found that the 1980 consent decree was comprehensive and supplanted the 1977 desegregation plan, even though it made no specific reference to the due process rights of principals.** Since the principals were not entitled to further protection, the school board was entitled to summary judgment and the court affirmed the district court's judgment. *Ahern v. Bd. of Educ. of City of Chicago*, 133 F.3d 975 (7th Cir.1998).

IV. RELIGIOUS DISCRIMINATION

Discrimination on the basis of religion is also forbidden by Title VII. However, § 702 of Title VII, 42 U.S.C. § 2000e-1, exempts religious organizations from this command. The U.S. Supreme Court has held that an employer's duty under Title VII is discharged by making a reasonable accommodation of an employee's religious needs, but no duty to accommodate arises where it would work an undue hardship upon the employer.

◆   In a U.S. Supreme Court case, a Connecticut high school teacher sued his school district under Title VII. He belonged to a church that required members to refrain from secular employment during designated holy days. This required the teacher to miss approximately six school days each year for religious purposes. The district's collective bargaining agreement allowed only three days of paid leave for religious observation. The agreement also allowed three days paid leave for "necessary personal business" which, the district said, could not be used for religious purposes. **The teacher repeatedly asked to be granted permission to use three days of his "necessary personal business" leave for religious purposes.** He also offered to pay for a substitute teacher if the school board would pay him for the extra days that he missed. These alternatives were turned down by the school board. When all administrative alternatives were exhausted, he filed a lawsuit alleging that the school board's policy regarding "necessary personal business" leave was discriminatory on the basis of religion. A U.S. district court dismissed the teacher's lawsuit and he appealed. The U.S. Court of Appeals, Second Circuit, said that the school board was bound to accept one of the teacher's proposed solutions unless "that accommodation causes undue hardship on the employer's conduct of his business."

On appeal, the U.S. Supreme Court modified the appellate court's decision. It decided that the school district was not required to accept the teacher's proposals even if acceptance would not result in "undue hardship." **The school board was only bound to offer a fair and reasonable accommodation of the teacher's**

religious needs. The bargaining agreement policy of allowing three days paid leave for religious purposes, but excluding additional days of "necessary personal business" leave if needed for religious purposes, would *not* be reasonable, explained the Court, if paid leave was provided "for all purposes *except* religious ones." Because none of the lower courts had decided whether the "necessary personal business" leave policy had been administered fairly in the past, the case was remanded for a determination of that question. *Ansonia Bd. of Educ. v. Philbrook*, 479 U.S. 60, 107 S.Ct 367, 93 L.Ed.2d 305 (1986). On remand, it was determined that the accommodation was reasonable. *Philbrook v. Ansonia Bd. of Educ.*, 925 F.2d 47 (2d Cir.1991).

◆   An Idaho school administrator claimed that his school district conducted a reorganization by which he was the only employee who lost his job. He stated that he was Catholic, while most of his co-workers were members of the Church of Jesus Christ of Latter Day Saints. His replacement was a member of the Church of Jesus Christ of Latter Day Saints with lower financial management qualifications that his own and was allegedly paid a higher salary. The administrator alleged that the district was not in a financial position that required a reduction in force and that the consolidation of positions caused by the reorganization resulted in increased costs. He sued the district in a federal district court for religious discrimination under Title VII and the Idaho Civil Rights Act. The court awarded summary judgment to the district and the administrator appealed. **The Ninth Circuit found sufficient evidence of pretext by the district to avoid summary judgment on the religious discrimination claim**. While this aspect of the case was returned to the district court for further consideration, the court affirmed other trial court rulings in the district's favor. *White v. Blackfoot School Dist. No. 55*, No. 99-35820, 2001 WL 294028 (9th Cir. 2001).

◆   **According to a tenured teacher, an Illinois school board, through her supervisors, began to treat her unfavorably after she reported receiving anti-Semitic hate mail**. She reported receiving the mail to her supervisor and the police, who were able to identify some school employees as "prime suspects," but otherwise failed to close the incident. The teacher complained that the school board's investigation was inadequate and later claimed that the board responded by reassigning her to work under the supervision of one of the suspected perpetrators and then refused to transfer her. Although the teacher received an unsatisfactory performance rating with a remediation plan, she brought an internal appeal and succeeded in having the rating upgraded. After commencing EEOC charges against the school board, she initiated a federal district court action against the board, alleging she had been the victim of discrimination based on religion. The district court dismissed the case.

On appeal, the Seventh Circuit stated that a materially adverse action depends upon the particular fact situation and may include claims of failure to investigate harassment claims. The district court had improperly found that the alleged ineffective investigation could not adversely affect the teacher's employment. The district court had in effect insisted upon additional factual allegations of adverse harm. **According to the circuit court, it was likely that being assigned to work under a person considered a prime suspect in a hate mail incident affected the**

conditions of employment. The district court had also failed to recognize the board's refusal to transfer claim as an adverse employment action. Even though the teacher had successfully challenged the unsatisfactory employment rating and the threat of a remediation plan, this information had been reported to the state board of education and had the potential to affect tangible employment benefits. Because the district court had prematurely concluded that the teacher did not suffer any adverse employment action, its judgment was reversed and remanded. *Bernstein v. Bd. of Educ. of School Dist. 200*, 191 F.3d 455 (7th Cir.1999).

◆   After her first two years of employment for a Missouri school district, a second grade teacher wrote each of her students a letter referring to a magic rock. The letter included a rock that each student was to rub while saying positive statements about him or herself. After receiving complaints from local clergy members, the principal recommended to the school board that the teacher's contract not be renewed. **The board voted not to renew the teacher's contract, and she filed a federal district court action against the school district, claiming religious discrimination** in violation of Title VII of the Civil Rights Act of 1964. The court conducted a trial after which a jury returned a finding of religious discrimination, but the court denied the teacher's motion seeking reinstatement. Both parties appealed.

The Eighth Circuit held that a complaining party in a Title VII case may proceed under a mixed motive analysis by establishing that religion was a motivating factor in an adverse employment decision. Even though other motives may have existed, the trial court had properly allowed the case to proceed under the mixed motive analysis, and **there was sufficient evidence for the jury to find that the decision had been motivated by religious concerns**. Although reinstatement is the preferred remedy in unlawful employment termination cases, it is inadvisable where no working relationship may be reestablished between the school district and employee. The district court had properly denied reinstatement. *Cowan v. Strafford R-VI School Dist.*, 140 F.3d 1153 (8th Cir.1998).

◆   An Illinois elementary school custodian complained that certain staff members were trying to get rid of him. He exhibited behavior, including threats, which caused the school's principal to fear for her personal safety. The principal called a meeting with the employee, a union representative and the school district's personnel director. The custodian brought a Bible to the meeting, interrupting the meeting with references to it. After the meeting, **the district placed the custodian on a paid leave of absence pending a psychiatric examination**. A psychiatrist diagnosed the custodian with paranoid psychotic symptoms which could predispose an individual to violent behavior. The district later allowed the custodian to return to work.

The custodian filed a federal district court action against the district, asserting ADA and Title VII claims. The court rejected his argument that the psychiatric examination requirement violated the ADA. The district had shown that the examination was job-related and consistent with business necessity since there was concern for the safety of others at the elementary school. The ADA prohibits only medical examinations that are not job-related and does not prohibit an employer from inquiring into an employee's ability to perform job-related functions. **The Title VII claim was also baseless, since the district had never raised any issue**

of religious expression. The custodian failed to raise the issue by making religious references. The court granted the district's summary judgment motion. *Miller v. Champaign Community Unit School Dist.*, 983 F.Supp. 1201 (C.D.Ill. 1997).

◆   Two Texas school bus drivers belonged to a religious group that required abstention from work on the Sabbath and annual attendance at 10-day feasts in designated cities. **The school district accommodated the drivers' requests to attend the feasts for four years, allowing them to take a week off from work**. However, the following year, the district rejected their request for eight consecutive working days off, allowing them to take only five. The district fired the employees when they disregarded the notice and took an eight-day leave. They filed a lawsuit against the district in a federal district court, asserting Title VII and related claims. The court noted that an employer violates Title VII unless it is able to demonstrate that it cannot reasonably accommodate the employee's religious practice without undue hardship. **The court then stated that the decision to allow only five days off instead of eight did not reasonably accommodate the employees. However, there was substantial evidence that such an accommodation would have created an undue hardship**. The court granted the district's motion for summary judgment. *Favero v. Huntsville Indep. School Dist.*, 939 F.Supp. 1281 (S.D.Tex. 1996).

V. AGE DISCRIMINATION

The use of age as a criterion for employment is forbidden by federal law with respect to persons ages 40 and above. The Age Discrimination in Employment Act of 1967 (ADEA), 29 U.S.C. § 621 et seq., is part of the Fair Labor Standards Act. It applies to institutions which have 20 or more employees and which "affect interstate commerce." Also, the ADEA contains an exception allowing the use of age as an employment criterion "where age is a bona fide occupational qualification reasonably necessary to the normal operation of the particular business."

◆   The ADEA, originally enacted in 1967, prohibits employment discrimination against individuals because of their age. The Fair Labor Standards Amendments of 1974 extended the act's substantive requirements to the states. **The U.S. Court of Appeals, Eleventh Circuit, consolidated three Florida cases filed against public employers and found that Congress did not effectively abrogate Eleventh Amendment immunity when it amended the ADEA**. Two of the cases consolidated by the Eleventh Circuit involved actions by current and former university employees against public universities. The other case involved the Florida Department of Corrections. The Supreme Court agreed to hear the consolidated cases.

The court explained that the Eleventh Amendment prohibits federal suits against non-consenting states. Congress may abrogate state immunity only by making its intention unmistakably clear in statutory language, and only then as a valid exercise of constitutional authority. In this case, Congress had clearly stated its intent to abrogate Eleventh Amendment immunity by subjecting the states to potential liability for monetary damages in suits filed by individual employees.

However, the court held that Congress lacked the power to do so when it amended the ADEA in 1974. Under the applicable legal standard, the court determined the ADEA as amended was not appropriate legislation under Section 5 of the Fourteenth Amendment, because its substantive requirements were found disproportionate to any perceived unconstitutional conduct by the states. The amended ADEA was out of proportion to its supposed remedial objective because it purported to prevent discrimination that was not protected by the Equal Protection Clause. Congress identified no pattern of age discrimination by the states and had no reason to believe that state and local governments were unconstitutionally discriminating against their employees on the basis of age. Therefore, **Congress exceeded its authority under the 14th Amendment when it included state employees within the coverage of the ADEA.** *Kimel v. Florida Bd. of Regents*, 528 U.S. 62, 120 S.Ct. 631, 145 L.Ed.2d 522 (2000). ·

◆   Roger Reeves worked for Sanderson Plumbing for 40 years before being terminated. **Reeves filed suit under the ADEA, claiming the reason he was terminated was his age**. At trial, the company argued that it fired Reeves because he had failed to maintain accurate attendance records, but Reeves countered with evidence that his record-keeping was proper and, contrary to the company's assertions, he had never falsified any information. A jury agreed with Reeves, awarding him $98,000 in damages. On appeal, the Fifth Circuit found the evidence sufficient to show that Sanderson Plumbing's explanation for the termination was pretextual, but not enough to prove intentional discrimination. Although Reeves introduced additional evidence that the person who fired him said he "was so old [he] must have come over on the Mayflower," and that he "was too damn old to do [his] job," those comments were not made in the context of termination and could not prove intent. The circuit court directed the district court to enter judgment in favor of Sanderson Plumbing.

On appeal, **the U.S. Supreme Court concluded that once Reeves offered substantial evidence from which a jury could conclude that Sanderson Plumbing's explanation for the termination was not the real reason he was fired, the jury was then free to infer intentional discrimination and hold Sanderson liable**. According to the Supreme Court, the circuit court wrongly confined its review of the verdict to derogatory age-related comments that the director of Sanderson's manufacturing operations made to Reeves and to evidence that the director had singled Reeves out for harsher treatment than younger employees. The Fifth Circuit "believed that only this additional evidence of discrimination was relevant to whether the jury's verdict should stand," Justice O'Connor wrote for the majority. "In so reasoning, the Court of Appeals misconceived the evidentiary burden borne by plaintiffs who attempt to prove intentional discrimination through indirect evidence." The Supreme Court disagreed, finding the circuit court improperly discounted the record as a whole, ignoring critical evidence that the director treated an employee who was substantially younger than Reeves more leniently and that even though two other company officials joined him in the termination recommendation, the director had final authority over all company decisions. *Reeves v. Sanderson Plumbing Products*, 530 U.S. 133, 120 S.Ct. 2097, 147 L.Ed.2d 105 (2000).

♦   A Connecticut school district sought a part-time high school art teacher and stated that the appropriate candidate should have a degree in art education. A 64-year-old applicant held both bachelor's and master's degrees in art education. He had more than 21 years of teaching experience in high school art instruction and had worked for five years at a high school in the district prior to applying for the job. The board ultimately selected a 42-year-old applicant with four years of teaching experience and a bachelor's degree in fine arts. The teacher believed he had superior qualifications to those of the selected candidate and contacted school officials, who explained that he was considered the least qualified of those who participated in a second round of interviews. He then filed a complaint against the board with the Connecticut Commission on Human Rights and Opportunities. The board explained in CCHRO proceedings that the teacher was not selected for the position because he had interviewed poorly and was unfamiliar with teaching methods from the Connecticut Competency Instrument. **The teacher sued the board in a federal district court for violation of the Age Discrimination in Employment Act**, and for gender discrimination in violation of Title VI of the Civil Rights Act of 1964 and Title IX of the Education Amendments of 1972.

The court awarded summary judgment to the board and the teacher appealed to the Second Circuit, which noted that on paper, the teacher was more qualified for the position that the selected candidate. The selected candidate lacked the prerequisite art education degree and had far less teaching experience than the teacher. The search committee's credibility was brought into question by the need to relax its educational requirements and the assertion that a teacher with 21 years of experience lacked familiarity with basic teaching competencies, especially given his recent long-term employment by the board. The board's credibility was further tarnished by the revelation that none of the teaching candidates had been familiar with the Connecticut Competency Instrument. **The apparent destruction of the written screening committee ballots, which should have been maintained for two years under Title VII regulations, was by itself adequate grounds to deny the board's summary judgment motion**. This was true because the circumstances indicated that they might have been intentionally destroyed. The court reversed and remanded the case. *Byrnie v. Town of Cromwell, Bd. of Educ.*, 243 F.3d 93 (2d Cir. 2001).

♦   **The Gary Community School Corporation offered early retirement benefits** to teachers and administrators aged 58 to 61. Those who retired on their fifty-eighth birthday qualified for 48 months of benefits, and received continuing health insurance coverage. However, **benefits decreased for each month an employee delayed retiring until age 62, when eligibility for payments terminated**. Teachers and administrators who qualified for the incentive but chose to keep working after reaching age 58 filed an ADEA action against the school corporation in federal district court. The court determined that the employees were entitled to summary judgment on the question of liability, then conducted a trial after which it awarded them damages based on the amount of benefits they would have received had they retired at 58.

The school corporation appealed to the U.S. Court of Appeals, Seventh Circuit, which stated that the ADEA bars employers from discriminating against any person in the compensation, terms, conditions or privileges of employment due to age. An employer offering an early retirement incentive must make benefits available on nondiscriminatory terms. The court held that withholding an early retirement inducement on the basis of age was the type of discrimination that the ADEA was enacted to remedy. **The amount of available benefits varied according to age and no other factor, putting those employees over 58 at a disadvantage.** Although the ADEA permits "bridge" payments to help employees through a gap between early retirement and social security eligibility, the school corporation had not implemented the early retirement incentive with this intent. There was no merit to the corporation's argument that the employees were required to prove that it intended to discriminate against them. The circuit court substantially affirmed the district court decision. *Solon v. Gary Community School Corp.*, 180 F.3d 844 (7th Cir.1999).

◆   A New York school district and the association representing its teachers entered into a collective bargaining agreement providing for an early retirement incentive plan. Teachers attaining the age of 55 with at least 20 years of credited service in the state teacher's retirement system and with at least ten consecutive full years of service in the district were entitled to receive $12,500 in cash plus an amount equal to half of their accumulated sick leave. In order to accept the early retirement incentive, teachers were required to retire at the conclusion of the school year during which they became 55 by submitting a letter of resignation no later than January 1. **A group of teachers filed a federal district court action against the school board, claiming that the plan's eligibility requirements violated the ADEA.** The court dismissed as premature claims filed by teachers who had not yet retired and upheld the plan requirements under the ADEA. The teachers appealed to the U.S. Court of Appeals, Second Circuit.

The court affirmed the judgment dismissing the unretired teachers' claims since they were speculative. It disagreed with the district court's grounds for dismissing the ADEA claim, which had focused on seniority, not age. **The court noted that a 1990 ADEA amendment permits voluntary early retirement incentive plans that are consistent with the ADEA's purpose** of prohibiting age discrimination. In this case, the plan complied with the ADEA since it was voluntary, allowed teachers sufficient time to consider retirement and did not discriminate on the basis of age. The plan gave each teacher an opportunity to receive a cash payment without coercion. The court affirmed the judgment for the school board. *Auerbach v. Bd. of Educ. of Harborfields Central School Dist. of Greenlawn*, 136 F.3d 104 (2d Cir.1998).

◆   A Wisconsin technical college advertised for an instructor of psychology, listing the minimum criteria as a masters' degree in psychology with a sociology minor preferred. The college received 29 applications, of which the top 10 were numerically rated. Only the three highest-rated candidates received interviews. The fifth-rated applicant was a 55-year-old male with a doctorate degree in teaching with a psychology minor and relatively little teaching experience. **He claimed that the college's hiring practices were biased in favor of young women,** observing that the three top-ranked candidates were all women and that only one was over 40. He sued the college in a federal district court for violations of federal age discrimination laws. The court entered summary judgment for the college, and the applicant appealed to the U.S. Court of Appeals, Seventh Circuit. The court agreed with the applicant that it was only necessary for him to show some evidence that the college's reasons for rejecting his application were pretextual. However, **his presence among the job finalists undermined his age discrimination theory, and although there were irregularities in the college's hiring policies, there was no evidence of discrimination**. The court affirmed the summary judgment order for the college. *Senner v. Northcentral Technical College*, 113 F.3d 750 (7th Cir.1997).

◆   An Illinois speech language pathologist worked for a school district for 30 years. She considered an early retirement incentive program enacted by the state legislature that allowed teachers and administrators over the age of 50 to receive extra pension credit. Although she met the program's eligibility requirements, she was only interested in retiring if she could continue to work for the district in some capacity. She negotiated for part-time work, but the district never made an official commitment to rehire her. **She accepted the early retirement incentive at the last possible opportunity after filing an application for part-time work and indicating her willingness to work after retiring**. Although the district hired several younger employees as speech language pathologists for the following school year, it did not contact the retiree.

She filed a federal district court action against the school district for age discrimination and the court considered a summary judgment motion by the school board and named officials. The court found some evidence that the school district's refusal to consider the retiree as a part-time employee was based on its perception of older employees as short-term workers who could not be depended upon for a commitment to the district. The court also found evidence that the district was continuing to deny her request for part-time work in retaliation for filing an age discrimination complaint against it. **Because there was a genuine issue of fact concerning the district's motivation for failing to rehire the retiree as a part-time worker, the court denied the summary judgment motion by the school board and officials**. *Kastel v. Winnetka Bd. of Educ., Dist. 36*, 975 F.Supp. 1072 (N.D.Ill.1997).

◆   An Indiana high school teacher/football coach filed an age discrimination complaint against his local education agency. The parties settled, but the coach later claimed that the agency retaliated against him for filing the complaint by giving him poor employment performance reviews. He asserted that the agency's conduct created a hostile work environment in violation of the ADEA. He filed a lawsuit against the agency and several other employees in the U.S. District Court for the Northern District of Indiana, which considered dismissal motions filed by the defendants. **The court refused to dismiss the teacher's hostile work environment lawsuit. Such a lawsuit was permissible under the ADEA because the conditions alleged by the teacher suggested that a hostile environment existed**. EEOC regulations require employers to maintain a work environment that is free of harassment. The court then granted summary judgment motions filed by two administrative employees who could not be found liable for the harassment. The court allowed the teacher to seek compensatory damages, but held that the ADEA did not permit an award of punitive damages. The court also dismissed the teacher's state law complaint for intentional infliction of emotional distress. *Eggleston v. South Bend Community School Corp.*, 858 F.Supp. 841 (N.D.Ind.1994).

VI. DISABILITY DISCRIMINATION

A. Rehabilitation Act of 1973

Section 504 of the Rehabilitation Act of 1973 prohibits any employer who receives federal funding from discriminating against an "otherwise qualified individual with a disability." Section 504 provides that no otherwise qualified individual with a disability shall, solely by reason of his or her disability, be denied employment. An otherwise qualified person with a disability is one who can perform the "essential functions" of the job "with reasonable accommodation" of the person's disability by the employer. Employers are relieved of the duty to reasonably accommodate if to do so would create undue hardship.

◆   The U.S. Supreme Court ruled that tuberculosis and other contagious diseases are to be considered disabilities under § 504 of the Rehabilitation Act. The law defines an individual with a disability as "any person who (i) has a physical or mental impairment which substantially limits one or more of such person's major life activities, (ii) has a record of such impairment or (iii) is regarded as having such an impairment." It defines "physical impairment" as disorders affecting, among other things, the respiratory system and defines "major life activities" as "functions such as caring for one's self ... and working." **The case involved a Florida elementary school teacher who was discharged because of the continued recurrence of tuberculosis.** The teacher sued the school board under § 504 but a U.S. district court dismissed her claims. The U.S. Court of Appeals, Eleventh Circuit, reversed the district court's decision and held that persons with contagious diseases fall within § 504's coverage. The school board appealed to the U.S. Supreme Court.

The Supreme Court ruled that tuberculosis was a disability under § 504 because it affected the respiratory system and the ability to work (a major life activity). The school board contended that in defining an individual with a disability under § 504, the contagious effects of a disease can be distinguished from the disease's physical effects. However, the Court reasoned that the teacher's contagion and her physical impairment both resulted from the same condition: tuberculosis. **It would be unfair to allow an employer to distinguish between a disease's potential effect on others and its effect on the employee in order to justify discriminatory treatment.** Allowing discrimination based on the contagious effects of a physical impairment would be inconsistent with the underlying purpose of § 504. The Supreme Court remanded the case to the district court to determine whether the teacher was "otherwise qualified" for her job and whether the school board could reasonably accommodate her as an employee. *School Board of Nassau County v. Arline*, 480 U.S. 273, 107 S.Ct. 1123, 94 L.Ed.2d 307 (1987).

On remand, the Florida federal district court held that the teacher was "otherwise qualified" to teach. **The teacher posed no threat of transmitting tuberculosis** to her students. The court ordered her reinstatement or a front-pay award of $768,724 representing her earnings until retirement. *Arline v. School Bd. of Nassau County*, 692 F.Supp. 1286 (M.D.Fla.1988).

◆   **A Connecticut fourth grade teacher was arrested for possession of co-caine and drug paraphernalia. He avoided felony charges by receiving accel-erated rehabilitation**. His school district notified him his employment contract would be terminated for moral misconduct and conduct which seriously compro-mised his effectiveness as a role model and employee. The teacher requested a hearing and admitted drug possession. Although the hearing officer recommended reinstatement for the following school year, the school board voted to terminate his contract for moral misconduct and other good and sufficient cause. The teacher appealed to a Connecticut superior court, which held that he was unprotected by § 504 of the Rehabilitation Act because he had not been discharged for a reason solely related to his disability. The teacher appealed to the Appellate Court of Connecticut.

The court observed that § 504 of the Rehabilitation Act requires a complaining party to prove that he is otherwise qualified for the position sought and is being rejected solely by reason of a disability. **Although prior substance abuse may be recognized as a disability under the Rehabilitation Act in some cases, having a disability alone is not enough to gain protection under the act**. In this case, the teacher could not show that his discharge had been solely because of his disability, since he had been arrested and charged with felonious activity that would have disqualified him from his employment despite his disability. The school board had not abused its discretion by characterizing his illegal activities as moral misconduct and by ruling that they were unprotected under federal law or the state constitution. The court affirmed the judgment for the board. *Gedney v. Bd. of Educ. of Town of Groton*, 47 Conn.App. 297, 703 A.2d 804 (1997).

◆   A clerical employee of the University of Arizona had carpal tunnel syndrome and myofascial pain syndrome, which prevented her from performing her heavy word processing duties. **She became unable to perform her work despite accommodations provided by the university and requested reassignment to a position with less word processing work**. The university considered the transfer request under its general personnel policy by requiring her to go through a competitive hiring process. She was not reassigned and the university discharged her. She filed a federal district court action against the university for violations of the Americans with Disabilities Act (ADA), § 504 of the Rehabilitation Act and Arizona law. The court considered cross-motions for summary judgment by the parties, and rejected the university's claim that the ADA does not mandate affirmative action efforts by employers.

The court held that the ADA and § 504 are comprehensive antidiscrimination laws designed to prohibit discrimination on the basis of disability through the requirement of reasonable accommodation. Reasonable accommodation, contrary to the university's claim, requires employers to evaluate possible ways to structure work for individuals with disabilities. **The university had failed to demonstrate that it had conducted any analysis to determine whether reassignment of the employee was reasonable and whether it presented an undue hardship** to the university. Because undue hardship was the university's only possible defense for failing to make a reasonable accommodation in this case, the employee was entitled to summary judgment. *Ransom v. State of Arizona Bd. of Regents*, 983 F.Supp. 895 (D.Ariz.1997).

◆   A disabled part-time instructional aide at an Ohio community college experienced problems with his supervisor and coworkers. **He stated that they demonstrated negative attitudes toward his disability, and he complained that one coworker called him names and made offensive statements about him** to her class. The community college responded by transferring his supervisor to another office and admonishing the coworker against making derogatory comments. The community college had a policy of limiting its part-time employees to 1,040 hours of work during each fiscal year. The instructional aide and several coworkers were laid off after exceeding the hour limit. The aide filed a complaint with the U.S. Department of Education, Office for Civil Rights, which investigated the matter and determined that it was without merit. The aide nonetheless filed a lawsuit in a federal district court against the college under § 504 of the Rehabilitation Act of 1973.

The U.S. District Court for the Northern District of Ohio stated that in order to prevail in a discrimination claim for hostile work environment under the Rehabilitation Act, the complaining party must demonstrate repeated discriminatory conduct by a defendant that is tolerated and condoned by management. In this case, **the aide's supervisors had taken corrective measures in response to his complaints. Accordingly, there was insufficient evidence of a hostile work environment.** The court also held that the layoff action had not been discriminatory because there was evidence that the aide had exceeded the permitted number of hours for part-time employees and this was a legitimate reason for the layoff. The court granted summary judgment to the community college. *Spells v. Cuyahoga Community College*, 889 F.Supp. 1023 (N.D.Ohio 1994). The U.S. Court of Appeals, Sixth Circuit, affirmed the district court decision. *Spells v. Cuyahoga Community College*, 51 F.3d 273 (6th Cir.1995).

◆   The Omaha School District demoted two diabetic school van drivers to van aide positions at lower pay rates. The drivers sued the school district in the U.S. District Court for the District of Nebraska, claiming violations of § 504 of the Rehabilitation Act of 1973, 29 U.S.C. § 794. The court granted motions to dismiss the lawsuit, and the drivers appealed to the U.S. Court of Appeals, Eighth Circuit. **The court of appeals held that the drivers had shown that their disabilities could be reasonably accommodated and that they were at low risk for hypoglycemic episodes.** Because they had demonstrated a material fact issue under the Rehabilitation Act, summary judgment was inappropriate.

On remand, the district court determined that the drivers were Type II insulin-using diabetics who had an appreciable risk of developing hypoglycemic symptoms without warning. Because this constituted a danger to students and others using public roads, there was no reasonable accommodation that could be offered by the school district. Accordingly, the Rehabilitation Act afforded no protection to the drivers. The drivers appealed again to the Eighth Circuit, which found that the district court's factual findings were not clearly erroneous. **Because hypoglycemia created an increased risk of sudden and unexpected vision loss and loss of consciousness, the district court's decision that the van drivers presented a danger to themselves and others was supported by the evidence.** The court of appeals affirmed the district court's judgment. *Wood v. Omaha School Dist.*, 25 F.3d 667 (8th Cir.1994).

B. Americans with Disabilities Act

The Americans with Disabilities Act (ADA) expands disability coverage to most employers with at least 15 employees in both public and private institutions. The same legal analysis used in § 504 Rehabilitation Act cases applies to ADA cases. In 1998, the Supreme Court held that a person who was HIV-positive was entitled to the protections of the ADA despite the fact that she was not yet symptomatic. *Bragdon v. Abbott*, 524 U.S. 624, 118 S.Ct. 2196, 141 L.Ed.2d 540.

◆   In two ADA disability cases decided during the 1998-99 term, **the Supreme Court concluded that the question of whether an impairment is "substantially limiting" as defined by the ADA should be made with reference to any mitigating measures**. This holding expressly contradicts established EEOC guidelines. In the first case, twin sisters with uncorrected vision of 20/200 or worse but corrected vision of 20/20 or better were denied jobs as global airline pilots with a commercial airline because their uncorrected vision did not meet the airline's minimum uncorrected vision standard. The sisters filed an ADA claim against the airline, which was dismissed by a federal district court. On appeal, the U.S. Court of Appeals, Tenth Circuit, affirmed.

The Supreme Court agreed with the lower court decisions, finding the sisters had not demonstrated they were disabled under the ADA. The court stated that mitigating measures had to be taken into account when evaluating whether an individual was disabled, and that, **because glasses or contacts corrected the sisters' vision to 20/20 or better they were not substantially limited in a major life activity**. The sisters were also not regarded as disabled, as there was no evidence that the airline perceived them as substantially limited in a major life activity. *Sutton v. United Airlines, Inc.,* 527 U.S. 471, 119 S.Ct. 2139, 144 L.Ed.2d 450 (1999).

In the second case, the Supreme Court concluded that a mechanic with high blood pressure who was fired from his job was not disabled under the ADA. **Because the mechanic was able to control his high blood pressure with medication, he was not substantially limited in a major life activity**. The court did not address the issue of whether the mechanic would be considered disabled while taking his medication. The mechanic was also not regarded as disabled. At most, the employer regarded the mechanic as unable to perform the job of mechanic because it believed his high blood pressure exceeded the U.S. Department of Transportation's requirements for drivers of commercial motor vehicles. *Murphy v. United Parcel Service, Inc.,* 527 U.S. 516, 119 S.Ct. 2133, 144 L.Ed.2d 484 (1999).

◆   Congress exceeded its authority by allowing monetary damage awards against the states in Americans with Disabilities Act cases, according to a U.S. Supreme Court decision. The Court held that Congress did not identify a history and pattern of irrational employment discrimination against individuals with disabilities by the states when it enacted the ADA, and therefore, states were entitled to Eleventh Amendment immunity from such claims. As a result, **two state employees were unsuccessful in their attempt to recover money damages under the ADA from their state employer for disability discrimination they claimed to have been subjected to**. *Board of Trustees of University of Alabama et al. v. Garrett et al.,* 531 U.S. 356, 121 S.Ct. 955, 148 L.Ed.2d 866 (2001).

❖   A groundskeeper severely injured her leg while on the job. She obtained a limited return-to-work release. **The district's employment director rejected her return to work under these restrictions, stating, "[W]e don't take limited releases."** The district allowed the groundskeeper to take 100 days of unpaid leave, but declined her request to use 23 days of unused vacation and sick leave, despite a district policy permitting this usage. The director then asked for the groundskeeper's resignation, stating that the groundskeeper could apply for re-employment if she obtained a full release. The groundskeeper resigned, and three weeks later obtained a full work release. The district repeatedly turned her down for open groundskeeping and maintenance positions. She sued the school district in federal district court under the ADA. The court awarded summary judgment to the district on the claims of discrimination on the basis of disability and denied the district's motion for summary judgment on the groundskeeper's claim that the district discriminated against her because it regarded her as disabled. A jury awarded the groundskeeper more than $237,000 in damages, but the court granted a post-trial motion by the district for judgment and a new trial.

The groundskeeper appealed to the U.S. Court of Appeals, Ninth Circuit, which found that the district court improperly drew inferences in the district's favor and made credibility determinations that only the jury was entitled to make. There was sufficient evidence to support the belief that the district considered the groundskeeper to be disabled. A jury verdict must be upheld if supported by substantial evidence. There was undisputed evidence that the district turned the groundskeeper down for re-employment 13 times after she obtained a full return-to-work release. **The district's policy against "partial releases" was itself a violation of the ADA and discriminated against individuals with disabilities**. A "fully healed" policy permitted employers to avoid the ADA's individual assessment requirement, which requires a determination of whether an applicant is able to perform the essential functions of a job either with or without reasonable accommodation. The jury was entitled to conclude that the director's explanations were a pretext for unlawful discrimination, and the district court committed error by granting the school district's post-trial motion. The Ninth Circuit reversed and remanded the case for entry of a judgment consistent with the jury verdict. *Johnson v. Paradise Valley Unified Sch. Dist.*, 251 F.3d 1222 (9th Cir. 2001).

❖   When the immediate supervisor of a Chicago School Board health services administrator learned that a district bus driver had died of meningitis, she instructed her staff "to go into a crisis intervention mode," expecting a tremendous media and public inquiry. The administrator failed to show up for a staff meeting called by her supervisor and called in sick the following three days. **The administrator met with a physician who diagnosed her as having anxiety and hypertension-new onset** and recommended that she take several weeks off from work. The supervisor met with the district's chief of specialized services, characterizing the administrator's conduct as abandonment of her responsibilities during a crisis, and citing her for failing to personally contact her to arrange for others to cover her responsibilities during the crisis. The administrator met with the chief but refused to provide her with the physician's phone number, stating that she had no right to speak with him. **The chief discharged the administrator for insubordination** and the administrator sued the school board in a federal district court for discrimination in violation of Title VII of the Civil Rights Act of 1964 and the Americans with Disabilities Act.

The board moved for summary judgment, arguing that the administrator was discharged for her absence during the meningitis crisis and for failing to contact her supervisor to explain her condition and arrange for the completion of her work by other employees. The court stated that an employer need only supply an honest answer to defeat a Title VII claim for discrimination where an employee claims to have been discharged for pretextual reasons. It is unnecessary for the employer's reason to be reasonable. The administrator failed to show that she was fired for anything but insubordination. She did not show that her high blood pressure and anxiety substantially limited any major life activity. **The court found that the administrator was not a person with a disability as defined by the ADA, and determined that the board's reasons for discharging her were not character-ized by pretext**. The board's motion for summary judgment was granted. *Lee v. Chicago School Reform Board of Trustees*, No. 00 C 178, 2001 WL 709455 (N.D.Ill. 2001).

♦   After a seven-year employee was observed drinking beer while on duty at an elementary school, he was allowed to keep his job under a "last chance agreement" requiring him to complete an alcohol rehabilitation program, accept a four-week suspension without pay and submit to alcohol and drug testing upon request for two years. The district later rejected the employee for a part-time bus driver/garage worker position, even though he was the most senior applicant. He filed a grievance under the collective bargaining agreement between his union and the district and won the position. **An arbitrator found that the board did not demonstrate that the employee posed a safety threat**. The board appealed to an Ohio trial court, which reversed and vacated the arbitration award. The Ohio Court of Appeals reversed that decision and reinstated the arbitrator's award, finding that the arbitrator had carefully balanced the competing concerns of safety and seniority.

The employee sued the board in a federal district court, asserting violations of federal and state laws prohibiting disability discrimination. The court awarded summary judgment to the board and the employee appealed to the Sixth Circuit, which noted that his request to be awarded the jobs he sought was now moot. The only issue was whether he should receive compensatory and punitive damages, including back pay due to discrimination. The court found that in order to prevail under the ADA, the employee was required to show that he had a disability, was otherwise qualified to perform the essential functions of the job, suffered an adverse employment action and was replaced by a nondisabled person. The district court awarded summary judgment to the board because it found that the employee had no disability, whether perceived or real. The circuit court held that there was a distinction between taking an adverse job action for unacceptable misconduct and taking action solely because of a disability, even if the misconduct was caused by the disability. **An employer may hold an alcoholic employee to the same performance and behavior standards to which it holds other employees**. The circuit court agreed with the board, ruling that the ADA did not protect the employee from his own bad judgment and did not force the board to hire him as a school bus driver. There was a serious risk that he would drink on the job again and subject the board to potential liability. The court affirmed the district court's judgment. *Martin v. Barnesville Exempted Village School District Bd. of Educ.*, 209 F.3d 931 (6th Cir. 2000).

◆   A school librarian was diagnosed with tinnitus, a condition that caused him to hear continuous loud ringing and often caused nervousness and agitation. The school board promoted him several times. In 1994, the librarian was promoted to the position of Coordinator of Media Center, Testing and Research. **Soon after the librarian was promoted, his tinnitus worsened, and he sought a transfer to an environment with more background noise**, since sufficient ambient or background noise masked the ringing sound. The superintendent of schools denied the librarian's request, but offered to allow him to close his door and play music, place a television in his office, or move his office to a noisier area. He rejected each of these proposals and took sick leave for the remaining four months of the school year. The board eliminated his position due to budget cuts, and he eventually accepted a transfer to an elementary school librarian position that resulted in a pay decrease. He then sued the school board in a federal district court for employment discrimination under the ADA. The court granted summary judgment to the board on the grounds that it had provided the librarian with a reasonable accommodation.

He appealed to the U.S. Court of Appeals, asserting that the board had discriminated against him by not transferring him to any vacant principal or assistant principal positions and by failing to engage in the informal, interactive process for identifying reasonable accommodations contemplated by the ADA. The circuit court noted that the librarian had received over a year of paid sick and sabbatical leave, as well as numerous options for creating more background noise. The board had also employed him in a new position and transferred him to an elementary school where there was sufficient noise to accommodate his disability. **The ADA does not require an employer to give an employee with a disability a job of choice or a promotion as a reasonable accommodation**. The librarian failed to demonstrate any discriminatory motive by the school board in transferring him and failing to offer him employment as a principal or assistant principal. The circuit court affirmed the order for summary judgment. *Allen v. Rapides Parish School Bd.*, 204 F.3d 619 (5th Cir. 2000).

◆   When the behavior of a long time Michigan teacher drastically changed, his employing school board began to informally evaluate his fitness for teaching. A psychologist determined that the teacher had a possible psychiatric disorder that justified formal assessment. The superintendent recommended suspending the teacher pending mental and physical exams. The teacher failed to participate in the requested exams, and the board discharged him for misconduct and insubordination. The state tenure commission modified the punishment to a three-year suspension without pay. The teacher brought an unsuccessful action against the board in the state court system that was resolved in the board's favor. The teacher then sued the school district and superintendent in a federal district court for disability discrimination under the ADA and state law. **The teacher asserted that the board regarded him as disabled and had illegally suspended him for refusing to submit to mental and physical examinations** to determine his fitness for duty. The district court awarded summary judgment to the district.

The teacher appealed to the Sixth Circuit, which observed that in order to succeed in a disability discrimination case, the teacher would have to show that the district treated him as having an impairment that substantially limited one or more major life activities, that he was otherwise qualified to teach, and that he was suspended because the district regarded him as having a disability. According to the court, **an employer must be able to determine the cause of aberrant employee behavior. Requiring the employee to see a psychologist before returning to work did not violate the ADA**. A request for examination does not meet the ADA threshold for perceived disability because it does not prove that the employer perceives that the employee has an impairment that substantially limits a major life activity. Since inability to perform a particular job does not constitute a substantial limitation of a major life activity, deterioration of performance at a single job cannot constitute disability under the ADA. While post-hiring demands for examinations can only be made where they are job-related and consistent with business necessity, the examinations ordered for the teacher met the standard established by the ADA and EEOC regulations. Since the reasons supporting the board's request for the examinations were reasonable, the request was not an adverse job action and did not prove discrimination. The board offered legitimate, nondiscriminatory reasons for the action, and the court affirmed the judgment for the school district and superintendent. *Sullivan v. River Valley School Dist.,* 197 F.3d 804 (6th Cir.1999).

◆   A teacher was the department head for foreign languages at a district high school for nine years, during which she engaged in an ongoing dispute with three teachers under her supervision. The school administration recommended that the teacher be removed because of her inability to resolve departmental problems. **The teacher attributed the escalating dispute and the resulting employment action to disability discrimination** on the basis of her morbid obesity and sued the school board in a federal district court.

Although she alleged that her condition prevented her from walking quickly or for long distances, the court held that she was not disabled within the meaning of the ADA and was therefore not protected by it. The court awarded summary judgment to the board and the teacher appealed to the U.S. Court of Appeals, Fourth Circuit. The court rejected the teacher's claim that school administrators retaliated against her for asserting her rights under the ADA. It accepted the board's explanation that the adverse employment action was taken because of the unresolved conflict between the teacher and her subordinates. **The circuit court also agreed with the district court that the teacher's morbid obesity was not a disability as defined by the ADA**. The district court decision was affirmed. *Pepperman v. Montgomery County Bd. of Educ.*, 201 F.3d 436 (4th Cir. 1999).

◆   After 10 years of working at a particular high school, a teacher was placed on a remediation plan under which she was subject to further evaluations. She completed two semesters of work under the plan, and then took sick leave after receiving unsatisfactory marks. **The teacher was diagnosed as having a clinical depressive disorder and took a one-year medical leave** under a plan that required her to complete the remediation plan upon her return. When the teacher sought to return to work, she requested a transfer to another district facility, based on her psychiatrist's finding that her condition would deteriorate if she returned to a stressful situation. Another counselor wrote the district a letter attributing the teacher's depression to the "toxic state of relationship" between the teacher and school administrators. The district refused to grant her request for a transfer and she sought other employment.

She then commenced a federal district court action against the school district, alleging discrimination in violation of the ADA.

The court stated that in order to establish a disability under the ADA, the employee claiming ADA protection must have a known physical or mental limitation that limits a major life activity. The teacher claimed that depression limited her major life activities, including work. The court stated that the presence of a disability alone is insufficient to establish ADA coverage. Even if the teacher showed that she had depression, she did not advance any evidence that her clinical disorder substantially limited her ability to work. The court rejected the teacher's assertion that she was entitled to the reasonable accommodation of a job transfer because the high level of stress at the school exacerbated her condition. This demonstrated that she was only prevented from working at her assigned school. **Many courts have rejected claims by employees asserting that job-related stress caused them to be disabled under the ADA. The ADA applies only where the individual is prevented from working in a wide range of jobs**, according to the court. The school district's motion for summary judgment was granted. *Osika v. Bd. of Educ. for Bremen Community High Schools, Cook County Dist. 228*, 1999 U.S. Dist. LEXIS 17996 (N.D. Ill. 1999).

◆ A behavior specialist worked in his school district's exceptional student education department for over 12 years in a position that required him to drive to different schools to meet with students and design their individual classroom behavior management programs. He was injured in an automobile accident and missed three weeks of work. He returned to work for the rest of the school year, but was reassigned to a hospital homebound position that required driving to meet with four to five different students each day. The behavior specialist requested reinstatement to his previous position. The school board denied his request and **he took a two-year medical leave of absence, during which he received sick pay and disability benefits** from his private disability carrier and the Social Security Administration.

The behavior specialist then sued the school district in a federal district court, asserting that the board failed to reasonably accommodate his injuries, improperly forced him to use benefits, demoted and harassed him, and retaliated against him in violation of the ADA and state disability law. The district moved for summary judgment, arguing that the behavior specialist now claimed to be qualified to accept employment, even though he had previously received disability benefits for being totally disabled. The court held that a claimant's assertion of total disability must be reconciled with a later claim to ADA protection. ADA coverage requires an employee to have the ability to perform essential functions of a job. **Because the behavior specialist was unable to reconcile his earlier assertion of total disability with his present claim of ability to accept employment, the court found that he was not a qualified individual with a disability** as defined by the ADA. Therefore, the district was entitled to summary judgment. *Jammer v. School Dist. of Palm Beach County, Florida*, No. 978663 CIVHURLEYLYNCH (S.D. Fla. 1999).

◆ When a Georgia special education teacher who worked in psychoeducation classrooms for students with severe behavioral problems learned that he was

HIV-positive, he advised his principal. **School officials believed that there was a risk of blood contact with his students due to their behavior problems, and transferred him to a classroom attended by students with mild disorders.** Although the teacher claimed that the transfer was a demotion, his salary, benefits and seniority were unchanged. He filed a discrimination complaint against the district with the federal Equal Employment Opportunity Commission (EEOC), which enforces the ADA and other federal civil rights laws. The EEOC issued the teacher a right to sue letter and he commenced an ADA and Rehabilitation Act lawsuit against the district in a federal district court. The court held a trial and determined that the teacher's infection rendered him disabled, but that the risk of transmission to students was remote and theoretical. It found that he had suffered an adverse employment action and issued a permanent order requiring the school district to reinstate the teacher. The district appealed to the U.S. Court of Appeals, Eleventh Circuit.

The court of appeals noted that the district court had failed to balance the relevant safety considerations in finding that the teacher presented only a remote risk to the students. The injunctive order requiring reinstatement was therefore vacated for further proceedings. The district court had also failed to support its finding of adverse employment action with appropriate facts, instead accepting the teacher's subjective belief that the transfer was an adverse employment action. An objective standard was appropriate for determining whether the action was a discriminatory demotion, and the case was reversed and remanded. *Doe v. DeKalb County School Dist.*, 145 F.3d 1441 (11th Cir. 1998).

♦   The U.S. Court of Appeals, Seventh Circuit, held that an Indiana school might be liable for violating the ADA where it failed to offer reasonable accommodations to an employee with a mental disability. The school argued that it had not been required to offer the employee a reasonable accommodation since he had never asked for one, but **the court noted that the regulations interpreting the ADA state that in some situations, it may be necessary for an employer to initiate an informal, interactive process with an employee to determine an appropriate accommodation.** This is especially true when the employee suffers from a mental disability and may have difficulty articulating what he or she needs. Here, the school was well aware of the employee's mental disability but made no effort to find out what he needed to enable him to work. The court reversed and remanded the district court decision. *Bultemeyer v. Fort Wayne Community Schools*, 100 F.3d 1281 (7th Cir. 1996).

C. State Statutes

♦   **A wheelchair-bound Arkansas teacher with disabilities** asserted that her employing school district and superintendent made inadequate accommodations to enable her to continue her employment, and that those offered to her caused her physical injuries and emotional distress. She **sued the district and superintendent in a state circuit court for compensatory and punitive damages, pain and suffering, emotional distress and mental anguish,** claiming that the superintendent made derogatory comments about her disability. The district and superintendent moved to dismiss the action, asserting immunity from suit under Article 5,

Section 20 of the Arkansas Constitution. The court denied the motion, ruling that school districts are not entitled to immunity under the provision.

The district and superintendent appealed to the Arkansas Supreme Court, which stated that when a complaint alleges an action against the state, a trial court has no jurisdiction. Even where the state is not a named party, the payment of monetary damages from the state treasury would violate constitutional principles of sovereign immunity. The court noted in previous cases that school districts are political subdivisions of the state that are not state agencies. The definition of political subdivision embraced school districts, since they operated schools in their territory, purchased and held title to real property and had charge of maintenance. Unlike school districts, state agencies such as the department of education enjoyed immunity. **School districts themselves were considered creatures of the state that could not avail themselves of constitutional immunity safeguards**. State law granted immunity to political subdivisions that was not as comprehensive as that provided under the Arkansas Constitution. This protection limited immunity to the extent that they were covered by liability insurance, prohibiting recovery for any excess over that amount. The trial court properly denied the motion to dismiss the case brought by the district and superintendent under the state constitution, and the state supreme court affirmed the trial court's decision. *Dermott Special School District v. Johnson*, 32 S.W.3d 477 (Ark. 2000).

◆   A visually impaired Illinois social worker applied for work at an alternative high school for students with behavior disorders. School officials determined that the applicant should have a two-day trial observation period prior to an employment decision. **When the evaluators noticed that she failed to detect cues from students which indicated the possibility of imminent violent behavior, the school decided not to hire her**. The applicant filed a complaint against school officials with the state human rights commission, asserting discrimination on the basis of her visual disabilities. The commission found that the applicant had failed to demonstrate her ability to interpret inappropriate gestures and cues by the students and that she had never before worked with behavior disordered students. It also found that her visual impairment interfered with her ability to recognize impending aggressive situations, and that the employment decision was unrelated to her disability.

The applicant appealed to the Appellate Court of Illinois, Second District, which found that **she was inexperienced with the behavior disordered population and that her application had been denied on the basis of legitimate safety concerns**. She failed to show her ability to perform the job and failed to demonstrate that she had not been hired for reasons related to her disability. The court rejected the applicant's argument that the school failed to offer her reasonable accommodations. An employer's duty to provide reasonable accommodations does not attach until an employee asserts the ability to perform essential job functions if afforded a reasonable accommodation. Since the applicant presented no evidence that she had even asked for a reasonable accommodation, the court affirmed the commission's decision dismissing the complaint. *Truger v. Dep't of Human Rights*, 688 N.E.2d 1209 (Ill.App.2d Dist.1997).

◆   A Nevada elementary school music instructor volunteered as a helping dog trainer. The volunteer work required her to acclimate a helping dog to its future master's home and public environment. This included having the dog lie down or sleep next to her for extended time periods. **The instructor asked her employer for permission to bring a golden retriever she was training to class each day to lie down or sleep under her desk. The school district denied the request**, stating that this would create a distraction and that students might be afraid of or allergic to the dog. The teacher filed a complaint against the school district in a state trial court under a Nevada law making it an unlawful practice for a place of public accommodation to refuse admittance to a person with a helping dog or service animal. The court granted the instructor's request for a temporary order allowing her to bring the dog to class pending further consideration, subject to any serious difficulties or dangers created by the presence of the dog at school. The district appealed to the Supreme Court of Nevada.

The state supreme court observed that **the district had refused to negotiate a reasonable compromise with the music instructor, despite the mandatory language of the statute requiring a place of public accommodation to allow a training dog**. The district court had correctly granted the instructor's request for an injunction, as there was a high probability that she would succeed on the merits of her claim since the school was a place of public accommodation and she was a trainer of helping dogs. If a legitimate health concern could be proven, the employer would be entitled to place reasonable restrictions on her right to train the helping dog as necessary to prevent health problems. The court affirmed the trial court order. *Clark County School Dist. v. Buchanan*, 924 P.2d 716 (Nev.1996).

◆   A New Hampshire high school Spanish teacher suffered from chronic asthma. Over a six-year period, he missed an average of 22 school days because of his condition. He was the only full-time Spanish teacher in the district. **He was informed by letter his contract would not be renewed.** After receiving the letter, he contacted a specialist in respiratory disorders who prescribed a new course of treatment. The specialist asserted that this new treatment would effectively control the teacher's respiratory problems. The school district, however, went through with the teacher's planned nonrenewal. The teacher appealed, claiming that the nonrenewal violated federal and state disability discrimination laws. The State Board of Education affirmed the nonrenewal, and the teacher sought review from the New Hampshire Supreme Court. The supreme court noted that the teacher fell within the protection of the state handicap discrimination law. **Since the school district conceded that he was a competent teacher, and presented no medical evidence that the attacks would continue, the teacher satisfied the requirements of New Hampshire law, and was ordered reinstated.** *Petition of Dunlap*, 604 A.2d 945 (N.H.1991), *rehearing denied* (N.H.1992).

CHAPTER SEVEN

Termination, Resignation and Retirement

I.   DECLINING ENROLLMENT AND BUDGET REDUCTION

In cases of layoffs and employment termination due to economic factors, school districts are bound to observe seniority rights and teacher qualifications when selecting employees who will be retained. For more cases involving employee tenure rights, see Chapter Eight of this volume.

A.   Declining Enrollment Dismissals

◆   Several teachers in Pennsylvania were laid off due to declining enrollment and realignment. The discharged teachers brought an action challenging their layoffs. **Teachers with more seniority were fired and a teacher with less seniority was retained** to be the coordinator of a program for gifted students. The superintendent chose the less senior employee because she had been involved with the program from the start and had a greater breadth of experience with arts and humanities. Further, the less senior employee had a greater ability to interact with the students and with the talented people within the community. A state trial court ruled in favor of the school district, stating that retaining a less senior employee did not violate the statute. The teachers appealed to the Supreme Court of Pennsylvania which stated that **in a realignment school districts have no choice but to replace less senior employees with more senior ones who carry proper certification**. The benefit of giving school districts discretion to make appointments on the basis of a person's qualifications is still limited by a requirement that retentions be based on seniority and certification. This method protects higher salaried long tenured employees from removal simply to save the district money and also provides an incentive for employees to broaden their professional abilities. The supreme court decided that since the teachers in this case were dismissed seven years earlier, an order for reinstatement would not be appropriate. A monetary award would be appropriate for lost wages. The court of appeals reversed the trial court's decision. *Dallap v. Sharon City Sch. Dist.*, 571 A.2d 368 (Pa.1990).

◆   A Minnesota school district sought to place a fulltime social studies teacher on unrequested leave of absence due to declining enrollment. The teacher requested and received a hearing, but she was still placed on unrequested leave. She sought judicial review of that decision, and the case came before the Court of Appeals of Minnesota. The district, while acknowledging that realignment of teaching positions would be reasonable and practical, stated that under the provisions of the collective bargaining agreement, it did not have a duty to realign to save the teacher's position. The court of appeals held that Minnesota law required the district to realign. Further, the district had conceded that realignment was practical and reasonable. **The court** thus **ordered the district to reinstate the teacher and realign teaching positions to preserve the teacher's continuing contract rights**. *Matter of Bristol*, 451 N.W.2d 883 (Minn.App.1990).

B. Termination for Budgetary Reasons

◆   A Minnesota school district employed an administrator as a finance and business director for 16 years. He signed employment contracts for the first 13 years, and during the two of them, the contracts referred to a statute governing teacher termination. For the last three years of his employment, the administrator had no written employment agreement. **The board ultimately resolved to discontinue his contract because of financial limitations.** Although the resolution discontinued the position immediately, the administrator claimed that he was entitled to his salary for the remaining four months of the school year under the teacher termination statute and the school district's employment manual. The administrator filed a state court action against the board, seeking reinstatement and back pay. The court held for the board and the administrator appealed.

A state appeals court stated that the teacher termination statute excluded the administrative position from its coverage because the statute pertained only to professional employees who were required to hold a state license. The administrator acknowledged that he was not licensed by the state education agency, but argued that the references to it in his prior written contracts entitled him to the law's protections. The appeals court rejected the administrator's arguments, finding that contractual provisions did not override statutory licensure requirements and that they pertained only to past years not at issue in this case. **Although definite employment terms contained in an employment manual may become part of an employment contract, the district manual in this case did not create rights of reinstatement or displacement.** While the manual might have bound the district to show that it had good cause for the administrator's termination, it did not incorporate the protections of the teacher termination statute for administrators. The court held that the administrator was entitled to be paid through the end of the school year and remanded the case for determination of the amount. *Herdegen v. School Board of Independent School District No. 482*, No. C6 00-783, 2000 Minn. App. Lexis 1154 (Minn. App. 2000).

◆   The Arkansas Supreme Court held that a full-time non-probationary cook whose position was being eliminated was entitled to notice and a hearing as mandated by the state Public School Employee Fair Hearing Act, despite her employer's claim that her position was being eliminated due to budget constraints. The court held that even though the employment relationship may be terminated at the will of either party to an employment contract, Arkansas employees remain entitled to the notice provisions of state law. **Even though the board could terminate the cook's employment for any reason, she was still entitled to adequate notice and hearing protections** prior to the action. *Gould Pub. Schools v. Dobbs*, 338 Ark. 28, 993 S.W.2d 500 (Ark.1999).

◆   A certified Alabama teacher with approximately 10 years of experience sought employment with several Alabama school systems. A teacher/coach at one district advised him that he had been hired by the school principal, and that the teacher/coach had received this message via the principal from the district superintendent. The teacher reported for work the next morning and was introduced at a meeting attended by all school principals and teachers in the system and a school board member.

302 TERMINATION, RESIGNATION AND RETIREMENT   Ch. 7

Within a week, the principal advised the teacher that his position had been eliminated due to budget cuts. The teacher filed a lawsuit against the school district in an Alabama circuit court, seeking reinstatement with damages in an amount representing his expected salary for the full school year. The court conducted a trial and awarded him an amount representing his expected salary until the time he accepted employment with another district. The parties appealed to the Supreme Court of Alabama.

The school board argued that the teacher had never actually been hired since the Alabama Code requires a superintendent to nominate a teacher for appointment in writing. Because the teacher had never been appointed for employment, the board could not be liable for an enforceable employment contract. The teacher argued that he had given up other job possibilities, moved to the city and rented a home and was entitled to be paid for an entire year because he had been wrongfully terminated. **The court agreed with the teacher that the board was prohibited from denying the existence of an employment contract, since he had been misled into thinking he was hired**. However, the trial court had properly limited the damage award to the actual period of unemployment he had suffered. *Talladega City Bd. of Educ. v. Yancy*, 682 So.2d 33 (Ala.1996).

◆ The Chicago school board reduced its subdistricts from 23 to 11 by combining some of them. **Thirteen subdistrict superintendents lost their jobs** because of the change, and they sued the board in an Illinois trial court, seeking injunctive relief and damages. They claimed that the Illinois School Reform Act established a contract of employment with them. They alleged that the reduction in force had deprived them of property without due process of law. The Appellate Court of Illinois, First District, Fifth Division, reversed the trial court's decision to grant the school board summary judgment. **Although the board had the power to change its subdistricts, the statute created a contract with the superintendents by operation of law** which bound the school board. *Kaszubowski v. Bd. of Educ. of City of Chicago*, 618 N.E.2d 609 (Ill.App.1st Dist.1993).

C. Reinstatement and Recall

◆ Because of declining student enrollment levels, a school district laid off a number of employees. A high school that experienced severe disciplinary problems temporarily closed and four new positions were created to help address student discipline when the school reopened. The district did not rehire the laid off employees for any of the new positions. The laid off employees sued the district in a state trial court for violation of the Pennsylvania School Code. The court held that at the time the positions were filled, one or more of the laid off employees had seniority for each of them. **It ordered the district to hire the most senior laid off employee for each position, retroactive to the position hire date**. The district and replacement employees appealed to the Pennsylvania Commonwealth Court, asserting that the laid off employees were required to pursue their available administrative and collective bargaining remedies prior to filing a lawsuit.

The commonwealth court held that the trial court maintained the discretion to hear the case since the labor union had not filed a grievance on behalf of any of the employees and it had concurrent jurisdiction to hear the case. With the exception of one position requiring special certification, it also rejected the district's assertion that the replacement employees were more qualified for the new positions than the laid off employees. **Although the educational needs of a school district may outweigh seniority as an employment consideration, the district in this case had failed to show that the new positions required any special certification or other criteria that justified the appointment of less experienced employees.** Since three of the laid off employees demonstrated the proper certification for one of the new positions and had greater seniority than the selected replacement employees, the court affirmed the judgment in their cases. The fourth position required special certification and the district obtained an experienced, qualified employee to fill it. With the exception of this one position, the court affirmed the judgment for the laid off employees. *Davis v. Chester Upland School District*, 754 A.2d 733 (Pa. Commw. 2000).

◆   A Minnesota social studies teacher was placed on unrequested leave of absence (ULA). Twice he was denied reinstatement when the school district reestablished positions and recalled two less senior teachers to fill them. The teacher brought a declaratory judgment action seeking to force the district to realign teachers with less seniority to make his reinstatement possible. The trial court held for the district and the teacher successfully appealed. The district then appealed to the Supreme Court of Minnesota. Holding that protection of teachers' seniority rights was paramount, **the supreme court held that the most senior teacher on ULA was to be recalled first, either for his former position if open, or after reasonable realignment to another position for which he was licensed**. The court ordered the district to realign positions and reinstate the teacher, and affirmed the appellate court's decision. *Harms v. Indep. School Dist. No. 300*, 450 N.W.2d 571 (Minn.1990).

II. EXCESSIVE ABSENCE AND TARDINESS

Either excessive absence or tardiness will constitute valid grounds for discipline, but written warnings should be given to the employee in advance of any disciplinary action.

◆   **A Rhode Island school system notified 15 probationary teachers that they would not earn tenure because of excessive absences.** The probationary teachers complained that their absences were authorized under the collective bargaining agreement of the parties and the state Leave Act, which entitles employees to 13 consecutive work weeks of parental or family leave in any two calendar years without loss of seniority or benefits. They filed an administrative complaint against the school committee with the state commissioner of education, who found that the denial of tenure had been appropriate. However, he concluded that the absences would not halt the consecutive years of service requirement so as to require the teachers to begin their probationary periods all over again. Any completed years of service would not be forfeited. The parties appealed to the state board of education, which affirmed the decision. The parties then petitioned the Supreme Court of Rhode Island for review.

The court rejected the teachers' argument that the local school committee was powerless to develop a rule concerning excessive absences and had done so without adequate notice. **The court deemed the teachers to be on notice that a substantial**

number of absences during a probationary period, in this case 27 or more, **would adversely affect their claims to tenure**. Each of the teachers had been offered another one-year teaching contract, and under the commissioner's reasonable interpretation of the tenure law, no teacher would forfeit any service credits earned prior to taking leave. Because the commissioner's ruling appropriately reconciled the state tenure and leave acts, the court affirmed his decision. *Asadoorian v. Warwick School Committee*, 691 A.2d 573 (R.I.1997).

◆   A Virginia high school security guard was absent 49 days in one school year. She took leave for family and personal illnesses or court appearances with the approval of her supervisors. However, **when a new principal was appointed, he notified the security guard that further absences would result in employment termination**. The guard was absent five more times, for a total of twelve absences in the first 47 days of school. The principal suspended the guard and the school board voted to terminate her employment. A Virginia trial court reversed the board's decision and the board appealed to the Supreme Court of Virginia. The supreme court observed that one of the stated reasons for firing the guard was the compromised nature of security and safety at the high school due to her excessive absences. It rejected the trial court's finding that she had been improperly fired for abuse of sick leave even though she had obtained approval for the leave requests. **Because the record showed that employment termination was warranted due to the guard's failure to comply with repeated warnings, the court affirmed the board's action**. *School Bd. of City of Norfolk v. Wescott*, 492 S.E.2d 146 (Va.1997).

◆   A Florida school board fired a teacher for absence without leave, wilful neglect of duty and misconduct in office. The district also withheld over $3,600 from her final paycheck for the unexcused absences. She requested an administrative hearing, which resulted in a recommendation for reinstatement without backpay. The hearing officer concluded that the school board had failed to prove wilful neglect of duty and that the teacher was only absent without leave for six hours, justifying the withholding of only $147. The school board rejected the recommendation and fired the teacher for wilful neglect of duty and absence without leave, authorizing the deduction of $3,272 from her final check. The teacher appealed to the Florida District Court of Appeal, Second District, which determined that the school board had violated a Florida statute that limited a school board's discretion to overturn hearing officer decisions. **The school board's decision to increase the penalties recommended by the hearing officer constituted an impermissible substitution of judgment**, and the court reversed and remanded its decision. *Dunham v. Highlands County School Bd.*, 652 So.2d 894 (Fla.App.2d Dist.1995).

III. IMMORALITY AND OTHER MISCONDUCT

School employees can be discharged for a wide variety of conduct, including conduct deemed immoral or inappropriate. In particular, a teacher may be discharged for conduct affecting his or her fitness to teach or ability to be a good role model. However, termination of employment has been limited by the courts in some contexts, such as homosexuality, language, and drug or alcohol abuse.

A. Sexual Misconduct

Sexual misconduct includes sexual harassment in the form of comments and contact. Generally, substantiated sexual misconduct will lead to termination of employment based upon a finding of immoral conduct.

◆   A physical education teacher was suspended for inappropriate conduct with female students during two school years. After reading newspaper accounts of the incident, two former students claimed he had abused them decades earlier. The district conducted further investigations and held a second disciplinary proceeding against the teacher. For the second time, the district charged him with immoral conduct and conduct unbecoming a teacher. The hearing officer rejected his assertion that the charge was time-barred, since New York law specifically excepts charges based on criminal conduct from an otherwise applicable three-year limit on actions. Instead of appealing the hearing officer's decision, the teacher filed a federal district court action against the school district, asserting due process violations. The court granted summary judgment to the district and a named official, and the teacher appealed to the U.S. Court of Appeals, Second Circuit.

The court found that **while the teacher had a property interest in his continued employment, requiring the district to provide him with certain due process protections, the delay in prosecution of the action against him did not create actual prejudice**. Contrary to his argument, the passage of time did not hamper his defense. The time lapse had the same comparative disadvantages to all involved parties. The court declined the teacher's invitation to presume that the passage of time created actual prejudice to him. The court also dismissed the teacher's claims regarding the disclosure of information from his disciplinary hearing to the media as meritless. *DeMichele v. Greenburgh Central School Dist.*, 167 F.3d 784 (2d Cir.1999).

◆   The state of Arizona filed criminal charges against a teacher who was suspected of inappropriate behavior and sexual conduct with three of his former students. The school district notified the teacher of its intention to fire him pending a hearing. The teacher requested a stay of the dismissal hearing until the criminal matter was resolved, but the board rejected his request. Instead, it advised the teacher that it would not penalize him for failing to testify at his employment termination hearing. **The teacher filed an action in a state trial court, seeking to obtain a stay of the termination hearing**. The court held for the school district, and the teacher appealed to the Court of Appeals of Arizona. On appeal, the teacher argued that the board placed him in a position in which he had to choose between his Fifth Amendment privilege against self-incrimination and his entitlement to further employment with the school district. The court rejected this argument, noting that the board had assured him that his silence in the administrative investigation could not be held against him. **Because the school board had not abused its discretion, the trial court had properly affirmed its denial of the request for a stay**. *Chadwick v. Superior Court, County of Maricopa*, 908 P.2d 4 (Ariz.App.Div.1 1995).

◆   A Montana school board received two letters alleging sexual misconduct by its school superintendent and later received similar complaints by a former employee and a graduate of the high school. The allegations became well known in the small community the district served, and the superintendent was forced to resign. **Although criminal charges against the superintendent were dismissed, the Montana Office of Public Instruction** (OPI) **refused to renew his teaching certificate**, finding that he was not of good moral character as required by Montana law. The superintendent requested a hearing at which the hearing examiner found that he was not of good moral and professional character, based upon the conflicting testimony of two alleged victims and the corroborating testimony of an expert witness. The state board of public education adopted the hearing officer's findings, but a Montana trial court reversed the decision. The OPI appealed to the Supreme Court of Montana.

On appeal, the OPI argued that the testimony of the expert witness who had presented evidence at the hearing was properly admitted. This evidence was intended to make coherent the otherwise inconsistent testimony of the alleged victims by generalizing that victims of sexual abuse frequently block out memories. According to that generalization, the conflicting testimony could be accepted because these witnesses fit the profile of other sexual abuse victims. **The supreme court held that the district court had properly disregarded the expert's bolstering of inconsistent testimony**. The supreme court affirmed the district court's finding that the board's decision was based upon improper evidence and was clearly erroneous. *In the Matter of Renewal of the Teaching Certificate of Thompson*, 893 P.2d 301 (Mont.1995).

◆   A tenured music teacher at a California middle school was accused of repeatedly sexually harassing female students. The school district suspended the teacher and began dismissal proceedings against him on the basis of immoral conduct. The state education commission conducted a hearing and determined that the teacher had not engaged in immoral conduct. It ordered reinstatement of the teacher with backpay. The district appealed the decision to a California superior court, which reversed the commission's decision, finding that the evidence supported dismissal of the teacher. The teacher appealed to the California Court of Appeal, Second District. The court reviewed the evidence, finding a number of incidents of inappropriate touching, hugging, sexual comments and other unwanted behavior by the teacher. Contrary to the commission's finding that the alleged conduct was not immoral, **the court determined that sexually harassing behavior could be construed as immoral under the statute. Proof of immoral conduct could demonstrate unfitness to teach upon consideration of the likelihood of adverse effect** on students or other teachers. In this case, the repeated and pervasive nature of the conduct supported dismissal. The court affirmed the judgment for the school district. *Governing Board of ABC Unified School Dist. v. Haar*, 33 Cal.Rptr.2d 744 (Cal.App.2d Dist.1994).

B. Other Misconduct

Other forms of misconduct that may lead to termination of employment include conduct characterized as immoral, criminal conduct, and neglect of duty. Neglect of duty usually involves a failure to perform the particular duties of the position.

1. Immoral Conduct

◆   **A Missouri school district terminated the contract of a probationary teacher for immoral conduct after he was confronted by police officers for hiding a 14-year-old girl in his apartment** late one night. The school board conducted a hearing at which it determined that the girl had come to his apartment without parental permission and that the teacher had refused to allow investigating officers into his apartment without a search warrant after denying her presence there. This constituted immoral conduct under state law. The board terminated the teacher's contract, and he appealed to a Missouri circuit court. After the court affirmed the board's decision, he appealed to the Missouri Court of Appeals, Southern Division. The court noted that while the teacher was not a permanent employee, he was entitled to notice and a hearing under state law, which the board had provided. The school board's decision was within its authority and had been supported by the evidence. **The teacher's misconduct and poor judgment created reasonable concern about his moral character**, and the court affirmed the dismissal action. *Hamm v. Poplar Bluff R-1 School Dist.*, 955 S.W.2d 27 (Mo.App.S.D.1997).

◆   An Idaho teacher impregnated a 15-year-old student. Prior to the birth of the child, the teacher and the student's father signed a confidential agreement under which the teacher was required to resign his position prior to the beginning of the following school semester. Meanwhile, he applied for employment with an Alaska school district, and accepted a job there. Ten years later, the district received notice from the student of the prior relationship and conducted an investigation. The Alaska district then terminated the teacher's employment on grounds that his prior conduct constituted immorality and substantial noncompliance with school law. The teacher appealed to an Alaska trial court, which granted the school district's summary judgment motion. The teacher appealed to the Supreme Court of Alaska. On appeal, the teacher argued that conduct prior to being hired by the Alaska district could not constitute grounds for dismissal. The Alaska supreme court disagreed, stating that such a policy would immunize from punishment a teacher who had engaged in prior illegal or immoral conduct and successfully concealed it. **The teacher's prior immoral conduct and failure to disclose his criminal behavior provided ample evidence that the teacher's employment had been properly terminated**. *Toney v. Fairbanks North Star Borough School Dist., Bd. of Educ.*, 881 P.2d 1112 (Alaska 1994).

◆   A New York physical education instructor married a former member of his volleyball team shortly after she graduated from high school. The school board then investigated his prior relationships with members of the team and removed him from his position as coach, refused to appoint him coach of the boys' team, and denied him tenure at the end of his probationary period. The former coach filed a lawsuit against the school board and several of its officials in the U.S. District Court for the Northern District of New York, asserting a violation of his constitutional right to marry and claiming damage to his reputation. The court awarded summary judgment to the school board and the former coach appealed to the U.S. Court of Appeals, Second Circuit. **The court of appeals held that public employees** claiming constitutional violations by their employers must demonstrate evidence of unfavorable employment action that is substantially motivated by the employee's constitutionally protected conduct. The former coach had presented only conclusory allegations of the board's decision and there was insufficient evidence that the board sought to penalize him because of the marriage. The court affirmed the judgment for the board. *Finnegan v. Bd. of Educ. of City School Dist. of Troy*, 30 F.3d 273 (2d Cir.1994).

◆   A Kansas high school teacher permitted several students to make a videotape as part of a social time for a student who was transferring. The school board learned of the tape and claimed that the incident demonstrated lack of classroom control and that material in the video constituted sexual harassment. **The board terminated the teacher's employment, but its decision was vacated by a due process hearing committee, which found no substantial evidence of good cause for termination.** The Court of Appeals of Kansas affirmed the committee's decision, finding that substantial evidence supported its decision. No female student had complained of sexual harassment and the videotape incident was apparently isolated. The teacher was reinstated with backpay. *Unif. School Dist. No. 434, Osage County v. Hubbard*, 868 P.2d 1240 (Kan.App.1994).

2.   Criminal Conduct

◆   A Tennessee school experienced eight incidents during a two-year period in which Ritalin was reported missing from prescription bottles being held for students. Local police installed a video surveillance camera in the school office, where medication was held and dispensed by the school secretary. Officials planted children's aspirin in a prescription bottle labeled "Methylphenidate," (the chemical name for Ritalin and placed it in the secretary's desk. A surveillance tape caught a teacher reaching into the secretary's drawer and slipping pills into her pocket. The teacher had been employed by the district for 19 years and had an unblemished record. When a police detective asked her if she had taken the pills, she denied doing so. **The superintendent recommended dismissal for conduct unbecoming a member of the teaching profession, namely dishonesty and unreliability.** The board voted to discharge the teacher, and she appealed to a Tennessee chancery court. In pretrial proceedings, the school board obtained a protective order from the court, preventing the teacher from obtaining the files of six other tenured teachers who had separated from the district. The court agreed with the board that the teacher had not been deprived of due process, that the discharge was not disproportionate to the offense, and that the finding of guilt was not arbitrary or capricious.

The teacher appealed to the Tennessee Court of Appeals, where she asserted that she never denied taking the pills and that the board could not dismiss her without proving every charge against her. The court disagreed, finding that it was sufficient for the board to advise her of the charges and of the possibility that she would be dismissed. The notice she received made her fully aware that her job was at stake. **While a teacher's employment record is a relevant consideration in determining the penalty for a lapse in judgment, the offense was not a minor one.** The teacher compounded the offense by destroying evidence. The school board was entitled to discharge her and was not arbitrary and capricious in doing so. The panel rejected the teacher's argument that the trial court's denial of her discovery requests violated the state Public Records Act. The chancery court judge had properly found the requests improper on grounds of relevance, confidentiality or privilege, and the court affirmed the judgment. *Lannom v. Bd. of Educ. for Metropolitan Gov't, Nashville and Davidson County*, 2000 Tenn. App. Lexis 133 (Tenn. App. 2000).

◆   **The New Jersey Division of Youth and Family Services** (DYFS) **investigated abuse allegations** against 14 Newark school district employees **and determined that while abuse was not substantiated in any case, there was evidence that some children were harmed and that specific corrective action must be taken** against certain employees. The employees filed a state court action asserting due process violations, because the findings reported to the district could result in adverse employment action without the opportunity for their participation in a hearing or other forum.

The Superior Court of New Jersey, Appellate Division, held that the DYFS was required by law to investigate and report child abuse complaints against a teacher to the teacher's employer. This was true even where abuse was not substantiated but some negative information was included in a report. However, **state school laws did not confer authority on the DYFS to recommend corrective action or remedial action** for a district to take against an employee in response to DYFS findings. School districts retained independent judgment about DYFS reports and could then decide whether to take disciplinary action. There was no merit to the argument that the employees suffered a due process violation as a result of the DYFS investigations despite the lack of a DYFS hearing. Tenured teachers were still entitled to state school law due process procedures. The use of information obtained through a DYFS investigation in a school disciplinary action did not create the right to a DYFS hearing, and the employees were not deprived of due process. *In the Matter of Allegation of Physical Abuse Concerning L.R. at First Middle School*, 321 N.J.Super. 444, 729 A.2d 463 (N.J.Super.App.Div.1999).

◆   **A teacher was investigated by law officers, but not charged with a crime, for possessing candid pictures of teenagers that had been taken in his home**. The school board decided to suspend the teacher with pay based on conduct unbecoming a teacher under New York Education Law § 3020-a, despite the lack of criminal charges. It also removed him from his extracurricular assignments. A hearing panel dismissed the charges and ordered him restored to his duties. He sued the district and its board in a federal district court for First Amendment violations, intentional infliction of emotional distress and other personal injuries.

The court dismissed all claims against the board, because there is no cause of action under 42 U.S.C. § 1983 for damages against a school board or individual school board members in their individual capacities. There was also no showing of emotional distress that was outrageous in character. There was no basis for the teacher's due process claims, because the school district had complied with state law procedures in suspending him with pay pending a hearing. He remained an employee of the district and was deprived of no property interest. He had received a hearing at which he had the ability to present evidence, was represented by counsel and had the opportunity to call and cross-examine witnesses. The court disagreed with the teacher's assertion that the board acted unreasonably in view of the dismissal of criminal charges against him. **It was reasonable for the board to take action in the interest of student safety because he was a teacher and coach of students in the same age range as the persons appearing in the photos**. *Montefusco v. Nassau County*, 39 F.Supp.2d 231 (E.D.N.Y.1999).

◆   A teacher who was a successful high school basketball coach led his team to a state championship. However, a parent complained about his discipline of a student, successfully campaigned for a seat on the school board, and joined other board members in calling for the coach's resignation. The board learned that the coach had a criminal record and had been imprisoned in Kentucky for criminal trespass and disorderly conduct. Rumors circulated in the district that the coach was a rapist who was a danger to students. **He was suspended pending charges of accepting a bribe from a gym shoe company and eventually was laid off**. The coach commenced a federal district court action against the school board for constitutional rights violations. He included a claim against his teachers' association for breach of the duty of fair representation.

The court dismissed the case, and the coach appealed to the Seventh Circuit, which held that the coach had failed to demonstrate that any public official had defamed him. The evidence of rumors was insufficient to show a false assertion of fact by any board member. The coach's constitutional property rights claim also failed because he could not show the absence of state-law remedies to redress the claimed misconduct of board members. **The reduction in force did not support his claim for intentional infliction of emotional distress because the action was not outrageous**. The coach could not sue his teachers' association for breach of the duty of fair representation, since federal labor law excludes political subdivisions, including school boards, from coverage. The court affirmed the dismissal of the lawsuit. *Strasburger v. Bd. of Educ., Hardin County Community School Dist. No. 1*, 143 F.3d 351 (7th Cir.1998).

◆   A North Carolina mathematics teacher with 15 years of experience entered a pool room with a 12-gauge shotgun and a .38 caliber pistol. He was arrested and subsequently pled guilty to trespassing. The matter was well publicized in the local area and the county school board voted to dismiss him. **The order affirming the dismissal stated that the teacher's ability to function as a teacher and role model had been seriously impaired**. The dismissal was approved under a North Carolina statute allowing dismissal for immorality or other cause constituting grounds for revocation of a teacher's license. The teacher appealed to a North Carolina county court, which affirmed the decision. The teacher then appealed to the Court of Appeals of North Carolina, where he claimed that the dismissal statute was unconstitutionally vague for failing to give teachers fair warning of what conduct was prohibited and failing to require a nexus between misconduct and teaching performance. The court found that the statutory term "immorality" may be properly viewed in the context of the teacher's employment, and is directly related to a teacher's fitness for service. **Immorality means such conduct that by common judgment reflects on a teacher's fitness to teach**. A reasonable teacher of ordinary intelligence would understand that entering a crowded pool room with firearms would reflect on the ability to effectively serve as a teacher and role model.

The law was not unconstitutionally vague and the court affirmed the dismissal action. *Barringer v. Caldwell County Bd. of Educ.*, 473 S.E.2d 435 (N.C.App. 1996).

◆   The Alabama legislature passed a law allowing the revocation of a teaching certificate when the teacher has been found guilty of immoral conduct or unbecoming or indecent behavior. **Three teachers who were subject to potential teaching certificate revocation because of criminal convictions filed a lawsuit against the state superintendent of education** in the U.S. District Court for the Middle District of Alabama, alleging that the statute was unconstitutionally void for vagueness. The court agreed with the teachers that the statutory terms "immoral conduct" and "unbecoming or indecent behavior" were susceptible to different interpretations. However, reading the statutory terms in conjunction with prior decisions of the Alabama Supreme Court, any vagueness in these terms was clarified by precise judicial construction. Under established law, **immoral conduct implied an unfitness to teach**. Under this limiting construction, the state superintendent could revoke a teaching certificate only if the conduct or behavior indicated that the teacher was unfit to teach. The statute was upheld as not unconstitutionally void for vagueness. *Alford v. Ingram*, 931 F.Supp. 768 (M.D.Ala. 1996).

◆   The wife of the director of maintenance for a Texas school district advised authorities that she believed her husband was stealing school property. The sheriff's department executed a search warrant and school property was found in the employee's home. Although a grand jury indicted the employee on theft charges, the wife became unwilling to testify and the indictments were dismissed. The school board held a hearing and voted to fire the employee for misconduct. The state commissioner of education upheld the board's decision. **The local school board then formulated a policy prohibiting its contractors from employing former school district employees at school worksites.** The former employee alleged that this rule caused him to lose his job with a contractor. He sued the district, school officials and law officers in a Texas trial court for malicious prosecution, invasion of privacy, tortious interference with contract and civil conspiracy. He claimed that the board's termination action and vendor exclusion policy violated his constitutional rights. The court dismissed the lawsuit and the former employee appealed to the Court of Appeals of Texas, which found no error in the decision. **The facts indicated that school officials and law enforcement officers were merely carrying out their duties and were not guilty of malicious prosecution, civil conspiracy, invasion of privacy or interference with contract rights.** The board had provided adequate due process protections concerning the termination and the vendor exclusion policy. The court affirmed the dismissal of the lawsuit. *Closs v. Goose Creek Consol. Indep. School Dist.*, 874 S.W.2d 859 (Tex.App.–Texarkana 1994).

3. Neglect of Duty

◆   A shop teacher who had no history of disciplinary charges came to school one day in his wife's car and parked it outside his classroom. After leaving work for the day, **he discovered that a gun was missing from the car and concluded that it had been stolen while he was at school**. The teacher reported the theft to school officials and the sheriff's department. The district superintendent placed the teacher on paid leave of absence and the board held a hearing to consider his case. **The board voted to dismiss the teacher for neglect of duty**, even though it had no policy prohibiting teachers from possessing guns concealed within motor vehicles while on a school campus. The teacher appealed to a state district court, which affirmed the board's decision. The state court of appeal affirmed the dismissal action, and the teacher appealed to the Louisiana Supreme Court.

According to the state supreme court, neglect of duty is a permissible ground for termination of a teacher's employment. Teachers may be dismissed for willful neglect of duty for a specific action or failure to act in contravention of a direct order or identifiable school policy. The court of appeal had erroneously found that the teacher could be dismissed for willful neglect of duty if he had some knowledge that his conduct was contrary to school policy "based on 'general knowledge' concerning the responsibility and conduct of teachers." The supreme court found that the record only showed the teacher had made a mistake and probably endangered students by bringing the gun to the school campus in a vehicle. However, this did not rise to the level of a failure to follow orders or an identifiable school policy. **The board failed to prove by substantial evidence that the teacher acted with willful neglect**. The court reversed the lower court decisions and reinstated the teacher, with salary and benefits. *Howard v. West Baton Rouge Parish School Board*, No. 00-C-3234, 2001 WL 744448 (La. 2001).

◆   An administrator was suspended and reprimanded for insubordination and not getting along with a teacher during his service as an elementary school principal. After being suspended, he filed his first Equal Employment Opportunity Commission (EEOC) claim, which he later withdrew. He became active in unionizing district administrative employees, and was eventually reassigned to serve as an assistant high school principal. He filed a second EEOC claim, alleging that the reassignment was discriminatory and a reprimand he received was retaliatory. A federal district court granted summary judgment to the school district and superintendent in that action, finding legitimate, nondiscriminatory reasons for the reassignment. The administrator continued having difficulties and received poor evaluations. The principal's refusal to change an evaluation led to a third EEOC claim alleging age discrimination, sex discrimination and retaliation. **The board then voted to discharge the administrator for failing to work required hours, inability to work with district employees, and failure to perform his duties**. The administrator filed a second district court action, challenging his termination. The district court granted the school board's motion for summary judgment, and the administrator appealed.

The Tenth Circuit upheld the decision to terminate the administrator's employment, finding he failed to establish a prima facie case of retaliation. The board established legitimate, nonretaliatory reasons for discharging the administrator, and there was no evidence the offered reasons were merely a pretext. **The administrator's involvement in protected activity had no bearing on the board's termination decision, as the individual who recommended terminating the administrator was the president of the union** he was involved in. The district court decision was upheld. *Grady v. Shawnee Pub. School Dist.*, 166 F.3d 347 (10th Cir. 1998).

◆   A relative of a Washington school maintenance employee brought a BB rifle to the employee's workplace and requested that he repair it. The employee repaired the gun, then tested it by firing at a target placed against the inside wall of the maintenance facility. The school district discharged the employee because of the incident and he appealed to a Washington superior court. The court affirmed the action and the employee appealed further to the Court of Appeals of Washington. The court held that under state law, **sufficient cause for discharge exists where an employee's performance deficiencies are unremediable and materially and substantially affect performance, or lack any positive aspect or legitimate professional purpose**. In this case, because the firing of the weapon lacked any legitimate professional purpose, it had not been necessary for the district to provide the employee a warning. The court also rejected the employee's claim that he was entitled to receive a copy of the district's gun free policy since he was the employee who had posted gun-free school zone warnings on school grounds and was aware of the policy. *Wolf v. Columbia School Dist. No. 400*, 938 P.2d 357 (Wash.App.Div.3 1997).

◆   A custodian employed by a Minnesota special school district often allowed students to remain in the school after school hours. **He played flashlight tag and had water fights with fourth graders and allowed two sixth graders to go on the roof**. The school principal suspended the custodian immediately when he learned of these incidents and, following an investigation, determined that the custodian should not come in contact with children. The custodian had a criminal record with convictions for trespassing, burglary and invasion of privacy, and was also a suspect in several rape cases. The district recommended discharge and conducted a veterans preference hearing under the state Veterans Preference Act. An administrative law judge determined that the custodian's behavior was misconduct. **A veterans preference board held the discharge inappropriate**, and appeal reached the Supreme Court of Minnesota.

The custodian claimed that extenuating circumstances existed which should preclude discharge, including his excellent work record, the lack of progressive disciplinary action by the school district and the absence of school rules governing proper staff interaction with students. He also claimed that the sanction was too harsh for the offense, that other employees had engaged in similar acts without being discharged and that the action had been based in part upon unproven allegations of rape. **The supreme court held that the custodian had committed numerous acts of misconduct that were sufficiently serious to warrant immediate discharge**. *Wagner v. Minneapolis Pub. Schools, Special School Dist. No. 1*, 569 N.W.2d 529 (Minn.1997).

◆   **A Louisiana bus driver failed to notice that a five-year-old special education student had been left behind on the bus**. The student was to get off at the bus driver's last stop but instead fell asleep under a seat and awoke when the bus driver had returned to her home. The child was found wandering around the bus driver's neighborhood. The principal recommended to the superintendent that the bus driver be suspended without pay for 30 days and the superintendent adopted this recommendation. After 30 days, the assistant superintendent recommended that the bus driver's employment be terminated and the superintendent adopted this recommendation as well. Following a full hearing, the termination was upheld. The bus driver appealed to the school board, which affirmed the superintendent's decision and, subsequently, the bus driver appealed the board's decision to a Louisiana trial court. The trial court ruled in favor of the school board, and the bus driver then appealed to the Louisiana Court of Appeal. **The court of appeal stated that sufficient evidence existed to find that the bus driver had neglected her duty. It affirmed the trial court's decision and upheld her discharge**. *McLaughlin v. Jefferson Parish Sch. Bd.*, 560 So.2d 585 (La.App.5th Cir.1990).

C.   Homosexuality, Bisexuality and Transsexuality

Homosexuality among teachers has been the subject of a number of lawsuits dealing with dismissal. The courts generally agree that homosexuality *per se*, absent a flaunting of sexual preference, does not constitute grounds for dismissal or for not hiring a teacher. In *Bowers v. Hardwick*, 106 S.Ct. 2841 (1986), however, the U.S. Supreme Court held that the privacy rights found in the U.S. Constitution do not protect homosexual sodomy.

◆   A Massachusetts school superintendent terminated the employment of a school custodian for inappropriate behavior and conduct unbecoming a school employee. **The action resulted from the employee's arrest for engaging in homosexual activities in a public park and his failure to report for work on his next shift because of his arrest**. Although the criminal charge was dismissed, the matter was reported in a local newspaper. The employee appealed the discharge to the state Civil Service Commission, which conducted a hearing. A hearing officer determined that there was no connection between the incident leading to the arrest and the custodian's employment by the school district except for the unexcused one-day absence from work. The commission modified the discipline to a one-year suspension, and the school committee initiated a state court action against the commission and employee, seeking reversal of the administrative decision. The court reversed the commission's order, and the employee appealed to the Appeals Court of Massachusetts. The court observed that the commission had correctly found that there was no significant nexus between the employee's conduct in the park and his employment. **There was no evidence that the employee presented a threat to students and the commission had correctly found that the discharge had been unrelated to his fitness to perform his job duties**. The court vacated the trial court judgment and affirmed the commission's order. *School Comm. of Brockton v. Civil Service Comm'n*, 43 Mass.App.Ct. 486, 684 N.E.2d 620 (1997).

◆   A teacher was dismissed for immorality by his Oregon school district after a police officer observed him engaging in homosexual intercourse in a booth at an adult bookstore. The Fair Dismissal Appeals Board (FDAB), a review board composed of teachers, administrators and school board members, found that sexual intercourse in a public place offended the moral standards of the school community and the people of the state of Oregon. The board ruled that the teacher was guilty of immorality under Oregon law and upheld his dismissal. **Following a series of appeals, the supreme court issued its decision holding that teacher**

"immorality" should not be defined by reference to community standards. The court proposed two possible immorality definitions but left to the FDAB the ultimate decision as to which of the two definitions to adopt. The FDAB was ordered to decide on a definition and then hear the teacher's case. *Ross v. Springfield School Dist. No. 19*, 716 P.2d 724 (Or.1986).

D. Inappropriate Language

Where objectionable language has been used in the classroom resulting in attempted dismissals of teachers, the courts generally look at the surrounding circumstances and consider the culpability of the teachers involved. If the language had a definite educational purpose and was not used merely for its own sake or if the teacher could not have prevented the language from being used, dismissal will usually not be upheld.

◆   A school board brought disciplinary charges against a high school teacher arising from an incident involving the student literary magazine. The parties settled their dispute under an agreement by which the teacher agreed to refrain from the use of unapproved reading materials and to obtain the principal's approval before using controversial materials. The agreement was to be sealed and not used unless a similar incident arose. A few years later, **students reported that the teacher discussed the topic of "phallogocentrism" and used the words "penis" and clitoris" in a classroom discussion**. The matter was submitted to arbitration and a hearing officer found that the evidence did not support the charges of conduct unbecoming a teacher and insubordination. However, the teacher was fined $3,000 and issued a letter of reprimand as a disciplinary measure.

A New York trial court confirmed the hearing officer's determination but found it was an error to impose a fine as well as a reprimand. It ordered a rehearing limited to the issue of the appropriate penalty, and the teacher appealed to the New York Supreme Court, Appellate Division. The court observed that there was an extensive history between the parties and that the teacher was adequately notified of his need to de-emphasize the sexual aspects of his classroom discussions. There was no merit to the teacher's contention that his academic freedom required protection. Even though teachers have rights to choose methodology under principles of academic freedom, the court held that **school officials must be permitted to establish and apply their curriculum in order to transmit community values, in a manner complying with the First Amendment**. The teacher received fair notice that his prior choice of materials offended community values and there was no basis for vacating the hearing officer's decision. The court affirmed the judgment for the board. *In the Matter of Arbitration Between Bernstein and Norwich City Sch. Dist. Bd. of Educ.*, 726 N.Y.S.2d 474 (N.Y. App. Div. 2001).

◆   A Missouri high school teacher with over 20 years of experience in her school district taught an English class that included a drama segment. **She allowed students to write, perform, and videotape plays that contained extensive profanity**. She neither encouraged nor discouraged the use of profanity by students and was aware that the school student discipline code prohibited student profanity. Based on the videotape of the plays, the district superintendent charged the teacher with wilful or persistent violation of education board regulations and recommended employment termination. The school board held a hearing and voted to terminate the teacher's employment for wilful or persistent violations of school policy. The teacher filed a lawsuit against the school district in the U.S. District Court for the Eastern District of Missouri, which reversed the school board's order and ordered the district to reinstate the teacher. On appeal to the U.S. Court of Appeals, Eighth Circuit, the court overturned the judgment, finding that the teacher received sufficient notice of board policies. **The disciplinary code prohibited student profanity with no exception for creative speech** by students. The district court erroneously found no legitimate academic interest in prohibiting student profanity, and the judgment on the First Amendment claim was reversed. Although there had been references to race by the superintendent and board members during the consideration of the teacher's contract, the court held that the decision was not racially motivated. *Lacks v. Ferguson Reorganized School Dist., R-2*, 147 F.3d 718 (8th Cir.1998).

E. Drug or Alcohol Abuse

Dismissal for drug or alcohol abuse has been at the center of a number of cases. Usually, the seriousness of the offense as well as the continuation of abuse are factors weighed by courts in making their decisions.

◆   A continuing contract elementary school teacher engaged in an alcohol-related binge for three days after the end of a school year. The school board initiated an investigation of the teacher, and a hearing officer determined that since the events concerned were all privately conducted, there should be no sanctions. Nevertheless, the board dismissed the teacher for incompetence and misconduct. The teacher appealed to the Florida District Court of Appeal, which reversed the dismissal. Here, **a tenured teacher had "exhibited a human weakness to a few persons for a few days during a troubled time in her life." This was not enough to warrant dismissal**. The teacher was ordered reinstated. *Clark v. School Bd. of Lake County*, 596 So.2d 735 (Fla.App.5th Dist.1992).

◆   Two 15-year-old girls testified at a grand jury hearing that they had smoked marijuana at the apartment of two brothers who were also teachers. The teachers both pleaded guilty to the misdemeanor of unlawful transactions with a minor. **The board of education took statements from the girls and discharged the teachers**. The issue before the Kentucky Supreme Court was whether the teachers could be dismissed for acts committed during off-duty hours, in the summer, and in the privacy of their own apartment. The court noted, "[a] teacher is held to a standard of personal conduct which does not permit the commission of immoral or criminal acts because of the harmful impression made on the students." **The court decided that the brothers' misconduct was serious and of an immoral and criminal nature**. It said that there was "a direct connection between the misconduct and the teachers' work," and held that the teachers' dismissals were proper because their actions constituted "conduct unbecoming a teacher." *Bd. of Educ. v. Wood*, 717 S.W.2d 837 (Ky.1986).

♦   The Missouri Court of Appeals upheld the dismissal of a tenured teacher due to problems stemming from his habitual abuse of alcohol. **At the dismissal hearing conducted by the school board, the evidence established that the teacher had a serious alcoholism condition** dating back several years. On many occasions he had been in the presence of students while intoxicated, and at least once, he was discovered by other school personnel on school grounds in a state of intoxication. Although he had spent 25 days at an alcohol treatment program, a substitute teacher later discovered a half-full bottle of vodka in his desk drawer, which he admitted to having consumed on school grounds. He was also involved in two alcohol-related automobile accidents, one of which occurred only 36 minutes after he left school in the afternoon and which found him with a blood alcohol content of .25 percent. **The court held that this evidence justified the school board's conclusion that the teacher had a "physical or mental condition unfitting him to instruct or associate with children," as set forth by Missouri law**, and upheld the dismissal. *Christy v. Bd. of Educ.*, 694 S.W.2d 280 (Mo.App.1985).

IV. INCOMPETENCE

Incompetence usually suffices as a reason for dismissal provided the proper procedures are followed.

A. Teaching Deficiencies

♦   A South Dakota school district contracted for 15 years with a community health nurse to provide sex education for elementary students. After a video presentation by the nurse, a teacher with 29 years of experience in the district solicited questions from a group of boys, as had been the established practice for 15 years. **The teacher responded to a question about homosexual practices in explicit language**, prompting complaints from parents. The school board then notified the teacher of a hearing to consider his discharge for incompetence. At the hearing, the school superintendent testified that the teacher's ability to perform his duties had been affected and the board voted to discharge him. A South Dakota circuit court upheld the discharge.

The teacher appealed to the Supreme Court of South Dakota, which noted that incompetence has been described as arising from a course of conduct, series of incidents or habitual failure to perform work with the degree of skill usually displayed by persons regularly employed in such work. **Although a single incident may be sufficient to support a finding of incompetency, the teacher's conduct here did not rise to that level since there was no showing that his teaching ability had been impaired or that students were detrimentally affected**. The school administration had abdicated control over the sex education program and no school officials ever took any steps to place limits upon it. The teacher had participated in the questioning for the past 15 years without incident. Accordingly, one ill-advised answer did not support the finding of incompetence. The court reversed and remanded the case for reinstatement of the teacher. *Collins v. Faith School Dist. No. 46-2*, 574 N.W.2d 889 (S.D.1998).

◆   A high school science teacher was accused of joking about menstrual periods, making obscene gestures at students and making inappropriate jokes and comments. Although the county superintendent was presented with evidence of at least seven such incidents, she determined that the board had failed to establish the teacher's incompetence or unfitness to teach. The state superintendent of public instruction reversed the county superintendent's order, and a state district court affirmed the decision. On appeal, the Supreme Court of Montana observed that **each of the incidents constituted inappropriate conduct by the teacher and indicated his unfitness to continue teaching**. Because the county superintendent had improperly applied the law in this case, the court affirmed the discharge action. *Baldridge v. Bd. of Trustees, Rosebud County School Dist. No. 19, Colstrip, Montana*, 951 P.2d 1343 (Mont.1997).

◆   An Arkansas elementary school teacher taught gifted and talented students in music and reading classes. **In April of her second year at the school, the superintendent of schools recommended that her contract not be renewed and the school board accepted the recommendation**. However, the board failed to comply with state statutory notification requirements and the teacher filed a complaint against the district for failing to comply with the requirements. The board reversed itself and awarded her a new contract, despite her allegedly poor performance and complaints from parents. During the summer, the school superintendent resumed his attempts to terminate the teacher's contract and suspended her with pay prior to the resumption of classes. A hearing was conducted and the school board voted to terminate her contract.

The teacher appealed to a state circuit court which dismissed the complaint. The teacher then appealed to the Supreme Court of Arkansas, seeking reinstatement and back wages. The court observed that the Arkansas Teacher Fair Dismissal Act requires strict compliance with its provisions and provides for the automatic renewal of any teacher's contract where the teacher is not given notice of nonrenewal prior to May 1 of a contract year. In this case, **the school district had attempted to correct its prior defective nonrenewal action after a contract had been awarded for the subsequent school year**. Because there was no conduct in the current school year which would justify employment termination, the board could not terminate the current contract. Although conduct in a prior year may be relevant in a nonrenewal decision, it cannot form the exclusive basis for the termination of a current contract. The court reversed and remanded the case. *Hannon v. Armorel School Dist. No. 9*, 946 S.W.2d 950 (Ark.1997).

◆   **A Louisiana school board demoted a tenured special education teacher to a paraprofessional position for failing to control his behavior-disordered and emotionally disturbed students**. The school administration based the action on 39 charges of incompetence and wilful neglect of duty. The teacher challenged the demotion, and at a school board hearing sought to present evidence of misbehavior by his special education students in other classes and to admit testimony by special education authorities that misbehavior from students in behavior-disordered and emotionally disturbed classifications was to be expected. The board refused to consider this testimony and upheld 20 of the charges for wilful neglect of duty, but dropped the incompetence charges. A Louisiana trial court ordered the board to reinstate the teacher with his full salary and awarded him attorney's fees. The board appealed to the Court of Appeal of Louisiana, Fourth Circuit.

The court held that under Louisiana law, wilful neglect of duty is a permissible statutory ground for demotion of a teacher. **Demotion on this basis must be supported by evidence that the teacher has deliberately violated a direct order or an identifiable school policy.** The evidence in this case indicated that the teacher had not wilfully violated any direct order or identifiable school policy. Because no testimony indicated wilful misconduct, and the incompetence charges had been dropped, the trial court order reinstating the teacher was affirmed. The additional evidence that the teacher had sought to introduce was relevant and had been improperly excluded. The court reversed the award of attorney's fees, but otherwise affirmed the trial court decision. *Coleman v. Orleans Parish School Bd.*, 688 So.2d 1312 (La.App.4th Cir.1997).

◆   **A Missouri school district fired a teacher with 17 years of experience after she failed to comply with specific recommendations to improve her performance.** During her last years of employment, supervisory employees determined that her classroom management and student disciplinary methods needed improvement. They indicated the problems on her evaluations, and discussed them with her. School administrators determined that she had not complied with their recommendations and the school board voted to fire her. The teacher appealed to a Missouri trial court, alleging substantive and procedural violations by the district. The court ordered the board to reinstate her and the district appealed to the Missouri Court of Appeals, Southern District. On appeal, the teacher complained that prior evaluations indicated that she was competent and that the district had created the conditions for her discharge by placing her in charge of a class composed disproportionately of boys and students with disabilities. The court observed that the teacher had received several evaluations indicating a need to improve her classroom management. **There was substantial evidence that her performance was unacceptable. The teacher had failed to comply with curative recommendations** and there was no merit to her argument that the district had engineered her termination by putting her in charge of the school's only third grade class. The district had violated no procedural or substantive due process rights and the court reversed and remanded the trial court decision. *Newcomb v. Humansville R-IV School Dist.,* 908 S.W.2d 821 (Mo.App.S.D.1995).

B. Procedural Problems

◆   After students in a teacher's math classes scored poorly on proficiency tests, she was transferred to a music teaching position. She asserted that the administration refused to help her and that she received no special education support, even though many of her students were enrolled in special education programs. The principal instructed the teacher to observe a class at another school to obtain an effective classroom model. He then rated her performance unsatisfactory in several areas and gave her two books on student discipline. **The teacher received satisfactory remarks on a second evaluation, but problems in some areas persisted, including her continued failure to institute an effective discipline plan.** The principal presented her with a plan for improvement in each deficient area, and the school board did not renew her contract.

The teacher appealed the non-renewal to an Ohio trial court, which found the plan for improvement specific enough to put her on notice of the need for change. She appealed to the Ohio Court of Appeals, asserting that the board violated a state law requiring that teacher evaluations include a written report with specific recommendations for necessary performance improvements. The law also requires identification of the means by which the teacher may obtain assistance in making such improvements. The appeals court rejected the teacher's assertion that the plan for improvement parroted definitions contained in the applicable collective bargaining agreement. **Recommendations are "specific" under Ohio law if they alert a reasonable person of the need for change**. The statute did not burden school boards with the duty to assure that every teacher fully appreciated each suggestion. **The improvement plans were sufficiently specific as they related to the teacher's problem areas and the principal had attempted to assist her**. The court affirmed the contract non-renewal. *Springer v. Bd. of Educ. of Cleveland Heights–Univ. Heights High School*, 2000 Ohio App. LEXIS 920 (Ohio App. 2000).

◆   Two students videotaped a teacher's science class and delivered the tape to the school board for use in disciplinary proceedings against the teacher. The teacher and her labor association demanded that the board not view or rely upon the tape. The board suspended the students from school as allowed by the California Education Code and agreed to await a court ruling on the legality of viewing the tape. **The teacher and association filed a superior court action for an order prohibiting the school board and district from viewing, showing and distributing the tape**. The court denied a request for a preliminary order and the teacher and association petitioned the court of appeal for review.

The court of appeal observed that the state Education Code prohibited students and others from bringing any electronic listening or recording device into a classroom without the prior consent of the teacher and principal of the school. Violation of the section constituted grounds for misdemeanor charges and appropriate school disciplinary action. However, the same section contained a paragraph protecting rights arising from use of electronic listening or recording devices under other provisions of law. **The court found that while the section provided for sanctions against violators, it did not prohibit the use of an illegally made student recording by a school board in a teacher disciplinary action**. A state criminal law prohibiting the use of evidence obtained through the eavesdropping upon or recording of a confidential communication was of no help to the teacher, since the recording had been made in a public classroom and was not a confidential communication. Neither the Education Code nor California privacy law prohibited the board's use of the illegally obtained videotape and the teacher had no privacy expectation regarding her classroom communications. The court denied the petition. *Evens v. Superior Court of Los Angeles County*, 77 Cal.App.4th 320 (1999).

◆   A Kansas school board decided not to renew the contract of an elementary and middle school principal after she had been employed by the district for four years. **The board gave her written reasons for the action including her lack of leadership, organizational skills, and a resulting distrust of her among school staff**. The board permitted her to respond, and then adopted a resolution affirming the action. The principal appealed to a Kansas district court, which held that the board had acted arbitrarily and denied her right to due process by failing to show good cause for nonrenewal. The board appealed to the Supreme Court of Kansas, which distinguished the statute for teacher tenure from the state administrators' act. The court observed that the administrators' act contained no provision requiring good cause for the contract termination of public school administrators, creating an at-will employment relationship for public school principals. **The administrators' act had none of the good cause requirements present in the teacher tenure act, and the court was unwilling to imply a good cause requirement for principals**. Because the school board had complied with the applicable statute, the principal's due process argument was meritless. There was also no merit to her claim that she was entitled to an evaluation during the year of her contract nonrenewal since this requirement applies only if the reason for nonrenewal is incompetence. Because the reasons stated by the board did not include incompetence, the board was not required to perform an evaluation during the year of nonrenewal. The court reversed and remanded the district court decision. *Brown v. Bd. of Educ. Unified School Dist. No. 333*, 928 P.2d 57 (Kan.1996).

◆   A five-year-old Louisiana kindergarten student with a behavior disorder exhibited several incidents of disruptive conduct within a one-week period. The student's classroom teacher brought him to the principal's office on a day when he was experiencing severe behavior problems. **The principal bound the student to a desk with rope and duct tape and placed him in the doorway of her office**. Several teachers and other school employees observed the student crying there for approximately two hours, when he was finally allowed to return to his class. The school board voted to demote the principal for incompetence, and she appealed to a Louisiana district court, which affirmed the board's action. The principal then appealed to the Court of Appeal of Louisiana, First Circuit.

The principal advanced several arguments supporting her position that the vote to demote her was improper. She claimed that one board member was biased against her due to political differences with her husband. She also alleged that the trial court had made evidentiary errors concerning her right to cross-examine witnesses and obtain the student's medical records. The court found no merit to these arguments, finding that the overwhelming majority of the board had found in favor of demotion and that the single vote of the board member was not evidence of bias. **The principal had been afforded the due process to which she was entitled** and had not been deprived of her due process rights by the presentation of tape recorded statements by adverse witnesses at her hearing. There was no merit to her argument that she should be entitled to receive the student's medical records, as they were irrelevant to the issue of her actions. Because there was substantial evidence that the principal was incompetent, the court affirmed the decision to demote her. *Sylvester v. Cancienne*, 664 So.2d 1259 (La.App.1st Cir.1995).

V.   INSUBORDINATION

Courts will generally uphold the discharge of school employees if insubordination can be proven. However, where a charge of insubordination is based upon an employee's spoken words or writings, a school district must be careful

to avoid disciplining the employee for speaking on matters of "public concern,"
which are matters protected by the First Amendment's free speech guarantees.

◆   Several teacher aides worked for a board of cooperative educational services. A
BOCES representative instructed them that they should report any concerns about
classroom matters to the supervisor of special education or school principal. Within
one month, **the aides became aware of bizarre and inappropriate sexual conduct
by a teacher toward a student**. They did not report the misconduct for over one
month, and then brought it to the attention of a union representative, not a BOCES
supervisor. The union representative informed BOCES of the report and BOCES
discharged the aides for insubordination.

The aides filed improper-practice charges against BOCES with the New York
Public Employment Relations Board, asserting that the BOCES violated the state
Civil Service Law by discharging them for reporting a teacher's suspected misconduct to their union representative, instead of a BOCES supervisor. An administrative
law judge found that the BOCES committed an improper practice because the report
by the aides was protected conduct. The Public Employment Relations Board
reversed and dismissed the charges and the aides appealed to the New York Supreme
Court, Appellate Division. The court held that the PERB and administrative law
judge had correctly found that the aides were engaged in protected activity when they
consulted with their union representative. However, **their discharges had not
been improperly motivated, since there were legitimate educational and
business reasons for the actions**. The evidence indicated that BOCES had discharged the aides for failing to follow a supervisor's directive and jeopardizing the
safety of a child under their supervision, not for engaging in protected conduct. The
court confirmed the PERB decision. *Hoey et al. v. New York State Public
Employment Relations Board*, 725 N.Y.S.2d 449 (N.Y. App. Div. 2001).

◆   A Colorado language arts teacher received occasional disciplinary notices,
although no formal disciplinary proceedings were ever brought against him until he
showed the film *1900* to his logic and debate class. The R-rated film depicts nudity,
sexual conduct, drug use and violence. After a parent complained, the principal
placed the teacher on administrative leave. **The district superintendent recommended dismissal for insubordination, neglect of duty and other good cause**
for violation of a district policy requiring teachers to provide their principals with
20 days' prior written notice before using a controversial learning resource. A
hearing officer recommended retaining the teacher since the district had failed to
publish its policy to teachers and the other charges would not warrant dismissal. The
school board unanimously resolved to dismiss the teacher. He appealed to the
Colorado Court of Appeals, which reversed, finding the teacher lacked formal
notice of the policy and that the other alleged misconduct was insufficient to justify
dismissal. The board appealed to the Supreme Court of Colorado.

The state supreme court reversed, stating that the teacher violated the controversial learning resources policy, and that no First Amendment violation occurred.
Schools can regulate the curriculum, as long as the regulation is "reasonably related
to a legitimate pedagogical concern," without violating the First Amendment. The
policy established a reasonable method of regulating possibly inappropriate materials,
therefore, it did not violate the First Amendment. The supreme court rejected the

teacher's assertion that the policy was overbroad and vague, finding no evidence to support this assertion. **Although the teacher may have lacked formal notice of the policy, he had reasonable notice, given his knowledge that prior approval was required before using controversial materials within his classroom**. Accordingly, no due process violation occurred. The dismissal of the teacher was upheld. *Board of Educ. of Jefferson County Sch. Dist. R-1 v. Wilder,* 960 P.2d 695 (Colo. 1998).

◆   A Florida art teacher served in Dade County public schools for 24 years and was described as a talented and caring teacher. However, school officials observed a pattern of insubordination during the last 14 years of her employment. She sent a religious letter to a faculty member, gave pocket Bibles to her students, and sent numerous unwanted gifts and messages to a school principal. Following complaints about the teacher's unprofessional demeanor, she was given a detailed improvement plan. **After she refused to complete the plan, the school board suspended her for gross insubordination and wilful neglect of duties**. An administrative law judge affirmed the board's subsequent decision to discharge the teacher and she appealed to the Florida District Court of Appeal. When the court affirmed the judgment, the teacher filed a separate lawsuit against the school board in the U.S. District Court for the Southern District of Florida, asserting religious discrimination in violation of Title VII of the Civil Rights Act of 1964 and violations of her First Amendment speech rights.

The board moved for summary judgment on grounds that the federal lawsuit was barred by the prior state court judgment. **The court held that since the teacher received a full and fair opportunity to present all her claims in a state forum, she could not relitigate them even as part of a different cause of action in federal court**. The religious discrimination claim had been fully considered at the state level. Even though the state court action had not been based upon Title VII or the First Amendment, the proceedings involved the same parties and identical issues. The court awarded summary judgment to the school system. *Tuma v. Dade County Pub. Schools,* 989 F.Supp. 1471 (S.D.Fla.1998).

◆   An Alabama school board reorganized its district, combining its high schools and a vocational school into a single facility. It notified affected teachers of their upcoming employment transfers prior to the commencement of the school year. The new facility was not completed at the start of the school year, and teachers and students continued to report to old facilities until instructed otherwise. **After several months, the board ordered an auto mechanics teacher to report to the new facility. He** claimed that the new facility was not secure enough to protect his tools and equipment, and **refused to report** there. Administrators scheduled a meeting at which the teacher voiced his concerns. The teacher then stated that he would report to the new facility. When he failed to do so, the school board voted to terminate his contract. The state tenure commission affirmed the dismissal and appeal reached the Court of Civil Appeals of Alabama. The court of appeals found that the teacher's termination for insubordination and neglect of duty was justifiable under state law. **Insubordination was defined as "the wilful refusal of a teacher to obey an order that a superior officer is entitled to have obeyed so long as such order is reasonably related to the duties of the teacher."** Because the order to report to the new school was reasonable, the teacher's refusal to report there after receiving two reprimands constituted insubordination. The court affirmed his dismissal. *Stephens v. Alabama State Tenure Comm'n*, 634 So.2d 549 (Ala.Civ.App.1993).

◆   A Kansas teacher scheduled a job interview in a Texas district and requested leave for that day. The principal denied the request because it was during the last week of the school year. The teacher went to the interview anyway and had his wife call in sick for him. Later that day, the principal of the district where he had interviewed called the principal of the school where the teacher worked asking for a recommendation. The principal, upon learning that the teacher had interviewed in Texas on the day he called in sick, called the teacher to his office and told him to leave school property. He was later fired for insubordination. After a hearing, the board approved the termination. The teacher appealed to a trial court for review of the board's decision. The court affirmed the board's termination of the teacher. The teacher then appealed to the Court of Appeals of Kansas. Insubordination is defined as a wilful or intentional disregard of reasonable instructions. **The court held that a single incident of insubordination can be sufficient to justify termination. It stated that the teacher's act of calling in sick in order to attend a job interview was insubordination and justified his termination**. *Gaylord v. Bd. of Educ., School Dist. 218*, 794 P.2d 307 (Kan.App.1990).

◆   A South Dakota teacher requested leave of absence for personal reasons. **While on leave, he took a teaching position in Alaska**. In April, he filed a written notice of his intent to return to the South Dakota school. Although positions were open for which he was qualified, the school board refused to hire him. He then contacted his union representative and attempted to file a grievance with the board. The board informed him that he could not file a grievance because he was no longer considered an employee of the district. He then appealed to the state Department of Labor, Labor and Management Division, where the board maintained that he deceived it as to his reasons for his leave of absence. However, he was never told there were conditions or limits on the leave, nor that he was prohibited from teaching while on leave. His leave of absence was never rescinded, and he was never advised that he had violated the terms of the leave until he was refused employment upon returning to the district. After the department concluded that he did not deceive the superintendent or the board, **the Supreme Court of South Dakota determined that the leave of absence was valid** on its face. It was authorized by the school board, his request was presented to and approved by the board, he was never informed he had violated the terms of his leave, and the board took no action to rescind or otherwise invalidate it. Therefore, the district did not carry its burden of proving deceit. *Rininger v. Bennett County School Dist.*, 468 N.W.2d 423 (S.D.1991).

◆   A Florida school principal disagreed with the school's head custodian about whether to renew another custodian's contract. The principal considered the head custodian's conduct concerning this disagreement to be impolite and disrespectful, so he terminated the custodian's employment. The school board upheld the termination, but the District Court of Appeal of Florida reversed. The head custodian was supposedly fired for gross insubordination in accordance with Florida law.

However, **the court stated that while the head custodian's behavior may have been disrespectful, there was no competent substantial evidence that the custodian refused to obey a direct order of the principal**. If the principal had given the custodian a letter of warning directly instructing him to cease his disruptive actions the result would have been different. The head custodian was reinstated for the remainder of the term of his annual contract. *Rosario v. Burke*, 605 So.2d 523 (Fla.App.2d Dist.1992).

VI. RESIGNATION AND RETIREMENT

Generally, once an employee tenders a resignation to the superintendent or school board, it may not be withdrawn unless the board approves of the reinstatement.

A. Resignation

◆   A Connecticut high school male teacher wrote flirtatious notes and a birthday card to a 16-year-old female student. The student showed the notes to her parents and they complained to the school's principal. He advised the teacher to refrain from any contact with the student pending an investigation, but the teacher instead approached the student to ask why she had reported him. He was then suspended with pay, and the school board voted to consider termination of his contract. The teacher agreed to resign in exchange for a severance pay package under which his resignation took effect after one year. During the year, the teacher sought to revoke his resignation, claiming that he had been forced to quit while suffering from depression and stress. **The revocation was not accepted, so the teacher filed a lawsuit against the school board** in a Connecticut trial court. **The court awarded judgment to the board** and the teacher appealed to the Appellate Court of Connecticut. The court of appeals determined that the trial court's ruling should be affirmed. *Geren v. Bd. of Educ. of the Town of Brookfield*, 36 Conn.App. 282, 650 A.2d 616 (1994).

◆   An Alabama woman was the secretary of a school for twelve years. After she was notified that she would be going from the position of secretary to that of a teacher's aide, **she delivered a letter of resignation to the principal that was accepted**. A replacement secretary was hired and began working. Two weeks later, the secretary attempted to rescind her resignation. However, one week later the board formally accepted her resignation. She filed a complaint in an Alabama trial court requesting that the board reinstate her. The court found for the school board. The secretary appealed to the Court of Civil Appeals of Alabama. She contended that her resignation was improperly accepted because it had been previously withdrawn. However, the appellate court disagreed and determined that **because the board had relied on her letter by hiring a replacement, it had accepted her resignation despite the informality**. *Mitchell v. Jackson County Bd. of Educ.*, 582 So.2d 1128 (Ala.Civ.App.1991).

◆   A Massachusetts teacher submitted her resignation to the district superintendent. The district found a replacement and the teacher went to work at another school district. After two days of work, she decided that the position was not what she had expected. She requested her old district to take no action on her letter of resignation. She stated that she was ready to resume her teaching duties. The district refused to withdraw the resignation and the teacher sued seeking reinstatement. The trial court entered judgment in favor of the teacher and the district appealed. The Supreme Judicial Court of Massachusetts held that **the teacher's attempt to withdraw her letter of resignation had no legal effect since the board did not actually need to take any action on a resignation**. The court vacated the trial court's decision and entered judgment for the school committee. *Sinkevich v. School Committee of Raynham*, 530 N.E.2d 173 (Mass.1988).

B. Retirement

The Age Discrimination in Employment Act of 1967 (ADEA) and the Fourteenth Amendment's Equal Protection Clause provide evaluation standards for public school employee retirement. Please see Chapter Six, Section V, for cases brought under the ADEA. Where the ADEA is inapplicable (for example, where the employer maintains fewer than 20 employees), state law takes effect.

◆   Three classroom teachers notified their district in 1997 that they would accept early retirement benefits the following year under the 1995-1997 master contract between the organization and school board. The board and organization negotiated a master contract for 1997-2000 that dramatically reduced early retirement benefits. **The retirees brought a state court action against the organization for breach of the duty of fair representation, and against the board for breach of contract for failing to pay benefits under the 1995-1997 contract**. An Indiana trial court dismissed the complaint, ruling that it should have been filed with the Indiana Education Employment Relations Board.

A court of appeals reversed the trial court judgment and the Indiana Supreme Court agreed to review the case. It held that the trial court correctly held that **the retirees needed to exhaust their available administrative remedies by filing their unfair-representation claims with the IEERB**. The state Certificated Educational Employee Bargaining Act recognized the right of school employees to organize and collectively bargain through employee associations, creating a method to resolve labor disputes through the IEERB. However, this ruling did not mean that the trial court had no jurisdiction over the breach-of-contract claim. **The IEERB had no power to consider the breach-of-contract claim** concerning the board's liability for early retirement benefits. By dismissing the breach of contract claim, the trial court had effectively denied the retirees the only forum in which the claim could be heard. The state supreme court ordered the trial court to retain jurisdiction over the breach-of-contract claim, suspending any action on it until the IEERB made a final decision on the retirees' unfair-representation claim. *Fratus v. Marion Community Schs. Bd. of Trustees*, No. 27S02-0005-CV-295, 2001 WL 615171 (Ind. 2001).

◆   A Pennsylvania teacher advised his school district that he wished to retire only two days in advance of the proposed effective date. The teacher submitted a written notice and quit reporting to work. He was removed from the district payroll, signed an additional document verifying his employment separation and began receiving retirement benefits. **Several weeks after giving notice, but before any school board resolution approving his resignation, the teacher attempted to rescind his retirement** by written request. The district declined to accept the rescission letter, and the teacher filed a lawsuit against the district in a Pennsylvania trial court. The court held for the school district, and the teacher appealed to the Commonwealth Court of Pennsylvania. The court observed that nothing in Pennsylvania law required any school board resolution to accept or reject a voluntary retirement. **The court noted that a requirement in Pennsylvania law that delayed the effective date of a written resignation for 60 days did not apply in cases of retirement**. It also stated that the teacher had referred to his "retirement" several times in his own correspondence. The commonwealth court affirmed the trial court's decision. *Bowman v. School Dist. of Philadelphia*, 661 A.2d 913 (Pa.Commw.1995).

◆   The Pennsylvania Public School Employees' Retirement System permits public school teachers to purchase service credit for work performed in public schools. **Three public school teachers who had formerly worked for private schools sought to purchase service credit for their work at approved private schools**. The state Public School Employees' Retirement Board denied the request, and the teachers appealed to the Commonwealth Court of Pennsylvania. On appeal, the teachers argued that they should be entitled to purchase credit in the system because the private schools were subject to regulation by the state education department. They also argued that they were entitled to purchase credit because private schools were reimbursed by the education department for teaching exceptional students placed in private schools by public school districts. The commonwealth court determined that state regulation was insufficient to confer public school status upon private schools. **The legislative intent of the retirement code provision was to benefit public school employees, and the teachers' private school employment did not relate to public employment. Accordingly, the court affirmed the retirement board's order denying the purchase of service credit**. *Cain v. Pub. School Employees' Retirement System*, 651 A.2d 660 (Pa.Commw.1994).

◆   A tenured secretary gave early notice of her intent to retire to a school district so that she could gain additional benefits under a collective bargaining agreement. The district accepted. After her husband died and her child fell ill, she requested a two-year extension of her intended retirement date. **The school board conditioned its acceptance of the request on a satisfactory job performance evaluation**. A problem later developed which eventually led to a denial of the requested extension. The secretary appealed, arguing that none of the other 17 recent extensions had been subject to such conditions. The issue reached the Supreme Court of New Jersey. The court held that the dispute must be resolved in light of the parties' mutual intent. The collective bargaining agreement addressed notification of intent to retire, but did not address whether it could be modified. Therefore, the court ruled that the board's past practices evidenced the parties' intent. Specifically, **the board's almost rubber stamp acceptances of other extension requests was held to have had the legal effect of notice to employees that the notices could be rescinded**. The court noted, however, that the limited scope of this decision did not extend to cases of a board's reliance and estoppel, nor did it apply where an alteration in past practices was adequately distinguished. The cause was remanded for a determination of damages. *Hall v. Bd. of Educ.*, 593 A.2d 304 (N.J.1991).

◆   **New Jersey law allowed institutions of higher education within the state the discretion to retire tenured faculty at age 70.** A group of previously and currently tenured faculty members at various New Jersey state colleges sued, claiming that the statute which granted that discretion was unconstitutional because it amounted to discrimination on the basis of age. They claimed that such discrimination violated the Equal Protection and Due Process Clauses of the Fourteenth Amendment and similar provisions of the New Jersey state constitution. The state claimed that the statute violated neither constitution and moved for summary judgment. The U.S. District Court for the District of New Jersey stated that in order to withstand constitutional scrutiny, statutes which make classifications based on age must be rationally related to a legitimate governmental interest. **Making way for the young, planning for the future, creating greater diversity, injecting new energy, reducing costs, and similar interests all supported the statute.** Even though these same bases are often used to support acts of age discrimination, they were sufficient to support the statute against constitutional challenge. *Freund v. Florio*, 795 F.Supp. 702 (D.N.J.1992).

C. Retirement Benefits

◆   A custodian applied for early retirement benefits after working for 30 years. The district's early retirement policy provided an explicit formula for calculating benefits, but left the school board with discretion to determine terms of payment and to "phase out" or repeal the policy with two years' prior notice. The board rejected the custodian's application for benefits without stating a reason. It invited him to rescind his resignation and continue working, but he commenced a Colorado trial court action against the district, board and individual board members. **The court awarded summary judgment to the custodian, ruling that the district policy created an implied contract** that allowed no discretion to deny benefits.

The board appealed to the court of appeals, arguing that it had complete discretion to phase out the policy without prior notice to employees. The court agreed with the custodian that changing the early retirement policy was a significant district action that could not be done simply by voting against an application for benefits. **The district was required to confer with groups and individuals affected by the phase-out before denying individual applications.** There had been no official announcement about the policy until a year after the board denied the employee's application, when it deleted the policy. Despite this ruling, the court held that the board could still avoid making early retirement payments to the employee if paying him would violate its state law obligation to refrain from deficit spending. The court remanded the case to the trial court to determine whether the district had the means to pay the benefits without spending in excess of appropriations. *Shaw v. Sargent School Dist. No. RE-33-J*, 21 P.3d 446 (Colo. App. 2001).

◆   The South Carolina legislature enacted an appropriations act authorizing a one-time retirement incentive bonus for public employees. The act established certain minimum requirements for service credit and age, and set mandatory dates for employees to make an irrevocable election to receive the incentive. One school district adopted the retirement incentive plan, with the additional requirement that employees work through the end of the current school year to be eligible. Although the requirement was stated in a memorandum distributed to all employees, **one school district employee retired in October of the current school year but claimed entitlement to the retirement incentive.** When the district refused to pay the incentive, she filed a lawsuit against it in a South Carolina circuit court. The court held that she was not entitled to receive the incentive, and she appealed to the Supreme Court of South Carolina. The court observed that South Carolina law authorizes school districts to prescribe necessary rules and regulations that are not inconsistent with state law. In general, additional regulations by a municipality that are not as broad as state law and are not inconsistent with the law may be reconciled where either is silent as to express or implied conditions. **Because the school district regulation did not conflict with state law, the employee was not entitled to the incentive bonus.** *Wright v. Richland County School Dist. Two*, 486 S.E.2d 740 (S.C.1997).

◆   A Rhode Island statute requires the full payment of teacher salaries where teachers are absent because of injuries resulting from an assault at work. The statute, however, requires injured teachers to apply to the Rhode Island employees retirement system for appropriate benefits at the conclusion of one year. One teacher injured in a student assault received her full salary under the law for one year, reduced by the receipt of workers' compensation benefits. At the conclusion of the year, she obtained a declaratory judgment from a Rhode Island superior court that her right to a full salary continued despite her failure to apply to the retirement system for appropriate benefits. The school committee appealed to the Supreme Court of Rhode Island, which held that **the statute requires a disabled employee to apply to the Rhode Island employees retirement system for appropriate benefits and the teacher's failure to do so cut off her entitlement to further full salary benefits.** The court reversed and remanded the circuit court judgment. *Woonsocket Teachers' Guild Local Union 951, AFT v. Woonsocket School Comm.*, 694 A.2d 727 (R.I.1997).

◆   The Maine public employee retirement system provides benefits for teachers and other employees based upon fixed contributions to the system. **Retiring employees may qualify for a pension in one of several ways,** including the reaching of the statutory retirement age with service requirements of a specified duration. The state legislature responded to a budget crisis in 1993 by increasing required member contributions, capping salary increases for inclusion in the calculation of benefits, delaying a cost-of-living adjustment, increasing the regular retirement age, increasing the penalty for early retirement and eliminating the use of sick or vacation pay for computing retirement benefits. The Maine Education Association and a group of public school teachers filed a federal district court action against state officials, seeking a declaration that the amendments violated the Contract Clause of the Constitution. The court ruled that the amendments violated the Contract Clause as to certain plan members who had satisfied the age and service requirements.

State officials appealed to the U.S. Court of Appeals, First Circuit, which held that a state legislature must clearly intend to bind itself in a contractual matter before a Contract Clause action may be brought. Absent a clear indication of intent to be bound, the presumption is that a law merely declares a policy to be pursued. Here, **the state of Maine had not unmistakably shown its intention to create enforceable private contract rights with respect to the modification of employee retirement benefits prior to an employee's actual retirement.** The amendments did not attempt to revoke retirement benefits earned by those teachers who had already retired and there was no Contract Clause violation. The court reversed the district court decision. *Parker v. Wakelin*, 123 F.3d 1 (1st Cir.1997).

♦   A Pennsylvania teacher participated in a 29-day strike during a school year that limited his total work days for the calendar year to 163. Because the state public school employees' retirement code requires 180 full day sessions of work or 1,000 hours of employment in a year for the attainment of a full year of credited service, **the employee received only .91 years of service for the year in which the strike occurred.** A state hearing examiner determined that because the state defined a full year as either 180 days or 1,000 hours of employment, and the employee had actually worked 1,222 hours during the strike year, he was entitled to a full year of service credit. An administrative board affirmed the decision, but the Commonwealth Court of Pennsylvania reversed that decision and the employee appealed to the Supreme Court of Pennsylvania. The court determined that **the statute should not be construed as providing credit for days that teachers did not work or contribute into the state retirement fund.** The commonwealth court had properly ruled that the board's regulation was contrary to the statute since the legislature did not intend a full school year to encompass only 1,000 hours of work, but instead contemplated 180 days. The court held the regulation invalid and affirmed the commonwealth court order. *Commonwealth of Pennsylvania, PSERS v. Pennsylvania School Boards Ass'n, Inc.*, 682 A.2d 291 (Pa.1996).

♦   The Maine State Retirement System calculates teacher retirement benefits on the basis of average final compensation. Compensation includes salaries and wages, but does not include payments for more than 30 days of unused, accumulated or accrued sick leave. State law excludes from consideration as compensation any other payment that is not for actual services rendered. Twenty-three Maine teachers received payments for up to 30 days of unused, accumulated sick leave as a retirement incentive. **The retirement system notified each of them that their retirement benefits had erroneously included up to 30 days of sick leave in the calculation of benefits.** Some of the retirees claimed that they had retired only because they were advised that their sick leave payments would be factored into their retirement benefit calculation. They filed a lawsuit against the state retirement system in a state trial court, seeking an order that would require inclusion of sick leave in their benefit calculations. The court held for the retirement system, and the retirees appealed to the Supreme Judicial Court of Maine.

The court found that while the statute allowed up to 30 days of earned sick leave to be included in compensation for the calculation of benefits, **an exclusion in the statute for other payments that were not for actual services rendered was applicable to defeat the retirees' claim that unused sick leave should be**

included as earnable compensation. The state board of retirement had permissibly interpreted this clause of the statute as not including any fringe benefits paid as inducements to retirement. However, because some of the retirees alleged that they had been induced to retire with the understanding that unused sick leave would be included into their retirement benefit calculations, these employees were entitled to reconsideration. The court vacated and remanded this aspect of the trial court decision. *Berry v. Bd. of Trustees, Maine State Retirement System*, 663 A.2d 14 (Me.1995).

◆   The Oklahoma legislature passed an act making education employees eligible for the state employees group health insurance program. School districts were required to either provide coverage for their employees under the plan or to obtain other insurance that was comparable. Because the act increased the number of employees eligible for the state plan by almost 56,000, **the act transferred almost $40 million from the state teachers retirement system to the education employees group insurance reserve fund**. To offset this transfer, the act also provided for the diversion of increased revenues from state gross production taxes on natural gas to the teachers retirement system. A group of school employees filed a lawsuit against the state and education employees group insurance program in a state trial court, claiming that their pension rights were compromised by the legislation. The court determined that the act was constitutional, and the employees appealed to the Supreme Court of Oklahoma. **The court stated that under Oklahoma law, public employee pension rights were contractually based and were treated as trust funds which the legislature could modify if necessary and reasonable**. The transfer of funds from the teachers retirement system did not prejudice the employees because the act called for an increase of revenues from the gross production tax. The act did not violate the state constitution and the changes it mandated were reasonable and necessary. *Taylor v. State and Educ. Employees Group Ins. Program*, 897 P.2d 275 (Okla.1995).

VII. UNEMPLOYMENT BENEFITS

Generally, where a school employee has worked a specified minimum amount of time, unemployment benefits will be available. However, if the employee has committed misconduct resulting in dismissal for cause, benefits are properly denied or lowered.

A. Eligibility Requirements

◆   A Missouri school district responded to a loss in revenue by assigning a tenured teacher who was certified in music and English to teach two band classes for which she claimed to have no experience or expertise. **She resigned after informing the school board by letter that the assignment required considerable time beyond classroom instruction and constituted an excessive teaching load**. She filed a claim for unemployment compensation benefits in which she stated that her employment separation was caused by lack of work. Her claim was initially approved, but an appeals board reversed the determination, finding that she had voluntarily separated from work without good cause attributable to her work or

employer. The state labor and industrial relations commission affirmed the decision, and appeal reached the Missouri Court of Appeals, Southern District. **The
court adopted the commission's order, reasoning that claimants have an
affirmative obligation to attempt to resolve work-related problems prior to
abandoning employment**. A claimant must act in good faith before a finding of
good cause to leave employment may be found. The court rejected the teacher's
assertion that the changed working conditions created good cause or established
good faith on her behalf. It affirmed the denial of benefits. *Standefer v. Missouri
Div. of Labor and Industrial Relations Comm'n*, 959 S.W.2d 479
(Mo.App.S.D.1998).

◆   A Rhode Island teacher was laid off after three years of employment and began
receiving unemployment compensation benefits. **She accepted substitute teaching assignments from two school districts which partially set off some of her
unemployment benefits**. She filed a claim for additional benefits based on the lack
of available work during the school Christmas break, which was denied by the state
Department of Employment and Training (DET). Her later claim for additional
unemployment benefits for the summer was also denied on the basis of a state law
preclusion for the payment of benefits to school employees during holidays and
summer breaks. A Rhode Island trial court found that the claims for additional
benefits had been properly denied, but it reversed the decision concerning previously awarded benefits. DET appealed to the Supreme Court of Rhode Island,
arguing that the acceptance of substitute teaching work resulted in the denial of
unemployment benefits, even for benefits previously awarded for prior fulltime
work. The supreme court disagreed with the DET, finding that **the teacher's
substitute teaching income had been properly deducted from her unemployment compensation benefits**. The teacher was not precluded from receiving
previously-awarded benefits based on her prior fulltime employment since she
remained eligible for these benefits under state law. *Brouillette v. Dep't of
Employment and Training*, 677 A.2d 1344 (R.I.1996).

◆   A West Virginia custodian worked for his school district during the summer
months as a painter for several years. The school board did not offer him employment for the summer break one year, and he filed a claim for unemployment
compensation benefits. The West Virginia Department of Employment Security
declared **the employee disqualified from benefits on the basis of the existence
of reasonable assurances that he would be working for the school board that
fall** as a custodian. The department's board of review reversed this decision, finding
that the employee was entitled to receive benefits since he had worked for the
school district in prior summers and was effectively laid off. This decision was
affirmed by a West Virginia circuit court and the education board appealed to the
Supreme Court of Appeals of West Virginia. The court held that **service personnel
employed by school boards are ineligible for unemployment compensation
benefits unless they hold a second, separate contract for the summer months,
or show the existence of a continuing contractual relationship**. Since the
employee had failed to show that he had a continuing contract for the summer break,
he was not entitled to receive benefits and the circuit court decision was reversed.
Raleigh County Bd. of Educ. v. Gatson, 468 S.E.2d 923 (W.Va.1996).

◆   A Rhode Island school committee voted not to renew the employment contracts of eight teachers because of the anticipated return from leave of several more senior teachers. The committee also voted not to renew the contract of the least senior of three speech pathologists employed by the district. The district's deputy superintendent advised the teachers that he expected at least 20 vacancies the following school year. **The superintendent of schools sent a letter to each teacher advising them that they could expect reemployment the following year**. The teachers and the speech pathologist filed claims for unemployment compensation that were denied on the basis of reasonable assurances of being reemployed the following year. The employees appealed to a Rhode Island district court, which held that the unemployment compensation board's decisions were clearly erroneous. The state board appealed to the Supreme Court of Rhode Island. The court observed that the state unemployment compensation statute distinguished between school employees who were unemployed, and those who were temporarily out of work because of holidays or summer break. **Teachers who were currently under contract or who received reasonable assurances of employment for the upcoming school year were ineligible for unemployment benefits**. There was sufficient evidence in the record that the teachers had received reasonable assurances of reemployment. The speech pathologist's claim was distinguishable because her certification was limited to speech pathology and she had not received assurances from the district that she would be reemployed. She was entitled to receive unemployment compensation benefits. *Baker v. Dep't of Employment and Training Bd. of Review*, 637 A.2d 360 (R.I. 1994).

B. Misconduct

◆   A Mississippi high school teacher showed his anatomy class a movie about alligator control. The school principal warned him that the film was unrelated to the subject matter of the class and stated that any films presented to a class must relate to class subject matter. Several weeks later, the teacher wished to reward his students for working hard by allowing them to vote on a film to watch in class. The students voted to watch *Silence of the Lambs*, an R-rated movie. A student brought the film and the class watched the first 45 minutes of it, with the rest to be seen the following day. However, parents complained. **The teacher resigned under pressure and filed a claim for unemployment compensation benefits** with the state employment security commission. The commission denied the application based on the misconduct section of state law. The teacher appealed to a state trial court, which reversed. The commission appealed to the Supreme Court of Mississippi.

The court commented that the display of an R-rated movie to students under the age of 17 demonstrated poor judgment. The teacher had been warned that any films presented to classes must relate to class subject matter. The film did not relate to any course work. **Because the teacher had intentionally disregarded the principal's warning and failed to preview the movie, there was substantial evidence to uphold the commissioner's determination that he was guilty of misconduct** under the state code. The trial court order awarding unemployment compensation benefits was reversed. *Mississippi Employment Security Comm'n v. Harris*, 672 So.2d 739 (Miss. 1996).

♦   A Pennsylvania teacher was frequently absent or late for work and other teachers and some students occasionally noticed alcohol on his breath. The school district learned that he had been convicted of three charges of driving under the influence of alcohol. It fired him for immorality and persistent neglect of duties and he applied for unemployment compensation benefits. After the claim was denied, the Commonwealth Court of Pennsylvania held that **because there was substantial evidence that the teacher's misconduct was wilful and had directly affected his ability to teach, the denial of unemployment benefits was justified**. Under previous Pennsylvania decisions, teachers are held to a higher standard of conduct than other unemployment compensation applicants. *Altemus v. Unemployment Compensation Bd. of Review*, 681 A.2d 866 (Pa.Commw.1996).

♦   A New York school district hired a probationary teacher to teach business education for a three-year probationary term. The district informed her that her continued employment with the district was contingent upon her taking and passing the National Teacher's Examination (NTE). Although the NTE consists of three separate parts, the teacher chose to take only one part, which she failed. She was again told that she had to take and pass the NTE to continue working in the district. However, the next time the test was offered, she registered for only two of the three parts. She was then discharged. When she sought unemployment insurance benefits, the New York Supreme Court, Appellate Division, found that **she had voluntarily engaged in conduct which eliminated any possibility that she could keep her employment. Accordingly, she was disqualified from receiving unemployment insurance benefits**. *Matter of Ambrose,* 595 N.Y.S.2d 126 (A.D.3d Dep't 1993).

♦   A woman worked for a Vermont school as a secretary in the housekeeping and maintenance departments. During the course of her employment, the head of maintenance (her supervisor) made sexual advances toward her on at least three occasions. Although the employee objected to and fended off the supervisor's harassment, she never told anyone else of the offending behavior. She quit, but when she sought unemployment compensation the Vermont Employment Security Board denied her benefits. The board stated that the school's business manager had no knowledge of the harassment. Therefore, he had no opportunity to remedy the problem. The Vermont Supreme Court stated that knowledge may be imputed to the employer in situations where the harassment took place at the office, during working hours, and was carried out by someone with the authority to hire, fire, promote and discipline. This conclusion was also bolstered by the fact that the school had an inadequate procedure for dealing with acts of sexual harassment. **The court reversed the board's conclusion that sexual harassment could not be attributable to the school because of lack of notice. It remanded for a determination on whether the employee quit for good cause given the circumstances**. *Allen v. Dep't of Employment Training*, 618 A.2d 1317 (Vt.1992).

VIII. WRONGFUL DISCHARGE

Nontenured teachers and administrators can be discharged upon expiration of their contracts. If the employees have been hired at will, they can be fired for any reason or no reason at all. However, an improper motive—one that violates state law or public policy—will result in a finding of wrongful discharge.

♦   During her fourth year of employment by a New York school district, a teacher was called on to testify before an impartial hearing officer in proceedings held under the Individuals with Disabilities Education Act. She gave testimony that supported the position advocated by the student's parent, who was successful in the IDEA proceedings. Almost five years later, **the district superintendent of instruction notified the teacher by letter that she would be terminated from her position** as a home instruction teacher. The letter referred to the teacher's "record of instruction" and stated that she had refused to turn in a grade for a student, failed to respond to repeated requests for work samples by the same student and failed to schedule an appointment with the superintendent. The school district discharged the teacher several months later.

Over two years after the receipt of her discharge notice, and over seven years after she testified in the IDEA hearing, the teacher sued the school district in a federal district court for retaliatory discharge. She asserted that the district discharged her because of her testimony at the hearing, in violation of her speech rights under the First Amendment and her Due Process and Equal Protection rights under the Fourteenth Amendment. She also advanced state law claims for defamation, intentional infliction of emotional distress, breach of contract and wrongful discharge. **A federal district court conducted a hearing on the district's motion to dismiss the teacher's amended complaint and determined that she had failed to state a claim for deprivation of her constitutional rights**. It also dismissed her state law claims in conformity with federal rules. The teacher appealed to the Second Circuit, which affirmed the judgment for the same reasons given by the district court. She failed to make out a claim for retaliation under the First Amendment or show that the district deprived her of any Due Process rights under the Fourteenth Amendment. Her claims of hostile work environment were time-barred. *Reynolds v. Board of Education of Wappingers Central School District*, 208 F.3d 203 (2d Cir. 2000).

♦   An employee of a Washington college could only be disciplined "for cause" under the applicable collective bargaining agreement. The employee received favorable employment evaluations until she was assigned a new supervisor. Before her third grievance under the CBA was resolved, she was discharged. She ultimately obtained a favorable arbitration award in a grievance action contesting her termination. The arbitrator ordered the college to reinstate her, as she was not terminated for cause following progressive discipline. The employee filed a total of four unfair labor practice complaints before the state Public Employment Relations Commission (PERC), complaining of retaliation and challenging her discharge. Before resolution of the PERC claims, **the employee sued the college and four officials in a state superior court for wrongful discharge in violation of public policy, defamation and First Amendment violations** via 42 U.S.C. § 1983. The court granted summary judgment to the college on the wrongful discharge claim for failing to exhaust remedies with the PERC and the § 1983 claim. After trial, the court found no public element in her speech and dismissed the § 1983 claims against the officials. The state court of appeals affirmed, and the Supreme Court of Washington granted review concerning the wrongful discharge issue.

The court examined case law from many other jurisdictions, noting that while contractual and statutory remedies afforded to certain employees may redress violations of the underlying employment relationship, these remedies do not protect against violations of public policy. It found erroneous the assumption that contractual employees do not require such protection. The tort of wrongful discharge for violation of public policy was independent of the terms of employment and protected a strong state interest in preventing employers from imposing improper employment conditions on employees. Although the PERC was authorized to redress certain wrongs arising from public employment contracts, it had no authority to award damages for wrongful discharge tort actions. **The court found that the public policy against retaliatory discharge applied with equal force to both at-will and contractual employees, and found it unnecessary to distinguish between these groups in tort cases**. It held that a cause of action for wrongful discharge in violation of public policy exists when an employee is fired for exercising a legal right or privilege. In this case, the employee asserted that she was wrongfully discharged in violation of her protected legal right to file grievances. It was unnecessary for her to exhaust administrative remedies before the PERC, because it lacked authority to decide tort claims. Thus, the lower court judgments to the contrary were reversed. The court rejected the employee's assertion that the First Amendment protected her speech where her statements concerned only her personal interest, and not that of the public. Her grievances arose from personal matters that were unprotected by the First Amendment. According to the state supreme court, the trial court properly dismissed the employee's § 1983 claims against the college and officials. The court reversed the summary dismissal of the wrongful termination claim and remanded the case to the superior court for trial. *Smith v. Bates Technical College*, 991 P.2d 1135 (Wash. 2000).

◆ A teacher made numerous complaints about safety and air quality in his classroom. After an air quality test revealed that the classroom was safe, the principal recommended that the district not rehire the teacher. The teacher sued the school board in a New Jersey trial court for retaliatory discharge in violation of the CEPA. The court set aside a $60,000 jury verdict in the teacher's favor, finding no CEPA violation. **The New Jersey Superior Court, Appellate Division, reversed the judgment and reinstated the award, holding that punitive damages might be available**. The Supreme Court of New Jersey affirmed the appellate division's judgment without ruling specifically on the punitive damage question. The case returned to the trial court, which dismissed the punitive damage claim. The appellate division again reversed the trial court, finding that punitive damages were available where there was evidence of actual participation in wrongful conduct by supervisory government officials such as the principal and superintendent. The court remanded the case, noting that the long passage of time clouded the issue of reinstatement of employment as a possible remedy. The case reached the state's supreme court for the second time, where it again refused to rule on the issue of the availability of punitive damages against a public employer under the CEPA. However, the court held that the appellate division's first opinion constituted the controlling law of the case, which was binding on the trial court. The appellate division's judgment was affirmed, and the matter returned to the trial court for a jury trial on the punitive damage issue. *Abbamont v. Piscataway Township Bd. of Educ.*, 163 N.J. 15, 746 A.2d 997 (N.J. 1999).

◆   A payroll clerk asserted that the district superintendent and her immediate supervisor retaliated against her after she attempted to make appropriate tax withholdings from the superintendent's paycheck. **She** further **alleged** that when she contacted the IRS for advice and sought to document her actions, **the superintendent and supervisor retaliated against her by refusing to communicate and placing unnecessary pressure on her, forcing her to quit**. A Wisconsin trial court awarded summary judgment to the school district and the clerk appealed.

The court of appeals stated that both parties to an employment contract for an indefinite term are generally free to sever the relationship. This is known as the rule of employment at will. However, certain exceptions exist where an employee is discharged in a manner that violates a fundamental and well-defined public policy described in existing law. An employee claiming constructive discharge must make an additional showing that working conditions were so intolerable that a reasonable person would have been compelled to resign. In this case, **the employee had described sufficient facts to support her claim that her supervisors had made her workplace so intolerable that a reasonable person would be forced to resign**, and whether these facts created a constructive discharge that violated public policy. Because the trial court should have allowed a jury to consider these questions, the court reversed and remanded the case. *Strozinsky v. School Dist. of Brown Deer*, 597 N.W.2d 773 (Wis.App.1999).

◆   The state of West Virginia adopted a policy prohibiting school personnel from using tobacco products. A county education board further banned the use of tobacco in all school buildings and on school grounds along with prohibiting school personnel from using tobacco in the presence of students during any school-related activities. The board's policy called for discipline including suspension or dismissal for employees who violated the policy. A motorist reported that she observed a bus driver smoking a cigarette while he was driving students to school. **The district transportation director observed cigarette ashes on the floor of the driver's bus and suspended him pending an investigation**. The driver denied smoking on the bus route and stated that he had apparently been seen with a white pen in his mouth. The school board conducted a hearing after which it voted to discharge the driver.

The driver then filed a grievance before the West Virginia Education and State Employees Grievance Board. **An administrative law judge deemed unreliable the motorist's testimony and credited testimony by two students who stated that the driver had not been smoking**. As a result, the driver was reinstated, and the school board appealed to a West Virginia circuit court. The court reversed the decision and upheld the discharge action, and the driver appealed to the Supreme Court of Appeals of West Virginia. The court held that a circuit court should give deference to administrative findings of fact. **Administrative credibility determinations are binding unless patently without basis in the record**. In this case, the circuit court judge had erroneously substituted his judgment for that of the administrative law judge, and the supreme court of appeals reversed and remanded the case. *Bd. of Educ. of County of Wood v. Johnson*, 497 S.E.2d 778 (W.Va.1997).

◆   A South Carolina administrative clerk's relationship with her school district deteriorated after her husband was fired by the district. The district began to document employment violations by the clerk including excessive tardiness, dishonesty, disrespectful behavior and destroying morale by complaining about supervisors and her job. She filed an unsuccessful grievance, then claimed that the district retaliated against her by taking away her telephone and restricting her use of the copy machine. The clerk began communicating with a local taxpayers' association and attempted to document improper school district expenditures. The district fired the clerk for tardiness, misuse of leave, misuse of office time and equipment, and dishonesty. **She filed a lawsuit against the district in a South Carolina trial court, claiming retaliatory discharge in violation of the state Whistleblower Act**. A jury awarded the clerk $150,000 and the court denied the district's post-trial motions to overturn the verdict. The district appealed to the Court of Appeals of South Carolina.

The court of appeals observed that the state Whistleblower Act protected from retaliatory discharge employees who reported violations of state or federal laws or regulations to expose governmental corruption, waste, fraud, negligence or mismanagement. An employee could claim coverage under the act where the reporting was made in good faith and was based on probable cause to believe that the employee's actions were protected. Although there was evidence that if proven, the employee's poor work performance justified the termination action, the jury had made a factual determination based on appropriate evidence and inferences. **The court determined that the jury could have reasonably reached its conclusion that the termination had been in retaliation for whistleblowing activities and affirmed the trial court decision**. *Ludlam v. School Dist. of Greenville County*, 455 S.E.2d 177 (S.C.App.1995).

◆   A New Jersey school administrator was employed under a three-year contract. The school administrator claimed that the superintendent falsely charged him with misconduct. The superintendent recommended termination of the administrator's contract, and the board ratified his decision. The administrator filed a lawsuit against the superintendent, board and individual board members in a New Jersey trial court for breach of contract, denial of tenure, violation of the state Conscientious Employee Protection Act (CEPA) and interference with his employment contract. **The court ruled that the board had terminated the contract without cause and that the superintendent had interfered with it**. The court awarded the administrator $750,000 in economic damages against the board and superintendent and emotional distress damages of $560,000, including damages for litigation-induced stress. The administrator was also entitled to $50,000 in punitive damages. The board appealed to the New Jersey Superior Court, Appellate Division, which affirmed the damage awards for punitive and emotional distress but reversed the economic damage award. The board appealed to the Supreme Court of New Jersey.

The court determined that litigation-induced stress was not an appropriate element of damages. This was because stress and anxiety are a normal part of litigation and the administrator himself had filed the lawsuit. Although the administrator had been fired without cause before attaining tenure, it was inappropriate to base the economic damage award on the theory that he would have achieved tenure had he not been fired. **Wrongful termination cannot result in the attainment of tenure, and the award of economic damages based on this expectancy was inappropriate**. The case was reversed and remanded for reconsideration of each component of the damage award. *Picogna v. Bd. of Educ. of the Township of Cherry Hill*, 143 N.J. 391, 671 A.2d 1035 (1996).

◆   A North Carolina teacher was employed to teach health and physical education. However, **her principal reassigned her to a coordinator position and allegedly placed her in a small office in the girls' locker room, where the temperature was 90 to 100 degrees**. The teacher complained that these and other conditions were so intolerable that she was forced to resign. She sued the board of education, principal and several others in a North Carolina trial court for intentional infliction of emotional distress, constructive wrongful discharge, malicious interference with contract and punitive damages. The court granted summary judgment motions by the school board and individuals, and the teacher appealed to the Court of Appeals of North Carolina. The court of appeals agreed that it was within the trial court's discretion to hold that the conduct in this case did not amount to extreme and outrageous behavior. Insults and indignities did not support a claim for intentional infliction of emotional distress. **There was no evidence of malicious interference with contract and no legitimate claim for constructive wrongful discharge**. Because all the other claims were dismissed, there was no basis for the punitive damages claim. The court affirmed the summary judgment order of the trial court. *Wagoner v. Elkin City Schools' Bd. of Educ.*, 440 S.E.2d 119 (N.C. App. 1994).

IX. DEFAMATION AND SLANDER

In the school employment context, defamation and slander claims usually arise when a school board member or high-level administrator makes negative statements about former employees to the press or members of the public. If the parties have signed either a confidentiality agreement or a settlement agreement that includes a confidentiality provision, and derogatory statements are made, state law may allow a cause of action for defamation or slander.

◆   **A Canadian teacher wrote a letter to the principal of a New Jersey high school complaining about the behavior of a New Jersey teacher during a trip to Spain**. The principal showed the letter to the teacher, who divulged its contents to her students. She was not fired or suspended from her teaching position and was permitted to chaperone other student trips. Despite the lack of district sanction, the teacher sued the Canadian teacher and his school in a New Jersey court for defamation, asserting that she had suffered loss of earnings and grievous mental injury. The court awarded summary judgment to the Canadian teacher and school, finding that the letter was not defamatory and that the New Jersey teacher failed to allege damages. The New Jersey Superior Court, Appellate Division, affirmed the judgment, finding that in order to prevail in a defamation action, the complaining party must prove injury to reputation, financial loss or extreme emotional distress.

The teacher appealed to the New Jersey Supreme Court, where she argued that even if the letter involved the public interest, she had been improperly deprived of the opportunity to demonstrate that it had been motivated by malice. The court observed that defamation law requires balancing the competing interests in reputation and the protection of free speech. When allegedly defamatory remarks involve the public interest, there is a high burden of proof to show actionable defamation. Damages will not be presumed in such cases, and the complaining party must demonstrate that the defendant published the statement with knowledge of its falsity and reckless disregard for whether it was false or not. There is a strong public interest in the behavior of teachers, especially regarding their conduct with students. **The letter was addressed to this subject and the court held that in view of the teacher's role, she was required to allege monetary damage or loss of reputation, not just embarrassment.** Teachers are aware that they will be subject to evaluation by principals, parents, administrators and peers. The New Jersey teacher failed to allege any specific harm to her reputation and incurred no medical expenses. She had also communicated the contents of the letter to students and others. Because summary judgment was an appropriate disposition of a meritless defamation suit, the court affirmed the judgment for the Canadian teacher and school. *Rocci v. Ecole Secondaire MacDonald-Cartier*, 165 N.J. 149, 755 A.2d 583 (2000).

◆   A Texas education service center discharged about 50 family service workers from the Head Start program. The administrator of the center granted an interview to a television station that included a statement that the employees were discharged "because they 'lacked the proper skills and training'" and "were responsible for poor performance of delivering services to Head Start recipients." **Twelve of the former employees sued the administrator in a Texas county court for defamation. The administrator moved for summary judgment on the basis of absolute immunity** under the state Education Code and on grounds of qualified immunity, asserting that her statements were true and without malice. The court denied her motion and she appealed to the Texas Court of Appeals.

The appeals court stated that the Texas Education Code provides immunity for professional employees of school districts for any act, incident to or within the scope of their duties, involving the exercise of judgment or discretion. Professional employees include superintendents, principals, teachers, supervisors, social workers, counselors, nurses and other certificated persons required to exercise discretion. Regional education service center employees were accorded immunity to the same extent as school district employees and volunteers. The court found that the administrator had been instructed by her immediate supervisor to respond to questions from the media concerning the discharged employees. Since she was required to answer the questions, the assignment was within the scope of her duties. The administrator's actions in this case were not ministerial. According to the court, ministerial acts are generally those that are based on formal rules or regulations providing clear guidelines. In contrast, discretionary acts are those involving personal deliberation, decision-making and judgment. **The administrator received no clear guidance from her supervisor about handling the media, and what she actually said in the interview was left to her judgment and discretion.** Because the administrator conclusively proved that the formulation of her media response was discretionary, she was entitled to summary judgment on the basis of immunity. *Enriquez v. Khouri*, 13 S.W.3d 458 (Tex. App. 2000).

◆   Certain employees of a charter school challenged school operations and made suggestions about teaching techniques and student performance. They addressed a series of board meetings and some filed grievances. The employees alleged that the school administrator retaliated against them by downgrading their employment evaluations after they asserted personal speech, association and grievance rights. They later submitted resignations, but attempted to rescind them when the school administrator resigned. The employees claimed that they were discharged without just cause when the board declined to accept their rescission letters. A local newspaper reported that school officials were suggesting that the former employees had caused "unfortunate problems" at the school and that there was just cause to discharge them. **The employees sued the charter school, school district, board chairman and former school administrator in a federal district court, asserting civil rights violations and defamation claims** based on statements to the newspaper and letters to parents advising them about the resignations.

The court held that the employees failed to state due process claims for damage to reputation under the U.S. Constitution. The statements to the newspaper by school officials were not false or stigmatizing, alleging only that there were unfortunate problems at the school. The letters to parents had simply indicated that it was unfortunate that the employees had resigned, and made no false statements. The letters did not implicate any dishonesty or immorality by the employees that would deprive them of any liberty interest in name or reputation. The court summarily dismissed the claims brought by the employees for misrepresentation because they failed to meet federal court specificity requirements. The claims for intentional infliction of emotional distress against the board, district and chairman were dismissed because discharge from employment, without more, does not constitute outrageous conduct that would support a claim for emotional distress. The court observed that there is no private cause of action under the Colorado Constitution for damages resulting from violations of speech and association rights, as the employees had alleged. There was no state law equivalent to 42 U.S.C. § 1983 upon which to enforce such claims. The employees were not entitled to have their personnel files and evaluations purged under the state constitution. **The court held that the former employees failed to allege defamation since the challenged statements were "neither scurrilous nor inflammatory," and would not cause damage or subject them to ridicule.** It dismissed all the claims for which the officials sought summary judgment, including those for defamation, speech, association and due process violations, misrepresentation, intentional infliction of emotional distress and punitive damages. In addition, the chairman was entitled to an award of attorney's fees. *Brammer-Heolter v. Twin Peaks Charter Academy*, 81 F.Supp.2d 1090 (D. Colo. 2000).

◆   During the ninth grade, a student had worked as a part-time maintenance worker for his school system. The student went on to graduate and other employment, with the goal of a teaching career. **He learned that a school board member said that he had "worked for the district in maintenance, but he was such a bad worker that we had to fire him."** The graduate sued in state court for slander after the board member refused to retract the statement. During a pretrial deposition, the graduate was asked if he believed that his reputation had actually been injured because of the board member's statement. He responded "[a]t the present time, no." Finding that he had acknowledged that his reputation was not actually injured, the trial court granted a summary judgment motion to the board and board member.

The graduate appealed to the Wisconsin Court of Appeals, which recited the general rule that **a statement or publication is defamatory if it tends to harm the reputation of another person in a way that lowers the estimation of the person in the community or deters third parties from associating with him.** The graduate's admission in pretrial proceedings that his reputation had not yet been harmed destroyed his claim, since evidence of lowered reputation in the community is a necessary element of a slander claim. Slander is not actionable without proof of actual damages, subject to some limited exceptions that were not applicable in this case. The court disagreed with the graduate's argument that his desire to be a teacher in the community made the board member's statement more harmful than it would be otherwise or that the board member's status drew unusual attention in the community to it. The court of appeals affirmed the trial court judgment for the school board and the board member. *Janusz v. Olen*, 234 Wis.2d 149, 610 N.W.2d 511 (Wis. App. 2000).

◆   A Colorado school board investigated a sexual harassment claim filed by a female employee against the superintendent and asked for his resignation based on the investigator's findings. **He agreed to resign under a confidential agreement by which there would be "no disparaging public comments or remarks made by either party."** The board paid him in excess of $278,000 for benefits and unused vacation pay and as consideration for his release of any age discrimination or other claims against the district. A newspaper reported the financial settlement and revealed that the superintendent had been accused of sexual harassment. A "source" quoted by the newspaper stated that the rumors of harassment had a basis and that "I'm very glad we let him go." The article also attributed statements to school board members that the district might face lawsuits because of the superintendent's conduct. The superintendent responded by suing the district and board members in state court for breach of the settlement agreement. The court awarded summary judgment to the district and board members, and the Court of Appeals of Colorado affirmed the decision.

On appeal, the state supreme court noted that the agreement required the parties to refrain from making disparaging public remarks. In particular, the district and its board members were prohibited from saying anything about the sexual harassment charges and making comments inconsistent with the announcement that the superintendent's resignation was for "personal reasons." The speech rights of board members did not invalidate the agreement, nor was there any public policy reason for disallowing it. **Finding no state law, constitutional or public policy reason for not enforcing the agreement, the state supreme court reversed and remanded** the appeals court decision awarding summary judgment to the school defendants. *Pierce v. St. Vrain Valley School Dist.*, 981 P.2d 600 (Colo.1999).

◆   An Ohio school district attempted to discharge a custodian for alleged misconduct with students. He was also engaged in a personal feud with the superintendent. The district and custodian reached a confidential settlement under which the custodian agreed to resign in exchange for a financial settlement, withdrawal of his grievances and expunction of certain information from his personnel file. During the board meeting at which the settlement was approved, **the superintendent read a prepared statement to members of the press and was quoted as saying that the board had "gotten rid of a bad employee."** The custodian brought a state court defamation action against the superintendent and district, also asserting a breach of contract claim. The court denied summary judgment to the board and superintendent and they appealed to the Court of Appeals of Ohio, Ninth District.

The court reviewed an Ohio statute providing immunity to political subdivisions and their employees in certain cases. It held that the custodian failed to specify evidence affirmatively demonstrating personal liability by the superintendent. Employees of political subdivisions are generally immune from personal liability unless they act outside the scope of their responsibilities or act maliciously or in bad faith. Because the custodian had made no such allegations, the superintendent was entitled to summary judgment and this part of the trial court decision was reversed. According to the court, **the district had been erroneously deprived of summary judgment on the issue of liability for defamation and slander as the result of alleged intentional conduct by the superintendent**. According to the court, state law prohibited intentional liability suits against political subdivisions, imposing liability only for negligent conduct. The court found that the superintendent's statements were not negligent because he had reasonable grounds to believe that the settlement resulted in removing a bad employee from the school. Since the superintendent's conduct did not amount to negligent publication, the district was entitled to summary judgment. However, the trial court had correctly denied summary judgment to the superintendent and board on the breach of contract claim. The court rejected their argument that the settlement agreement was a public document that could not be withheld from public review. The custodian claimed that the superintendent's statements were outside the scope of the settlement agreement itself, raising a genuine issue that the statements were not permitted by the agreement. *Bays v. Northwestern Local School Dist.*, 1999 Ohio App. LEXIS 3343 (Ohio App. 9th Dist. 1999).

CHAPTER EIGHT

Tenure and Due Process

I. STATE TENURE STATUTES

State tenure statutes often impose specific probationary periods or service requirements before an employee will be granted tenure. Disputes occasionally arise in crediting employees with service time, particularly where the employee has only worked part-time or has been absent from employment due to leave.

A. Tenure Status

◆   Near the conclusion of a foreign language teacher's third year of employment, the superintendent appointed her to a tenured position, effective the beginning of the next school year. The teacher then admitted violating the school's zero-tolerance policy against the consumption of alcohol at school-sponsored events. Three days before the teacher was to receive her tenured appointment, the superintendent of schools offered to extend her probationary period for an additional year. She declined the offer, and **the board rescinded her "conditional tenure appointment"** and terminated her employment. The teacher sued, asserting that she received tenure at the end of her third year of probationary employment, not the beginning of the following school year. A state trial court dismissed the case and a state appellate division court affirmed. The New York Court of Appeals agreed to review the case, and consolidated it with that of a special education teacher who received notice three months before the end of her probationary period that her services would be discontinued at the end of the year. The superintendent of the special education teacher's district erroneously submitted her name with those of 32 others who were being recommended for tenure. **The board approved her for tenure, but rescinded its action after learning of the mistake**. The special education teacher sued the district in a federal district court, which denied a motion to dismiss the case. The U.S. Court of Appeals, Second Circuit, determined that the case depended upon unsettled questions of New York law that required consideration by the state's highest court.

After consolidating the cases, the state court of appeals held that Section 2509 of the state Education Law distinguished between probationary teachers, who can be terminated without a hearing at any time for any reason, and tenured teachers, who are subject to dismissal only after formal disciplinary hearings. The law authorized boards to award tenure before the expiration of a teacher's probationary period, specifically allowing superintendents to recommend a teacher for tenure at the end of the period, or up to six months before that time. **The court held that a board resolution granting tenure to a probationary teacher as of a future date confers tenure to the teacher only as of the specified date**. The law contemplated that school boards would await the conclusion of the full three-year probationary period before making a binding tenure decision. This helps ensure that only qualified teachers were hired into tenured positions. A conditional tenure award provides teachers and school districts with notice of a board's intention to confer tenure upon completion of the school year, allowing the parties to plan for the upcoming year. The court affirmed the decision against the foreign-language teacher and certified an answer to the Second Circuit in favor of the special education teacher's school district. Neither teacher was entitled to tenure. *Remus v. Board of Educ. for Tonawanda City School Dist. v. Schenectady City School Dist.*, 727 N.Y.S.2d 43, 750 N.E.2d 1091 (N.Y. 2001).

◆   A teacher worked as a probationary music teacher for two years in a Nevada district after teaching in California for many years and being properly accredited by that state. During his third year in the Nevada district, he received a notice that his employment would be terminated unless he remedied a technical defect in his teaching license application within four days. The district then discharged the teacher after he failed to remedy the defect in the time allotted. It rehired him a few days later after he provided the necessary documentation and reapplied for his position, but **it reclassified him as a probationary teacher for the rest of the school year and the following year**. The teacher commenced a declaratory judgment action in a state district court, asserting that his Nevada school employment had never been actually terminated and that he was entitled to post-probationary status. He argued in the alternative that the district never effectively terminated his employment because it failed to follow state notice and hearing requirements when it gave him only four days to correct the defective certification forms.

The trial court awarded the teacher summary judgment and the school district appealed to the Supreme Court of Nevada, which held that the teacher was entitled to post-probationary status. Under state law, he was entitled to 15 days' notice prior to employment termination plus notice of the right to a hearing. The district had given him only four days of notice without any opportunity for a hearing. Without regard to whether the teacher was properly licensed, **the district had employed him as a post-probationary teacher for over a year. The court affirmed the trial court's ruling that he was entitled to statutory procedures and protections**. There was no merit to the district's argument that the dispute should have first been submitted to arbitration. The teacher's discharge was a fiction and he was an employee of the district at the time of the alleged reinstatement. Even if the case arose under the collective bargaining agreement, the court had jurisdiction to consider questions of statutory law raised by the teacher. The district court properly granted summary judgment to the teacher based on the fact that he was not effectively terminated and did not lose his post-probationary teaching status. *Clark County School District v. Riley*, 14 P.3d 22 (Nev. 2000).

◆   A New York principal was appointed to a position at an elementary school. **Although her three-year probationary appointment was extended by a year, the school superintendent denied her tenure**, resulting in the termination of her employment. The teacher filed a federal district court action against the school board, asserting that the superintendent had discriminated against her based on her race in violation of Title VII of the Civil Rights Act of 1964. The court held for the board, and the principal appealed to the Second Circuit.

According to the circuit court, the tenure decisions of New York superintendents are final. The alleged discrimination pertained to the superintendent's initial tenure denial in 1991, not to later administrative appeals of that determination which took place in 1992. Thus, her appeal seeking damages under the 1991 amendments to Title VII was legally flawed. Because the amendments were not retroactive, she was unable to recover any damages under the statute. **The circuit court found no reason to reverse the district court's extensive findings in support of the tenure denial. The principal's performance was manifestly deficient, and she received frequent notices of her poor performance**. The deficiencies noted by the supervisor included specific examples of continuing neglect for her duties, including failure to provide for the safety and welfare of students, submit timely reports and use standard procedures. *Joseph v. New York City Bd. of Educ.*, 171 F.3d 87 (2d Cir. 1999).

◆   Prior to becoming an administrator, an individual worked as a teacher and guidance counselor in the Marlington, Ohio school district. During his last year of employment, the teacher was awarded a continuing contract of employment. This contract was never reduced to writing. Shortly thereafter, the teacher accepted an administrative position with the Osnaburg, Ohio, school district. When the Osnaburg district failed to renew the administrator's contract, the administrator sued the district in state court, claiming he was a tenured teacher who was entitled to continuing service status. **The court determined that since the teacher had obtained continuing service status in Marlington, he had tenure rights in Osnaburg**. The local education association filed a separate suit, seeking a declaration preventing the teacher from reentering the bargaining unit. The administrator counter-claimed against the education association, claiming representatives of the association defamed him during a board meeting. A state trial court granted summary judgment to the education association with respect to the administrator's defamation claims. On appeal, the suits were consolidated. The Court of Appeals of Ohio affirmed the trial court ruling regarding the teacher's tenure status, and reversed the dismissal of the defamation claims.

The dispute was appealed to the Supreme Court of Ohio, which also concluded that the teacher was entitled to continuing service status. The failure of the parties to execute a written employment contract did not void the Marlington contract and state law did not require a teacher to accept a continuing contract of employment once a school board voted to award one. **The teacher attained continuing service status during his employment with the Marlington school district, and did not waive this status by accepting employment as an administrator in the Osnaburg school district** the same year. This portion of the appeals court decision was upheld. The appeals court ruling regarding the defamation claim was also affirmed, as the administrator was not a public official for purposes of his defamation claim. *East Canton Educ. Ass'n v. McIntosh,* 85 Ohio St.3d 465 (Ohio 1999).

◆   An Oklahoma school district offered a probationary teacher a temporary contract for the following school year as she neared the completion of her third year of employment. The district declined to offer her a permanent contract due to performance concerns. **Under Oklahoma law, teachers gain tenure after the completion of three consecutive complete school years under a written teaching contract.** The temporary contract contained a resignation clause effective at the end of the school year and a waiver of the teacher's right to further notice for contract termination. At the end of her fourth year of employment, the board decided not to renew the temporary contract and she sued the school district in an Oklahoma trial court for an order compelling tenured status. The court granted the district's summary judgment motion, but the Oklahoma Court of Civil Appeals reversed the decision. The Supreme Court of Oklahoma agreed to review the case, and held that the teacher was not tenured either before or after completion of the temporary contract. Since she was untenured, the school district could permissibly offer her the temporary contract instead of simply not rehiring her. **Teachers employed under temporary contracts are exempt from the state tenure law, and the court rejected the teacher's assertion that she was entitled to tenure rights prior to the completion of three years of employment under a written contract.** The court affirmed the district court judgment. *Scheer v. Indep. School Dist. No. I-26, Ottawa County, Okla.,* 1997 OK 115, 948 P.2d 275 (Okla.1997).

◆   New York Education Law requires teachers to serve a three-year probationary period in order to gain tenure. An amendment to the law allows regular substitutes to earn credit towards tenure, but does not define "regular substitute." A special education teacher served as a substitute for a New York school district for two terms when other employees took child care leaves for unspecified time periods. Although the substitute received a probationary teaching position after the employees returned, the school agency decided not to renew her position just prior to the expiration of the three-year probationary term. **The substitute filed an action in a New York trial court to annul the agency's determination, arguing that she had acquired tenure based on her substitute service** prior to the probationary appointment. The court granted her petition and reinstated her as a full-time tenured teacher.

The appellate division reversed, and the teacher appealed to the Court of Appeals of New York. The court found that while the Education Law failed to define the statutory term "regular substitute," **a teacher is entitled to earn credit for continuously performing the duties of a regular substitute for at least one term in the teacher's original area of employment**. This is without regard to whether the employer designates the substitute as a regular substitute or a per diem substitute since the nature of the service and not the employer's designation carries legal significance. The court reinstated the trial court judgment in favor of the teacher. *In the Matter of Speichler v. Bd. of Cooperative Educ. Services*, 90 N.Y.2d 110, 659 N.Y.S.2d 199, 681 N.E.2d 366 (1997).

◆   **The Court of Civil Appeals of Alabama held that a teacher who instructed alternative programs for expectant mothers was not entitled to tenure under the state tenure law**. In order to qualify for tenure under the law, teachers must serve for three consecutive school years under a written contract and be re-employed for a fourth school year. Although the teacher in this case had instructed alternative classes fulltime in academic areas such as mathematics, science and social studies, she had served under a written contract for only one of the six years she was employed by the school board. The adult education programs were not public school programs within the meaning of the tenure act and she was not entitled to tenure. *Nelson v. Etowah County Bd. of Educ.*, 703 So.2d 413 (Ala.Civ.App.1997).

◆   Virginia law requires teachers to serve a three-year probationary period before attaining continuing contract status. A Virginia librarian who was covered under the statutory definition of teacher performed about four years of work for a school district during a seven-year time period, missing substantial amounts of time due to a work-related injury. She did not perform the work in three consecutive years. **When she was not rehired by the school board, she filed a lawsuit** against it in the U.S. District Court for the Western District of Virginia, **claiming to have obtained the statutory right to continuing contract status and entitlement to the position**. The court granted the librarian's summary judgment motion for an order reinstating her with backpay, attorney's fees and costs. The board appealed to the U.S. Court of Appeals, Fourth Circuit, which certified a question about the statute to the Supreme Court of Virginia.

The librarian argued that she was entitled to tenure because the statutory language required only that she enter into three employment contracts and that there was no statutory requirement to perform substantial teaching services. The board argued that state board of education regulations interpreted the statute as requiring a teacher to complete a probationary work period of three consecutive years before attaining tenure. The court agreed with the board's interpretation of the statute, holding that **continuing contract status could be earned only after completing a probationary period of three consecutive years**. It answered the Fourth Circuit's question in the board's favor. *Corns v. School Bd. of Russell County*, 454 S.E.2d 728 (Va.1995). The Fourth Circuit then entered judgment for the school board, reversing the district court. *Corns v. Russell County Virginia School Bd.*, 52 F.3d 56 (4th Cir.1995).

◆   A Missouri teacher worked part-time for 18 years and enjoyed annual salary increases. The state general assembly amended the Teacher Tenure Act by allowing part-time teachers to accrue prorated credit toward tenure. The following year, **the teacher's school district offered her a fulltime contract, but indicated that it was probationary rather than permanent,** and decreased the teacher's compensation to an amount equivalent to a first year teacher's salary. The teacher signed the contract and submitted a letter protesting her salary decrease and demotion to probationary status. She then sued the district in a Missouri trial court, which ruled that she was entitled to a permanent contract, but not a salary increase. Both parties appealed, and after the Court of Appeals of Missouri affirmed the trial court decision, the matter was transferred to the Supreme Court of Missouri.

The court agreed with the teacher that she should be given retroactive credit toward permanent status for the years she had worked part-time. **Because the teacher had worked approximately 18 years part-time prior to the amendments to the tenure act, she had accrued more than five years toward permanent status.** The court affirmed this part of the trial court's decision. It then reversed the trial court's determination that the teacher was not entitled to a salary increase. The contract did not indicate the teacher's salary level, but the custom of the parties was to grant a step increase for each year worked. Because fixed practices that exist for a sufficient duration to become custom may be implied as contractual terms, the teacher was entitled to a salary increase. *Dial v. Lathrop R-II School Dist.*, 871 S.W.2d 444 (Mo. 1994).

B. Tenure Rights

Once tenure has been granted, certain privileges apply to tenured employees such as protection from dismissal. Although the privileges vary from state to state depending upon state statutes, tenured teachers generally have the right to "bump" less experienced teachers in a reduction in force action. For a more general discussion of Termination, see Chapter Seven.

1. Reductions in Force

◆   A teacher was certificated with endorsements for teaching English, social studies and sciences and taught seventh grade social studies until his position was eliminated. He was reassigned to a computer applications class and other duties during the next two school years, with no reduction in benefits or salary. Within two years, **the board reinstated a seventh grade social studies teaching position, for which the teacher applied, but did not receive.** The teacher petitioned the state commissioner of education, asserting that the district violated his tenure and seniority rights when it refused to place him in the open social studies position. The commissioner held that the district had properly transferred the teacher to a position for which he was certified and that no reduction in force took place. The state education board reversed the commissioner's decision, finding that a reduction in force had occurred and ordering the local board to reassign the teacher to the social studies position.

The local board appealed to the Superior Court of New Jersey, Appellate Division, where it argued that no reduction in force occurred when the position was abolished, since there had been no layoff of teaching staff and this is a prerequisite to the creation of a preferred eligibility list under state law. **The court agreed with the local board, finding that the teacher's seniority rights were not triggered. Although the board had abolished the position, it had reassigned the teacher to teach different subjects within his certification without any reduction in salary or benefits.** The court rejected his argument that this implicated the state tenure law, since school boards maintain the managerial prerogative to transfer staff by a majority vote, even if the transfer is involuntary. The transfer was not a demotion because the teacher's new duties were within the scope of his certification. The reasons stated by the board for the reassignment were permissible and abolishment of the position did not trigger the teacher's seniority rights. The court reversed the state board's decision for the teacher. *Carpenito v. Bd. of Educ. of Borough of Rumson*, 322 N.J.Super. 522, 731 A.2d 538 (N.J.App.Div. 1999).

◆   An Oklahoma school superintendent advised his school board that the district should eliminate four teaching positions to reduce the annual budget by $120,000. The board eliminated a driver education position occupied by a tenured teacher with 19 years of experience. **The district retained some nontenured, probationary teachers who instructed classes in academic areas in which the tenured teacher was also certified to teach.** He filed a lawsuit against the school district in an Oklahoma district court, claiming breach of employment contract. The court granted summary judgment to the school district, and the Court of Appeals of Oklahoma affirmed. The teacher appealed to the Supreme Court of Oklahoma. The court stated that school boards were allowed to exercise discretion when making necessary reductions in force but were required to conform their actions to the state tenure act. **Although boards were allowed to make necessary economic adjustments, they were required to retain tenured teachers before rehiring nontenured or probationary teachers pursuant to any reduction in force.** Because the tenured teacher presented evidence that he was certified to teach in other areas and also showed that the school district could have accommodated him through minimal efforts, the summary judgment order had been improper and the case was reversed and remanded. *Barton v. Indep. School Dist. No. I-99, Custer County*, 914 P.2d 1041 (Okla.1996).

◆   A New York local education board abolished the position of school nurse teacher and refused to allow the incumbent to displace any less senior health teachers. **The board claimed that the nurse teacher was neither tenured** under New York law **nor certified to teach health.** The teacher, who had taught health and health-related topics at district schools for 15 years, filed a lawsuit in a New York trial court seeking reinstatement. The court ordered the board to reinstate the teacher and the board appealed to the New York Supreme Court, Appellate Division. The court found error in the trial court's order to reinstate the teacher. **The law did not require placement of a teacher having seniority rights unless a vacancy was presently available in a similar position.** The nurse teacher had not successfully alleged that a vacancy existed for which she was qualified. However, the teacher had gained tenure by operation of law by teaching health classes in excess of the two-year probationary period under state law. The case was reversed and remanded to the trial court for a hearing and further determination of whether a vacancy existed in health instruction. If the teacher could show that a vacancy existed, she would be entitled to position. *Freeman v. Bd. of Educ. of Hempstead School Dist.*, 616 N.Y.S.2d 911 (A.D.2d Dep't 1994).

2.   Other Substantive Rights

◆   A Missouri school district signed permanent, indefinite term employment contracts with a select group of teachers that included a ten percent salary increase for performing one month's extra work. **The extended duty contracts were intended to reward desirable teachers with pay in excess of the district salary schedule** by allowing them to come in before the school year to order supplies, clean and repair equipment, develop curriculums and perform other non-teaching duties. When the school district reported an operating deficit, the program was discontinued. A number of teachers claimed that the action violated the state Teacher Tenure Act. They argued that the extra month had become a contract term that could not be unilaterally modified. A Missouri circuit court held for the school district, and the teachers appealed to the Missouri Court of Appeals, Western District. **The court held that the activities undertaken by the teachers during the extra month did not come under the coverage of the tenure act**. The activities did not require a teaching certificate and no instruction of students took place during these times. The board's action was a legitimate response to a reduced budget. The court of appeals affirmed the circuit court's decision. *Campbell v. Reorganized School Dist. No. 1*, 904 S.W.2d 18 (Mo.App.W.D.1995).

◆   A New York board of education hired a teacher to teach business education. The teacher also had certification in driver and safety education. Years later, his position as a high school business teacher was eliminated as part of the district's reduction in force. Driver's education courses were cut and the remaining business classes were assigned to a more senior teacher. New York law, however, allowed the teacher to "bump" a teacher having less seniority within his tenure area, i.e. the general secondary school area. Since there were less-senior teachers within his tenure area (teaching subjects he was not certified to teach) the school district fired a tenured and certified secondary science teacher and moved the business teacher into that position. **It then began incompetency proceedings against him for lack of certification, but the teacher sued the district** in a state trial court for backpay and continuing pay during the pendency of the incompetency proceedings. A New York trial court concluded that the board of education did not have the authority to suspend the teacher without pay, but an appellate division court reversed. The teacher then appealed to the New York Court of Appeals. **The Court of Appeals stated that pay is a substantive right that cannot be taken away except pursuant to explicit statutory or collective bargaining authorization**. The court stated that qualified teachers must be paid. It also stated that the board could not equate teacher qualification with certification in a specific subject area. Since the teacher was certified on the day he was suspended, he was qualified under New York law and, therefore, had to be paid. *Winter v. Bd. of Educ. for Rhinebeck Central School Dist.*, 588 N.E.2d 32 (N.Y.1992).

C. Collective Bargaining Agreements

Controversies occasionally arise between state labor and education statutes and collective bargaining agreements, particularly in areas such as due process and contract renewal. Sometimes the statutes or agreements contain peremptory language which guides the court by stating the preference for what should be applied. For more cases addressing collective bargaining agreements, see Chapter 9.

1. Due Process

◆   In the final year of a Spanish teacher's three-year contract, the school's principal recommended that the teacher not be rehired based on classroom evaluations, and the school board did not renew the contract. The teacher requested a written statement of the reasons for the board's failure to rehire him. The board provided a statement that advised the teacher that the contract was terminated according to the terms of the collective bargaining agreement. **The teacher was not allowed to make an oral presentation at the termination hearing.** He claimed that he was entitled to introduce witnesses and cross-examine evaluators who had performed in-class observations under an Ohio statute. He argued that the statute took precedence over the collective bargaining agreement and sued the board in an Ohio county court. The court held for the board, and the teacher appealed to the Court of Appeals of Ohio, Fourth District.

The court of appeals reasoned that even though the collective bargaining agreement had lapsed prior to the teacher's final year, the school board and collective bargaining association had continued to act according to its terms and were deemed to have acquiesced to them. Under contract law, where parties continue to act as though a contract is valid, the status quo continues, and contract terms prevail as long as neither party expresses an intent not to be bound by the contract. **The terms of the lapsed contract took precedence over the provisions of the Ohio statute during the interim period, and the board had fully complied with them.** The trial court decision for the school board was affirmed. *Young v. Washington Local School Dist. Bd. of Educ.*, 619 N.E.2d 62 (Ohio App.4th Dist.1993).

◆   Three public school teachers received unfavorable classroom observation reports from a Maryland board of education. The teachers filed grievances pursuant to their collective bargaining agreement, seeking final and binding arbitration. However, the county education board obtained a Maryland trial court order staying arbitration and requiring the teachers to exhaust their remedies before the state education board. Although the hearing officer ruled that the observation report dispute was a subject which constituted a controversy or dispute under § 4-205(c) of the Maryland Education Article, **the state education board ultimately ruled that classroom observation disputes were purely local matters which were appealable only to local superintendents.** This result was affirmed by the Maryland trial court and the teachers appealed to the Court of Special Appeals of Maryland. The court of special appeals determined that the state board's position was inconsistent with the legislative purpose of Maryland Education Article §§ 2-205 and 4-205, the latter of which provided for rights of appeal in Maryland

courts from unfavorable local decisions. **The unfavorable classroom observation reports were appealable controversies or disputes, and the case was
remanded to the trial court with directions to reverse the decision of the state
education board and for a consideration of the merits** of each case. *Strother v.
Bd. of Educ. of Howard County*, 623 A.2d 717 (Md.App.1993).

2. Contract Renewal

◆   An Ohio school board employed a tutor to instruct small groups of students with
learning disabilities. It paid her at a specified hourly rate for five hours per day. The
following school year, the workload was reduced to two hours per day, and the tutor
refused to accept additional work instructing homebound students. **The board gave
the tutor an unsatisfactory performance evaluation and advised her that she
would not be reemployed the following year**. The tutor filed a lawsuit against the
school board in an Ohio trial court, claiming entitlement to compensation at the
wage rate specified by state law, and seeking an order that the reduction in hours was
an illegal wage decrease. The court granted summary judgment to the school board,
and the tutor appealed to the Supreme Court of Ohio. The court stated that according
to Ohio law, **the terms of a collective bargaining agreement supersede the
general provisions of state statutes**. Because the tutor was bound by the terms of
the applicable collective bargaining agreement, she was not entitled to a higher rate
than that specified in the agreement. She was not a salaried employee, and the
reduction in hours did not violate state law. The trial court judgment was affirmed.
State ex rel. Burch v. Sheffield-Sheffield Lake City School Dist. Bd. of Educ., 75
Ohio St.3d 216, 661 N.E.2d 1086 (1996).

◆   A Washington law limits the duration of the employment term of each school
district employee to one year. Another statute allows public employee collective
bargaining agreements to remain in effect for up to three years. A school district and
the labor organization representing its bus drivers entered into a collective bargaining agreement that limited the district's right to discipline or discharge employees
by requiring justifiable cause. **The district refused to renew the contract of an
experienced driver at the end of a school year, claiming that just cause was not
required** since the action was for contract nonrenewal rather than discharge. The
union filed a demand for arbitration, and the district responded by filing a lawsuit
against the union in a Washington trial court. The court granted the district's
summary judgment motion, and the driver and union appealed to the Supreme Court
of Washington.
     The court stated that the one-year term limitation for school employees must
be read in conjunction with the law recognizing the right of public employees to
enter into collective bargaining agreements which exceed one year. **The collective
bargaining law contained a supremacy clause that prevailed over inconsistent laws**. The statute did not conflict with the school district employment statute,
which only governed individual employment contracts and did not limit the ability
of unions and school districts to negotiate just cause terms in collective bargaining
agreements. **Since the reason for terminating the driver's employment involved consideration of the collective bargaining agreement, the case was
reversed and remanded for arbitration**. *Peninsula School Dist. No. 401 v. Pub.
School Employees of Peninsula*, 924 P.2d 13 (Wash.1996).

♦   New Jersey education law was amended to allow local education boards to negotiate collective bargaining agreements of up to three years for teachers. After the amendments took effect, an education board and the collective bargaining representative of its teachers negotiated a three-year agreement calling for annual salary increases. **When the contract expired, the parties were unable to agree upon a new contract, and the teachers' association demanded pay increases based on the expired salary guide**. The board adjusted the salaries, but petitioned the state commission of education for an order declaring that the increase was prohibited by the amended statute. An administrative law judge determined that state education law preempted labor law and prohibited a salary increase beyond the date of the contract. The commissioner reversed this decision, and this decision was later affirmed by the state education board and the New Jersey Superior Court, Appellate Division. The Supreme Court of New Jersey granted review.

On appeal, the teachers' association argued that under state labor law, employers were prohibited from unilaterally altering the status quo concerning mandatory bargaining topics without first bargaining to impasse. The court determined that in the case of teachers, the specific provisions of education law preempted labor law. **Because the amended statute expressly limited the duration of contracts between school boards and teachers to three years, the extension of the contractual salary increases to a fourth year violated the law**. This part of the appellate court's decision was reversed, but because non-teaching employees were bound by the provisions of labor law, the appellate division judgment pertaining to non-teachers was affirmed. *Bd. of Educ. of Township of Neptune v. Neptune Township Educ. Ass'n*, 144 N.J. 16, 675 A.2d 611 (1996).

D. State Regulatory Authority

Even though state statutes may grant employees specific tenure rights, state legislatures still retain the power to amend the statutes or create additional statutes which may affect the status of employees. Through legislative enactments, state legislatures may eliminate positions, create new positions, or modify tenure requirements and privileges.

♦   The superintendent of the Lowell, Massachusetts, schools advised a principal in writing that he would be dismissed for inefficiency, insubordination and conduct unbecoming a principal. After obtaining advice from counsel, the superintendent revoked his decision and sent another letter advising the principal that his contract would not be renewed after the school year. **The principal demanded arbitration, asserting that because he had served in his position for more than three years, he was a "tenured principal"** whose contract required renewal in the absence of good cause. He filed a Massachusetts superior court action against the city of Lowell, seeking a declaration that his contract had to be renewed because of the good cause requirement and asserting his entitlement to a hearing.

The court awarded summary judgment to the city, and the principal appealed to the Massachusetts Court of Appeals, which noted that the Massachusetts Education Reform Act of 1993 removed the procedural protections he claimed. The act eliminated the involvement of a school committee in the decision against renewing a principal's employment contract, also removing principal collective bargaining rights. **Principals, superintendents and other managerial personnel were** reclassified as contractual employees, and they were no longer insulated from contract nonrenewals. It was permissible to simply let a principal's contract expire, as dismissal was not the same as a contract nonrenewal. The court explained that the 1993 act recognized that principals were logically distinct from teachers and other staff and enjoyed different rights and responsibilities. Although the amended law created specific procedural safeguards for teachers, principals were excluded from the definition of "teacher." Under the reform legislation, principals now had a managerial role and they did not enjoy the same procedural protections as teachers. The court affirmed the judgment for the city. *Downing v. City of Lowell*, 50 Mass.App.Ct. 779, 741 N.E.2d 469 (Mass. App. 2001).

◆   The Tennessee Educational Improvement Act of 1992 (EIA) abolished the office of county superintendent of public instruction. The EIA authorized each local education board to employ a director of schools to perform the superintendent's former duties. The stated purpose of the legislation was to shift the duties of a former elected office to an administrative position filled by the local education board. **A county and its board of commissioners filed suit in a state trial court against state officials including the governor, seeking a declaration that the EIA violated the state constitution**, which prohibits the filling of a county office except by an election or action by the county commission. The court upheld the legislation except for a provision limiting local school board service eligibility to residents of the area served by the same local education agency. The county appealed to the Court of Appeals of Tennessee, Western Section.

The court stated that **the constitutionality of the EIA depended on whether the director of schools was a county officeholder, who must be elected, or a county employee, who could be appointed**. It noted that the county superintendent's position had been legislatively created, not constitutionally created. Therefore, the legislature had the power to abolish the position. The legislation was not impermissibly vague and was not preempted by an earlier home rule act which generally prohibits legislation which is local in form or effect. The court affirmed the trial court judgment finding the EIA constitutional, and reversed its determination concerning school board membership eligibility. *County of Shelby v. McWherter*, 936 S.W.2d 923 (Tenn.App. W. Sec. 1996).

◆   New York Education Law § 1709[22] prevents school districts from operating cafeteria programs that are not completely self-sustaining. One district submitted a budget proposal to voters that included a $60,000 breakfast and lunch program. The proposal was defeated three times. **The district then hired an outside food service to comply with the statute causing a district cafeteria employee to lose her job**. The employee filed an improper labor practice charge against the district through her collective bargaining organization. The state Public Employment Relations Board (PERB) upheld the improper labor practice charge and ordered the employee reinstated with backpay and full benefits. It also ordered the private contract voided. The district appealed to a New York trial court, which transferred the matter to the New York Supreme Court, Appellate Division, Third Department. On appeal, the court agreed with the district's argument that **state education law required it to terminate the school lunch program and hire a private food service because of the school budget defeat and consequent**

imposition of a contingency budget. The employee was not entitled to reinstatement through collective bargaining because the elimination of her job was the result of operation of law and not school district discretion. The court annulled the PERB action. *Germantown Central School Dist. v. PERB*, 613 N.Y.S.2d 957 (A.D.3d Dep't 1994).

II. DUE PROCESS REQUIREMENTS

State tenure laws create property rights in public employment that vest school employees with certain procedural rights. These rights vary from state to state according to the type of personnel action. In cases of employment termination, tenured school employees are generally entitled to notice and an opportunity to respond to the charges, a hearing with the right to confront and cross-examine witnesses, and the right to be represented by counsel. These and other related procedural protections are referred to as due process rights.

◆   Two U.S. Supreme Court decisions, *Board of Regents v. Roth*, 408 U.S. 564, 92 S.Ct. 2701, 33 L.Ed.2d 548 (1972), and *Perry v. Sindermann*, 408 U.S. 593, 92 S.Ct. 2694, 33 L.Ed.2d 570 (1972), help define the due process rights of teachers. The *Roth* case explained that **in order for a teacher to be entitled to due process, the teacher must have a "liberty" or "property" interest at stake**. The teacher in *Roth* was hired at a Wisconsin university for a fixed contract term of one year. At the end of the year, he was informed that he would not be rehired. No hearing was provided and no reason was given for the decision not to rehire. In dismissing the teacher's due process claims, the Supreme Court stated that no liberty interest was implicated because in declining to rehire the teacher, the university had not made any charge against him such as incompetence or immorality. Such a charge would have made it difficult for the teacher to gain employment elsewhere and thus would have deprived him of liberty. **As no reason was given for the nonrenewal of his contract, the teacher's liberty interest in future employment was not impaired and he was not entitled to a hearing on these grounds**. The Court declared that because the teacher had not acquired tenure he possessed no property interest in continued employment at the university. To be sure, the teacher had a property interest in employment during the term of his one-year contract, but upon its expiration the teacher's property interest ceased to exist. The Court stated: "To have a property interest in a benefit, a person clearly must have more than an abstract need or desire for it. He must have more than a unilateral expectation of it. He must, instead, have a legitimate claim of entitlement to it."

The *Sindermann* case involved a teacher employed at a Texas university for four years under a series of one-year contracts. When he was not rehired for a fifth year, he brought suit contending that due process required a dismissal hearing. The Supreme Court held that "a person's interest in a benefit is a 'property' interest for due process purposes if there are such rules and mutually explicit understandings that support his claim of entitlement to the benefit that he may invoke at a hearing." **Because the teacher had been employed at the university for four years, the Court felt that he might have acquired a protectible property interest in continued employment**. The case was remanded to the trial court to determine whether there was an unwritten "common law" of tenure at the university. If so, the teacher would be entitled to a dismissal hearing.

Roth and *Sindermann* emphasize, first, that there must be an independent source for a liberty or property interest to exist. Such interests are not created by the Constitution, but arise by employment contract or by operation of state tenure laws. Second, if a liberty or property interest is not established, no requirement of due process exists under the Fourteenth Amendment. Third, if a teacher possesses a liberty or property interest in employment, then due process is required and the teacher may not be dismissed without a hearing. A tenured teacher, or an untenured teacher during the term of his or her contract, possesses a property interest in continued employment. An untenured teacher who is not rehired after expiration of his or her contract is entitled to a due process hearing if the decision not to rehire is accompanied by a finding of incompetence or immorality, because the teacher's liberty of employment would be impaired by such a finding.

A. Property Interest

As *Roth* and *Sindermann* point out, a liberty or property interest in employment must exist before attachment of procedural due process rights. A common source for creating a property interest arises from state tenure statutes that often create property interests for particular employees who meet the statutory requirements. However, probationary employees or at-will employees generally do not enjoy due process protections.

♦   A principal's first-year evaluation expressed concerns and she received a preliminary notice of contract nonrenewal during her second year. At the hearing she requested, the board renewed her contract. At the start of the principal's third year, a new district administrator developed a formal assistance plan for the principal. During the same school year, a group of five or six students violently and aggressively assaulted a student. When the principal called law enforcement and suspended the students, parents of the disciplined students began to actively denounce her. The district administrator initially voiced support for the principal, and he recommended renewal of the principal's contract for two years. When a complaining parent reported that the closed board vote renewing the principal's contract violated the state open-meetings law, the board rescinded its action and held a second meeting to consider the contract renewal. By the time the board met again, it was bound by state law to renew the contract, and it did so. However, all district employees were notified that the board had revised the principal's title and job description. Subsequently, **the principal resigned, stating that the removal of her main job duties amounted to a constructive discharge**.

She sued the school district, school board, and district administrator in federal district court, asserting violation of an asserted constitutional property right in continued employment duties, constructive discharge and violation of her liberty interest in her reputation. The court awarded summary judgment to the board and administrator, and the principal appealed to the Seventh Circuit, which noted that a constitutional property right in employment arises from state laws and contractual relationships, not the Constitution. Wisconsin law provided that a principal must perform administrative and leadership responsibilities and receive preliminary notices of non-renewal. The law and the principal's contract did not encompass any right to perform particular job duties. The district did not transfer the principal and she retained her title and salary. **Her expectation of retaining certain job duties did not create a protectable property interest**. While the court stated that the principal was the victim of a cowardly and politically motivated school board that failed to support her, she had no constitutionally protected claims against the board, district or administrator. Her constructive-discharge claim failed because she had abruptly resigned and had declined the opportunity to participate in the creation of her new job duties. There was no violation of her liberty interest in reputation because **a charge of mismanagement or incompetence does not rise to a constitutionally protected level**. The court affirmed the district court's judgment. *Ulichny v. Merton Community School Dist.*, 249 F.3d 686 (7th Cir. 2001).

◆   A student was found dead in a school swimming pool the day after a nontenured, part-time lifeguard and a tenured teacher had been supervising the student's class. No one observed the student in the pool at the end of class, but there was evidence that his clothing had been left near the pool. **The Chicago school board investigated the incident, and transferred the teacher to non-teaching duties pending the outcome**. It discharged the lifeguard without a hearing and never recalled him to work. The board served the teacher with charges of violating board rules, but soon decided to reinstate him to his duties. Because of anger and unrest among parents and students, the board delayed reinstating the teacher for several months, and he missed coaching opportunities and supplemental pay as a result. Both employees sued the school district in a federal district court for civil rights violations. A federal district court awarded summary judgment to the board on the lifeguard's claims, finding that he kept a community-college teaching position he maintained while employed by the board and that he did not present any evidence that he was turned down for other jobs. The court denied summary judgment to the board on the teacher's claims, ruling that his temporary reassignment constituted a "removal" from his position under Illinois law.

The parties appealed to the U.S. Court of Appeals, Seventh Circuit, which agreed with the district court's disposition of the lifeguard's claims. The lifeguard admitted that he was not discharged from his community college position and was not turned down for other potential employment. The court disagreed with the teacher that his temporary job reassignment was a tangible loss of employment opportunities, even though he had lost income under his supplemental contracts. The board's action did not deprive him of constitutional property interests in employment because he was not "removed" from his position, as used in Illinois tenure statutes. In order for removal to occur, there must be a permanent reduction in job duties. The teacher received his full teaching salary during his reassignment and was notified that he would be restored to his duties within two months. **It was foreseeable that the teacher would receive a temporary reassignment when a serious safety incident occurred, and the temporary removal did not implicate a constitutional property right**. The temporary loss of income from coaching contracts did not trigger his due process rights, since he did not enjoy tenure rights in these assignments. The temporary reassignment was a reasonable response to a difficult situation, and school officials were entitled to qualified immunity from the teacher's claims. The court reversed this aspect of the district court judgment. *Townsend v. Vallas*, 256 F.3d 661 (7th Cir. 2001).

◆   A long-term probationary teacher was identified as being present while a cheat sheet was prepared to improve student performance on citywide reading and math tests. The school district reassigned her to nonteaching duties in another school. The teacher denied the allegations against her at a disciplinary hearing, but the district held that she had violated school policies by cheating during the standardized tests and failing to report to her supervisors that the cheat sheets were prepared in her presence. The district placed a strong letter of reprimand in her employment file and instructed her principal to assign her an unsatisfactory performance evaluation. The teacher filed a notice of claim against the city, special commissioner and two investigators for defamation and violation of her civil rights. The commissioner issued a supplemental report accusing her of helping students cheat during testing, pressuring other teachers to do the same, and assaulting another teacher. The district provided the teacher a second hearing at which the district affirmed its earlier findings and **the superintendent of schools denied her certification of probation, disqualifying her from district employment**.

The teacher sued the district, superintendent, school board and board chancellor in a federal district court for violating her due process rights and terminating her employment in retaliation for filing a notice of claim. The board moved to dismiss the complaint, asserting that she was a probationary employee with no constitutionally protected due process rights. The court held that a civil rights plaintiff attempting to show a due process violation must identify a protected interest and a deprivation of that interest without the provision of the constitutional minimum procedures. **When state law defines an employment position as probationary, the employee lacks a legal claim of entitlement and has no property interest in continued employment**. Unlike permanent employees, probationary employees have no property rights in their position and may be lawfully discharged without a hearing. This was true even though the teacher had worked for the district for ten years. Although the district's accusations impugned the teacher's honesty, touching on her constitutional liberty interest in reputation, she had an adequate state remedy to redress these allegations in Article 78 of the New York Civil Practice Law and Rules. Because Article 78 provided for a hearing and redress that was adequate to meet due process requirements, there was no constitutional violation that remained to be remedied in a federal civil rights action. The court dismissed the teacher's constitutional claims, but allowed her 30 days to come forward with sufficient facts to avoid dismissal of her retaliation claim. *Rivera v. Community School Dist. Nine*, 145 F.Supp.2d 302 (S.D.N.Y. 2001).

◆   Two teachers received annual stipends for performing coaching duties. The district notified them that their coaching assignments and stipends would not be renewed for the following school year. The teachers sued the district in an Idaho trial court for reinstatement to their coaching positions and other relief. They alleged violation of their statutory rights to due process under Idaho law; violation of their federal due process rights under 42 U.S.C. § 1983 and the Idaho Constitution; and breach of their written contracts. The court ordered the district to reinstate the teacher who coached the basketball team for the season. The parties moved the court for summary judgment. The trial court found that while the teachers did not have any property interest in their extra-duty assignments under Idaho law, a clause in the master contract between the district and their education association prohibited termination, discharge or other adverse action in the absence of just cause. **The just cause language was incorporated into their individual contracts, creating a property interest in the extra-duty assignments**. The court granted judgment to the teachers, finding that the district had violated their state and federal due process rights and breached their contract rights under the master and individual contracts.

The school district appealed from an order requiring reinstatement of the teachers to their extra duties, with an award of $4,598 to the volleyball coach. The Idaho Supreme Court held **that in order to create a property interest in a benefit, such as public employment, a person must have more than an expectation in it. The person must, instead, have a legitimate claim of entitlement to the benefit**. The contracts between the school district and teachers regarding extra duties created a property interest in those assignments that was constitutionally protected. The individual employment contracts covered both classroom and extra-duty assignments, and the same rights applied to the coaching duties as to the classroom duties. The master contract protected the teachers from a reduction in compensation in the absence of just cause. Since the district failed to provide the teachers with notice and a hearing prior to the reduction in compensation, it violated their due process rights. The award of damages for the volleyball teacher was not barred by the Idaho Tort Claims Act, since the claim was based on breach of contractual rights. The award of injunctive relief to the basketball coach was not an abuse of discretion. The state supreme court affirmed the trial court's decision. *Farner v. Idaho Falls School District No. 91*, 17 P.3d 281 (Idaho 2000).

♦   An administrator for the Houston school district lobbied for higher pay during the 13 years she served as community services director for the district homebound program. She asserted that her duties resembled those of a large school principal and that she was accordingly entitled to a pay increase. During the administrator's final year of employment, the school district agreed to raise her pay, but she decided to retire and sued the district in state court. **Among her claims was one that asserted a constitutional right to be paid at the large school principal pay rate** for the 12 previous years of employment.

The court awarded summary judgment to the school district and the administrator appealed to the court of appeals, which rejected her argument that various writings created a property interest in higher pay that was protected by the Constitution. These included a memorandum from the superintendent, district salary manuals and letters of recommendation. The court found that the documents did not arise under state law, and could not form the basis of a constitutionally protected right. **There was no merit to the administrator's claim that she was entitled to back pay under the theory that there was a constitutionally guaranteed property interest in correct salary**. The court rejected her other claims as meritless and affirmed the order for summary judgment. *Jackson v. Houston Indep. School Dist.*, 994 S.W.2d 396 (Tex.App. 1999).

♦   The Texas Term Contract Nonrenewal Act confers procedural protections and mandates automatic contract renewal for teachers in the absence of proper notice. **The act requires school districts to furnish written notice and an opportunity for a hearing when the district fails to renew a teacher's contract**. A Texas school district failed to rehire an experienced school nurse without stating a reason for its decision or providing an opportunity for a hearing. The nurse claimed that she was "certified" within the meaning of the Term Contract Nonrenewal Act because the state board of education's regulations required a school nurse to hold either a provisional school nurse certificate or a current registration with the state board of nurse examiners. **The state commissioner of education ruled that the nurse was not protected by the nonrenewal act** because she was not a teacher within the definition of the act. The Court of Appeals of Texas affirmed. The nurse appealed to the Supreme Court of Texas.

The supreme court observed that the nonrenewal act protected teachers, a term that was defined as superintendents, principals, supervisors, teachers, counselors and other fulltime professionals, who were required to hold a valid certificate or teaching permit. Although all school nurses were required to be registered by the state board of nurse examiners, not all school nurses were required to have a provisional school nurse certificate. Although state board regulations made it possible for school nurses to obtain a certificate, the statute did not require certification. **Because the nonrenewal act distinguished between employees who were required to hold certificates and those who were not, the commissioner of education had properly ruled that the nurse was not entitled to the act's protections**. *Dodd v. Meno*, 870 S.W.2d 4 (Tex.1994).

◆   A Mississippi school district employed a school librarian under a one year contract. She volunteered to temporarily teach an alternative class made up of students with disciplinary problems. A student left his desk while she was writing on the blackboard with her back to the class. When she turned around, the student startled her and she slapped him. The school district suspended her for the rest of the school year for unprofessional conduct and brutal treatment of a student. The board conducted a hearing and voted to uphold the suspension. The librarian appealed to a Mississippi trial court, which determined that because the slap was unintentional, it could not be brutal treatment. The court awarded the librarian backpay of almost $6,000 and found the board's decision arbitrary and capricious. **While the court considered the case, the board notified the librarian of its intention not to renew her contract**. She filed a lawsuit against the school board and its members in the U.S. District Court for the Northern District of Mississippi, claiming constitutional violations. The court considered the board and members' summary judgment motion.

The court observed that the librarian's constitutional complaint pertained only to the nonrenewal of her contract, and not the suspension. Claims for constitutional rights violations are analyzed on the basis of whether state officials comply with state statutes. In this case, **Mississippi law did not confer a property interest in continued employment** to the librarian. State school administrators are not required to demonstrate good cause in declining to renew employment contracts. There was evidence that the board did not violate the librarian's constitutional liberty interest in her reputation and future employment prospects. **The hearing satisfied minimal constitutional requirements** and the school board and its members were entitled to summary judgment. *Pruett v. Dumas*, 914 F.Supp. 133 (N.D.Miss.1996).

B. Notice

In most cases, adequate notice includes a statement of the reasons for the action and time to respond. This affords the employee an opportunity to take remedial action or prepare a defense.

♦ **During a teacher's third year of employment, her school principal wrote her a letter advising her that he would not recommend renewal of her contract due to classroom management problems.** The board granted the teacher's request for an informal hearing. At the hearing, the teacher and her attorney appeared, and the board considered testimony from various individuals. The principal recommended nonrenewal for failure to maintain appropriate student participation and behavior and deficient classroom management skills. The board deliberated in a closed session, then recessed. The parties agreed to extend the deadline for a hearing and final action beyond the statutory limit. The board's attorney wrote two letters to the teacher's attorney in the intervening weeks indicating the date of a final hearing, and the board published a notice of the final hearing in a local newspaper. The teacher and her attorney declined to attend the final board meeting. During the meeting, the board again went into a closed session to discuss the case. It voted against renewal of the teacher's contract after returning to open session, and she petitioned a state district court for review. The court affirmed the board's action, finding that the teacher was a probationary employee who had received proper notice and a hearing on her contract. Her due process rights had not been violated by the board's closed session deliberations because state law required only that formal action for contract nonrenewal take place in an open session of the school board.

The teacher appealed to the Nebraska Supreme Court, which found sufficient evidence upholding the board's decision. The principal had evaluated her and had provided a written growth plan for the year. He had notified her of classroom management problems, which included improper references to some students as "the upper group" and to others as "challenge" students. The court found no requirement in state law that a probationary teacher receive notice that a performance deficiency is of such magnitude that failure to remedy it could lead to contract nonrenewal. The board had complied with statutory observation and evaluation requirements. **School officials had complied with the notice and hearing requirements of state law by providing the teacher with written notices of the informal and formal hearings and by honoring her request for an open informal hearing.** Although state law required that a formal vote on contract nonrenewal take place in an open session, the law did not require that board deliberations take place in open session. Public meeting laws specifically do not apply to a board's judicial functions with respect to employment matters. The board had received no new evidence at the formal hearing. Rather, it had only continued to make its deliberations in the closed session. The court affirmed the district court judgment for the school board. *McQuinn v. Douglas County School District No. 66 et al.*, 259 Neb. 720, 612 N.W.2d 198 (2000).

♦ California law requires school boards to notify administrative and supervisory employees 45 days in advance of the end of their current term of nonrenewal of their contract. An assistant school superintendent nearing the end of her two-year contract was in informal communication with a board member who advised her that the board had not discussed the renewal of her contract. However, the school superintendent served her with a notice 45 days in advance of her contract expiration that her contract was nearing expiration. **After the assistant superintendent's request to appear before the board was denied, the board voted to ratify the superintendent's notice, only four days prior to expiration of her contract**. The board then offered her a one-year contract, which she rejected and the board excluded her from returning to her position. The assistant superintendent sued the school district in a California trial court, which dismissed the action. On appeal, the California Court of Appeal observed that California law requires the automatic reemployment of an administrative or supervisory employee under the same terms and conditions as the current contract if no timely notice is given. In this case, **the board had taken no action until four days prior to the expiration of the contract, and its ratification of the superintendent's notice had no legal effect**. Accordingly, the court reversed the trial court's judgment and held that the assistant superintendent was entitled to reemployment for another two years, under the same terms and conditions as her original contract. *Jenkins v. Inglewood Unified School Dist.*, 41 Cal.Rptr.2d 80 (Cal.App.2d Dist.1995).

♦   **An Alabama second grade teacher with 23 years of experience received notice of her employing school board's intention to discharge her for incompetency, neglect of duty and other good causes**. Specified reasons for the termination action were that she failed to maintain classroom discipline, failed to properly administer and monitor achievement tests, failed to make and carry out lesson plans and otherwise failed to comply with state teaching requirements. The board voted to terminate the teacher's employment, and she appealed to the state teacher tenure commission, which affirmed the decision. The teacher appealed to an Alabama circuit court, which affirmed the administrative decisions. She appealed to the Court of Civil Appeals of Alabama. The teacher argued that the notice of termination failed to state that student test scores would be presented at the termination hearing to establish the claim of incompetence and that she had been deprived of notice that classroom discipline incidents dating back several years would be used against her. **The court found that the state tenure law required the board to provide a detailed statement of the reasons for termination, but did not require a detailed statement of the evidence that would be presented at a hearing**. The trial court had properly found that the notice was adequate, and numerous incidents demonstrating incompetence and inability to maintain classroom order were sufficient to justify employment termination. The court affirmed the trial court judgment for the school board. *Dunson v. Alabama State Tenure Comm'n*, 653 So.2d 995 (Ala.Civ.App.1994). The Supreme Court of Alabama denied further appeal. *Ex Parte Dunson*, 653 So.2d 1001 (Ala.1995).

♦   Ohio law required school boards to give notification to school administrators on or before the last day of March of the year in which the contract expired if the district did not intend to rehire the administrator. One section of the statute stated that nothing prevented a board of education from making a final decision to employ or fail to renew an administrator's contract. **An Ohio school district failed to give**

the required written notice to an assistant principal, and eliminated her position along with those of 10 others. The assistant principal accepted a high school teaching assignment, but petitioned an Ohio court for an order requiring the school board to issue her a two-year contract as an assistant principal with backpay and fringe benefits. The court granted summary judgment to the school board and the administrator appealed to the Supreme Court of Ohio. **The court determined that the conflict between statutory sections should be resolved in favor of the school board.** Even though the board had failed to comply with the notice statute, its ability to nonrenew the contract was not undermined. The language of the statute vesting the board with final authority was distinct from a similar statute governing teacher contracts, which the assistant principal had relied upon in her argument. The legislature would have used the same language from the teacher statute if it had intended the same result. The administrator failed to demonstrate her right to reappointment and the court affirmed the decision in favor of the school board. *State ex rel. Cassels v. Dayton City School Dist. Bd. of Educ.*, 69 Ohio St.3d 217, 631 N.E.2d 150 (1994).

◆   A Mississippi school board voted to reemploy a number of teachers and counselors for the following school year despite acknowledging that a reduction in staff would be necessary over the next three years due to budget shortfalls. **At the end of the school year, the board learned of a $400,000 budget shortfall and sent notice to a guidance counselor that he would not be rehired the following year because of a staff reduction.** A hearing officer determined that the school district's financial crisis constituted good cause for contract termination. A Mississippi trial court reversed this decision and awarded damages to the counselor. The district appealed to the Supreme Court of Mississippi. The supreme court observed that in states such as Iowa and Massachusetts, budgetary restraints could serve as just cause for termination of employee contracts because their tenure statutes did not differentiate between contract termination and nonrenewal. Mississippi's termination, suspension, and contract renewal statutes made a clear distinction between discharges and contract nonrenewals. **Because the school board did not provide written notice to the guidance counselor of its intention not to renew his contract as required by the state employment procedures law, it was liable for the employment contract.** Its budgetary problems could not constitute good cause for suspension or removal under the statute. The court affirmed the trial court's damage award. *Byrd v. Greene County School Dist.*, 633 So.2d 1018 (Miss.1994).

C. Hearing

Tenured employees must be given a fair and impartial hearing, conducted in accordance with statutory procedural safeguards, if a property or a liberty interest exists or if the dismissal involves a stigma upon the character of the teacher.

1. Minimum Requirements

Dismissal of tenured teachers requires a hearing because of their property interest in employment which cannot be taken away without due process of law.

However, a number of cases address the adequacy of hearings and whether the type of employment involved requires a hearing.

◆   A police officer employed by a Pennsylvania state university was arrested in a drug raid and charged with several felony counts related to marijuana possession and distribution. State police notified the university of the arrest and charges, and the university's human resources director immediately suspended the officer without pay pursuant to a state executive order requiring such action where a state employee is formally charged with a felony. Although the criminal charges were dismissed, university officials demoted the officer because of the felony charges. The university did not inform the officer that it had obtained his confession from police records and he was thus unable to fully respond to damaging statements in the police reports. **He filed a federal district court action against university officials for failing to provide him with notice and an opportunity to be heard before his suspension without pay**. The court granted summary judgment to the officials, but the U.S. Court of Appeals, Third Circuit, reversed and remanded the case.

The U.S. Supreme Court agreed to review the case, and stated that the court of appeals had improperly held that a suspended public employee must always receive a paid suspension under *Cleveland Bd. of Educ. v. Loudermill*, 470 U.S. 532 (1985), below. **The Court held that the university did not violate due process by refusing to pay a suspended employee charged with a felony pending a hearing**. It accepted the officials' argument that the Pennsylvania executive order made any presuspension hearing useless, since the filing of charges established an independent basis for believing that the officer had committed a felony. The Court noted that the officer here faced only a temporary suspension without pay, and not employment termination as in *Loudermill*. The Court reversed and remanded the court of appeals' judgment for consideration of the officer's arguments concerning a postsuspension hearing. *Gilbert v. Homar*, 520 U.S. 924, 117 S.Ct. 1807, 138 L.Ed.2d 120 (1997).

◆   In two consolidated cases, the U.S. Supreme Court considered what pretermination process must be afforded a public employee who can be discharged only for cause. In the first case, a security guard hired by a school board stated on his job application that he had never been convicted of a felony. Upon discovering that he had in fact been convicted of grand larceny, the school board summarily dismissed him for dishonesty in filling out the job application. He was not afforded an opportunity to respond to the dishonesty charge or to challenge the dismissal until nine months later. In the second case, a school bus mechanic was fired because he had failed an eye examination. The mechanic appealed his dismissal after the fact because he had not been afforded a pretermination hearing. **The Supreme Court held that because the employees possessed a property right in their employment, they were entitled to a pretermination opportunity to at least respond to the charges against them**. The pretermination hearing need not fully resolve the propriety of the discharge, but should be a check against mistaken decisions. The Court held that in this case the employees were entitled to a pretermination opportunity to respond, coupled with a full-blown administrative hearing at a later time. *Cleveland Bd. of Educ. v. Loudermill*, 470 U.S. 532, 105 S.Ct. 1487, 84 L.Ed.2d 494 (1985).

◆   Missouri elementary school administrators determined that a teacher had many communication problems. After giving her warnings, the administrators imposed a professional development plan upon her, requiring her to attend teaching workshops and to read materials on communication and instruction. Later assessments determined that the teacher's performance was still deficient and that she had difficulty maintaining classroom discipline. After further meetings and warnings, **the administrators issued the teacher a warning letter in compliance with the state tenure act advising her that formal charges would be brought unless improvement was made** within 120 days. The administrators then videotaped class sessions instructed by the teacher and met to discuss them with her. Although the teacher's deadline was extended, **the administrators ultimately recommended termination**. The school board approved the dismissal, and a Missouri circuit court affirmed its decision. The teacher appealed to the Missouri Court of Appeals, Eastern District.

The court of appeals observed that the state tenure act mandated the procedure for removing teachers for incompetency, inefficiency or insubordination. The teacher must receive a written warning specifying the grounds for action, which may result in charges if the grounds are not removed within a probationary period of at least 30 days. Teachers are then entitled to confer with the superintendent. The court rejected the teacher's argument that the board had not acted in good faith under the tenure act. **Administrators had made many efforts to help improve her performance and gave her more than the minimum time required by statute to comply with the development plan.** The court affirmed the board's decision. *Johnson v. Francis Howell R-3 Bd. of Educ.*, 868 S.W.2d 191 (Mo.App.E.D.1994).

2. Hearing Procedures

Usually when a hearing has been inadequate or unfair or where there has been evidence of bias, the courts will require that procedural problems be corrected prior to dismissal or demotion. On occasion, courts have also ordered reinstatement.

◆   A Kentucky teacher served for 12 years prior to the district's initiation of a discharge action, which was based on evidence that he initiated a conversation with students about circumcision and penis size. The district provided him with an opportunity to respond to the incident, and he acknowledged the conversation with students. **The district notified him of his statutory right to appeal the termination decision within 10 days, and provided him with a hearing that lasted 13 days**. The teacher was represented by counsel, called witnesses and presented evidence challenging the decision. He complained that one of his witnesses could not appear for medical reasons, but the hearing officer refused to delay the proceedings. The hearing officer upheld the teacher's termination.

The teacher appealed the adverse administrative decision to a federal district court, asserting violation of his due process rights. The court first determined that the employee had a property interest in his position that was entitled to constitutional protection. He was protected by state tenure law, and **the district satisfied due process requirements by providing him with the opportunity to challenge the termination action both before and after it took place**. Although the pre-termination due process had been limited to the opportunity to respond to the charges, the teacher received an elaborate post-termination hearing where he was represented by counsel and had a full opportunity to present evidence in his own behalf. The unavailability of a single witness did not prevent the teacher from presenting his defense, and was not caused by the school district. The Due Process Clause of the Fourteenth Amendment requires only that a hearing be granted at a meaningful time and in a meaningful manner. There was no reason to delay the extensive hearing. The school district had a vital and legitimate interest in protecting students from teachers who exposed them to sexually explicit conversations. The court awarded summary judgment to the district on the federal claims and remanded the state law claims to a state court. *Lafferty v. Board of Educ. of Floyd County*, 133 F.Supp.2d 941 (E.D. Ky. 2001).

◆   **Under a California statute, teachers who challenged suspension or discharge actions were required to pay for half the costs of the hearings in the event of an unsuccessful appeal.** A teacher who had demanded a hearing to contest his discharge for unfitness for service and immoral conduct was billed almost $8,000 for half the cost of an administrative hearing. When the teacher did not pay the bill, the state threatened to offset his state income taxes to recover the amount. The teacher, along with the California Teachers Association, obtained a California trial court order enjoining the tax offset and holding the statutory provision unconstitutional.

The Court of Appeal of California affirmed the judgment and state officials appealed to the state supreme court, which found the statute a unique and unprecedented departure from the tradition of publicly funded judges and administrative hearing tribunals. It held that the state, having monopolized the process for teacher disciplinary hearings, was required to provide teachers with meaningful hearing opportunities. **The law had a chilling effect on the exercise of due process rights by teachers, since it presented strong financial disincentives against the pursuit of an administrative hearing**. The law was at odds with the principle of free access to the courts and was not justified by any proper legislative goal. The law placed the burden of half the cost of an administrative appeal on those teachers who were ultimately unsuccessful, rather than on those who advanced frivolous or meritless appeals, and penalized those teachers who lost at the administrative hearing level without regard for the reasonableness of the appeal. This forced teachers to predict in advance how the commission would rule on their cases—a practical impossibility. Because the law burdened teacher due process rights, and because the interest of teachers in due process outweighed any state interest in protecting scarce resources, the court affirmed the judgment. *California Teachers Ass'n v. State of California*, 20 Cal.4th 327, 975 P.2d 622 (Cal.1999).

◆   Georgia school administrators investigated allegations by students that a teacher in the school system had made sexual advances toward them. The school superintendent reported the matter to the Georgia Professional Practices Commission, which conducted an investigation. The commission recommended that the school board immediately place the teacher on administrative leave and begin a dismissal action. The school board then voted to terminate the teacher's contract. The commission requested a second investigation concerning the revocation of the teacher's teaching certificate. **The teacher filed a state court lawsuit against the**

commission, seeking injunctive relief to prevent the taking of any action against his teaching certificate prior to a hearing. The court granted summary judgment to the commission, and the teacher appealed to the Supreme Court of Georgia. The commission subsequently held an administrative hearing at which a formal recommendation was made that his certificate be suspended. The supreme court then determined that the commission had complied with state law by providing the teacher with a hearing prior to the suspension of the certificate. State law authorizes investigations for allegations that a teacher has violated ethical or professional standards and authorizes the commission to recommend warnings, reprimands, suspensions or the termination of teaching certificates. **The court found that the statutory scheme satisfied procedural due process since teachers were allowed a hearing before the commission could impose actual sanctions.** The court affirmed the judgment for the commission. *Gee v. Professional Practices Comm'n,* 491 S.E.2d 375 (Ga.1997).

◆   An Ohio school district fired a high school custodian for suspected drug dealing and sexually suggestive behavior with students. The custodian filed a grievance under the collective bargaining agreement between his union and the district. A former student at the school was called to give evidence concerning drug dealing at the arbitration hearing. She claimed to be afraid of the custodian. Accordingly, **the arbitrator permitted her to testify from a separate room via closed-circuit video screen by which she was subjected to direct and cross-examination.** The cross-examination yielded evidence that the custodian had not actually threatened her. The arbitrator determined that the sexual misconduct charge was insufficient to warrant employment termination, but that the former student's testimony established the custodian's involvement in a drug deal. The grievance was denied, and appeal reached the Supreme Court of Ohio. The supreme court determined that **while deprivation of a property right such as public employment mandated due process, there was no explicit right to confrontation and cross-examination in a public employee's pretermination or post-termination hearing.** The purpose of due process was to protect substantial rights, but the same procedures were not mandated in every case. The custodian's right to present evidence and to conduct cross-examination was outweighed by the state's interest in securing necessary testimony. The student had a reasonable fear of reprisal and the arbitrator's action had been appropriate. The court declined to rule that a face-to-face confrontation was an absolute requirement of due process and it reinstated the arbitrator's decision. *Ohio Ass'n of Pub. School Employees v. Lakewood City School Dist. Bd. of Educ.,* 68 Ohio St.3d 175, 624 N.E.2d 1043 (1994).

3. Impartiality

◆   A high school principal received satisfactory evaluations but was assigned areas of concern during his first three years of employment. The district superintendent issued him an unsatisfactory rating at the end of his fourth year, based on failure to maintain good working relationships with staff, failure to act professionally on a number of occasions and lack of cooperation in working toward district and instructional or management goals. The school board voted unanimously to demote the principal to a teaching position. In response to the principal's request, the board conducted an evidentiary hearing, and again voted to demote him. The principal petitioned the state secretary of education, arguing that the board's vote was not supported by substantial evidence. **He claimed that a board member was married to a district secretary who had testified against him at the evidentiary hearing and that potential bias existed** because of their marital relationship. The secretary held that the decision to demote the principal was justified and that while allowing the board member to participate in the voting despite his relationship to the school secretary was imprudent, his participation did not violate the school code. The secretary's *de novo* review of the case cured any potential for bias in the school board proceedings.

The principal appealed to the Commonwealth Court of Pennsylvania, which vacated the secretary's order, ruling that the principal had been denied due process because of the appearance of bias created by the board member's presence in board deliberations. The school district appealed to the Supreme Court of Pennsylvania, which observed that the state secretary of education is vested with the authority to hear appeals by employees who are aggrieved by school board actions. State law gives the secretary the authority to conduct a *de novo* review of proceedings, whether or not additional testimony is taken. Aggrieved employees receive an opportunity to have the facts of their cases reheard in an independent forum in which the board acts only as a prosecutor. Minimum requirements of due process demand that a case be heard by a neutral fact finder at some stage of the proceedings. **Although school board proceedings have an inherent potential for bias because of a board's dual prosecutorial and judicial roles, independent review by the secretary ensured that the requirements of due process were satisfied.** Since the principal received all the process he was due, the court reversed and remanded the commonwealth court's decision. *Katruska v. Bethlehem Center School Dist.*, 767 A.2d 1051 (Pa. 2001).

◆   In 1985, a New York board of education initiated disciplinary charges against a teacher with more than 25 years of experience in the district. The charges alleged both incompetence and insubordination. Consistent with New York law, the teacher chose a hearing panel member, the board of education chose a hearing panel member, and those two designees in turn chose a third person to serve as panel chairperson. At the conclusion of the proceedings, the panel unanimously found the teacher not guilty of incompetence but, by a two to one vote, determined that she was guilty of insubordination and recommended termination. The board of education dismissed the teacher. Three days later, the teacher learned that the board of education had violated New York law by paying the panel member it had nominated an additional $100 per day to serve on the panel. **The teacher claimed that the compensation scheme violated her right to have an impartial decisionmaker under the Due Process Clause of the U.S. Constitution.** A New York appellate court concluded that the board of education's actions violated the teacher's rights. The school board appealed to the Court of Appeals of New York.

The court of appeals stated that it was not necessary to address the constitutional issues because the case could be resolved on other grounds. **The board of education's material departure from the mandatory provision of New York law constituted error entitling the teacher to relief.** While not all deviations from statutory procedures justify the reversal of an administrative determination, when the procedure provided is mandatory and the rule is intended to prevent bias and financial influence, the failure to follow those procedures results in at least the appearance of an unfair hearing. Accordingly, the determination had to be vacated. The court of appeals ordered a new hearing. *Syquia v. Bd. of Educ. of the Harpursville Central School Dist.*, 591 N.Y.S.2d 996 (N.Y. 1992).

◆   A fifth grade teacher at a Florida elementary school was suspended for ten days without pay for misconduct. The misconduct was based upon several incidents of misconduct including using the word "bitch" in class. The teacher appealed her suspension, claiming that not only was the evidence insufficient to support her suspension, but also that the school's attorney had inappropriately played a dual role during the misconduct hearing before the school board. According to the teacher's argument, the attorney acted as both the prosecutor and as the school board's legal advisor. **The Florida Court of Appeal vacated the suspension and ordered a new hearing. It agreed with the teacher, stating that due process requires an administrative board, such as a school board, conducting disciplinary proceedings to designate one person to act as its legal advisor and a different person to fulfill the role of prosecutor.** Since a new hearing was to be held, the evidence would be reheard. However, the court stated that the teacher's use of the word "bitch," used by the teacher in the sense of "to complain," could not legally constitute conduct so serious as to impair the individual's effectiveness in the school system. *Forehand v. School Bd. of Gulf County*, 600 So.2d 1187 (Fla. App. 1st Dist. 1992).

◆   A Connecticut teacher was arrested and charged with electronic eavesdropping. He was suspended with pay. Following a trial, he was acquitted of the charges against him. Thereafter, the school board voted to consider terminating him. The teacher requested a hearing and an impartial panel was chosen. The panel concluded that the evidence was sufficient to support a termination. However, the majority of the panel believed that the evidence of criminal wrongdoing was inadmissible because of Connecticut's Erasure Act, which erases the court and police records of criminal proceedings when the accused is acquitted. Prior to the meeting of the board to vote on the panel's recommendation, **the teacher filed a motion to disqualify four members of the board for personal bias or conflict of interest.** The board denied the motion and voted to terminate the teacher. The board issued a written opinion in which it stated that the undisputed evidence was sufficient to justify termination for moral misconduct. The teacher unsuccessfully appealed to a Connecticut trial court and further appealed to the Connecticut Supreme Court. On appeal, the court held that the erasure act was limited to court documents and police reports. Since the disputed testimony did not fall into either of these categories, it was admissible and provided a sufficient basis for termination. The teacher's remaining argument that four members of the board were biased against him was also rejected. **The court held that the teacher needed to show actual bias, not merely a presumption of bias based on past altercations.** The court upheld the lower court's decision affirming the termination of the teacher. *Rado v. Bd. of Educ. of the Borough of Naugatuck*, 583 A.2d 102 (Conn. 1990).

CHAPTER NINE

Labor Relations

I. PROFESSIONAL ASSOCIATIONS

School employees are entitled to form professional associations to represent their employment interests. Once elected, professional associations become exclusive collective bargaining agents for their members and have a legal duty to fairly represent all association members. The association also may collect agency fees from both members and nonmembers. However, strict requirements exist for the collection of agency fees from nonmembers in order to limit the use of the funds to collective bargaining activity rather than other association interests such as political support.

A. Representation

◆ In a 5-to-4 decision, **the U.S. Supreme Court upheld a collective bargaining agreement between an Indiana school board and the local teacher union which provided that the teacher union, to the exclusion of a rival union, had access to the school district's internal mail and delivery system.** The rival union challenged the denial of access to the mail system on grounds that the restriction violated free speech rights under the First Amendment and the Equal Protection Clause of the Fourteenth Amendment. The Supreme Court held that since the interschool mail system was not a public forum generally available for use by the public, access to it could be reasonably restricted without violating either free speech or equal protection rights. The Court noted the special responsibilities of the exclusive bargaining representative and the fact that other channels of communication remained available to the rival union. *Perry Educ. Ass'n v. Perry Local Educators' Ass'n*, 460 U.S. 37, 103 S.Ct. 948, 74 L.Ed.2d 794 (1983).

◆   In another U.S. Supreme Court case, Minnesota community college faculty members brought suit against the State Board for Community Colleges. **The faculty alleged that a state statute requiring public employers to engage in official exchanges of views only with their professional employees' exclusive representatives on certain policy questions violated their First Amendment rights**. Under the statute, public employers were required to bargain only with the employees' exclusive bargaining representative. The statute gave professional employees, such as college faculty members, the right to "meet and confer" with the employer on matters outside the scope of the collective bargaining agreement. The faculty members objected to the "meet and confer" provision, saying that rights of professional employees within the bargaining unit who were not members of the exclusive representative were violated. **The Supreme Court held that the "meet and confer" provision did not violate the faculty members' constitutional rights**. There was no constitutional right to force public employers to listen to the members' views. The fact that an academic setting was involved did not give them any special constitutional right to a voice in the employer's policymaking decisions. Further, the state had a legitimate interest in ensuring that its public employer heard one voice presenting the majority view of its professional employees on employment related policy questions. *Minnesota Comm. College Ass'n v. Knight*, 465 U.S. 271, 104 S.Ct. 1058, 79 L.Ed.2d 299 (1984).

◆   Each of five district cafeterias had its own on-site manager, who did not have hiring, firing, promotional or disciplinary authority. The district also employed maintenance and custodial workers to perform various tasks. Employees in these classes received comparable health and retirement benefits and received vacation, sick leave and other compensated time off. All employees in these classifications were paid on an hourly basis. The employees sought representation by a labor organization and elected a collective bargaining representative. The school district challenged the inclusion of all three employment classifications in the proposed bargaining unit before the Pennsylvania Labor Relations Board. **A PLRB hearing examiner held that the appropriate bargaining unit included all full-time and regular part-time custodians, maintenance workers and cafeteria workers**, including the cafeteria managers. The PLRB issued an order and notice of election, and the proposed association won a majority of votes. The district appealed a PLRB order certifying the association to a Pennsylvania trial court, which affirmed. The district then appealed to the Pennsylvania Commonwealth Court.

The commonwealth court determined the PLRB had correctly found many similarities among the different employee classifications. Each group performed "blue collar duties," received similar health and pension benefits, and was compensated on an hourly basis. Significantly, the employees had expressed the desire to be in the same bargaining unit. In determining the appropriateness of a collective bargaining unit, the PLRB was required to find that employees had an identifiable community of interests and evaluate the possible effect of over-fragmentization. An identifiable community of interest did not require perfect uniformity among these factors and conditions, and the board did not err in its findings. **It was clearly the desire of the employees to be represented by one union, and though their work was performed in different areas, it was generally blue-collar in nature and required no special certification**. Because the cafeteria managers were not supervisors within the meaning of state law, the PLRB did not err in finding that they were rank-and-file employees who were appropriately included in the collective bargaining unit. The trial court decision upholding the PLRB order was affirmed. *West Perry School District v. PLRB*, 752 A.2d 461 (Pa. Commw. 2000).

◆ The Michigan legislature amended state law by limiting the authority of state education associations to veto local bargaining unit decisions concerning tentative collective bargaining agreements. **The Michigan Education Association and state AFL-CIO filed lawsuits against state officials** in Michigan circuit courts, each **seeking a declaration that the amended law was unconstitutional**. The cases were consolidated and the court held that two provisions of the amended act were unconstitutional because they violated due process by imposing fines upon unions for the unauthorized actions of individuals. It also ruled that the act's mandatory injunction provision violated the separation of powers doctrine. The court upheld remaining aspects of the legislation, including a prohibition on the veto power of statewide labor associations in local bargaining unit decisions. The labor organizations appealed this part of the decision to the Michigan Court of Appeals, which affirmed the decision. The AFL-CIO and education association appealed to the Supreme Court of Michigan. **A plurality of the court held that the prohibition on state association veto powers did not violate the First Amendment speech rights of the associations. Their ability to advise and assist local units was not a legal power that could be enforced against local units**. The power to compel local bargaining units to adhere to state association policies was not guaranteed by the First Amendment. The court refrained from finding the legislation unconstitutional. *Michigan State AFL-CIO v. Employment Relations Comm'n*, 551 N.W.2d 165 (Mich.1996).

◆ A number of instructors worked for an Ohio public school board as special education and English as a second language tutors. They held valid teaching certificates and worked on an as-needed basis at hourly rates. Their salary levels were not equivalent to teachers in the district and they were not members of the bargaining unit representing teachers who worked in district schools. After several years, the tutors were brought into the bargaining unit under a separate wage schedule and they became aware of Ohio state court decisions that interpreted teacher wage statutes as also applying to tutors. **The tutors filed a petition for an order to compel the school board to pay them back wages for the difference between their actual pay and teachers' salaries prior to joining the collective bargaining association**. The court denied the petition and the tutors appealed to the Supreme Court of Ohio.

The supreme court held that tutors were "teachers" under Ohio law and were therefore entitled to the same pay where they were employed by a school board and were providing instruction to students. The court of appeals had properly held that the tutors had no right to back pay under the collective bargaining agreements for the period prior to joining the union. However, **an Ohio statute that applied in the absence of a collective bargaining agreement required payment in accordance with applicable teacher wage schedules**. Accordingly, the tutors had a right to receive the difference between the amounts they were actually paid and the amount that would have been due under the teachers' salary schedule after joining the teachers' union. The court reversed and remanded the case. *State ex rel. Chavis v. Sycamore City School Dist. Bd. of Educ.*, 71 Ohio St.3d 26, 641 N.E.2d 188 (1994).

B. Agency Fees

◆   **The exclusive bargaining representative of the faculty at a state college in Michigan entered into an agency-shop arrangement with the college requiring nonunion bargaining unit employees to pay a service or agency fee equivalent to a union member's dues**. Employees who objected to particular uses by the unions of their service fee brought suit under 42 U.S.C. § 1983, claiming that using the fees for purposes other than negotiating and administering the collective bargaining agreement violated their First and Fourteenth Amendment rights. A federal district court held that certain collective bargaining expenses were chargeable to the dissenting employees, the U.S. Court of Appeals affirmed and the U.S. Supreme Court granted certiorari. The Court first noted that chargeable activities must be "germane" to collective bargaining activity and be justified by the policy interest of avoiding "free riders" who benefit from union efforts without paying for union services. It then stated that **the local union could charge the objecting employees for their *pro rata* share of costs associated with chargeable activities of its state and national affiliates, even if those activities did not directly benefit the local bargaining unit**. The local could even charge the dissenters for expenses incident to preparation for a strike which would be illegal under Michigan law. However, lobbying activities and public relations efforts were not chargeable to the objecting employees. The Court affirmed in part and reversed in part the lower courts' decisions and remanded the case. *Lehnert v. Ferris Faculty Ass'n*, 500 U.S. 507, 111 S.Ct. 1950, 114 L.Ed.2d 572 (1991).

◆   Detroit teachers elected a labor association to become their exclusive collective bargaining representative, and it instituted an agency shop agreement. **A group of teachers filed a class action lawsuit in a Michigan trial court, stating that they would not pay dues or agency fees because of their opposition to collective bargaining** in the public sector. They specifically disapproved of the union's political and social activities, which they claimed were unrelated to the collective bargaining process. The teachers argued that the agency shop agreement violated state law and the First and Fourteenth Amendments. The case was dismissed by the trial court and was eventually appealed to the U.S. Supreme Court on the federal constitutional issues.

The Supreme Court drew on its earlier private sector decisions concerning labor relations and noted that compelled support of collective bargaining representatives implicated teacher First Amendment rights to free speech and association and religious freedom. However, some constitutional infringement was justified in the interest of peaceful labor relations. As long as the union acted to promote the cause of its membership, individual members were not free to withdraw their financial support. The Court agreed with the teachers that **compelled agency fees**

should not be used to support political views and candidates that were unrelated to collective bargaining issues. Because the state court had dismissed the case without a trial, the teachers had not received the opportunity to make specific allegations that their contributions were being used to support activities with which they disagreed. There was no evidentiary record and the Court remanded the case. If the teachers could prove a First Amendment violation, they were entitled to relief in the form of an injunction or a *pro rata* refund of fees being used for such purposes. *Abood v. Detroit Bd. of Educ.*, 431 U.S. 209, 97 S.Ct. 1782, 52 L.Ed.2d 261 (1977).

◆   In a later case, the Supreme Court found that the Chicago Teachers Union had not adequately protected the free speech rights of nonunion teachers. In 1982, the Chicago school board and the teachers' union agreed to deduct "proportionate share payments" from the paychecks of any nonunion employee. The deduction was fixed at 95 percent of the dues for union members, and no explanation was given as to how that figure was reached. This method of deduction was held to violate First Amendment freedom of speech protections. **To guard against the possibility of nonunion teachers' service fee payments being used for political purposes disagreeable to the nonmembers, the Supreme Court ruled that there must be an adequate accounting and explanation of the basis for the deduction**. In case of challenge, there must be an opportunity for a reasonably prompt decision by an impartial decisionmaker as to whether any part of the service fee deduction has gone to fund political causes. Any amount that was reasonably in dispute must be held in an escrow account during pendency of the challenge. *Chicago Teachers Union v. Hudson*, 475 U.S. 292, 106 S.Ct. 1066, 89 L.Ed.2d 232 (1986).

◆   Non-union members of an Indiana school district were given three options for paying fair share fees, and the collective bargaining agreement called for arbitration of disputed fees. One of the options for fair sharing reduced fair share fees by the estimated amount of fees attributable to matters not related to collective bargaining. Another option allowed objectors to obtain an arbitrator's decision before any amount of fair share dues were paid. Fair share fees were about 20 percent less than full union dues. **A group of non-union teachers sued, asserting constitutional rights violations and complaining that the fair share method spelled out in the collective bargaining agreement did not correspond to the standards set forth by the U.S. Supreme Court** in *Chicago Teachers Union v. Hudson*, above. The trial court held the fair share provision unconstitutional, and severed it from the collective bargaining agreement.

The union appealed to an Indiana court of appeals, which noted that the disputed provision did not require nonmember teachers to pay the full amount of union dues, nor did it require them to await a refund of costs that were unrelated to collective bargaining. **The court agreed with the union that the collective bargaining provision was constitutionally adequate. The collective bargaining agreement included a very specific explanation of the fair share fee**. Moreover, the union made no attempt to collect disputed fair share fees until after the decision of an impartial arbitrator. The union provided non-member teachers with detailed and voluminous information concerning expenditures that satisfied the standard set forth in *Chicago Teachers Union*. The collective bargaining agreement provided for arbitration of disputed amounts, and there was no need for escrowing funds since no disputed amounts were ever collected until after arbitration. Because the trial court had improperly found unconstitutional the fair share system described in the collective bargaining agreement, the court of appeals reversed and remanded the case. *Whitley County Teachers Ass'n v. Bauer*, 718 N.E.2d 1181 (Ind.Ct.App. 1999).

◆ A teachers union that represented employees of a New Hampshire school district collected agency fees from non-union member bargaining unit employees via involuntary payroll deductions. A non-union member employee objected to the involuntary payroll deduction and filed a wage claim against the school district with the state department of labor. The teachers union responded by filing a New Hampshire superior court action against the employee in which it sought a declaration that the mandatory payment of agency fees, and the use of involuntary payroll deductions to collect agency fees, was legal. **The court held that compulsory agency fees were lawful** as part of a public sector collective bargaining agreement, **but that collection of the fees by payroll deduction violated state law**. The employee appealed to the Supreme Court of New Hampshire.

The state supreme court found that New Hampshire law authorized agency fees as a mandatory subject of collective bargaining. This was because they were included within a broad category of terms and conditions of employment sanctioned by the legislature as appropriate for negotiation in public sector collective bargaining agreements. The court rejected the employee's argument that the mandatory collection of agency fees improperly encouraged union membership and constituted an unfair labor practice. Even though agency fees are only marginally lower that full union dues, the fair allocation of agency fees to pay the costs of representation did not provide employees with an incentive to join a union. The court held that agency fees were not prohibited and affirmed the judgment. *Nashua Teachers Union v. Nashua School Dist.*, 707 A.2d 448 (N.H. 1998).

◆ In a 1992 case, the Indiana Court of Appeals required labor associations to affirmatively prove that agency fees are chargeable. **A group of bargaining unit employees who were not union members refused to pay the agency fee** assessed by their collective bargaining representative. The labor association filed a lawsuit against the employees to collect the fees in an Indiana trial court which granted its summary judgment motion. On appeal, the Court of Appeals of Indiana rejected the teachers' argument that the association had failed to affirmatively prove its chargeable expenses. Union officials had required their staffs to complete time sheets indicating both chargeable and nonchargeable expenses. It was appropriate for the union to assess a percentage of its overhead costs, and these costs had also been affirmatively proven as chargeable. **The association had proven that its chargeable expenses were related to collective bargaining and not significantly burdensome**. The court affirmed summary judgment for the labor association. *DeBaets v. National Educ. Ass'n–South Bend*, 657 N.E.2d 1236 (Ind.App.1995).

◆ The Michigan Education Association (MEA) represents Michigan school and college employees as their exclusive bargaining representative. A group of nonunion employees who were required to pay the MEA agency for its representational services objected to the MEA's notice of required services. **The notice advised nonmember employees of the amount of the agency fee with an explanation of its expenditures. It gave nonunion members 30 days to file a written objection**, and provided a form and prepaid business reply envelope in which to return the form. Nonunion members who objected to the amount of the agency fee could request that the entire amount be escrowed until the legality of the fee was determined by an arbitrator. The objecting employees filed a lawsuit against the MEA and the National Education Association in the U.S. District Court for the Western District of Michigan, which granted the MEA's motion to dismiss the lawsuit. The employees appealed to the U.S. Court of Appeals, Sixth Circuit, which remanded the case for reconsideration in view of the U.S. Supreme Court's decision in *Lehnert v. Ferris Faculty Ass'n*, above. The district court again granted the union's dismissal motion and the employees appealed to the Sixth Circuit. **The court of appeals found no constitutional violation in the MEA's notification procedures. It provided all nonmember employees with an explanation of their agency fee calculation and provided a clear procedure for objecting parties to appeal**. Because the notice accurately informed the nonunion members about the fee, there was no constitutional violation and the court of appeals affirmed the district court's judgment. *Jibson v. Michigan Educ. Ass'n–NEA*, 30 F.3d 723 (6th Cir.1994).

II. COLLECTIVE BARGAINING AGREEMENTS

Federal labor law imposes an obligation upon employers to bargain with duly elected collective bargaining representatives over the terms and conditions of employment. School districts and employees become bound by the terms of their agreements and failure to abide by them constitutes an unfair labor practice. For cases discussing the interaction between state labor and education statutes and collective bargaining agreements, see Chapter 8, Section I.C.

A. Compensation

◆   A union collective-bargaining agent who represented the employees of two schools owned and operated by the U.S. Army, submitted proposals asking for mileage reimbursement, paid leave, and salary increases on behalf of the schools' employees. The schools refused to negotiate, stating that under Title VII of the Civil Service Reform Act of 1978 they were not required to negotiate these matters. The union filed a complaint with the Federal Labor Relations Authority (FLRA) which held that the union's proposals were negotiable. The schools appealed to the U.S. Court of Appeals, Eleventh Circuit, which upheld the FLRA's decision. The schools then appealed to the U.S. Supreme Court. **Title VII of the Civil Service Reform Act defines conditions of employment as matters "affecting working conditions" but excludes matters relating to prohibited political activities, classification of positions, and those specifically provided for by federal statute.** The Court determined that the union's proposals were "conditions of employment." The Supreme Court, affirming the district court's decision, held that the schools were required to negotiate salary increases and fringe benefits. *Fort Stewart Schools v. Federal Labor Relations Authority*, 495 U.S. 641, 110 S.Ct. 2043, 109 L.Ed.2d 659 (1990).

◆   A Kansas school district and National Education Association-Topeka (NEA-T) negotiated a series of professional agreements providing for an employee health insurance fringe benefit. Under the initial agreement, employees who opted out of group coverage received a cash payment. This was later reduced to the difference between a single low option plan and the cash payment amount. A rider governed the distribution of any divisible surplus resulting from a lower usage of insurance benefits than expected at the time the premiums were calculated. The school district contracted with NEA-T to offer an employee cafeteria plan. The health insurer refunded the district over $1.7 million to the district as a divisible surplus. The district notified employees about the surplus, and ultimately decided to retain almost $1 million for a stabilization fund to adjust future premiums. The rest of the refund was distributed to plan participants. **The NEA-T sued the district in a state trial court on behalf of participant/employees, asserting that they were entitled to the entire surplus**. The court found that the case required a determination of whether the fringe benefit plan was a part of total employee compensation, requiring interpretation of the professional agreement by an arbitrator.

In response to the district's motion to amend the judgment, the court agreed to delete its order remanding the case to an arbitrator. The NEA-T appealed to the Kansas Supreme Court.

The state supreme court rejected the NEA-T's arguments in favor of returning the full surplus to employees, noting that the rider did not entitle employees to the surplus and that the insurer had properly refunded the surplus directly to the district. The cafeteria plan did not dictate the entitlement to the surplus, since employee rights under it were contingent on definitions from the professional agreement. **A school board policy calling for return of premium refunds to insured employees did not create any entitlement**, since the rider was the governing contract with regard to the distribution of surpluses. Resolution of the ultimate question in this case required interpreting the professional agreement. The court found incorrect the assertion by the NEA-T that any other document obligated the district to pay the surplus to employees. Under the express terms of the agreement, any employee claiming a violation was required to present a written grievance within 15 days of the act or occurrence forming the basis for the complaint. Since no such grievance had ever been filed by the NEA-T or any employee, arbitration was no longer an option. A party making no attempt to enforce mandatory contractual grievance procedures is barred from a lawsuit to enforce the contract. The NEA-T was also precluded from bringing a wrongful conversion claim to recover the surplus funds, and the court affirmed the judgment for the school district. *NEA-Topeka v. Unified School Dist. No. 501*, 269 Kan. 534, 7 P.3d 1174 (Kan. 2000).

◆   A group of trainers were employed by the San Antonio school district to work with high school and middle school coaches and athletes to prevent injuries and rehabilitate injured athletes. **The trainers worked an average of 60 hours per week and sought overtime pay. The school district refused** to pay overtime, asserting that the trainers worked in a bona fide professional capacity and were not entitled to overtime compensation for time worked in excess of 40 hours per week. A federal district court granted summary judgment to the trainers and awarded them liquidated damages, finding they were not exempt professionals under the FLSA and its regulations.

The trainers appealed to the Fifth Circuit, which applied the regulatory short test of 29 CFR Part 541.3, which considers the level of training and specialization required by the work being considered, as well as whether the employee consistently exercises discretion and judgment in his performance. The court agreed with the district court's finding that the requirement of 15 hours of specific college courses met the first prong. However, the panel rejected the district court's finding that the trainers worked under the supervision of a physician and therefore did not exercise discretion as contemplated under the exception. While standard procedures and guidelines were in place to assist the trainers, they were required to respond to emergencies, take responsibility for communications among parents, physicians and coaches, and determine the status of athletes. The district court had erroneously relied upon a reference in the trainers' job description indicating that they worked under the supervision and direction of the team physician. In reality, they applied discretionary skills when assessing injuries to determine player status at times when no physician was present and with no expectation of physician intervention. **This independent application of judgment satisfied the discretionary prong of the FLSA short test, and the court reversed the district court judgment in favor of the trainers**. *Owsley v. San Antonio Indep. School Dist.*, 187 F.3d 521 (5th Cir. 1999).

◆ A Tennessee school district and the union representing its teachers negotiated a collective bargaining agreement containing a salary schedule that added a local supplement to state minimum salary levels. **The union claimed that the school district improperly calculated local salary supplements to the state minimum salary for those employees with prior teaching experience outside the district**, instead imposing a five-year experience limitation on their out-of-district experience. In those cases, the district used a composite salary schedule rather than simply adding the local supplement to the state minimum. The union filed a lawsuit against the school board in a Tennessee chancery court, seeking a declaration that the limitation on credit for non-county teaching experience was unlawful. The court held for the board, and the union appealed to the Court of Appeals of Tennessee, Eastern Section.

The court observed that state law permits local education agencies to supplement salaries with local funds. Local agencies are permitted to establish a schedule that considers college preparation, but not teaching experience. State law therefore allows the negotiation of salary supplements according to experience. The trial court had permissibly held that **the school board could limit non-county experience in determining the local salary supplement**. However, the court agreed with the union that **the composite schedule utilized by the school board improperly negated any experience earned outside the school system**. The court reversed and remanded this part of the trial court decision with instructions to declare that the salary schedule must add the local supplement to the required state minimum. *Knox County Educ. Ass'n v. Knox County Bd. of Educ.*, 953 S.W.2d 686 (Tenn.App.E.Sec. 1997).

◆ Eleven Ohio school employees who worked as tutors were excluded from a collective bargaining unit representing classroom teachers in their district. The tutors were paid less than teachers, even though they held teaching certificates and were therefore entitled to be paid the same as teachers under Ohio law. **When they sought to join the bargaining unit represented by the teachers association, it declined to assist them** in their efforts. The school superintendent then requested that the association bargain on their behalf. The association refused, and the school board filed an unfair labor practice charge against the association with the State Employment Relations Board (SERB). The SERB dismissed the claim because the tutors were not represented by the association. An Ohio trial court refused to consider the school board's appeal for lack of jurisdiction and the Supreme Court of Ohio agreed to review the case. The court observed that **since the tutors held teaching certificates, they were entitled to be paid in accordance with the applicable teacher salary schedule**. *State ex rel. Kabert v. Shaker Heights City School Dist. Bd. of Educ.*, 78 Ohio St.3d 37, 676 N.E.2d 101 (1997).

B. Positions

◆   The Ohio legislature enacted a statute requiring state universities to adopt faculty workload policies and made the policies an inappropriate subject for collective bargaining. Any policy adopted by a university board of trustees under the law prevailed over the contrary provisions of a collective bargaining agreement. One state university adopted a workload policy pursuant to the statute and notified the representative of its professors that it would not bargain over the policy. **The professors' union sued the university in a state court, seeking an order that the statute violated the equal protection rights of public employees**. The Supreme Court of Ohio found that the collective bargaining exemption was not rationally related to the state's interest in encouraging public university professors to spend less time researching in favor of more time teaching.

The U.S. Supreme Court accepted the university's petition for review, and held that the Ohio Supreme Court applied the wrong Equal Protection Clause standard of review. In Equal Protection Clause cases that do not involve fundamental rights or suspect classifications of persons, there need only be a rational relationship between disparity of treatment and some legitimate government purpose. Under the circumstances presented in this case, the disputed Ohio statute met the rational relationship standard. **The state legislature could properly conclude that collective bargaining would interfere with the legitimate goal of achieving uniformity in faculty workloads**. The Ohio Supreme Court decision was reversed and remanded. *Central State Univ. v. American Ass'n of Univ. Professors, Central State Univ. Chapter,* 526 U.S. 124, 119 S.Ct. 1162 143 L.Ed.2d 227 (1999).

On remand, the Ohio Supreme Court acknowledged that the standards of review for the Equal Protection Clauses of the state and federal constitutions are functionally equivalent. Imposing greater judicial scrutiny to Equal Protection claims arising under the state constitution than upon those arising under the federal counterpart would needlessly confuse Equal Protection jurisprudence. **The legislation did not violate the Ohio Constitution because it bore a rational relationship to the legitimate governmental interest of encouraging undergraduate teaching**. The court also rejected the professors' claim that the law violated another state constitutional section providing that laws may be passed fixing and regulating hours of labor, minimum wages and other areas of employee welfare. The section is a broad grant of authority to the legislature, not a limitation on its power to enact labor legislation. The general assembly routinely enacted legislation limiting employee rights, in addition to laws that improved employee working conditions. *American Ass'n of Univ. Professors, Central State Univ. Chapter v. Central State Univ.,* 87 Ohio St.3d 55, 717 N.E.2d 286 (Ohio 1999).

◆   Fourteen employees of an Ohio school district were employed as bus drivers and mechanics under a collective bargaining agreement through which the board maintained its authority over matters of inherent managerial policy, including the right to determine adequacy of the work force and to lay off, promote, retain or transfer employees. At the conclusion of a contract year, **the board contracted with a private company to perform all student transportation services. The board passed a resolution abolishing all bus driver and mechanic positions and laid off the employees occupying those positions**. The employees then accepted employment with the private company to perform the same work. Some of them filed a grievance against the school board. The school superintendent denied the grievance and the employees' association demanded that the board honor its existing statutory employment contracts. When the board declined, the association appealed to the Ohio Court of Appeals, which held that the terms of the CBA prevailed over the employees' statutory protections and ruled that the board's actions were appropriate under the agreement.

The association appealed to the state supreme court, which observed that Ohio law provides certain protections for nonteaching employees. Employment termination can only be for express reasons, and layoffs are not specifically authorized by law. In the absence of a specific contractual agreement, the law prohibited the board from abolishing positions and laying off nonteaching personnel. An agreement must specifically exclude statutory rights in order to negate them. The language of the contract in this case described a general layoff and recall provision and did not preempt the job security provisions of the law. Had the parties intended to accomplish this result, they could have included such language in the contract. **The board had invoked the layoff provision in a manner that was unauthorized by the agreement or by the law** when it discharged the employees and contracted with the private company for the same services. If the board maintained such authority, the employees' statutory rights would be nullified. The court reversed the judgment and granted an order requiring reinstatement of the employees. *State ex rel. Ohio Association of Public School Employees/AFSCME, Local 4, AFL-CIO v. Batavia Local School District Board of Education*, 89 Ohio St. 191, 729 N.E.2d 743 (Ohio 2000).

◆   A school district subcontracted its printing services to a Board of Cooperative Education Services (BOCES) district with the consent of its only printing employee, who continued performing his duties in the same shop. Under the arrangement, he performed the printing services for two school districts, rather than one, and became a member of the BOCES district's bargaining unit. The employee association representing certain school district employees filed an improper practice charge. **An administrative law judge held that the district committed an improper practice by unilaterally subcontracting out printing services performed exclusively by a bargaining unit employee**. He also held that printing services were not covered by Education Law § 1950(4)(d) and not exempt from the law's mandatory collective bargaining requirement. On appeal, the PERB reversed and dismissed the improper practice charge, ruling that Section 1950(4)(d) applied to contracts for shared noninstructional services and that the state education commissioner had approved the agreement. A New York trial court affirmed the PERB decision, but an appellate division court reversed.

The court of appeals agreed to review the decision, and first determined that printing was a service falling within the scope of Section 1950(4)(d). That section of the law gave BOCES districts the authority to provide services to other districts on a cooperative basis. Because printing was not within the statutory list of prohibited services, and was the type of service that promoted the policy behind the BOCES statute, the court held that printing was a service that the education commissioner could approve on a cooperative basis through BOCES districts. The court then analyzed whether the statute permitted school districts to subcontract printing services without first submitting the issue to collective bargaining. While the BOCES statute did not refer to collective bargaining, it was apparent from the statute's strict timetable that schools needed to plan for the provision of services no later than Feb. 1 for programs beginning in September. Section 1950(4)(d) did not include job protection provisions for public employees whose jobs were transferred to BOCES districts under shared services contracts. **The broad state law recognition that BOCES program takeovers were to be considered transfers implied that an action taken pursuant to Section 1950(4)(d) was not subject to collective bargaining**. Accordingly, the court held that the school district's decision to subcontract its printing services to the BOCES district was not subject to mandatory collective bargaining. *In the Matter of Vestal Employees Ass'n, NEA/NY v. Public Employment Relations Bd. of State of New York*, 94 N.Y.2d 409, 727 N.E.2d 122 (N.Y. Sup. 2000).

◆   The management rights article of the CBA between a school district and its maintenance workers recognized the right of the district to direct operations, determine the method and means of operations, determine work hours and schedules, supervise, manage and control the work force and to hire, promote, transfer and lay off employees. It also reserved all rights and responsibilities not specified in the agreement in accordance with state law. **The union** representing district custodial and maintenance employees **filed an unfair labor practices complaint after the district announced that bargaining unit employees would be laid off and their duties transferred to a private company**.

The PELRB held that the district's action was an unfair labor practice and the district appealed to the state supreme court. The court found that **while the district maintained certain management prerogatives to change the amount or nature of work performed by the bargaining unit, it could not lawfully discharge all bargaining unit employees during the term of a collective bargaining agreement in favor of a subcontracting arrangement** with private companies to perform the same work. There was no support for this action under the parties' contract or state law, despite the district's finding that the action would save about $91,000 annually. The district was obligated to bargain with the union over the matter and its unilateral action was an unfair labor practice. *Appeal of Hillsboro-Deering School Dist.*, 737 A.2d 1098 (N.H.1999).

◆   **Twenty-seven administrators of a Nebraska school district,** including principals, assistant principals and special services employees, **sought a determination from the state commission of industrial relations that they made up an appropriate collective bargaining unit.** The commission approved the bargaining unit as appropriate and ordered an election. The school district appealed to the Court of Appeals of Nebraska, and the court affirmed the commission's order. The district appealed to the Supreme Court of Nebraska, which considered several Nebraska laws concerning employee labor relations, including **one that forbids the inclusion of supervisors in any bargaining unit that includes employees under their supervision.** Because there was evidence that the assistant principals were supervised by the principals, the court reversed and remanded the case. *Papillion/LaVista Schools Principals and Supervisors Org. v. Papillion/LaVista School Dist., School Dist. No. 27,* 252 Neb. 308, 562 N.W.2d 335 (1997).

◆   An Illinois cooperative special education district provided special education services for 37 member school districts. The special district independently hired its own teachers under a CBA that was separate from those between its member districts and their employees. **The CBA between the special district and its employees provided that if a member district took back any special education programs, the member district had to notify the special district of new positions created** by the action so that the special district could advertise the job openings to tenured special district employees. One member district took back certain special education programs that had been previously delegated to the special district but failed to advise the special district of three teaching vacancies created by the action. The union representing employees in the special district filed a grievance and submitted the matter for arbitration. The member district responded by seeking a declaratory judgment from a state court that it had no contractual responsibility to hire displaced employees of the special district. The court dismissed the case and an arbitrator held for the special district and union.

The Illinois Educational Labor Relations Board rejected the special district union's unfair labor practice charge, and the union appealed to the Appellate Court of Illinois, First District. The court affirmed the board's order, finding that **the special district had no authority to bind member districts to the CBA between the special district and its employees.** It agreed with the member district that such an interpretation would violate the member district's collective bargaining agreement with its own employees, noting that no special district teacher had lost employment due to the take back action. *SEDOL Teachers Union v. IELRB,* 668 N.E.2d 1117 (Ill.App.1st Dist.1996).

◆   A Connecticut teacher filed a grievance when the position of English department head, which he had applied for, was filled by a less senior teacher. The teachers' CBA required that when two candidates for a position were equally qualified, the position should go to the most senior teacher. **An arbitrator ordered the school district to promote the teacher to the position. In response, the school district eliminated the department head position.** The teacher filed an unfair labor practice complaint with the state labor relations board. The board ordered the school district to reinstate the position and appoint the teacher to it. The school district appealed the board's decision to a Connecticut trial court. The trial court held that the elimination of a teaching position was a discretionary act of the school board and that the labor relations board could not order the district to reinstate the position. The labor relations board appealed to the Supreme Court of Connecticut.

On appeal, the board of education admitted that its sole reason for eliminating the position was to prevent the teacher from holding a position for which the board believed he was not qualified. It argued that because the arbitrator's decision concerned only the teacher's entitlement to the position when it did exist, the subsequent elimination of the position, which was a discretionary act, was not an unfair labor practice. The labor board argued that the school board's action constituted a refusal to participate in good faith in mediation and arbitration, and was an unfair labor practice in violation of Connecticut law. **The court examined the relevant statutes and concluded that the school board's action was an unfair labor practice**. The court reversed the judgment of the trial court and dismissed the board of education's appeal. *Bd. of Educ. of Town of Thomaston v. State Bd. of Labor Relations*, 584 A.2d 1172 (Conn.1991).

C. Other Terms and Conditions

♦ **The Chicago Board of education extended spousal health benefits to domestic partners who were of the same sex** as an employee if they met certain requirements, including a minimum age, duration of cohabitation and joint home ownership with their partner. A female Chicago school employee lived with the same man for over 20 years. Although the couple had two children, they never married. The employee received health benefits from the board but was unable to cover her domestic partner because of the same-sex requirement. She sued the board in a federal district court, alleging that the board policy violated her right to equal protection of the laws.

The district court dismissed the lawsuit for failure to state a claim, and the employee appealed to the Seventh Circuit. The board argued that its policy was adopted to encourage the hiring of homosexual teachers. These teachers were expected to provide support for homosexual students, and would encourage all students to be tolerant and accepting of lesbian and gay students. The board asserted that it was more important to recognize unmarried homosexual couples than heterosexual couples, since the latter could marry and the former were unable to do so under Illinois law. While the court stated that the board had adopted an argument that many people might find shocking, it was not its role to determine the soundness of local government policies tolerating or endorsing homosexuality. The court also stated that the efficacy of the policy was doubtful. **Limited efficacy and the political nature of the policy did not make the board's action irrational. It was rational for the board to refuse to extend benefits to unmarried opposite-sex domestic partners**. The court affirmed the judgment for the school board. *Irizarry v. Board of Educ. of City of Chicago*, No. 00-3216, 2001 WL 506985 (7th Cir. 2001).

♦ A collective bargaining agreement between a Wisconsin school district and its teachers' association provided for employee coverage under one of three group health plans. One of the options included family coverage for designated family partners and their dependent children, and described the criteria for qualification as a family partner. **Resident taxpayers sued** the school district, school board president and teachers' association in a state court, **seeking an order that the district lacked the statutory authority to enter into an agreement providing for family partner coverage**. They asserted that a state law authorized health insurance benefits only for school employees and officers and their spouses and dependent children, and that no other law authorized the district to provide benefits to unmarried partners of school district employees. The taxpayers further asserted that the district was prohibited from using public funds for this purpose. The court denied the taxpayers' request for declaratory and injunctive relief and they appealed to the Wisconsin Court of Appeals.

The appeals court analyzed Wis. Stat. § 66.185, which authorized school districts to pay the health insurance premiums of retirees and employees and their spouses and dependent children. The law provided that "nothing in the statutes shall be construed to limit the authority of the state or municipalities" to pay insurance premiums for employees, their spouses and dependents. The statute did not prohibit the district from providing insurance benefits for other persons, and the appeals court looked at other statutes granting districts the power to sue and be sued, levy and collect taxes, and perform other functions required to operate a public school system. The appeals court rejected the taxpayers' argument that Wis. Stat. § 66.185 and other state laws indicated a legislative intent to limit the authority of school districts to exercise their broad powers. There was no conflict among these statutes, and **the district had the power to provide health insurance benefits to designated family partners of teachers covered by the CBA**. The court affirmed the judgment for the district and school officials. *Pritchard v. Madison Metropolitan School District*, 242 Wis.2d 301, 625 N.W.2d 613 (Wis. App. 2001).

◆   A school district sought to fill a head coaching vacancy through a screening committee and considered three internal applicants, who were all members of the teachers' association. The job was offered to an assistant principal and athletic director employed by the school system who was not an association member. An applicant who was not selected for the job, despite being an association member, filed a grievance against the school board, asserting that it had violated the CBA. **An arbitrator agreed with the association and member, finding the position should have been given to a member of the association**. After an Ohio county court directed the board to employ the association member as the coach, the board appealed to the Ohio Court of Appeals.

The appeals court noted that while Ohio courts must show considerable deference to arbitrators, an award is legitimate only if it "draws its essence from the collective bargaining agreement." According to the court, an arbitrator departs from the essence of an agreement when an award conflicts with its express terms, or is without rational support. The agreement in this case excluded from the bargaining unit all substitutes, part-time tutors, "persons employed for supplemental duties" under an Ohio statute and various administrative positions. The arbitrator had improperly focused on the past practice of the district and ignored contractual terms. His premise that the coaching job was a bargaining unit position was not grounded on the collective bargaining agreement, and the board was not obligated to fill the vacancy according to the arbitration award. **Since coaching positions were**

not bargaining unit positions, the arbitrator's decision was irrational and had to be reversed. *Clearview Education Association OEA/NEA v. Clearview Local School District Board of Education*, 751 N.E.2d 494 (Ohio App. 2001).

◆   When a school district and its teacher's association failed to reach agreement on a contract for 1997–1999, efforts to mediate the dispute by the Wisconsin Employment Relations Commission were also unsuccessful. The district implemented a qualified economic offer and teachers worked for more than a year with no contract. The parties ratified tentative agreements for 1997–1999 and 1999–2001, but the teachers' association nullified them because they exceeded the two year limit on collective bargaining agreements created by Wis. Stat. § 111.70(4)(cn). The parties then ratified separate agreements for the contracts, presenting voters with the option of either rejecting or accepting both agreements. **Teachers who objected to the result petitioned the WERC to challenge both CBAs, asserting that the contract ratification resulted in one three-year contract** that violated § 111.70(4)(cn). The WERC found that the parties had validly agreed to two two-year contracts, but a Wisconsin circuit court reversed that decision.

The WERC appealed to the Court of Appeals of Wisconsin, which rejected the objecting teachers' argument that the effect of the integrated vote was a three-year contract. **There was substantial evidence that the parties intended to reach agreement on separate two-year contracts**. The statute did not address the ratification process and separate ballots were not required. A key public policy underlying § 111.70(4)(cn) was to make CBAs coincide with the state's two-year budget cycle. The court held that integrated CBAs did not contravene the legislative purposes of the statute or the long-standing practice of allowing deadlocked parties to settle contract disputes for an outstanding year while reaching agreement on later contracts. The court reversed the judgment. *Hoffman v. Wisconsin Employment Relations Comm'n*, 625 N.W.2d 906 (Wis. App. 2001).

◆   A Pennsylvania school board unilaterally raised the requirements for achieving the student honor roll by one-quarter grade point, in an effort to improve statewide educational quality and accountability. The local education association filed a grievance against the district under the collective bargaining agreement. **The arbitrator held that the board violated the CBA, finding that the parties were obligated to work jointly to develop all policies and procedures**. A state trial court agreed with the district that the new policy had been adopted pursuant to the board's inherent managerial prerogatives and vacated the arbitration award.

The association appealed to the commonwealth court, which noted that review of an arbitration award is limited to the "essence test," which affords broad deference to an arbitrator's award. The court held that state law does not require public employers to bargain away matters of inherent managerial policy, including areas of discretion or policy in the employer's functions and programs, standards of service, budget, technology, organizational structure, and personnel matters. The association acknowledged that the setting of honor-roll standards was a matter of inherent managerial policy that was subject only to permissive bargaining, but argued that the district had expressly bargained away this right in the CBA. The court disagreed, finding that the CBA clearly limited the subjects selected for bargaining to those mandated by law, including wages, hours, and other terms and conditions of employment. **The arbitrator had ignored the relevant articles of the CBA preserving the board's right to develop and adopt management policies for the district without the association's participation**. Since the arbitration award did not draw its essence from the CBA, the trial court had properly vacated it, and the court affirmed the judgment for the school district. *Rochester Area School Dist. v. Rochester Educ. Ass'n*, 747 A.2d 971 (Pa. Commw. 2000).

◆   A New Hampshire teacher filed a grievance under the applicable collective bargaining agreement after his contract was renewed with reservations. The principal's recommendation stated that the teacher must improve his interpersonal relations in order to be rehired. **The principal, and later the superintendent and district, refused to arbitrate the matter,** but the state public employee labor relations board held that it was a proper subject of arbitration.

   The district appealed to the state supreme court, which observed that a presumption of arbitrability existed because the CBA contained an arbitration clause. The agreement provided that all reprimands and other disciplinary action must be for just cause only. Disciplinary action was not defined in the agreement. The court agreed with the district that the principal's evaluation and recommendation simply notified the teacher of areas in which he needed improvement. Because the principal was without authority to fire the teacher or otherwise impose penalties, his actions did not constitute disciplinary action under the agreement. The court held that the superintendent had a far greater scope of powers than the principal. Because the superintendent had also warned the teacher of potential contract nonrenewal in the event that his performance in specific areas did not improve, the teacher was entitled to proceed to arbitration of his case. *Appeal of Lincoln-Woodstock Cooperative School Dist.*, 143 N.H. 598, 731 A.2d 992 (N.H.1999).

◆   After sustaining work related injuries, two certified teachers sought workers' compensation benefits, and filed a state court action when their requests for benefits were denied. Their employing school board sought summary judgment, stating that the teachers were ineligible for compensation under the applicable collective bargaining agreement. The board further asserted that the issue of workers' compensation coverage was rejected in the parties' contract negotiations. The teachers asserted that workers' compensation benefits must be available to all board employees, since they had been made available to a group of non-professional, non-union board employees some years prior to the current actions. A Tennessee trial court denied the board's summary judgment motions in both cases, and the board appealed to the state supreme court. According to the high court, **Tennessee law allowed exempt entities to elect for the provision of coverage and to delineate their workforces by departments and divisions. The school board had validly divided its workforce, and was entitled to provide coverage to its unrepresented non-professional employees, while declining to cover certified teachers who were represented by a union**. *Muhlheim v. Knox County Bd. of Educ.*, 2 S.W.3d 927 (Tenn. 1999).

◆   A Wisconsin school district established a pilot program calling for teachers to contact parents during the first few weeks of the school year. The program was designed to increase the promotion rate among ninth graders. **The teacher's association advised the district that the calls would create a burden upon teachers that could not be unilaterally imposed**. The union filed a prohibited practice complaint with the state employment relations commission, asserting that the district had a duty to bargain over the program. The commission dismissed the complaint, finding that calling parents had no impact on teacher wages, hours or employment conditions.

A state circuit court affirmed the commission's decision, and the teacher's association appealed to the Court of Appeals of Wisconsin. **The commission found that telephoning parents is fairly within the scope of a teacher's regular job duties**. The calling of parents required only five to six hours of teacher time during the first two weeks of school and did not adversely affect their wages, hours or working conditions. Telephone contact with parents was expected of teachers and did not represent a new duty. The court affirmed the judgment in favor of the school district. *Madison Teachers, Inc. v. Wisconsin Employment Relations Commission,* 580 N.W.2d 375 (Wis.App. 1998).

◆   The Buffalo Teachers Federation and a negotiating team for the Buffalo Board of Education approved a collective bargaining agreement that was ratified by the teachers federation. However, **the board refused to approve the agreement and the federation filed an improper labor practice charge** against the board with the state Public Employment Relations Board (PERB), asserting that the school district's chief negotiator sought to undermine the agreement. The PERB affirmed the improper practice charge and ordered the district to execute a document embodying the agreements reached by the parties, but did not order the board to implement the collective bargaining agreement. The board passed a resolution to execute such a document, then notified the teachers federation that the agreement was not legislatively approved as required by state law. It sought a state court order that it was under no obligation to approve the funding necessary for salary increases reflected in the agreement.

The Court of Appeals of New York agreed to review the case and determined **that the board had no right to an additional legislative approval role and did not retain any residual statutory powers that would frustrate an otherwise valid agreement**. A statutory reference to legislative approval did not concern the board's delegated powers. No further approval of the agreement was required and the board had exhausted its authority in agreeing to execute the contract. The court ordered the board to implement the salary increases reflected in the collective bargaining agreement, retroactive to its effective date. *Bd. of Educ. for the City School Dist. of Buffalo v. Buffalo Teachers Fed'n, Inc.,* 89 N.Y.2d 370, 653 N.Y.S.2d 250, 675 N.E.2d 1202 (1996).

◆   A New Jersey school board adopted a 186-day school calendar providing for three additional makeup days for school closings due to weather emergencies. Because of severe weather, schools in the district were closed for 12 days during the school year and the school superintendent proposed eliminating several school holidays including the spring break, with additional make-up days to be added to the end of the school year. Although he notified parents and employees of the proposed changes, he presented the changes to the school board without consulting the employees' labor organization. After the board unilaterally adopted a revised calendar, **the employees' association filed an unfair labor practices complaint against the board, alleging that the changes affected terms and conditions of employment that could not be unilaterally changed by the board**. A hearing officer dismissed the complaint and the state public employment relations commission declined to review it.

The association appealed to the Superior Court of New Jersey, Appellate Division. The court noted that the establishment of a school calendar is a traditional management decision that is not a term or condition of employment. However, even non-negotiable management decisions may have an effect on terms and conditions of employment that are negotiable. **The court stated that a case-by-case analysis must be applied to non-negotiable management decisions to determine whether negotiating their impact upon employees would significantly or substantially encroach upon a management prerogative**. Because the hearing officer had not conducted such an analysis in this case, the court reversed and remanded the case to the employment relations commission. *Piscataway Township Educ. Ass'n v. Piscataway Township Bd. of Educ.*, 307 N.J.Super. 263, 704 A.2d 981 (App.Div.1998).

◆   The collective bargaining agreement between a New Hampshire city education board and the union representing city school custodians expired without any automatic renewal provision. The agreement had provided for full-time employment for represented employees at a specified wage rate. During contract renegotiations, **the city announced a reorganization under which full-time custodians would be laid off and replaced by part-time employees** who would perform the same work in 20 hours per week at over two dollars per hour less than the contract rate and without benefits. The union filed an unfair labor practice charge against the city board, asserting that the layoff and hiring of part-time employees amounted to a unilateral change in the conditions of employment in violation of the collective bargaining agreement. The Supreme Court of New Hampshire found that **the reorganization was a mandatory subject of collective bargaining because it was not reserved to the exclusive managerial authority of the board, it affected terms and conditions of employment** rather than broad managerial policy, and it did not involve governmental functions. The primary effect of the reorganization was to unilaterally change the wage and hour agreement of the parties, while the actual job duties of custodial employees remained the same. *Appeal of City of Nashua Bd. of Educ.*, 695 A.2d 647 (N.H.1997).

◆   A Wisconsin school district and the union representing its teachers negotiated a contract that did not state the minimum usable increment of sick leave. As an unwritten policy, the district allowed employees to use sick leave in one-hour increments. The contract contained a management clause, purporting to reserve the board's right to establish reasonable work rules and a "zipper clause" stating that supplemental amendments and past practices were not binding on either party. When the contract expired, the parties were unable to reach a new agreement. The district then unilaterally changed its leave policy so that sick leave was limited to minimum half-day (four-hour) increments. **The union filed a complaint** with the Wisconsin Employment Relations Commission (WERC), **claiming that the unilateral** change in sick leave policy was a prohibited practice. The WERC agreed with the union, and the district appealed to a Wisconsin trial court. The court affirmed the WERC's decision and the district appealed to the Court of Appeals of Wisconsin. The court of appeals stated that zipper clauses did not authorize unilateral changes in employment practices and that the normal function of the clause was to maintain the status quo, not to facilitate change. **Because sick leave was a matter that was mandatorily subject to collective bargaining, the district was not authorized to unilaterally change the sick leave policy between contracts**. The district could not rely on the management contract to enforce the sick leave policy change for the same reason. The court affirmed the judgment for the union. *St. Croix Falls School Dist. v. Wisconsin Employment Relations Comm'n*, 522 N.W.2d 507 (Wis.App.1994).

III. GRIEVANCES AND ARBITRATION

Collective bargaining agreements contain grievance procedures for the resolution of contractual items on which the parties cannot agree. Where the item in contention concerns the interpretation of the agreement, the school board must enter into arbitration with the teachers' union if it is called for in the collective bargaining agreement.

A. Arbitrability

◆ The superintendent of the Peabody (Massachusetts) School Committee rejected three teacher transfer requests. The teachers' union filed separate grievances on their behalf under the collective bargaining agreement between the union and school committee. Three arbitrators held independent grievance hearings and each of them ordered the committee to make the requested transfer, **finding that the failure to approve a transfer in each case was not based on just cause under the CBA.** The committee appealed to a Massachusetts superior court, which consolidated the cases and vacated the awards on grounds that the grievances were not arbitrable under the state Educational Reform Act.

The union appealed to the Massachusetts Appeals Court, arguing that the transfer provisions of the CBA validly established a seniority-based procedure for voluntary and involuntary teacher transfers that vested managerial authority solely in the superintendent. The court determined that the CBA made transfers subject solely to the approval or recommendation of the superintendent, and did not recognize the statutory approval rights of the principals of schools into which teachers intended to transfer. **According to the court, a CBA relating to a nondelegable managerial right created by a statute was not enforceable**. Since the transfer provision in this case conflicted with the Educational Reform Act, and the ERA applied to transfers, the arbitrators had exceeded their powers in each case by construing the transfer provisions. The arbitration awards had to be vacated. *Peabody School Committee v. Peabody Federation of Teachers, Local 1289, AFT, AFL-CIO*, 748 N.E.2d 992 (Mass. App. Ct. 2001).

◆ A Vermont school district created a position for a vocational teacher by merging two half-time positions in its special education program. The teacher was not licensed to teach special education but obtained a waiver for the year. He received his special education certificate during the year and received a contract for the following year. However, the superintendent of schools advised the teacher that the position would be eliminated because a half-time teacher was returning from leave and another half-time position was to be eliminated. When another special education teacher resigned, creating a vacancy, the district passed over the teacher and he pursued a grievance against it under the applicable collective bargaining agreement. **The teacher's union argued that the school board had violated reduction in force rights** in this and other cases by using one-year employment contracts in violation of the collective bargaining agreement. An arbitrator reinstated the teacher to a full-time position with seniority and back wages without making a specific wage calculation.

The school district reinstated the teacher but contested the back wage order, and the union petitioned a state trial court to confirm the arbitration award. The court granted the petition and awarded the teacher over $32,000. **The school board appealed to the Supreme Court of Vermont, which rejected its argument that the arbitration award could not be enforced because it did not reduce the back pay award to a specific amount.** At the time of the award, it was impossible to know how much pay would be due the teacher. The question of the wage award was properly before the arbitrator and not the courts. The court affirmed the arbitration award and remanded the wage calculation question to the arbitrator. *Springfield Teachers Ass'n v. Springfield School Directors*, 705 A.2d 541 (Vt.1997).

◆   A Maine high school 10th grade course curriculum included a novel entitled *Bastard Out of Carolina*. The superintendent of schools received a parental complaint about the book's sexually explicit content and **the school board voted to remove it from the curriculum unless the school developed a plan to teach the book in conjunction with another approved novel** addressing similar themes in a manner calculated to accord the books equal treatment and allow students to choose between them. In accordance with existing board policy, the board required parental notification prior to teaching the book. An English teacher filed a grievance against the school district based on the board's action. The grievance proceeded to arbitration over the school district's objection, with the district claiming that the use of books was a management right and an educational policy decision that was not a subject of collective bargaining. The arbitrator held that because there was a possibility that teachers could be disciplined for failing to comply with the board's conditions, the conditions did not constitute educational policy decisions but were properly the subject of arbitration as affecting teacher working conditions.

The school district petitioned a Maine superior court to vacate the arbitration award. The court denied the petition, and the district appealed to the Supreme Judicial Court of Maine. The court stated that **educational policy decisions are not subject to grievance and arbitration procedures, even though they can affect the working conditions of teachers**. The incidental effect on teaching presented by the board's action did not transform educational policy decisions into arbitrable teacher working conditions. Accordingly, the court agreed with the school district that the matter should not have been arbitrated and it vacated and remanded the superior court order. *School Admin. Dist. No. 58 v. Mount Abram Teachers Ass'n*, 704 A.2d 349 (Me.1997).

◆   A New Jersey elementary school principal who was employed by the same school district for 31 years requested a paid medical leave of absence. The board initially approved a five-week leave, but granted him repeated extensions for over one year, until he retired. **The school board then notified the principal that his salary increment for the year would be withheld due to excessive absence** in accordance with New Jersey law and the applicable collective bargaining agreement. The principal's union demanded arbitration but the school board sought to restrain it. The state Public Employment Relations Commission (PERC) found that arbitration was proper under a state law which subjects salary withholding appeals to arbitration when the withholding is based on predominantly disciplinary reasons. The board appealed to the Superior Court of New Jersey, Appellate Division, where it argued that the salary withholding related predominantly to evaluation, and was therefore appealable to the state education commissioner. The court held that the PERC was vested with the power to determine whether a proceeding was predominantly disciplinary or evaluative. The PERC properly found that the principal's case was predominantly disciplinary as there had been no evaluation of his performance during the year he had taken leave. **Because the case was properly set for arbitration, the court affirmed the PERC's order.** *Edison Township Bd. of Educ., Middlesex County v. Edison Township Principals and Supervisors Ass'n,* 304 N.J.Super. 459, 701 A.2d 459 (App.Div.1997).

◆   A union representing kitchen helpers employed by a Pennsylvania school district filed a grievance against the district under the collective bargaining agreement, **asserting that the district had unilaterally changed its method of wage payment from a yearly salary basis to an hourly basis.** The arbitrator held for the union and ordered the district to pay the employees for their remaining time in the current school year. The district complied, but in two later school years failed to pay the employees on an annual salary basis. The union filed a Pennsylvania trial court action against the school district, seeking an order directing it to pay unpaid wages. The court granted the school district's summary judgment motion, ruling that it was without jurisdiction to accept the case because refusal to comply with a binding arbitration award is an unfair labor practice that is within the jurisdiction of the state labor relations board. The union appealed to the Commonwealth Court of Pennsylvania, which held that the state labor relations board had jurisdiction over the case even though the dispute arose after the arbitration award. **State courts had only limited jurisdiction to enforce unfair labor practice orders, and the dispute was not properly before the court.** The court vacated and remanded the case, with the effect of dismissing the complaint. *Hotel and Restaurant Employees Int'l Union Local No. 391, AFL-CIO v. School Dist. of Allentown City,* 702 A.2d 16 (Pa.Commw.1997).

◆   A Rhode Island labor organization representing teachers of English as a second language disputed a memorandum from the director of the program requiring them to submit copies of their lesson plans to the director each month. **The union argued that this procedure constituted a unilateral change in working conditions** that violated the collective bargaining agreement. Its request for arbitration was denied by the local school committee, which stated that the appropriate recourse was appeal to the state education commissioner. A Rhode Island trial court determined that the lesson plan memorandum constituted a management prerogative that was not subject to arbitration. The union appealed to the Supreme Court of Rhode Island. According to the supreme court, **the English as a second language program** was mandated by state law. It **was subject to the state education department's rules and regulations, and the committee had a necessary oversight and evaluation role in day-to-day operations** of the program. The school committee did not have the power to bargain away statutory responsibilities and the trial court had properly found that there was no arbitrable grievance. *Pawtucket School Comm. v. Pawtucket Teachers' Alliance, Local No. 930*, 652 A.2d 970 (R.I.1995).

B. Standard of Review

◆   **In a case involving an employer's challenge to an arbitration award reinstating a truck driver who failed two drug tests in a 16-month period, the U.S. Supreme Court held that no public policy reason required the court to overturn the arbitration award in the driver's favor.** The arbitration award constituted an agreement of the parties and its rehabilitation provisions were consistent with federal labor law. After the driver tested positive for marijuana a second time, and an arbitrator refused to allow the employer to discharge the driver, the employer brought a federal district court action against the driver's collective bargaining association seeking to vacate the second arbitration award, arguing that it violated a strong public policy against the operation of dangerous machinery by drug users. A district court held that the driver's conditional reinstatement did not violate that policy and the U.S. Court of Appeals for the Fourth Circuit affirmed. On appeal to the U.S. Supreme Court, the Court initially noted that because the parties had bargained for the arbitrator's construction of the CBA, the decision would only be set aside in the rare case in which it did not "draw its essence from the contract." According to the Court, although U.S. Department of Transportation regulations and federal transportation laws required the testing of those in safety-sensitive jobs for drug use, they did not prohibit the reinstatement of a person in such a position for failing random drug tests on one or even two occasions. Moreover, the award's rehabilitative aspects were consistent with the federal transportation law regime, since it required the driver to participate in substance abuse treatment and continue undergoing testing. The Supreme Court affirmed the lower court decisions, allowing the arbitration award to stand. *Eastern Associated Coal Corp. v. United Mine Workers of America 17 et al.*, 531 U.S. 57, 121 S.Ct. 462, 148 L.Ed.2d 354 (2000).

◆   **A school nurse filed a grievance against the school committee after a principal ordered her to administer medication to a special education student**. Her collective bargaining association argued that any increase in her workload was not covered by the collective bargaining agreement and that the nonemergency medication of special education students attending the collaborative program located at the school was not permitted. According to the association, the matter had to be negotiated by the parties and the collaborative program was not a party to the agreement. An arbitrator held that a school administrator could not order the nurse to dispense medication to a student who was not a member of the regular student body. A Rhode Island superior court confirmed the arbitrator's decision, and the school committee appealed.

The Rhode Island Supreme Court observed that an arbitrator exceeds his or her powers by resolving a non-arbitrable dispute or by making an award that does not draw its essence from the agreement, is not based on a plausible interpretation of the contract, manifestly disregards a contractual provision or reaches an irrational result. The school district had a non-delegable managerial duty to provide health services to students attending the collaborative education program. The arbitrator was powerless to address the issue because a ruling against the district would cause a violation of state law. The district was bound by state law to operate a school health program and to provide special education programs. These duties were non-delegable and could not be bargained away in a CBA. State law and regulations stated that special education students in the collaborative program were within the public school system and entitled to receive health services. There was no collective bargaining provision limiting the provision of services to students within the exclusive control of the school district. **The principal acted according to law when he ordered the nurse to provide medication to the student.** The arbitration award contradicted a collective bargaining agreement provision stating that the parties maintained the common goal of providing public education to all children. The court vacated and remanded the award. *Woonsocket Teachers' Guild, Local 951, AFT v. Woonsocket School Comm.*, 770 A.2d 834 (R.I. 2001).

◆   After a student mooned the camera during a class trip picture, the teacher chaperoning the trip advised the student that if he showed up in the picture, he would be held accountable. Several weeks later, the teacher informed the student's guidance counselor of the student's conduct during the trip and that the picture showed the student mooning the camera. The student was expelled and the teacher was suspended for taking an inappropriate picture and failing to report serious student misconduct. **The teacher's collective bargaining association filed a grievance and obtained a favorable ruling, based on the arbitrator's finding that the school board did not have good and just cause for disciplining the teacher**. The board appealed to an Ohio trial court, which vacated the arbitration award on the ground that the arbitrator failed to consider critical issues and had exceeded his authority.

The association appealed to the Court of Appeals of Ohio, which observed that judicial review of arbitration awards is extremely limited. Under state law, courts may vacate arbitration awards only where arbitrators exceed their powers. **So long as an award "draws its essence" from the applicable collective bargaining agreement, a reviewing court must affirm the award and may not substitute its judgment for that of the arbitrator**. In this case, the arbitrator had carefully considered all the issues necessary to resolve the case. The decision drew its essence from the parties' collective bargaining agreement and the trial court lacked any basis for vacating the award. The court held that the arbitrator had acted within his authority and reversed the judgment. *Princeton City School Dist. Bd. of Educ. v. Princeton Ass'n of Classroom Educators, OEA/NEA*, 731 N.E.2d 186 (Ohio App. 1st Dist. 1999).

◆   A Pennsylvania bus driver abandoned his vehicle while returning to school with a busload of seventh and eighth graders who had been to a theater. He left the bus to confront a motorist who was shouting obscenities and threatening him. Prior to exiting the bus, the driver turned the engine off and set the parking brake. He returned to the bus within approximately 15 seconds. The school district conducted an investigation and determined that the driver had intentionally abandoned the students. It fired the driver and he filed a grievance through his union. **An arbitrator sustained the grievance, finding that the driver's behavior constituted negligence rather than intentional misconduct**. He reduced the disciplinary action from employment termination to a 90-day suspension. The school district filed a Pennsylvania county court action to vacate the arbitration award, but the court denied the petition. The district then appealed to the Commonwealth Court of Pennsylvania, where it argued that the trial court had misapplied the law.

The commonwealth court disagreed, stating that the trial court had applied the proper standard of law. Contrary to the district's assertion that its decision was a core responsibility that was entitled to due deference, the decision involved the interpretation of a collective bargaining agreement. Accordingly, the appropriate standard of review was contained in the state arbitration act. **The arbitrator had properly decided to refashion a remedy once it was determined that the driver had committed mere negligence and not wilful misconduct**. Where an arbitrator determines that no cause for dismissal exists and the collective bargaining agreement does not forbid the modification of a school district penalty, the arbitrator may modify the discipline. The commonwealth court affirmed the denial of the petition. *Upper St. Clair School Dist. v. Upper St. Clair Educ. Support Personnel Ass'n*, 649 A.2d 470 (Pa.Commw.1994).

◆   A tenured New Jersey teacher supervised special education students in a high school resource room. She missed 55 days during one four-month period due to surgery and another 27 days because of injuries received in a train accident. Because the students required special attention and supervision, the teacher's frequent absences created difficulty. **The teacher was denied a salary increase for the following school year based on her record of absences**. The district asserted that the withholding of the salary raise was for predominantly educational reasons. The state Public Employment Relations Commission (PERC) determined that the withholding was for predominantly disciplinary reasons and was therefore arbitrable under the applicable collective bargaining agreement. **An arbitrator then determined that the withholding of the salary increase had been arbitrary and capricious** because it was based only on the number of absences without regard for the reasons for absence. Appeal reached the Supreme Court of New Jersey.

The teacher's labor association argued that the arbitrator had properly applied the just cause standard of review because the denial of the salary raise was based on disciplinary reasons. The district argued that the arbitrator had improperly imposed this standard of review because it was not contained within the collective bargaining agreement. The court determined that the weight of labor relations authority held that the just cause standard was properly used even if not specified in the agreement. **Because the PERC had determined that the denial of the raise had been based on discipline, the arbitrator was bound by this determination and had applied the correct legal standard**. Accordingly, the arbitrator's decision was affirmed. *Scotch Plains-Fanwood Bd. of Educ. v. Scotch Plains-Fanwood Educ. Ass'n*, 139 N.J. 141, 651 A.2d 1018 (N.J. 1995).

C. Association Duties and Rights

◆   A Tennessee middle school guidance counselor attempted to break up a fight between some students and was struck in the face by one of them. She suffered a permanent head injury and filed a personal injury lawsuit against the local education agency, asserting claims for negligence, civil rights violations and assault and battery. She included a third-party beneficiary claim against the agency for breach of the employment agreement existing between the agency and the Metropolitan Nashville Education Association, which represented agency employees. **She claimed that the collective bargaining agreement required the employer to discipline the student, warn her of his previous record of criminal activity, train teachers to intervene in student fights, provide trained security personnel at schools and make individual student records available** to teachers. The court granted summary judgment to the education agency. The teacher appealed to the Court of Appeals of Tennessee, Western Section.

   The court reviewed contract language contained in the collective bargaining agreement and found that it did not create the legal duty that the teacher asserted as the basis of her lawsuit. The school's student code did not specify the punishment to be imposed for violations and gave the school principal only limited powers to punish students. Because of the time delays inherent in student disciplinary cases, the student who had inflicted the injury in this case could not have been disciplined for his prior behavior in the manner claimed by the teacher so as to ensure his absence from school on the day of the injury. Since the employment contract created no legal duty to provide the safeguards claimed by the teacher, the court affirmed the summary judgment order. *Warren v. Metropolitan Gov't of Nashville and Davidson County*, 955 S.W.2d 618 (Tenn.App.1997).

◆   A Pennsylvania school district contracted with a Tennessee corporation to operate an elementary school for five years. The association representing employees at the school filed a motion in a Pennsylvania court to enjoin the district from entering into any private contract to provide teaching services. The court granted the request for a preliminary order, and the Commonwealth Court of Pennsylvania affirmed the order. The district appealed to the Supreme Court of Pennsylvania, which remanded the case for further proceedings. The district requested approval from the state Department of Education to alter its program at the elementary school. It informed the department that the contractor would hire its own teachers and that several district employees would be laid off. **The secretary of the department approved the request to alter the elementary program, but held that any layoff must comply with state tenure law**.

   The teachers association asserted that the secretary's action was an administrative adjudication in which it had a right to intervene. It contested both the department's refusal to allow its intervention and the approval of the program alteration by filing a petition with the commonwealth court. The court observed that no statute afforded the association any right to intervene in the request to alter the program. The secretary's order had specifically referred to the district's obligation to comply with state laws preserving teacher seniority and there was no adverse effect on the public that would justify intervention by the association. **The association had no substantial or immediate interest at stake and was not an aggrieved party**

entitled to intervene in the action. The court granted the district's motion to dismiss the petition. *Wilkinsburg Educ. Ass'n v. School Dist. of Wilkinsburg*, 690 A.2d 1252 (Pa.Commw.1996).

IV. STRIKES

The purpose of state legislation to prohibit or limit strikes by public employees is to protect the public and not to circumvent meaningful collective bargaining. Courts have upheld punitive actions taken against unlawfully striking teachers and their unions.

◆   Wisconsin education law prohibited strikes by teachers. Under state law, school boards had sole authority to make hiring and firing decisions and were required to negotiate employment terms and conditions with authorized collective bargaining representatives. When contract negotiations between teachers and their local school board became protracted, the teachers called a strike. The board attempted to end the strike, noting it was in direct violation of state law. When the teachers refused to return to work, the board held disciplinary hearings and fired the striking teachers. **The teachers appealed to the Wisconsin courts, arguing that the school board was not an impartial decisionmaker and that their discharges had violated their due process rights**. The Wisconsin Supreme Court ruled that due process under the Fourteenth Amendment required that the teachers' conduct and the board's response to that conduct be evaluated by an impartial decisionmaker and that the board itself was not sufficiently impartial to make the decision to discharge the teachers. The board appealed to the U.S. Supreme Court.

The Supreme Court reversed the Wisconsin Supreme Court decision and held that **there was no evidence that the board could not make an impartial decision in determining to discharge the teachers**. The mere fact that the board was involved in negotiations with the teachers did not support a claim of bias. The board was the only body vested with statutory authority to employ and dismiss teachers and participation in negotiations with the teachers was required by law. This involvement prior to the decision to discharge the teachers was not a sufficient showing of bias to disqualify the board as a decisionmaker under the Due Process Clause of the Fourteenth Amendment. *Hortonville Joint School Dist. No. 1 v. Hortonville Educ. Ass'n*, 426 U.S. 482, 96 S.Ct. 2308, 49 L.Ed.2d 1 (1976).

◆   The association representing teachers at an Illinois school district declared a strike that lasted almost two months. A settlement was reached which called for modification of the school calendar to eliminate the winter and spring breaks. The superintendent of schools agreed to honor requests for leave during the normal winter break for teachers who could document that their travel arrangements had been completed on the basis of the original calendar. The superintendent disapproved of a vacation leave request by a teacher of students with learning disabilities, even though she submitted documentation that her travel arrangements had been made early in the school year. **She was charged with insubordination and abandonment of her job duties when she went on leave, and association representatives were prohibited from representing her** at a meeting at which the board voted to dismiss her.

An administrative hearing officer held that the teacher had been improperly discharged under the superintendent's oral policy and that her due process rights had been violated by the board's refusal to allow her representatives to appear at the board meeting. An Illinois circuit court affirmed the decision, and the school board appealed to the Appellate Court of Illinois. The court found no error by the hearing officer or circuit court in determining that the teacher had been denied her due process rights. **Due process requires notice, an explanation of the charges and an opportunity to respond to them, which the district had failed to provide.** There was substantial evidence that the leave policy was arbitrary and not uniformly applied, and the court affirmed the judgment for the teacher. *Bd. of Educ. of Round Lake Area Schools v. Community Unit School Dist. No. 116*, 685 N.E.2d 412 (Ill.App.2d Dist.1997).

♦   A Pennsylvania school district and the education association representing its teachers were unable to reach a new agreement upon the expiration of their collective bargaining agreement. After six months, the association called a two-day strike that ended with an agreement to extend the terms of the expired agreement. As the school year reached its end, the association called a second strike because of continuing unsuccessful negotiations. **The strike jeopardized the district's ability to provide 180 days of instruction per year as required by the state public school code.** The state secretary of education filed a complaint against the association in a Pennsylvania county court for a preliminary order to compel a return to work because the district had provided only 163 days of instruction for the year. The court granted the request and ordered the association and school board to engage in court-monitored bargaining. The district and board appealed to the Commonwealth Court of Pennsylvania, which ruled that the trial court had no authority to order the parties to bargain. The secretary appealed to the Supreme Court of Pennsylvania. On appeal, the board and district argued that the state Public Employee Relations Act did not grant state courts the authority to order negotiations between parties to collective bargaining agreements. **The court ruled that the Public Employee Relations Act must be read in conjunction with the state public school code, which empowers the secretary of education to compel a return to work in order to provide at least 180 days of instruction annually.** Because the trial court had correctly construed the statutes together in ordering the parties to resume bargaining, its order was affirmed. *Carroll v. Ringgold Educ. Ass'n*, 680 A.2d 1137 (Pa.1996).

♦   Teachers in a Michigan school district went on a strike that resulted in a 14-day school closure that was never made up during the school year. As a consequence, school was open only 166 days of the 180 days required by Michigan law. The district was able to keep its special education program open for the minimum required 230 days. **Michigan's state school aid act called for the deduction of a prorated amount of total state aid for each day a district failed to hold school when the district did not meet the 180-day requirement.** The state department of education required the district to forfeit over $1.6 million, including in its calculations the district's special education program budget and federal insurance collection act (FICA) payments made by the state to the district. These items accounted for over $408,000 of the total reduction. The district filed a lawsuit in a state court against the department of education to challenge the reduction, but the court held for the department. The district appealed to the Court of Appeals of Michigan. **The court of appeals held that the state legislature had not intended to penalize school districts that met the special education requirement merely because they failed to meet the requirement for general education programs**. This would be inconsistent with and beyond the purpose of the statutory scheme, which addressed regular and special education in different sections. It was also improper for the department to withhold FICA reimbursement for unpaid salaries, because this had been taken into account by the district's nonpayment of salaries during the strike. The court of appeals reversed and remanded the trial court's decision. *School Dist. of the City of Pontiac v. Dep't of Educ.*, 516 N.W.2d 516 (Mich.App.1994).

◆   Indiana law prohibits public school teachers from striking. Unions representing South Bend public school teachers nonetheless elected to strike in February 1994. The local education agency sought temporary and permanent injunctions from an Indiana trial court to prohibit the strike. The court issued the order, but the teachers went out on strike. **The education agency sought a trial court order for contempt against the teachers, then requested a contempt order against the unions for violating the temporary restraining order**. The court allowed the unions a one-day continuance upon request, then conducted a hearing on a Sunday and found the unions in contempt for violating the temporary restraining order. It fined the local association $25,000 and the state teachers' association $175,000. The unions appealed to the Indiana Court of Appeals, which determined that **the trial court had properly exercised its jurisdiction to issue contempt citations**. There was no merit to the unions' argument that the local education agency had violated the state Open Door Law by failing to specify that it would discuss filing a lawsuit against the unions in a notice concerning the executive session. There was also no merit to the argument of the unions that they had not received enough time to respond to the temporary order. The civil contempt orders granted the unions an opportunity to purge themselves of the contempt fines, and satisfied the requirements for civil contempt. The court of appeals affirmed the trial court orders for contempt. *National Educ. Ass'n-South Bend v. South Bend Community School Corp.*, 655 N.E.2d 516 (Ind.App.1995).

◆   A group of West Virginia teachers began a strike to protest the failure of the local government to enact a wage and benefit package to their satisfaction. The local board of education filed suit in a West Virginia trial court and the judge granted it injunctive relief. The teachers then appealed to the Supreme Court of Appeals of West Virginia. The court noted that the trial court had ruled correctly on the current law in West Virginia, and looked to see if it was not time to change that law. **The current law held that the strike was illegal in the absence of legislation requiring the public employer to recognize the association as a union**. Other jurisdictions outside West Virginia had recently changed their laws allowing public employees to form unions. In the jurisdictions allowing unions, contracts were formed by negotiation. In West Virginia contracts are formed solely by the legislative body. When contracts are formed this way, allowing public employees to strike would give them excessive bargaining leverage and threaten the public welfare. These factors would continue to be problems in West Virginia unless a legislative act changed the process. **In order to avoid irreparable harm to the public welfare, teachers in West Virginia would not be recognized as a union and therefore would not be allowed to strike**. The supreme court upheld the decision of the trial court. *Jefferson Cty. Bd. of Educ. v. Educ. Ass'n*, 393 S.E.2d 653 (W.Va.1990).

CHAPTER TEN

School Operations

I.   BUDGET AND FINANCE

According to the U.S. Supreme Court, education is not a fundamental right under the federal Constitution. However, state constitutional provisions for public education mandate adequate state financing for public education. Unlike race, economic status is not a suspect class for the purpose of constitutional analysis and, in some cases, claims based on financial disparity among school districts have been dismissed because courts have not applied strict scrutiny to their analyses of the disparities.

A. Taxation And Equal Educational Opportunity

The U.S. Supreme Court sharply limited educational financing claims based on the Equal Protection Clause of the U.S. Constitution when it held that education is not a fundamental right in *San Antonio School Dist. v. Rodriguez*, 411 U.S. 1, 93 S.Ct. 1278, 36 L.Ed.2d 16 (1973). Litigation of constitutional challenges to school funding systems has shifted to state courts, which continue to consider financial equity claims under state constitutions. The most typical state court challenges to school financing systems occur when differing tax bases result in disparities among school district revenues within the state.

◆   In 1970, a group representing students in poor urban school districts sued New Jersey education officials to enforce the state constitutional requirement that the legislature provide for a thorough and efficient public school system. The litigation prompted a series of legislative attempts at equitable funding and the remediation of educational deficiencies in poor districts. The court declared such legislation unconstitutional in 1975, 1985 and 1994. In a 1997 decision, the court upheld much of the Comprehensive Educational Improvement Financing Act of 1996, which provided for substantive educational standards. However, the court rejected the act's reliance on a model school district to determine funding standards and remanded the case. **The remand order required the state to immediately increase funds in special needs districts to achieve funding equity**. It also addressed the need for supplemental programs and facilities improvement in all public schools. The trial court issued a report and recommendation, and the case returned to the supreme court, which approved many of the proposals made by the state education commissioner. Some of the reforms included whole-school re-form, full-day kindergarten and half-day preschool programs, alternative schools, accountability measures, school-to-work programs and college transition pro-grams. The court approved of procedures and standards to enable individual schools to obtain necessary funds and initiate managerial authority over school construction and funding measures. The commissioner was authorized to secure necessary funds for poor school districts, which could also finance construction through indirect market participation. The court remanded the case for further remedial relief. *Abbott by Abbott v. Burke*, 153 N.J. 480, 710 A.2d 450 (1998).

In response to allegations that the state education department failed to fully implement the 1998 decision, the New Jersey Supreme Court held that **discrepancies in the implementation of its 1998 order were the result of misunderstandings, not bad faith. The court issued further guidance to the**

parties for implementation of reforms, and found that the state's use of community care providers staffed by uncertified teachers violated its order to establish quality preschool programs. The state education commissioner was required to ensure that programs were adequately funded and to assist the schools in meeting transportation, service, support and resource needs. The commissioner and education department failed to establish substantive standards describing the educational content of preschool programs as required by the 1998 mandate. Staff assistance teams established by the commissioner were no substitute for educational standards and the department was ordered to adopt standards by April 17, 2000. According to the court, the department's regulations excessively delayed staffing every preschool classroom with a fully qualified teacher. The state was required to clarify the regulations and eliminate the disparity among preschool programs. The court ordered the state to adopt rules requiring uncertified teachers to obtain certification within four years and that new teachers be college graduates. The state was ordered to comply with the 1-to-15 teacher-to-student ratio established by the trial court. **The court urged the parties to resolve funding issues expeditiously, in view of the districts' claim that the state failed to comply with the 1998 mandate by denying funding for facilities improvements**. The court disagreed with the districts that judicial oversight was required to ensure state compliance with the quality preschool network established by state law. *Abbott by Abbott v. Burke*, 163 N.J. 95, 748 A.2d 82 (2000).

◆   A group representing 40 poor school districts in South Carolina filed a state circuit court action against the state and a number of named officials alleging violations of state law and the state and federal constitutions. **The complaint included assertions that the education system was under-funded and violated the equal protection rights of students in poor districts because of the funding mechanism** employed by state law. The plaintiffs asserted that the funding method resulted in an inadequate education for students attending school in these districts. The circuit court dismissed the action, and the group appealed to the South Carolina Supreme Court.

The state supreme court affirmed the dismissal of the constitutional equal protection claims. The court also upheld the portion of the circuit court's decision which found state education law did not create a private cause of action for students, due to the fact that the state education law was not created for the special benefit of any private party, but for the benefit of the public. Despite these findings, the supreme court concluded that **the education clause of the South Carolina constitution required the general assembly to provide the opportunity for each student in the state to receive a minimally adequate education**. The legislature had previously acknowledged the need to guarantee each public school student the availability of minimum educational programs and services. While the court stated that it would not dictate appropriate programs for public schools, it had the authority to define the outlines of the state constitutional mandate, and reversed and remanded the case. *Abbeville County School Dist. v. State of South Carolina*, 335 S.C. 58, 515 S.E.2d 535 (S.C. 1999).

◆   A class of persons representing students from East St. Louis, Illinois, sued state education officials and the local school district in state court, asserting that due to official mismanagement and neglect, schools in the district were in wretched disrepair, unsanitary, vermin infested and unsafe. The complaint further stated that **local officials failed to provide an adequate instructional program, which resulted in high drop out rates and low test scores, and that state officials failed to rectify the problems**. The state trial court dismissed the complaint, but the Appellate Court of Illinois allowed the class to amend its complaint to allege more specific claims that might survive pretrial dismissal under various legal theories, including violations of the state and U.S. constitutions and state law.

On appeal to the Supreme Court of Illinois, the court rejected the class' argument that the state constitution created a right to a minimally adequate education that would allow a lawsuit against state or local officials. The court refused to interpret questions of educational quality, finding this was an issue for the legislature. The court had previously held that the state constitution's education article does not allow for such judicial intervention. **There was no merit to the due process claims brought by the class, since the constitution does not create affirmative rights for students and the alleged inaction of school officials did not place students in danger**. The Due Process Clause does not create a right to a safe school environment. The class also failed to allege that specific students were actually injured by the squalid conditions present in district schools. The state constitution's Due Process Clause similarly failed to create an enforceable right. The state school code claim had technical defects that rendered it an insufficient basis for relief. However, the supreme court ruled that the class should be allowed to amend the complaint in order to state specific official acts or omissions and identify the specific statutory violations which might entitle the class to relief. The class was given an opportunity to appropriately re-plead the case. *Lewis E. v. Spagnola,* 186 Ill.2d 198, 710 N.E.2d 798 (Ill. 1998).

◆   A group of public school parents and students, and an organization of 26 Louisiana school districts brought state court actions against various state entities and officials, challenging the Louisiana school funding methods. **The cases were consolidated and the court rejected arguments by the state officials that the complaints failed to state an appropriate claim for relief**. The officials appealed to the Court of Appeal of Louisiana, First District. The court reversed the trial court decision and dismissed the consolidated actions. The complaining parties obtained an order from the state supreme court remanding the case to the court of appeal for further briefing, argument and an opinion.

While rejecting the officials' assertion that the state court system was powerless to address the cases, the court found no evidence that the state's funding formula discriminated against the residents of individual school districts with fewer taxable resources. The equal protection claims thus failed. The court rejected the complaining parties' assertion that state officials had failed to appropriate sufficient funds to ensure a minimum educational foundation program as required by the Louisiana Constitution, which does not require the legislature to provide for adequate, sufficient, or otherwise measurable funding standards for students and local districts. **The evidence indicated that state officials had performed their statutory duty to develop a funding formula, determine the cost of a minimum foundation program of education and equitably allocate funds among local districts**. The case was reversed and remanded. *Charlet v. Legislature of State of Louisiana, et al.,* 713 So.2d 1199 (La.App.1st Cir.1998).

◆   In 1994, the Supreme Court of Arizona held that the state's educational financing system violated the state constitution because it directly caused substantial capital facility disparities among school districts in the state. The system relied extensively on local property taxes, created arbitrary school district boundaries and made only partial attempts at funding equalization. The supreme court struck down a 1996 amendment to the financing system, and in 1997, the legislature established the Assistance to Build Classrooms Fund (ABC). **The state governor filed an Arizona superior court action seeking a declaration that the 1997 amendments complied with the supreme court's 1994 mandate**. The court denied the governor's motion, and she appealed to the state supreme court.

The supreme court held that the ABC legislation failed to remedy the system's excessive reliance upon local property taxes at the school district level, which varied enormously among districts. The legislation created a small fund which had no relationship to the capital needs of any district and which did not equalize funding. It imposed vastly different tax burdens on residents of different districts and did not set standards for adequate capital facilities. The system improperly allowed voters within school district areas to opt against funding adequate capital facilities by choosing not to issue bonds. **Because the ABC legislation violated the state constitutional requirement for uniform public school facilities, the court declared it unconstitutional and suggested that the legislature resolve continuing funding problems by abandoning heavy reliance upon property taxation** in favor of funding by a sales tax, income tax or statewide property tax. *Hull v. Albrecht*, 950 P.2d 1141 (Ariz.1997).

◆   Students and parents residing in relatively poor North Carolina school districts filed a lawsuit against state education officials, claiming that their districts received insufficient funding from the state and from local taxes. They argued that **the students in these districts received a constitutionally inadequate education and were deprived of equal educational opportunities** because of the great disparity between the education available in wealthier districts and poorer districts. Students and parents residing in wealthier districts joined the action, contending that the state violated the constitution and state laws by failing to provide supplemental educational resources and by failing to ensure that their schools had sufficient resources to provide adequate and equal educational opportunities. A North Carolina superior court denied motions by the state officials to dismiss the lawsuit, but the North Carolina Court of Appeals reversed its decision. The Supreme Court of North Carolina agreed to review the case.

The court held that the North Carolina Constitution imposes a qualitative standard that requires an adequate education for all public school students. The court of appeals had erroneously reversed the superior court order denying relief to the state officials on that claim. While the state constitution requires equal access to a sound basic education, it does not require substantially equal funding among all school districts. Accordingly, the current funding provisions of state law did not violate the state constitution. Students and parents from wealthier districts were entitled to show that the state supplemental funding system was unrelated to legitimate educational purposes, and **the students and parents from the poorer school districts were entitled to demonstrate state-level violations of state education law**. The court reversed the decision in part and remanded the case. *Leandro v. State of North Carolina*, 488 S.E.2d 249 (N.C.1997).

◆   Five New Hampshire school districts and several resident students, taxpayers and parents filed a state court action against the state and governor, alleging that the state's public education finance system violated the New Hampshire Constitution. The court dismissed the petition, but the Supreme Court of New Hampshire reversed the decision, ruling that the state had a duty to provide a constitutionally adequate public education through adequate funding. It remanded the case for a trial. **The trial court determined that New Hampshire school districts were providing students with a constitutionally adequate education and that the school funding system did not violate the equal protection rights** of the complaining parties under the state constitution. The complaining parties appealed to the Supreme Court of New Hampshire.

The court found that New Hampshire public schools depended upon local funding to the extent that the state ranked last in the nation in percentage of direct support by the state for public education. State legislation placed the responsibility for providing public education on local school districts, forcing some property-poor districts to tax their residents at rates of up to four times the amount assessed by property-rich districts. **The court found that the school tax was a state, rather than a local, tax which had to be both proportionate and reasonable in order to comply with the New Hampshire Constitution.** It held that the current school tax was disproportionate and unreasonable based upon the 400 percent disparity in local tax rates. Because a constitutionally adequate public education is a fundamental right under the state constitution, the court reversed the judgment and stayed further proceedings pending legislative action. *Claremont School Dist. v. Governor*, 703 A.2d 1353 (N.H.1997).

◆   A group of Florida citizens and taxpayers filed a complaint against the state, governor, and others in a state trial court alleging that the state educational finance system violated the Florida Constitution. The complaint alleged that state education programs were insufficient to allow certain students to gain proficiency in the English language and that economically deprived, gifted, disabled and mentally handicapped students received inadequate special programs. The complaining parties alleged that students in property-poor counties received an inadequate education due to insufficient funding and that these districts were unable to perform their constitutional duties because of inappropriate actions by the state legislature. **The Supreme Court of Florida rejected the complaining parties' argument that the uniformity requirement mandated equal funding among school districts.** This goal was impossible in practice. Consideration of the question of adequacy would require the court to usurp the legislature's role, and the separation of powers provision of the state constitution precluded the court from granting the relief sought by the complaining parties. *Coalition for Adequacy and Fairness in School Funding, Inc. v. Chiles*, 680 So.2d 400 (Fla.1996).

◆   The Rhode Island General Assembly reduced the primary public education funding program for each public school district entitlement that was not fully funded. **Three Rhode Island school districts** that were affected by the reduction **filed a lawsuit against state officials** in a Rhode Island trial court, **seeking an order that the state's public school financing method was unconstitutional.** The court determined that the financing system violated the Education, Equal

Protection and Due Process Clauses of the Rhode Island Constitution. The state officials appealed to the Supreme Court of Rhode Island. The supreme court stated that the trial court had wrongly determined that the Education Clause of the state constitution guaranteed state residents an equal, adequate and meaningful education. The state had historically relied upon local revenues in funding its public schools, and the evidence indicated that Rhode Island's educational financing method was among the most equitable in the nation. **The complaining school districts were unable to demonstrate any violation of the Due Process and Equal Protection Clauses of the state constitution, and any disparities in state funding did not rise to the level of a constitutional violation**. The court reversed and remanded the trial court decision. *City of Pawtucket v. Sundlun*, 662 A.2d 40 (R.I.1995).

B. Property Taxes and Other Local Funding Issues

◆   As a result of increased enrollment, **a Pennsylvania school board approved a program providing for a district-financed tuition scholarship for any student legally residing in the district for attendance at any private school or non-district public school**. The board action endorsed parental choice and empowerment, and asserted that increased competition would spur school improvement to the community's benefit. A group of resident taxpayers filed a declaratory judgment action against the district in the state court system. The trial court agreed with the taxpayers and granted their motion for judgment on the pleadings, ruling that the district lacked authority to implement the plan.

The district and board appealed to the Commonwealth Court of Pennsylvania, which rejected the assertion by the board that the plan was impliedly authorized by the Pennsylvania School Code. The court reasoned that because school districts are created by legislation, they have no power except that authorized by express statutory grant and necessary implication. The School Code did not expressly authorize reimbursement of tuition and fees. The court rejected the argument that the broad grant of authority found in 24 P.S. § 5-501 created implied authority for the plan. **While the section authorized district expenditures for building, maintaining and equipping schools, it required too great a leap of logic to conclude that school districts should provide financial incentives not to attend public schools**. Where a district found its financing insufficient, its options were to either obtain a court order, or follow procedures established by the secretary of education. The legislature did not authorize tuition payments to parents in the situation presented in this case, as it had in other circumstances, and there was no implied authority for the district plan. A statewide program resembling the district's plan was struck down by the U.S. Supreme Court in 1973 in *Sloan v. Lemon*, 413 U.S. 825 (1973). The school district had clearly acted outside the scope of its statutory authority, and the court affirmed the trial court order enjoining the district from implementing or enforcing the plan. *Giacomucci v. Southeast Delco School Dist.*, 742 A.2d 1165 (Pa.Commw.1999).

◆   A North Carolina statute requires counties to distribute the proportion of *ad valorem* taxes levied on a taxing district's behalf by a county to the individual taxing district. Another code section allows counties to make discretionary appropriations to county school districts on an "average daily student membership" basis. One North Carolina county had two school districts, one serving most of the county and another serving a city with 16 percent of the entire county's average daily membership. Voters in the city school district approved a supplemental tax. Voters in a county high school attendance area also approved a supplemental tax, but it was later repealed. After the repeal, **some resident taxpayers alleged that the county schools would no longer receive a portion of residual sales taxes generated by the supplemental tax** in violation of state law and the North Carolina Constitution. The taxpayers filed a state court action against the county. The court held for the county, and the taxpayers appealed to the Court of Appeals of North Carolina. **The court held that the county had correctly followed state law by declining to apportion the residual sales taxes raised by the supplemental tax according to the *ad valorem* method.** The court rejected the taxpayers' claim that residual sales tax proceeds should be distributed to the districts on an average daily membership basis, since this claim rested on a general statute and the more specific *ad valorem* statute applied. *Banks v. County of Buncombe*, 494 S.E.2d 791 (N.C.App.1998).

◆   Voters in a Maryland county approved an amendment to the county charter in 1978 which prohibited the county council from establishing tax rates that exceeded those in effect during the 1978–79 tax year, except for additional revenues from new construction or other previously untaxed property. **The limitation prevented the council from increasing its property tax revenues**, and several organizations and individuals filed a complaint in a Maryland county court for a declaration and order that the amendment violated state law and the Maryland Constitution. The court granted the requested order, and a group of individuals aligned with the county appealed to the Court of Appeals of Maryland. **The court determined that the charter provision improperly restricted the council's legal authority to set an appropriate tax rate.** This was inconsistent with Maryland general laws and the state constitution. Since the council had the legal authority to assess, levy and collect taxes and annually set the tax rate, the court affirmed the trial court decision. *Hertelendy v. Bd. of Educ. of Talbot County*, 344 Md. 676, 690 A.2d 503 (1997).

◆   Alaska school districts are organized into municipal school districts or regional educational attendance areas (REAAs). State educational funding laws treat districts and REAAs differently. REAAs are prohibited by the state constitution from levying their own taxes. In order to compensate for this, **state law reimburses REAAs for 98 percent of their school construction project costs, while municipal school districts receive only 70 percent of their construction funds** from the state. An Alaska municipality and municipal school district joined several residents in a state court lawsuit against the state, governor and commissioner of education, asserting that the school construction aid statute was unconstitutional. They also asserted that the tax on their real and personal property and the lack of any taxation on residents in REAAs violated their equal protection rights. The court granted summary judgment to the state and officials, and the taxpayers, municipality and school district appealed to the Supreme Court of Alaska.

The court stated that the taxpayers failed to present evidence that the disparity in local contributions affected student education interests or that disparities in contribution rates translated into disparities in educational opportunities. They also failed to present evidence that there was an actual disparity in state aid for school construction, or that municipal students and taxpayers were disadvantaged relative to REAA residents. **The legislature had accommodated the prohibition on REAAs to levy taxes, and the different treatment did not violate equal protection rights**. The court reversed the trial court's decision to assess costs against the taxpayers, but otherwise affirmed the decision. *Matanuska-Susitna Borough School Dist. v. State of Alaska*, 931 P.2d 391 (Alaska 1997).

◆   **The city of Atlanta and the Atlanta Independent School System entered into a revenue sharing agreement under which the school system received 30 percent of the city's local option sales tax receipts**. The Georgia Constitution requires the financing of state school systems by local ad valorem taxes. A resident taxpayer filed a lawsuit against the school system and city in a Georgia superior court, seeking a declaration that the agreement was unconstitutional and seeking an order for repayment of amounts paid under the agreement. The court held the agreement unconstitutional, but refused to award relief in the form of a repayment. The taxpayer appealed to the Supreme Court of Georgia. **The court noted that the state constitution established ad valorem taxation as the exclusive financing method for public schools** in the state. It disagreed with the system's argument that the agreement had to be upheld as an inter-governmental agreement that was authorized by the Georgia Constitution. Because repayment of the amounts received by the system from the city would require satisfaction of a judgment from ad valorem taxes, the trial court had properly denied an order for repayment and the supreme court affirmed its judgment. *Atlanta Indep. School System v. Lane*, 469 S.E.2d 22 (Ga. 1996).

C. Federal Funding

◆   A Utah school district agreed in 1975 to provide educational services to Native American students residing in one of the most remote areas of the U.S. In 1994, **resident students filed a lawsuit** against the school district in a federal district court, **claiming that it had violated the decree and failed to provide them with secondary schools** in violation of the Constitution and Title VI of the Civil Rights Act of 1964. The court denied a summary judgment motion filed by the school district, deferring consideration of whether the district had been discriminatory in its actions. However, it accepted the district's claim that the state, federal and tribal governments shared the responsibility to provide services to students residing in the area.

Parties including the U.S., the Navajo Nation, the school board, the state of Utah and the students and parents agreed to present a consent decree to the court. The court approved the decree, which provided for the creation of joint committees composed of the school board and representatives of the class of students for the development of appropriate bilingual education, special education and curriculum. The district agreed to incorporate a Native American cultural awareness program into its curriculum, and to hold a bond election to fund additional classroom facilities. **The parties** also **agreed to use their best efforts to obtain funding to build an elementary school for students residing in the Monument Valley**

area of Arizona and Utah. The Navajo Nation agreed to use its best efforts to obtain reduced water and power rates for a proposed elementary school. The agreement contained an elaborate dispute resolution process and a plan for continuing cooperation among the parties. *Sinajini v. Bd. of Educ. of San Juan County School Dist.*, 964 F.Supp. 319 (D.Utah 1997).

◆   Two Arizona school districts and several students attending district schools filed a lawsuit against the Arizona Superintendent of Public Instruction in the U.S. District Court for the District of Arizona, **asserting that an Arizona funding equalization statute violated the federal Impact Aid Law and the U.S. Constitution.** The Arizona law required county treasurers within the state to return a portion of each school district's ending cash balance to a state fund for equalization of revenues among rich and poor districts. Because the superintendent interpreted the law as including federal Impact Aid revenues in the districts' overall financial resources, some of these funds had to be returned under the state law. The districts and students argued that this violated the Supremacy Clause of the Constitution as well as the Impact Aid Law. The court dismissed the case, finding that the districts and students had no legal standing to bring the action. The students and districts appealed to the U.S. Court of Appeals, Ninth Circuit, which observed the general rule that a political subdivision may not bring a lawsuit against the state of which it is a part. **Because the school districts were Arizona state political subdivisions, they were without legal standing to advance any action against the state.** The students also failed to show that they had standing since they had not proven that they had suffered a concrete and particularized injury or that they would suffer tangible harm from a decrease in Impact Aid funding. The court affirmed the judgment dismissing the lawsuit. *Indian Oasis-Baboquivari Unified School Dist. No. 40 v. Kirk*, 91 F.3d 1240 (9th Cir.1996).

◆   The Perkins Vocational Education Act authorizes federal grants to the states to assist them with vocational education programs. **The receipt of Perkins Act funding requires each state to maintain or increase its annual level of financial support for vocational education** within the state. An audit conducted by the U.S. Department of Education determined that Pennsylvania failed to maintain appropriate funding levels for two fiscal years. The department demanded a refund of over $3 million and the state appealed to the federal Office of Administrative Law Judges. An administrative law judge held for the department, and denied the state's request for an evidentiary hearing. The state appealed to the U.S. Court of Appeals, Third Circuit. The court agreed with the administrative determination that **the state was not entitled to an evidentiary hearing because there was sufficient evidence that the state had not complied with Perkins Act requirements** and the written record was adequate to resolve all factual issues. The court also rejected the state's argument that compliance with Perkins Act requirements infringed upon its authority to interpret its own laws. The federal act, and not state law, defined what constituted vocational education under the act. This did not infringe upon the state's sovereign authority. The court affirmed the administrative decision for the department of education. *State of Pennsylvania v. Riley*, 84 F.3d 125 (3d Cir.1996).

◆   The U.S. Supreme Court ruled that the Secretary of Education has the authority to demand a refund of misused funds granted to states under Title I of the Elementary and Secondary Education Act of 1965. Title I provides funding for local education agencies to prepare economically underprivileged children for school. Recipient states must provide assurances to the secretary that local educational agencies will spend the funds only on qualifying programs. After federal auditors determined that the states of New Jersey and Pennsylvania had misapplied funds, the secretary ordered those states to refund to the federal government the amount of the misapplied funds. Both states appealed to the U.S. Court of Appeals, Third Circuit, arguing that the secretary exceeded his statutory authority in ordering the refunds. **The Supreme Court stated that Title I, as originally enacted, gave the federal government a right to demand repayment once liability was established.** The 1978 amendments to Title I were designed merely to clarify the secretary's legal authority and responsibility to audit recipient states' programs and to specify the procedures to be used in the collection of any debts. *Bell v. New Jersey*, 461 U.S. 773, 103 S.Ct. 2187, 76 L.Ed.2d 312 (1983). The U.S. Supreme Court also held that the 1978 amendments' new, relaxed standards concerning local schools' eligibility to receive Title I funds could not be applied retroactively. *Bennett v. New Jersey*, 470 U.S. 632, 105 S.Ct. 1555, 84 L.Ed.2d 572 (1985). In a companion case, the Court held that the state of Kentucky's lack of bad faith was irrelevant in assessing its liability to repay misused Title I funds. *Bennett v. Kentucky Dep't of Educ.*, 470 U.S. 656, 105 S.Ct. 1544, 84 L.Ed.2d 590 (1985).

D. State Funding

◆   In 1997, the Ohio Supreme Court held that Ohio public schools were neither thorough nor efficient, as required by the state constitution. There was evidence that the lack of sufficient funding adversely affected academic performance. Under the state's School Foundation Program, the General Assembly had provided for funding to local school districts on the basis of political and budgetary considerations without regard to actual local operating costs. **The court declared a number of specific statutory provisions unconstitutional and directed the General Assembly to devise a new funding system** that would provide for facilities in good repair, with necessary supplies and materials. *DeRolph v. State of Ohio*, 78 Ohio St.3d 193, 677 N.E.2d 733 (1997). On remand, the trial court held a hearing on the General Assembly's efforts to create a new funding method. The court held that the state had failed to implement a complete overhaul of the school financing system and failed to meet its burden of proof that the system was constitutional.

The state appealed to the state supreme court, which held that the General Assembly was required to address the problem of school financing. Funding difficulties continued to flow from the state's excessive reliance on local revenue. This ran counter to the U.S. Constitution's requirement that there be a statewide system of public schools. **A system that relied heavily on property taxation was by nature arbitrary, since there was no connection between local property valuation and actual educational needs.** The court held that a "thorough system" meant that every school district had sufficient operating funds. An "efficient system" was one in which every school district had enough teachers, sound buildings that complied with state fire and building codes, and sufficient equipment to provide students with educational opportunities. Despite a series of efforts by the General Assembly to remedy the inadequacy in funding, the current statutory formula was almost identical to its predecessor. The legislature had failed to eliminate the scheme of forced borrowing that existed in former law. Any system that required borrowing against future funds to meet ordinary expenses was not a thorough and efficient system. **Property taxes could no longer be the primary means of providing for a thorough and efficient system of schools**. The court stated that the legislature must resolve the problem of over-reliance on local property taxes. The legislature was also directed to avoid requiring school districts to seek additional tax increases to make up for lost revenues. The state's efforts to increase accountability in schools through increased academic standards amounted to unfunded mandates. Students were required to earn more credits to graduate and schools would now receive report cards evaluating their performance, yet the system continued to provide inadequate funding. The court declined to intervene as requested by the plaintiffs, expressing confidence that the governor and legislature would continue to take actions to bring the state funding system into compliance with the constitutional mandate. *DeRolph et al. v. State of Ohio et al.*, 91 Ohio St.3d 1274, 747 N.E.2d 823 (Ohio 2000).

◆   **The Florida Opportunity Scholarship Program provides that parents of public school students may request scholarships for children to attend private schools, if the children are assigned to public schools that receive a performance grade of "F"** for two years in a four-year period. Opportunity scholarships result in parental assignment of vouchers for attendance at private schools or higher-performing public schools. The statute creating the OSP was enacted in 1999, but some schools were assigned "F" grades based on their performance in prior years and some students received vouchers for the 1999-2000 school year. Voucher opponents filed separate actions against state officials shortly after the legislation creating the OSP was signed into law. The trial court consolidated the actions, which were filed by groups such as the Florida Teaching Profession-NEA, American Civil Liberties Union, Anti-Defamation League and NAACP. Although the groups challenged the OSP under the Establishment Clause and an analogous state law religion clause, the court considered only whether it was constitutional under the state constitution's education clause, which requires that adequate provision be made for a uniform, efficient, safe, secure and high quality system of free public schools. The court agreed with the plaintiffs that the state constitution's education clause, Article IX, § 1, provided the exclusive manner for the state to provide public education. It held that the legislature was prohibited from providing education in any other manner than through the public school system.

State officials appealed to the Court of Appeal of Florida, First District, asserting that the trial court had denied them due process and a fair trial by entering a judgment without a trial or consideration of evidence and that the law creating OSP was not unconstitutional on its face. After ruling that the state's procedural complaint was correct but of no real consequence, the court proceeded to the constitutional claim. It observed that the Florida Constitution acts as a limitation upon, rather than a grant of, power. A law should not be held invalid unless it is clearly unconstitutional. The trial court had found that Article IX, Section One of the state constitution prohibited state-funded private school scholarships by implication. The court of appeal rejected this theory, holding that **since nothing in the constitutional provision expressly prohibited the Legislature from "the well-delineated use of public funds for private school education," the state could do so to fulfill its mandate to provide for the education of all children in Florida**. The trial court improperly held that Article IX, Section One made the public school system the exclusive means for the state to fulfill its requirement to make adequate provision for education, and the court of appeal reversed and remanded the case. It declined to address the remaining constitutional arguments asserted by the anti-voucher groups, since the trial court had yet to make any ruling on them. *Holmes v. Bush, et al.,* 767 So.2d 668 (Fla.App. 1st Dist. 2000).

◆   The Ohio General Assembly adopted the Cleveland School Voucher Program in 1995, in response to a federal district court order placing the Cleveland School District under the direct control of the state superintendent of public instruction due to local board mismanagement. **The voucher program pertained only to the Cleveland school system and provided for public financing of up to $2,500 in scholarships for attendance at participating public or private schools,** including religiously affiliated schools or public schools in adjacent districts. The program placed no controls on how schools could use program funds. No public schools enrolled in the program. The Ohio Supreme Court struck down the program on state constitutional grounds in *Simmons-Harris v. Goff,* 86 Ohio St.3d 1, 711 N.E.2d 203 (Ohio 1999). The general assembly reauthorized the program in time for the 1999–2000 school year, and a new lawsuit was initiated challenging the program. The court enjoined operation of the program on a preliminary basis days before the start of the 1999–2000 school year. State officials appealed to the Sixth Circuit, which did not immediately enter an order. The U.S. Supreme Court granted the state's motion to allow program participants to attend their participating schools that year, pending final disposition by the Sixth Circuit. **The district court then permanently enjoined the state from administering the program** under *Committee for Public Education and Religious Liberty v. Nyquist,* 413 U.S. 756 (1973). In *Nyquist,* the U.S. Supreme Court held that direct aid from states to sectarian schools "in whatever form is invalid." It found the Cleveland school voucher program indistinguishable from the program struck down in *Nyquist,* because only private schools received funds and the vast majority of schools were sectarian.

State officials appealed again to the Sixth Circuit, which found the *Nyquist* decision similar to the Cleveland case. Under both the New York and Cleveland programs, parents received government funds to pay for private schools, the great majority of which were sectarian. The Cleveland program placed no restrictions on the use of funds and had no means of guaranteeing that they would be used for secular, neutral, and non-ideological purposes. The Sixth Circuit found no evidence that the use of vouchers was a neutral form of state assistance that excused direct state funding of religious institutions. Instead, the program discouraged participation by non-religious schools and limited the schools to which parents could apply for funding. No public school participated in the program, nor were places available in suburban public schools for students seeking transfers. The circuit court rejected the state's argument that the government-religious nexus was broken by the idea of parental choice. Their choice was instead limited to the overwhelmingly sectarian private schools that could afford the tuition restrictions placed on them by the program. The circuit court held that **the program was calculated to attract religious institutions and chose its beneficiaries by non-neutral criteria. It had the primary effect of advancing religion, constituted an endorsement of religion and was a direct monetary subsidy to religious institutions** that was prohibited by the Establishment Clause. *Simmons-Harris v. Zelman*, 234 F.3d 945 (6th Cir. 2000).

◆   The Pennsylvania Constitution requires the state General Assembly to provide for a thorough and efficient system of public education, which Pennsylvania courts have construed as an affirmative duty. The School District of Philadelphia is the only school district in Pennsylvania without the direct power to levy local school taxes, but the city is vested with discretionary power to levy necessary taxes. **The City and School District of Philadelphia and civic organizations joined Philadelphia students and parents in suing the Commonwealth of Pennsylvania, the General Assembly, governor and other executive officers, seeking a declaratory ruling that the assembly must appropriate more funds for Philadelphia schools**. It requested a declaration that the commonwealth had failed to fulfill its constitutional obligation to provide for an adequate system of public schools in Philadelphia, and an order that the assembly amend the present school financing scheme to account for the inability of Philadelphia's tax base to generate sufficient revenues. Officials of the state legislative and executive branches sought dismissal of the lawsuit in the Commonwealth Court of Pennsylvania. The court found that while the state constitution mandated a thorough and efficient system of public education, there was no individual right of students to a particular level or quality of education. **In considering state public school legislation, courts are prohibited from inquiring into the reason, wisdom or expediency of legislative policy or the scope of educational activity**. The court was unable to judicially define what constituted an adequate education or what funding level was adequate for public school programs. Because these matters were exclusively within the assembly's powers, the state legislators and executives had correctly argued that the case was nonjusticiable, and the court dismissed the petition.

The complaining parties appealed to the Pennsylvania Supreme Court, which held that **the issue of school funding appropriations is a political question that is inappropriate for resolution by the courts**. According to the court, the state constitutional requirement of a thorough and efficient education did not confer upon students an individual right to a particular level or quality of education, but instead imposed a duty upon the Pennsylvania legislature to provide for a thorough and efficient system throughout the state. So long as the legislative scheme for financing education had a reasonable relationship to providing for the maintenance of public schools, the General Assembly's duty was fulfilled, the state high court held, affirming the judgment for the state. *Marrero v. Commonwealth of Pennsylvania*, 559 Pa. 14, 739 A.2d 110 (1999).

◆   Illinois amended its state tax law in 1999 with Public Law 91-0009, the Education Expense Credit Act, enacted as 1999 Illinois S.B. 1075 and codified at 35 ILCS 5/201. **The law permits a tax credit of up to $500 for taxpayers for the**

educational expenses of qualified students. In order to obtain the credit, the taxpayer must be an Illinois resident and the parent or legal guardian of a student under the age of 21 who is a full time student in any public or nonpublic elementary or secondary school complying with specified requirements. Nothing in the law requires a student to attend any particular school in order for a taxpayer to obtain the credit. The expenses for which the credit may be obtained are costs in excess of $250 incurred for tuition, book fees and lab fees at the school where a qualifying student is enrolled. Taxpayers and objecting groups sued state officials, including the director of the department of revenue in Franklin County Circuit Court, asserting violations of the Illinois Constitution.

The court issued a brief memorandum decision and final order dismissing the complaint. It found that in addition to the general presumption of constitutionality accorded to legislative pronouncements, **the legislature is entitled to broad latitude in tax classification matters**. It then found that the Illinois statute was similar in all material ways to the Minnesota law at issue in *Mueller v. Allen*, 453 U.S. 388 (1983). In that case, the U.S. Supreme Court upheld a state law allowing taxpayers to deduct certain tuition, transportation and educational expenses incurred in sending children to public or private schools. According to the court, the Illinois law passed constitutional muster under *Mueller*. Based on this authority, the court dismissed the case. *Griffith v. Bower*, No. 99-CH-0049 (Ill.Cir. Franklin County 1999).

◆   Vermont law requires school districts that do not maintain schools to pay the tuition for resident students to attend approved public schools in other districts or an approved independent school selected by parents. Until 1997, one district without a high school authorized tuition payments only for nonsectarian schools. It then adopted a policy allowing tuition reimbursement for the costs of sectarian schools. The parents of 15 students residing in the district selected one parochial school for attendance that required instruction in theology prior to graduation. The school also required students to attend mass on some occasions. **The state education commissioner terminated state assistance to the district when it voted to reimburse the parents of students who attended the parochial school**. The district sued the commissioner and state education department in a Vermont superior court, which held that the payments violated the federal Establishment Clause and the Compelled Support Clause of the Vermont Constitution.

The district appealed to the Supreme Court of Vermont, which declined to evaluate the case under the U.S. Constitution, instead focusing on the Compelled Support Clause of the Vermont Constitution. The court observed that no state law or department rule discussed payment for sectarian education, and that **the method for tuition payment selected by the district in this case would result in the impermissible comingling of public and private funds and the expenditure of public funds for religious education**. It stated that the Compelled Support Clause prohibits compelled worship, church attendance or support of any place of worship contrary to the dictates of a person's conscience. The district argued that the sectarian school was not a place of worship and that the state constitutional provision did not pertain to religious education. The court stated that the Compelled Support Clause also pertained to "any place of worship," which could include a school. The Vermont Supreme Court criticized the Supreme Court of Wisconsin's

1998 opinion upholding the constitutionality of the Milwaukee School Choice Program, and refused to apply it to the present case. The court held that allowing the district to pay tuition for parochial school students would result in a direct state payment for religious instruction that violated the state constitution. This was primarily because of the lack of any restriction on the schools' expenditure of public funds once they were received. The court rejected the argument that parental choice in the selection of the sectarian school precluded a finding that the payments to sectarian schools made them constitutional. It affirmed the superior court judgment for the education commissioner and state education department. *Chittenden Town School Dist. v. Vermont Dep't of Educ.*, 169 Vt. 310, 738 A.2d 539 (1999).

◆   Under Maine law, students who live in districts that do not maintain schools may attend public schools in other districts at their home district's expense or obtain direct state funding to attend qualified private schools. Approximately half the school districts in the state lack separate school facilities. The law excludes sectarian schools from participating in the tuition program. A group of parents sued the state education department and education commissioner in federal court, asserting that the exclusion of sectarian schools from the program violated their constitutional rights. **The district court held that while parents were allowed to send their children to sectarian schools, they were not entitled to require taxpayers to subsidize that choice.** The parents appealed to the U.S. Court of Appeals, First Circuit, where they argued that the program violated the Establishment Clause by excluding them from the program on the basis of their religious viewpoint.

Relying on the U.S. Supreme Court's decision in *Committee for Public Education and Religious Liberty v. Nyquist*, 413 U.S. 756 (1973), the court found that direct tuition payments by a state to sectarian schools violate the Establishment Clause. The First Circuit agreed with the Supreme Judicial Court of Maine, which upheld the exclusion of religious school students from the program in *Bagley v. Raymond School Dep't,* below. The state had a paramount interest in avoiding Establishment Clause violations. The First Circuit refused to apply a line of recent U.S. Supreme Court decisions allowing government funding in the context of target grants available to limited populations for specific purposes. The parents' claims that their rights under the Equal Protection, Free Exercise, Speech and Due Process Clauses of the Constitution had been violated were also rejected. **The court stated that there was no restriction on the use of tuition funds once received by the schools, and that the exclusion of religious schools from the program did not prevent any student from attending a sectarian school.** The state was not required to pay for sectarian education in order to protect individual rights. The district court judgment was affirmed. *Strout v. Albanese,* 178 F.3d 57 (1st Cir. 1999).

◆   Maine's education tuition law provides that local school districts that do not maintain their own schools must pay the tuition of resident students so that they may attend private schools or public schools located in other districts. Only half of the districts in the state maintain their own schools. Districts may contract with one public school to take all of their students, or pay tuition to public and private schools that will accept them. District payments under the second option go directly to the school at which a resident student is accepted. In 1981, the state legislature excluded religious schools from the tuition program, finding that their inclusion would violated the Establishment Clause. **A town which did not maintain its own schools denied tuition requests by five families with children enrolled at a Catholic high school.** The parents sued the town, state education board and commissioner of education in a state superior court, asserting that the exclusion of religious schools from the tuition program violated their constitutional rights. A group of taxpayers and the Maine Civil Liberties Union joined the action, siding with state officials. The court granted summary judgment to the town and officials.

The families appealed to the Maine Supreme Judicial Court, which observed that unlike recent state supreme court decisions allowing private schools to benefit from public funding legislation in other states, the Maine tuition program excluded religious schools from participating in the state's existing program. **Exclusion of religious schools from the program did not violate the families' rights under the Free Exercise Clause, since failure to receive state funding did not impair their ability to obtain religious instruction for their children.** The exclusion did not violate the Establishment Clause, and to the contrary, the legislature had enacted the exclusion to prevent violation of the Establishment Clause. Otherwise, the program would require direct government payments to religious schools, with no safeguards to ensure that state funding was used only for secular purposes. According to the court, while the U.S. Supreme Court now applies a different analysis to Establishment Clause cases than the one which prompted the 1981 legislative change, it has never approved of direct state payments to religious schools, which would have the impermissible effect of advancing religion. There was no merit to the argument of the families that the exclusion of religious schools from the program created an equal protection violation. While the law treated religious schools differently than non-religious schools, the state justified the exclusion in order to comply with the Establishment Clause. The court affirmed the judgment for the town and state officials. *Bagley v. Raymond School Dep't,* 728 A.2d 127 (Me.1999).

♦ **The Wisconsin legislature enacted the Milwaukee Parental Choice Program in 1989 to allow moderate to low-income resident students to attend any nonsectarian private school located in the city at public expense.** The state issued direct payments to the parents of participating students but required them to endorse their checks to a private school. The program was amended in 1995 to greatly increase the number of participating students and allow attendance at sectarian schools. Groups of taxpayers, teachers, parents and civic organizations challenged the program's constitutionality in two state court actions brought against the state superintendent of public instruction and other officials. The cases were consolidated by a Wisconsin trial court, which found that the amended program violated the Wisconsin Constitution. The state appealed to the Court of Appeals of Wisconsin, which held that the program violated the religious establishment provisions of the state constitution

The Supreme Court of Wisconsin granted the state's petition for review, and considered the case under both the Wisconsin and U.S. Constitutions. It held that **the program had a secular purpose of providing low-income students with opportunities to receive an education outside the Milwaukee public school** system in a manner that did not have a primary effect of advancing religion, was religiously neutral and did not lead to religious indoctrination. Religious school attendance came only as the result of individual private choices by parents. Because state administration of the program required no oversight beyond existing efforts to monitor the quality of education provided at private schools, the program did not excessively entangle the state with religion. The court upheld the program under the Establishment Clause and on three additional state constitutional grounds. It was also not an unconstitutional private or local bill because its experimental nature was of statewide importance and it did not violate state constitutional uniformity and public purpose provisions. The court rejected arguments that the program violated student equal protection rights and found it constitutional in its entirety. *Jackson v. Benson*, 578 N.W.2d 602 (Wis.1998), *cert. denied*, 119 S.Ct. 466, 142 L.Ed.2d 419 (1998).

◆   **A relatively wealthy Texas school district wanted to opt out of the state statutory wealth equalization provisions.** The district's per-student wealth exceeded the maximum amount allowed under recent amendments to state law that required districts with such excesses to take actions including consolidation with other districts, detachment of territory and purchasing average daily attendance credits. The district was required to pay the state over $815,000 under the attendance credit option and commenced a state court action against the state education agency and commissioner of education seeking permission to opt out. The court joined as parties two of the 127 districts which sought to intervene in the suit. The trial court rejected the complaining school district's assertion that the wealth equalization provisions of state law were included as "requirements and prohibitions" of the code that could be exempted by the state education agency. Judgment was awarded in favor of the agency and commissioner, and the district appealed.

A state appeals court reviewed the history of educational funding litigation and legislation, which had resulted in several state supreme court opinions and legislative amendments since 1989. The state educational financing laws that had emerged from the cycle of court decisions and legislative amendments were distinct from the 1990 legislation that provided for the exemption sought by the complaining district. Although that law permitted districts that showed their ability to teach skills to be excused from many state regulatory requirements, **there was no legislative intent to excuse any district from the wealth equalization provisions of state law**. The district's argument would spoil the efficiency sought by the wealth equalization provisions of state law, as an estimated cost of $56 million in funds recaptured from similarly situated districts. The wealth equalization provision was not one of the requirements and prohibitions from which exemplary districts could obtain exemption. The trial court judgment was affirmed. *Miami Indep. Sch. Dist. v. Moses,* 989 S.W.2d 871 (Tex.App.–Austin 1999).

◆   The Pennsylvania Department of Public Welfare contracted with a private children and youth agency to operate a day treatment program located in the Bethlehem Area School District. The program served students attending school in the Bethlehem district and nonresident students who had been ordered into treatment by the county juvenile court. **The facility had an educational component for which the agency sought reimbursement from the Bethlehem school district.**

When the district refused, the agency filed a state court petition seeking an order requiring the district to either pay for the educational services provided by the facility to nonresident students or provide the services to students regardless of their residency. The court granted the requested order, and the school district appealed to the Commonwealth Court of Pennsylvania.

On appeal, the school district argued that state law imposed no duty upon it to pay for the education of nonresident students, but created an option to provide or purchase services for its own students while the home districts of nonresident students were required to pay for the education of those students. The court disagreed, finding that **the school district had an obligation to provide for the educational component of all students attending the day treatment program**. The option it had under state law was to either provide the services or to pay another district to provide them. Because the provision of education to all students assigned to a day treatment program is the responsibility of the school district in which the program is located, the court affirmed the judgment. *Community Service Foundation, Inc. v. Bethlehem Area School Dist.*, 706 A.2d 882 (Pa.Commw.1998).

◆   An Indiana school board entered into an agreement with a non-public high school to operate an alternative school, paying it $2,334 per semester for each student enrolled in the program. **The teachers' association and a group of taxpayers with children attending schools in the district commenced a state court action** against the state department of education, state board of education, local educational agency and high school, **challenging the agreement**. The complaint sought recovery of monies paid under the agreement, asserting that the Indiana Constitution and state law prohibited the argument. The court granted motions to dismiss the case filed by the school entities, and the complaining parties appealed to the Court of Appeals of Indiana.

The court held that in order to attain standing to bring a lawsuit, a party must demonstrate a personal stake in the outcome of the case, and show an immediate threat of a direct injury as a result of the conduct at issue. The parents claimed that they would suffer direct injury due to the agreement, since public money used to fund the high school would result in less money for other programs attended by their children. The court disagreed, finding no threat of a direct injury to them as a result of the school board's action. **Taxpayers typically have only a general interest in the spending of public funds that is common to all members of the public, and the taxpayers in this case had no personal stake in the expenditure of funds**. Since the taxpayers had no standing, the court affirmed the dismissal of the case. *Fort Wayne Educ. Ass'n v. Indiana Dep't of Educ.*, 692 N.E.2d 902 (Ind.App.1998).

◆   **A suburban Detroit school district contracted with a private entity to provide alternative education to students at an academy located within the city of Detroit and its school district**. The academy was attended almost entirely by students residing within the Detroit Public School area, and the Detroit school board filed a state court action against the suburban school board, seeking an order against the operation of the academy and a ruling that the suburban district could not count Detroit residents who attended the school for state aid purposes. Both parties moved the court for summary disposition, and the trial court held for the suburban school board. The Detroit board appealed to the Court of Appeals of Michigan, which observed that the state school aid act provides that a school district must have the approval of a student's residence district to count the student in membership and receive state nonresident aid. **The suburban district was not entitled to receive any state aid payments for students residing in Detroit since it did not have the approval of the Detroit Public Schools**. Detroit students enrolled in the academy were not enrolled in a district other than their own residence district for the purposes of state aid payments. The court reversed and remanded the trial court's decision. *Bd. of Educ. of Detroit Pub. Schools v. Bd. of Educ. of Romulus Community Schools*, 575 N.W.2d 90 (Mich.App.1997).

◆   A group of Missouri school districts and students filed a lawsuit in state court challenging the state's system of calculating public school revenues. According to the complaint, the current system violated the Missouri constitution's requirement that 25 percent of state revenues be expended for education. The group argued that federal funds should be included in the calculation of state revenues when construing the constitutional requirement. Under that argument, the state had failed to allocate the necessary revenue for public schools. A 1986 amendment to the state constitution stated that once deposited into the state treasury, federal funds retained their character and were not considered as state funds. When the $3.8 billion in federal funds received by Missouri for the year were excluded from consideration as part of the state's $11.9 billion total receipts, **the state had expended more than 25 percent of state revenues for education as required by the constitution**. The court affirmed the trial court judgment for the state. *Committee for Educational Equality v. State of Missouri*, 967 S.W.2d 62 (Mo.1998).

◆   The Michigan Constitution was amended in 1978 by a complex system of revenue and tax limits on state and local government. As a result, the state can only change state revenues in an amount based on changes in personal income in the state and is prohibited from either requiring any new or expanded activity by local governments without full state financing or from reducing the proportion of state assistance to local government units. Local government units are prohibited from levying any new taxes or increasing existing taxes above authorized rates without the approval of local voters. **A group of resident taxpayers filed a lawsuit against state education and finance officials, asserting that the state violated the amendments by failing to maintain the state-financed portion of the necessary costs of required activities**. A second group of taxpayers and Michigan school districts filed another action seeking a money judgment for the school districts on the basis of the state's failure to maintain funding required by the amendments.

The Court of Appeals of Michigan consolidated the cases and issued a judgment favorable to the taxpayers and districts. The state appealed to the Supreme Court of Michigan, where it argued that it was not required to comply with the constitutional mandate concerning special education, special education transportation, and state-matched school lunch payments, since these programs were federal rather than state mandates. **The supreme court observed that the programs identified by the state were also covered by comparable state legislation and therefore were not excluded federal mandates**. The court substantially affirmed the judgment of the court of appeals, but modified the remedy so that the state would be liable for monetary damages to be distributed to the plaintiff school districts or taxpayers within the prevailing districts. *Durant v. State of Michigan*, 566 N.W.2d 272 (Mich.1997).

◆   Nebraska maintains several categories of school districts. Class I districts have only elementary grades, Class VI districts have only high schools and all other classes maintain grades K-12. In 1991, the state amended its laws to require Class I districts to affiliate themselves with a district providing K-12 education or a Class VI district. Prior to the amendment, property owners in all Class I districts paid only the taxes required to support the Class I district and the Class VI district into which its students advanced. Under the amended statute, Class I school districts became grouped together into a Class VI system composed of one high school and each of the elementary schools feeding into that high school. **Funds for Class VI schools were drawn from a common levy certified by the county and distributed to the Class I districts in proportion to their budget requirements**. A Nebraska taxpayer filed a lawsuit against the state department of education in the Supreme Court of Nebraska, claiming violations of the Nebraska Constitution.

The taxpayer argued that the amendment constituted a commutation of property tax by diverting his property taxes to other Class I districts, benefited residents of other Class I districts in an unconstitutional manner, and violated the state constitutional requirement for uniform taxation. He also claimed that the amendment established a property tax for state purposes, which was expressly prohibited by the state constitution. The supreme court rejected each of these arguments, noting that the taxes supported the taxpayer's own district and each of the Class I districts feeding into the high school. **The amended statute provided for uniform taxation within each Class VI system and involved no tax increase which might violate the uniformity clause of the state constitution**. Because local education officials maintained their autonomy, the tax supported local purposes and did not benefit taxpayers in other Class I districts. The court found the amendments constitutional. *Swanson v. State of Nebraska, Dep't of Educ.*, 249 Neb. 466, 544 N.W.2d 333 (1996).

◆   **The 1996–1997 Florida General Appropriations Act contained a proviso allowing district school boards to divert up to 20 percent of funds appropriated to categorical programs for other uses**. The proviso language was included despite existing Florida statutes limiting the expenditure of categorical program funds to those specific programs, including instructional materials, student transportation and inservice training. The governor petitioned the Supreme Court of Florida for an order to expunge the proviso language from the general appropriations act as unconstitutional. The court observed that the Florida Constitution states that appropriations for public officers and other current state expenses shall not contain provisions on other subjects. The court had previously ruled that this limitation forbids an appropriations bill from amending an existing statute on any other subject than appropriations.

Because the proviso language attempted to amend existing statutes on a subject other than appropriations, the court found it unconstitutional. Existing statutes created categorical programs that were previously funded to provide for instructional materials, student transportation and inservice training with mandatory language for expenditures in the identified programs. The Florida Administrative

Code further limited these expenditures by requiring that any funds not expended by a school district during a fiscal year be carried forward to the following fiscal year for the same categorical purpose. **The court directed the secretary of state to expunge the unconstitutional language and ordered the state comptroller to ensure that the expunction was reflected in state financial operations.** *Chiles v. Milligan*, 682 So.2d 74 (Fla.1996).

E. Student Fees and Tuition

1. Transportation Fees

◆   North Dakota statutes authorized thinly populated school districts to reorganize into larger districts for efficiency. Reorganized districts had to provide for student transportation to and from their homes. **School districts choosing not to reorganize were authorized by statute to charge students a portion of their costs for transportation.** Parents of a nine-year-old student refused to sign a transportation contract with the school district. The family was near or at the poverty level. Claiming inability to pay the fee, the family made private transportation arrangements that were more costly than the school's fee. The parents sued the school district in a North Dakota trial court for an order to prevent the school district from collecting the fee on grounds that it violated the state constitution and Equal Protection Clause. After losing at the trial court level, the parents appealed to the North Dakota Supreme Court which upheld the lower court decision on state and federal constitutional grounds. The U.S. Supreme Court upheld the statute's validity. The parents claimed that the user fee for bus service unconstitutionally deprived poor persons of minimum access to education and placed an unconstitutional obstacle on education for poor students. The Court noted that the student continued to attend school during the time she claimed she was denied access to the school bus. The Equal Protection Clause does not require free transportation. Education is not a fundamental right under the U.S. Constitution. **The Court upheld the statute because it bore a reasonable relationship to the state's legitimate objective of encouraging local school districts to provide bus service.** Payment of bus fees was not directly imposed by the statute. The statute did not discriminate against any class and did not interfere with any constitutional rights. *Kadrmas v. Dickinson Pub. Schools*, 487 U.S. 450, 108 S.Ct. 2481, 101 L.Ed.2d 399 (1988).

◆   New York education law permits local school districts to establish mileage thresholds for providing transportation to public school students that are below the statutory thresholds. The distance is to be measured by the nearest available route from home to school. One New York school district furnished transportation for kindergartners who lived one half mile or more from the nearest school, and to elementary students who lived at least one mile away. **A group of parents objected to the measurement from their homes to a particular school by use of a walkway** through a public park and some privately-owned property, contending that the walkway was not a "route" under state law. They filed a lawsuit against the district in the New York Supreme Court, Nassau County, seeking an order directing the district to determine the distance along public highways. The court determined that the walkway was publicly maintained since town employees cleared snow from the pathway and otherwise maintained it, and the district furnished a crossing guard at appropriate times. **The court also noted that the district could bus kindergartners while refusing to transport elementary students**. State law permitted but did not require school boards to provide kindergarten instruction, and kindergartners did not attend mandatory full time day programs. For this reason, it was permissible to provide transportation to them on different terms than those extended to elementary students. The court dismissed the parents' petition. *Arlyn Oaks Civic Ass'n v. Brucia*, 654 N.Y.S.2d 1016 (N.Y.Sup.–Nassau County 1997).

◆   A Kentucky school board furnished bus transportation and allowed students to attend schools that were outside their attendance area but within the same district. However, to limit class sizes, **the board instituted a revised transportation policy that permitted students to attend schools within the district but outside their attendance areas only if they utilized private transportation**. The parent of a student affected by the change filed a lawsuit in a Kentucky trial court, claiming that the transportation policy was arbitrary, capricious and unreasonable and violated his constitutional rights to due process. The court granted summary judgment to the school board and the parent appealed to the Kentucky Court of Appeals. The court of appeals affirmed the trial court's judgment, finding that the board's decision was not arbitrary, capricious or unreasonable. The due process rights of students and parents had been protected by numerous public meetings held during the policy revision. Its impact on students already availing themselves of the policy was mitigated by the use of a grandfather clause. **Any change in school policies might have an adverse impact on some students, but some such impacts could not be avoided**. The court affirmed the trial court's decision. *Swift v. Breckinridge County Bd. of Educ.*, 878 S.W.2d 810 (Ky.App.1994).

2. Tuition and Other Fees

◆   The Supreme Court upheld an activity fee assessed to all students of a university, finding that the university assessed the fee to facilitate the free and open exchange of ideas among students. Objecting students could insist upon certain safeguards to mitigate the compelled support of expressive activities. Even though the student activities fund was not a traditional public forum, the case was controlled by the standard from public forum cases including *Widmar v. Vincent*, 454 U.S. 263 (1981), and *Lamb's Chapel v. Center Moriches Union Free School Dist.*, 508 U.S. 384 (1993). The standard of germane speech from *Abood* and *Keller* gave insufficient protection to objecting students and the university program. To insist upon germaneness to the university's mission would contravene the program's purpose of encouraging a wide range of speech. The Court held that although the fees would subsidize speech that some students would find objectionable, the Constitution did not compel a requirement that the university refund student fees. Viewpoint neutrality was the proper standard for the protection of the rights of the objecting students, as set forth in *Rosenberger v. Rector and Visitors of Univ. of Virginia*, 515 U.S. 819 (1995). The Court held that **the university could require students to support the extracurricular speech of other students in a viewpoint-neutral manner, and observed that the parties had stipulated, in this case, that the program was viewpoint neutral**. The university had wide latitude to adjust its extracurricular speech programs to accommodate students. The Court reversed the judgment of the Seventh Circuit, and remanded the case for further proceedings on the issue of the student referendum. The record required further development on whether a referendum by students undermined constitutional protection for viewpoint neutrality. *Board of Regents of Univ. of Wisconsin System v. Southworth,* 529 U.S. 217, 120 S.Ct. 1346, 146 L.Ed.2d 193 (2000).

♦   The University of Virginia collected a mandatory $14 student activity fee from full-time students each semester. The fees supported extracurricular activities that were related to the educational purposes of the university. University-recognized student groups could apply for funding by the activities fund, although not all groups requested funds. University guidelines excluded religious groups from student funding. A university-recognized student group published a Christian newspaper for which it sought $5,862 from the activities fund for printing costs. **The student council denied funding because the group's activities were deemed religious under university guidelines**. After exhausting appeals within the university, group members filed a lawsuit against the university in the U.S. District Court for the Western District of Virginia, claiming constitutional rights violations. The court granted summary judgment to the university, and its decision was affirmed by the U.S. Court of Appeals, Fourth Circuit. The students appealed to the U.S. Supreme Court.

The Court observed that government entities must abstain from regulating speech on the basis of the speaker's opinion. Upon establishing a limited public forum, state entities must respect the forum by refraining from the exclusion of speech based upon content. **Because the university had opened a limited public forum by paying other third-party contractors on behalf of student groups, it could not deny the religious group's claim for funds on the basis of its viewpoint**. Allowing payment of the group's printing costs amounted to a policy of government neutrality for different viewpoints. The Court distinguished the student fee from a general tax and placed emphasis on the indirect nature of the benefit. The Court reversed the lower court decisions, ruling that access to public school facilities on a neutral basis does not violate the Establishment Clause of the First Amendment. *Rosenberger v. Rector and Visitors of Univ. of Virginia,* 515 U.S. 819, 115 S.Ct. 2510, 132 L.Ed.2d 700 (1995).

♦   A 13-year-old U.S. citizen who was born in Texas resided with his parents in Mexico until he was sent to live with his aunt in Illinois. The aunt's school district of residence refused to recognize documents from his parents granting custody to the aunt, stating that only an American court could confer legal guardianship rights to the aunt. Because the parents were unable to enter the U.S., the district denied the student's application for tuition-free enrollment. The aunt obtained the assistance of a congressman, and the Illinois State Board of Education requested that the student be enrolled without tuition. The local board rejected the request and affirmed the denial of enrollment. **The aunt obtained a temporary restraining order from an Illinois circuit court allowing the immediate enrollment of the student**. The court then made the order permanent and the district appealed to the Appellate Court of Illinois, First District.

The court observed that the Illinois Constitution confers the right to tuition-free education upon resident students. **A child presumptively resides in the** school district where his parents reside; however, this presumption may be rebutted by circumstances including the permanency of the student's residence, the extent to which the parents exercise care, custody and control over the student and the presence of non-educational reasons for living apart from the parents. There was evidence in this case that the student was not applying for residence in the district solely for educational purposes, and contrary evidence that he had moved to Illinois to escape economic and social hardships in Mexico. Because there was sufficient evidence to support the circuit court decision, the court affirmed it. *Joel R. v. Bd. of Educ. of Mannheim School Dist. 83, Cook County, Illinois*, 686 N.E.2d 650 (Ill.App.1st Dist.1997).

◆   North Carolina statutes permit local education boards to charge tuition to students who do not reside within the school's administrative unit or district. **A school district determined that a student who resided in its administrative area was not properly domiciled within the territory and attempted to charge tuition to her parents**. The district filed a lawsuit in a North Carolina trial court to recover tuition from her parents. The court held for the parents and the school district appealed to the Court of Appeals of North Carolina, which observed the distinction between residence and domicile. Residence was defined as an actual place of abode while domicile was a permanent, established home. It was possible for a student to reside in a place other than with his or her parents and therefore have different places of domicile and residence. In this case, **the student resided within the school's administrative unit and could not be assessed tuition charges**. The court remanded the case for the entry of judgment for the parents. *Chapel Hill-Carrboro City Schools System v. Chavioux*, 446 S.E.2d 612 (N.C.App.1994).

◆   Another North Carolina case involving the same statute arose where a school district had imposed exit fees on students. A small, rural North Carolina county with rapidly declining enrollment experienced a significant loss of students because of transfers to schools in other counties. **The county board of education passed a student transfer policy that imposed an exit fee of $200 for resident student transfers to different districts**. The parent of a student who transferred out of the school unit filed a lawsuit in a North Carolina trial court for an injunction against enforcement of the policy. The court granted the injunction and the school board appealed to the Court of Appeals of North Carolina. The court of appeals found no statutory support for the policy. The statute authorized tuition only for students who did not reside within a particular school district. Because there was no authority for the exit fee, the court affirmed the permanent injunction against enforcing the policy. *Streeter v. Greene County Bd. of Educ.*, 446 S.E.2d 107 (N.C.App.1994).

F.   Private Contractors

◆   An Illinois school district solicited bids to replace the boilers in a junior high school. Although the project pertained only to installation, **the board rejected the lowest bid because the contractor who submitted it was located 75 miles from the school site** and board members believed that it would be unable to respond appropriately to service calls. The contractor filed a lawsuit against the school board in an Illinois circuit court, which ordered the board to award the contract to the contractor since it was the low bidder. The district appealed to the Illinois Appellate

Court, where it argued that state law requires public agencies to award contracts to the lowest responsible bidder, but only in conformity with specifications, delivery terms, quality and serviceability. It claimed that the statutory term serviceability referred to a contractor's ability to provide service. **The court rejected this assertion, stating that serviceability refers only to the dependability of the implement or product being installed.** The court affirmed the judgment for the contractor. *Doyle Plumbing and Heating Co. v. Bd. of Educ., Quincy Pub. School Dist. No. 172*, 683 N.E.2d 530 (Ill.App.4th Dist.1997).

◆   A New Mexico school board invited bids on a project to re-roof five buildings. The board selected a contractor that had submitted the low bid on several items, even though it did not submit a complete bid for the entire project. A disappointed bidder filed a lawsuit against the school board in a state trial court, seeking a declaration that it was the lowest responsive bidder and was entitled to the contract. The court agreed with the bidder, and ordered the board to void the contract with the selected bidder. The selected bidder then sought payment for its expenses under the contract, plus a profit. When the school district failed to pay this amount, the selected bidder filed another lawsuit against the district in a state court, seeking payment. The court granted the district's summary judgment motion. The contractor appealed to the Court of Appeals of New Mexico, which considered the district's argument that state law required partial payments to a terminated contractor only where a local public body declares a contract illegal. **The court of appeals stated that because the trial court had instructed the school board to void the contract, it had been set aside by a local agency, satisfying statutory language requiring compensation of the selected bidder.** The court reversed and remanded the district court judgment. *Hamilton Roofing Co. of Carlsbad, Inc. v. Carlsbad Municipal Schools Bd. of Educ.*, 1997-NMCA-053, 941 P.2d 515 (N.M.App.1997).

◆   The Pennsylvania Milk Marketing Law established a state administrative board with the power to fix minimum wholesale and retail milk prices in the state. The law required the board to base minimum prices upon market conditions affecting the local milk industry including the amount necessary to yield a reasonable profit for producers. **The school district of Philadelphia claimed that the Milk Marketing Law resulted in an overcharge by producers of $1 million annually** for milk supplied to its students. The district challenged a board order fixing minimum prices at a level that the district asserted was over three cents too high for each half-pint unit. The district and a consumer organization appealed the board order to the Commonwealth Court of Pennsylvania.

The district argued that the law violated the Commerce Clause of the U.S. Constitution, which prohibits states from imposing unjustifiable burdens on interstate commerce. **The court upheld the law, finding that the minimum pricing scheme took many appropriate economic factors into consideration, did not discriminate against out-of-state dealers, and did not unduly burden interstate commerce.** The law was geographically neutral, and in the contested action, the board had considered information from one out-of-state producer in setting the price. The law placed only an incidental burden on interstate commerce, and the board had provided all interested parties with the appropriate level of due process in setting the new minimum price. The court rejected the district's argument that the board should have placed more emphasis on the ability of consumers to pay the new minimum price. *School Dist. of Philadelphia v. Pennsylvania Milk Marketing Bd.*, 683 A.2d 972 (Pa.Commw.1996).

◆   An Arizona school board ordered a contractor to stop working on a project for over two months because of problems obtaining building permits. The contractor claimed that the board breached its contract. The contractor filed for arbitration under a contractual clause, and an Arizona trial court refused to stay arbitration. **The Arizona Court of Appeals held that an Arizona statute preserved the contractor's right to arbitrate delay-related claims, but that all procurement-related claims must be resolved under procedures specified by the board**. The Supreme Court of Arizona reinstated the trial court's decision, ruling that the board had exceeded its authority by adopting a contractual remedy procedure in contravention of the statute. The contractor was entitled to arbitrate all of its claims, plus its attorneys' fees and costs. *Canon School Dist. No. 50 v. W.E.S. Const. Co., Inc.*, 869 P.2d 500 (Ariz.1994).

◆   An Indiana community school solicited bids for its school bus contract. The day after bids were received, the school board adopted an affirmative action form. Two weeks later, the board rejected all bids for the contract, declared an emergency rebidding and changed a specification. **A bus company that had served the school for at least 16 years submitted bids both times and alleged that it was the lowest responsible bidder**. The school board awarded the contract to another bidder, and the bus company sought review in an Indiana trial court. The court ruled that the board's failure to give any notice of the changed specification violated Indiana's public bidding statute. It enjoined the board from granting any bid based on this faulty procedure and remanded the case to the board. The bus company appealed this decision, claiming that there should be no remand and that it should have been awarded the contract as the lowest responsible bidder.

The Court of Appeals of Indiana, Second District, held that the trial court had properly enjoined the board from awarding the contract because of its irregular bidding procedure. It further held that the trial court could only remand the case to the board for further proceedings. The bus company's argument that it should be automatically awarded the contract due to its prior low bid was without merit. Under Indiana law, only the school board could properly make the decision to award a contract. The court of appeals affirmed the trial court's decision, remanding the case to the school board for solicitation of new bids under the proper procedure. *M & M Bus Co., Inc. v. Muncie Community School Corp.*, 627 N.E.2d 862 (Ind.App.2d Dist.1994).

II. DESEGREGATION

In Brown v. Board of Education, *347 U.S. 483, 74 S.Ct. 686, 98 L.Ed. 873 (1954), the U.S. Supreme Court declared unconstitutional separate but equal systems of segregation in public schools. Fourteen years after its landmark decision in Brown, the Court responded to widespread resistance by school districts to federal court desegregation orders by ruling that segregation must be eliminated "root and branch." Green v. County School Bd. of New Kent*

County, *391 U.S. 430, 88 S.Ct. 1689, 20 L.Ed.2d 716 (1968). By 1992, the Court had undergone a major political and ideological shift and consequently declared that formerly segregated, dual school districts could be released from federal court supervision upon a demonstration of good faith compliance with a desegregation decree where the "vestiges of past discrimination have been eliminated to the extent practicable."* Freeman v. Pitts, *503 U.S. 467, 112 S.Ct. 1430, 118 L.Ed.2d 108 (1992). Courts still rely on the factors identified by* Green *in determining whether a district should be declared unitary and released from federal court supervision, but subject to the reduced standard of scrutiny stated in* Freeman, Bd. of Educ. of Oklahoma City Pub. Schools v. Dowell, *498 U.S. 237, 111 S.Ct. 630, 112 L.Ed.2d 715 (1991), and* Missouri v. Jenkins, *495 U.S. 33, 110 S.Ct. 1651, 109 L.Ed.2d 31 (1990).*

A. Release from Federal Court Supervision

The test for releasing a school system from federal court supervision as stated by the Supreme Court in *Freeman* and *Dowell* is whether there has been compliance with the decree, whether retention of the case by the court is necessary or practicable to achieve compliance with the decree, and whether the school district has demonstrated a good faith commitment to the desegregation decree to the public and to African-American parents and students. The *Freeman* decision is also important for approving the concept of the withdrawal of federal court supervision in stages as partial unitary status is achieved with respect to specific programs and areas including facilities, faculty and staff assignments, extracurricular activities, transportation and student assignments.

♦   In 1969, a Georgia school system was enjoined by a federal district court from discriminating on the basis of race and was required to close all legally recognized black schools. The system complied and the case remained inactive until the 1970s. In 1983, **the plaintiff class returned to court contending that the school system improperly limited minority transfers to a predominantly white school and that the proposed expansion of a white high school would perpetuate segregation**. The district court ruled that the school system had achieved unitary status, and did not have a discriminatory intent in deciding to expand the high school. The U.S. Court of Appeals, Eleventh Circuit, reversed, stating that the school system could not be declared unitary without a hearing, and that until it was declared unitary, its intent was immaterial. On remand, the district court held that the school system had not yet achieved unitary status. The school system would achieve unitary status when all schools possessed minority staffs within 15 percent of the system average. However, the court refused to impose additional duties on the school system in the areas of student assignment, transportation, and extracurricular activities. Both parties appealed the ruling.

The court of appeals stated that the system had not discharged its duty in the areas of student assignment, transportation, and extracurricular activities by closing all legally recognized black schools in response to the 1969 order. The court stated that the system would not achieve unitary status until it maintained at least three years of racial equality in the six categories set out in *Green*: student assignment, faculty, staff, transportation, extracurricular activities, and facilities. The court of appeals ordered the district court to require the system to file a plan in accordance with its opinion. The U.S. Supreme Court, however, held on appeal that the *Green* framework did not need to be applied as construed by the court of appeals. **Through relinquishing control in areas deemed to be unitary, a court and school district may more effectively concentrate on the areas in need of further attention. The Court held that the "incremental" approach was constitutional**, and that a court may declare that it will order no further remedy in any area which is found to be unitary. The order of the court of appeals was reversed, and the case was remanded to the district court. *Freeman v. Pitts,* 503 U.S. 467, 112 S.Ct. 1430, 118 L.Ed.2d 108 (1992).

On remand from the Supreme Court and the Eleventh Circuit, the district court accepted the Supreme Court's invitation to consider the three remaining issues that prevented a finding of unitariness and release from federal court jurisdiction. The court considered further evidence in three areas: faculty assignments, resource allocation and good faith by the school district. The district presented evidence that there was no greater than a 15 percent variation in minority staff rates among district schools and that district spending per student was also within an acceptable range. **The court rejected the complaining parties' evidence that the district continued to discriminate in its resource allocation and that an unacceptable gap persisted in student achievement which could not be explained by nonracial factors**. The court characterized the complaining parties' evidence as not demonstrating a pattern of discrimination or absence of good faith by the district. It therefore granted the district's motion to be released from federal court jurisdiction. *Mills v. Freeman*, 942 F.Supp. 1449 (N.D.Ga.1996).

♦ In 1972, a federal district court issued an injunction imposing a desegregation plan on Oklahoma City public schools. In 1977, the court found that the school district had achieved unitary status and issued an order terminating the case. In 1984, because of an increase in young black students, which would result in them being bused farther away, the board adopted the Student Reassignment Plan (SRP). The SRP assigned students who were in grades K-4 to their neighborhood schools, but continued busing for grades 5-12. The parents who had brought the original desegregation case filed a motion to reopen the case, claiming that the SRP was a return to segregation. **The federal district court refused to reopen the case and held that its 1977 finding that the school district was unitary could not be relitigated**. The parents appealed to the U.S. Court of Appeals, Tenth Circuit. The court held that the trial court's 1977 finding was binding, but this did not mean that the 1972 injunction itself was terminated. The case was remanded to determine if the injunction should be lifted. On remand, the trial court found that the SRP was not designed with discriminatory intent and ordered the injunction lifted. The case was again appealed to the U.S. Court of Appeals which reversed the lower court's decision. The school board then petitioned the U.S. Supreme Court for review and its petition was granted.

The Supreme Court first determined that the 1977 order did not dissolve the desegregation decree and that the district court's finding that the school district was unitary was too ambiguous to bar the parents from challenging later actions by the board. However, the Court stressed that supervision of local school districts by the federal courts was meant as a temporary means to remedy past discrimination. The Court remanded the case and instructed the trial court to determine whether the school district had complied with constitutional requirements when it adopted the SRP. *Bd. of Educ. of Oklahoma City Public Schools v. Dowell*, 498 U.S. 237, 111 S.Ct. 630, 112 L.Ed.2d 715 (1991).

On remand, the district court reaffirmed its prior findings without allowing additional hearings. It ruled that the parties had already received a full opportunity to present their evidence and adopted the school board's proposed order almost verbatim. The court of appeals affirmed the district court's decision, ruling that it had not violated the Supreme Court's remand instructions by failing to hold a new hearing and by adopting the board's proposed order. The school board had complied with the desegregation decree and maintained a unitary school system. **Because the school board met its burden of showing that the current racial imbalance at its schools was not traceable to prior violations, the court affirmed the district court's decision**. *Dowell v. Bd. of Educ. of Oklahoma City Pub. Schools*, 8 F.3d 1501 (10th Cir.1993).

◆ A group of citizens filed an action in 1989 on behalf of black and Hispanic students who claimed intentional discrimination by the Rockford Board of Education that resulted in racially segregated schools. The city had been the subject of earlier desegregation litigation and had operated under a remedial decree as early as 1973. A federal court held in 1994 that the board engaged in intentional race discrimination. **In 1996, the court fashioned a complex remedial decree** that was vacated in large part by the U.S. Court of Appeals, Seventh Circuit, due to the imposition of racial quotas on employees, classroom composition, student tracking and cheerleading squads. **The board moved the district court to dissolve the decree, arguing that it had fully complied** with the objectives of the decree and that remaining inequalities in educational achievement could not be attributed to its own illegal conduct. A federal magistrate judge ruled that some of the provisions of the decree must remain in effect for at least six more years.

The board appealed to the Seventh Circuit, which noted that the decree had cost the district $238 million through 1999 and that the parties' legal fees alone were almost $20 million. It said **the Rockford schools were now less segregated than those in any previous case in which a system was declared unitary** by a court. The minority composition range established by the magistrate was tighter than that imposed in most desegregation cases, requiring that each school's minority population deviate no more than 15 percentage points from that of the district's overall minority population. The court rejected the complaining parties' assertion that the decree should remain in effect an additional 15 years, stating the decree was not intended to operate in perpetuity, and the state and its subdivisions had a right to restoration of control over its institutions once its objectives were achieved. Although minority educational achievement lagged behind that of white students, the court found that the board had no legal duty to remove vestiges of societal discrimination for which it was not responsible. Factors such as poverty, parents' education and employment, peer pressure, and ethnic culture might be created or exacerbated by discrimination, but the board had no federal constitutional duty to remedy them. There was no evidence of bad faith by the board and the court reversed and remanded the case with instructions to grant the relief it requested. *People Who Care v. Rockford Board of Education*, 246 F.3d 1073 (7th Cir. 2001).

◆   The Muscogee County, Georgia, public school system responded to a federal court order to desegregate its schools in 1971 with a student assignment plan intended to achieve racial balance in its schools. In just two years, 57 of 64 county schools were within 10 percent of the target racial balance. However, **demographic changes in the 1980s changed the racial composition of county schools,** and by 1991, several racially identifiable schools existed. The school board implemented neighborhood school and majority-to-minority transfer plans to address the resegregation problem. A federal court declared the system unitary, releasing it from federal court jurisdiction.

The students appealed to the U.S. Court of Appeals, Eleventh Circuit, arguing that the district court decision declaring the system unitary was erroneous. The court of appeals stated that a district court must divest itself of jurisdiction where the constitutional violation has been remedied by the elimination of the vestiges of past discrimination to the extent practicable, and school officials have demonstrated good faith compliance with a desegregation plan. In this case, **the board had responded to dramatic demographic changes in the county by developing good faith plans that demonstrated a commitment to the desegregation plan.** The board had complied with all court orders and eliminated vestiges of past discrimination to the extent practicable. The court affirmed the final case dismissal and declaration of unitary status. *Lockett v. Bd. of Educ. of Muscogee County School Dist., Georgia,* 111 F.3d 839 (11th Cir.1997).

◆   The state of Missouri established two vocational education systems for the St. Louis metropolitan area during the mid-1960s. One of the systems served the county and the other served the city of St. Louis. **A federal district court held that the dual system created a racially segregated vocational education system.** It directed the state, U.S. government and the city board to develop a consolidation or merger plan for the separate systems. The parties reached an agreement that refrained from the creation of a consolidated, integrated vocational school system but permitted the county and city systems to operate their own schools and set racial goals for a five-year period during which the state would provide funding. By 1991, the court designated the county school system as the sole provider of vocational education for the area and ordered the state to pay interdistrict transportation and other costs.

The court then authorized the creation of the St. Louis Career Education District to ensure a quality, integrated vocational education system for the area. The following year, the county district filed a motion seeking a declaration that the system had achieved unitary status, which the district court denied. The state and county district appealed to the U.S. Court of Appeals, Eighth Circuit, which held that the county district had not achieved unitary status. **The district would be required to show that it had eliminated all vestiges of the prior unconstitutional segregated system before federal court jurisdiction could be relinquished.** The court remanded the case to the district court for a formal hearing. *Liddell by Liddell v. Bd. of Educ. of City of St. Louis,* 121 F.3d 1201 (8th Cir.1997).

◆   In 1952, the Supreme Court of Delaware ordered the desegregation of certain schools previously attended only by white students. An appeal of this decision to the U.S. Supreme Court was consolidated with *Brown v. Bd. of Educ.,* in which the Court first held that the racial segregation of public schools violated the Equal Protection Clause. The case was remanded to the Supreme Court of Delaware. **Because many Delaware schools remained racially identifiable, the U.S. District Court for the District of Delaware assumed jurisdiction of the case and in 1978 issued a remedial decree calling for interdistrict remedies** among four school districts in northern New Castle County. The court held in 1995 that each of the districts had achieved unitary status and a group representing students attending district schools appealed to the U.S. Court of Appeals, Third Circuit.

The court stated that the test for discontinuing federal supervision of school districts under desegregation decrees is whether the vestiges of past discrimination have been eliminated to the extent practicable. In this case, **the school districts had been ordered to consolidate urban and suburban districts and had achieved some of the most racially balanced schools in the nation through student reassignment**. The court rejected the argument that unlawful segregation persisted within specific schools, classrooms and programs, including special education programs. The U.S. Supreme Court has held that no particular racial balance must be achieved in each school, grade or classroom before a school system may be declared unitary. Because there was no evidence linking current racially identifiable conditions to the prior segregated system, the court of appeals affirmed the district court order that the districts had achieved unitary status. *Coalition To Save Our Children v. State Bd. of Educ. of the State of Delaware*, 90 F.3d 752 (3d Cir. 1996).

◆   Mississippi maintained a dual system of public education at the university level—one set of universities for whites, and another set for blacks. In 1981, the State Board of Trustees issued "Mission Statements" to remedy this, classifying the three flagship historically white institutions (HWI) as "comprehensive" universities, redesignating one of the historically black institutions (HBI) as an "urban" university and characterizing the rest as "regional" institutions. However, the universities remained racially identifiable. **A federal district court found that state policies need merely be racially neutral, developed in good faith, and not contribute to the racial identifiability of each institution**. The court held that Mississippi was currently fulfilling its duty to desegregate. The U.S. Court of Appeals, Fifth Circuit, affirmed. The U.S. Supreme Court granted review.

The Supreme Court held that the district court had applied the wrong legal standard in ruling that Mississippi had brought itself into compliance with the Equal Protection Clause. **If a state perpetuates policies and practices traceable to its prior dual system that continue to have segregative effects, and such policies are without sound educational justification and can be practicably eliminated, the policies violate the Clause**. This is true even if the state has abolished the legal requirement that the races be separated and has established neutral policies. The proper inquiry is whether existing racial identifiability is attributable to the state. Because the district court's standard did not ask the appropriate questions, the court of appeals had erred in affirming the judgment. Applying the proper standard, several surviving aspects of Mississippi's prior dual system were constitutionally suspect. First, the use of higher minimum ACT composite scores at the HWIs, along with the state's refusal to consider high school grade performance was suspect. Second, the unnecessary duplication of programs at HBIs and HWIs was suspect. Third, the mission statements' reflection of previous policies to perpetuate racial separation was suspect. Finally, the state's policy of operating eight universities had to be examined to determine if it was educationally justifiable. *U.S. v. Fordice*, 505 U.S. 717, 112 S.Ct. 2727, 120 L.Ed.2d 575 (1992).

On remand to the U.S. District Court for the Northern District of Mississippi, the court entered a remedial decree prohibiting the state from maintaining remnants of the prior segregated system and mandating specific relief in areas of admissions and funding. However, the court refused to order the relief requested by the complaining parties which would significantly increase the number of African-Americans accepted for regular admission at state universities. The complaining parties claimed that the district court order's reliance on a summer remedial program to boost African-American admissions was inappropriate and the parties appealed to the U.S. Court of Appeals, Fifth Circuit. **The court agreed with the complaining parties that the district court's order affirming the elimination of many remedial courses had to be reconsidered, along with its finding that use of college entrance scores as a criterion for scholarships was not traceable to the illegal system of segregation**. The court remanded for clarification the status of a proposal to merge two universities to eliminate unnecessary program duplication, as well as questions of increasing the other-race presence at two HBIs and issues of accreditation and funding. The court affirmed many aspects of the district court decision as consistent with the *Fordice* decision, significantly affirming its decision to maintain admissions standards that ensured educational soundness. *Ayers v. Fordice*, 111 F.3d 1183 (5th Cir.1997).

B. Compliance with Desegregation Orders

After a court finds a school district or other government agency liable for maintaining racially segregated facilities, the agency becomes subject to the jurisdiction of the court and court orders requiring remedial action. Many desegregation orders come in the form of a consent decree, which is a court-approved agreement of the parties to implement particular desegregation programs.

◆   The San Francisco Unified School District (SFUSD) joined the San Francisco NAACP in a 1983 consent decree that prohibited any of nine specified ethnic groups from making up more than 45 percent of the students in any school. The decree also required at least four ethnic groups to be represented in each school. Eleven years later, three students of Chinese descent alleged that SFUSD rejected their requests to attend their school of choice because each school had reached its limit for students of Chinese descent under the decree. They sued SFUSD in a federal district court, seeking an order that the decree violated their constitutional rights. **The court rejected the students' assertion that the decree was unconstitutional at the present time, since there was evidence of past discrimination by SFUSD**. Because the class had agreed to the consent decree, there was no issue as to its present binding effect. However, there was a question as to its continuing appropriation, and the court denied the students' summary judgment motion.

The students appealed to the Ninth Circuit, petitioning the court for an order that would prevent the matter from proceeding to a scheduled trial. The court upheld the district court's finding that the consent decree was binding upon the students with regard to its appropriateness in 1983. It had also correctly left open for consideration at trial the question of the continuing propriety of the decree, in view of SFUSD's history of discrimination against students of Chinese ancestry and evidence that vestiges of segregation remained in its schools. **At trial, SFUSD would have the burden of demonstrating that the racial quotas imposed by the consent decree were narrowly tailored to further a compelling government interest**. *Ho by Ho v. San Francisco Unified School Dist.*, 147 F.3d 854 (9th Cir.1998).

◆   A Maryland school district that was under federal court supervision to desegregate its schools had over 4,500 students on waiting lists for its magnet programs. Less than ten percent of the waiting lists were made up of non-African American students, creating the possibility that students on magnet waiting lists would not be placed within the court's desegregation guidelines. **The school board resolved to seek the court's permission to allow the admission of 330 African-American students to magnet programs without regard to racial guidelines**. The complaining parties in the desegregation lawsuit learned from media reports that the board intended to modify the magnet school admission guidelines, and filed a motion in the court for a scheduling order. The court issued the order and required the board to file a motion for leave to modify the magnet school admission guidelines for the upcoming school year.

The board filed the motion and presented evidence of the expected difficulty in complying with the magnet school component of the desegregation plan, given the increase in African-American students in the school system, the budgetary limits on magnet school recruiting, and the increased numbers of Asian and Latino students in the school system. The court stated that the board's resolution had seriously limited the opportunity of the court and the complaining parties to meaningfully review its actions. However, admitting only 330 African-American students to the magnet program for the present school year would not significantly harm the process of desegregating county schools. **The court approved the limited admission of students into the magnet program for the coming school year without regard for its admission guidelines**. *Vaughns v. Bd. of Educ. of Prince George's County*, 941 F.Supp. 579 (D.Md.1996).

C. Liability Issues

Courts that review the actions of government officials in desegregation cases may find that liability exists for civil rights violations where actions by the officials foreseeably perpetuate racial segregation in schools. Relief for constitutional violations may be apportioned among government agencies and school district entities since there may be liability at state, county and local levels.

1. Government Liability

◆   Student assignments in Boston schools were under federal court supervision from 1974 until 1987. A court order required the examination schools to set aside 35 percent of each entering class for students of African-American and Hispanic descent. In 1987, the First Circuit held that student assignment in the school system was no longer segregated. The city's examination schools retained the policy even after federal district court supervision ended. The policy was modified in response to a 1995 reverse discrimination suit. **The modified policy admitted the top 50 percent of applicants, but allowed the consideration of racial or ethnic categories for the remaining half of the class**. A white applicant who was not admitted to the school, but would have been admitted if not for the modified policy, filed a federal district court action against the school committee, asserting constitutional rights violation. The court upheld the school's admission policy as furthering a compelling government interest in student diversity.

The student appealed to the U.S. Court of Appeals, First Circuit, which held that student diversity itself is not a compelling government interest that could justify a race-based selection policy. Strong constitutional scrutiny applies whenever a government entity attempts to draw distinction based on race, and diversity did not satisfy the standard. **The school system had been declared unitary over 10 years previously and the policy could not be justified in the name of redressing past vestiges of discrimination**. The district court had impermissibly credited certain anecdotal evidence, including testimony that the policy was required to address an achievement gap between minority and white students. Because the policy violated the equal protection rights of the white applicant, she was entitled to be admitted to the Latin School, and the court reversed the judgment. *Wessman v. Gittens*, 160 F.3d 790 (1st Cir.1998).

◆   A federal district court declared the Akron City School District unitary in 1980. The Ohio legislature passed state open enrollment laws, permitting students to transfer to adjacent school districts that have agreed by resolution to allow transfers. Districts can block student transfers to maintain appropriate racial balances. **The Akron school board implemented a policy prohibiting the transfer of white students to other districts** in order to maintain an appropriate racial balance in its schools. A group representing white parents and students from Akron who wished to transfer out of the district filed a lawsuit against the district in a federal court seeking a declaration that the policy was unconstitutional and an order prohibiting its enforcement. The court considered the group's motion for a preliminary order. The court stated that the policy created a racial classification that was subject to strict judicial scrutiny, requiring the district to justify the policy by showing that it was necessary to further a compelling state interest. **The district failed to demonstrate that a disproportionate number of white students were taking advantage of the transfer law or that the policy was necessary to maintain an appropriate racial balance** in Akron schools. The district had successfully defended its status as a unitary school district in federal court, removing doubt that it was guilty of past discrimination against minority students. The evidence did not indicate a massive transfer of white students from district schools, and the policy was too drastic to meet the perceived threat of white flight. The court granted the group's request for a preliminary injunction prohibiting the board from enforcing the policy. *Equal Open Enrollment Ass'n v. Bd. of Educ. of Akron City School Dist.*, 937 F.Supp. 700 (N.D.Ohio 1996).

2.   Interdistrict Remedies

◆   Busing has been utilized by many school districts in order to achieve racial balance. Courts have affirmed intradistrict school district desegregation plans that have included busing. See *Columbus Bd. of Educ. v. Penick*, 443 U.S. 449, 99 S.Ct.

2941, 61 L.Ed.2d 666 (1979). However, in the landmark Detroit school busing case, **the U.S. Supreme Court rejected a plan which would have required multi-district, interdistrict busing**. The Court said that there was no evidence that the districts outside Detroit which were included in the plan either themselves operated segregated school systems or by their actions affected segregation in other districts. The Court went on to say that absent some interdistrict constitutional violations with interdistrict effects, racial segregation existing in one district could not be remedied by interdistrict solutions. *Milliken v. Bradley*, 418 U.S. 717, 94 S.Ct. 311, 41 L.Ed.2d 1069 (1974).

♦   In 1979, **a federal district court required the interdistrict busing of students between primarily black Indianapolis public schools and primarily white public schools in local suburban areas**. The court found that Indianapolis Public School District (IPSD) boundaries were deliberately maintained to preserve segregated schools and that the city's housing authority refused to build public housing that would encourage desegregation. Years later, the Indianapolis school board moved the court to lift the busing injunction, observing that the lawsuit was 30 years old and claiming that the district had achieved unitary status. The court denied the motion, and ordered all kindergarten students in designated sections of the city to participate in mandatory busing, rescinding an earlier order permitting parents to select busing at their option. IPSD appealed to the U.S. Court of Appeals, Seventh Circuit. **The court held that the school board should have received an opportunity to present evidence at a hearing to consider whether the order should be dissolved**. The district court had erroneously denied the board this opportunity. In addition, the district court had improperly modified the decree to include the compulsory busing of kindergartners. The court vacated and remanded the case, so that the district court could develop a record based upon an evidentiary hearing. *U.S. v. Bd. of School Commissioners of City of Indianapolis*, 128 F.3d 507 (7th Cir.1997).

♦   An Arkansas parent filed a lawsuit against four Arkansas school districts and state education officials in the U.S. District Court for the Eastern District of Arkansas, claiming that their actions intentionally caused the districts to remain racially segregated. **He asserted that a statute permitting students to transfer out of their residence school districts had been used to resegregate schools which had formerly been under federal court supervision**. One of the districts had gone from a racial composition of 80 percent black and 20 percent white to 97 percent black and three percent white. The parent requested consolidation of the four districts, creation of magnet schools and other programs to improve the racial balance of county schools. The court entered judgment for the school districts and officials, and the parent appealed to the U.S. Court of Appeals, Eighth Circuit.
   The court held that the district court could reasonably have found that the transfer statute had not been the cause of the present racial imbalances in the four school districts. Evidence indicated that many transfers had been revoked among the districts under another statute prohibiting transfers that had an adverse effect on racial balances in school districts that were formerly under court supervision. There was contrary evidence that resegregation was caused by changing demographics and the lack of job opportunities in the region. Because there was no evidence of an interdistrict violation of the constitutional rights of students, the

court affirmed the district court order dismissing the case. *Edgerson on Behalf of Edgerson v. Clinton*, 86 F.3d 833 (8th Cir.1996).

◆   Montgomery County, Alabama, schools were under federal court supervision from 1964 to 1993, when the U.S. District Court for the Middle District of Alabama declared county schools unitary. During the years of court supervision, the Majority to Minority Transfer Program enabled students to freely transfer to schools where the student's race was in the minority. After the declaration of unity, the school system retained the transfer program, but revised it in response to concerns of athletic recruiting in predominately African-American schools. **Under the new transfer policy students would lose a year of eligibility under the majority to minority transfer program**. This policy complied with the rules used by the state athletic association. A group of African-American students who wished to transfer to predominately white schools objected to the amended policy and claimed that it discriminated against them on the basis of race. The district court issued a temporary restraining order against enforcement of the transfer policy, then conducted a trial.

The court reviewed the policy in conjunction with the county's history of court supervision. The board had a legitimate and substantial justification for prohibiting athletic recruitment at its high schools, since this practice had a negative effect on predominately African-American schools. **Even though African-American athletes might be disproportionately affected by the transfer policy, the legitimate school interest in curtailing athletic recruitment outweighed this interest**. The result of enforcing the transfer policy brought the county schools into conformity with state athletic association rules and there was no evidence of intentional discrimination by the board. *Young by and through Young v. Montgomery County Bd. of Educ.*, 922 F.Supp. 544 (M.D.Ala.1996).

3. Budget Issues

◆   In 1977, the Kansas City, Missouri, School District (KCMSD), its school board and a group of resident students sued the State of Missouri and a number of suburban Kansas City school districts in the U.S. District Court for the Western District of Missouri, claiming that the state had caused and perpetuated racial segregation in Kansas City schools. Following realignment of the parties to make the KCMSD a nominal defendant, **the district court held that the state and KCMSD were liable for an intradistrict constitutional violation**. The defendants were ordered to eliminate all vestiges of state-imposed segregation. Because the district's student population was almost 70 percent African-American, the district court ordered a wide range of quality education plans which converted every high school and middle school, and some elementary schools, into magnet schools to attract white students. This action was based upon the court's finding that KCMSD student achievement levels still lagged behind national averages in some grades. **The state contested its court-ordered responsibility to help fund capital improvements for KCMSD schools. It also contested district court orders requiring it to share in the cost of teacher salary increases and quality education plans**.

The U.S. Court of Appeals, Eighth Circuit, affirmed the district court orders. The state appealed to the U.S. Supreme Court. The Court observed that the district court's remedial plan had been based on a budget that exceeded KCMSD's authority to tax. There was a lack of evidence in the district court record to substantiate the theory that continuing lack of academic achievement in the district was the result of past segregation. **The Court determined that the district court had exceeded its authority by ordering the construction of a superior school system to attract white students from suburban and private schools**. Its mandate was to remove the racial identity of KCMSD schools, and the interdistrict remedy went beyond the intradistrict violation. The magnet district concept of KCMSD schools could not be supported by the existence of white flight and the district court orders for state contribution to salary increases, quality education programs and capital improvements were reversed. *Missouri v. Jenkins*, 115 S.Ct. 2038, 132 L.Ed.2d 63 (1995). See also *Missouri v. Jenkins*, 495 U.S. 33, 110 S.Ct. 1651, 109 L.Ed.2d 31 (1990), where in earlier stages of the litigation, the Court prevented the district court from imposing a property tax increase, ruling that relief should be directed against local authorities who could then impose the tax increase.

The district court established a remedial plan and budget for the 1996–1997 school year and ordered the phaseout of a voluntary interdistrict transfer program involving 13 students in a suburban district. The state of Missouri appealed these aspects of the decision to the U.S. Court of Appeals, Eighth Circuit, and the class representing African-American students in Kansas City schools cross-appealed an order prohibiting the use of desegregation funds to market magnet school programs to private school students. **The court approved of the marketing and recruiting efforts directed at nonminority private school students**, finding nothing in the Supreme Court's decision preventing it. **It also approved of the continued funding of the interdistrict program while present enrollees continued their education**. The court approved the inclusion of an extended day program within the 1996–1997 budget. However, it remanded to the district court certain remedial and budgetary issues concerning the retention of permanent substitutes at district schools. *Jenkins by Jenkins v. State of Missouri*, 103 F.3d 731 (8th Cir.1997).

On appeal, the full Eighth Circuit reversed the district court's determination that the district had achieved unitary status, finding the court acted improperly in not holding a hearing to allow both sides to present evidence on the issue prior to issuing a ruling. Due process required a hearing before the district court could make a decision regarding the unitary status of the school system. According to the court, both parties should have been given notice and an opportunity to prepare for the unitary hearing instead of the district court issuing a sua sponte ruling. The district court decision was reversed. *Jenkins by Jenkins v. State of Missouri*, 216 F.3d 720 (8th Cir. 2000).

◆   A group of African-American students filed a lawsuit against a South Carolina school district in 1962, seeking an order to compel the desegregation of its schools. The U.S. District Court for the District of South Carolina entered an order in 1970 requiring the district to implement a desegregation plan. The U.S. intervened in the case in 1990, claiming that the school district violated the 1970 order by maintaining segregated schools. **The school district filed a motion to join the state of South Carolina, claiming that it was partly responsible for perpetuating segregated schools**. The court rejected the state's claim for Eleventh Amendment immunity and approved a consent order resolving several remedial issues. It ordered the state defendants to participate in desegregation remedies, fund necessary transportation services and pay 15 percent of the capital costs and operating expenses of implementing the desegregation order. The state appealed to the U.S. Court of Appeals, Fourth Circuit.

The court held that had the U.S. or the original plaintiffs filed the claim against the state, the district court could have apportioned relief between the school district and state. However, **because only the school district had sought relief against the state, the district court could not order any relief against the state.** Because the U.S. and the original plaintiffs had failed to name the state as a defendant, there was no basis for the school district's claim against the state for contribution. The court reversed the district court judgment pertaining to the imposition of liability on the state, but otherwise affirmed its judgment. *Stanley v. Darlington County School Dist.*, 84 F.3d 707 (4th Cir.1996).

Prior to the release of the court of appeals' decision, the school district revised the selection and admission process for a new magnet school by eliminating a set-aside of seats from the school's attendance zone and the initial requirement for a 50/50 student racial composition. The U.S. objected to the revised selection and admission criteria, and the court held a hearing to consider the revisions It determined that the school board had ignored research by the magnet school task force and disregarded expert opinions in imposing the revisions. **Evidence indicated that a 50/50 racial composition was important to prevent a racial identity in the community which might stigmatize the school.** It was also important for resident students to enjoy the benefits of the school to engage community support. Because the school board action removed all desegregation mechanisms from the selection and admission criteria, it jeopardized the success of the magnet school and the orderly desegregation of the district. The court found the district in default of its obligation to establish a magnet school and held that its prior interim order remained in effect. *Stanley v. Darlington County School Dist.*, 915 F.Supp. 764 (D.S.C.1996).

III. SCHOOL DISTRICT OPERATIONS

School district powers are defined by state laws, and actions exceeding statutory directives may be set aside by a reviewing court. If state law provides, school district territories may be altered by annexation and detachment where economics or demographics make such action necessary.

A. School Closing and District Dissolution Issues

◆   A New Jersey regional high school district served six municipalities. Five of the municipal education boards and governing bodies applied to the county school superintendent to dissolve the district under a state law allowing for such action where any constituent district suffers an excessive debt burden, an efficient school system cannot be maintained, insufficient students will be left in any constituent district, or for any other reason which the regional board may deem sufficient. **The superintendent issued a report recommending against dissolution, but four of the constituent education boards and governing bodies obtained approval by the state education commissioner for permission to hold a referendum to dissolve the regional district.** A district with a tax levy per student that was only half the average amount of the other districts objected to the commissioner's order. A majority of regional voters elected to dissolve the regional district, and the objecting district appealed to the Superior Court of New Jersey, Appellate Division.

The court held that none of the three enumerated statutory reasons for denying a referendum were satisfied here. **The objecting district also failed to show that the dissolution was inconsistent with the state's obligation to assure the maintenance of a thorough and efficient school system**. The lack of a sufficient tax base by the objecting district was not a policy reflected in the statute, and the commissioner's decision was affirmed. The court also rejected the complaining district's argument that the action violated the state open public meetings act because it had failed to promptly challenge the board's action until it actually filed the lawsuit after the election. *In re Dissolution of Union County Regional High School Dist. No. 1*, 298 N.J.Super. 1, 688 A.2d 1082 (1997).

◆   The North Carolina General Assembly passed legislation consolidating three school systems in Guilford County, and provided for a county referendum vote to select a merger plan that would take effect two years after the legislation was passed. Before voters were presented with the referendum, the Guilford County School Board, one of the three constituent school boards of the proposed consolidated district, extended the contract of its superintendent for two years beyond the date of the prospective merger. The contract extension provided that the superintendent would be entitled to additional compensation in the event of a merger. Voters ratified the merger, and the constituent district school boards ceased to exist. **Eleven days before the defunct Guilford board's dissolution, it agreed to pay the superintendent $275,000 as additional compensation** and issued a check to him in this amount. The new board for the consolidated system sought a return of these funds, but was unsuccessful and discontinued its efforts.

A group of resident taxpayers brought an action against the new school board and the former superintendent to recover the funds. A North Carolina trial court granted summary judgment to the taxpayers, ordering the superintendent to pay the new board $275,000 plus interest. The superintendent appealed to the Court of Appeals of North Carolina. **The court held that the defunct board had acted without actual authority and that the settlement with the superintendent was unenforceable**. Adoption of the merger act impliedly repealed the defunct board's ability to enter into contracts after the effective date of the merger. The court rejected the superintendent's claim that the taxpayers had no standing to advance the action, and the decision to grant them summary judgment was affirmed. *Guilford County Bd. of Comm'rs v. Trogdon*, 478 S.E.2d 643 (N.C.App.1996).

◆   A Kentucky school board operated two high schools in different parts of the same county. **The board determined that, because of declining enrollment and older facilities, one of the high schools should be closed**. The board held several public hearings to consider its options. When it adopted a plan to close one of the schools, a group of county residents filed a complaint in a Kentucky trial court claiming that the decision was arbitrary and capricious, and that it violated provisions of the Kentucky Constitution. The trial court granted their request for a restraining order prohibiting the school board from taking any action to close the school pending a hearing. It then ordered the school board to reconsider its prior order in an open meeting. The board considered public comments and voted to close the school immediately. The trial court rejected the residents' motion for a new restraining order, dissolved the previous order and set aside the order prohibiting the board from implementing its prior decision to close the school. On appeal, **the Court of Appeals of Kentucky held that the school board had complied with all applicable provisions of Kentucky law in making its decision to close the school**. The board had complied with the state Open Meetings Act in publishing notice of the rescheduled hearing, and the constitutional complaint was without merit. The trial court decision was affirmed and the Supreme Court of Kentucky denied review of the case. *Coppage v. Ohio County Bd. of Educ.*, 860 S.W.2d 779 (Ky.App.1992).

B. Redistricting and Zoning

◆   A New York school district provided special education services at private, religious schools to students with disabilities who were members of the Satmar Hasidic group. The group's religious beliefs include segregation of school-aged boys and girls, and separation from mainstream society. A U.S. Supreme Court decision in 1985 prohibited the state from paying public school teachers for teaching on parochial school grounds. See *Aguilar v. Felton*, Chapter Thirteen, Section V.B., below. Hasidic children were then sent to public schools while the group continued to challenge the matter. **The state legislature passed a statute establishing a new, separate school district entirely within the Hasidic community. The district provided only special education services**, and Hasidic regular education students continued to attend private religious schools. New York taxpayers and an association of state school officials sought and obtained a state trial court declaration that the statute was unconstitutional. The New York Court of Appeals held that the statute conveyed a message of government endorsement of religion in violation of the Establishment Clause of the U.S. Constitution. The U.S. Supreme Court agreed to review the matter.

The Supreme Court held that a state may not delegate authority to a group chosen by religion. Although the statute did not expressly identify the Hasidim as recipients of governmental authority, it had clearly been passed to benefit them. The result was a purposeful and forbidden fusion of governmental and religious functions. **The creation of a school district for the religious community violated the Establishment Clause**. The legislation extended a special franchise to the Hasidim that violated the constitutional requirement of religious neutrality by the government. The statute crossed "the line from permissible accommodation to impermissible establishment," and the Supreme Court affirmed the judgment of the court of appeals. *Bd. of Educ. of Kiryas Joel Village School Dist. v. Grumet*, 512 U.S. 687, 114 S.Ct. 2481, 129 L.Ed.2d 546 (1994).

Eleven days later, the legislature repealed the law and passed new legislation allowing municipalities to establish their own school districts upon the satisfaction of several criteria. Noting that these criteria had the effect of restoring the Hasidic school district, the taxpayers renewed their state law challenge. A state trial court upheld the act. The taxpayers appealed to the New York Supreme Court, Appellate Division, where they argued that the new legislative criteria for authorizing school districts created the same result as under the prior unconstitutional law. The court agreed, and observed that one of the criteria was apparently meaningless and had been included only to limit the applicability of the statute and afford special treatment to village residents. **The legislation had no educational purpose, was not generally applicable and had been enacted as a subterfuge** to avoid the prior U.S. Supreme Court decision. The trial court decision was reversed and remanded, and the court declared the statute unconstitutional under the Establishment Clause. *Grumet v. Cuomo*, 647 N.Y.S.2d 565 (A.D.3d Dep't 1996).

A state appellate court agreed to review the case, and found that **despite the neutral statutory criteria in the amendments, the Hasidic village was the only municipality that could ever avail itself of the amendments**. Because the law applied only to municipalities in existence as of the effective date of the amendments, no other municipality could become eligible for redistricting, and the legislation impermissibly favored the Satmar sect. Since the law could be perceived as being for the sole benefit of the sect, the court affirmed the judgment for the taxpayers. *Grumet v. Cuomo*, 90 N.Y.2d 57, 659 N.Y.S.2d 173, 681 N.E.2d 340 (1997).

After a decision by the New York Supreme Court, Appellate Division invalidating the statute, the case reached the New York Court of Appeals, which held that despite the fact that the 1997 law was facially neutral with respect to religion, its effect only benefited Kiryas Joel residents, and its potential benefit extended to only one other district in the state. **Since other religious groups would be unable to benefit from the law in the manner enjoyed by the Satmar sect of Kiryas Joel, the law was not neutral in effect**, and violated the Establishment Clause. The law lacked a secular purpose, and had the primary effect of advancing religion. *Grumet v. Pataki,* 93 N.Y.2d 677, 720 N.E.2d 66 (N.Y. 1999).

◆   The Oklahoma Alcoholic Beverage Laws Enforcement Commission issued a liquor license to an applicant who proposed locating a liquor store on the same block and within 300 feet of a high school. **The action was approved even though a state law prohibits a retail liquor store from being located within 300 feet of a church or public school**. The commission granted the license before a group of objecting citizens was able to obtain a special court order to prohibit the licensure. The protesting citizens then amended their state court complaint against the director of the commission under the Oklahoma Administrative Procedures Act. The court dismissed the case, ruling that the citizens had no legal standing to contest the agency action. The Oklahoma Court of Appeals affirmed, and the citizens appealed to the Supreme Court of Oklahoma.

The court reviewed the applicable statutes and found that **even though the commission's action violated the law, the statutory scheme that created the commission did not permit intervening citizens to challenge the issuance of a liquor license**. The trial court decision on that issue was affirmed; however, parents of children residing within an affected school district had legal standing to protest the granting of a license in potential violation of Oklahoma law. This right arose under another state law which permits a state district court to compel a state agency to perform a specific duty arising from its statutory duties, or to enjoin the breach of an official duty. The district court decision was affirmed without prejudice, with the effect of allowing further proceedings for the parents to challenge the action. *Bird v. Willis*, 927 P.2d 547 (Okla.1996).

◆   A group of Wisconsin residents petitioned for the detachment of their property from the school district in which the property was located, seeking attachment to adjoining districts. The adjoining districts approved the petitions, but the residence district denied them. **The residents appealed to the state school district boundary appeal board, which allowed the detachment of many property parcels even though they did not share a common boundary with the attaching school districts**, creating "island parcels." The district that lost the property appealed to a Wisconsin circuit court, which affirmed the board's decision. The Wisconsin Court of Appeals affirmed the circuit court decision, and the school district appealed to the Supreme Court of Wisconsin.

The court found that a 1981 amendment to Wisconsin law deleted a reference to boundary lines in school district property detachment cases. Although there was ambiguity in the amended statute, the court agreed with the board's interpretation, which permitted non-contiguous property annexation. While common borders were no longer an issue in detachment and annexation cases, the board was required by the legislation to consider the geographical characteristics of the affected school districts, travel time, student educational needs, potential adverse effects on curricular and extracurricular programs and the fiscal effects of proposed reorganizations. **Because the evidence indicated that the board's decision was within its discretion and jurisdiction, the court approved of the detachment of property.** *Stockbridge School Dist. v. Dep't of Pub. Instruction School Dist. Boundary Appeal Bd.*, 550 N.W.2d 96 (Wis.1996).

◆   Thirteen Texas students attended school in a school district adjoining their district of residence without officially transferring. The Texas Education Agency had previously refused requests by other students residing in the same subdivision to transfer to the adjoining district as violative of a federal district court desegregation order. When the adjoining district discovered that the students were attending its schools without official transfers, it threatened to charge them tuition. **Residents of the subdivision sought detachment of the subdivision from their district and annexation to the adjoining district**. The state commissioner of education ordered the detachment of the subdivision, but on appeal, a Texas district court reversed and remanded the case with instructions to deny the proposed action. The subdivision and annexing school district appealed to the Court of Appeals of Texas, Austin, which determined that the commissioner's sole duty had been to determine whether the proposed boundary change would violate the federal court order. **Although the action resulted in a 2.5 percent decrease in the white student population in the ceding district, and the annexing district had a higher rate of white attendance, the proposed boundary change did not violate the federal court order**. This was because the proposed boundary change would not create, maintain, reinforce, renew or encourage a dual school system. Both systems were presently unitary. The court rejected the ceding district's argument that the detachment would lead to the defection of other white subdivisions to the annexing district. *Texas Educ. Agency v. Goodrich Indep. School Dist.*, 898 S.W.2d 954 (Tex.App.–Austin 1995).

IV. SCHOOL BOARDS

School boards are vested with the authority to manage school districts in accordance with state laws. State laws also define election and meeting requirements, which must be strictly complied with to avoid potential reversal of an improper board action by a reviewing court.

A. Membership

1.   Appointments, Elections, Residency and Recall

◆   The Voting Rights Act of 1965 was enacted to eradicate certain widespread discriminatory voting practices. Section 2 of the act bars all states and their political subdivisions from maintaining discriminatory voting practices, standards or procedures. Violation of this section may be shown where the electoral system is not open to equal participation because of race. **Section 5 of the act is limited in scope to particular states and their political subdivisions that are identified as covered jurisdictions. It prohibits the passing of new discriminatory laws as soon as old ones are struck down** by freezing election procedures in covered jurisdictions unless the changes are nondiscriminatory.

A Louisiana school board that was covered under § 5 addressed population disparities revealed in the 1990 census by adopting a plan similar to one adopted by the parish's governing body that preserved a white majority in each of its twelve single member districts. The board rejected a proposal by the local NAACP that would have created two districts with a majority of African-American voters. **The board complied with § 5 procedures by applying for preclearance** from the U.S. District Court for the District of Columbia. A three judge panel granted the preclearance request, and the U.S. Attorney General's office appealed to the U.S. Supreme Court, where it joined with the NAACP in arguing that a change in voting practices that violates the § 2 prohibition on discriminatory voting practices also constitutes an independent reason to deny preclearance under § 5. The Court rejected this argument, stating that the board would be improperly burdened by this presumption. The sections addressed different voting policy concerns and nothing in the statute justified presuming that a violation of § 2 was sufficient for denying preclearance under § 5. However, some of the evidence presented in support of a § 2 claim might be relevant in a § 5 proceeding. **Because the district court had failed to consider evidence of the dilutive impact of the board's redistricting plan, the Court vacated the judgment and remanded the case.** *Reno v. Bossier Parish School Bd.*, 520 U.S. 471, 117 S.Ct. 1491, 137 L.Ed.2d 73 (1997).

On remand, the district court again granted preclearance to the board, and the Attorney General again petitioned the Supreme Court for review. In an opinion authored by Justice Antonin Scalia, the Court rejected the board's preliminary challenge based on mootness, noting that even if the plan at issue was never used again, it would serve as the baseline for future preclearance matters. In then considered the Attorney General's argument that the district court had improperly found no evidence of discriminatory intent, and that Section Five of the Voting Rights Act must be construed to prohibit preclearance of a redistricting plan enacted with a discriminatory but non-retrogressive purpose. The Court declined to address the evidentiary question, finding that resolution of the Section Five issue required affirmation of the district court decision. **The Court stated that Section Five requires a covered jurisdiction to demonstrate that a proposed change does not have the purpose and will not have the effect of denying or abridging the right to vote on account of race or color.** In a 1976 case, the Court construed this clause as applying only to "retrogressive effects." Under this construction, the clause could not be construed to mean discrimination in general. The Court explained that Section Five preclearance proceedings are unique, dealing only with specific changes to voting procedures. Failure to grant preclearance to a redistricting proposal may result in the preservation of the status quo, no matter how discriminatory that might be. In contrast, Section Two actions commonly involve changes to the status quo itself, requiring comparison with a hypothetical alternative used to assess the existence of discrimination. The Court declined to blur the distinction between Section Five and Section Two cases, noting that denying preclearance to a non-retrogressive plan would risk leaving in effect a discriminatory status quo, perhaps even more discriminatory than the proposed change. **Holding that Section Five does not prohibit preclearance of a redistricting plan enacted with a discriminatory but non-retrogressive purpose, the Court affirmed** the district court judgment. *Reno v. Bossier Parish School Bd.*, 528 U.S. 320, 120 S.Ct. 866, 145 L.Ed.2d 845 (2000).

◆   Section 5 of the Voting Rights Act of 1965 requires covered jurisdictions to obtain preclearance from the U.S. District Court for the District of Columbia or the U.S. Attorney General prior to the implementation of any state change affecting voting. Texas is a covered jurisdiction under § 5. **The Texas legislature enacted a comprehensive statutory scheme for holding local school boards accountable to the state for student achievement.** The law contains ten possible sanctions which can be imposed on school districts for failing to meet legislative standards governing the assessment of academic skills, development of academic performance indicators, determination of accreditation status and the imposition of accreditation sanctions. The two most drastic sanctions, appointment of a master or of a management team to oversee school district operations, requires the exhaustion of the lesser sanctions first. **In compliance with § 5, Texas requested administrative preclearance** for the amendments. The attorney general approved most of the sanctions as not affecting voting, but determined that the appointment of a master or management team could result in a § 5 violation.

Texas appealed to the U.S. District Court for the District of Columbia, which held that the claim was not ripe for adjudication. **The U.S. Supreme Court agreed to review the case, and stated the general rule that a claim is not ripe for adjudication if it rests upon contingent future events that may not actually occur.** Texas had not identified any school district in the state which might become subject to the appointment of a master or management team and was not required to implement the sanctions until one of the remedies already approved by the attorney general had been exhausted. Because the issue presented was speculative and unfit for judicial review, the Court affirmed the judgment. *Texas v. U.S.*, 523 U.S. 296, 118 S.Ct. 1257, 140 L.Ed.2d 406 (1998).

◆   The president of an Illinois teacher association prepared union notices endorsing three candidates who were running in an upcoming school board election. She used school paper and copying equipment to prepare the notices and distributed them to union representatives at other district schools using the district's internal mail system. Two candidates for school board vacancies who were not endorsed by the union learned of the mailing and complained about it to the district superintendent, who responded that they could distribute their campaign literature by regular mail. Following the election, the union reimbursed the district for the direct costs of the notices. **The nonendorsed candidates sued the school district and teacher association in a federal district court, alleging First and Fourteenth Amendment violations**. The court granted summary judgment to the district and association, and the candidates appealed to the U.S. Court of Appeals, Seventh Circuit.

The candidates argued that the district was precluded from restricting the use of its equipment and facilities to union-endorsed candidates while denying use to others. **The court of appeals held that the teacher association was entitled to use the internal mail system because of its status as the exclusive representative of school employees, and not because of the viewpoint of its communication**. The district did not sponsor or endorse any candidate, but had lawfully restricted use of the mail system to its employees' recognized bargaining agent for internal communications. Because the facilitation of the association's communications did not violate any constitutional rights of the candidates, the court affirmed the judgment. *Davidson v. Community Consol. School Dist. 181*, 130 F.3d 265 (7th Cir.1997).

♦   The Tennessee Constitution requires that all popularly-elected county officials, including school board members, be elected by all voters within the county. In addition, Tennessee adopted the state Education Improvement Act, which mandates that a school board be popularly elected. Shelby County, Tennessee, which encompasses the city of Memphis, has two school districts, one of which serves only Memphis residents. The county enacted an electoral plan calling for the election of county board members from seven single member districts throughout the entire county. As a result, **Memphis residents could vote in county education board elections, even though students from Memphis attended school in a different system**. The county board of commissioners filed a federal district court action against state officials including the attorney general, seeking a declaration that the Education Improvement Act violated the Fourteenth Amendment rights of county voters who did not reside in Memphis. The court agreed with the commissioners, and the state officials appealed to the U.S. Court of Appeals, Sixth Circuit.

The court stated that the courts have established a number of factors to determine whether nondistrict voters have a substantial interest in school board elections. These included the degree to which one district finances the other, the voting strength of district voters, the potential for crossover students and joint programs between school districts. In this case, Memphis voters did not substantially finance the county school district, and they outnumbered county voters by three to one. There was very little crossover of students and a negligible number of joint programs between city and county districts. Applying these factors, **the court determined that the Education Improvement Act was unconstitutional as applied to county school board voters because it improperly diluted votes and placed the majority of votes in the hands of out-of-district voters**. The court affirmed the district court's judgment. *Bd. of County Commissioners of Shelby County, Tennessee v. Burson*, 121 F.3d 244 (6th Cir.1997).

◆   A 1990 Arizona law allowed school district governing boards to implement alternative election systems for electing board members in districts where the total minority enrollment was at least 25 percent of total enrollment and average daily attendance was at least 1,000 students. **One school district voted to change from an at-large system to a single member system and held an election employing a single member ward system** to fill three of five board positions. After the election, a group of voters challenged the validity of the ward system, claiming that the law was unconstitutional and that the election result was invalid. The court agreed, declared the statute unconstitutional and reinstated the prior incumbents to their board positions pending a special election using the at-large system. The unseated board members appealed to the Court of Appeals of Arizona, which found that the statute required close judicial review since it was explicitly race-based. Under this standard, **the state was unable to identify a compelling interest that would justify the racial classification as there was no evidence of historic racial discrimination**, only the threat of a lawsuit because of the existence of past litigation involving two other school districts. The law was unconstitutional in its entirety. However, the court modified the trial court's order, determining that the incumbents should not have been reinstated. The proper remedy was the ordering of a future election. *McComb v. Superior Court of State of Arizona, County of Maricopa*, 943 P.2d 878 (Ariz.App.Div.1 1997).

2.   Misconduct, Conflict of Interest and Nepotism

◆   After a teacher won a four-year term as a school board member, the board sought to disqualify her from service while she continued her teaching duties. It alternatively sought to prevent her from receiving her teaching salary while serving as a board member. According to the board, Kansas law, board policy and the common law doctrine of incompatibility of office prohibited the dual service. **A state district court held that while state law prohibited certain persons from school board membership, it did not specifically exclude teachers**. The court also found that the board's policy prohibiting members from receiving compensation for employment by the district was void as an unlawful attempt to determine who was qualified to serve as a board member. The school board appealed to the Kansas Supreme Court.

According to the state supreme court, the district court had erroneously found that the teacher was not subject to disqualification from board membership simply because teachers were not specifically listed among those excluded from serving as board members in Kan. Stat. Ann. § 72-8202. In the absence of legislative authority, the court analyzed the case under the common law doctrine of incompatibility of office, which considers whether the nature and duties of two offices render it improper as a matter of public policy for one person to retain both positions. The high court relied on authority from decisions out of Wyoming and New Jersey holding that the offices of teacher and board member are demonstrably incompatible with the common law rule. Under the dual-service arrangement, the teacher occupied one position that was subordinate to the other. She was both employer and employee, and in the first capacity sat on a policy-making body that negotiated with the employees' collective bargaining representative. This presented a clear conflict of interest that could not be remedied. She was subject to discipline by the board as a teacher and could be fired by it in certain circumstances. The principal who evaluated her answered directly to the board and "her board duties, her actions, no matter how well-intentioned, will be colored by the conflict inherent in her two positions." **Because the fulfillment of one office by the teacher was invariably at odds with the other, the offices were incompatible and the dual arrangement was prohibited.** Applying equitable principles, the court found that her employment as a teacher endured despite her election to the board and disqualified her from serving on the board. *Unified School District No. 501, Shawnee County, Kansas v. Baker*, 269 Kan. 239, 6 P.2d 848 (Kan. 2000).

◆   A Georgia citizen complained that three elected school board members had participated in decisions affecting the compensation and benefits of their spouses, who were employees of the school system, alleging that the participation betrayed the public trust in violation of the Georgia constitution. The individual also asserted that the board members' recent election of a new superintendent was improper because the new superintendent would "be beholden to the [board members] and would reciprocate by granting [their] spouses additional privileges, compensation or benefits." **A Georgia trial court dismissed the complaint** for failure to state a claim upon which relief could be granted, **finding no enforceable duty among the board members to refrain from voting on matters that might affect the financial interests of their spouses** as school board employees.

The citizen appealed to the Georgia Supreme Court, which affirmed the trial court's decision in all respects. The constitutional provision at issue stated that "[p]ublic officers are the trustees and servants of the people and at all times amenable to them." This broad language had been construed in other cases as prohibiting a public officer from financially benefiting as the result of performing official duties. In this case, the alleged benefit to the board members' spouses was speculative, and the language of the constitution did not support the citizen's construction. **There was no precedent for the position that the familial relationship of locally elected school officials disqualified them from participating in school operations decisions.** Under the citizen's argument, the spouse of any school system employee would be precluded from serving the school board of that system based on speculative presumption. The ineligibility criteria of state law did not include familial relationships, and the trial court had properly dismissed the complaint. If any of the board members actually violated a duty to ensure the integrity of the local school system by intentionally acting to the benefit of a spouse, the public trust would be breached. However, such action was not presumed under the law or the Georgia Constitution. *Ianicelli v. McNeely*, 272 Ga. 234, 527 S.E.2d 189 (2000).

◆   An Iowa school board member publicly denounced an assessment test given to all eleventh grade students in the district that was intended to measure problem solving abilities and competence. The board member stated that the test, which was a graduation requirement, improperly reflected an outcome-based educational philosophy. The district responded by copyrighting the test and ordering the dissenting board member to return her copies of it. She refused to return the copies and requested test scoring information. The district custodian of records denied the request under the confidentiality exception to the state public records act. The board passed a resolution vesting the superintendent with discretion to determine whether materials should be released to a school board member. The dissenting board member filed an action in a state district court for release of the testing materials. **The court ruled that the materials were confidential records that were excluded from the public records act** and enjoined the dissenting board member from copying, distributing or disseminating the testing materials. She appealed to the Supreme Court of Iowa.

The court held that **the tests were confidential records even though they had already been released** to the board member and were available for public inspection as the result of the copyright action. Records do not lose their confidential nature because of a limited release of information. The custodian of records had exercised his discretion in a reasonable manner by withholding the further release of testing materials. However, **the board member was entitled to receive the information since she needed the information in her capacity as a board member**. The court held that the board's policy limiting her access to the information was improper and reversed the part of the district court order prohibiting disclosure of the information to her. The court modified the decision by enjoining her from any further dissemination of confidential materials. *Gabrilson v. Flynn*, 554 N.W.2d 267 (Iowa 1996).

♦   The Kentucky General Assembly established school-based councils to oversee individual school operations while preserving the role of the school board as the authority over each school district in the state. **The legislation contained an anti-nepotism clause prohibiting school district employees or their spouses from serving as parent members of school-based councils**, which are composed of two parents, three teachers and the principal or administrator of each school. Two parent members of school-based councils gained election despite the fact that their spouses were employed at a district grade school. They challenged their removal actions by the state department of education in a Kentucky circuit court, seeking a declaratory judgment and order prohibiting their removal. The court determined that the anti-nepotism provision was unconstitutional, and the state department of education appealed to the Supreme Court of Kentucky. The court observed that the trial court had subjected the statute to an improper level of scrutiny. Parents were not a suspect class who enjoyed a constitutionally protected fundamental right to serve on school councils. **There was a clear indication in the amendment that the legislature intended to eradicate nepotism within school districts, and the amendment was not unconstitutional**. The court reversed the circuit court decision. *Kentucky Dep't of Educ. v. Risner*, 913 S.W.2d 327 (Ky.1996).

♦   A Virginia teacher worked for a county school board for six years. Following a 13-year absence from teaching, she reapplied to the board for employment. However, during her absence, her brother-in-law was elected chairman of the board. **Because the Virginia Code prohibited the employment of a person related to a board member, her employment application was denied**. The teacher filed a lawsuit against the board in a Virginia trial court, claiming that she was entitled to an exception applicable "to any person within such relationship who has been (i) regularly employed ... by any school board prior to the taking of office of any member of such board." The court held for the school board, and the teacher appealed to the Supreme Court of Virginia. The supreme court noted that the legislature had used the present perfect tense in the statute, indicating action beginning in the past and continuing to the present. This required an interpretation that **persons seeking to avail themselves of the exception be employed by the school board at the time the conflict of interest arose**. Because the teacher was not employed by the board at the time her brother-in-law was elected chairman, she could not avail herself of the exception, and the trial court had properly held for the school board. *Williams v. Augusta County School Bd.*, 445 S.E.2d 118 (Va.1994).

B. School Board Powers and Duties

♦   A school district assigned a six-year-old student to a different elementary school than that attended by his older sister. His parents alleged that if he was not allowed to transfer, each of their three children would attend different schools. Moreover, the six-year-old's assigned school was not as close to home as the school attended by his sister, and he would be required to walk home from his bus stop along a complex, potentially hazardous route. The school board denied the transfer request and the parents commenced a county circuit court action for an order preventing the board from refusing to allow the transfer. **The court agreed with the school board that it did not act arbitrarily by denying the transfer**. However, it found that **denying the requested transfer when space became available would be arbitrary and capricious**. The court entered a judgment allowing the transfer when space allowed.

The district appealed to the state supreme court, which reviewed Miss. Code Ann. § 37-15-15, which details a number of considerations for school boards when making student assignments. Included items were the educational needs and welfare of the child, the welfare and best interests of all students attending the school and the availability of school facilities. **The court agreed with the parents that the district failed to comply with § 37-15-15, which requires school districts to make assignments on an individual basis by considering the listed factors**. The school superintendent admitted in his testimony that the district considered only its attendance   zones   when   denying   the   transfer   application. Contrary testimony of the district's director of student services indicated that the district had considered district policy when declining the transfer application. This supported the circuit court's finding that the board did not arbitrarily deny the transfer application at the time it was made. The court also agreed with the circuit court that the district would be acting arbitrarily and capriciously if it continued to deny the transfer when space became available in the school the parents wanted the student to attend. It appeared that the district had liberally allowed transfers within district schools in the past, and that its current policy provided that it honor transfer requests "at the end of a school year or sooner, if educationally sound, or at the request of their parents," under stated guidelines. Since the student had by now completed his year at school, a transfer would comply with district policy and the continuing denial of a transfer when space became available would be arbitrary and capricious. The court affirmed the circuit court decision for the family. *Pascagoula Municipal Separate School District v. Barton et al.*, 776 So.2d 683 (Miss. 2001).

◆   A Virginia school board drafted a bylaw that attempted to prohibit personal attacks during meetings. The bylaw was designed to preserve decorum and order during school board meetings and to ensure that the board could transact its business with minimal disruption. Part of the bylaw created regulations governing the public comment portion of meetings. **One regulation instructed potential speakers to avoid "attacks or accusations regarding the honesty, character, integrity or other like personal attributes of any identified individual or group."** A man who requested time to speak during a public comment period of a board meeting expressed concerns about the conduct of school officials. The board chairman attempted to cut short his presentation because it exceeded the time allotment, but then allowed him to conclude his remarks.

The man sued the board and chairman in a federal district court for constitutional rights violations. The court stated that the standard for reviewing prior restraint of speech depends upon the type of forum in which the speech is to occur. In this case, the board had created a limited public forum. In a limited public forum, regulations may be drawn to restrict the time, place and manner of protected speech, so long as they are content-neutral, narrowly tailored to serve a significant government interest and leave open adequate channels for communication. The board argued the regulation was content-neutral, because it only prohibited attacks targeted at school officials in their personal capacities. The court rejected the board's arguments, observing that the First Amendment affords its broadest protection to political expression in order to promote the exchange of ideas and the will of the people. **A policy that deters individuals from speaking out on issues of public importance violates the First Amendment. The contested regulation had the effect of chilling any speech critical of school officials**. The regulation prevented public debate in violation of the First Amendment, and the court ordered it stricken from the board's bylaws. *Bach v. School Board of City of Virginia Beach*, 139 F.Supp.2d 738 (E.D. Va. 2001).

◆   The Tuscaloosa City, Alabama, school board solicited bids to manage its transportation services and then entered into a multi-year contract with a private transportation company. Under the contract, all affected board employees were given the option of accepting employment with the company or remaining school board employees on the same terms as they previously enjoyed. The company was to assume direct control over all bus drivers and transportation support personnel, and the company retained control over its employees and was required to resolve complaints from parents. Moreover, school board employees working under the company's direction were required to abide by the company's work and safety rules, schedules, employee handbook and over-all supervision. The Alabama Education Association sued the school board in a state trial court, asserting that the contractual arrangement was a scheme devised to reduce the number of board employees and deny benefits to support personnel. **The court held that the contract was illegal, as it violated state laws prohibiting the expenditure of the appropriated funds for salaries of personnel not under the direct control, employment or supervision of local education boards**.

The board appealed to the Alabama Supreme Court, where it argued that the contract was justified by the need to replace its aging fleet of school buses, save transportation expenses and increase its liability insurance coverage. The court examined relevant state laws and noted that city education boards were vested with "all powers necessary or proper for the administration and management" of their schools. The board's decision to enter into the contract was consistent with the interest of students in city schools, according to the court. The contract did not violate state budget acts by calling for payment of a set fee for transportation services. There was no merit to the association's claim that the contract violated state law by allowing the company's employees to provide their services to the board, even though they did not participate in state public employee benefit systems such as retirement and health insurance. These employees were also excluded from the protections of the state fair dismissal act. However, the contract violated state law by requiring the board to pay the salaries of personnel not under its own direct control and supervision. **The board's inability to pay its employees from legislatively allocated funds violated state law by denying the employees legal rights or benefits, including the procedures of the Fair Dismissal Act**. Since the board exceeded its statutory powers by entering into the contract, the supreme court affirmed the trial court judgment for the association. *Laidlaw Transit Inc. v. Alabama Education Association et al.*, 769 So.2d 872 (Ala. 2000).

◆   An Illinois school district did not violate the constitutional rights of a parent who challenged the district's dress code. An appellate court held that **a policy banning the parent from school functions for a year was narrowly tailored to serve the district's interest in avoiding disruption**. The board barred the parent from school events for a full year for alleged violations of board policy prohibiting any act intended to disrupt or impede school-sponsored activities after the parent's challenge to the board's dress code policy included a demonstration involving a toy gun and a pocketknife. The court observed that while the First Amendment covers expressive conduct as well as written and spoken words, a state may impose reasonable restrictions on the time, place and manner of constitutionally protected conduct in a public forum. In this case, **the board's policy addressed the conduct of the public while on school property, applying to any person without regard to the person's ideas or views. It thus satisfied constitutional requirements for content neutrality**. The policy was narrowly tailored to serve the significant government interest of restricting disruptions of school-related activities and conduct that impeded such activities. Since the policy did not ban any particular type of expression at a given place or time, it left open alternative channels of communication. *Nuding v. Board of Education of Cerro Gordo Community Unit School District No. 100 et al.*, 313 Ill.App.3d 344, 730 N.E.2d 96 (Ill. App. 4th Dist. 2000).

◆   The Illinois School Code allows school districts to petition the state education board for waiver or modification of statutory requirements. State board actions may then be disapproved by the General Assembly within a specified time period. **The Chicago school board applied for a waiver from the requirement that all students participate in daily physical education classes**. The application was submitted to the state school board in connection with the city board's effort to improve academic performance in its high schools. The state board approved the request under a plan by which physical education became an elective class. The General Assembly took no action to disapprove the waiver request. A group of taxpayers, parents, teachers and the Chicago Teachers Union sued the city board in a state circuit court for declaratory and injunctive relief prohibiting implementation of the plan on grounds that it encroached upon the legislative and executive powers in violation of the separation of powers doctrine. The court dismissed the Chicago Teachers Union and parents from the action, but held that two physical education teachers and two taxpayers had legal standing to mount the challenge. It agreed with them that the waiver statute was invalid and granted their request for an order enjoining the city board from waiving physical education requirements for high school juniors and seniors.

The city board appealed directly to the Supreme Court of Illinois, arguing that the teachers and taxpayers lacked legal standing to maintain the action, requiring dismissal of the case. **The court found speculative the teachers' claim that the waiver would reduce the need for physical education teachers.** Physical education classes remained available, but would no longer be required. The board had the power to excuse students from physical education classes on a case-by-case basis and could accomplish the same objective even without securing a waiver under state law. The teachers had not sustained any direct injury from the challenged statement and the circuit court should have dismissed them for lack of standing. The state supreme court also held that the taxpayers had no claim to standing under a state law allowing taxpayers to enjoin the disbursement of public funds by any officer of the state government. This law was inapplicable, since the board was not an officer of the government. The circuit court had erroneously allowed the case to proceed and the state supreme court reversed. *Chicago Teachers Union, Local 1 v. Bd. of Educ. of City of Chicago*, 189 Ill.2d 200, 724 N.E.2d 914 (2000).

◆   An Iowa school board member sued the district superintendent, board and remaining members after she was assessed $138.53 by the superintendent's office for locating and retrieving documents pertaining to a report that was still being prepared by a board committee. **The board member** also **objected to the superintendent's action of seeking legal advice without prior board approval.** A state trial court granted summary judgment to the board and superintendent, upholding board policies establishing a retrieval fee and allowing the superintendent to obtain legal advice without board approval.

On appeal, the Supreme Court of Iowa noted that state law provides for a retrieval charge if processing a request for documents exceeds 30 minutes of staff time. However, the school district was not permitted to charge the board member for retrieving records that she was entitled to inspect. Therefore, that portion of the trial court decision was revered. The aspect of the district court decision which upheld the board policy allowing the superintendent to seek legal advice without the board's approval was affirmed. **The court rejected the board member's assertion that state law limited a school board's ability to hire a private law firm,** since the law had been specifically amended to permit boards to hire attorneys as necessary. *Rathmann v. Bd. of Directors of Davenport Community School Dist.*, 580 N.W.2d 773 (Iowa 1998).

◆   The District of Columbia Superior Court found that District of Columbia public school officials violated their statutory duty to address widespread violations of the D.C. Fire Prevention Code by allowing unsafe conditions in district schools. **It issued an order requiring the fire chief to conduct periodic inspections of**

public school buildings and to abate fire code violations by ordering the immediate closing of buildings with life-threatening fire code violations. The court issued over 50 remedial orders in a three-year period to compel compliance with the original court order and maintained ongoing supervision to enforce its injunction. Prior to the opening of the 1997-1998 school year, the court denied a joint request by the district and fire chief to permit 50 schools to open despite scheduled roof replacement and repair work which could threaten the safety of students and staff. The parties appealed to the District of Columbia Court of Appeals. The court found that the superior court had not usurped the authority of the fire chief by rejecting his determination that the repair work did not require the closure of school buildings. There was evidence that propane tanks, ladders and scaffolding at over 50 schools created a danger to students and staff. **The superior court had appropriately found substantial evidence of recent fire code violations and unsafe conditions at the school buildings**. The court of appeals affirmed the lower court judgment. *Parents United For D.C. Pub. Schools v. Dist. of Columbia*, 699 A.2d 1121 (D.C.App.1997).

◆   The Oklahoma School Code allows students to transfer to schools outside their residence districts upon the approval of the education boards in both the residence and receiving districts. Graduating seniors in counties having a population in excess of a specified number who are previously enrolled in the school district to which they wish to transfer are exempt from the requirement of approval by the receiving district. **A student who attended a public school as a transfer student for 11 years applied again for attendance in the receiving school district for his senior year**. However, the district denied his application for transfer, and the student's parents appealed to a county district court. The court found that the receiving district had no discretion to deny the transfer. The receiving district appealed to the Supreme Court of Oklahoma. On appeal, the receiving district argued that transfers under the law were discretionary except for the limited circumstances listed in the statute and that the approval of both the residence and receiving districts was required. The court disagreed, finding that **where a previously transferred student seeks a transfer for a senior year and the requirements of law are otherwise met, a receiving district has no discretion to disapprove a transfer request**. Because the district was within a county that was in excess of the specified population level and had allowed the student to transfer into the district for 11 straight years, it had no discretion to disapprove the transfer request. The court affirmed the judgment for the student. *Hill v. Bd. of Educ., Dist. I–009, Jones, Oklahoma*, 1997 OK 111, 944 P.2d 930 (Okla.1997).

◆   The Kentucky General Assembly amended state education law to remove an education board's control over the termination of a teacher contract upon a superintendent's recommendation. The amendment requires a three-member tribunal, consisting of a teacher, administrator and a lay person residing outside the school district, to conduct an impartial hearing upon a teacher's request to review a proposed contract termination. **The amendment failed to specify a board's right to appeal an unfavorable decision by a tribunal**. A teacher whose contract was recommended for termination appealed to a tribunal, which reversed the superintendent's decision and held that the teacher was entitled to reinstatement with back wages. A Kentucky circuit court rejected the board's appeal, finding that it had no appeal rights under the amended legislation. The Court of Appeals of Kentucky reversed the decision, and the teacher appealed to the Supreme Court of Kentucky.

On appeal, the teacher claimed that the statute could not be enlarged to include appeal rights which were not incorporated in the amendment. The board asserted that it had an inherent right to appeal an agency decision under prior decisions of state courts and the Kentucky Constitution. **The court agreed with the board, finding that an aggrieved party, including a corporation or administrative body, had the ability to seek judicial review of arbitrary administrative decisions,** which may always be reviewed by a court. Because the amendment removed the education board's quasi-judicial function in employment termination cases, the board was now a complaining party before a tribunal. The court affirmed the court of appeals' decision. *Reis v. Campbell County Bd. of Educ.,* 938 S.W.2d 880 (Ky.1996).

C. Open Meeting Laws

◆   A teacher alleged that his school board violated the open-meetings act when it failed to place the matter of his contract non-renewal on the agenda for a meeting at which it considered evidence, testimony and arguments by counsel. The board took no action on the contract, but voted not to renew it in a properly noticed meeting held two weeks later. **The teacher asserted that the non-renewal vote at the second meeting was invalid because of the lack of adequate public notice for the first meeting**. He argued that his contract was automatically renewed the day after the first meeting because the school district failed to hold a valid hearing within 15 days of his request for one. The teacher sued the school district in a Texas district court, which awarded summary judgment to the district.

He appealed to the Texas Court of Appeals, asserting that the failure to provide adequate public notice of the first hearing violated the open-meetings law. The court noted that the Texas Government Code provides that a final action, decision or vote on a matter deliberated in a closed session must be conducted in an open meeting. **The open-meetings act distinguished between meetings at which only deliberations take place and those at which decisions are made. If a meeting involves only deliberation, a governmental entity does not violate the law by closing the meeting**. In this case, the board did not vote or take any final action on the teacher's employment contract at the first meeting. It conducted an open hearing at which the teacher was permitted to introduce evidence, present testimony and offer the arguments of his counsel. The district properly notified the public of the second meeting held two weeks later, where it voted to terminate his contract in an open session. The court held that the first meeting was not the type of governmental action that could be invalidated by a court because it did not involve a decision of some kind. It rejected the teacher's argument that his contract was automatically renewed the day after the first hearing and that the board had no evidence upon which to terminate his contract at the second hearing because of a due process violation by the district. The court held that the open-meetings act was not a legislative means for service of legal process and had no due process implications. There was no fundamental unfairness issue, and the court affirmed the judgment for the school district. *Hill v. Palestine Independent School District*, No. 12-00-00101-CV, 2000 WL 1737531 (Tex. App. 2000).

◆   The Education Empowerment Act is a Pennsylvania law providing for the development of school district improvement plans within 30 days of a district being placed on the Education Empowerment List. "Empowerment teams," made up of school board members, school employees and administrators, parents, and community members, have 120 days to transmit a final improvement plan to the state department of education. **A newspaper publisher sought access to empowerment team meetings in two districts with histories of low student performance that had been placed on the Education Empowerment List**. The publisher asserted that the teams were "agencies" under the Pennsylvania Sunshine Act, which requires public agencies to take official action and deliberate in public meetings. In separate trial court proceedings, a state common pleas court ordered the teams to open their meetings to the public and to make minutes of past meetings available to the public.

The empowerment teams appealed to the Pennsylvania Commonwealth Court, which consolidated the actions and reviewed the language of the Education Empowerment and Sunshine Acts. It determined that the empowerment teams were "agencies" under the Sunshine Act. This conclusion was based on the facts that: the empowerment teams were established for the limited purpose of devising school district improvement plans setting forth specific goals and methods for improving educational performance; they were authorized to take official action, even if they served only as consultants to the school board; they decided and deliberated on specific methods and goals for improving educational performance as described in the improvement plans; and school boards were powerless to alter their recommendations. The teams were de facto school boards because they decided and deliberated official policy. Therefore, the Sunshine Act applied to team meetings and deliberations. The court held that **the preliminary injunctions ordered by the trial court were essential to avoid the immediate and irreparable harm of denying the public an opportunity to witness team decisions that were very important to the public interest**. The public was entitled to access to the minutes of meetings held prior to the trial court orders. The commonwealth court affirmed the orders. *Patriot-News Company v. Empowerment Team of the Harrisburg School District et al.*, 763 A.2d 539 (Pa. Commw. 2000).

◆   After an incident with an aide, school officials proposed suspending the involved student and placed a letter in the aide's personnel file for initiating the incident. The aide then became fearful that her reputation might be harmed by the incident. **The school board's attorney notified the family that the student's suspension hearing would be closed**, and the board voted to close the hearing pursuant to Iowa law. The suspension was stayed and the family sued the school board in an Iowa district court for violations of the state open meetings act. The court held that the board's closure action was void and it enjoined the board from making future violations. It also awarded the family $3,000 in attorneys' fees.

The board appealed to the Supreme Court of Iowa, which held that **the open meetings law required an open proceeding upon request by a student or parent**. Meetings may not be closed unless they are intended to evaluate the professional competency of an employee or to make employment actions such as hiring and discharge. Since no exception applied under the open meetings act, the court affirmed the district court judgment, including the award of attorneys' fees. *Schumacher v. Lisbon School Bd.*, 582 N.W.2d 183 (Iowa 1998).

◆   The Connecticut Freedom of Information Act generally requires state agencies to conduct their meetings in public, but excludes strategy meetings and negotiations with respect to collective bargaining. A union representing teachers employed by a Connecticut school board filed grievances against the board for unfair labor practices. The board and union agreed to close the meetings to the public, and **individuals representing a local newspaper filed a complaint with the state freedom of information commission, seeking access to the hearings**. After the commission held that the grievance sessions should have been open to the public, the union appealed to a state trial court. The court agreed with the union that the grievance proceedings were part of the collective bargaining process and reversed the commission's order. This decision was affirmed by the Appellate Court of Connecticut.

The individuals appealed to the Supreme Court of Connecticut, which noted that collective bargaining grievances may be separated into two aspects: the first being the fact-finding portion, and the second being the decisionmaking portion. **The public should be guaranteed access to the fact-finding parts of grievance hearings, but could be lawfully excluded from decisionmaking negotiations and settlement talks** in the later stages of a grievance proceeding. The court reversed and remanded the lower court judgments, holding that in the future, grievance proceedings must be open to the public for hearings where testimony and evidence would be received from witnesses. *Waterbury Teachers Ass'n v. Freedom of Information Comm'n*, 240 Conn. 835, 694 A.2d 1241 (1997).

◆   The Michigan Open Meetings Act contains an exception allowing closed sessions for strategy and negotiations related to a collective bargaining agreement. An education board considered a contract for its teachers at an open meeting, but closed the session to discuss negotiations with the union. One of the board members stated that any vote in closed session violated the law and walked out of the room. He filed a complaint against the other board members in a Michigan trial court for violations of the open meetings act. The court granted summary judgment to the other board members, and the dissenting member appealed to the Court of Appeals of Michigan, where he argued that any voting in closed session was forbidden by the act. **The court of appeals observed that the act specifically permitted the consideration of collective bargaining negotiations in closed sessions** and that a straw poll of board members did not constitute a vote or decision as defined by the law. The trial court had properly granted summary judgment to the other board members. *Moore v. Fennville Pub. Schools Bd. of Educ.*, 566 N.W.2d 31 (Mich.App.1997).

◆   The West Virginia Open Governmental Proceedings Act requires that all meetings of any government body, including a school board, be open to the public. The law defines a meeting as the convening of a quorum of a public body in order to make or deliberate toward a decision on any matter. The day before an important school consolidation and closing vote, four of the five members of a West Virginia school board met for two hours with the superintendent of schools and his assistants to consider information relevant to the vote. The following day, the consolidation and closure matters were approved without extensive discussion. Opponents of the action filed a petition against the board in a West Virginia trial court, **seeking an order setting aside the vote under the Open Governmental Proceedings Act and requiring the board to post notices of the intended action at all schools which might be affected** by the vote. The court granted the petition and set aside the board's action. The board appealed to the Supreme Court of Appeals of West Virginia.

The court observed that the state law applied to discussions leading up to a decision as well as to actual voting. **Each of the statutory requirements had been satisfied in this case, as four of the five board members were present** and had discussions at a "meeting" as defined by the act. There was no good faith exception to the act as claimed by the board members and the lack of formality at the meeting had no bearing on whether the board had violated the act. The court affirmed the trial court order setting aside the board action, and held that the board could be properly required to reconsider the matter in an open meeting. The trial court had correctly required the board to post notices of the action at all schools that would be affected by the vote. *McComas v. Bd. of Educ. of Fayette County*, 475 S.E.2d 280 (W.Va.1996).

V.   REFORM LEGISLATION

♦   The Pennsylvania legislature enacted the Education Empowerment Act (EEA) in 2000, authorizing the state education secretary to place school districts with a history of low test scores on an "Education Empowerment List." Placement on the list required districts to form a team to develop an improvement plan approved by the state education secretary. If a district failed to meet its plan goals within three years, it would be designated an "education empowerment district," requiring its board to surrender all powers and duties, except the levying of taxes, to a board of control appointed by the secretary. Local boards resumed control after a district no longer had a history of low test performance. **The EEA treated the Harrisburg school district differently by immediately certifying it as an education empowerment district under a board of control**. Unlike other boards of control, the Harrisburg board was to be appointed by the city's mayor, who also appointed the district's education empowerment team. The board obtained an order from the Pennsylvania Commonwealth Court that the EEA was unconstitutional special legislation that violated equal protection by treating Harrisburg differently than other districts and placing it under a board of control appointed by the mayor. The Supreme Court of Pennsylvania affirmed. The legislature then enacted a law amending the EEA by eliminating its reference to "the city of the third class which contains the permanent seat of government." It redefined the class of districts subject to mayoral control as those with a population in excess of 45,000 and a history of "extraordinarily low test performance."

The Harrisburg school district petitioned the commonwealth court for a declaration that the new amendment to the EEA was special or local legislation that violated the state constitution and the Equal Protection Clause of the U.S. Constitution. The court agreed with the district on three of its five claims. The legislature was permitted to create classifications among local governments, but not on artificial or irrelevant distinctions such as the ones relied on in the amended EEA. The number and irregularity of the distinctions contained in the amendment indicated that they were irrelevant and artificial. Even if "extraordinarily low test performance" was a valid distinction, there was no real educational distinction making it necessary to immediately place the district under a board of control, when the situation would be just as grave for students in other failing districts. No apparent reason existed for establishing the criteria for the class, and the court held on a preliminary basis that the EEA violated the state constitutional prohibition on special or local legislation. **The court agreed with the district that the amended EEA violated its equal protection rights, since there was no apparent reason for treating the district differently from other similarly situated districts**. By giving the mayor the power to appoint a board of control, the legislature violated the city's home rule charter. While the court agreed with the commonwealth that the amended EEA did not improperly delegate the district's power to levy taxes and did not remove board members from their offices, the court agreed with the three other district objections. *Harrisburg Sch. Dist. v. Hickok*, No. 550 M.D. 2000 (Pa. Commw. 2001).

♦ **In an earlier EEA case, a group of taxpayers, teachers and parents challenged the portion of the act that allowed districts with a history of low performance for two years as of the effective date of the act and were financially distressed to be placed under a special board of control** that assumed control of district business in place of the school board until a sound financial structure could be established. The Chester Upland School District was found to be financially distressed in 1992 and came under the control of a special board. When the EEA took effect, its financially distressed condition automatically brought it under the supervision of a control board, without the opportunity to appoint a local team to devise an improvement plan or a three-year period to improve test scores and meet plan goals. The plaintiffs sued the governor and secretary of education in the Pennsylvania Commonwealth Court, alleging that the immediate control provisions of EEA were unconstitutional. The plaintiffs parties asserted that the legislation unconstitutionally singled out the district as a special class of one.

The court considered the petition for review by the complaining parties and the preliminary objections of state officials who argued that the case did not state a claim upon which relief could be granted. It agreed with the complaining parties that the EEA created a constitutionally impermissible closed class consisting only of the Chester Upland School District. The classification was not genuine, and there was a strong likelihood that the provision would be declared unconstitutional in a proceeding for a permanent order. However, the state officials were correct in arguing that the EEA did not violate constitutional restrictions on the levying of taxes by local authorities, since control boards did not exercise this power. The court agreed with the complaining parties that the EEA violated the Equal Protection Clauses of both the Pennsylvania and U.S. Constitutions. **The legislation singled out the Chester Upland district based solely on its "financially distressed" designation, without providing any reason for such treatment. Because the**

**EEA treated the district differently from the class of other potential empow-
erment districts, the court granted the petition for review** and denied the
commonwealth's objections with the exception of the local-taxation issue. *Warren v.
Ridge*, 762 A.2d 1126 (Pa. Commw. 2000).

CHAPTER ELEVEN

Academic Practices

I. CHARTER SCHOOLS

State legislatures have responded to public demands for improving public schools and student achievement levels by authorizing charter schools and other innovative educational approaches. Charter schools employ special curriculums under a plan approved by public school boards and permit the delegation of certain management functions to non-school district entities, including private entities. State and local educators must have final authority over charter school boards and each school charter must comply with statutory requirements.

A. Legislation

◆ The U.S. Bureau of Indian Affairs funded 10 charter schools with money from the Indian School Equalization Program for school maintenance and operations under the federal Tribally Controlled Schools Act of 1988. Under the terms of a "deduct statute," **the Arizona basic state aid to charter schools was reduced by the amount of state and federal funds the school received for maintenance and operations**. The schools received no state equalization assistance, since the BIA maintenance and operations funding for each school exceeded the amount that would have been provided as basic state aid. Several charter schools and their students initiated state court actions against Arizona and certain officials, arguing the "deduct statute" was preempted by federal law, and violated their Equal Protection rights and federal laws, including Title VI of the Civil Rights Act of 1964. The court awarded summary judgment in favor of the state and officials, and the schools and students appealed.

The Arizona Court of Appeals held that the deduct statute did not violate the plaintiffs' equal protection rights. The equal protection clauses of the Arizona and U.S. constitutions required only that the state treat similarly situated individuals equally and create reasonable classifications of people. BIA-funded charter schools were not similarly situated to other charter schools. They received maintenance and operations funds from government sources that exceeded state equalization assistance. The BIA provided a free education to American Indian students attending these schools, and **if the state did not reduce school funding under the deduct statute, it would violate the equal protection rights of students attending non-BIA-funded charter schools**. In the event that the BIA decreased or eliminated funding for the schools, the state would make up the difference with supporting funds. There was no evidence that BIA-funded schools suffered as a result of application of the deduct statute, since they would always receive maintenance and operations funding that equaled or exceeded the amount received by other charter schools. The schools and students failed to state a claim under Title VI. The deduct statute also did not violate the federal Pastor Amendment, which prohibits the payment of federal charter school stimulus funds for states that include Indian School Equalization Program funding in state assistance calculations. This was because charter schools were not "states" or political subdivisions under the amendment. The amendment was not intended to preclude charter schools from applying directly to the federal government for funds. The court affirmed the judgment for the state. *Salt River Pima-Maricopa Indian Community School et al. v. State of Arizona*, 23 P.3d 103 (Ariz. App. 2001).

◆   The Utah Legislature enacted the Charter Schools Act in 1998. The act authorized a three-year pilot program for eight charter schools that would function as part of the public education system under the state board's supervision. **The Utah School Boards Association challenged the act in a proceeding before the state board, arguing that it conflicted with the state constitution**. The state board rejected the association's challenge, and the association commenced a state court action against the board. The board moved for summary judgment, arguing that the state constitution did not prevent it from directly controlling specific schools or programs authorized by the legislature, because the greater power of "general control" included the lesser power of specific control. The court denied the association's cross-motion for summary judgment, and held for the board.

The association appealed to the Utah Supreme Court, where it renewed its arguments that the legislature had exceeded its constitutional authority to delegate powers to the state board and that the board could act only in ways that affected the entire education system. The act required the board to exceed its authority in a number of ways, including the consideration of charter applications, negotiations with applicants for terms and conditions of school operations, termination of charters and the redirection of local revenues. The court found that the legislature had limited powers to create laws for the establishment and maintenance of the state public education system. The terms "general control and supervision" meant the direction and management of all aspects of operations. The association's argument was unreasonable, as the state board had always managed separate educational programs in different ways. It created accreditation rules for elementary, junior high and middle schools that were different from those for secondary and special schools. It managed vocational and athletic programs differently than its educational programs. The board was vested with the constitutional authority to direct and manage all aspects of public education under the laws established by the legislature. The charter schools legislation was intended to improve and customize the education system and **the state constitution did not prohibit the legislature from authorizing the board to exercise control and supervision under it**. The court affirmed the trial court decision in favor of the state board. *Utah School Boards Association v. Utah State Board of Education*, 17 P.3d 1125 (Utah 2001).

◆   Three school boards charged that New Jersey's 1995 charter school legislation was unconstitutional for several reasons. A state court upheld the act, and the school boards appealed to the state supreme court, which analyzed the act under the state constitutional requirement that the legislature provide for a thorough and efficient system of free public schools. The act expressed a legislative intent to improve public learning, increase available educational choice, encourage innovation, establish a new form of accountability, require measured outcomes and provide for teacher improvement and opportunity. The act provided for charter school approval and funding at a level that could be determined by the commissioner but was presumed to be 90 percent of the local levy budget per pupil in the school district. **The supreme court reasoned that the choice to include charter schools in the range of educational options was permissible so long as it did not violate the thorough and efficient system of education requirement of the state constitution**. According to the court, the act adequately provided for the maintenance of nonsegregated public schools through various measures. The funding mechanism presumptively assigned to each charter school an amount equal to 90 percent of the local levy budget per pupil in the school district for each specific grade level. This amount was subject to adjustment by the commissioner at the time of approval in an amount not exceeding 100 percent of the local levy budget per pupil and could also be set at a lower rate at the commissioner's discretion. The commissioner could set the amount to be forwarded by the school district of residence to a charter school in a way that would comply with the thorough and efficient mandate of the New Jersey Constitution. None of the districts had alleged that its ability to meet constitutional obligations was presently affected. The court also upheld state regulations arising under the charter schools act that established a two-step application and review procedure. Under the regulatory scheme, the commissioner was permitted to process the application in an orderly fashion. The review process was a reasonable implementation of the statute and was efficient and practical. For these reasons the state supreme court upheld the charter school legislation. *In the Matter of Grant of Charter School Application of Englewood on Palisades Charter School*, 164 N.J. 316, 753 A.2d 687 (2000).

◆   **Taxpayers who objected to the California Charter Schools Act sued the state board of education, seeking an order that would prohibit the board from issuing charters** and spending funds on charter schools. The taxpayers asserted the act violated provisions of the state constitution requiring state control over public education and prohibiting public funding of religion, among others. A California superior court denied the petition and the objectors appealed.

The court of appeal noted that important restraints on charter schools were written into the act, including nonsectarian program requirements, nondiscriminatory hiring and admissions policies, and a prohibition on conversion of private schools into charter schools. Charter schools are required to meet statewide performance standards, and public officials may revoke charters for failing to meet stated requirements. Charters can only be approved through local school districts, which maintain continuing oversight and monitoring powers over charter schools. The law did not amount to abdication of state control over essential educational functions. The law was a valid exercise of discretion aimed at improving education in the state. **The creation of charter schools did not create a dual public school system** that would violate the state constitution. Funding for charter schools was comparable to that of other public schools. **There was no violation of a state constitutional provision prohibiting the transfer of any part of the public school system to another authority, or another section prohibiting the appropriation of public funds for sectarian schools.** The court rejected the taxpayers' claim that the initial charter schools legislation was an unconstitutional delegation of legislative powers to the state board and other chartering authorities. The court characterized the legislation as a policy decision to give parents, teachers and community members the opportunity to set up operationally independent public schools to improve learning, promote educational innovation and achieve related public education goals. The court held that the act reflected a reasonable grant of legislative power to administrative agencies that did not violate the Constitution, and affirmed the judgment. *Wilson v. State Bd. of Educ.*, 75 Cal.App.4th 1125 (Cal.App.1 Dist.1999).

◆   The Colorado legislature adopted a charter schools act in 1993. The statutory charter application procedure culminated with review by the state board of education. The legislation specified that any second appeal of the denial of a charter application to the state board would be final. The state board was required to instruct the local board of the district in which the charter school would be located to approve a charter application if the denial of the application was contrary to the public interest. The Denver Board of Education rejected a charter school application. **The state board remanded the application to the Denver board with instructions to reconsider** the disputed issues. **The Denver board again denied the application** and the applicants appealed again to the state board. The state board ordered the establishment of the charter school, but required the parties to submit status reports and did not compel the Denver board to approve the application in its entirety. The applicants applied to a Colorado district court to enforce the state board's order. The court granted the requested order, and the Denver board appealed. A court of appeals reversed and remanded, finding the order was unenforceable because it did not compel approval for the complete application.

On appeal to the Colorado Supreme Court, the court analyzed the state charter schools act under the education article of the Colorado Constitution, which the court found vested the state board with general supervisory powers, providing a precedent for designation of the state board as the final arbiter of education disputes. The court held that the role of local education boards to control instruction may be restricted or limited by law, and was to be balanced by reviewing courts with the state board's general supervisory powers. **The charter schools act's allocation of powers between the state board and local boards was constitutionally permissible**. The court determined that the state board was authorized to substitute its judgment for that of a local board. In this case, the state board had exceeded its authority in requiring the parties to submit status reports. That portion of the appeals court decision was reversed. The court characterized the second appeal portion of the charter schools act as a constitutional effort by the legislature to create educational opportunities for innovation and reform by combining local initiative with state and local educational policy expertise. The state board's authority to approve charter school applications made it necessary for local boards and applicants to resolve outstanding issues. The disputed application had a number of deficiencies, and the state board order to approve the charter did not invalidate the local board's concerns. The court stated the local board and applicants should have resolved the outstanding concerns in order to develop a valid charter. The court remanded the dispute to the Colorado school board for modification of the board's order. *Board of Educ. of School Dist. No. 1, Denver v. Booth, et al.*, 984 P.2d 639 (Colo. 1999).

◆   The Michigan Legislature amended the state school code in 1993 to allow charter schools, also known as public school academies. Academy applications must be approved by an authorizing body, which can only be a public school entity, such as a school board, community college board or public university governing board. An authorizing body must oversee the application and administration of public school academies and approve their boards of directors. Authorizing bodies have the power to revoke public school academy contracts. **A group of citizens and two members of the state board of education filed a lawsuit in a state circuit court to challenge the constitutionality of the charter schools act**. The court declared the act unconstitutional, finding that public school academies were not under the immediate, exclusive control of the state and were not public schools because they were not governed by publicly elected bodies. The Court of Appeals of Michigan affirmed the circuit court decision, and state officials appealed to the Supreme Court of Michigan.

The supreme court observed that the Michigan Constitution does not mandate the exclusive control of public schools by the state or by local school districts. **Public school academies were under the ultimate control of public school officials, since the officials could revoke charters for violation of the state school code and controlled the application process**. The state constitution vested the legislature with the responsibility for public schools and it could lawfully delegate the selection of academy school directors. The act specifically prohibited any religious organization from organizing an academy. Because the legislation did not violate the state constitution, the court vacated and remanded the case. *Council of Organizations and Others for Education About Parochiaid, Inc. v. Governor of Michigan*, 566 N.W.2d 208 (Mich.1997).

B. Applications

◆   The Harrisburg, Pennsylvania, school board held a public hearing on a charter school application submitted by the Mosaica Charter School of Harrisburg.

The school was to be owned by a for-profit company. The board denied the application, but failed to send the school a written notice stating the reasons for denial, as required by law. The charter school revised its application and resubmitted it, but the board took no action during the required statutory time period. The charter school appeal board denied a petition by resident taxpayers to intervene in the case, then ordered the district to approve the application. The district did not approve the charter and appealed the appeal board's order to the commonwealth court.

The Pennsylvania Commonwealth Court consolidated the case with an appeal by the taxpayers. It held that the modified charter application contained many revisions, and the district was required to take action on it within 45 days. The district was not authorized to make an informal decision that would excuse it from taking timely action. **The court rejected the district's assertion that the charter school management agreement unlawfully vested control of the school in a for-profit company**. The charter school law allowed charters only for schools organized as public, non-profit corporations. However, nothing prevented a for-profit entity from submitting a charter school application or contracting to perform a charter school's management and administrative functions. The law granted the management and operation of charter schools to boards of trustees who were public officials vested with the authority to make decisions about budgeting, curriculum and operations. **So long as the school itself was not operated as a for-profit entity, the trustees had real and substantial authority and responsibility for educational decisions**. There was no evidence that the arrangement between Mosaica and the charter school deprived school trustees of their statutory powers. No trustee was a Mosaica employee or had any financial interest in the company. The applicants had satisfied the law's requirement that the charter school enjoy community support. The court approved the appeal board's order requiring the district to grant the charter, and determined the board had properly denied the taxpayers' request to intervene. *Brackbill v. Ron Brown Charter Sch.*, No. 3220 C.D. 1999, 3281 C.D. 1999, 20,711, 2001 WL 540237 (Pa. Commw. 2001).

◆   The Roosevelt Union Free School District's schools were primarily made up of minority students and had significant curricular and financial problems since at least 1995. The district board opposed the operation of a charter school, asserting that this would exacerbate ongoing financial problems and have a devastating impact on the district's ability to deliver educational programs and services to students in its regular schools. The board projected that the charter school would cause a net loss in tax revenue that would make necessary a 13 percent district property tax increase. The trustees of the State University of New York nonetheless approved a charter application. The school board sued the trustees in a state trial court, **claiming the charter application violated the Charter Schools Act because it contained insufficient evidence of community support and made inaccurate representations about the financial consequences of school operations**. The board also asserted that the Charter Schools Act was unconstitutional. The court denied the board's motion for an order that would block the school's opening and granted motions in favor of the trustees to dismiss the board as a party to the action due to lack of capacity.

The board appealed to the New York Supreme Court, Appellate Division, which agreed that the board had the capacity to challenge administrative decisions of the trustees. However, it did not have the capacity to mount a constitutional challenge against the Charter Schools Act. The court noted that a school district is "a creature and subdivision of the State," and had only an expectancy or hope of preserving funds appropriated to it under state law. The board had no proprietary interest in state funds because if a student did not attend a district school, the district had no right to that student. **Once a charter agreement was consummated by applicants and the trustees, the issuance of the charter was a foregone conclusion**, since the state board of regents could then only make recommendations and was powerless to disapprove an application. The appellate court modified the trial court judgment. *Board of Education of Roosevelt Union Free School District v. Board of Trustees of the State University of New York*, 723 N.Y.S.2d 262 (N.Y. App. Div., 3d Dep't 2001).

◆   A community school board denied a charter school application on grounds that it contained inadequate financial and facility plans. The proposal was the sponsoring foundation's third attempt, and the prior two proposals were rejected at both the local and state levels. The foundation petitioned the state board for review, and it reversed the local board's decision. The local board's appeal reached the Illinois Appellate Court, which determined **the state board had the explicit power to reverse a local board decision regarding a charter school application if the board found a proposal in compliance with the state charter school law, and in the best interests of the students who would attend the school**. The law vested the state board with the authority to carry out and accomplish the objectives of the act and it could approve a proposal that substantially complied with the act. Proposals for charter schools were to identify at least two sites that were potentially available to a charter facility by the time the school was to open and contain a proposed budget indicating that the school was economically sound for both the school and local school district. In this case, although the proposal conformed to only 13 of 15 statutory factors, there was evidence that the sponsoring foundation intended to meet the remaining two requirements within a specified time period. The foundation indicated that four sites were potentially available as of the time the charter school was to open and that budgetary documentation would be updated 30 days prior to the opening of the school. The state board did not commit an error in considering evidence regarding spending assumptions that diverged from those used by the local board, and the court affirmed the judgment. *Board of Education of Community Consolidated School District No. 59 v. Illinois State Board of Education*, 317 Ill.App.3d 790, 740 N.E.2d 428 (Ill. App. 2000).

◆   Three school districts denied a petition for a regional charter school for reasons including: lack of demonstrated, sustainable support by teachers, parents, students and community members; failure to demonstrate capability of support and planning; lack of information required by state law; and failure to show how the school would serve as a model for other public schools. One of the districts also found that the application did not demonstrate a need for a charter school, failed to offer evidence of compliance with the Americans with Disabilities Act, offered an insufficient curriculum and had financing, implementation and administrative problems. **The state charter school appeal board agreed with the school districts that the application failed to show sustainable support by teachers, parents, students and community members** and denied the application.

The applicants appealed to the Pennsylvania Commonwealth Court, which observed that the charter school appeal board was charged with exclusive review powers over appeals from local school board decisions. Accordingly, **the board's decision was to be affirmed in the absence of a violation of law or the U.S. Constitution or for lack of substantial evidence**. There was no merit to the applicants' assertion that the board had violated a state law requiring it to render a decision within 60 days of an initial meeting to consider a local board decision. The law required the board to meet and review the record of a local board decision within 30 days of acceptance of the appeal, and then to issue a written decision within 60 days of affirming or denying the appeal. In this case, the board issued a written decision 46 days after affirming the decision of the local boards. The court further determined the appeal board did not act inappropriately in denying the applicants' request to supplement the record with additional evidence. There was no error in denying the application and the court affirmed the board's decision. *Shenango Valley Regional Charter School v. Hermitage School Dist.*, 756 A.2d 1191 (Pa. Commw. 2000).

◆   A local school board found that a charter application would not improve student learning, increase learning opportunities or encourage teaching innovations under a plan to hold the school accountable for meeting measurable academic standards, as required by the Charter School Law. Accordingly, the board rejected the application. **The Charter School Appeal Board** (CAB) **reversed the local board's decision and granted the charter**, and the school district appealed to the Pennsylvania Commonwealth Court. The court held that the Charter School Law delayed the right of the applicants to appeal the denial of the charter within a two-year statutory moratorium. Thus, the CAB had not improperly considered the appeal. The court rejected the school district's argument that the CAB was bound to apply a high level of deference to its decision. The law required the CAB to give appropriate consideration to a local board's findings, but did not mandate a particular standard of review. Accordingly, the CAB was permitted to conduct a new hearing on the matter and was not bound by the local board's findings of fact. The local board was incorrect in its assertion that CAB acted arbitrarily by determining that charter school facilities do not have to be reviewed and approved by a local board prior to the opening of the charter school In this case, the charter applicants had proposed opening the school in a strip mall, which the local board claimed was totally inappropriate and presented a substantial risk to the safety and welfare of students. **The CAB found instead that the Charter School Law exempted charter schools from public school regulations, including those governing student health and safety.** It also found no evidence that small classroom sizes created health or safety concerns and that bus access and space for recreation had been arranged. The application was acceptable at the time it was submitted and there was no merit to the school district's claim that two years later, the application could be denied based on the passage of time. The CAB could not deny the appeal based on the possibility that the particular facility might no longer be available. The court affirmed the CAB's decision in favor of the charter school applicants. *Souderton Area School District v. Souderton Charter School Collaborative*, 764 A.2d 688 (Pa. Commw. 2000).

◆   A South Carolina school board denied a charter school application based on the failure of the applicants to show that the school would have facilities that met statutory state health and safety requirements by the proposed start up time. The application failed to meet the civil rights requirements of state law because it did not comply with a 1970 desegregation agreement. The application additionally failed to satisfy state law provisions governing the racial composition of school districts. A trial court upheld the school board's decision and the applicants appealed.

The South Carolina Supreme Court noted that there was evidence that the charter school application did not meet state statutory requirements for showing that the proposed school will be economically sound. **Because the applicants had relied on speculative revenue sources, the board had not rejected the application arbitrarily. The court upheld the charter denial on the additional ground that the application adversely affected other students in the district by failing to identify prospective students and creating a racially identifiable school**. Finding that the trial court had properly upheld the local board's decision, the supreme court affirmed the judgment. However, it remanded an appeal brought by the state attorney general's office challenging the validity of a charter schools act provision requiring that the racial composition of a charter school not deviate from that of the district by more than ten percent. *Beaufort County Bd. of Educ. v. Lighthouse Charter School Comm.*, 335 S.C. 230, 516 S.E.2d 655 (S.C.1999).

◆   **A non-sectarian private school in rural Arizona received conditional approval for charter status from the state education board**. However, the board received complaints from local residents about the lifestyle and beliefs of those associated with the school. A background check revealed that the school's director of education had a bad credit history and the board voted to deny the charter on that basis. The school moved for a rehearing after the director and another employee resigned from its board of directors. However, the board again denied the charter application. The school and director appealed to a state superior court, which affirmed the charter denial, ruling that the board acted within its discretion when it considered creditworthiness as an application criteria.

The school and director appealed to the Court of Appeals of Arizona, which held that state law requires administrative orders to be adequately supported by sufficient findings of fact and conclusions of law. **Because the board had not based its final order upon adequate factual findings and conclusions of law, the charter application was remanded for further consideration**. The school should have received the opportunity to revise its application after the credit history issue arose. However, the court affirmed the trial court judgment concerning additional matters on appeal, including the question of whether creditworthiness was a proper requirement for consideration by the board. The board had the power to add criteria to those listed in the statute in order to make appropriate decisions. There was no merit to other statutory and constitutional claims advanced by the school and director. The court affirmed that aspect of the trial court's judgment. *Shelby School v. Arizona State Bd. of Educ.*, 962 P.2d 230 (Ariz.App.Div.1 1998).

C. Operation

◆   A Florida school received a charter for the 1997–98 school year to serve a small population of at-risk students in grades K–4. **The charter was renewed the following year, but the school board, which had sponsored the school, denied renewal** for the 1999–2000 school year. The state education board rejected the determination and remanded it for further consideration. The school board conducted a hearing and held that the school failed to meet requirements for student performance and progress and did not perform required assessments. The school appealed to the Florida Court of Appeal, Fourth District.

The court found evidence that the school was unable to show that its program provided adequate learning opportunities for students. Students at the school had the lowest standardized test score results in the state. Even when compared to other schools serving at-risk students, **the school's performance was unacceptably low and its continued operation presented an unreasonably high risk to students**. The progress and performance goals of the school projected continuing failure for its academic program through 2003. There was further evidence of declining community and parental support for the school, poor attendance at directors' meetings and other evidence of improper school governance. The school had operated at a deficit during its last year and improperly expended revenue. Expert witnesses testified that there was significant doubt that the school had appropriately tested students, including excessive reliance on "failure free" reading tests. There was an overall downturn of student performance on the tests that were actually performed, and evidence indicated that the school failed in comparison to comparable public schools. Because continued operation of the school was contrary to the best interests of its students, the court affirmed the board's decision. *Orange Avenue Charter School v. St. Lucie County School Bd.*, 763 So.2d 531 (Fla. App. 4th Dist. 2000).

◆   Mosaica Academy was granted charter school status by the Bensalem School District. State law provides that charter schools notify the county of residence of each nonresident charter school student of the share of state funds to which the school is entitled to receive on behalf of the non-resident students who attend. In the event of a county board's default, the commonwealth department of education will provide the funds to the school and withhold the same amount from the county. **The Philadelphia school district refused a per diem funding request to cover the cost of students residing in Philadelphia who wanted to attend the charter school**, and further challenged the validity of the school's charter.   The state department of education determined that Mosaica's charter application was in order and directed the Philadelphia school district to make the per diem payments to Mosaica on behalf of the Philadelphia residents. However, the Philadelphia district refused. Mosaica also requested transportation for the students residing in the Philadelphia district. The Philadelphia school district refused the request, and Mosaica commenced a state court action against the commonwealth education department and Philadelphia school board, seeking declaratory relief in the form of payment of the per diem, plus the cost of student transportation. The parties entered into a court-approved consent agreement prior to the start of the 1998-99 school year. Under the agreement, the Philadelphia district agreed to provide transportation costs for Philadelphia students attending the school. Pending further proceedings, the state department of education agreed to withhold distribution of funds to Philadelphia in order to reflect the per diem amount due Mosaica. The Philadelphia school district was not obligated by the agreement to pay the per diem. *Mosaica Academy Charter School v. Commonwealth of Pennsylvania, Dep't of Educ.*, No. 803 M.D. 1998 (Pa.Commw.1998).

◆   A citizens' group sued the City of Jersey City and related parties in state court for an order barring the city's mayor from using revenue bonds to finance a community education facility that was to house a charter school. The court granted a motion by the city to dismiss the case. On appeal, the appellate division court held that the action was time barred. The citizens had failed to file the action until after the lapse of a 20-day time period applicable to bond ordinances. **Even if the challenge had been timely filed, the construction of the community education facility did not violate state law**. Although charter schools were prohibited from constructing facilities with public funds under state law, the construction of the facility in this case was an undertaking of the city. The facility would not be owned by the school, which would lease space from the facility at fair market value. This use did not violate state law and the court affirmed the judgment for the city and officials. *Jersey City Educ. Ass'n v. City of Jersey City*, 316 N.J.Super. 245, 720 A.2d 356 (App.Div.1998).

II. CURRICULUM AND GRADING

Because state laws vest local education authorities with considerable discretion in academic, curricular and grading issues, these matters are infrequently litigated. Courts reviewing complaints about public school curriculum and grading matters do not subject official decisions to close judicial scrutiny. For additional cases concerning challenges to curriculum choices on religious grounds, please see Chapter Two, Section I.B.1. Curricular challenges on the basis of academic freedom are found in Chapter Three, Section III.C.

A. Curriculum

◆   A workforce training program under which students performed unpaid work on a school construction project for class credit survived a union-led challenge asserting that the failure to pay students prevailing wages for work performed violated New York Labor Law. A state court held that the students were not employees as defined by the state Labor Law, which required the classification of all employees on state-funded public works to be either journeymen or apprentices individually registered in a state-approved skills training program. Only the contractors' employees on public work projects met this definition. **The court found it significant that students were not hired or paid for their work, did not work a regular work day and performed no work without direct and constant supervision**. The completion of their construction technology class was not the equivalent of wages, and the court annulled the commissioner's decision in favor of the union. *In the Matter of Onondaga-Cortland-Madison Bd. of Coop. Educ. Servs. v. McGowan*, 2001 N.Y. Slip Op. 05401, 2001 WL 669918 (A.D., 3d Dep't 2001).

◆   In 1998, California voters approved of Proposition 227, a legislative initiative amending the state education code. **The amendment called for replacing the state's existing bilingual educational system with programs designed to teach English and other subjects to limited English proficient (LEP) students in the English language.** Proposition 227 requires that LEP students receive instruction through "sheltered English immersion," under which English instruction is provided during a temporary transition period that is normally one year or less. Five students filed a federal court action against state officers including the governor, asserting that the act was unconstitutional and violated the federal Equal Educational Opportunities Act (EEOA) of 1974, which prohibits the denial of equal educational opportunities to individuals based on characteristics including national origin.

The court first observed that the requirements of the new law had yet to be incorporated into any school district's curriculum and the state board of education had yet to enact any regulations or programs pursuant to the law. **The court held that while the EEOA requires educational agencies to take appropriate action to overcome language barriers that impede equal access by students, it does not create an affirmative duty by the states to adopt a particular educational system.** Evidence indicated that English immersion was a legitimate educational theory, and education experts are in disagreement about the best program for LEP students. The amended act itself allowed for different educational choices and did not violate the EEOA. The court rejected constitutional challenges to the amended law under the Supremacy Clause and Equal Protection Clause. **Neither federal law nor the Constitution requires the provision of bilingual education.** There was no showing of intentional discrimination sufficient to violate Title VI of the Civil Rights Act of 1964 or the Equal Protection Clause, and the court denied the petition for relief from implementation of the act. *Valeria G. v. Wilson*, 12 F.Supp.2d 1007 (N.D.Cal.1998).

Several months later, the court denied a motion to dismiss the case filed by intervening parties who are opposed to bilingual education. The court also denied a motion for judgment by the class representing students claimed to have been adversely affected by Proposition 227. These decisions were based on the court's inability to determine whether any of the parties were entitled to judgment at the time the motions were filed. *Valeria G. v. Wilson*, No. C-98-2252-CAL (N.D.Cal. 1999).

◆   A federal district court upheld the constitutionality of § 320 of Proposition 227, a California law requiring the instruction of limited English proficiency (LEP) students through immersion in the English language. **The statute provides legal recourse for parents of LEP students to sue teachers, administrators, and school board members who "willfully and repeatedly" refuse to provide English language instruction.** The court rejected arguments by the California Teachers Association (CTA) that the section violated teacher speech rights and was unconstitutionally vague. The CTA, along with teachers, administrators, and affiliated interest groups, sued the state education board and its members, seeking to enjoin enforcement of § 320. The CTA moved the court for summary judgment, and the state board responded with its own summary judgment motion.

The court observed that Prop. 227 was drafted to ensure that all children in California public schools be taught English as rapidly as possible. Since the act only refers to teaching and instruction, the court rejected the CTA's free speech violation claim, noting that teachers are required to follow the curriculum and do not enjoy strong First Amendment protection in the classroom. **Prop. 227 does not prohibit the use of non-English languages outside the classroom and in emergency or disciplinary contexts, as the teachers had claimed**. Also, the act does not restrict the use of other languages at parent-teacher conferences and other situations for which the teachers expressed concern, the court found. The law was not unconstitutionally vague in its mandate to conduct classroom instruction overwhelmingly in English, said the court, which awarded summary judgment to the state education board. *California Teachers Ass'n v. Davis,* 64 F.Supp.2d 945 (C.D. Cal. 1999).

◆   Proposition 227, a 1998 California voter initiative, created a new law requiring the instruction of limited English proficiency (LEP) students through immersion in the English language. Prior law provided for bilingual instruction in many cases. The legislation created by Prop. 227 allows parents to obtain a waiver from English immersion for specified reasons, but contains no other exceptions. Even before the provisions of Prop. 227 were passed into law, three Bay-area school districts sought waivers from its provisions. **While the legislation provided for parental waivers from mandated English immersion instruction, it did not specifically include a provision allowing districts to obtain such waivers**. The state education board held that it had no authority to grant waivers to school districts. However, a state trial court attempted to reconcile the lack of any language in Prop. 227 regarding the general waiver procedure, and held that the state board had to consider the applications. The board appealed to the state appellate court.

The panel noted that the stated purpose of Prop. 227 was to teach English to all children in California public schools as rapidly and effectively as possible. Parents were provided with a right to sue if their children were not provided English-only instruction, except when they specifically sought a waiver. **The legislative history of the act indicated the intent to give parents the decision-making authority for teaching LEP students, rather than leave it with school boards and administrators**. In order to preserve this legislative intent, the court of appeal held that the general waiver provision of state law was inapplicable to school district requests for waivers from English-only instruction. The core elements of LEP instruction were specifically excepted from the waiver procedure, alienating LEP education choice from school district control. The court of appeal vacated the trial court's order and remanded the case. *McLaughlin v. State Bd. of Educ.,* 75 Cal.App.4th 196 (Cal. App. 1st Dist. 1999).

◆   A New York school district allowed high school students who had recently received training as AIDS peer educators to present information on AIDS prevention to elementary and middle school students. A parent observed a presentation and complained to the district superintendent about its sexually explicit content and failure to stress abstinence and the dangers of high-risk behavior. As a result of her complaint and others, **the school board passed a resolution limiting peer education presentations to after-school hours in which students would be allowed to participate only with parental permission**. The board also formed a health advisory council and resolved that parental requests to remove children from AIDS education segments would be honored pursuant to the state-mandated curriculum.

The parent petitioned the state commissioner of education for a formal hearing, which was dismissed as untimely. The commissioner also held that the parent lacked legal standing to contest the board's resolution because parents retained the right to remove their children from AIDS education programs and she was not aggrieved by the resolution. A New York trial court affirmed the commissioner's order, and the parent appealed to the New York Supreme Court, Appellate Division, which held that **the parent had no statutory right to a hearing before the commissioner and had not been deprived of due process**. There was no merit to her assertion that she was entitled to a trial since no factual issues remained in dispute and the trial court had the authority to make a ruling on the case. The commissioner had not acted arbitrarily or capriciously in finding the action time barred, and the court affirmed the judgment. *In the Matter of Akshar v. Mills*, 671 N.Y.S.2d 856 (A.D. 3d Dep't 1998).

◆   The Oregon Educational Act for the 21st Century restructured the state's public schools by imposing a rigorous academic program upon them with periodic student assessments, the development of alternative learning environments, the establishment of early childhood programs and an emphasis on work-related learning experiences. The act was passed with the legislative intent to have students learn and succeed in a rigorous academic program. **A Christian fundamentalist organization challenged the act, asserting that the act represented a constitutionally impermissible encroachment on free thinking by students and infringed upon parental child-rearing rights** in violation of the First and Fourteenth Amendments. A district court granted summary judgment to the school officials, and the complaining parties appealed to the Ninth Circuit.

The court noted the absence of a single constitutional rights violation as a result of the state's application of the act. The students and parents had submitted only hypothetical evidence of unconstitutional action and had alleged no concrete harm. The parents could allege no tangible threat of injury and had no standing to pursue their parental rights claims. **While the students had standing to bring the action by alleging a threat of injury to their speech rights, the court rejected their claim that the act coercively violated their "freedom of mind."** Nothing in the act compelled students to adopt state-approved viewpoints. The court affirmed the summary judgment order for the school officials. *Tennison v. Paulus*, 144 F.3d 1285 (9th Cir.1998).

◆   **The Indiana legislature enacted the Improvement in Student Achievement in School Cities Act to remedy problems in Indianapolis public schools**, including low student achievement on statewide tests, high remediation rates and poor graduation and attendance rates. The law required the school system to develop and implement a plan to improve student achievement, including general guidelines for teachers and administrators and an awards program for outstanding performance. Educators in each school were required to develop school plans conforming to the city school board plan. Although the school board approved an initial draft of the plan, it failed to finalize the draft, stating that it required input from parents and educators. The Indianapolis Education Association (IEA) and the Indiana State Teachers Association (ISTA) filed a declaratory action in a state superior court, seeking a ruling that the board plan did not comply with the law.

The court denied the requested relief and the board amended the plan twice. The court awarded summary judgment to the school board, and the ISTA and IEA appealed to the Court of Appeals of Indiana, where they argued that their authority to control school policy had been improperly diluted by the board plan. The court observed that local educators at individual schools were required to ensure compliance with the board plan. Accordingly, even though some teachers were not given copies of their school plan prior to a formal vote on it, this did not reflect an illegality in the board plan. **The court rejected claims by the ISTA and IEA that the plan impermissibly required teacher evaluations based on student remediation and attendance rates**. The statute permitted reliance on these criteria, and the court affirmed the judgment. *Indiana State Teachers Ass'n v. Bd. of School Commissioners of City of Indianapolis*, 693 N.E.2d 972 (Ind.App.1998).

✦ **A Massachusetts school district conditioned the approval of home education plans on home visits that were intended to provide school authorities with the opportunity to observe and evaluate the home instructional process**. Two families in the district notified school officials of their intent to instruct their children at home. Three of the parents had teaching certificates and the fourth had a master's degree in Christian education. They refused to consent to home observation and evaluation, instead suing the district in state court for a declaration and order that the local requirement violated state law and the state constitution.

A state trial court upheld the conditional approval requirement and the families appealed to the state supreme court, which examined the state compulsory attendance law. The law exempts from its requirements those students who are being "instructed in a manner approved in advance by the superintendent or school committee," and also authorizes approved home education. According to the court, the right to home instruction is subject to the state interest in seeing that home-schooled students receive an education. School officials can enforce reasonable educational requirements like those applicable to private schools, such as insisting on approval of home education plans, requiring certain course work and minimum hours of instruction, examining teacher competency, and periodic evaluation of student progress. **The state compulsory education law did not mandate home visits, and court deemed them not essential to the approval of a home education plan**. The requirement did not protect the state's interest in education and thus could not be made a condition to approval of a home education plan. The court expressed no opinion on whether home visits could be required if a child was not making satisfactory progress. The court vacated the trial court judgment and held that the school system could not condition approval of home education plans upon the home visit requirement. *Brunelle v. Lynn Public Schools*, 428 Mass. 512, 702 N.E.2d 1182 (1998).

✦ A member of a religious group whose beliefs included the avoidance of modern technology purchased a building formerly housing a Minnesota public school. He proposed that the school district lease the school from him for use as a modified curriculum public school. The district agreed to open the school. However, the curriculum of the school was not modified even though only members of the religious group attended it. Parents of students attending the school requested that no computers or other modern technology be used at the school. The district complied under a Minnesota law allowing parents to review public school instructional material and to request curricular exceptions and alternative instruction. **Two taxpayers filed a federal district court action against the school district, seeking a declaration and order that operation of the school violated the Establishment Clause of the First Amendment.** The court agreed with the taxpayers and permanently enjoined the district from operating the school in conformity with religious preferences.

The school district and board members appealed to the U.S. Court of Appeals, Eighth Circuit, which observed that the district had established the school primarily for financial reasons including the possibility of losing substantial state funding if members of the group withdrew their children from the district. The district was also able to reduce transportation and classroom costs by operating the school. **The accommodation of parental requests to conform the curriculum to their religious beliefs had been made pursuant to a religiously-neutral state law that served secular purposes, did not advance religion or endorse any particular religion.** The school was open to all students and the benefits to the religious group were incidental and secondary to the provision of a secular education. Because the operation of the school did not violate either the U.S. or Minnesota Constitutions, the court vacated and remanded the case. *Stark v. Indep. School Dist.*, 123 F.3d 1068 (8th Cir.1997).

♦   Massachusetts high school administrators contracted with a private speaker to make a presentation about AIDS awareness. The program included sexually explicit speech and behavior, including skits, joking and audience participation. No advance notice of the presentation was given to parents and there was no opportunity for students to be excused. **Two students who attended the program objected to its content and claimed that they had been compelled to attend against their will** in violation of their constitutional privacy rights. They also stated that the presentation violated their right to an educational environment that was free from sexual harassment. They joined their parents in filing a lawsuit against the speaker and school officials who participated in the decision to hire her in the U.S. District Court for the District of Massachusetts. The court dismissed the complaint and the students appealed to the U.S. Court of Appeals, First Circuit.

The court found that the judicial standard for the type of violation alleged by the students was very high and required evidence of behavior that shocks the conscience. **The failure to provide a parental opt-out feature was not a shocking deprivation of constitutional rights** and was not a due process violation. In addition, no fundamental privacy right to be free from exposure to offensive language exists. The parents failed to show that school officials violated their constitutional rights by showing a serious intrusion into their child rearing rights. **Parents do not have a constitutional right to dictate curricular matters** to public school administrators or prescribe what the state may teach to their children. The claim was also insufficient to constitute a Title IX complaint for sexual harassment since no reasonable person would have understood the program to create a hostile environment. The court affirmed the district court judgment for the school officials. *Brown v. Hot, Sexy and Safer Productions, Inc.*, 68 F.3d 525 (1st Cir.1995).

♦ A New York school district required its students to perform 40 hours of community service prior to graduation. The requirement culminated in a senior class entitled "Managing your Future," in which students discussed the career implications of their community service work and told where the service was performed. **A student and his parents filed a lawsuit against the school district** in the U.S. District Court for the Southern District of New York, **seeking a declaration that the program violated the constitutional rights of parents to direct the upbringing and education of their children, and the Thirteenth Amendment prohibition against involuntary servitude.** The parties brought cross-motions for summary judgment. The court rejected the argument by the parents that the program violated their rights to direct and control the upbringing of their children. As there was no constitutionally protected parental right to allow students to opt out of an educational curriculum for purely secular reasons, and any such ruling by the court would violate the right of local educational authorities to perform their duties, the court granted the school district's motion for summary judgment.

The family appealed to the U.S. Court of Appeals, Second Circuit. The court agreed with the district court that the community service program in no way resembled involuntary servitude and did not implicate the Thirteenth Amendment. The work was not severe or exploitative and the program had a constitutionally permissible educational purpose. **Although the parents had a liberty interest in raising their children that was recognized under the Fourteenth Amendment, they had failed to express religious objections to the program, and the court was unwilling to extend constitutional protection to their purely secular claim.** The program was reasonably related to the state's legitimate function of educating students and did not violate any privacy interest. The court affirmed the judgment for the school district. *Immediato v. Rye Neck School Dist.*, 73 F.3d 454 (2d Cir.1996).

♦ A California school district contracted with a limited partnership to show current events video productions in its schools. **The 12-minute videos included two minutes of commercial advertising. The contract contained an opt-out feature** for students who wanted to avoid viewing the production. The superintendent, a parent, a student organization and two teachers filed a lawsuit against the district seeking an order to void the contract, plus other declaratory relief. The court denied the request for a preliminary injunction, and determined that the mere presence of commercial advertising in public schools was not illegal. Although there had been no evidence of direct coercion in this case, the court retained jurisdiction over the matter and permanently enjoined the showing of commercial broadcasting unless strictly voluntary standards were implemented. The order also required maintenance of the opt-out feature and a supervised alternative activity during times in which the program was shown. Appeal reached the California Court of Appeal, Sixth District.

The court of appeal determined that the decision to permit commercial broadcasting in schools was within the discretion of local school boards. The

incidental use of commercial broadcasting within a larger presentation of educational materials was also permissible. The opt-out feature prevented students from being compelled to watch advertising in the classroom. The trial court had correctly found that the school board could enter into a contract for showing commercial broadcasting. However, it was unnecessary for the trial court to issue the injunction establishing procedures for opt-out or to retain jurisdiction. The court affirmed the trial court decision with modifications. *Dawson v. East Side Union High School Dist.*, 34 Cal.Rptr.2d 108 (Cal.App.6th Dist.1994).

◆   A group of African-American public school students attending New York city schools filed a lawsuit in the U.S. District Court for the Southern District of New York alleging that the city's public school curriculum injured African-American students because of a systematic bias against them. They stated that the curriculum distorted and demeaned the historical role of African-Americans and failed to include their important contributions. **The students sought a declaration that the curriculum was discriminatory and an order directing the school board to revise its curriculum to reflect African-American contributions**. The school board and other defendants brought a motion to dismiss the lawsuit on the grounds of government immunity and failure to state a claim under 42 U.S.C. § 1983 and other federal statutes.

The court observed that the Eleventh Amendment to the U.S. Constitution did not entitle the state and its agencies, including the school board, to immunity in this case because Congress had explicitly exposed them to suit under Title VI of the Civil Rights Act of 1964. However, in order to prevail in a § 1983 lawsuit, intentional discrimination must be proven and it must be established that the defendants' discriminatory purpose was a motivating factor in its actions. According to the court, no such intentional purpose could be discerned from the school board's actions. **It was impermissible for the court to infer discrimination from the alleged failure to incorporate African-American features in the curriculum**. The court dismissed the § 1983 complaint for failure to adequately allege intentional discrimination. The court also dismissed the students' Title VI complaint because neither the statute nor its regulations extended to curricular content. *Grimes v. Sobol*, 832 F.Supp. 704 (S.D.N.Y.1993).

B. Grading

◆   A middle school music teacher assigned three students conduct grades of "needs improvement" or "unsatisfactory." Each set of parents complained to the teacher and principal about the poor conduct grades, which made the students ineligible for honor society membership and school field trips. **The principal then changed the grades to "satisfactory" without consulting the teacher**, allowing the students to regain their eligibility for lost privileges. The teacher filed a complaint through the grievance procedure, asserting that the grade change was improper. The grievance was denied at all three levels, culminating with the school board. The teacher and his collective bargaining association filed a state superior court action against the district and principal, seeking declaratory and injunctive relief. The court ordered the reinstatement of the original grades assigned by the teacher and the district and principal appealed to the California Court of Appeal, Second District.

Initially, the appeals court rejected arguments that the action had to be dismissed on the procedural ground that use of the grievance procedure had been improper. The district was not prejudiced by its own failure to invoke statutory procedures applicable to grade changes nor was error committed when the students' parents were not joined as parties. **The California Education Code provides that a grade assigned by a classroom teacher is final and can be changed only in limited circumstances such as a clerical or mechanical mistake, or where the assignment is characterized by bad faith or incompetency.** The court rejected the district's argument that the code section did not apply to citizenship grades. Performance in a secondary school has both academic and behavior components that are graded separately and become part of a student's permanent record. Citizenship grades reflected a teacher's assessment of student performance for cooperation, attitude and effort and there was no reason to believe that the California Legislature meant to distinguish them from academic marks. The court agreed with the superior court's finding that even if citizenship marks were not considered grades, the district had exceeded its authority in changing them. Under another provision of the Education Code, parents can request the change of a school record for inaccuracy or where the record is based on an unsubstantiated personal conclusion or inference outside the observer's area of competence. Since none of these circumstances was present, the district had exceeded its authority in changing the citizenship grades. **Citizenship marks were dependent on first-hand observation and an administrator's bowing to pressure to change them was to be avoided.** *Las Virgenes Educators Association v. Las Virgenes Unified School District,* 102 Cal.Rptr.2d 901 (Cal. App. 2000).

◆   A Texas student filed a federal district court action against his football coach, claiming that the coach unfairly disciplined him and encouraged other athletic department members to harass and intimidate him. **He also complained that he had been arbitrarily assigned a low grade in one class section and that a school employee had released information about him to a local newspaper** in violation of the Family Educational Rights and Privacy Act and state law. The U.S. District Court for the Southern District of Texas held that the student had no constitutional interest in the disputed grade and that the release of information to a local newspaper which did not mention the student by name did not violate the federal privacy act. The court awarded summary judgment to the school district and coach and remanded the state law claims to a Texas state court.

The court then granted summary judgment to the school district on state law claims for intentional infliction of emotional distress and conspiracy to intentionally inflict emotional distress claims. However, it severed the claims against the coach and vacated a prior summary judgment order for him upon the family's reconsideration motion. The Texas Court of Appeals affirmed this decision, and the coach appealed to the Supreme Court of Texas. **The supreme court found that the coach was entitled to immunity under the same statutory section which had afforded governmental immunity to the school district.** Because the section unequivocally provided immunity for all actions against an employee where a governmental entity obtains a judgment involving the same subject matter, the court reversed the decision. *Newman v. Obersteller,* 960 S.W.2d 621 (Tex.1997).

◆   A Dallas high school math teacher alleged that his principal instructed him to give a student-athlete a passing grade in his class, even though the student was failing the class. After the teacher refused to change the grade, the principal allowed the student to transfer out of the teacher's class. The Texas Education Agency (TEA) investigated the school's grading policies on the basis of an anonymous tip, and the school was disqualified from the state football playoffs. **The school district then transferred the teacher to a middle school, placed him on probation for a year, froze his salary, assigned him an unsatisfactory performance rating and prohibited him from teaching math.** An administrative panel upheld the school board's decision, but the TEA reversed the decision. Although prevailing in the TEA action, the teacher resigned from teaching and filed a Texas district court action against the school district and certain school officials, including the principal. The court granted judgment to the school district and officials, and the teacher appealed to the Court of Appeals of Texas, Dallas.

The court agreed with the school district that **the teacher had no constitutional right to refuse to assign a grade to a student as instructed by his supervisor. This was not an example of academic freedom protected by the First Amendment**, because the assignment of a grade is not a teacher method. Accordingly, the district could not be held liable for maintaining a policy or custom of causing constitutional injuries and enjoyed immunity from the tort injuries alleged by the teacher under the Texas Tort Claims Act. The teacher also failed to allege that he had been subjected to intolerable working conditions that would support a constructive discharge claim. The court affirmed the judgment for the district and officials. *Bates v. Dallas Indep. School Dist.*, 952 S.W.2d 543 (Tex.App.–Dallas 1997).

◆   A Louisiana high school senior missed many history and algebra classes because of personal medical problems. Her progress reports indicated failure in both subjects. The history teacher refused to accept overdue assignments and assigned the student an F. Although the algebra teacher stated at one point during the semester that she had never failed a senior, she assigned the student an F for algebra and the student was not allowed to graduate with her class. **She filed a lawsuit against the school board in a Louisiana district court, asserting outrageous behavior on behalf of school employees that caused her emotional distress, humiliation and embarrassment.** The court granted summary judgment to the school board, and the student appealed to the Court of Appeal of Louisiana, First Circuit.

The student claimed that she should have been allowed to demonstrate the intent of school district employees to cause her emotional distress. **The court found no evidence of extreme and outrageous conduct, which is required to recover damages for intentional infliction of emotional distress.** Evidence indicated that the student had been graded and evaluated on the same scale as other students in the district and that her progress reports indicated she was failing both classes. The negligent infliction of emotional distress claim also failed because the school district had no legal duty to allow the makeup of missed assignments and tests. The history teacher was permitted to insist upon the timely submission of work. The court affirmed the judgment for the school board. *Barrino v. East Baton Rouge Parish School Bd.*, 697 So.2d 27 (La.App.1st Cir.1997).

◆   **A North Carolina high school changed its method of selecting honor students** when a newly appointed principal determined that the existing method was in conflict with school board policy. The new method ranked students using a weighted semester grade average. As a result of the change in policy, one student dropped from first to fourth in her class standing and was not selected valedictorian of her graduating class. The student's parents appealed the decision to implement the semester average formula, but were advised by the superintendent of schools that the new system was fair and in compliance with school board policy. This decision was affirmed by the board of education, and the student filed a lawsuit against the board in a North Carolina trial court for negligent infliction of emotional distress, with additional constitutional claims. The court granted the board's summary judgment motion, and the student appealed to the Court of Appeals of North Carolina. On appeal, the student presented evidence that an advisor had told her that she was first in her class during the year of the change in policy and claimed that the board had interfered with her "right to be valedictorian of her senior class." The board argued that the method of determining class ranking was made under the authority of the school board, that the student and her family were advised of the change in procedure and that all students were subject to the same procedure. **Because the student had not alleged that the district's calculations were incorrect or different from any other student's computation, there had been no error by the trial court in dismissing the claim for negligent infliction of emotional distress**. The court of appeals affirmed the trial court's judgment. *Townsend v. Bd. of Educ. of Robeson County*, 454 S.E.2d 817 (N.C.App.1995).

III. STUDENT RECORDS

The Family Educational Rights and Privacy Act of 1974 (FERPA), 20 U.S.C. § 1232g, establishes student and parent rights with regard to student records. Unlike Title VI, Title IX, § 504 and other federal civil rights statutes, FERPA applies to the entire institution and not only to the "program or activity" receiving federal funding. Educators should be familiar with FERPA and it's implementing regulations, which are found at 34 CFR Part 99. FERPA's major requirements are that student records be kept confidential, that parents be allowed access to their children's educational records, and that parents be allowed to challenge information kept in their children's records. Students who are 18 years of age or older have all the rights granted to parents. The states have enacted analogous laws that further define student privacy rights.

◆   According to the Tenth Circuit, **an Oklahoma school district violated the Family Education Rights and Privacy Act by allowing elementary school students to grade each other's tests and call out the results in class**. Although the practice violated the law, it did not violate student constitutional privacy rights and the district and its employees were entitled to immunity for monetary damages. *Falvo v. Owasso Indep. School Dist.*, 233 F.3d 1203 (10th Cir. 2000).

Editor's Note: In the first half of 2001, the U.S. Supreme Court accepted a petition for certiorari filed in this case. The Court is expected to hear oral arguments and release a decision during the 2001-2002 term.

◆   An elementary school student was disciplined for verbally and physically abusing other students. **The school district notified the parents of several victims and witnesses by sending memorandums** to the parents of the affected students and student witnesses. The district communications revealed to parents that the incidents had occurred and that the student was accused of verbally and physically abusing others. The district also reported that each child had been questioned about the incident, that each had reported abuse of some kind by the student and that the student had been advised "that if he had been abusive, he must stop such behavior immediately." The district suspended the student for 10 days, and his parents sued the school district and school officials in a federal district court, asserting civil rights violations under the state and federal constitutions; § 504 of the Rehabilitation Act; the Family Education Rights and Privacy Act; and state law. The court dismissed the complaint and the parents appealed to the U.S. Court of Appeals for the 10th Circuit.

The panel affirmed the district court' judgment on the constitutional claims, the § 504 claim, the interference with parental rights claim and the claim based on injury to reputation. The 10th Circuit held that the parents' privacy claims failed because **the disclosure of information about their son to the parents of student victims and witnesses did not constitute prohibited disclosures of an "educational record" under the Family Education Rights and Privacy Act**, 20 U.S.C. § 1232g. Although the district court had found that FERPA does not create a private right of action under 42 U.S.C. § 1983, the 10th Circuit had recently held that such a cause of action was permitted. The court held that the district memorandums did not violate FERPA because "the contemporaneous disclosure to the parents of a victimized child of the results of any investigation and resulting disciplinary actions taken against an alleged child perpetrator does not constitute release of an 'education record' within the meaning of 20 U.S.C. § 1232g." If this were not the case, educators would lack the ability to assure parents of affected students that they were taking adequate steps to protect children. The court stated that the targeted, discrete disclosure of this information to the parents of victims did not resemble the broad, routinized disclosure of student grades in *Falvo,* above, and was permissible under FERPA. The court found it unnecessary to address the issue of whether the contemporaneous disclosure of information to the parents of witnesses, as opposed to victims, was permitted under FERPA. The memorandums in this case did not disclose anything that qualified as an education record under the act. No court interpreting FERPA had ever held that the limited kind of information conveyed by the district in this case was an education record. The district court had properly dismissed the case and the 10th Circuit affirmed the judgment. *Jensen v. Reeves,* 246 F.3d 681 (10th Cir. 2001).

◆   **A Kentucky news reporter made open-records requests to inspect and copy a school district's student disciplinary hearing records** for 1990 through 1996, seeking the school of origin and the reason for each disciplinary action. The superintendent of schools initially denied the request, but later provided the reporter with copies of board minutes concerning expulsion votes, with all other information redacted. The state attorney general concluded that the Kentucky Open Records Act required disclosure without redacting the school name and category of offense. A county circuit court held that the requested information was excluded from the Open Records Act because it was an "educational record" under FERPA and an analogous state law.

An appeals court reversed the circuit court decision, and the school district appealed to the Kentucky Supreme Court, which noted that FERPA defined "educational records" as materials containing information directly related to a student. **The definition of "personally identifiable information" included name, address and personal characteristics that made a student's identity easily traceable.** Courts have held that **records pertaining to a single student meet these criteria, but statistical compilations do not**. The information requested by the reporter did not directly relate to a particular student and was not an educational record under FERPA. Because the requested information did not meet the FERPA definition of educational record, it was not exempt from disclosure under the Open Records Act, which generally favors public disclosure of records. The act stated that no exemption existed for the "disclosure of statistical information not descriptive of any readily identifiable person." The state high court affirmed the appeals court decision, requiring the district to release the records of student disciplinary hearings without redacting the names of the schools and the offenses appearing in the records. *Hardin County Schools v. Foster*, 40 S.W.3d 865 (Ky. 2001).

◆   A child with numerous health problems, including cerebral palsy, was placed in foster care. Three school district employees who worked at the foster home became concerned about the foster home environment and wrote a letter supporting the guardian *ad litem's* advocacy for the child in an ongoing custody dispute. A copy of the letter was faxed to the county child protection agency, but it declined to investigate. However, the agency forwarded a copy of the letter to the professional association that issued the foster parents' license. The association performed an investigation, found no areas of concern and relicensed the parents with a recommendation to increase their capacity. The parents filed an administrative action against the school district, seeking to rescind the letter. **An administrative law judge recommended that the letter be rescinded and destroyed**, and the commissioner issued an order adopting the recommendation. The school district appealed to the Minnesota Court of Appeals, asserting that the letter was a confidential mandated report that was outside the commissioner's jurisdiction.

The court stated that if a letter is classified as a confidential mandated report of child neglect or abuse under Minn. Stat. § 626.556(7), the commissioner of administration has no jurisdiction to hear the dispute. Under § 626.556(7), a confidential mandated report is "any report received by the local welfare agency, police department, or county sheriff pursuant to this section." However, if it was not a confidential mandated report, it was public or private government data, which the parents had the right to challenge under another chapter of state law. In that case, the commissioner acquired jurisdiction to order the correction of factual errors and conclusions. The court held that the letter was written to the child's guardian *ad litem* in connection with a custody dispute. The district employees did not send it to a local welfare or law enforcement agency and it did not indicate that it was a "report." The employees were child-care professionals who were presumed to know their obligation to report abuse and neglect to a welfare or law enforcement agency, not a guardian *ad litem*. There was no merit to the district's assertion that faxing the letter to the county child protection agency after mailing it to the guardian transformed it into a report. **Because the letter was not a mandated report of abuse or neglect, it was government data** coming under the commissioner's jurisdiction. The allegations contained in the letter were based on the observations of the district employees, and its accuracy or completeness was not communicated to the agency. The court affirmed the order requiring the district to rescind and destroy the letter. *In the Matter of the Appeal of the Determination of the Responsible Authority for the South Washington County School District 833*, 620 N.W.2d 45 (Minn. App. 2000).

♦   The parents of a high school student wrote the school principal a letter explaining that disclosure of some information contained in the student's school records would violate federal privacy laws and referred to a disciplinary incident involving the student. **When the student applied for college attendance and scholarships, the family discovered that their letter had been included with school transcript information**. The family sued the school district and three school administrators in state court, asserting negligence, constitutional rights violations and violation of FERPA.

The court considered a dismissal motion by the school defendants, and first observed that FERPA does not provide a private cause of action for students to sue school districts. Therefore, the family's claim under FERPA was preempted. The court also rejected the family's attempt to recover damages for FERPA violations by way of 42 U.S.C. § 1983. This was because there was no assertion that the school district had a policy or practice of denying parents or students access to educational records under FERPA or that it released records without the required consent. There was evidence that the school complied with FERPA by allowing the parents to include explanatory material in the student's records. The letter was apparently an attempt to explain the student's actions and assert his rights, rather than a reference to the disputed disciplinary action. **FERPA specifically allows the inclusion of disciplinary records in a student's education records and allows dissemination of this information to other schools that have legitimate educational interests in student behavior**. The court rejected the family's claim that school officials violated the family's constitutional rights, since there is no generalized right to privacy. The letter contained no substantive private information, and did not form the basis for a federal privacy action. The family's state law claims were barred for failure to comply with the notice provisions of the Indiana Tort Claims Act. The court entered judgment in favor of the defendants. *Meury v. Eagle-Union Community School Corp.*, 714 N.E.2d 233 (Ind. App. 1999).

♦   A Minnesota student had boasted to classmates that he would have sex with a district paraprofessional and her daughter. The paraprofessional supervised the in-school suspension (ISS) and behavior rooms where the student was often sent for discipline. The school's assistant principal suspended the student for 10 days after observing an incident in the school cafeteria in which the student claimed before a group of students that he had had sex with one of the students. School employees then learned that he had been charged with raping the paraprofessional's daughter. The assistant principal scheduled a meeting with the student's parents and invited the paraprofessional so that she could explain that ISS was no longer possible in view of the student's behavior. The parents requested that the student not attend the meeting. The parents demanded homebound instruction, which the school agreed to provide. However, the parents left the meeting without receiving written notice of a suspension, as required by Minnesota law. The principal later mailed the notice. The student remained in homebound instruction after the end of his suspension, and he graduated from a different school system the following year. **He sued the assistant principal, the paraprofessional, his former school district and its superintendent in a federal district court, claiming many state and federal law violations**.

The court dismissed the student's state law claim for revealing educational data to the paraprofessional, finding little reason to show that the school's behavior room supervisor was not entitled to receive a behavior-related record. Despite the occurrence of a technical violation of the state fair dismissal act, the suspension notice had been mailed on the same day as the meeting and there were no grounds for awarding damages. The court also dismissed the student's claim that the district violated its student manual and that the manual created a contract that could be legally enforced. While the student had been excluded from the suspension conference, he had received an opportunity to present his side of the story as required by *Goss v. Lopez*, 419 U.S. 565 (1975). Despite the technical violation of his procedural rights in personally presenting his story, he was not prejudiced in any way. The court found that even if the student had denied the conduct, he would have still been suspended. The court found no basis for any damage claim as the result of FERPA violations. While the court recognized the possibility of a cause of action under 42 U.S.C. § 1983 for FERPA violations, **the student failed to show that the school district maintained a policy or practice of violating FERPA by improperly releasing student data without written parental consent**. A one-time violation was insufficient to show the existence of a policy or practice. The court granted the school district and employees' motion for summary judgment. *Achman v. Chisago Lakes Indep. School Dist. No. 2144*, 45 F.Supp.2d 664 (D.Minn.1999).

◆   The Ohio Department of Education (ODE) administers the Ohio Proficiency Test to high school seniors to ensure that they have requisite knowledge in selected academic areas. Ohio State University also administered a statewide test to high school students that was developed to accelerate the modernization of vocational education in the state. Part of that test was developed and owned by a private entity. Both tests used a new format each time a test was administered and the tests were owned in part by the state agencies that administered them. **An Ohio student who had taken both examinations requested access to the tests after they had been administered**. The ODE refused to release test information for review unless the student signed a nondisclosure agreement. The family refused to sign the agreement and instead commenced a state court action to compel state education officials to release relevant portions of both tests pursuant to the state Public Records Act.

The Supreme Court of Ohio accepted jurisdiction over the case and found that **the state-owned parts of both tests were considered public records within the meaning of state law. Further, none of the exceptions to the state law presumption in favor of public disclosure applied**. The student sought release of the information for educational purposes and did not seek to use it for a commercial purpose. A state law that prohibits assisting a student in cheating on proficiency tests was not applicable to this case. The student was entitled to an order for disclosure of the requested information. However, the portion of the test devised by the private entity was not a public record and was not subject to release. *State ex rel. Rea v. Ohio Dep't of Educ.*, 81 Ohio St.3d 527, 692 N.E.2d 596 (1998).

◆   A California student was sexually assaulted by three other students on a high school campus. A newspaper publisher obtained information, including the assailants' names, from the records of the juvenile court proceedings resulting from the assault. The victim's attorney initiated a settlement with the school district to confidentially resolve the district's civil liability arising from the assault. The school district tendered its defense to its insurance carrier and the parties reached a settlement. The agreement was approved by a California superior court, which sealed the file. The publishing company unsuccessfully moved the court to unseal the record. It appealed to the California Court of Appeal, Fourth District, which found that the student's privacy interests did not exceed the public's right of access to information concerning school district accountability. The court rejected the student's claim that releasing to the public the amount of the settlement would result in mental anguish. **Because the student failed to show a compelling interest in concealing the amount of the settlement, the court ordered the superior court to vacate its prior order and unseal the court record.** *Copley Press, Inc. v. Superior Court of San Diego County*, 74 Cal.Rptr.2d 69 (Cal.App.4th Dist.1998).

◆   The Virginia Freedom of Information Act requires the public disclosure of all nonexempt official government records. A statutory exception gives records custodians discretion concerning scholastic records which contain information about identifiable individuals that are maintained by a public agency. **The editor of a Virginia high school student newspaper requested the individual total vote counts for each candidate in a school election**, which had been furnished only to student candidates. The school principal and a teacher who acted as the student government advisor denied the request under the state freedom of information act, expressing concern that release of the information might embarrass students who did not gain election. The student editor filed a petition against the school board in a Virginia circuit court, seeking disclosure. The court held that the scholastic records exemption applied, and the editor appealed to the Supreme Court of Virginia. The court found that each of the statutory elements applied to the requested records, since they contained information about students and were maintained by a public educational agency. **Because the principal and teacher were not required to disclose the information, the records were exempt from public disclosure**, and the circuit court decision was affirmed. *Wall v. Fairfax County School Bd.*, 475 S.E.2d 803 (Va.1996).

◆   A Delaware school district disciplined a music teacher for harassing female students. The teacher filed a grievance against the district under the applicable collective bargaining agreement, which required just cause for any disciplinary action against a teacher. **The district refused to disclose the names of complaining students and witnesses to the teacher's union**, and it filed an unfair labor practice complaint against the district with the state Employment Relations Board.

The board ruled that the district had an unconditional duty to disclose student names to the union and had committed an unfair labor practice. The district appealed to a Delaware trial court, which held that the district's failure to first consult with parents before refusing to disclose student identities constituted an unfair labor practice. However, parents had a right to receive advance notice of any disclosure of student names and the board order calling for an unconditional duty of disclosure had been improper.

The union appealed to the Supreme Court of Delaware, which held that the district's failure to first obtain parental consent before denying the request for information constituted an unfair labor practice. It also agreed with the trial court that the remedy imposed by the employment relations board violated the rights of parents to make fundamental decisions for their children prior to any disclosure of information. The court substantially affirmed the trial court decision, but refused to rule on whether parents retained an unconditional right to refuse disclosure of a child's name, since this issue was not required to resolve the dispute and called for an advisory opinion. *Colonial Educ. Ass'n v. Bd. of Educ. of Colonial School Dist.*, 685 A.2d 361 (Del. 1996).

◆ **The Texas Open Records Act contains an exception for disclosure of documents that are related to the deliberative process of inter or intra-agency policymaking**. The exception protects from public disclosure any memorandums that would not be discoverable in litigation. The parent of a Texas student questioned a low grade received by the student for conduct in her choir class. He requested all documents, notes, letters and summaries of conversations concerning his complaint, but the custodian of records for the school district refused to release them, citing the deliberative process exception. The state attorney general issued an opinion letter stating that the documents should not be exempt from public disclosure. The school district and records custodian filed a lawsuit in a Texas trial court, seeking a declaratory judgment that they were entitled to privacy. The court found that the documents would be discoverable in litigation but were exempt as related to the deliberative process. The Texas Court of Appeals, Houston, found that **the documents related to the implementation of existing policy and not the making of any new policy. Since they would otherwise be discoverable in litigation, the exception did not apply and the parent was entitled to receive copies.** *Lett v. Klein Indep. School Dist.*, 917 S.W.2d 455 (Tex.App.–Houston 1996).

IV. TESTING

Placement testing, exit examinations, and achievement tests may be used to assist in the determination of classroom assignments and eligibility for graduation, provided that the test results are not a reflection of past racial segregation policies, the testing is accurate, and the results of the tests are open to public scrutiny.

◆ **A class of Indiana students with disabilities challenged the Indiana graduation qualifying examination**. One subclass of students asserted that the state violated their due process rights by making the Graduation Qualifying Examination (GQE) a graduation requirement beginning in 2000. The students were previously exempted from the examination and did not receive instruction in the tested material. A second subclass of students claimed denial of testing accommodations and adaptations in violation of the Individuals with Disabilities Education Act. They alleged that the state denied them permission to use the accommodations called for in their individualized education programs during the test. The court refused to certify one subclass for failing to first exhaust administrative remedies and rejected a proposal for certification of all students who asserted lack of accommodation. The Indiana Court of Appeals reversed and remanded in response to the students' appeal.

On remand, the trial court entered judgment for the state, and the students appealed again. The court of appeals held that the students had a property interest in the award of a diploma if they met all graduation requirements. This interest was protected by the right to due process, requiring adequate notice of the examination and exposure to the material being tested. However, the state had provided school districts with at least five years' notice about the GQE and the students learned of it at least three years in advance. The trial court did not erroneously find that this notice was adequate, in view of the multiple opportunities provided to students for remediation and retaking the GQE, if necessary.

The court found that the students received exposure to the curriculum tested on the GQE. There was evidence that school systems were required to align their curriculum with state standards as of 1996. The trial court properly found that the remedy for failing to teach students the subjects tested on the GQE was remediation, not to award diplomas. The IDEA does not require such a result, mandating only that students with disabilities receive specialized and individualized services. **The state did not violate the IDEA by failing to honor accommodations specified in IEPs where they would affect the validity of GQE results**. It permitted accommodations such as sign language responses, use of Braille, special lighting and furniture, large type and individual or small group testing. However, it prohibited accommodations in the form of reading questions designed to measure reading comprehension or allowing unlimited testing time. The state was not required to provide all accommodations specified in IEPs during the GQE. It affirmed the trial court judgment for the state. *Rene v. Reed*, No. 49A02-0007-CV-433, 2001 WL 688228 (Ind. App. 2001).

♦   Twelve New York high schools were part of a consortium of county high schools, which in 1995 received a five-year variance to develop student achievement assessments as an alternative to the state Regents examination. The following year, the schools were designated "twenty-first century schools" under the state's Twenty First Century School Act. They remained under local board control, and retained the exemption from Regents examinations. After the New York Legislature enacted the Charter Schools Act in 1998, the schools pursued "fast track conversion" applications by which they agreed to charters that were consistent with state law. Among the provisions of the Charter Schools Act was that students take Regents examinations to the same extent required of other public school students. **The chancellor of New York City schools assured the new charter schools that their exemption from Regents examinations could continue** pending review by the state assessment panel and approval by the state education commissioner. The charters were approved, but when the schools applied for extension of the variance from student participation in Regents examinations, they were denied a one-year extension because they received their charters under the condition that students would take the examinations. The schools sued the commissioner, asserting unlawful revocation of their twenty-first century school designations.

The trial court entered judgment for the commissioner and the schools appealed to the New York Supreme Court, Appellate Division, which noted that the case hinged on inconsistencies between provisions of the Twenty-First Century School Act and the Charter Schools Act. While the twenty-first century schools had no legal existence apart from a school district, charter schools were separate legal entities acting independently of a school district under the control of a board of trustees. Twenty-first century schools were subject to district rules and regulations and could use only certified teachers, but charter schools were exempt from most public school laws, regulations and certification requirements and were governed by their own charters. **Charter Schools Act provisions were governing and controlling in the event of any inconsistency with other state or local laws, rules or regulations. Its participation requirement for state Regents examinations was incorporated in each school's charter**, therefore the schools were not entitled to exclude students from the Regents examinations. The schools were entitled to a variance from the Regents examination only until the revised examination was in place, and no waiver from the English portion of the examination was ever granted. The court affirmed the judgment for the commissioner. *In the Matter of International High School: A Charter School at LaGuardia Community College v. Mills*, 715 N.Y.S.2d 490 (A.D. 2000).

◆   The Texas Assessment of Academic Skills (TAAS) has been administered to all Texas students since 1990 to measure student mastery of the state-mandated curriculum. Passing the tenth grade test is a requirement for graduation. **Groups representing Texas minority students sued the Texas Education Agency (TEA), asserting that the exit level TAAS exam had a disparate impact on minority students** in violation of the Due Process Clause of the 14th Amendment and federal law. The court dismissed many of the plaintiffs' claims, then held a trial on the claims brought under Title VI of the Civil Rights Act of 1964 and the Due Process Clause.

The court accepted evidence that minority failure rates on the TAAS exam were much higher than those for majority students, but noted that minority students were rapidly narrowing the passing-rate gap. It held that the TAAS exam did not disadvantage minority students. Students failing any portion of the exam receive concentrated, targeted educational remediation. The court accepted the TEA's evidence that school accountability and mandated remediation helped to address the effects of prior discrimination in Texas. **Cumulative pass rates did not demonstrate a severe disparate impact on minority students** for the classes of 1996, 1997, and 1998. The exam provided the state with an objective way to assess student mastery of the skills and knowledge required for graduation. **The selection of a 70 percent exam passing score was not arbitrary and bore a relationship to the state's legitimate goals, as was the use of the TAAS exam as a graduation requirement**. The student groups failed to identify equally effective alternatives to the use of the TAAS exam for achieving the state's goals of holding students, teachers, and schools accountable for teaching, learning, and ensuring equal opportunity to learn. The court held that the exam did not violate student due process interests because it was not fundamentally unfair to minority students. The exam reliably measured what it purported to measure and met accepted standards for curricular validity. Students had adequate notice and opportunity to learn all covered subject matter and disparities in test scores did not result from flawed testing or administration. TAAS exit exam administration addressed educational inequalities and did not violate Title VI regulations or the Due Process Clause, according to the court. Judgment was granted to the TEA. *GI Forum v. Texas Education Agency*, 87 F.Supp.2d 667 (W.D.Tex. 2000).

◆   Two African-American students sued the Montgomery County, Alabama, school board and its individual members in a federal district court, seeking permission to participate in graduation ceremonies. They had satisfied their course requirements but had failed the state-mandated exit examination, despite four opportunities to do so. **The students contended that the school board, without properly notifying them of the consequences of failing the test, was refusing to let them partici-pate in graduation ceremonies, even though special education students and certain others could participate** by walking across the stage and receiving certificates of attendance. They argued that the exit exam was racially biased and had an overwhelmingly disparate impact on African-American students.

The court held that the exit exam, which is not a local policy but rather a graduation requirement of the state education board, did not violate student equal protection rights. Although 36 of 37 students who were not allowed to participate in graduation ceremonies were African-American, the remaining 1,142 African-American students in the county had passed the test. **The court found no constitu-tionally protected interest to participate in graduation ceremonies**. The claim of inadequate notice about the policy was undercut by evidence that the two students named as parties had acknowledged receipt of copies of the code of good student behavior. These acknowledgments had been returned to their schools as part of the district policy noted above. The court stated that the students had met the legal standard for their Title VI claim by demonstrating that the policy had an adverse effect upon them. However, they had received up to four opportunities to take the exam and were not required to re-take the exam sections they had passed. **The court found no Title VI violation because the exam was justified by substantial, legitimate government interests**. There was an important government interest in denying the students permission to walk at the graduation ceremony and the court denied their application for a temporary order. *L.I. by Wanda I. v. Montgomery County School Bd.*, No. CV-98-A-597-N (N.D.Ala.1998).

◆   **A Texas student who attended a non-accredited private religious institu-tion transferred to a public school that required her to take proficiency tests**, at her own expense, for each of the course credits she wished to transfer. The student and her parents sued the school district in the U.S. District Court for the Western District of Texas, challenging the policy on grounds including violation of the Free Exercise and Equal Protection Clauses.

The court held that the policy did not violate the Free Exercise Clause of the U.S. Constitution because the plaintiffs failed to demonstrate how it burdened their right to the free exercise of religion. The family admitted that it had no religious objection to the policy. Even had the family raised religious objections, the court stated, the policy would still be a valid, religion-neutral policy of general applicability because it applied to all students without regard to the nature of their prior education. The court granted the school summary judgment on this claim. With regard to the equal protection claim, the court found that **the testing policy did not treat one group of individuals differently from any other group because any student coming to the school from a non-accredited school would be subject to the policy**. The policy did not infringe on any fundamental right, or burden a suspect class of people but was instead rationally related to a legitimate state interest. The school was also entitled to summary judgment on this claim. *Hubbard v. Buffalo Indep. School Dist.*, 20 F.Supp.2d 1012 (W.D.Tex.1998).

◆   The Kentucky Education Reform Act was passed by the state legislature in response to the Supreme Court of Kentucky's decision in *Rose v. Council for Better Education, Inc.*, Ky., 790 S.W.2d 186 (1989), a landmark decision declaring the state education system unconstitutional on state constitutional grounds. The KERA mandated shared responsibilities among state and local governments, students and teachers to improve public education in Kentucky. It established a student assessment examination to evaluate each school district's progress in reaching KERA goals. **Although KERA did not specifically permit districts to require passing the assessment examination as a prerequisite for advancement or graduation, one district resolved that each student must complete the examination prior to graduation or advancing to the next grade**. A family that objected to the examination on religious grounds refused to allow their children to take it, and the district failed to promote one student and refused to award a diploma to the other. The family commenced a state court action against the board, asserting that its policy violated their constitutional privacy, free exercise of religion, parental and due process rights.

The court dismissed the constitutional claims, but held that the examination should be open for public review. The family appealed to the Kentucky Court of Appeals, which found nothing in the examination that invaded student religious beliefs or discriminated on the basis of religion. The examination had a secular purpose that furthered the provision of an efficient education system as required by the *Rose* decision. State laws empowered local boards to impose additional graduation requirements upon students beyond those specified by law. **Local boards were accountable for their performance and there was a sufficiently compelling need for them to require all students to take the examination**. The court affirmed the trial court judgment upholding the constitutionality of the examination and the board policy requiring all students to take it. However, it reversed the part of the trial court judgment requiring the exam to be open to public inspection. It restricted inspection of the examination for the limited purposes of the lawsuit. *Triplett v. Livingston County Bd. of Educ.*, 967 S.W.2d 25 (Ky.App. 1997).

◆   **A North Carolina school board adopted a student accountability policy providing that students in grades three through eight who failed a state-**

developed standardized test would be retained in their grade instead of promoted the following school year. The policy contained a waiver for students who achieved passing grades during the school year as long as they obtained teacher and principal approval. A group of students and their parents filed a federal district court action against school officials, challenging the constitutionality of the board's policy. The court rejected the group's assertion that students would suffer irreparable harm if they were retained in a grade for failing to pass the test. The complaint was based on speculative injuries including low self-esteem, negative school attitudes and a reduced chance of succeeding in school. The students failed to present the court with cognizable constitutional claims, since **a student who was not promoted to the next grade would be given a remedial year to catch up on skills in which future performance could be enhanced.** Public policy discourages a federal court from substituting its judgment for that of publicly elected school board members. The policy employed rational means to further a legitimate academic purpose. The court denied a motion by the group for a preliminary order that would prohibit the use of the standardized test. *Erik V. by and through Catherine V. v. Causby,* 977 F.Supp. 384 (E.D.N.C.1997).

◆   Louisiana required all public school graduating seniors to pass a graduate exit examination (GEE) in order to get their diplomas. Private school students were not required to take the test. Five public school students who had completed their required coursework but failed the GEE prior to the end of their senior year sued the state Board of Elementary and Secondary Education (BESE) in a Louisiana trial court, seeking a declaration that the policy was invalid and an order requiring the awarding of their diplomas. The court issued a preliminary order prohibiting BESE from withholding the diplomas. BESE appealed to the Court of Appeal of Louisiana, First Circuit. The court found that the GEE requirement was permissible under BESE's broad discretionary power to supervise public education. The policy did not violate the U.S. Constitution's Equal Protection Clause, even though the test was not administered to private school students. BESE had no authority to control private school curriculums or to set examination requirements without violating the rights of parents who sent their children to private schools. **Although public and private school students were treated differently as a result of BESE's inability to administer the GEE test to private school students, the court of appeal upheld the testing requirement because it was rationally related to the goal of insuring minimum competency in public school graduates.** *Rankins v. Louisiana State Bd. of Elementary and Secondary Educ.,* 637 So.2d 548 (La.App.1st Cir.1994).

V.   EDUCATIONAL MALPRACTICE

Claims of educational malpractice have, for the most part, failed. Only Montana has recognized the claim as a legal cause of action. Courts have been reluctant to interfere with a school's internal operations.

◆   A group of parents sued the Denver Public Schools and its superintendent in a state court for contractual, statutory and constitutional violations for failure to provide students with a quality education. The complaint asserted that the school system failed to provide course books, failed to control student conduct through adequate discipline, improperly used credit waivers to inflate graduation rates, maintained a pattern of poorly performing schools, and used "dumbed-down" standards for measuring school performance. **It also alleged damages for intellectual and emotional harm, diminuation of educational and career opportunities, discrimination, and asserted that parents were forced to send their children to private or alternative schools**. The trial court granted the board's motion to dismiss the case on grounds that the constitutional and statutory claims were not justiciable. It agreed with the board that the contract claim failed because no contractual relationship existed between public schools and their students.

The court of appeals agreed to review the contract claim, and distinguished the case from cases involving contractual breach claims against private schools. Contract claims attacking the general quality of education have been rejected because they are not truly based in contract but instead seek damages for educational malpractice. **Public school students, unlike those attending private schools, have not individually contracted with their school systems for specific educational services and cannot assert claims for breach of contract**. There was no legally enforceable promise to provide a curriculum, books or other educational services in this case. The court held that the matter was political in nature and not within the power of the courts to decide. No court in the nation has recognized a breach of contract claim rooted in legislative policy, and the court affirmed the judgment for the school board and superintendent. *Denver Parents Association v. Denver Bd. of Educ.*, 10 P.3d 662 (Colo.App. 2000).

◆   A Connecticut school purchased and implemented a teaching method called "responsive classroom method" from a private Massachusetts foundation. **Students at the school commenced a state court negligence action against the school board, alleging that implementation of the method created an atmosphere of disruptiveness and violence** and that meaningful learning did not take place at the school. The complaint further alleged educational malpractice and the intentional infliction of emotional distress. The court granted the board's motion to strike the nine-count complaint.

On appeal, the students argued that a cause of action for educational malpractice exists in at least two situations. According to the students, educational malpractice is an appropriate claim where it is shown that an institution has breached a contract for educational services or fails to fulfill specific contractual promises. The court held that the allegations in this case were personal injury claims that did not allege a breach of contract. **The trial court had properly stricken the tort-based claims for educational malpractice**, according to the appeals court. However, the complaint alleged conduct exceeding all bounds usually tolerated in society, and thus met the minimal standards for an intentional infliction of emotional distress claim. Only a jury could determine whether the claims were true, and the appeals court reversed this part of the trial court decision. *Bell v. Bd. of Educ. of City of West Haven*, 55 Conn.App. 400, 739 A.2d 321 (Conn. App.1999).

◆   A second-grade Michigan student hanged himself the night after viewing a film at school featuring the attempted suicide of a young disabled character who eventually learns to overcome his disability. The student's estate filed a lawsuit in a Michigan trial court against the school district, school superintendent, members of the board of education, principal, teacher, staff members and the distributor and producer of the film *Nobody's Useless*. The court held that the distributor and producer had no duty to state the age-appropriateness of the film, and that **the school principal, teachers, and other school staff had no duty to refrain from showing the film to second graders**. However, the court denied a motion by the district, school board and superintendent for summary disposition on the grounds of absolute governmental immunity. The case reached the Court of Appeals of Michigan.

The court of appeals held that Michigan's governmental immunity statute applied to the board members, the superintendent and the district. The school district was a governmental entity performing duties contemplated in the immunity statute. Likewise, school board members and the superintendent were entitled to absolute governmental immunity. **The court affirmed the finding of the lack of a duty to refrain from showing the film to a second grader. This theory was rooted in educational malpractice, a claim that the court refused to recognize**. Any lawsuit based upon educational malpractice was impossible to prove and unreasonably burdensome to the educational system. The court also affirmed the lack of liability by the film's producer and distributor. *Nalepa v. Plymouth-Canton Community School Dist.*, 525 N.W.2d 897 (Mich.App.1994).

CHAPTER TWELVE

Students with Disabilities

I. STATE AND LOCAL RESPONSIBILITIES UNDER THE IDEA

The Individuals with Disabilities Education Act (IDEA) is the major federal legislation pertaining to the education of students with disabilities. It provides federal funding to local education agencies through grants to the states. To receive IDEA funds, states must demonstrate that they maintain a policy that assures that all children with disabilities have access to a free appropriate public education. In 1997, Congress enacted Public Law 105–17, the Individuals with Disabilities Education Act Amendments of 1997. Included in the amendments are a revised funding formula based on a state's child population and child poverty level; requirements for the least restrictive environment for the placement of students, and the requirement that the states use methods of distributing IDEA funds that ensure compliance with those requirements.

After the enactment of the IDEA Amendments of 1997, the Secretary of Education issued regulations to implement the new statute. The regulations incorporate the statutory changes of the 1997 Amendments, including a shift in focus to heighten attention to improving results for children with disabilities, and promoting early identification and early provision of services, as well as ensuring access. The outcome-oriented approach of the 1997 Amendments and their regulations expands the act's basic guarantee of access to educational services.

A. Generally

The educational program of a student with disabilities must be individually tailored to the needs of the student. The IDEA accomplishes this by requiring an individualized education program (IEP) for each student with a disability to be prepared by school staff with the participation of the student's parents or guardian and at least one of the student's present teachers. The IEP is subject to annual review. The IDEA also requires that students with disabilities receive instruction in the least restrictive appropriate environment; in other words, they must be educated in regular classes to the extent possible. This is also known as mainstreaming.

The IDEA defines children with disabilities as those having mental retardation, hearing impairments including deafness, speech or language impairments, visual impairments including blindness, serious emotional disturbance, orthopedic impairments, autism, traumatic brain injury, other health impairments, and specific learning disabilities, who, by reason of their disabilities, are in need of special education and related services. See 20 U.S.C. § 1401(3). For further definitions, see 34 CFR Part 300.7. The IDEA imposes an affirmative duty on the states, through local education agencies, to provide eligible students with a free appropriate public education, defined as special education and related services provided at public expense that meet state educational agency standards in conformity with an IEP. Local educational agencies receiving IDEA funds must include satisfactory assurances that they are identifying and providing special education services to all students with disabilities residing within the local jurisdiction, regardless of the severity of the disability. Local educational agencies (LEAs) must identify, locate and evaluate students in need of special education and related services and establish a goal of providing full educational opportunities to all their students with disabilities with the participation and consultation of the parents of each student. The method of ensuring that each student with a disability receives a free appropriate public education is the provision of an IEP to be reviewed at least once a year. IDEA regulations require the inclusion of transition services in the IEP of each student with a disability no later than the age of 16, or earlier if appropriate, as in the case of students who are at risk of dropping out. See 34 CFR Part 300.347.

Related services are defined as "transportation, and such developmental, corrective, and other supportive services (including speech pathology and audiology, psychological services, physical and occupational therapy, recreation, including therapeutic recreation, social work services, counseling services, including rehabilitation counseling, and medical services, except that such medical services shall be for diagnostic and evaluation purposes only) as may be required to assist a child with a disability to benefit from special education, and includes the early identification and assessment of disabling conditions in children." See 20 U.S.C.

§ 1401(22). While medical services are excluded from the definition of related services, they are not excluded insofar as they may be needed by a child for diagnostic and evaluative purposes. Psychological services are related services and thus are to be provided free of charge by school districts to students with disabilities who require such services.

Because the IDEA's only qualitative standard for the provision of special education and related services is that they "meet the standards of the state educational agency," the courts have refrained from extensive review of contested IEPs, focusing instead on the protection of IDEA procedural rights. In the following case, the U.S. Supreme Court ruled that the IDEA establishes a basic floor of opportunity for students with disabilities, and imposes no requirement on LEAs to maximize their potential.

◆   A New York student with hearing impairments sought the provision of a sign language interpreter from her school district. She had residual hearing and was an excellent lipreader, which allowed her to attain above average grades and to advance through school easily. **The student's parents requested the services of a sign language interpreter at school district expense, arguing that the IDEA required the district to maximize her potential**. The U.S. District Court for the Southern District of New York held that the disparity between the student's achievement and her potential to perform as she would if not for her disability deprived her of a free appropriate public education. This decision was affirmed by the U.S. Court of Appeals, Second Circuit, and the U.S. Supreme Court agreed to review the case.

The court reviewed the IDEA's legislative history and **found no requirement that public schools maximize the potential of each student with a disability**. The opportunities provided to each student by their school varied from student to student. The IDEA was primarily designed to guarantee access to students with disabilities to allow them to meaningfully benefit from public education. The IDEA protected the right to access by means of its procedural protections, including the annual IEP meeting and review process. The Court was unwilling to recognize the substantive requirement urged by the parents in this case. **In IDEA cases, courts were to limit their inquiry to whether the school had complied with IDEA procedural protections, and whether the IEP was reasonably calculated to enable the student to receive educational benefits**. *Bd. of Educ. v. Rowley*, 458 U.S. 176, 102 S.Ct. 3034, 73 L.Ed.2d 690 (1982).

◆   In a dispute over the placement of a student with cerebral palsy, a learning impairment and a visual deficit in a private academy, the court agreed with the academy that its rule that students with disabilities perform at least at a fifth grade level before being placed in mainstream classes was not directly subject to IDEA standards. It relied on a 1989 Office for Special Education Programs policy letter interpreting the general standards under the IDEA for private schools serving eligible students with disabilities. The letter stated that private schools are not bound by the same admission and discipline policies applicable to public schools. According to the court, **the IDEA and its regulations apply only to state and local agencies, and expressly contemplate that federal IEP and LRE requirements**

will be enforced by a public agency when it places a student in a private school. Even when a private school conducts and revises IEPs, the public agency remains responsible for IDEA compliance. The student had no IDEA cause of action against the academy and the district court had improperly found that it was a local education agency under the IDEA. A local education agency is by definition a public entity, and must be an agency, as opposed to a school. The agreement between the district and academy created only a negotiating procedure, and was not a vehicle for IDEA enforcement against the academy. The circuit court vacated the district court's order, noting that the student might still have IDEA claims against the district and state education department. The academy also prevailed with respect to the Section 504 claim, since its performance requirement was a legitimate academic policy with respect to all students, regardless of disability. The student was unable to meet the academy's legitimate program requirements of performing at a fifth-grade level and was not a qualified individual with a disability under the Rehabilitation Act. Section 504 does not require institutions to lower their academic standards. *St. Johnsbury Academy v. D.H.*, 240 F.3d 163 (2d Cir. 2001).

◆   The Washington legislature enacted a law in 1998 providing for the education of juveniles incarcerated in adult prisons. After two school districts began providing services at correctional facilities under the new law, **a group of inmates brought a class-action lawsuit** in the state court system against Washington state, the school districts, and a number of state officials, **alleging that the various entities failed to provide special education services in violation of state and federal law, including constitutional violations**. The court granted summary judgment to the inmates on their state-law claims and invalidated the 1998 legislation as unconstitutional because it failed to provide special educational opportunities. The court dismissed all of the federal claims, and the parties appealed unfavorable aspects of the decision to the Washington Supreme Court.

The state supreme court observed that the 1998 legislation, not the state's basic and special education acts, determined the outcome of the state-law claims. The legislature had specifically acted to exempt incarcerated juveniles from the state compulsory school attendance law. The state special education law did not specifically address the education of juveniles incarcerated in adult facilities. It ensured educational opportunities "for all children with disabilities who are not institutionalized." **Inmates were outside the state's school system and were exempt from the provisions of the state special education act**. The court rejected the inmates' argument that the state constitution required basic and special education for all inmates in adult prisons up to the age of 22. The provision of education to inmates up to the age of 18 satisfied the U.S. Constitution. The 1998 legislation did not violate the Washington Constitution, since the court found that the state had no obligation to provide an identical education to all children within the state. The court rejected the inmates' assertion that the state had a duty under the IDEA to provide special education to students with disabilities under the age of 22. IDEA language specifically exempts the states from their duty to provide special education services "where its application would be inconsistent with state law or practice" for students age 18 through 21. It also exempted those students who were not identified as disabled or did not have IEPs prior to incarceration. **The state was not required to provide special education services to students over the age of 18 if it did not**

also provide education services to students without disabilities in this age group. Since the 1998 law clearly stated that inmates were entitled to education until the age of 18, the trial court had properly dismissed the inmates' IDEA claim. The school districts were not required by state law or the Washington Constitution to provide educational services to juvenile inmates, and the trial court had properly dismissed the claims against them. *Tunstall v. Bergeson*, 5 P.3d 691 (Wash. 2000).

◆   A New Jersey student was identified as needing speech therapy. His parents decided to educate him at home and requested speech therapy from the district. The district rejected the request, stating that the student did not attend a public or nonpublic school. The state department of education denied mediation and due process hearing requests by the parents, and they commenced a state court action against the district in which the department intervened. The trial court found that the student was entitled to a pro rata allocation of federal funds available for New Jersey nonpublic school students. It also held that the department had improperly engaged in rulemaking in violation of the state administrative procedure act when it created its regulatory definition of "nonpublic school." Moreover, **the department and district violated the student's equal protection right to receive special education under the New Jersey Constitution**. The court ordered the department and district to reimburse the family for weekly speech therapy sessions.

On appeal, the New Jersey Superior Court, Appellate Division, noted that the IDEA allows school districts to treat nonpublic-school students and home-schooled students differently. IDEA regulations state that local districts must provide services to students in "private schools" under a specific funding formula. Because the student was not attending a "nonpublic school," he was not included in this calculation. Under the IDEA, state law determines whether a home-schooled student is enrolled in a "private school." New Jersey did not include home schooling within the definition of "nonpublic school" and there was no indication that the Legislature intended to provide services to students elsewhere than school. The appeals court observed that **the amended IDEA creates no individual entitlement to funds and allows the states to differentiate among students who attend nonpublic schools and those who are educated at home**. State law, the IDEA and the OSEP opinion letter provided a clear statutory basis for the exclusion of home schooling from the definition of "nonpublic school" in department regulations. Although it was permissible for New Jersey school districts to differentiate between nonpublic-school students and those who received home education, **the district had violated the student's equal protection rights by refusing entirely to provide him with services**, even after his parents agreed to follow a recommended treatment plan that was to take place at a public school in the district. Because the district did not provide the student with services it provided for other students who needed speech therapy services, and they would be delivered at the same cost to the district, the district violated the student's equal protection rights. The appeals court affirmed the trial court's decision regarding the alleged equal protection violation. *Forstrom v. Byrne et al.*, 775 A.2d 65 (N.J. App. Div. 2001).

◆   A student with Down syndrome who was 20 years old received instruction in a learning support environment for two-thirds of the school day under an IEP. **His** parents requested that the school IEP team allow him to participate in graduation ceremonies at the end of the school year, even though he would not graduate at that time. The district refused the request, and the parents requested a special education due process hearing. A special education hearing officer upheld the district policy requiring students to complete all local and state graduation requirements, including IEPs, before participating in graduation ceremonies. A state special education appeals panel reversed and ordered the district to allow the student to participate.

The district appealed to the Pennsylvania Commonwealth Court, arguing that it was vested with discretion to develop its own criteria for participation in graduation ceremonies, and that its decision to exclude the student was a valid exercise of its discretion. The court agreed, observing that the state general assembly had vested local districts with the authority to establish graduation requirements and confer diplomas upon those who complete the requirements. **Any ceremony celebrating the completion of these requirements, and the decision to award a diploma, was within the local district's educational policy discretion**. The family did not dispute that the student was not yet eligible to receive a diploma, and the appellate panel had improperly found the district policy requiring students to complete an appropriate instructional program before receiving a diploma void for vagueness. Both state and federal special education law mandated that the student receive instruction under his IEP and it was appropriate that he complete requirements beyond those required of students without disabilities before becoming eligible to graduate and receive a diploma. The district's policy did not violate the IDEA, and was applied uniformly to all students, regardless of disability. The practical effect of the IDEA was to give students with disabilities the right to an IEP, not a right to graduate with his or her peers. The court reversed the appeals panel's decision. *Woodland Hills School District v. S.F.*, 747 A.2d 433 (Pa. Commw. 2000).

◆   At age three, the school district a student resided in assumed responsibility for providing him with educational services. The district and family disagreed about continuing a learning center program and beginning a public school program, and disputed whether the program should be integrated. The family attacked an initial integrated public school program placement because of the school's inadequately trained staff. After the student was reevaluated, the program included increased staff training. The parents alleged that the training never took place, and requested a hearing before the state board of special education appeals. The hearing officer issued a preliminary order that called for improving the placement, but declined the parents' request for an off-site program. They sought federal district court review. The court denied their request for an immediate, off-site placement of the student, and then appointed a neutral expert who recommended placement in a district school with some changes in the program. The district implemented the changes, but the student eventually transferred. **The family sought compensatory and punitive damages against the district for IDEA violations under 42 U.S.C. § 1983**.

The district court noted that § 1983 does not create substantive rights, but instead provides a vehicle for persons to obtain monetary damages for civil rights violations. The IDEA was amended in 1986 to allow plaintiffs in IDEA actions to seek remedies available under the Constitution and other federal laws, but the courts have disagreed on the availability of damages under § 1983 for IDEA violations. Section 1983 liability has been found in cases of alleged misconduct of constitutional proportions, but not for mere statutory violations. **The intent of Congress in amending the IDEA could not be seen as allowing a § 1983 claim whenever a school district and family disagreed about an educational placement.** In this case, the family failed to claim that the alleged civil rights violations by the school district were the product of a custom or practice. Because the allegations did not meet this threshold for § 1983 liability, the court dismissed the claim. The parents were entitled to an award of attorney's fees, since they were prevailing parties in an IDEA action. The court reduced the amount of fees claimed by the family, but required the district to pay about half the amount claimed. *Andrew S. v. School Comm. of Town of Greenfield*, 59 F.Supp.2d 237 (D.Mass.1999).

◆   A regular education student's intelligence was measured at the ninety-fifth percentile, yet his test scores were very low and his reading ability tested in the second percentile. During the third grade, an independent consultant concluded that the student had a learning disability. The school's child study team (CST) noted the discrepancy between the student's test scores and abilities, and his anxieties about his academic performance, but refused to identify him as learning disabled. Four years later, the CST agreed to classify the student as perceptually impaired and devised an IEP for him. The IEP included Orton Gillingham instruction in reading and spelling, with resource center instruction in three other subjects. The student made minimal progress through the eighth grade. At that point, the CST proposed an IEP that called for the student's removal from regular education academic classes except for gym. **The parents asked for a due process hearing, seeking a district funded private placement.** A state administrative law judge concluded that the district IEP was inappropriate, and ordered the district to pay the student's tuition at a private school selected by the parents. Both parties appealed to a federal district court, which reversed the administrative decision.

On appeal by the parents to the Third Circuit, the court rejected the district court's conclusion that the IDEA only requires an IEP to provide a student with more than trivial educational benefit. According to the circuit court, **the IDEA calls for more than a trivial benefit and requires a satisfactory IEP to provide meaningful educational benefit.** This portion of the district court decision was vacated and remanded for reconsideration, as was the award of reimbursement for the private school costs. The district court was also instructed to reconsider the student's claims for compensatory education, fees and costs and IDEA damages under Section 1983. *Ridgewood Bd. of Educ. v. N.E.*, 172 F.3d 238 (3d Cir. 1999).

◆   The parent of a 22-year-old student with severe autism had a history of filing administrative complaints with the Massachusetts Bureau of Special Education Appeals. **During the student's last year of attendance in district schools, another complaint was filed with the BSEA, alleging the district failed to implement the student's IEPs throughout his high school career.** A hearing officer concluded that the district had implemented and complied with the student's IEPs. The family appealed to federal district court, arguing that the student did not receive any significant benefits from his four-year high school program. As relief, the family sought five years of compensatory education and $100,000 in punitive damages.

The court took judicial notice of the previous complaints, and barred the parent from raising any of those claims again. Although the administrative decision had not been issued within the required 45 days, the court concluded this delay did not prejudice the student, as it did not deprive him of any benefits or remedies to which he was entitled. The court identified three guidelines courts should use when evaluating whether an IEP had been implemented. **A district fails to implement a student's IEP when: 1) the failure to implement is complete; 2) there is a variance from the program described in the IEP that deprives the student of a FAPE; and 3) the student does not make progress toward IEP goals.** In this case, the student was challenging the implementation of a compilation of IEP documents that had been amended and modified with new proposals during the course of his final year of school. Review of these documents indicated that the IEP was implemented. Applying the three-part framework for evaluating the implementation of IEPs, the court concluded that the district had not completely failed to implement the student's IEPs. There was no support for the student's assertion that he did not make progress toward his IEP goals, or that the IDEA requires the complete realization of all IEP goals. Because the services offered by the school district provided the student a FAPE, the court granted the district's motion for summary judgment. *Ross v. Framingham School Comm.,* 44 F.Supp.2d 104 (D.Mass. 1999).

◆   A 13-year-old student with profound deafness moved from Idaho to a small town in Arizona. The Arizona school district contacted the district in Idaho in which he had attended school and relied in part on his records there in making a placement decision. **The Arizona district determined** that it did not have the resources to provide the student with a full-day immersion program in American sign language, which was identified as an educational requirement. It therefore determined **that the student should be placed at the Arizona School for the Deaf and Blind** (ASDB), a residential facility located 280 miles away. The student's parents argued that the placement selected by the district failed to consider the continuum of alternative placements required by the IDEA and failed to comply with the IDEA's mainstreaming requirement. When the parents insisted on mainstreaming the student at district schools, the district's special education coordinator initiated an impartial IDEA hearing at which the hearing officer agreed that the student should be placed at ASDB. The Arizona Department of Education affirmed the hearing officer's decision, and the parents appealed to the U.S. Court of Appeals, Ninth Circuit.

The parents argued that the district had failed to comply with the IDEA by failing to consider a continuum of alternative placements and by selecting an overly restrictive placement that did not provide for mainstreaming. The court stated that it had been appropriate for the district to rely on the student's Idaho IEPs in reaching its decision. The district had considered alternative placements and reasonably concluded that mainstreaming did not allow the student to receive educational benefits. **The student had only primitive communication skills and he could not receive educational benefits in a regular classroom until he acquired greater communication skills.** This might be obtained from the intensive sign language training program available at ASDB. Because ASDB was the closest facility at which the student could obtain the services he required, it was appropriate under IDEA regulations at 34 CFR § 300.552(a)(3). The school district had complied with the IDEA in developing an IEP that was reasonably calculated to confer educational benefits, and the court of appeals affirmed the judgment for the school district. *Poolaw v. Bishop*, 67 F.3d 830 (9th Cir.1995).

B. Procedural Protections

The IDEA's most important sections describe mandatory procedures designed to safeguard the inclusion of students with disabilities in appropriate educational programs. The IDEA requires adequate notice to parents and opportunities for parental participation in the development of a student's special education program. During the pendency of a special education appeal, the student must remain in her then current educational program. Schools must provide students with a grievance procedure to challenge unfavorable special education decisions. Further appeal must be available to an impartial hearing officer, and the state education department may in turn review an administrative hearing decision. Only after the administrative review process is complete may an aggrieved party in an IDEA action appeal to a state or federal court.

◆   A student who was diagnosed with attention-deficit hyperactivity disorder, oppositional defiant disorder and depression attended private schools until the fifth grade, when an evaluation team concluded the student was eligible for "severe behavior handicap" services. **The parties arranged for a meeting, but never met at an IEP team meeting. A formal IEP was never prepared**, although the district proposed an internal placement, which the parents rejected. A school district official faxed them a draft IEP proposing the placement they had already rejected and that required them to pay for costs over their insurance coverage. The parents then enrolled the student in an out-of-state residential school without informing the school district. They requested a due process hearing midway through the student's seventh-grade year, seeking tuition reimbursement. A hearing officer held that the while the district did not hold an IEP conference, it could provide the student with a FAPE, and therefore, was not liable for tuition reimbursement. The family was not responsible for paying for any services under the proposed IEP since the resulting reduction in their lifetime medical insurance coverage would deprive the student of a FAPE. A review officer dismissed the case, and the parents appealed to a federal district court. The court affirmed the hearing officer's decision. Both parties appealed to the Sixth Circuit.

The circuit court concluded that the district had violated IDEA regulations requiring school districts to convene an IEP meeting within 30 calendar days of the determination that a student requires special education and related services. It had also violated Ohio administrative regulations requiring IEP conferences as soon as possible after officials initially suspect that a student has a disability. While the parties had met to consider the student's evaluation, there was no evidence that they addressed the additional items comprising a formal IEP meeting and no IEP was produced. The court rejected the district's assertion that it had failed to convene an IEP meeting because of the parents' lack of cooperation. IDEA regulations do not require that parents agree to a proposed placement before an IEP meeting can be held, but expressly provide for the development of an IEP without parental involvement if they refuse to participate. The court concluded that **because the district never held an IEP meeting, the parents were denied any meaningful opportunity to participate in the IEP process, as required by the IDEA. The lack of an IEP for the student during a full school year denied him access to specialized instruction and related services**. The procedural violations resulted in the substantive deprivation of the student's IDEA rights. The district had not even offered a free program, as the draft IEP asserted that it would only pay for costs beyond the parents' insurance coverage. The residential placement selected by the parents offered the student a therapist, psychiatrist and teacher-counselors, in small classes with frequent individual and group-therapy sessions. The parents were entitled to reimbursement since the district had defaulted on its IDEA obligations and the private school was a proper placement. *Knable ex rel. Knable v. Bexley City School District*, 238 F.3d 755 (6th Cir. 2001).

◆   In another case involving procedural violations and an IEP, a federal district court determined a school district violated the IDEA when it developed an IEP calling for three potential placements for a three-year-old student with developmental delays. **Although one of the placements identified in the IEP was appropriate and satisfied IDEA substantive requirements, the district's failure to present one coherent written placement offer violated the IDEA.** Parents had no expertise in evaluating educational programs and the district was required to select an appropriate placement designed to meet the unique needs of a student. The multiple placement offerings required the parent to ferret out the only appropriate one identified by the district. While discussion of possible placements during an IEP meeting was appropriate, the district could not abdicate its responsibility to make a specific offer by making a parent choose among several placements. This procedural violation resulted in the denial of a FAPE. The court affirmed the hearing officer's decision that the district was required to reimburse the mother for the costs of a private preschool placement, and rejected the district's claim that her conduct required the denial of all reimbursement. Although the IDEA emphasizes parental involvement and the mother had the right to be an aggressive advocate, her withholding of relevant information justified a reduction in the amount of reimbursement she claimed. The court affirmed the hearing officer's decision. *Glendale Unified School District v. Almasi*, 122 F.Supp.2d 1093 (C.D. Cal. 2000).

◆   A student with disabilities had a significant history of starting fires and aggressive behavior with peers. His IEP team recommended a full-time emotional support placement, which the parents alleged was never made. **Three months after the IEP was developed, the student started a fire in the cafeteria, and school personnel notified the police**. A delinquency petition was brought and the student was incarcerated. At due process, a hearing officer concluded that the district's report to police did not violate the IDEA. He held that he had no authority to grant the parents' request to place their son in another educational setting, as the student remained in a juvenile detention center. A state special education review panel did not disturb the hearing officer's decision and the parents appealed to a federal district court, seeking an order requiring the district to prepare an IEP offering their son a FAPE, plus compensatory services, reimbursement for an independent evaluation, and compensatory and punitive damages for IDEA violations under 42 U.S.C. § 1983.

The court noted that the U.S. Court of Appeals, Third Circuit, has ordered all Pennsylvania school districts to work with the state education department to ensure that students with disabilities receive appropriate services. The Third Circuit order requires districts to notify the department if no appropriate placement is expected for a student within 30 days. In this case, the district did not notify the department of its failure to obtain a placement for the student for more than three months. The district violated the order by failing to timely notify the state of its inability to provide the student with an appropriate placement for a period of more than 30 days. Since the district failed to provide the student with the services required by his IEP, it was liable to provide them for the two-month period representing the time it was first mandated to report a lack of placement through the date of his offense. **Under 20 U.S.C § 1415(k)(9), nothing prohibits a district from reporting a crime committed by a student with disabilities to appropriate authorities. The IDEA does not obligate school authorities to conduct a manifestation determination review before notifying authorities that a student with disabilities has committed a crime.** The court rejected the district's argument that the claim for failing to provide the student with services required by his IEP was barred due to failure to exhaust administrative remedies. After reviewing the IDEA's legislative history, the court held that Congress intended that claims asserting failure to provide IEP services be exempt from the administrative exhaustion requirement. Administrative exhaustion was no bar to the student's claim for damages under § 1983, which was based on underlying IDEA violations. The district was liable for the two-month period in which it failed to take required action to implement the student's IEP, and was not liable for failing to implement it once he was placed in juvenile detention. No punitive damages were available against a municipality under § 1983, so the court dismissed this claim. The court affirmed the special education review panel's decision. *Joseph M. v. Southeast Delco School District*, No. 99-4645, 2001 WL 283154 (E.D. Pa. 2001).

◆ During the seventh grade, **a student with ADHD, pervasive development disorder and a history of aggression and violent outbursts wrote a story for a class about a student who gets revenge on his school, designed a violent computer game and asked a classmate about getting guns.** After learning of the incident, the school suspended the student pending a manifestation determination committee/multidisciplinary committee (MDC) meeting. At the MDC meeting, **the district concluded that the student should not return to school.** The team discussed alternative sites, but because none were available, the mother suggested an "interim homebound placement." The school district agreed and promised weekly tutoring and social work therapy while searching for an alternative setting. The team concluded that the student's conduct was related to his disability. At no time during the meeting was the student's IEP, IEP goals, related services or behavior plan changed. The parents then requested a hearing, which the school and hearing officer considered to be a non-IDEA suspension hearing, but the parents believed was an IDEA proceeding. The parents were never told that the hearing officer was not an authorized IDEA hearing officer. The hearing officer held that the interim placement should remain in effect. The parents subsequently requested an IDEA due process hearing, at which a hearing officer awarded the parents their costs for counseling services.

The school district appealed to a federal district court, which held that the district's numerous procedural errors resulted in the denial of a FAPE. The notice for the MDC hearing did not indicate to the parents that the district was considering a change in placement. The district deprived the family of any meaningful opportunity to participate in the MDC. As the IHO found, the district was bound to address the student's behavior after determining that his conduct was related to his disability. Such a finding requires an IEP team to change the IEP, discuss ways to address behavioral problems, or consider what in-school remedies or services could address the behavior. The district instead removed the student from school without considering realistic alternatives. The district apparently intended only to remove him from school under the 45-day period specified under IDEA regulations for weapon and drug violations. It acknowledged the error in making such a removal and was limited to making an interim placement of 10 days or less. **The district violated the IDEA by offering an interim homebound setting without first seeking the expedited due process hearing procedure under 20 U.S.C. § 1415(k) for students posing a threat to themselves or others**. Had it done so, an IHO would have considered the appropriateness of the student's placement and other relevant factors, such as the LRE available for him. The district provided a non-IDEA suspension hearing over which the hearing officer had no true authority. According to the court, the district was more concerned with removing the student from school than complying with the IDEA. The IHO properly found that the defective notices and failure to propose a range of placements forced the family into accepting the homebound placement and denied the student a FAPE. The homebound program was not designed to meet the student's unique needs and was calculated to remove him from school. The parents were entitled to reimbursement for their counseling expenses and attorneys' fees. *Community Consolidated School District No. 93 v. John F.*, No. 00 CV 1347 (N.D. Ill. 2000).

◆   The New York City School Board of Education adopted a policy under which students were required to meet objective criteria for advancing to the next grade. Students not meeting promotional requirements received notices to attend a mandated summer program. The system adopted a regulation governing the suspension of students with disabilities that afforded them a hearing when they faced suspension from the summer program. However, the regulation did not provide for a manifestation determination review, as required by the IDEA. **The students alleged that they had been disciplined without required special education procedural protections** and sued the school board in a U.S. district court, seeking a preliminary order enjoining the enforcement of the policy for the 2000 summer session.

The court noted that a status report on the summer program characterized it as an integral part of the board's promotional policy, completion of which was the critical factor. Some of the students named in the complaint had already been suspended under the policy and faced the risk of being denied completion of the summer program. Despite the importance of the summer program, **the policy did not provide for alternative instruction of suspended students nor did it attempt to determine whether the conduct giving rise to discipline was related to the student's underlying disability**. The court found that the board's failure to follow statutorily required procedures created a substantial likelihood of harm to the students. An erroneous suspension and exclusion of a student from school would result in his or her inability to be promoted to the next grade. The students demonstrated that they were likely to succeed on the merits of their claim, as the policy appeared to violate both the IDEA and board regulations. Two of the main violations involved parental notification in the case of disciplinary removals and the provision of a manifestation determination review to decide whether the behavior leading to discipline was a manifestation of the student's disability. Certain procedural requirements of the board regulation were more stringent than those of the IDEA. The IDEA and its regulations state that the extensive disciplinary protections apply every school day that students are in attendance for instructional purposes. The summer program qualified under the regulatory definition. The court rejected the board's position that the IDEA did not apply to the summer program. For these reasons, the court granted the students' application for a temporary order enjoining the board from implementing the policy governing suspension of students during the 2000 summer session. *LIH ex rel. LH v. New York City Bd. of Educ.*, 103 F.Supp.2d 658 (E.D.N.Y. 2000).

◆   The Hawaii Department of Education utilizes parental notification procedures complying with IDEA requirements when evaluating students for special education. However, the department also provides for the evaluation of students who are not suspected of having a disability, but who exhibit achievement delays or adjustment difficulties requiring alternative teaching strategies. **The department did not require parental notification concerning these tests**, and three students claimed that the non-IDEA testing was selectively administered to students, which denied their rights to appropriate procedural safeguards. The U.S. District Court for the District of Hawaii granted summary judgment to the education department, and the families appealed to the U.S. Court of Appeals, Ninth Circuit.

The department claimed that the IDEA should not apply to the class of students represented in the action because they were not suspected of having disabilities nor were they being tested for special education eligibility. The court stated that the department's position denied students and parents their role in determining appropriate educational services where students were not currently receiving special education and related services. The IDEA was intended to create procedural protections to guard against the tendency of educators to make unilateral decisions concerning students with disabilities, and **the lack of notification to families about the non-IDEA tests gave the education department almost absolute control over procedures in a manner that did not comply with the IDEA and the Rehabilitation Act**. Because the parents were entitled to receive notice and an opportunity to participate in the evaluation and identification of student disabilities, the court reversed the summary judgment order and remanded the case. It ordered the department to notify parents whenever individualized testing of a student was contemplated, regardless of the purpose of the testing. *Pasatiempo v. Aizawa*, 103 F.3d 796 (9th Cir.1996).

◆   A Vermont student had a severe language disorder, learning disabilities and physical disabilities. Although she was mainstreamed into some regular classes while in junior high school, she received extensive special education in speech and language. Her school district refused to address her mother's objections to the size of the school, complexity of the classes and lack of coordination among teachers. Her mother asked the district to consider a private school placement but it refused and developed an IEP without the mother's participation and in the absence of the student's teachers. The IEP contained no language development program and the mother rejected it, requesting reevaluation and a private school placement. The district denied the requests and the mother placed the student at a private residential school. She requested a hearing and her request for tuition reimbursement was denied. **The district** then **failed to adopt an IEP for the next three years**. The mother sued the district for tuition reimbursement in the U.S. District Court for the District of Vermont.

The court found that **the school district had violated IDEA procedural requirements by failing to inform the mother of her rights, excluding her from IEP meetings, failing to conduct an evaluation and failing to adopt a formal IEP for over three years**. The court also found that draft IEPs prepared by the district failed to address the student's severe language problems, omitted goals and objectives from previous IEPs and did not consider the effect of the complex high school environment on the student. The private school placement selected by the mother was appropriate. Because the district had violated IDEA procedures and substantive requirements, and the district had failed to propose any nonresidential alternatives, the court awarded tuition reimbursement. *Briere v. Fair Haven Grade School Dist.*, 948 F.Supp. 1242 (D.Vt.1996).

II. PLACEMENT OF STUDENTS WITH DISABILITIES

The IDEA requires each local education agency (LEA) to identify and evaluate students with disabilities in its jurisdiction. After a school district identifies a student as disabled, it must develop an appropriate educational placement. The district must develop and implement an individualized education program (IEP) for each student with a disability in the district. The IEP must be calculated to provide an educational benefit and where possible, to mainstream the student with nondisabled students.

A. Identification and Evaluation

◆   A student with learning disabilities and an emotional disturbance, who never attended public schools, was enrolled in a private Connecticut school with a curriculum designed for students with learning disabilities. The parents did not contact the district before making the placement or request an evaluation of their son. When the family requested an evaluation over a year later, the district took over six months to complete it. During a meeting to discuss the student's educational program, his father expressed his intention to keep his son in the Connecticut facility for the rest of the school year and did not complain about the lengthy evaluation process. The district certified the student for special education services and proposed a public school placement. The parents commenced an IDEA action against the district, asserting they were entitled to private school reimbursement and claiming that the district had an insufficient child find plan under the IDEA. A federal district court found that **the district's child find plan called for the** dissemination of information to all area private schools, day-care centers, nursery schools, hospitals and other places where medical professionals were likely to encounter children with special education requirements. The district also made public service announcements in the local media and sent outreach personnel to PTA meetings and low-income communities.

The district court decision was appealed to the U.S. Court of Appeals, Sixth Circuit, which remanded the case for a trial. On remand, the district court found that the school district had made adequate child find efforts and denied the parents' request for private school tuition reimbursement. The parents appealed to the Sixth Circuit, which observed that they had never contacted the district about their son's placement before seeking reimbursement. The district's publicity campaign fulfilled its child find duties. **The IDEA's child find obligation requires districts to ensure that students in need of special education are identified and served. It does not require districts to pursue the parents of private school students who do not act upon available information**. Although the student's evaluation took six months to complete, the parents were not entitled to reimbursement on that basis. The court affirmed the district court judgment in favor of the school district. *Doe v. Metropolitan Nashville Public Schools*, No. 00-5027, 2001 WL 549431 (6th Cir. 2001).

◆   During a honors student's 10th grade year, his father contacted school officials, expressing concern about his son's emotional problems and drug use and asking for assistance. Prior to the father's request, the student was diagnosed with ADHD, bipolar disorder, obsessive-compulsive disorder and marijuana abuse. The parents unilaterally placed the student in a Connecticut therapeutic school, where he received treatment for his emotional problems. However, he continued to use marijuana and inhalants and was transferred to a residential drug treatment program in Utah. His behavior improved and he returned to the Connecticut school, where he completed 11th grade. The student re-enrolled in his public school for grade 12. **The parents requested an IDEA due process hearing, arguing that their request for assistance with identification of the student's problems created a duty on the school district to make an special education eligibility determination**. Moreover, they argued that the district's failure to make an eligibility determination denied the student a FAPE.

An administrative law judge agreed with the parents, finding that school officials' failure to identify the student as having a disability amounted to a procedural violation of the IDEA. The ALJ based this finding on the student's negative behavioral changes and academic decline. Because the district violated IDEA procedures, the ALJ found it fundamentally unfair to require the student to prove that he had a disability as a prerequisite to an award of tuition reimbursement for the Connecticut placement. The ALJ also held that the Connecticut placement was appropriate. The school district appealed to the U.S. District Court for the District of Maryland, which reversed. According to the district court, the ALJ had improperly held that a procedural violation alone can create a duty on the school district to reimburse the parents for the cost of private school tuition. **The district court** also **found that the student's behavior problems resulted not from an educational disability but from social maladjustment, as evidenced by his history of drug abuse. The student was not disabled under the IDEA** and the school district was entitled to summary judgment. The parents appealed to the Fourth Circuit, which affirmed the order for summary judgment in a brief memorandum decision that stated only that its decision was based on the reasoning of the district court. *Board of Education of Frederick County, Maryland v. JD III et al.*, 232 F.3d 886 (4th Cir. 2000).

◆   After a hazing incident at a private school, a student enrolled in public school. He received poor grades and did not interact well with other students. School officials repeatedly asked the student's mother for permission to evaluate him for special education. She provided written authorization for an evaluation but withdrew her consent at the initial evaluation session. The school implemented a general education intervention plan for the student. The following year, the student entered high school and school officials initially believed that he might be eligible for special education services. However, **the student's mother advised them that he was not experiencing academic problems and was not disabled**. The following year, the student's mother declined an offer to have the student placed in a special study hall because of his middle school performance. Later in the year, he was cut from the junior varsity basketball team and was repeatedly late for geometry class, in violation of school rules. After being reprimanded for frequent tardiness, school officials withdrew the student from his geometry class. Two days later, the mother asserted that the student had a disability and consented to an evaluation. However, she refused to sign an evaluation consent form and refused to provide supporting medical records.

  A hearing officer determined that the school system had not failed to identify the student as eligible for special education. School officials had made every effort to assist the student and gain parental permission to evaluate him. The school system did not violate the student's rights under § 504 of the Rehabilitation Act by applying the tardiness policy to him and cutting him from the basketball team. The state board of special education appeals affirmed the hearing officer's decision, and a federal district court awarded summary judgment to the school system. The parents appealed to the U.S. Court of Appeals, Seventh Circuit, which agreed with the hearing officer's findings that, in view of the student's improved academic performance, the neurologist's diagnosis of no learning disability, and the mother's resistance to the performing of an evaluation, the school system did not fail to identify the student as requiring special education. **Because Indiana special education regulations require written parental consent before any evaluation, there was no merit to the mother's claim that the system was responsible for evaluating and identifying the student as being in need of special education services over her objection**. There was also no merit to the student's § 504 claims, since there was evidence that the decisions to enforce the tardiness policy and cut him from the basketball team were non-discriminatory. The circuit court affirmed the judgment for the school system. *P.J. v. Eagle-Union Community School Corp.*, 202 F.3d 274 (7th Cir. 1999).

◆   A student experienced behavior problems while in grade ten at a parochial school. The parents then transferred the student to a public school for eleventh grade. The family returned intake forms to the new school asserting that the student had never been in any special classes or accelerated programs, including classes for learning or behavioral disabilities. The student appeared apathetic about school, and he received one failing grade. The family hired a private counselor who determined that the student had depression, but did not allow school employees access to this information. In February of the student's 11th grade year, after an incident of running away, the family enrolled him in an out-of-state residential treatment program. After six months, the family asked the district to evaluate the student, asserting that he was emotionally disturbed. The school district sought to have the student's private school records transferred, but the family never did so until almost one year later. In the meantime, the district sought and received time extensions from the state education department that relieved the district of its state law obligation to perform an evaluation within 90 days. By the time the records were forwarded to the district, the student, who was by then over 18, withdrew himself from the residential school. After an administrative hearing, **a hearing officer held that the school district had reason to know that the student was eligible for an exceptional educational needs evaluation and that he was a student with emotional disabilities who needed special education**. The private school provided the student with an appropriate educational program and educational benefits, and the district was ordered to pay for the student's educational costs and therapeutic expenses. A review officer reversed, finding the hearing officer's findings were unsupported by the record.

The family appealed to a federal district court, which agreed with the review officer that **the district had no reasonable cause to suspect that the student had exceptional educational needs. There was no violation of the IDEA's child find obligation and no evidence that district screening policies were deficient**. The most serious problems experienced by the student, falling asleep in school and receiving lower grades, did not indicate a disability, and the father had denied that they were caused by a disability. The student passed all but one of his classes and was receiving some educational benefit. District employees had no reasonable cause to suspect that the student was emotionally disabled or required special education. He was removed from district schools before the pre-referral screening process was complete, and the family resisted early screening efforts. The court held that the family had a strictly financial motive for seeking an emotionally disturbed classification and had blocked the district's good faith efforts to evaluate the student. The school district was awarded summary judgment in its favor. *Hoffman v. East Troy Community School Dist.*, 38 F.Supp.2d 750 (E.D. Wis. 1999).

◆ After a Texas school district disciplined a student for several incidents of misconduct, his parents prepared to transfer him to a private school and commenced an administrative claim against the school district requesting expunction of the discipline from the student's records, reimbursement for evaluation costs and private school tuition reimbursement. **The parents claimed the student was eligible for special education**, based on a disability, **and that the district had failed to evaluate the student prior to disciplining him**. The hearing officer held for the parents, ruling that the student was entitled to IDEA procedural protections that made his alternative placement inappropriate. The district brought a federal district court counterclaim to challenge the administrative findings when the family asserted claims for monetary damages.

The court held that the district was not obligated to perform a special education evaluation of the student prior to the disciplinary hearing. The student was not enrolled in any special education classes and no party had previously requested an evaluation. **The court recited language from the IDEA providing that students may be subject to the same discipline as applied to students without disabilities in the absence of knowledge that a child is disabled. The district had no knowledge that the student had a disability when it disciplined him**. The court rejected the assertion that assignment to an alternative placement for more than 10 days violated the IDEA. The district did not become aware of any need to evaluate the student for special education services until after his disruptive behavior occurred, and this part of the administrative decision was erroneous. The court issued an order remanding the case to the hearing officer for a determination of whether the district violated the IDEA by failing to evaluate or provide him with special education, but otherwise granted summary judgment to the district and denied summary judgment to the parents. *James C. v. Eanes Indep. School Dist.*, No. A-97-CA-745 JN (W.D.Tex.1999).

♦   When a gifted California student was in the fifth grade, a school district concluded he was not eligible for special education services because and learning disability he had did not interfere with his regular class performance. The student's family obtained private assessments indicating the student had attention deficit disorder. **After reviewing the private assessments, the district again denied the student special education services because he was performing adequately in regular classes**. A due process hearing resulted in a determination that the discrepancy between the student's ability and achievement was inconclusive, and that he did not qualify for special education because his regular education program, with modifications, was adequate. A federal district court affirmed the hearing officer's decision.

On appeal to the Ninth Circuit, the court observed that to qualify for IDEA protection under California law, "an individual with exceptional needs must have an impairment that requires instruction, services or both which cannot be provided with modification of the regular school program." A student with suspected learning disabilities also had to meet additional statutory criteria for "children with specific learning disabilities." Under California law, children who do not meet the additional criteria must be instructed in regular education programs. The court rejected the family's assertion that the student was eligible for special education because of the discrepancy between his test scores and achievement. **The family failed to demonstrate the student was not benefiting from his modified regular education program, therefore, the student was not entitled to special education services**. *Norton v. Orinda Union School Dist.*, 168 F.3d 500 (9th Cir. 1999).

♦   A New York student who was classified as speech impaired by her school district received special education services through her fourth grade year. She was placed in a remedial reading program through grade seven, and promoted to ninth grade despite failing multiple subjects in grades seven and eight. She then began to experience behavior problems and was hospitalized for depression at a psychiatric treatment facility. The student's emotional and behavior problems resumed after she returned to school and she was hospitalized again. The family followed the recommendations of a consultant and placed the student in an out-of-state residential treatment and education center. While thee, the student was diagnosed with conduct disorder and oppositional defiant disorder. The parents sought reimbursement from the district for the costs of the out-of-state placement. A district employee concluded that the student was depressed, but that special education was not necessary. **The district committee on special education formally concluded the student was ineligible for IDEA services, but recommended a referral under § 504 of the Rehabilitation Act**. The family rejected a comprehensive public school education plan proposed by the § 504 Committee and enrolled the student in a private program. At an administrative hearing requested by the family, a hearing officer confirmed the district's determination that the student was not considered disabled under the IDEA. A federal district court vacated the administrative decision, finding the student was emotionally disturbed as defined by both state and federal regulations. The school district was ordered to reimburse the family the costs of the private placement.

The district appealed to the U.S. Court of Appeals, Second Circuit, which held that the student had been deprived of appropriate IDEA services due to the school committee's failure to classify the student as eligible for IDEA services. The evidence indicated the student demonstrated an inability to learn that could not be explained solely by intellectual, sensory or health factors. This included her repetition of a grade, her previous receipt of special education services and her failing several subjects in the seventh and eighth grades. There was also evidence the student's performance improved in settings that addressed her emotional and behavioral problems. **Because the student's academic problems resulted at least in part from her emotional problems, and most of her medical evaluations indicated symptoms of depression that endured for several years, the district court properly deemed the student eligible for IDEA services**. The district court decision was upheld. *Muller on Behalf of Muller v. Committee on Special Education of East Islip Union Free School Dist.,* 145 F.3d 95 (2d Cir. 1999).

◆   A Montana student was diagnosed with a learning disability and attention deficit disorder. He was found eligible for special education services. Five years later, the student's family alleged that his school district failed to complete a triennial reevaluation as required by the IDEA and its regulations, failed to properly test and evaluate him, and improperly placed him with emotionally disturbed students. The parents requested a due process hearing, which resulted in a decision for the school district. The parents appealed to a Montana district court. The court dismissed the action and the family appealed to the Supreme Court of Montana. The court held that **the hearing officer could have reasonably determined that the absence of a reevaluation did not materially infringe upon the student's educational opportunities or deprive him of a FAPE**. The parents had not been deprived of an opportunity to participate in the development of the student's IEP and the alleged procedural inadequacies did not deprive him of a FAPE. The court affirmed the district court judgment dismissing the action. *Parini v. Missoula County High School, Dist. No. 1,* 944 P.2d 199 (Mont.1997).

◆   A South Dakota student with cerebral palsy had visual impairments, walked slowly with a walker or used a wheelchair and could not function independently in many aspects of personal life. Despite her impairments, she was an "A" student who participated in the school band, newspaper and public speaking program. Prior to her entry into ninth grade, **the district stated its intention to dismiss her from her special education program, based on the belief that she no longer required special education services under the IDEA**. A hearing examiner determined that the student remained eligible for IDEA services because the school district provided her with many special accommodations and related services not included in the IEP that had enabled her to achieve good grades.

The school district appealed to the U.S. Court of Appeals, Eighth Circuit, which stated that **if it were not for the specialized accommodations, instruction and services provided by the school district, the student's grades would be adversely affected**. The district had failed to incorporate the services it was providing the student into its written IEP and her need for the services had not ended. The student would be entitled to receive transition services from the school district until the age of 21 or her graduation date. The court affirmed the district court judgment. *Yankton School Dist. v. Schramm*, 93 F.3d 1369 (8th Cir.1996).

◆   A Texas student with learning disabilities and speech impairments received special education services from his public school district. After three years, a district reevaluation determined that he was no longer speech impaired but was learning disabled and entitled to IDEA placement and services. However, other students taunted him to the point that he was admitted to a psychiatric hospital. The student received homebound instruction the following school year. His parents believed that additional testing would further traumatize him and **they refused to allow the school district to conduct a scheduled triennial reevaluation**. A hearing officer decided that the school district could not be compelled to accept an independent assessment obtained by the parents. The U.S. District Court for the Eastern District of Texas reversed the administrative decision, finding that while school districts generally had the right to use their own personnel to reevaluate students, an exception existed where medical and psychological factors indicated that this would harm the student. The school district appealed to the U.S. Court of Appeals, Fifth Circuit.

The court observed that parents of students with disabilities who sought special education services were required to allow schools to conduct their own special education reevaluations. A public school district could not be compelled to rely solely on an independent evaluation of the parents' choosing. The exception that the district court had created to this rule was not contained in the IDEA and should not be recognized. Because the student's parents had refused to allow the school district to perform its own reevaluation, the student was not eligible for special education after the date his triennial reevaluation had been due. The court reversed and remanded the district court judgment. *Andress v. Cleveland Indep. School Dist.*, 64 F.3d 176 (5th Cir.1995).

◆   In 1969, California education officials implemented standardized IQ testing for determining the appropriate placements of educable mentally retarded (EMR) students. Within two years of the commencement of standardized testing, a class representing African-American students filed a lawsuit in the U.S. District Court for the Northern District of California, claiming that the overrepresentation of African-American students in EMR classrooms and the standardized testing violated the IDEA and Title VI of the Civil Rights Act of 1964. In 1979, the district court issued an injunction banning the use of IQ tests for evaluating EMR students and for students who attended classes that were the substantial equivalent of EMR classes. **The parties reached a settlement agreement that abolished the EMR category and banned the use of standardized tests to evaluate African-American students for any special education assessment**. Based on the settlement, the court entered an order in 1986 modifying the 1979 injunction.

Years later, another group of African-American students petitioned the district court for an order to vacate the injunction modification because they wanted to take IQ tests. The district court consolidated the case with the original action and vacated the 1986 modification, awarding summary judgment to the students seeking to be tested. Members of the original plaintiff class and the state superintendent of public instruction appealed the summary judgment order to the U.S. Court of Appeals, Ninth Circuit. The court of appeals affirmed the district court's decision to vacate the 1986 modification and reinstate the original order. It also affirmed the district court order for further proceedings to determine whether all special education classes were substantially equivalent to the EMR designation and whether IQ tests were effective in placing African-American students. **The new class of plaintiffs should not be bound by the prior judgment because its members had not been adequately represented by the original class. The 1986 ban on all IQ tests expanded the scope of the original injunction and was unsupported by the original factual findings**. These findings pertained only in the context of EMR placements. *Crawford v. Honig*, 37 F.3d 485 (9th Cir.1994).

B. Placement

◆   An Illinois student who was disruptive and frequently truant became a serious disciplinary problem. A psychologist determined that the student did not have a learning disability but suffered from depression, accompanied by substance abuse and a conduct disorder. **The student's mother objected to a proposal by the school district for the resumption of his placement in a therapeutic day school. Upon the boy's release from jail, she unilaterally placed him in a Maine residential school** under a program that did not provide him with psychological services and requested reimbursement from the district. School officials refused the request, and the mother commenced an administrative proceeding. A state hearing officer ordered the district to pay for the residential placement. The district appealed and a review officer reversed. A federal district court reversed the review officer's decision and the school district appealed to the U.S. Court of Appeals, Seventh Circuit.

The court noted that the review officer had found no evidence that the Maine facility provided a superior educational placement to that of the therapeutic day school. The review officer had properly determined that **the IDEA does not require a school district to pay for the confinement of a truant student**. The district court had improperly rejected the review officer's determination that the Maine residential school did not provide a FAPE to the student. The Maine school did not provide the student with psychological services, and did not offer treatment for his depression or conduct disorder. The court held that it only provided confinement, and was "a jail substitute." According to the court, the only difference between the therapeutic day school and the Maine school was its residential character. Moreover, the district court was obligated to defer to the review officer's decision, since he was presumed to have superior competence to that of federal courts in resolving educational policy matters. The court stated that the student's problems were primarily the result of improper socialization, as he had the intelligence to perform well in school and had no cognitive defects or disorders. **Residential placement was improper where it was not a necessary predicate for learning or where medical, social or emotional problems were separate from the learning process**. The court stated that the residential placement was appropriate for the student "only if confinement is a related service" under the IDEA. Since it was obviously not, the district court erroneously reversed the review officer's decision. *Dale M. v. Board of Education of Bradley Bourbonnais High School District No. 307*, 237 F.3d 813 (7th Cir. 2001).

♦   When a student with significant learning disabilities was in the eighth grade, her parents and local school system met to develop her IEP and placement for the ninth grade. For the first eight years of school, the student was enrolled in a private school, and **the parents wanted her placed in an out-of-state residential school. The district disagreed with the parents, recommending a non-residential public school's fundamental life skills program**. The parents rejected the district placement offer and enrolled their daughter in the residential school. At due process, an ALJ upheld the proposed district placement and denied the parents' request for tuition reimbursement. He determined that there had been no procedural violations of the IDEA and that the district's placement proposal afforded the student the opportunity to receive a FAPE. The parents then commenced a federal district court action against the school district for IDEA violations, adding claims under § 504 of the Rehabilitation Act and seeking an award of monetary damages under 42 U.S.C. § 1983.

The court referred the case to a federal magistrate judge, who considered the district's motion for summary judgment. The magistrate observed that the IDEA does not guarantee each student will receive an ideal educational opportunity. In this case, the only procedural error alleged was that the hearing officer had improperly imposed the burden of proof on the parents. The magistrate found this argument meritless, ruling that while the allocation of the burden of proof may determine the outcome in certain cases, it did not affect the outcome of this case. The evidence in favor of the school district was strong enough that it would have prevailed even if it had been allocated the burden of proof. **The district proved by a preponderance of evidence that its placement recommendation for the student's first year in high school would provide her with a FAPE**. Educators at the student's private school agreed that she needed fundamental skills instruction to prepare her for everyday life and that it would be difficult for her to attend a diploma-track program, as preferred by her parents. School officials strongly believed that a residential placement was unnecessary because the student was not a behavior problem and did not require that restrictive a placement. The magistrate held that the fundamental life skills curriculum at the public school would provide the student with educational benefit. The administrative decision was affirmed. Because the parents' IDEA claim failed, the closely related § 504 and § 1983 claims were not viable. *Steinberg v. Weast*, 132 F.Supp.2d 343 (D. Md. 2001).

♦   Although a student struggled in his public school placement and was required to repeat the first grade, he did not initially qualify for special education services. His parents obtained an independent evaluation and learned that the student had dyslexia and attention deficit disorder and enrolled him in a private school for second grade. The student returned to the public school system before the end of the year and was eventually referred to an admission, review and dismissal (ARD) committee, which identified reading and language deficiencies. The ARD committee recommended 10 hours per week in a reading and language resource room with an hour of weekly speech therapy. The student continued to experience some difficulties in grade four and received extended-year services and 25 hours of compensatory speech therapy. His parents objected to the district's failure to implement certain IEP modifications. For two months during the student's sixth grade year, the district failed to provide him with services in alphabetic phonics as it had previously agreed. His parents sought administrative review, and **a hearing officer found that the district failed to consistently or appropriately implement the IEP**. The parties then failed to agree upon an IEP for the student's seventh grade year and the parents withdrew him from public school in favor of a private placement.

The school district appealed to a federal district court, which granted its motion for summary judgment, finding that the student showed improvement in most areas of study and received educational benefit under the IDEA. The court dismissed the parents' counterclaim for private school compensatory services reimbursement, and the parents appealed to the Fifth Circuit, which discussed the IDEA's free appropriate public education requirement as described by the U.S. Supreme Court in *Bd. of Educ. v. Rowley*, 458 U.S. 176 (1982). **Under *Rowley*, an IEP need not maximize a student's educational potential; it must only be designed to meet the student's unique needs and provide the student with a basic floor of opportunity to receive educational benefits**. The court also discussed the test for appropriateness of an IEP under *Cypress-Fairbanks Indep. School Dist. v. Michael F.*, 118 F.3d 245 (5th Cir. 1997), which included assessment of whether education is provided in a coordinated and collaborative manner by key stakeholders and indicates that the student is receiving positive academic and nonacademic benefits. According to the circuit court, the district court properly determined that any shortcomings in the school district's implementation of the IEP were remedied by the compensatory services it offered, and the student received educational benefits. A student challenging the adequacy of an IEP must demonstrate more than a minimal failure to implement all elements of an IEP and must demonstrate that school authorities failed to implement substantial or significant IEP provisions. The district court also correctly relied on the student's increasing test scores during his public school education. **It was unnecessary for the student to improve in every academic area in order to receive educational benefit from his IEP**, and the district court properly held that the student received a FAPE in his public school placement. The parents' claim for private school reimbursement was properly rejected and the circuit court affirmed the judgment for the school district. *Houston Indep. School Dist. v. Bobby R.*, 200 F.3d 341 (5th Cir., 2000).

♦   When a preschool student was three years old, his parents started a home-based discrete trial training (DTT) program. The district prepared an IEP calling for preprimary impaired services with speech and language therapy that did not include DTT. A teacher voluntarily provided the student with DTT. A psychologist selected by the parents submitted a written proposal for a DTT program, including staff training at an IEP conference held when the student was five years old. The meeting was taped but never written into a formal IEP. The district's director of special education drafted a new proposal calling for placement in a mainstream kindergarten class, without DTT. At the next IEP conference, the parents objected to the proposed mainstream placement. They then initiated due process proceedings, and a local hearing officer decided in their favor. **A state hearing review officer reversed the decision, finding that the oral proposal was not an IEP and that the written one was valid and provided a FAPE designed to maximize the student's potential. The order denied the parents' request for reimbursement** for the cost of providing the home-based DTT program, and they appealed to a federal district court, asserting violations of state and federal law. The court granted the school district's motion for summary judgment, holding that the district had conducted a proper evaluation of the student and proposed an IEP designed to address his needs and attain his maximum potential, as required by state law. Because the IEP was appropriate, the court affirmed the decision not to award the parents reimbursement.

The parents appealed to the Sixth Circuit, which described the appropriate standard of review in special education cases arising under the IDEA. The court stated that if IDEA procedural requirements are met, greater deference is given to a district's placement decision. According to the court, the IDEA's requirement that the courts give "due weight" to administrative decisions means that courts should defer to administrative findings only when educational expertise is relevant and the decision is reasonable. There was no merit to the parents' argument that the taped IEP proceeding was a final IEP. State and federal laws indicate that an IEP is a written document, and there had been no writing in this case until the second IEP meeting. The parents were not entitled by law to attend the staff meetings occurring between the two IEP meetings, and staff members were entitled to discuss the student's IEP outside the presence of the parents. The district was not required to conduct a comprehensive evaluation at the time of the second IEP, since the parents' unilateral decision to decrease his school participation in favor of increased use of DTT did not amount to a change in placement. There was no statutory time limit for the district to recertify the student's autism diagnosis and any delay identified by the parents did not substantively deprive the student of appropriate services. **The IEP prepared by the school district took into account the unique needs of the student, set out his goals and included detailed daily schedules addressing each goal.** His program included group instruction and one-to-one therapy. The court affirmed the district court's finding that **the IEP was developed specifically to accommodate the student**. Because the IEP offered the student a FAPE, the remaining state and federal claims were properly dismissed. *Burilovich v. Bd. of Educ. of Lincoln Consol. Schools*, 208 F.3d 560 (6th Cir. 2000).

♦   A high school student with a significant sexual disorder was placed in a segregated program at a regional high school where he received speech, language, counseling, and transportation services. After the student improperly touched a classmate, his IEP was amended to require adult supervision at all times. The student was hospitalized and treated for ongoing pedophilic problems. **Although a treatment plan described the student as a sexually deviant youth who required intensive residential treatment, the school district refused to place the student in a residential placement,** claiming he was making educational progress within his district placement. The student's adoptive parents initiated child protection proceedings, and the student was committed to the custody of the state department of social services (DSS). Without notifying the school district, DSS placed him in a residential school for mentally disabled students with sexually offending behavior. The residential program included academic instruction, life skills instruction, and a relapse prevention plan. The district proposed placing the student at his former high school. A hearing officer determined the proposed IEP was inappropriate because it failed to address his sexual behavior. The residential placement was deemed appropriate.

A federal district court concluded that the district was obligated to address the student's sexual behaviors in his IEP, as those behaviors were related to his educational needs. **The combination of the student's disabilities made him eligible for special education, and the best method of addressing the student's disabilities was a residential placement.** Given the student's needs, his special education program had to include counseling and therapy, which were available at the residential school, but not the district school. The court rejected the school district's assertion that the student's inappropriate out-of-school behavior was not related to his educational performance. For these reasons, the district court ordered the school district to provide the student with a residential placement. *Mohawk Trail Regional School Dist. v. Shaun D.,* 35 F.Supp.2d 34 (D.Mass. 1999).

◆   A Missouri student with learning disabilities in reading and math attended a public school where he was instructed in regular education classes with resource room support for 20 percent of the school day. District personnel documented his apathy and lack of effort and reduced his resource room participation. At the end of the student's third grade school year, the parents rejected a proposed IEP pending a summer placement they had made at a private school. **The student made progress in the summer program, and the parents rejected the proposed public school IEP and unilaterally placed him in the private school,** where he remained through the following summer and school year. The family sought an administrative ruling that the private school placement was appropriate for both academic years and an award of tuition reimbursement. A hearing panel denied the family's claim for reimbursement, finding that the district had proposed a free appropriate public education. A state level review officer reversed the decision, finding that the IEPs proposed by the school district had not been appropriate. The hearing officer ordered reimbursement through the first year of private school attendance. The school district appealed to a federal district court. The court awarded reimbursement to the family for both academic years and one summer session.

The school district appealed to the U.S. Court of Appeals, Eighth Circuit, which determined that **the student had been making academic progress at the public school and that the IEP proposed by the school district had been calculated to provide him with educational benefits.** The court found that the parents had abruptly removed the student from the public school system, preventing the district from making an appropriate review of his IEP. The family was not entitled to reimbursement for any private school tuition or costs, or for interest on loans used to pay for the private school tuition. The court reversed the district court decision. *Fort Zumwalt School Dist. v. Clynes*, 119 F.3d 607 (8th Cir.1997).

◆   A Texas student with attention deficit hyperactivity disorder was initially classified as other health impaired by his school district. When he entered sixth grade, he was diagnosed as having Tourette's syndrome. His behavior problems increased during sixth grade and he frequently disrupted classes. The student's parents removed him from public school and placed him at a residential treatment center in Utah for several months. **Although the school's admissions, review and dismissal committee agreed to modify his IEP, it refused to approve the Utah placement or offer tuition reimbursement**. The student's parents filed an administrative appeal. A hearing officer held that the IEP was inappropriate and that the Utah placement was appropriate.

The U.S. Court of Appeals, Fifth Circuit, identified four factors that can help courts identify whether an IEP is reasonably calculated to provide a meaningful educational benefit under the IDEA. The factors include whether the IEP is individualized on the basis of a student's assessment and performance, is administered in the least restrictive environment, is provided by key service providers in a coordinated and collaborative manner, and confers positive academic and non-academic benefits. **The court stated that while the student continued to demonstrate behavioral problems, the IEP conferred significant academic and non-academic benefits upon him in the least restrictive environment and was appropriately individualized.** *Cypress-Fairbanks Indep. School Dist. v. Michael F.*, 118 F.3d 245 (5th Cir.1997).

◆   An 11-year-old student with autism engaged in daily screaming episodes and frequent incidents of hitting, pinching, kicking, biting and removing his clothes. During his outbursts, staff members had to calm and redirect him and spend additional time getting other students in his classes to focus after he was calmed. After initial placement in regular education classrooms, **his school district proposed a self-contained classroom for academic instruction and speech, with regular education for art, music, physical education and recess**. His parents rejected the placement proposal. A Virginia federal court held that he had to be mainstreamed under the IDEA. However, the U.S. Court of Appeals, Fourth Circuit, reversed, finding that the district court had disregarded overwhelming evidence that the student made no academic progress in regular classes and that separate, one-on-one instruction was appropriate for him. **The IDEA establishes a presumption in favor of inclusion in regular education classes, but explicitly states that inclusion is inappropriate when the nature or severity of the disability prevents satisfactory progress in regular classes.** *Hartmann v. Loudoun County Bd. of Educ.*, 118 F.3d 996 (4th Cir.1997).

◆   An 11-year-old Rhode Island student had a respiratory condition that required the use of a tracheal tube for breathing and the presence of a full-time nurse in case of a medical emergency. His parents met with school district representatives to discuss an appropriate IEP. **The parties agreed to an acceptable program, but the parents objected to implementation of the program at the location designated**

by the school district, which was a school located three miles from their home. They argued that the district should reassign its only full-time nurse from that school to the student's neighborhood school. They appealed an adverse administrative decision on the issue to the U.S. District Court for the District of Rhode Island.

The court refused to second-guess the school district's deployment of its only full-time nurse and rejected the parents' claim that she should be transferred to the neighborhood school. The U.S. Court of Appeals, First Circuit, affirmed, noting that the site selected by the school district was only three miles from the student's home and was readily accessible to the student. **The district's obligation to provide the student with a FAPE did not require an optimal placement or a change in district staffing decisions.** *Kevin G. by Robert G. v. Cranston School Comm.,* 130 F.3d 481 (1st Cir.1997).

◆   A Minnesota student with dyslexia received extended year services from the school district during the summer months, including one-to-one tutoring under the Orton-Gillingham instructional method. The student's mother requested continuation of the Orton-Gillingham method for the following school year, but the district declined to include it in the student's IEP. The U.S. Court of Appeals, Eighth Circuit, noted that despite the lack of grade-level achievement by the student in many critical skill areas, the IDEA does not require the best possible education or the achievement of outstanding results by students. As long as a student is benefiting from her education, there is no IDEA violation. **Educators are entitled to determine appropriate methodologies for carrying out IEPs which provide appropriate educational benefits.** *E.S. v. Indep. School Dist. No. 196,* 135 F.3d 566 (8th Cir.1998).

◆   A Connecticut student had serious social and emotional problems including hyperactivity, inability to interact with others and lack of self-confidence. Although she was in the average intelligence range, she failed to progress academically and met only four of 32 objectives stated in her IEP. A public school evaluator recommended placement in a residential facility, but the board refused the recommendation. However, the placement was arranged through the state Department of Child and Youth Services. The student attended the residential facility, where her academic and social skills improved. However, the school board maintained that the placement was non-academic and was made necessary by the student's mother's manipulative behavior. **The mother requested a due process hearing to obtain complete funding for the placement,** resulting in a decision favorable to the school board. The U.S. District Court for the District of Connecticut reversed the hearing officer's decision and granted the mother's summary judgment motion. The board appealed to the U.S. Court of Appeals, Second Circuit.

The court observed that, notwithstanding the non-academic reasons for the residential placement, the student had failed to progress in her public school placement and the school board had failed to take action to remedy her serious academic regression. **The residential placement was necessary to enable the student to obtain academic benefits, and it was appropriate for the board to fund the non-educational portion of the residential placement** despite the other factors that were present in the decision to place her there. The other factors did not relieve the school district of its obligation to pay for a necessary academic program, and the court affirmed the district court decision. *Mrs. B. v. Milford Bd. of Educ.*, 103 F.3d 1114 (2d Cir.1997).

◆   A Seattle student with a history of early neglect, physical and sexual abuse, abandonment and foster home placement had behavioral problems including physical and verbal aggression, tantrums, attention deficit and inappropriate adult affectional behavior. When her behavior problems escalated, she was hospitalized and was expelled from school for an entire semester. During this time, she received no educational services from her school district. Although the district found the student eligible for special education services, it rejected proposals by an independent child psychiatrist for residential schooling. The student's adoptive mother requested an administrative hearing and private tutoring pending the hearing. **The hearing officer ordered the district to provide tutoring services and to pay for a private residential placement**. The order was limited to educational costs. The school district appealed to the U.S. District Court for the Western District of Washington, which affirmed the administrative decision. The school district appealed to the U.S. Court of Appeals, Ninth Circuit.

The court agreed with administrative and district court findings that the school district had failed to include appropriate staff persons on the assessment team to identify the student's disabilities and assure an appropriate evaluation. The district had failed to appropriately consider expert recommendations for the Montana residence and disregarded medical testimony that such a placement was necessary. The evidence indicated that a mainstream program was inappropriate because the student was disruptive to the point of being expelled. **Residential placement was necessary for her to receive any meaningful educational benefit. The fact that the residence facility provided medical treatment did not invalidate the district's financial responsibility for educational services at the facility**. The administrative order had expressly limited school district liability to nonmedical costs. Because the district's proposed placement was inadequate and the residential facility was appropriate, the district court decision was affirmed. *Seattle School Dist., No. 1 v. B.S.*, 82 F.3d 1493 (9th Cir.1996).

C. Change in Placement

The IDEA requires school districts to provide parents of students with disabilities prior written notice of any proposed change in placement. If the parents wish to contest the change in placement, a hearing must be granted. The IDEA further requires that during the pendency of such review proceedings, the child is to remain in the then current educational placement. A long term suspension or expulsion of a student with a disability from school constitutes a "change in placement" for purposes of the IDEA.

The 1997 amendments to the IDEA allow the removal from classes of certain students with disabilities for placement in an alternative educational setting for an additional 45 days over the 10-day limit of prior law for carrying firearms, or for having, using, soliciting the sale of, or selling medication or illegal drugs. The IDEA now allows a hearing officer to order a change in placement if there is substantial evidence that maintenance of the current placement is substantially likely to result in injury to the child or others.

The 1997 amendments require an IEP team to review whether the child's inappropriate action was a manifestation of the disability, and allows a change of placement, with the parents' agreement, if the behavior is the result of the disability. The amendments provide for an immediate appeal to a hearing officer if the parents disagree with the determination or the changed educational placement. Where behavior is determined not to be a manifestation of the disability, the same disciplinary procedures applied to nondisabled children may be applied to children with disabilities. Also, if a local educational agency does not have knowledge that a child is disabled, it can impose the same discipline on the child that it would impose on a nondisabled child. A due process hearing is allowed if the parents disagree with these procedures. State and local educational agencies receiving IDEA assistance must now offer parents voluntary mediation for disputes over the provision of a free appropriate public education to children with disabilities.

◆   Two emotionally disturbed children in California were each suspended for five days for misbehavior that included destroying school property and assaulting and making sexual comments to other students. Pursuant to state law, **the suspensions were continued indefinitely during the pendency of expulsion proceedings**. The students sued the school district in U.S. district court contesting the extended suspensions on the ground that they violated the "stay put" provision of the IDEA which provides that a student must be kept in his or her "then current" educational placement during the pendency of proceedings which contemplate a change in placement. The district court issued an injunction preventing the expulsion, and the school district appealed.

The U.S. Court of Appeals, Ninth Circuit, determined that the **indefinite suspensions constituted a prohibited "change in placement" without notice under the IDEA and that there was no "dangerousness" exception to the IDEA's "stay put" provision**. It ruled that indefinite suspensions or expulsions of disabled children for misconduct arising out of their disabilities violated the IDEA. The court of appeals also ruled, however, that fixed suspensions of up to 30 school days did not constitute a "change in placement." It determined that a state must provide services directly to a disabled child when a local school district fails to do so. The California Superintendent of Public Instruction filed for a review by the U.S. Supreme Court on the issues of whether there was a dangerousness exception to the "stay put" provision and whether the state had to provide services directly when a local school district failed to do so.

The Supreme Court declared that the intended purpose of the "stay put" provision was to prevent schools from changing a child's educational placement over his or her parents' objection until all review proceedings were completed. While the IDEA provided for interim placements where parents and school officials were able to agree on one, no emergency exception for dangerous students was included. **Where a disabled student poses an immediate threat to the safety of others, school officials may temporarily suspend him or her for up to 10 school days**. The Court affirmed the court of appeals' decision that indefinite suspensions violated the "stay put" provision of the IDEA. It modified that court's decision on fixed suspensions by holding that suspensions up to 10 rather than up to 30 days do not constitute a change in placement. The Court also upheld the court of appeals' decision that states could be required to provide services directly to disabled students where a local school district fails to do so. *Honig v. Doe*, 484 U.S. 305, 108 S.Ct. 592, 98 L.Ed.2d 686 (1988).

◆   After a student with an emotional disturbance was tardy 20 times during one academic year and was disruptive in class, a family court truancy petition was filed. The family court denied a motion by the student's guardian to dismiss the petition, and placed the student under county supervision. The New York Supreme Court, Appellate Division, noted that the 1997 IDEA Amendments contain a provision prohibiting an interpretation of the IDEA that would prevent the reporting of crimes committed by students with disabilities or preventing law enforcement officers from exercising their duties. Even though the student had been accused of threatening other students, he was not charged with committing a crime and was not the subject of a juvenile delinquency petition. The truancy proceeding arose under the Family Court Article and the 1997 IDEA Amendments had no application in the case. **The court agreed with the guardian that the filing of the truancy petition triggered the stay put provision** and that the county failed to exhaust required IDEA and state special education administrative remedies prior to filing the petition. Accordingly, the court dismissed the petition.

School officials appealed to the New York Court of Appeals, which observed that the stay put provision requires that parents or guardians of students with disabilities receive written prior notice whenever an education agency proposes to initiate or change the identification, evaluation or educational placement of the student. According to the high court, the key phrase in this dispute was "change in educational placement," which is not defined in the IDEA. **The determination of whether a change in placement has occurred must be made on a case-by-case basis in which a number of factors are considered**: whether the student's IEP has been revised, whether the student will be educated with non-disabled students to the same extent as before, whether the student will have the same participation opportunities in nonacademic and extracurricular programs, and whether the new placement option is the same option on the continuum of alternative placements. The court also relied on authoritative guidance from the U.S. Department of Education indicating that a change in placement occurs when the substance of the student's educational program itself has been changed, so that the program has been materially altered. In this case, the school officials were not seeking a change of placement by filing the PINS petition. To the contrary, they sought to enforce his program through probation. Probation primarily sought to improve his attendance record and supervise his activities, not alter his educational services or placement. The student attended the same school, same classes and received the same type and level of services. Since no substantial and material change was effected by the filing of the PINS petition, the high court reversed and remanded the decision of the appellate division. In doing so, the panel rejected a blanket rule under which the stay put provision barred all PINS proceedings. *In the Matter of Beau "II,"* 715 N.Y.S.2d 686 (N.Y. 2000).

◆   A student attended a private special education school under an IEP formulated by the District of Columbia Public Schools. When the student's family moved to Pennsylvania, the new district evaluated him and proposed placing him in a learning support or combined learning/emotional support program. The family rejected these proposals and unilaterally enrolled the student in a private school. He remained there for 41 days before the family moved to New Jersey. The student's parents commenced Pennsylvania due process proceedings, seeking tuition reimbursement. They claimed that the IDEA's stay-put provision required the Pennsylvania district to accept the IEP developed in Washington, D.C. The hearing officer held that because state standards differ, the adoption of an IEP from another state would require the receiving state to approve of standards that would not necessarily be applicable under the receiving state's standards. The parents appealed to a federal district court, which reviewed the U.S. Department of Education's Office of Special Education Programs (OSEP) Policy Memorandum 96-5 for guidance. **The court agreed with the school district and hearing officer that a receiving school district is not required to accept an IEP drafted by a district in another state pending an appeal involving an intrastate transfer**. The Washington IEP was presumably based on local standards that did not necessarily comply with Pennsylvania special education standards. The IDEA does not impose nationwide standards on the states, but instead requires them to create and implement their own standards for students with disabilities. The court agreed with the OSEP policy memorandum that there is a distinction between intrastate and interstate transfers and held that the Pennsylvania district was not compelled to accept the Washington IEP. It rejected the family's alterative argument that Pennsylvania discriminated against students who transferred there from out of state.

The family appealed to the U.S. Court of Appeals, Third Circuit, arguing that the OSEP policy memorandum was not entitled to deference because it conflicted with the IDEA stay-put provision and Pennsylvania special education regulations. The circuit court observed that the stay-put provision does not specifically address student transfers between districts in different states. The OSEP policy memorandum and district court judgment were both based on sound reasoning, since the IDEA recognizes the traditional role of the states to determine their own educational standards. Under the IDEA, provision of a FAPE requires that special education and related services meet the standards of the state educational agency and that states have special education policies, procedures and programs consistent with their own standards. **The circuit court found it unlikely that Congress intended the stay-put provision to require a state to implement an IEP established in another state without first considering consistency with its own policies**. Where a parent unilaterally removes a student from a placement determined under state procedures, the stay-put provision is inoperative until the parties reach a new agreement. The Third Circuit held that the stay-put provision is inapplicable when a parent removes a student from an existing placement in favor of another placement not assigned through state procedures. Because the student was without a "then current educational placement" in Pennsylvania, he was not entitled to stay-put protection. Moreover, **whenever a student moves into a new state, the receiving state is not obligated to automatically effectuate a prior IEP from another state, and parents maintain the risk of unilateral private school placements.** The court affirmed the district court's decision that the school district was not required to preserve a private school placement for the student on the basis of the IEP prepared in Washington, D.C. The court found that even if it interpreted state or federal law in the manner urged by the parents, the stay-put provision was inapplicable in this case. This was because the family had moved to New Jersey at the time the due process hearing was requested and no pending proceeding existed in Pennsylvania. The school district took no action to alter or deny the student's right to a free appropriate public education, and the court affirmed the summary judgment order for the district. *Michael C. v. Radnor Township School Dist.*, 202 F.3d 642 (3d Cir. 2000).

◆   An 18-year-old Florida student with specific learning disabilities and attention deficit hyperactivity disorder attended a public school until he encountered problems with students and faculty members. The district then complied with his mother's request for an administrative transfer to a school outside his residential area. The administrative placement required the student to maintain good conduct and attendance, show satisfactory effort in classes and comply with the student code of conduct. His IEP remained in effect. The student experienced academic difficulties and was disciplined six times during his first semester at the new school. **The administrative placement was revoked on the basis of his failure to comply with the placement conditions, and he was returned to his residence district high school.**

The student's mother requested administrative review of the transfer without challenging the IEP or requesting any changes in his educational program. A hearing officer determined that the transfer was not a change in placement under the IDEA stay put provision and dismissed the action. The student appealed to the U.S. District Court for the Middle District of Florida, which observed that educational placement refers to a student's educational program and not the particular institution at which the program is implemented. **Because there had been no change to the IEP upon transfer to the new facility, the student had remained in his then current educational placement under the IDEA; his educational placement had not changed.** The court denied the student's motion for a temporary restraining order preventing the transfer. *Hill v. School Bd. for Pinellas County*, 954 F.Supp. 251 (M.D.Fla.1997).

◆   A Missouri student with multiple mental disabilities exhibited aggressive behavior toward students and teachers. She was placed in a public school's self-contained classroom. She was also enrolled in several regular education classrooms. Despite this placement, her aggressive behavior continued to the point that daily lesson plans were not completed and the parents of other students complained of the negative effect on their children. The student's IEP team reevaluated the placement. The parents objected to any change in placement and requested the imposition of the IDEA's stay put provision during the course of administrative proceedings. Shortly thereafter, the student hit another student on the head three times during art class. The school imposed a ten-day suspension, and the parents filed a lawsuit seeking to set it aside in the U.S. District Court for the Eastern District of Missouri. **The school district filed a counterclaim to remove the student from school during the revision of the IEP, based on the substantial risk of injury she presented to herself and others.** The court granted the district's motion for an order allowing it to remove the student from school. The parents appealed to the U.S. Court of Appeals, Eighth Circuit.

On appeal, the parents argued that the district court should have inquired into whether the student was "truly dangerous," based upon her capacity to inflict injury.

The court disagreed, determining that it was only necessary to determine whether a student with a disability posed a substantial risk of injury to herself or others. **There was substantial evidence in the record of a likelihood of injury based on almost daily episodes of aggressive behavior by the student**. Accordingly, removal of the student had been proper and temporary placement at a segregated facility for students with disabilities was appropriate. The court affirmed the lower court's decision for the school district. *Light v. Parkway C-2 School Dist.*, 41 F.3d 1223 (8th Cir.1994).

◆   A 15-year-old Washington student with Tourette's Syndrome and attention deficit hyperactivity disorder became increasingly uncontrollable and frequently disrupted classes with name-calling, profanity, explicit sexual comments, kicking and hitting. The school ultimately expelled him under an emergency order after he assaulted a staff member. **The student's parents agreed with the school's determination that he should be placed in a self-contained program off the school campus for individualized attention and a structured environment. The parents soon changed their minds** and requested a due process hearing to contest the interim placement and demand a new IEP. The parties were unable to agree upon a new IEP, and the parents insisted that the student return to regular classes for the rest of the school year. A 10-day due process hearing was held during the summer break, resulting in a determination that the school had complied with the IDEA. The parents appealed to the U.S. District Court for the Western District of Washington, which affirmed the administrative decision. The parents appealed to the U.S. Court of Appeals, Ninth Circuit.

The court held that **because the parents had initially agreed with the interim placement, it could be implemented without a current IEP and could be considered the student's "stay-put" placement for IDEA purposes**. The school district had complied with substantive requirements of the IDEA by placing the student in the interim placement that constituted the least restrictive environment in which he could receive educational benefits. Accordingly, the court of appeals affirmed the district court judgment. *Clyde K. v. Puyallup School Dist. No. 3*, 35 F.3d 1396 (9th Cir.1994).

III. RELATED SERVICES

Related services include sign language interpreters, transportation, speech pathology, psychological and counseling services, and physical and occupational therapy. The IDEA requires school districts to provide services that are necessary for students with disabilities to receive educational benefits, but excludes medical services from coverage except where required for evaluation or diagnostic purposes.

◆   An Iowa student suffered a spinal cord injury that left him quadriplegic and ventilator dependent. For several years, his family provided him with personal attendant services at school. A family member or nurse performed catheterization, tracheostomy suctioning, repositioning and respiratory observation during the school day. When the student entered the fifth grade, **his mother requested that**

the district provide him with continuous, one-on-one nursing services during the school day. The district refused, and the family filed a request for due
process. An administrative law judge determined that the school district was
obligated to reimburse the family for nursing costs incurred during the current
school year and provide the disputed services in the future. The school district
appealed to a federal district court, which granted summary judgment to the family.
The district appealed to the U.S. Court of Appeals, Eighth Circuit, which concluded
the disputed services were related services the district was obligated to provide
under the IDEA. Because the student required the services to benefit from his
education, the district was required to provide them. The district appealed to the U.S.
Supreme Court.

A majority of the Supreme Court affirmed the Eighth Circuit's opinion,
agreeing that the requested services were not medical services. The court based its
decision in the IDEA definition of related services, its previous holding in *Tatro,*
below, and the purpose of the IDEA to make special education available to all
disabled students. **Adopting a bright-line, physician/non-physician standard,
the court held that since the disputed services could be performed by someone
other than a physician, the district was obligated to provide them.** *Cedar
Rapids Community School Dist. v. Garret F. by Charlene F.,* 526 U.S. 66, 119
S.Ct. 992, 143 L.Ed.2d 154 (1999).

◆   **The U.S. Supreme Court ruled that clean intermittent catheterization
(CIC) is a related service not subject to the "medical service" exclusion of the
IDEA.** The parents of an eight-year-old girl born with spina bifida brought suit
against their local Texas school district after the district refused to provide CIC for
the child while she attended school. The parents pursued administrative and judicial
avenues to force the district to train staff to perform the simple procedure. After a
U.S. district court held against the parents, they appealed to the U.S. Court of
Appeals, Fifth Circuit, which reversed the district court ruling. The school district
then appealed to the U.S. Supreme Court. The Supreme Court affirmed the court of
appeals' ruling that clean intermittent catheterization is a supportive related service,
not a medical service excluded from the IDEA. *Irving Indep. School Dist. v. Tatro,*
468 U.S. 883, 104 S.Ct. 3371, 82 L.Ed.2d 664 (1984).

◆   An Arizona student attended a school for the deaf from grades one through five
and a public school from grades six through eight. During his public school
attendance, a sign language interpreter was provided by the school district. **The
student's parents enrolled him in a parochial high school for ninth grade, and
requested the school district to continue providing a sign language interpreter. The school district refused,** and the student's parents then sued it in the
U.S. District Court for the District of Arizona under the IDEA. The court granted the
school district's summary judgment motion. On appeal, the U.S. Court of Appeals,
Ninth Circuit, affirmed, stating that the placement of a public school employee in
a parochial school would create the appearance that the government was a joint
sponsor of the private school's activities. The U.S. Supreme Court granted the
parents' petition for a writ of certiorari.

The Supreme Court stated that the Establishment Clause did not completely
prohibit religious institutions from participating in publicly-sponsored benefits. If
this were the case, religious groups would not even enjoy police and fire protection

or have use of public roads and sidewalks. Government programs which neutrally provide benefits to broad classes of citizens are not subject to Establishment Clause prohibition simply because some religiously affiliated institutions receive "an attenuated financial benefit." **Providing a sign language interpreter under the IDEA was part of a general program for distribution of benefits in a neutral manner to qualified students**. A sign language interpreter, unlike an instructor or counselor, was ethically bound to transmit everything said in exactly the same way as it was intended. The Supreme Court reversed the court of appeals' decision. *Zobrest v. Catalina Foothills School Dist.,* 509 U.S. 1, 113 S.Ct. 2462, 125 L.Ed.2d 1 (1993).

♦   A county intermediate unit provided speech and language services to a parochial school student during his kindergarten year. It then notified the family that it intended to discontinue services to Diocesan schools. The student's mother submitted a written request to the school district special education director for necessary services. **A district** multidisciplinary team performed a comprehensive evaluation report and found the student eligible for speech and language therapy and **devised an IEP calling for biweekly speech/language therapy sessions on the condition that the student be exclusively enrolled in district schools**. The parents rejected the IEP and requested a due process hearing. A hearing officer held that the district was not obligated to provide the student with services while he was enrolled in a private school.

A state appeals panel affirmed the decision and the parents appealed to the Pennsylvania Commonwealth Court, which discussed 1997 amendments to the IDEA providing that public school agencies are not required to pay for private school special education costs if the agency has offered a FAPE. States are required only to spend proportionate amounts on special education services for students attending private schools, and private school students have no individual right to IDEA special education services. However, the parents did not seek tuition reimbursement, only the provision of speech/language therapy. **The court agreed with the parents that a state law, 24 Pa. Stat. § 5-502, prevented the district from denying their child services by reason of his attendance at a parochial school**. The family had a constitutionally protected right to determine where he should attend school. The IDEA did not relieve school districts of their obligation to provide services to students with disabilities, only from requiring them to provide services at nonpublic schools. The parents made no claim of an entitlement to services at their son's school. The court agreed with them that state and federal special education law did not permit school districts to dictate the conditions imposed on private school students in order to receive services. State law did not prevent dual enrollment of a student in a private school and a district gifted program such that the student had to forego the right to receive special education. State guidelines recommended dual enrollment as a "genuine opportunity for equitable participation." The 1997 IDEA Amendments did not change decades of educational jurisprudence, but instead clarified certain points related to unilaterally enrolled private school students. Services offered to private school students had to reflect a genuine opportunity to participate in programs, the court found, reversing the administrative decisions. *Veschi v. Northwestern Lehigh School District,* 772 A.2d 469 (Pa. Commw. 2001).

◆   After an Indiana student was released from a medical center, her parents contacted local school officials for a residential placement. The parties met at an IEP case conference and agreed that the student needed a residential placement. While the student awaited the outcome of the administrative process, she was placed in a psychiatric hospital for over sixth months. Shortly after the student was hospitalized, her parents filed a state court petition to have her involuntarily committed. The court accepted the petition and held that the student was mentally ill, schizoaffective, paranoid, suicidal, and required long-term education in a locked residential protective placement. She remained in the hospital for an additional five months, since the least restrictive appropriate facility had no available space. The hospital notified the court that she was no longer a threat to herself or others and recommended termination of her civil commitment. In a separate action, a class of Indiana students with disabilities and their parents sued the Indiana Department of Education, alleging that the department's long delays in residential placement matters violated the procedural protections of the IDEA. The parties settled that lawsuit under an order that provided a procedure for recovery of certain educational and related services costs from the state where there was a delay between the date of the IEP and the date of the placement. The state agreed to place eligible students in residential facilities within 30 days of the development of their IEPs, "except where special circumstances require otherwise." **The student and her parents joined the action and sought reimbursement for services she received while hospitalized**. The state board of special education appeals reversed an administrative decision in their favor, ruling that the hospitalization was not "education or related services" that required reimbursement.

A federal district court affirmed the appeals board order and the family appealed to the Seventh Circuit, arguing that the hospitalization costs were reimbursable under the settlement agreement. The court held that the hospitalization charges resulted from "special circumstances" as described in the settlement order, therefore, the delay in placing her in a residential facility, as called for in her IEP, did not violate the terms of the settlement agreement. Her IEP was designed for homebound services and contemplated a residential placement for her educational needs, not a placement based on medical treatment. The student's unstable condition made hospitalization necessary, and resulted in her inability to be placed at a residential facility. Medical services are not reimbursable under the IDEA unless they are for diagnostic or evaluative purposes, which was not the case here. **The hospital placement was for medical reasons related to the student's psychiatric crisis, therefore, reimbursement was not warranted**. The student's IEP team had unanimously concluded that she did not require hospitalization, and her parents had failed to challenge the adequacy of the IEP. Further, the parents did not request a new case conference, and the initiation of commitment proceedings was not an IDEA action. The hospital was not equipped to serve as an educational provider. The court affirmed the district court decision. *Butler v. Evans*, 225 F.3d 887 (7th Cir. 2000).

◆   The mother of a Rhode Island student who was profoundly retarded, paraplegic and required a ventilator requested a due process hearing challenging the student's IEP. The city school department prevailed in administrative proceedings, and the mother appealed. However, she voluntarily dismissed the action. At the time of the voluntary dismissal, an IEP team meeting was already one month overdue under a state special education law. A state education department compliance officer requested an IEP review meeting for the student. Although a meeting was held, it was not attended by any representative from the city school department. The state education department then initiated compliance proceedings against the city school department for failure to conduct an annual IEP review. Following a hearing, the education department authorized the compliance officer to take necessary action to develop a revised IEP. At a final hearing in the compliance action, the officer testified that nursing services were appropriate for the student in order to provide her with a safe environment in which to receive a FAPE. **The city later refused to pay for a full-time nurse to assist the student, and the commissioner deducted almost $55,000 from the city's operation aid to pay for nursing services** rendered to the student.

The city appealed the deduction to the state Board of Regents for Elementary and Secondary Education. The board denied the appeal, and the Rhode Island Supreme Court denied the city's subsequent petition. The case then came before the Rhode Island Superior Court, which found that the state's general laws authorized the commissioner to deduct funds from a city's operation aid for a violation or neglect of law, or for a municipality's violation or neglect of rules and regulations. State special education law required an annual meeting to review a student's IEP. In this case, the city had violated the law by failing to timely arrange for an IEP meeting, despite requests from the student's mother and the compliance officer. Withholding of funds by the commissioner had therefore been appropriate. The court then considered whether the provision of full-time nursing services while the student was weaned from her ventilator constituted "related services" under the IDEA. According to the court, "related services" included supportive services that may be required to assist a student with disabilities to benefit from special education. In this case, **the record indicated that full-time nursing services were necessary for the student to maintain her health and safety while she received public education**. She was a technology-dependant child who was in need of respiratory suctioning, special feeding, catheterization and a ventilator. The disputed services could be provided by a nurse and were thus not subject to the IDEA's medical services exclusion., *City of Warwick v. Rhode Island Dep't of Educ.*, No. PC 98-3189, 2000 WL 1879897 (R.I. Super. Ct. 2000).

◆   An Oregon student, who was blind and had cerebral palsy, initially attended public schools. There, he received physical therapy and services from a vision specialist, along with special equipment. His parents transferred him to a sectarian school. The district continued to provide him with braillers, computers, and other special equipment after the transfer, but declined to provide a vision specialist at the sectarian school. Instead, it provided the service at a nearby fire hall, with transportation. The family sued the school district and state superintendent of public instruction in a federal district court for an order requiring the district to furnish the services at the sectarian school. The court determined that the IDEA did not require the district to provide the services at the sectarian school. However, **a state regulation requiring the provision of services for private school students only in religiously neutral settings violated the student's rights under the Free Exercise, Establishment, and Equal Protection Clauses of the U.S. Constitution**. The district and superintendent appealed to the Ninth Circuit.

The Ninth Circuit held that the 1997 IDEA amendments do not require the provision of services on-site at a private school and affirmed that part of the judgment. It rejected the family's assertion that the state regulation violated the Free Exercise Clause. The regulation did not force the family to choose between enrolling the student in a sectarian school and forgoing the services, nor did it burden their free exercise of religion. Moreover, the regulation did not discriminate against religious school students or suppress religion or religious conduct. **The circuit court rejected the district court's holding that the regulation violated the Establishment Clause, because it did not result in entanglement between the state and religion.** Under *Zobrest v. Catalina Foothills School Dist.*, 509 U.S. 1 (1993), and *Agostini v. Felton*, 117 S.Ct. 1997 (1997), the presence of public school employees on private school grounds is not longer presumed to violate the U.S. Constitution, and the superintendent would not be required to perform a case-by-case analysis of whether particular school settings were religious. The Ninth Circuit also rejected the district court's finding that the regulation violated the Equal Protection Clause, finding that the district court applied the wrong standard of review. The district court had subjected the regulation to the strict scrutiny analysis, which was not warranted in this case, as students with disabilities are not regarded as a class of persons for which the strict scrutiny analysis is required. The court held that the regulation did not violate the family's constitutional rights, and reversed the judgment. *KDM v. Reedsport School Dist.*, 196 F.3d 1046 (9th Cir. 1999).

♦   A Missouri student with disabilities attended a private school. She sought language services and occupational, speech and physical therapy from her public school district. Although the district agreed to make these services available to her at a public school site, it refused to provide them at the private school. The student's parents filed an administrative complaint against the school district, resulting in a decision that the district did not violate the IDEA when it refused to provide on-site services. The U.S. District Court for the Eastern District of Missouri noted that IDEA regulations distinguish between students who are voluntarily placed at private schools by their parents and those placed at private schools through the public school IEP process. **Under IDEA regulations, educational agencies have discretion to determine the manner and extent of related services to be provided to private school students.** In this case, there was no evidence that occupational, speech and physical therapy services could not be appropriately provided at a public school site. These services would be more costly to provide at the private school. The district did not have to provide on-site services at the private school.

On appeal to the U.S. Court of Appeals, Eighth Circuit, **the circuit court concluded voluntarily enrolled private school students have no individual right to IDEA services.** Under IDEA 1997, districts are only obligated to spend a proportionate amount of federal IDEA funds on voluntarily enrolled private school students with disabilities. **Since the student had no individual right to services, she had no right to such services on-site at the parochial school,** and the relief sought by the parents could not be granted. The court further noted that Missouri law barred the provision of services by public school employees on the grounds of private schools. Despite questioning the constitutionality of this state law, the court refused to overrule it. *Foley v. Special School Dist. of St. Louis County,* 153 F.3d 863 (8th Cir. 1998).

◆   A student with brittle bone disease received physical and occupational therapy
from her school district until her parents placed her in a religious school. **Her
parents met with the district to develop an IEP, and requested that the
therapies take place at the religious school, rather than at their home,** to avoid
disruption of her daily schedule. The district refused the request, arguing that the
provision of on-site therapy services would constitute excessive entanglement
between church and state in violation of the Establishment Clause. A hearing officer
agreed with the district, and her decision was substantially affirmed by a state review
officer. The family appealed to a federal district court, which remanded the case for
further fact finding. On remand, the hearing officer concluded that the possibility
of excessive entanglement existed because of the increased supervisory time and
additional contact that would be required by district employees and religious school
staff if the services were provided on-site. The district court rejected this analysis
and granted summary judgment to the family. It noted that there was no issue of
entitlement to the services, which the student required. The parties only disagreed
on the location at which the services would be provided. The court stated that only
a minimal potential for religious entanglement existed in this case.

The school district appealed to the Sixth Circuit, which noted that the U.S.
Supreme Court's decision in *Agostini v. Felton*, 117 S.Ct. 1997 (1997), changed
the outcome of earlier cases in which the mere presence of a public school teacher
on parochial grounds was sufficient to create a constitutional violation. Under
Agostini, **a federally funded program does not violate the Establishment
Clause even if services are provided on parochial school grounds—as long as
the instruction is supplemental to regularly provided services, the funding is
awarded on neutral criteria and the program has adequate safeguards to
ensure secular instruction**. In this case, there was no evidence that the provision
of services by the school district would impermissibly supplant services already
provided by the religious school, and therefore there was no constitutional violation.
Peck by Peck v. Lansing School Dist., 148 F.3d 619 (6th Cir.1998).

◆   **A multiply disabled Indiana student was enrolled by her parents in a
private school. They requested the assistance of an on-site instructional
assistant.** The school district denied the request and the parents requested a hearing.
The hearing officer held that the school was not obligated to provide the student with
an instructional assistant at the private school. After a federal district court held that
IDEA regulations required the school district to provide related services to private
school students that were comparable to those received by public school students,
the school district appealed to the U.S. Court of Appeals, Seventh Circuit.

The court of appeals determined public schools need not provide voluntarily
placed private school students with related services that are comparable to those
received by public school students. School districts need only provide voluntarily
placed private school students with a genuine opportunity for equitable participation. The court reversed the district court judgment, but the U.S. Supreme Court
vacated and remanded the case for reconsideration in view of the IDEA Amendments
of 1997. The court then found that **the 1997 amendments relieve a local
education agency from the obligation to pay for a private school student's
special education and related services if the agency has made a FAPE
available and the parents voluntarily place the child in the private school**.
Because the school district had afforded the student a genuine opportunity to receive

a FAPE, the court again reversed the district court judgment. *K.R. by M.R. v. Anderson Community School Corp.*, 125 F.3d 1017 (7th Cir.1997).

◆   In a Louisiana case involving a student with a hearing impairment who was voluntarily enrolled at a parochial school and who was seeking on-site sign language interpretation services, the U.S. Court of Appeals, Fifth Circuit, held that **the IDEA does not require school districts to expend non-IDEA funds for students who are voluntarily enrolled in private schools. A local education agency must make a FAPE available to all disabled students and provide a proportionate share of IDEA funds to students voluntarily enrolled in private schools.** The court added that the IDEA Amendments Act of 1997 specified that an agency is required only to provide students voluntarily enrolled in private schools with a proportionate share of IDEA funding. Because the school district had offered the student an appropriate public school IEP, it was not required to provide him with an on-site interpreter. *Cefalu v. East Baton Rouge Parish School Bd.*, 117 F.3d 231 (5th Cir.1997).

◆   An Illinois preschool student had developmental disabilities as the result of a rare neurological-muscular disease. He used a wheelchair and had a tracheostomy tube to keep his airway clear. His parents filed an administrative complaint against the district when it refused to place him in a public early childhood center for students with disabilities that was operated by another school district. A hearing officer determined that the student was entitled to the placement and a review officer upheld the decision. **The school district** appealed to an Illinois circuit court and **refused to provide a nurse to perform tracheostomy suctioning while he rode the school bus.** The student's mother performed the suctioning and the parents initiated a separate action in a federal district court to require the district to provide a licensed nurse during bus rides.

The court considered the family's application for a temporary order requiring tracheostomy suctioning for bus rides pending further consideration of the case. The court observed that federal regulations published under the IDEA exclude medical services from the IDEA's definition of related services. **Excluded medical services are defined in the regulations as those that are provided by a physician. In this case, the services did not require a physician and could be performed by any individual with minimal training.** The U.S. Supreme Court has ruled that services that can be provided in the school setting by a nurse or qualified layperson are not subject to the medical services exclusion. Because it appeared that the student in this case required only a nurse, he was entitled to a preliminary order requiring the district to furnish tracheostomy suctioning during his bus rides. *Skelly v. Brookfield LaGrange Park School Dist. 95*, 968 F.Supp. 385 (N.D.Ill.1997).

IV. TUITION REIMBURSEMENT

If a public school district is unable to provide special education services to a student with a disability in its own facilities, it must locate an appropriate program in another school district, hospital or institution. When no public facility is adequate and a private placement is required, the school district becomes responsible for tuition and other costs. A provision of the 1997 IDEA Amendments allows public agencies to reduce or deny reimbursement to parents of a child placed in a private school by the parents without agency consent or referral if the parents fail to give at least 10 days notice of the intended placement, if the child was not made available to designated school employees for an assessment and evaluation before the child's removal from public school, or if a judge so rules.

◆   A South Carolina ninth-grader with a learning disability attended special education classes. Her parents disagreed with the individualized education program (IEP) established by their public school district. The IEP called for mainstreaming in regular education classes for most subjects. The student's parents requested a due process hearing under the IDEA. Meanwhile, they unilaterally placed the student in a private school. The hearing officer held that the IEP was adequate. After the student raised her reading comprehension three full grades in one year at the private school, the parents sued the school district for tuition reimbursement. The U.S. District Court for the District of South Carolina held that the educational program and achievement goals of the proposed IEP were "wholly inadequate" under the IDEA and that even though the private school did not comply with all IDEA requirements, it provided the student with an excellent education that complied with IDEA substantive requirements. It held that the parents were entitled to tuition reimbursement, a result that was upheld by the U.S. Court of Appeals, Fourth Circuit. The school district appealed to the U.S. Supreme Court.

The Supreme Court held that **the failure of the school district to provide an appropriate placement entitled the parents to tuition reimbursement** by the school district, **even though the private school was not on any state list of approved schools**. This was because the education provided to the student was determined by the district court to be appropriate. Moreover, South Carolina did not release a list of approved schools to the public. Under the IDEA, parents had a right to unilaterally place children in private schools. **To recover private school tuition costs, parents must show that the placement proposed by the school district violates the IDEA, and that the private school placement is appropriate**. The Supreme Court upheld the lower court decisions in favor of the parents. *Florence County School Dist. Four v. Carter*, 510 U.S. 7, 114 S.Ct. 361, 126 L.Ed.2d 284 (1993).

◆   The U.S. Supreme Court ruled that the parents of a child with a disability did not waive their claim for reimbursement of the expenses involved in unilaterally placing their child in a private school during the pendency of proceedings to review the child's IEP. The case involved a learning disabled child who was placed in a public school special education program against the wishes of his parents. **The parents requested a due process hearing and, prior to the resolution of their complaint, placed their child in a private residential school** recommended by specialists. The parents then sought reimbursement for their expenses. The U.S. Court of Appeals, First Circuit, found the IDEA provision against changing a child's placement during administrative proceedings to be "directory" rather than "mandatory." It decided that the "status quo" provision did not bar claims for reimbursement. The

Supreme Court subsequently held that to bar reimbursement claims in cases of unilateral parent placement was contrary to the IDEA, which favors proper interim placements for disabled children. The Court declared, however, that **parents who unilaterally change a child's placement during the pendency of proceedings do so at their own financial risk**. If the courts ultimately determine that a child's IEP is appropriate, the parents are barred from obtaining reimbursement for any interim period in which their child's placement violated the IDEA. The Supreme Court affirmed the appellate court ruling. *Burlington School Comm. v. Dep't of Educ.*, 471 U.S. 359, 105 S.Ct. 1996, 85 L.Ed.2d 385 (1985).

◆   A Maryland student was eligible for special education services and attended public schools under IEPs for three years. The parents agreed to an IEP proposed by the school system during March of a school year without mentioning that they had submitted an application on behalf of their son for admission to a private school. After the student was accepted by the private school, the family's attorney sent a letter to the public school principal, stating that the parents intended to place their son at the private school. He requested that the school system consider the private school as the appropriate placement. The parties met to discuss new evaluations, but the system maintained its recommendation for placement in a public school. The student attended the private school for the remainder of the year, and the parents commenced an administrative proceeding seeking tuition reimbursement. The system moved to dismiss the action, arguing that the IDEA required the parents to provide prior notice of the rejection of an IEP as a prerequisite to any reimbursement claim. An administrative law judge granted the motion, even though it was untimely filed, ruling that the parents did not comply with Section 8-413(i)(1), a provision of Maryland special education law that parallels 20 U.S.C. § 1412(a)(10)(C). **Both provisions**, among other things, **preclude private school tuition reimbursement for a unilateral parental placement unless the parents timely notify a school IEP team of a placement rejection and state the reasons** for the rejection.

The parents sued the school system and officials in a federal district court, which awarded summary judgment to the district and officials. The parents appealed to the Fourth Circuit, which held that the administrative law judge did not abuse her discretion in considering the system's late dismissal motion. Although the parents now asserted they had expressed reservations about signing the IEP, they did not inform school officials they were rejecting it. The letter from their attorney did not serve as a proper rejection, as it did not explain that they no longer considered the IEP legally adequate. The parents had thus waived the issue of whether they failed to provide timely notice of their son's enrollment in the private school. The circuit court rejected the parents' argument that the school system was required to show it was prejudiced by their failure to provide the rejection notice required by state and federal laws. **Section 8-413(i)(1) clearly explained the consequences of failing to provide timely notice of a student's private school enrollment, and the claim for tuition reimbursement was properly denied**. The system had provided the parents with notice of their procedural rights at an IEP meeting. They were not entitled to receive any additional notifications, and were not excused from providing appropriate notice of their decision. The court affirmed the summary judgment order for the school district. *Pollowitz v. Weast et al.*, No. CA-99-3118-S (4th Cir. 2001).

◆   Because a student with disabilities did not perform well in a district middle school, his parents removed him from the school in favor of a private placement. He was eventually transferred to a private residential placement in Connecticut. The parents requested reimbursement of the costs of the school and a reevaluation. Before an IEP was approved, the parents requested a hearing on their tuition reimbursement claim. The district later approved an IEP calling for a 45-day diagnostic placement, but the plan was not approved until after the hearing date. The board moved to dismiss the administrative proceeding on grounds that the family failed to provide it with a notice required by Maryland special education law. It cited a statute which provided in part that **parents who enrolled their children in nonpublic schools were not entitled to tuition reimbursement if they did "not provide to the county board prior written notice rejecting the program proposed by the county board, including the reason for the rejection, and stating an intention to enroll the student in a nonpublic school."** An administrative law judge granted the board's motion and the parents appealed to a federal district court. The court granted summary judgment to the board on grounds that the parents failed to comply with state special education law.

On appeal, the parents argued that the state law did not apply in their case, because the board had not proposed an IEP at the time they enrolled the student in the residential school. The court agreed with the parents, noting that **because there was no IEP for them to reject, the notice contemplated by the state law was impossible**. To preclude the parents from seeking reimbursement because they failed to give notice as specified in the statute would create an absurd result. The court construed the law as applying only when an IEP had actually been proposed by a school district prior to the time a student is enrolled in a nonpublic school. The court explained that this interpretation would not allow parents to bypass required steps for seeking a FAPE for their children within the public school context. This was because any entitlement to reimbursement could only result from a decision by an administrative hearing officer or court that a school district did not make a FAPE possible before the parents enrolled a student in a nonpublic school. Districts would still receive the opportunity to timely fashion appropriate educational programs for students with disabilities. The Fourth Circuit reversed the district court judgment and remanded the case for further proceedings. *Sandler et al. v. Hickey et al.*, 246 F.3d 667 (4th Cir. 2001).

◆   The First Circuit held that **school officials are precluded from seeking reimbursement from parents for a school year covered by an administrative decision ordering reimbursement**. It was thus unnecessary to award any relief to a Maine parent seeking protection from such reimbursement claims as a result of the district court's reversal of an administrative decision requiring the school committee to fund her disabled child's residential placement. Even if the student's IEPs for the 1998-1999 and 1999-2000 school years were deemed adequate, the parent would not be required to reimburse the committee for amounts it paid. *Rome School Committee v. Mrs. B.*, 247 F.3d 29 (1st Cir. 2001.)

◆   The parents of a seventh grader with attention deficit hyperactivity disorder, depression, a learning disability in written expression and difficulties processing verbal information unilaterally placed the student in a private summer program and, after he completed it, sought his placement at the private school. The district agreed that the school was appropriate but made the student's placement there contingent on entering into a contract with the school to ensure that it followed the student's IEP and remained accountable for him. The school and district were unable to reach an agreement and the parents filed a due process complaint, seeking reimbursement. **The hearing officer held that the private school placement was appropriate and that the parents were entitled to tuition and tutoring reimbursement** for the student's eighth-grade year. However, the placement was inappropriate for grade nine because of the private school's refusal to sign a contract with the school district and the parents' failure to provide necessary intake information. The administrative decision also denied the parents' request for reimbursement of psychological services. The parents appealed to a federal district court, which held that they were entitled to reimbursement for the costs of the ninth-grade private school placement and the psychological counseling services, along with attorneys' fees.

The district appealed to the Second Circuit, which held that the district court had failed to properly apply the correct analysis for evaluating tuition reimbursement cases. In these cases, **courts must first determine whether the school district's proposed placement is adequate under the IDEA. The district court had only considered whether the school district had a valid reason for rejecting the private placement, and did not evaluate the adequacy of the IEP team's proposals**. The court had then concluded that the lack of a contract between the district and the private school did not bar reimbursement. The Second Circuit held that this reasoning was flawed, since it ignored the analysis approved by the U.S. Supreme Court in *School Comm. of Burlington v. Department of Education of Massachusetts*, above. The Second Circuit vacated the portion of the judgment awarding reimbursement to the parents for grade nine and remanded the issue to the district court. The panel also reversed the award of reimbursement for psychological services. Under the IDEA, no-cost psychological counseling is required only if the services are required to assist the student to benefit from special education. Courts have uniformly barred psychological counseling reimbursement where parents unilaterally arrange for the services without first notifying their school boards of dissatisfaction with an IEP. The parents brought the issue to the district's attention about eight months after the services were obtained, making it impossible for the district to determine whether the expenditures were necessary. The court reversed the judgment awarding reimbursement for these costs. *M.C. v. Voluntown Bd. of Educ.*, 226 F.3d 60 (2d Cir. 2000).

◆   A student with spinal meningitis required constant medical care and supervision. He received special educational services at home, according to his IEP. **The parents moved the student to a licensed nursing facility located within the school district for non-educational reasons. The district discontinued the student's educational services** and the parents filed an administrative complaint. A hearing officer held that the parents were not entitled to relief because they had placed the student at the nursing facility without consulting school officials. The parents appealed to a state trial court, and the school district removed the case to a federal district court. The court held that state law and the IDEA required the district to provide services at the nursing facility.

The district appealed to the U.S. Court of Appeals, Eighth Circuit, which noted that the school district remained willing to provide the student with a FAPE at school facilities or at his home. The parents had chosen the nursing facility for non-educational reasons and had acted unilaterally, without the consent or approval of the student's IEP team. Their arguments were foreclosed by the 1997 amendments to the IDEA, which clarified that **local education agencies are not required to pay for the cost of a private school education if they have offered a FAPE to the student and the parents nonetheless make a voluntary private school placement**. Further, under Eighth Circuit precedent, parents who unilaterally place a student with disabilities in a private school or facility have no individual right under the IDEA to special education and related services, and no right to a federal court order mandating that those services be provided at a particular location. The court considered the parents' state law claim, which arose from a section of the Nebraska Special Education Act that requires school districts to provide visiting teachers for homebound students with disabilities. The section did not mandate the provision of on-site teaching services to homebound students; it only listed on-site teaching services as one of the authorized methods by which a school district may provide a FAPE to a student with disabilities. According to regulations published by the Nebraska Department of Education, school districts were not required to pay for the costs of educating a student with a disability at a non-public school or facility if the school district made a FAPE available at the student's home and the parents made a unilateral choice to place the student in the private facility. Since the district offered the student a FAPE, the district complied with the IDEA and Nebraska special education laws and regulations. The circuit court reversed the district court judgment. *Jasa v. Millard Public School Dist. No. 17*, 206 F.3d 813 (8th Cir. 2000).

◆   Because a student had a history of emotional and behavioral problems, his elementary school held a two-day evaluation and multi-disciplinary conference to develop a ninth grade IEP. School officials recommended placing him in a behavior disorder resource program with weekly social services. The student's mother disagreed with the proposal and unilaterally enrolled the student in a private parochial school that had no formal special education behavior disorder program. At the end of the school year, the mother re-enrolled him in district schools. However, **she placed him in a private residential school in Maine for the following year without consulting with the district, and sought reimbursement**. The district declined the request and the mother commenced administrative proceedings. The district obtained an order dismissing the request. Rather than appealing the decision to a second-level hearing officer as required by state law, the mother commenced a new action against the district for tuition reimbursement, which was denied by another administrative hearing officer. A second-level hearing officer affirmed on the merits. The mother appealed to a federal district court, which agreed with the school district that the first administrative decision precluded the mother from advancing the virtually identical claim in the second action. However, the court also ruled on the merits of the case, finding that the claim for tuition reimbursement was properly dismissed.

On appeal, the U.S. Court of Appeals, Seventh Circuit, held that the district court had appropriately considered the merits of the case, despite the district's assertion that the second action was barred by the first. Even though typically deemed "orders for summary judgment," district court decisions in actions filed under the IDEA are evaluated under a preponderance-of-the-evidence standard.

Courts considering IDEA administrative appeals must give due weight to administrative proceedings and refrain from substituting their judgment for that of administrative hearing officers who specialize in education. The mother was required to show only that the administrative findings were clearly erroneous. **The IDEA provides for a cooperative placement procedure** in which school officials, parents and others who are knowledgeable about the student meet and confer about the student's educational needs. School authorities are obligated to reimburse parents for private school tuition expenses only if a court ultimately determines that the private placement, and not the proposed IEP, is appropriate under the IDEA. Without some minimal cooperation from parents, schools cannot evaluate students with disabilities as contemplated by the IDEA. **The circuit court held that parents who fail to cooperate with a school district's attempts to evaluate children with disabilities and make unilateral private placements forfeit their claims for tuition reimbursement**. The district court correctly found that the mother did not cooperate with school officials by placing the student in an out-of-state residential school and declining to allow district officials to evaluate him in the state of Illinois. The circuit court affirmed the district court decision. *Patricia P. v. Bd. of Educ. of Oak Park and River Forest High School Dist. No. 200*, 203 F.3d 462 (7th Cir. 2000).

♦   Two gifted brothers with learning disabilities attended district schools for several years. Their parents became dissatisfied with both programs and obtained independent evaluations. The parties failed to reach any agreement on IEPs and the parents enrolled the students in a private school for students with learning disabilities. The school district sent the parents IDEA notices concerning due process hearings, but they did not request a hearing for either student for over one year. Even after the family initiated administrative proceedings against the district, the hearings did not take place for several months. As a result over two years elapsed from the time the students were placed in the private schools until the hearing officer rendered a decision. The hearing officer found that the IEPs proposed by the district were appropriate and denied the family's request for reimbursement. **A special education review panel reversed, finding that the district was liable for tuition reimbursement for proposing inadequate IEPs, but reducing the amount of liability because of unreasonable demands by the parents**. A federal district court affirmed the review panel's decision and the parties appealed to the Third Circuit.

The school district argued that the private school selected by the parents was inappropriate because it was not approved by the state of Pennsylvania. The court disagreed, observing that the U.S. Supreme Court's decision in *Florence County School Dist. Four v. Carter*, 510 U.S. 7 (1993), disposed of the notion that a non-approved school is always inappropriate. The court held that the private school placement was appropriate, affirming the district court's finding that it was not overly restrictive. However, **the Third Circuit reversed the district court's reduction in tuition reimbursement based on the parents' conduct**, which the lower court had characterized as "uncooperative and unreasonable." **The Third Circuit held that such a reduction in appropriate benefits would be contrary to the core IDEA policy of encouraging parental participation in special education decisions**. The circuit court approved of the reimbursement of private school tuition for both students as of the time the family requested the administrative hearings. The family was also entitled to reimbursement for the cost of independent evaluations for both students. The court affirmed the district court judgment, except for the limitation on tuition reimbursement for parental behavior. *Warren G.; Grant G. by and through Tom G. v. Cumberland County School Dist.*, 190 F.3d 80 (3d Cir.1999).

◆   The parents of a student with autism objected to a proposal calling for his placement in the district's early childhood cross-categorical classroom with speech and language therapy, social work services and occupational therapy. Instead, **the parents sought funding for the home-based ABA program they were already implementing for 35 to 40 hours per week**. When the district denied the request, the parents requested a due process hearing. The hearing officer found the district's proposed IEP inadequate. The IEP was insufficiently individualized to meet the student's unique needs and the district had apparently determined that the early childhood program was the only available school-based placement. A review officer upheld this decision, rejecting the district's argument that the dispute only involved appropriate methodology and holding that the IEP was not reasonably calculated to provide the student with educational benefit or progress at a rate that would allow for a successful transition to a regular classroom.

The district appealed to the U.S. District Court for the Northern District of Illinois, which ruled that the student was entitled to a homebound program pending full consideration of the case. The court also ordered the district to immediately revise his IEP and denied its request to obtain funding of the placement by the state education agency. The court then considered further motions of the parties concerning the merits of the administrative orders. According to the court, the dispute did not merely involve appropriate methodology. Staff members were unable to articulate a preferable methodology and apparently did not employ any teacher with significant training in the education of students with autism. The IEP was not sufficiently individualized for the student. There was evidence that the IEP process was hampered by the staff's inability to consider an ABA program and failure to sufficiently specify goals. **The district's proposal was incomplete and not reasonably calculated to enable the student to receive educational benefits in preschool or beyond**. In contrast, the homebound ABA program selected by the parents was reasonably calculated to provide such benefits, and the court affirmed the administrative orders approving the placement. **The court ordered the district to reimburse the parents for the full cost of 38-hour-per-week homebound ABA program**. The district was not entitled to reimbursement from the state based on the assertion that the homebound program was not approved by state regulations. Even though states bear the ultimate responsibility to ensure the implementation of IDEA goals and policies, the district's failure to provide an appropriate placement in this case could not be charged to the state. *T.H. v. Bd. of Educ. of Palatine Community Consol. School Dist. 15*, 55 F.Supp.2d 830 (N.D.Ill.1999).

◆   A Missouri student who had attended his neighborhood elementary school began seventh grade at a middle school. He came home after the first day of school with stomachaches, vomiting, crying and other physical symptoms that he continued to experience throughout the school year. A psychiatrist determined that he had general and separation anxiety but had no impediment to attending school. The student completed seventh grade, receiving mostly As and Bs and showing marked improvement in managing his anxiety. However, **he began to cry when he returned home from his first day in eighth grade, and his parents enrolled him in a private school without consulting the school district**. Over a year later, the parents requested reimbursement for the private school placement, which the school district denied. They commenced a federal district court action against the district for reimbursement of their costs. The court granted summary judgment to the district, finding that the student was not disabled within the meaning of the IDEA because his anxiety did not cause his academic performance to fall below his age level. The parents appealed to the U.S. Court of Appeals, Eighth Circuit.

The court observed that the parents had unilaterally transferred the student to the private school without informing the school district. The IDEA contains specific requirements for school administrators, parents and students regarding the formulation of IEPs. **The district had received no opportunity to provide an appropriate public education for the student through possible accommodations**. Because the district had been excluded from the parents' decision making process, reimbursement was inappropriate. The court affirmed the district court judgment without reaching the issue of whether the student was disabled within the meaning of the IDEA. *Schoenfeld v. Parkway School Dist.*, 138 F.3d 379 (8th Cir.1998).

◆   A Maryland student with learning disabilities attended a private day school through the eighth grade. His parents then requested an evaluation for him for special education services from the Baltimore City Public Schools (BCPS). BCPS failed to develop an IEP for the student and the parents unilaterally enrolled him in a private Connecticut residential school. The parents challenged the IEP later developed by the school district for a public school placement. The parties settled the dispute under an agreement by which BCPS agreed to pay a statutory portion of private school tuition as described in the Maryland Education Code. However, **the state of Maryland refused to pay a portion of the private school's cost because BCPS agreed to the placement without first obtaining the approval of the state coordinating council**. The parents filed an administrative challenge with the state board, which held that the state was responsible for its portion of the private school placement costs.

The parents then filed a federal district court action for enforcement against BCPS, the state school superintendent and the state education department. The court granted dismissal motions by the education officials and BCPS, and the parents appealed to the U.S. Court of Appeals, Fourth Circuit. The court agreed with the state hearing board that the IDEA applied to the dispute. **Because the IDEA places the ultimate responsibility upon the state education agency to ensure local education agency compliance with the IDEA, the state could not avoid its share of liability if the district court held on remand that relief was appropriate**. Either or both the state and BCPS could be held liable for the failure to provide a student with a free appropriate public education. The court vacated and remanded the case to the district court. *Gadsby by Gadsby v. Grasmick*, 109 F.3d 940 (4th Cir.1997).

V. COMPENSATORY EDUCATION

Compensatory education is the belated provision of necessary educational or related services to a student with a disability to which the student was entitled, but which the education agency failed to provide. Compensatory education is awarded to some students who are over the statutory age of entitlement (usually this is 21) to prohibit education agencies from indefinitely delaying the provision of necessary services until the student is beyond school age.

◆   The mother of a student with disabilities petitioned the West Virginia Supreme Court of Appeals for an order compelling the school district to provide her child with certain special education services she claimed he was entitled to under his IEP but had not received. After numerous court proceedings, a special master issued a report in favor of the mother, finding that the district did not perform its obligations under the IEP from 1993 to 1995. Moreover, **the district's performance of make-up services did not compensate the student for depriving him of them at the time they were actually required, justifying an award of compensatory education**. The district challenged the action in a federal district court, which first referred the case to mediation, then dismissed it because the district failed to exhaust its administrative remedies.

When mediation attempts failed, the mother moved the state court of appeals for relief based on allegations of "a 14-year history of inadequate, bad-faith malfeasance" by the district and sought a private placement for the student at the district's expense. She also sought a court-appointed monitor and reimbursement for the costs of services she had previously arranged for the student. The court stated that it intended a prompt hearing to determine whether the services provided to the child were adequate. The record supported the special master's finding that the district did not comply with its legal duty to provide the student with special education from 1993 to 1995, and that the corrective measures it took did not fully address the lack of services during the relevant time period. The record also supported her finding that a new IEP and medical evaluation were necessary. The court granted the mother's request for relief, ordering the parties to promptly create a new IEP. The mother was ordered to permit a full physical and psychological examination of her son. Any conflict was to be addressed in an appropriate trial court or administrative proceeding, not by further proceedings. **The district was responsible for providing special education services for two additional years beyond the student's statutory entitlement to compensate him for past service deficiencies**. *State of West Virginia ex rel. Justice v. Board of Education of County of Monongalia*, 539 S.E.2d 777 (W.Va. 2000).

◆   The parents of a 20-year-old student with disabilities requested a due process hearing to resolve a dispute with the school district over the district's diagnosis of the student as multiply disabled. The hearing resulted in an administrative order requiring the school district to conduct an evaluation and devise a new IEP. The parents disputed the resulting IEP and arranged for independent evaluations. The parents did not participate in further IEP and multidisciplinary team meetings and requested a second hearing. A hearing officer held for the school district and the parents appealed. A state appeals panel affirmed the hearing officer's decision that the appropriate classification of the student was physically disabled and mentally retarded, and denied the parents' request for reimbursement of the costs of the independent evaluations. **The appeals panel held that the IEPs for the student's three most recent school years were inadequate in the areas of transition planning and assistive technology**. As relief, the student was awarded over 600 hours of compensatory education.

The district appealed to a federal district court, which noted that in two-tiered administrative systems, courts should generally accord due weight to the appeals panel's findings, rather than those of the hearing officer, except for determining witness credibility. In examining the transition services issue, the court stated that the IDEA requires a statement of transition services for students no later than age 16. In this case, the transitional evaluation prepared by the school multidisciplinary team was inadequate because the team did not include personnel who had evaluated the student's transition needs. The district also failed to include aspects of transition planning in the student's IEP. The court adopted the panel's decision, finding that the IEP was not sufficiently tailored to meet the student's needs. The district had also improperly delayed providing assistive technology to the student. After identifying the student's needs in this area, no equipment was provided for over one year, and the student received inadequate training once the equipment was provided. Applying the Third Circuit's standard for awarding compensatory education, **the court found that the district knew or should have known that the student's IEP lacked appropriate transitional planning and assistive technology provisions. Accordingly, an award of compensatory education was appropriate**. The court modified the appeals panel decision by slightly decreasing the amount of compensatory education awarded, but otherwise upheld the appeals panel's decision. *East Penn School Dist. v. Scott B.*, 1999 WL 178363 (E.D.Pa.1999).

◆ A special school district within the Connecticut Department of Corrections failed to offer a student special education services during his incarceration. **An administrative hearing officer** found the special school district liable for over ten months of educational services during the student's period of incarceration and **ordered it to provide compensatory education at a private residential program after the student reached the age of 21**. The special school district appealed to the Superior Court of Connecticut, where it argued that even if it were required to pay for compensatory education, it should only be required to pay $28,000, the cost of custodial care in its own program, rather than the $116,200 amount charged by the private facility. The court upheld the hearing officer's decision as it pertained to the finding of liability. However, the hearing officer had abused her discretion by approving the placement in the private facility commencing after the student reached age 21. **This prospective placement, issued two years in advance of the time when services were to be provided, did not comply with the law**, and it would be necessary to convene a planning and placement team meeting to evaluate the student's needs when he turned 21. *State of Connecticut-Unified School Dist. No. 1 v. State Dep't of Educ.*, 45 Conn.Sup. 57, 699 A.2d 1077 (1997).

◆ An Illinois student with autism was unable to care for himself or speak as he approached age 21. Shortly before his birthday, **his parents requested a hearing under the IDEA to preserve his placement in a program for autistic students**

funded by his school district. The complaint sought compensatory education in the form of continued placement in the program under the IDEA stay put provision, pending the resolution of administrative proceedings. They claimed that the district had deprived the student of an appropriate placement prior to being placed in the program for autistic students. A hearing officer ordered the district to provide the student with six months of compensatory education, and the district appealed to the U.S. District Court for the Northern District of Illinois. Meanwhile, the court applied the IDEA stay put provision and ordered the school district to pay for the program for autistic students until after the student's 23rd birthday. The district appealed to the U.S. Court of Appeals, Seventh Circuit.

The court stated that while not specified in the IDEA, **compensatory education was appropriate in certain cases, even where the student had attained the age of 21. However, the stay put provision**, which preserves a student's placement pending IDEA proceedings, **was inapplicable to cases in which a student was beyond the age of statutory entitlement**. Otherwise, parents could file a claim for compensatory education just prior to the student's 21st birthday simply to preserve an educational placement. The district court order requiring the school district to preserve the student's placement was reversed. *Bd. of Educ. of Oak Park and River Forest High School Dist. 200 v. Illinois State Bd. of Educ.*, 79 F.3d 654 (7th Cir.1996).

VI. DISCRIMINATION

The Americans with Disabilities Act (ADA), 42 U.S.C. § 12101 et seq., and § 504 of the Rehabilitation Act of 1973, 29 U.S.C. § 794, are federal statutes that prohibit discrimination against persons with disabilities. Both statutes require schools and their employees to make reasonable accommodations for qualified individuals with disabilities, but no institution is required to lower its academic standards in order to do so. The Rehabilitation Act was the statute construed by the courts as prohibiting the exclusion of students with contagious diseases from public school attendance if they were otherwise qualified to attend and did not present a risk of harm to themselves or others. Federal courts have applied this rule to students with HIV. See Martinez v. School Bd. of Hillsboro County, 861 F.2d 1502 (11th Cir.1988), 711 F.Supp. 1066 (M.D.Fla.1989). For employment cases involving § 504 and the ADA, please see Chapter Six, Section VI.

◆   **A student with a form of dwarfism and another student with disabilities were left with an adult in an otherwise evacuated middle school for approximately 70 minutes during a bomb threat**. The student filed a disability discrimination complaint against the school board with the Office for Civil Rights, which resulted in an agreement calling for the board to adopt a new emergency preparedness plan. The parents dropped the case and the board adopted a policy regarding the evacuation of students with disabilities during emergencies. Within two months, an unscheduled fire alarm went off and the student was left alone for approximately two minutes. The student's math teacher stayed with her during the incident, while non-disabled students were evacuated. The family sued the school board in a federal district court, claiming that its actions during both evacuations violated § 504 and the ADA. The court denied the board's motion to dismiss, but later awarded it summary judgment. The court denied the family's motion to reconsider and they appealed to the Fourth Circuit.

The Fourth Circuit held that the motion for reconsideration had been properly denied. However, the OCR settlement was not a waiver of the student's federal civil rights under § 504 or the ADA. The right to file actions under these laws was a statutory right created by Congress that could not be barred without a knowing waiver. Since the settlement did not contain a waiver or release of rights under federal discrimination laws, the claims could not be dismissed on that basis. The district court had also considered the summary judgment motion under an erroneous standard, requiring proof of either bad faith or gross misjudgment. This standard was applicable in the context of the development of an IEP, but had no relevance in a case involving the emergency evacuation of a disabled student from a school building. The relevant consideration was whether the board denied the student access to safe evacuation procedures afforded to others. The student was not excluded from these procedures during the fire drill incident because the board had by then devised an emergency preparedness plan to safely evacuate students with disabilities during emergencies. The board was not liable for its conduct and summary judgment had been correct. However, **the student had been excluded from safe evacuation procedures during the bomb threat incident**, as the board had no reasonable plan to evacuate students with disabilities at that time. Because the board had discriminated against the student on the basis of her disabilities during the bomb threat, the district court order for summary judgment regarding this aspect of the student's claims was improper. **The appropriate remedy for the violation was an order requiring the board to develop and implement a reasonable plan of evacuation for students with disabilities**. Since it had already done this in response to the OCR proceeding, the student was not entitled to further relief. *Shirey v. City of Alexandria School Board*, 229 F.3d 1143 (4th Cir. 2000).

◆   An Iowa student with severe disabilities, including cerebral palsy and spastic quadriplegia, participated in the special education program of her regularly assigned, neighborhood school. She was transported there with a lift bus that traveled a special route for her. **Her parents sought to transfer her to a different school under an intra-district transfer program, and asked for special transportation, despite the program requirement that they furnish their own transportation**. The district approved the transfer but denied the transportation request. An administrative law judge held that the parents had established no need for special transportation beyond parental preference for a specific placement. A federal district court reversed the administrative decision, ruling that the district had impermissibly limited the student's opportunity to participate in the transfer program.

The district appealed to the Eighth Circuit, which observed that in § 504 cases, complaining students must demonstrate that there has been discrimination on the basis of disability. A defendant school district is entitled to show that the requested accommodation is unduly burdensome. This may be demonstrated by proof of undue financial and administrative burdens to the district, or by showing that the requested accommodations require fundamental alteration of a school program. The court found that the student was not denied the benefit of participating in the intra-district transfer program, since she was allowed to participate in it on the same terms as other applicants. There was no evidence of discrimination in the conduct of the transfer program, and the student was not denied access to it on the basis of her disability. Instead, her parents did not wish to comply with "the main condition of the program applicable to all students who wish[ed] to participate — parental transportation." **Requiring the district to spend additional funds on transportation for the transfer program would fundamentally alter this requirement, creating an undue burden on the school district.** The court reversed and remanded the district court decision. *Timothy H. and Brenda H. v. Cedar Rapids Comm. School Dist.*, 178 F.3d 968 (8th Cir.1999).

◆   A student who suffered recurrent sinus infections that caused frequent absences was accepted into her school's show choir. The choir director advised the student's father that continuing absences caused potential problems for her participation. The student was picked for a minor role in the spring play. She soon attempted suicide, allegedly in the belief that the director had intended that she fail her audition. She was diagnosed as having severe depression and placed on a treatment plan. The diagnosis was communicated to school staff, and after the student returned to school, the director announced to the entire class that the student would not be permitted to participate in the spring play. The student's mother intervened, arguing that the student's mental health and recovery required that she be allowed to continue participating. The school principal advised the director that she must either enforce a previously unenforced written absence policy, or allow all students to perform. **The director announced that she would enforce the attendance policy, which resulted in the student being denied permission to fully participate.** The family sued the director, principal, school board, and others in a state court for Americans with Disabilities Act violations and intentional infliction of emotional distress. The school defendants removed the case to a federal district court, which held that the student had not been discriminated against, and that she was excluded from full participation in the spring play for reasons other than her disability.

The family appealed to the Fourth Circuit, which held that the district court decision was based on a misunderstanding of the complaint. The complaint alleged that the exclusion of the student had occurred after the director was informed of the student's depression, and that the instructor had made the decision to exclude her based on the alleged disability. The complaint also stated that that the attendance policy was not uniformly enforced. These allegations were adequate to support federal disability discrimination claims. Alternatively, the complaint alleged that the policy was used as a pretext for unlawful discrimination. **The discriminatory application of a neutral rule, if proven, would be grounds for an ADA violation.** Because Congress expressly stated that Title VII remedies apply to ADA actions, the court agreed with the school employees that the ADA does not authorize any remedies against individuals for violations of its provisions. Only employers are liable for damages in Title VII actions, and the district court had properly dismissed the claims against the director and principal in their individual capacities. However, the district court had improperly dismissed the state law claim for intentional infliction of emotional distress, and that claim was reinstated. The court remanded the case for further proceedings. *Baird v. Rose*, 192 F.3d 462 (4th Cir. 1999).

◆   An Illinois school's athletic code of conduct called for partial loss of athletic eligibility following an alcohol-related violation and loss of eligibility for a full year after a second incident. The school revoked a student's athletic eligibility after he was involved in an alcohol-related auto accident, his second violation of the policy in a one-month period. **The student was later diagnosed as an alcoholic and requested reinstatement to sports eligibility**. The school superintendent and board denied his request, and his mother sued under the Americans with Disabilities Act and § 504 of the Rehabilitation Act.

The school board moved for judgment on the pleadings, noting that not even the student himself was aware of his alcoholism at the time of the incidents and that, therefore, discrimination could not have played a role in the decision to revoke his athletic eligibility. The court agreed, noting that in order to prevail on his federal disability discrimination claims, the student was required to show unlawful discrimination. **Even if school officials had been aware of the student's condition at the time of revocation, they would not have violated the law because the Rehabilitation Act expressly permits schools to punish students for using alcohol, and students with disabilities are subject to punishment to the same extent as others**. See 29 U.S.C. § 705(20)(C)(iv). The court also rejected the student's claim that school officials refused to grant reasonable accommodation to his disability. It held that the accommodation he requested was not a reasonable one, because it was at odds with the purposes behind the no-alcohol rule, which was intended to establish ideals of good sportsmanship and respect for rules and authority. The court awarded judgment to the board and officials. *Stearns v. Bd. of Educ. for Warren Township High School Dist. No. 121*, 1999 U.S. Dist. LEXIS 17981 (N.D. Ill. 1999).

◆   A Missouri elementary school student had a prescription from his doctor for daily dosages of Ritalin that far exceeded the recommended maximum dosage described in the *Physician's Desk Reference*. A nurse at his school administered part of the dosage to him during the school day for over one year until she consulted with a district nursing coordinator who believed that the dose was excessive. **The district's medication policy allowed school nurses to refuse to give any medication and to question and verify potentially inappropriate prescriptions**. Although the family obtained a second physician's opinion stating that the prescription was not harmful, the nurse did not resume administering the medication. School officials offered to allow the administration of the medication by a family member. The family filed a federal district court action against the school district, asserting that it had violated the Americans with Disabilities Act (ADA) and § 504 of the Rehabilitation Act. The court granted the family's request for a temporary restraining order, but refused to issue a preliminary injunction. The U.S. Court of Appeals, Eighth Circuit, affirmed the order.

The district court later granted summary judgment to the school district, and the family appealed again to the Eighth Circuit, which found no evidence that the student had been treated differently from others on the basis of disability. The district's medication policy was nondiscriminatory and aimed at protecting student health. It had offered alternatives which reasonably accommodated the student's disability. **The family offered no evidence that the district had implemented or enforced the policy because of the student's disability, and their proposed accommodations**

presented an undue burden to the district. The court affirmed the summary judgment order for the district. *Davis v. Francis Howell School Dist.*, 138 F.3d 754 (8th Cir.1998).

◆   A Tennessee student attended a private school from first grade through the first semester of her senior year in high school. She maintained a high grade point average and was a member of three school athletic teams. The student developed a blood disorder during her senior year. The disease put her at risk of spontaneous hemorrhaging and presented a risk of infection, anemia and life-threatening bleeding. The student cut herself in an art class. According to later accounts by school staff members, she became hysterical and used profanity. **The principal asked her to withdraw from the school, citing her lack of remorse for her behavior. The following day, he proposed alternatives to expulsion**. The student sought a preliminary injunction against the school in the U.S. District Court for the Middle District of Tennessee.

The student claimed that she was a qualified individual with a disability under the ADA, 42 U.S.C. § 12101 *et seq.*, and § 504 of the Rehabilitation Act, 29 U.S.C. § 794. She stated that the school had discriminated against her on the basis of her disability in violation of both acts. The court agreed that the student had a disability and that she was academically qualified to continue at the school. An expert witness for the student submitted evidence that an individual with her condition could be expected to react to an accident in an exaggerated manner. The school's failure to recognize and accommodate this reaction by "blind adherence" to its disciplinary standards resulted in violations of the ADA and § 504. According to the court, **discrimination could be found in the form of the rigid application of rules and policies which unreasonably excluded an otherwise qualified individual from receiving the benefits of an educational institution**. The student was entitled to a preliminary injunction prohibiting her expulsion. The court retained jurisdiction of the case for the remainder of the school year. *Thomas by and through Thomas v. Davidson Academy*, 846 F.Supp. 611 (M.D.Tenn.1994).

◆   Three students with hearing impairments required the use of sign-language interpreters in their classrooms. The Nebraska school district they attended provided a modified SEE-II system. However, the students used strict SEE-II signing systems at home, and their parents made numerous requests to use strict SEE-II systems at school. After the district refused to comply with their requests, **the parents filed an administrative complaint with the Nebraska Department of Education, where they alleged that the modified signing system did not provide their children with an adequate individualized special education program**. The hearing officer held for the school district, but imposed on it the requirement to develop IEPs for each student that called for interpreters during both academic and nonacademic activities. The parents appealed to the U.S. District Court for the District of Nebraska, which affirmed the administrative decision. The parents appealed to the U.S. Court of Appeals, Eighth Circuit.

On appeal, the parents renewed their argument that the IDEA and ADA required the district to provide their signing system of choice, rather than the one selected by the school district. They argued that the use of the modified SEE-II system amounted to failure to develop an appropriate IEP. They also claimed that the district violated the Americans with Disabilities Act (ADA) by depriving them of access to educational programs and discriminating against them. The court of appeals disagreed. There was no requirement under the IDEA for a school district to maximize the educational potential of each student. **Parents and students were not entitled to compel a school district to provide a specific signing system of choice as a related service. Although ADA regulations required a public entity to provide an auxiliary aid or service of choice to an individual with disabilities, the public entity was allowed to demonstrate that another effective means of communication existed**. The school district had complied with the ADA by providing the modified SEE-II system as an effective means of communication. The court affirmed the district court's decision. *Petersen v. Hastings Pub. Schools*, 31 F.3d 705 (8th Cir.1994).

CHAPTER THIRTEEN

Private Schools

I. PRIVATE SCHOOL EMPLOYMENT

State laws governing public school tenure are inapplicable to private schools and colleges. Private schools typically grant tenure according to their own employment policies. State and federal antidiscrimination laws apply to private schools employing at least 15 employees, unless the school has a bona fide reason for using discriminatory practices on the grounds of religion.

A. Employment Discrimination

◆   In a decision affecting private religious educational institutions, the U.S. Supreme Court ruled that such institutions may discriminate on the basis of religion in hiring for nonreligious jobs involving nonprofit activities. The case involved a man who worked at a Mormon church-operated gymnasium for 16 years. **After being discharged for failing to meet several church-related requirements for employment, he sued the church in a U.S. district court alleging religious discrimination in violation of Title VII**. The church moved for dismissal claiming that § 702 of Title VII exempted it from liability. The man claimed that if § 702 allowed religious employers to discriminate on religious grounds in hiring for nonreligious jobs, then Title VII would be in violation of the Establishment Clause of the First Amendment. The district court ruled for the man, and the church appealed directly to the U.S. Supreme Court.

The question before the Court was whether applying § 702 to the secular nonprofit activities of religious organizations violated the Establishment Clause. Section 702 provides that Title VII "shall not apply ... to a religious corporation, association [or] educational institution ... with respect to the employment of individuals of a particular religion to perform work connected with the carrying on by such [an organization] of its activities." In ruling for the church the Supreme Court applied the three-part test set out in *Lemon v. Kurtzman* (see § IV, C of this chapter). **The Supreme Court reversed the district court's decision and upheld the right of nonprofit religious employers to impose religious conditions for employment in nonreligious positions involving nonprofit activities.** *Corp. of the Presiding Bishop of the Church of Jesus Christ of Latter-Day Saints v. Amos*, 483 U.S. 327, 107 S.Ct. 2862, 97 L.Ed.2d 273 (1987).

◆   **Several employees of the Montrose Christian School filed two separate suits against the school** under Chapter 27 of the Montgomery County (Maryland) Code, **claiming they were fired because they were not Baptists**. Chapter 27 bars employers from discriminating against employees based on race, color, religious creed, ancestry, national origin, age, sex, marital status, handicap or sexual orientation. The statute includes an exemption for religious organizations, allowing them to hire employees of a particular religion "to perform purely religious functions." The plaintiffs had performed secular duties for the school, such as cafeteria work, bookkeeping and administrative duties as a teacher's aide. They alleged that the school was not able to fire them based on their religious creed because they did not perform "purely religious functions." In the first suit, a jury found that Montrose terminated the plaintiffs based on their religious affiliation and awarded them compensatory damages. In the second, similar suit, the trial court granted summary judgment to a former teacher's aide and awarded her $31,000 in damages and attorneys' fees.

On appeal, Montrose claimed the exemption provision of Chapter 27 violated the Free Exercise and Establishment Clauses of the First Amendment, as well as the Maryland Declaration of Rights. Montrose also claimed the exemption conflicted with state law prohibiting employment discrimination. Maryland exempts religious organizations from state laws prohibiting discrimination based on religion, but not including such actions does not mean the state authorized such activities, the court noted. As such, a conflict did not exist between the exemption and state law. The court rejected the school's charitable-immunity defense because charitable organizations are only immune from tort actions in Maryland, and statutory employment discrimination cases are based in contract law. Although it rejected the school's other defenses, **the court agreed that the exemption violated the Free Exercise and Establishment Clauses, as well as the Maryland Declaration of Rights.** In examining the language of the county statute, the court reasoned that giving religious organizations immunity from discrimination claims concerning the employment of workers with "purely religious" duties nullifies the exemption. Maryland case law holds that if a portion of a statute or enactment is found invalid, that portion should be severed. After the court deleted the portion of the exemption that specifies employees who perform "purely religious functions," **the statute was interpreted to allow religious organizations to make employment decisions based on religion for any employee.** In light of this new application of the exemption, the court held that the school did not violate state discrimination laws when it fired the plaintiffs. *Montrose Christian School Corp. et al. v. Walsh et al. v. Carver,* 363 Md. 565, 770 A.2d 111 (Md. 2001).

◆   An employee assistant counselor employed by a school run by an association based on the beliefs of the Roman Catholic Church was fired from her position. The school claimed the termination was the result of the elimination of the position. The counselor filed suit against the school, claiming her termination violated Montana discrimination law by firing her because of her marital status or gender. **According to the counselor, she was terminated due to her supervisor's disapproval of her cohabitation with a man who was not her husband.** Cohabitation between unmarried individuals is prohibited by the teachings of the Catholic Church. The counselor further contended that she was fired in retaliation for testifying in another discrimination suit brought against the school. A Montana district court entered summary judgment in favor of the school, finding the counselor's claim interfered with the school's free exercise rights under the U.S. Constitution.

On appeal to the Montana Supreme Court, the court determined that even if the school's proffered reason for firing the counselor was a pretext, the case was not about marital status or gender—it was about the code of conduct she agreed to follow when she signed her employment agreement with the school. The counselor fail to present case law suggesting the state's anti-discrimination laws prohibited discrimination based on conduct. The court noted **the counselor did not demonstrate that her situation involved a right that surmounted the school's First Amendment right to freely exercise its religion through its employment practices.** The grant of summary judgment in favor of the school was affirmed. *Parker-Bigback v. St. Labre School,* 7 P.3d 361 (Mont. 2000).

◆   A parochial school teacher's contract was renewed on an annual basis for 15 years, until **the principal decided not to renew it based on the belief that the teacher managed her classroom inadequately and demonstrated poor instructional skills.** At the time of the non-renewal, the teacher was 52 years old and had a history of hip problems. The teacher filed suit in federal district court, claiming her termination was the result of disability and age discrimination in violation of the ADA and ADEA.

In granting the school's motion for summary judgment, the court concluded that the teacher's ADA claim failed because her hip condition was not serious enough to substantially limit her major life activities. Even if the teacher was considered disabled within the meaning of the ADA, **she failed to establish that the legitimate, non-discriminatory reasons for her termination offered by the school, poor performance and failure to improve, were a pretext for discrimination** based on disability. The school was entitled to summary judgment on the teacher's ADEA claims for the same reasons. Although the teacher was within the statutorily protected age range and had been replaced by someone significantly younger, she offered no evidence that the legitimate reasons offered for her termination were a pretext for age discrimination. The court also granted summary judgment in favor of the school on the teacher's state law claims arising from her termination. *Brown v. Holy Name Church,* 80 F.Supp.2d 1261 (D. Wyo. 2000).

◆   A Catholic school principal gave a white first grade teacher poor work evaluations and allegedly told her that she "did not have the 'know how' to teach 'these children' and that [she] should be teaching in a suburban area where there are not problems." **The teacher** further **claimed that the principal schemed to fire white lay teachers and to replace them with Hispanic ones**, preferably Hispanic nuns from Argentina. After the teacher learned that the school had not renewed her employment contract, she filed a charge with the Equal Employment Opportunity Commission. The principal then retracted the non-renewal letter and offered her a position as a pre-kindergarten teacher for the following year. The teacher declined the position and sued the school for race discrimination under Title VII.

A New York federal court found neither direct nor circumstantial evidence of discrimination based on race. The teacher conceded that she thought the principal used the phrase "these children" to refer to the fact that the school's students were poor. Further, taken on its face, the comment constituted an administrator's assessment of the employee's strengths and nothing more. The court also concluded that the teacher did not support her allegation that the principal wanted to match the teaching population ethnically to the student body. The Argentinean nuns came to the parish to help in its religious ministry. No plans existed to replace the white teachers with the nuns, of whom only one was qualified to teach, and no teacher at the school lost his or her position to a nun. *Ticali v. Roman Catholic Diocese of Brooklyn,* 41 F.Supp.2d 249 (E.D.N.Y.1999).

◆   When the Indianapolis Department of Education gave a Catholic elementary school a poor review and put the school on a probationary status, the principal decided not to renew the contracts of three teachers who she believed were not performing at the level they should be. During the performance review of a 52-year-old teacher, the principal listed seven strengths but also noted nineteen weaknesses. The teacher was replaced by a younger instructor. The discharged teacher sued the Archdiocese for discrimination, alleging that her dismissal, as well as the dismissal of the other two teachers, violated the federal Age Discrimination in Employment Act. An Indiana federal court noted that **the teacher had to do more than show that** the nonrenewal of her contract was incorrect. She had to show that the reason for the nonrenewal was a pretext for discrimination. The court ruled that the mere ages of the older teachers' replacements did not demonstrate age discrimination. Further, the positive reviews of past principals at the school did not mean that the principal had discriminated against the teacher. Those reviews had expressed the same strengths listed by the principal here. The court conceded that the department's review did not specifically mention the teacher by name; however, the court found that the principal clearly believed the teacher was one of the people causing the poor review. The court ruled in favor of the Archdiocese. *Guinan v. Roman Catholic Archdiocese of Indianapolis*, 50 F.Supp.2d 845 (S.D.Ind.1999).

◆   A teacher employed by the Chesapeake Conference of the Seventh-day Adventist Church was not rehired. **The stated reasons for the refusal to rehire the teacher were insufficient enrollment and lack of funds**. The teacher sued the conference, claiming the employment action was motivated by other factors, including age and gender discrimination. A federal district court agreed with the conference that allowing the lawsuit would violate its religious rights under the Free Exercise Clause of the federal constitution, and the teacher appealed.

The Fourth Circuit applied the "primary duties test" to determine that the teacher's position was of a religious character and therefore beyond the court's jurisdiction. According to the court, **the bringing of federal claims against the conference would unconstitutionally infringe on its right to select spiritual leaders**. All teachers were required to belong to the church and their primary duty was to teach the Seventh-day Adventist faith to students through daily instruction, worship and prayer. Teachers performed the Conference's most important duty and its decisions regarding employment were protected from judicial scrutiny by the Free Exercise Clause. *Clapper v. Chesapeake Conference of Seventh-day Adventists*, 166 F.3d 1208 (4th Cir. 1998).

◆   A New Jersey archdiocese approved a plan to create a cosponsored school district to include several different parishes. A cosponsored Catholic elementary school was to replace a preexisting parish elementary school. The new school invited all interested administrators, faculty and staff from the original parish schools to apply for the position of principal. Three pastors were to make the final decision. After extensive interviews, **a Catholic nun was appointed to the position, displacing the principal of the preexisting parish elementary school** who had been employed under a series of one-year contracts. The school contended that the selection was guided by religious principle and made pursuant to the exercise of religious freedom. Although her contract had expired, the former principal filed a breach of contract lawsuit against the school in a New Jersey superior court. The superior court granted the school's motion for summary judgment based on the ecclesiastical abstention doctrine. The principal appealed to the Superior Court of New Jersey, Appellate Division.

The appellate division court held that the position of principal in the parochial school was a "ministerial" one because the principal was in charge of students' religious education. She supervised the teachers, played a significant role in curriculum development, was a liaison between the school and the religious community, and was the guiding force behind the school's spiritual mission. Thus, the selection of the nun to be the principal of the new school was an ecclesiastic decision precluding civil court review. Moreover, nothing in the principal's employment contract or in the school's policies and procedures consented to civil court jurisdiction in ecclesiastic matters. The court affirmed the dismissal of the claim. *Sabatino v. Saint Aloysius Parish*, 288 N.J.Super. 233, 672 A.2d 217 (1996).

B. Labor Relations

The courts have ruled that "pervasively religious" schools may be able to avoid any obligation to bargain with employees under the National Labor Relations Act (NLRA). This exception to the NLRA's coverage is based upon First Amendment religious freedom considerations. Managerial employees are not protected by the NLRA.

◆   The right of employees of a Catholic school system to form a collective bargaining unit was successfully challenged in a case decided by the U.S. Supreme Court. In this case, the unions were certified by the National Labor Relations Board (NLRB) as bargaining units but the diocese refused to bargain with them. The Court said that the religion clauses of the U.S. Constitution, which require religious organizations to finance their educational systems without governmental aid, also free the religious organizations of the inhibiting effect and impact of unionization of their teachers. **The Court agreed with the employers' contention that the threshold act of certification of the union would necessarily alter and infringe upon the religious character of parochial schools**, since this would mean that the bishop would no longer be the sole repository of authority as required by church law. Instead, he would have to share some decisionmaking with the union. This violated the religion clauses of the U.S. Constitution. *NLRB v. Catholic Bishop of Chicago*, 440 U.S. 490, 99 S.Ct. 1313, 59 L.Ed.2d 533 (1979).

◆   A Roman Catholic secondary school in New York City employed lay and religiously affiliated faculty and taught both secular and religious subjects. After a union began representing the lay faculty, the school administration and the union met repeatedly to negotiate the terms of a collective bargaining agreement. When those efforts failed, the union staged a strike. The school discharged the striking workers and ended negotiations. **The state Employment Relations Board** cited the school for alleged violations of the state Labor Relations Act. It **charged the school with refusing to bargain in good faith, and with improperly discharging and failing to reinstate striking employees**. The case came before the Court of Appeals of New York, which held that the state Labor Relations Act governed labor relations between the school and its lay faculty. The act was a facially neutral, universally applicable and secular regulatory regimen. It did not implicate religious conduct or beliefs, nor did it restrict or impose any burdens on religious belief or activities. The court held that the Establishment Clause argument failed because the state board's supervision over collective bargaining with respect to secular terms and conditions of employment was neither comprehensive nor continuing and did not entangle the state with religion. Here, **the government was not forcing the parties to agree on specific terms, but was ordering the employer to bargain**

in good faith on secular subjects. *New York State Employment Relations Board v. Christ the King Regional High School*, 90 N.Y.2d 244, 660 N.Y.S.2d 359, 682 N.E.2d 960 (1997).

❖   A group of elementary schools operated by the Catholic Diocese of Camden, New Jersey, employed a sizable number of lay teachers. A union representing lay teachers asserted that it was elected by a majority of the lay teachers employed in each of the schools. When it sought to have the schools recognize it as the collective bargaining representative of the lay teachers, a Board of Pastors, acting on behalf of the schools, informed the union that it would be recognized only if it signed a document that vested in the board complete and final authority to dictate the outcome of any dispute. It also prohibited the union from assessing dues or collecting agency fees from nonunion members. When the union refused to sign the document, the schools refused to recognize the union or to bargain collectively. **The union sued to compel the schools to recognize it as the collective bargaining representative of the lay teachers**. The court granted the schools' motion for summary judgment, and the Superior Court of New Jersey, Appellate Division, reversed.

On certification to the Supreme Court of New Jersey, the court examined the U.S. Supreme Court decision in *NLRB v. Catholic Bishop*, above. In that case, the Court ruled that the National Labor Relations Board (NLRB) did not have jurisdiction to require church-operated schools to grant recognition to unions as bargaining agents for their teachers. The Supreme Court of New Jersey noted that the schools' reliance on *Catholic Bishop* was misplaced because the case at issue here was distinguishable. The regulatory scheme of the National Labor Relations Act (NLRA) requires the NLRB to act as a monitor-referee and causes much more entanglement of government with religion than does the New Jersey Constitution. **The court held that requiring the schools to bargain would not violate the religion clauses of either the state or federal constitutions because the agreement between the diocese and the elected representative for the lay teachers would preserve the bishop's exclusive right to structure the schools and their philosophies.** The diocese had bargained with lay high school teachers in the past without either advancing or inhibiting religion. As long as the scope of collective bargaining was limited to secular issues such as wages and benefit plans, neutral criteria could be used to ensure that religion was neither advanced nor inhibited.

The court further noted that the Religious Freedom Restoration Act had recently been held unconstitutional by the U.S. Supreme Court in *City of Boerne v. Flores*, 521 U.S. 507, 117 S.Ct. 2157, 138 L.Ed.2d 624 (1997). Accordingly, the law in place prior to the enactment of that act would apply to this case. Using that analysis, **the schools could be required to bargain under New Jersey law because the state constitutional guarantee of the right to organize and bargain collectively for persons in private employment was neutral and of general application**. The state had a compelling interest in allowing the lay employees to unionize and to bargain collectively over secular terms and conditions of employment. The fact that this incidentally burdened the free exercise of religion did not violate the Free Exercise Clause. The court held that the schools were required to bargain with the union. *South Jersey Catholic School Teachers Organization v. St. Teresa of the Infant Jesus Church Elementary School*, 150 N.J. 575, 696 A.2d 709 (N.J.1997).

◆   Two teachers at a private Catholic elementary and secondary school in Pennsylvania attempted to organize a teachers union. Through an association of Catholic teachers, they filed a petition with the Pennsylvania Labor Relations Board (PLRB) to compel an election. **The teachers were fired and the association filed a second petition which was dismissed because the school was not a public employer and the teachers were not public employees** under the Public Employee Relations Act (PERA). The teachers appealed to a state trial court which reversed the PLRB. The school appealed to a commonwealth court which reversed the trial court's decision, finding that Catholic teachers are excluded from coverage by the PERA. The teachers appealed to the Supreme Court of Pennsylvania.

The court first noted that the U.S. Supreme Court ruled in *NLRB v. Catholic Bishop of Chicago*, above, that the NLRA does not apply to lay teachers employed at church-operated schools. However, because the NLRA and the PERA do not have the same scope, the court went on to consider the language of the PERA. It defines a public employee as any individual employed by a public employer but excludes employees at church facilities "when utilized primarily for religious purposes." A public employer includes the state and its political subdivisions as well as any religious institutions receiving funds from the state or federal government. Although the court noted that the definition of public employee was not completely clear, it agreed with the commonwealth court that the term "utilized primarily for religious purposes" modified church facilities rather than employees. Therefore, **because the teachers conceded that the school was operated primarily for religious purposes, they were excluded under the act**. However, the court additionally noted that even if this interpretation was not correct, the legislature had not affirmatively indicated its intention that teachers at religious schools be covered under the PERA. The court affirmed the commonwealth court's decision. *Ass'n of Catholic Teachers v. PLRB*, 692 A.2d 1039 (Pa.1997).

◆   A religious order operated a parochial school in Albany, New York. A union served as the collective bargaining representative of the school's lay teachers. Following the expiration of the union's collective bargaining agreement with the school in 1992, formal negotiations toward a successor agreement were begun. However, **the school then gave notice that it was withdrawing its recognition of the union** and that it would no longer collectively bargain with it. The union filed an unfair labor practice charge against the school with the state Employment Relations Board, which found that the school had violated the Labor Law by withdrawing its recognition of the union. It then sued the school in the New York Supreme Court seeking to enforce its order. The supreme court granted the petition, and the school appealed to the Supreme Court, Appellate Division.

The appellate division rejected the school's contention that the board's assertion of jurisdiction over it violated its Free Exercise and Establishment Clause rights under the First Amendment. The state Labor Relations Act was a facially neutral, universally applicable and secular regulatory regimen that did not violate the Free Exercise Clause. It did not impose any express or implied restriction or burden on religious beliefs or activities. Nor did the act violate the Establishment Clause. There was no excessive entanglement in the board's relationship with religious schools over mandatory subjects of bargaining. **Even though lay faculty members were expected to instill "Christian values" in their students, this did not** serve "to make the terms and conditions of their employment matters of church administration and thus purely of ecclesiastical concern." Also, the U.S. Supreme Court's decision in *NLRB v. Catholic Bishop of Chicago*, above, did not apply because the case involved a state agency exercising its jurisdiction over religiously affiliated schools. The court affirmed the lower court's decision that the school had to bargain collectively. *New York State Employment Relations Board v. Christian Brothers Academy*, 668 N.Y.S.2d 407 (A.D.3d Dep't 1998).

◆   In *NLRB v. Yeshiva University,* the U.S. Supreme Court held that in certain circumstances, faculty members at private educational institutions could be considered managerial employees. The Supreme Court's ruling was based on its conclusion that Yeshiva's faculty decided school curriculum, standards, tuition rates and admissions. The Court noted that its decision applied only to schools that were "like Yeshiva" and not to schools where the faculty exercised less control. **Schools where faculty members do not exercise binding managerial discretion do not fall within the scope of the managerial employee exclusion**. *NLRB v. Yeshiva Univ.*, 444 U.S. 672, 100 S.Ct. 856, 63 L.Ed.2d 115 (1980).

C. Termination from Employment

◆   During a mandatory faculty meeting, an administrator at a Christian day school made announcements concerning the school's problems with recruiting and retaining students. The administrator blamed "marginal" teachers for the problem, noting that they were "mean and cruel to the children," that they "spoke harshly and unkindly" to the students and "called them names." The administrator told the faculty that six to eight teachers would be terminated at the end of the school year, and that they would receive notices in their mailboxes. The next day, **a teacher received such a notice and sued the school and its administrators for defamation**. In moving for pretrial judgment, the school and its administrators asserted that the comments at the faculty meeting were not defamatory. Moreover, they argued, the information conveyed qualified as privileged.

A Pennsylvania federal court disagreed. **Although no specific teachers were named, the listeners could infer that the statements applied to the teachers whose contracts were not renewed**. Moreover, the statements had the potential to harm the teacher's reputation in the community. Thus, a possible defamatory meaning of the statements existed. The court concluded that the school and administrators failed to show that statements relating to a teacher's behavior in the classroom are privileged when published at a faculty meeting to explain why certain teachers' contracts will not be renewed. There was also a genuine issue as to whether the defendants abused any privilege by publishing the statements to the entire faculty, and by including matters not reasonably believed to be necessary for informing the faculty that certain teachers' contracts would not be renewed. Consequently, the court denied the school and administrators pretrial judgment. *MacCord v. Christian Academy*, 1998 U.S. Dist. LEXIS 19412 (E.D.Pa.1998).

◆   An Illinois corporation operating several private secular elementary schools hired a third grade Hebrew teacher and granted her application for tenure several years later. The school's code of practice essentially provided that tenured teachers could be fired only for cause. The school discharged her, following a pretermination hearing, for allegedly misrepresenting the reasons she returned late from a trip to Israel at the beginning of the 1990-1991 school year. The teacher filed a breach of contract lawsuit against the school in an Illinois trial court, seeking reinstatement to her position. The trial court held for the school, and the teacher appealed to the Appellate Court of Illinois. The appellate court held that employees working pursuant to personal service contracts are not entitled to reinstatement, an equitable remedy. As a matter of public policy, **courts generally avoid the friction that would be caused by compelling an employee to work, or an employer to retain somebody against their wishes**. Because the public school code did not apply to give the teacher statutory rights to employment, the trial court had properly dismissed the claim. *Chady v. Solomon Schechter Day Schools*, 645 N.E.2d 983 (Ill.App.1st Dist.1995).

II. STATE AND FEDERAL REGULATION

Private schools must meet many of the same regulations governing accreditation, compulsory attendance, and mandatory reporting for suspected abuse as public schools. Additionally, private schools enjoy certain tax exemptions from federal income taxes and state and local property taxes.

A. Accreditation

◆ A Florida business school was accredited by a council of independent schools and colleges. The council used a list of criteria in its accreditation decisions. In determining whether to continue accrediting the school, the council conducted an on-site evaluation and found that the school was not in compliance with a number of the listed criteria. Most importantly, less than 50 percent of the school's students had a high school diploma or its equivalent and the number of students enrolled in nonbusiness programs exceeded the number enrolled in business programs. **The school failed to adequately explain its noncompliance, the council suspended its accreditation and a review board approved** this decision. The school filed an emergency motion for injunctive relief in the U.S. District Court for the Southern District of Florida. The court noted that its review was limited to whether the council's decision was arbitrary and unreasonable or supported by substantial evidence. Although the school had originally reported that most of its students did not have high school diplomas, it later discovered that the report was wrong because of a computer error and actually less than 50 percent of its students were without a diploma. The school also argued that it believed its cosmetology and nursing programs qualified as business programs based on language in the council's accreditation manual and the practices of other accrediting agencies. **Because the school would not receive federal funding and would be closed if it did not receive accreditation, the court found that it would suffer irreparable harm,** which outweighed the harm that the council would suffer. The court also found that the school showed a substantial likelihood of success on the merits. It granted the preliminary injunction and remanded the case for further proceedings. *Florida College of Business v. Accrediting Council for Independent Colleges and Schools*, 954 F.Supp. 256 (S.D.Fla.1996).

✦   A group of Native American students took out federally guaranteed student loans in order to attend an Arizona technical institute which was accredited by two nationally recognized accrediting agencies. **The students filed suit against the institute and the agencies in federal district court, alleging that the agencies negligently accredited and monitored the institute,** causing them monetary damages. The district court dismissed their lawsuit and the students appealed to the U.S. Court of Appeals, Ninth Circuit. The court of appeals noted that to establish a cause of action for negligence under Arizona law, a plaintiff must establish that the defendant has a duty, recognized by law, to conform to a certain standard of conduct. This duty can be imposed when both the person to whom the duty is owed and the risk are foreseeable to a reasonable person. The students argued that it was foreseeable to the agencies that the negligent performance of their duties would cause the alleged damages. The court disagreed, finding that the students had not sufficiently shown that the agencies had given them false information. **It also found no Arizona cases that either recognized a duty of care in this type of situation or held that accrediting agencies owe a duty to students attending the institutions that they accredit.** The court affirmed the district court's decision. *Keams v. Tempe Technical Institute, Inc.,* 110 F.3d 44 (9th Cir.1997).

B. Mandatory Reporting

✦   A New York private school student spent summer vacations with her aunt and uncle in Pennsylvania and later, in New Jersey. The student told her social studies teacher that she had been sexually abused by her uncle. The teacher stated that there was nothing she could do since the uncle was in New Jersey, but if it happened again, the student should let her know. The teacher did not report the abuse and the student continued to visit her aunt and uncle. A year later, the student told a school counselor about the abuse. The counselor told the student's mother and a report was filed. **The student's parents filed suit** in state court against the school, **seeking to recover damages for the psychological trauma their daughter suffered** as a result of the teacher's failure to report a case of suspected child abuse. The school filed a motion to dismiss which the trial court granted, finding that the teacher had no common law duty to report the abuse and that she did not breach her statutory duty as a mandatory reporter of child sexual abuse. The parents appealed to the New York Supreme Court, Appellate Division.

The appellate court found that whether a teacher is required to report a case of suspected child sexual abuse was to be determined by the facts known to the teacher at the time he or she learns of the abuse. Considering that the teacher here knew that the student visited with her relatives on regular occasions and that her parents were not with her during these visits, the court held that **it would have been reasonable for the teacher to believe that the uncle fell under the statute as a "person legally responsible" for the student and that she was thus required to report the suspected abuse.** Furthermore, the mandatory reporter does not have to determine whether the abuser meets the technical definition of the statute. The reporter must simply report immediately any suspected child abuse. The court held that a reporter can be held liable for a breach of that duty even if it is eventually found that the abuse did not occur or that the abuse did not fall within the statute. The trial court's decision was reversed. *Kimberly S.M. v. Bradford Central School,* 649 N.Y.S.2d 588 (A.D.4th Dep't 1996).

◆   A student at a private religious school in Iowa run by a church was sexually abused by her father. Her family met with the parish priest for counseling. He was not a licensed counselor and in his role as priest, he focused on efforts to reunite the family. Although the student told him that her father hurt her, she did not expressly state that he sexually abused her. The student later had sessions with the school counselor. Even though she was being abused by her father at this time, she did not tell the counselor about the abuse until it had stopped, approximately three years later. At that time, the student sought counseling from a social worker who stated that the student's symptoms as an abused child were obvious. She also stated that the emotional problems of an abused child outweigh the need to preserve the family unit. **The student filed suit in state court against the priest, the church, the counselor and the school**, among others, alleging that the priest and the counselor failed to report the abuse and that the school and the church were vicariously liable for these omissions and had failed to adequately train their employees. The defendants filed a motion to dismiss, which the trial court granted and the student appealed to the Supreme Court of Iowa.

The court found that **the priest had no duty to report child abuse** even if he suspected it. As a clergyman, he was not a mandatory reporter of suspected child abuse under Iowa law. Although the court held that the school counselor was a mandatory reporter, it also found that she had no knowledge of the abuse until the student told her. The student argued that based on the testimony of the social worker, the counselor should have known about the abuse because the student was exhibiting obvious symptoms. The court agreed with the trial court that **the social worker's testimony did not create a jury issue with regard to whether the counselor should have known about the abuse**. Because the priest was not a mandatory reporter, the church could not be held vicariously liable for his inaction nor could it be held liable for failing to adequately train him. The counselor was a mandatory reporter and the school was required to provide her with two hours of initial training and additional training every five years. The counselor not only received this training but also was college-trained and professionally licensed. Thus, the school did not fail to adequately train her. Finding no liability on the part of the priest, the church, the counselor or the school, the court affirmed the motion to dismiss. *Wilson v. Darr*, 553 N.W.2d 579 (Iowa 1996).

C. Taxation

1. Federal Income Taxation

◆   Section 501(c)(3) of the Internal Revenue Code provides that "corporations ... organized and operated exclusively for religious, charitable ... or educational purposes" are entitled to tax exempt status. The Internal Revenue Service routinely granted tax exemptions under § 501(c)(3) to private schools regardless of whether they had racially discriminatory admissions policies. In 1970, however, **the IRS concluded that it could no longer grant tax-exempt status to racially discriminatory private schools because such schools were not "charitable" within the meaning of § 501(c)(3)**. Two private colleges whose racial admissions policies were rooted in their interpretations of the Bible sued to prevent the IRS from interpreting the federal tax laws in this manner. The Supreme Court rejected the colleges' challenge and upheld the IRS's interpretation. The Court's ruling was based on what it perceived as the strong public policy against racial discrimination in education. Because the colleges were operating in violation of that public policy, the colleges could not be considered to be "charitable" under § 501(c)(3). Thus, they were ineligible for tax exemptions. The court held that the denial of an exemption did not impermissibly burden the colleges' alleged religious freedom interest in practicing racial discrimination. *Bob Jones Univ. v. United States*, 461 U.S. 574, 103 S.Ct. 2017, 76 L.Ed.2d 157 (1983).

✦ Parents of black public school children sought a federal court order requiring the IRS to adopt more stringent standards for determining whether private schools had racially discriminatory admissions policies. The black parents claimed that the IRS standards were too lax, and that certain private schools were practicing racial discrimination and were nevertheless obtaining tax exemptions. **The Supreme Court dismissed the parents' claims, ruling that the parents and children had shown no injury to themselves as a result of the allegedly lax IRS standards**. None of the children had sought enrollment at the private schools involved, and the abstract stigma attached to living in a community with racially discriminatory private schools was also insufficient to show actual injury. Further, the parents' theory that denial of exempt status to such schools would result in greater white student enrollment in area public schools, and hence result in a greater degree of public school integration, was only speculation. *Allen v. Wright*, 468 U.S. 737, 104 S.Ct. 3315, 82 L.Ed.2d 556 (1984).

2. State and Local Taxation

✦ A Maine nonprofit corporation operated a summer camp for children of the Christian Science faith. Activities included supervised prayer, meditation and church services. Weekly tuition for the camp was roughly $400. A Maine statute exempted charitable institutions from real estate and personal property taxes. However, institutions that were operated primarily for the benefit of nonresidents were only entitled to a more limited tax benefit, and then only if the weekly charge for services did not exceed $30 per person. **Because most of the campers were not residents of the state and weekly tuition was over $30, the corporation was ineligible for any tax exemption**. It petitioned the town for a refund of the taxes it had paid, arguing that the exemption violated the Commerce Clause of the U.S. Constitution. The case reached the U.S. Supreme Court.

The Court noted that the Commerce Clause was designed to override restrictive and conflicting state commercial regulations that fostered local interests and prejudiced nonresidents. It found that the camp was engaged in commerce not only as a purchaser, but also as a provider of goods and services. **The Court also held that a real estate tax, like any other tax, could impermissibly burden interstate commerce and noted that if the exemption applied to for-profit entities, there would be no question of a Commerce Clause violation**. It found no reason why an entity's nonprofit status should exclude it from Commerce Clause coverage and noted that nonprofit institutions are subject to other laws regulating commerce as well as federal antitrust laws. Finally, the Court found that the town could not defend the statute by showing that it advanced a legitimate purpose that could not be obtained by reasonable, nondiscriminatory alternatives. *Camps Newfound/ Owatonna, Inc. v. Town of Harrison, Maine*, 520 U.S. 564, 117 S.Ct. 1590, 137 L.Ed.2d 852 (1997).

◆   The Illinois Education Association-NEA sued state officials in an Illinois county court for a declaration that 35 Ill. Comp. Stat. 5/201(m) violated the state constitution. **The law allowed taxpayers to take a $500 tax credit equal to 25 percent of the their "qualified education expenses" on behalf of a full-time K-12 student at a public or qualified nonpublic school**. "Qualified education expense" was defined as an amount in excess of $250 for tuition, book fees and lab fees. The complaining parties alleged the credit supported private religious schools, since public schools did not charge tuition or book and lab fees in excess of $250 per year for any student. They asserted the credit reduced state revenue and was the equivalent of a legislative appropriation for private schools, the vast majority of which were sectarian. The court dismissed the case, holding that money accruing from the credit did not constitute "public funds."

The complaining parties appealed to the Illinois Appellate Court, which rejected the complaining parties' argument that the term "public fund" has a broad, expansive meaning that includes tax credits. The credit was not an "appropriation," as they argued. The statute had the secular purpose of assisting parents with their educational costs and furthered the state interest of ensuring students were well educated. Private schools relieved taxpayers of the burden of educating students who would otherwise attend public schools. The credit was available to parents of public and private school children alike, and funds became available to private schools only as the result of private choices by parents. **Any attenuated benefit to private schools was created by a neutral tax program that was part of a general government program that did not unconstitutionally advance religion**. The tax credit did not create religious entanglement with the government, since its administration involved only a determination of whether expenses claimed by taxpayers were "qualified." This was no different than any number of other tax deductions and credits allowed by state law and did not foster excessive government entanglement with religion. The court rejected the complaining parties' arguments that the tax credit discriminated against low-income families and was not for public purposes. It affirmed the judgment for the state revenue director and department of revenue. *Toney et al. v. Bower et al.*, 744 N.E.2d 351 (Ill. App., 4th Dist. 2001).

◆   The Pottstown, Pennsylvania, School District and the borough of Pottstown petitioned the Montgomery County Board of Assessment Appeals to remove The Hill School's real estate tax exemption. Pennsylvania's Institutions of Purely Public Charity Act exempts certain charitable entities from paying real estate taxes. **The district**, which receives a portion of the funds assessed from the real estate tax, **argued that The Hill School's single-sex status disqualified it from the tax exemption**. The Hill School, located in Pottstown, Pa., was founded as an all-boys school, but began to admit female students in 1998. The borough and school district argued to the board of assessment that The Hill School was ineligible for the tax exemption during the years it admitted only boys because the exemption pertains to charities that benefit a "substantial and indefinite class of persons." The statute of limitations only allowed the borough and school district to challenge the exemption for the 1996 and 1997 school years. The board of assessment rejected the borough and district's claims. The plaintiffs brought the matter before the Montgomery County Court of Common Pleas.

The court initially ruled that the school did not qualify for the exemption before it admitted female students; however, on reconsideration, the court ruled in favor of The Hill School. The court found that applicable federal and state laws did not prohibit secondary or undergraduate private schools from admitting only male or female students. The court also noted that it knew of no relevant Pennsylvania case law that addressed whether a single-gender private school qualifies as an institution of purely public charity, and stated that a limitation on admissions to one sex did not prevent an institution from qualifying as a charity under the act. In affirming the assessment board's ruling, the court stated that The Hill School benefited an indefinite class before it admitted female students. **Since the school qualified as a charity under the act, it was entitled to the real estate tax exemption.** *Pottstown School District v. The Hill School,* No. 96-16925 (Pa. C.P. 2000).

◆   A not-for-profit educational institution in New Hampshire was taxed to the extent that the aggregate value of its dormitories, dining rooms and kitchens, as well as the land on which they sat, exceeded $150,000. The school petitioned a state trial court for an abatement of its taxes, arguing that the town could tax the aggregate value of the dormitories, dining rooms and kitchens in excess of $150,000, but could not tax the land on which those buildings stood. **The Supreme Court of New Hampshire determined that the school's dormitories, dining rooms and kitchens were taxable to the extent their value exceeded $150,000, but the land on which those building stood was not taxable.** *Brewster Academy v. Town of Wolfeboro,* 701 A.2d 1240 (N.H.1997).

III. PRIVATE SCHOOL STUDENT RIGHTS

Private school students do not enjoy the same level of constitutional protection as the courts have granted to public school students. Generally, courts have demonstrated a reluctance to interfere with private school academic and disciplinary policies. Federal discrimination and civil rights statutes also only provide limited protection. For example, civil rights cases attempting to assert private school liability under a constitutional theory or federal statutory right pursuant to 42 U.S.C. § 1983 require a determination that the school is a state actor. Although a private school may become a state actor based on performance of duties normally associated with government entities or close cooperation with the government, the U.S. Supreme Court in Rendell-Baker v. Kohn, *457 U.S. 830, 102 S.Ct. 2764, 73 L.Ed.2d 418 (1982), limited the circumstances in which an ostensibly private institution can be found to be acting "under the color of state law." In short, the level of constitutional protection afforded to private school students has been limited in a variety of contexts.*

A. Admissions and Other School Policies

Although the U.S. Supreme Court has applied 42 U.S.C. § 1981 to private schools, as illustrated in *Runyon v. McCrary,* below, to prohibit race discrimination, the Court noted that its holding did not extend to religious schools that practiced racial exclusion on religious grounds. Similarly, Title VI of the Civil Rights Act of 1964, 42 U.S.C. § 2000d, prohibits discrimination on the basis of race, color, or national origin but only applies to "programs or activities" receiving federal financial assistance. In the context of sex discrimination, Title IX applies to recipients of federal funding but also provides a specific exclusion which allows private undergraduate institutions to discriminate on the basis of sex in admissions. 20 U.S.C. § 1681(a)(1).

♦   In *Runyon v. McCrary*, the U.S. Supreme Court relied on 42 U.S.C. § 1981 to declare that blacks could not be excluded from all-white elementary schools. In this Virginia case, the parents of black students sought to enter into contractual relationships with private nonreligious schools for educational services advertised and offered to members of the general public. The students were denied admission because of their race. **The Supreme Court recognized that while parents have a First Amendment right to send their children to educational institutions which promote the belief that racial segregation is desirable, it does not follow that the practice of excluding racial minorities from such institutions is also protected by the same principle**. The school's argument that § 1981 does not govern private acts of racial discrimination was rejected. However, the Court observed that its holding did not extend to religious schools that practiced racial exclusion on religious grounds. *Runyon v. McCrary*, 427 U.S. 160, 96 S.Ct. 2586, 49 L.E.2d 415 (1976).

♦   A woman was enrolled in an occupational therapy program at a private New York college. To graduate, a student had to take the required number of credits and complete two placements. According to school policy, if a student left a placement without a supervisor's permission, he or she automatically failed the placement, and two failed field placements resulted in automatic termination from the program. During her final placement, the student had an argument with her supervisor, walked out and never returned. Two weeks later, she wrote a letter to the school stating that she was going to be evaluated for a learning disability and requesting accommodations. **Because she had already failed a placement before walking out of her final placement, the school responded that she had been automatically terminated from the program**. The student was later diagnosed with a mental disorder and requested that the college reconsider its decision. It refused and the student filed suit in the U.S. District Court for the Western District of New York, alleging violations of § 504 of the Rehabilitation Act and the Americans with Disabilities Act (ADA), among other claims. The college filed a motion to dismiss.

The court found that the student did not show that she was discharged because of her disability. According to the evidence, she was automatically dismissed from the program when she walked out of her last placement. At this time, the college did not know that she had a disability and it was not informed of her disability until after her termination. The student argued that her letter informing the college that she was being evaluated for a possible disability was adequate notification but the court disagreed. The letter merely stated that she was going to be evaluated, not that she was disabled. The student also argued that once the college was informed, it was required to readmit her into the program. **The court found that the college was not**

required to reconsider a nondiscriminatory decision. Because the student could not show as a matter of law that she was dismissed from the program because of her disability, she was not able to make out a *prima facie* case of discrimination under § 504 or the ADA. The college's motion to dismiss was granted. *Goodwin v. Keuka College*, 929 F.Supp. 90 (W.D.N.Y.1995).

◆   An Ohio statute required that all public schools administer proficiency tests to their students. The statute was then amended to include testing of all students, both public and private. The tests were first given in the ninth grade and each student had to pass by the end of the twelfth grade in order to graduate. The tests covered reading, writing, mathematics, science and citizenship. Failure to administer the tests would result in the loss of the school's charter. **A group of private secondary schools and an association of private schools filed suit** against the state in an Ohio federal district court, **alleging that the testing requirement violated their rights under the First and Fourteenth Amendments** to the U.S. Constitution and requesting injunctive relief prohibiting enforcement of the statute. The district court found for the state and the private schools appealed to the U.S. Court of Appeals, Sixth Circuit.

The schools argued that the statute infringed on a parent's Fourteenth Amendment right to direct, by choice of school, the education of his or her child. The statute, in effect, eradicated the distinction between public and private education and therefore the strict scrutiny standard should apply. The court of appeals applied the rational basis standard, finding that the state need only show that the testing requirement was rationally related to a legitimate governmental interest. **Since the state has an interest in ensuring that certain educational standards are met, the schools' rights were not compromised.** However, the court noted that a more intrusive testing requirement could displace a private school's discretion to design its own educational program. The court also found that **the schools' First Amendment rights were not violated because the testing requirement did not restrict the teaching of any particular material.** The court affirmed the district court's decision. *Ohio Ass'n of Independent Schools v. Goff*, 92 F.3d 419 (6th Cir.1996).

B. Athletics and Extra-Curricular Activities

◆   The Tennessee Secondary School Athletic Association is a not-for-profit corporation organized to regulate interscholastic sports among member schools. The TSSAA sanctioned one of its members, Brentwood Academy, after determining that the school violated the association's recruiting rules. **Brentwood, a parochial high school, then sued the TSSAA in a federal district court for constitutional rights violations under 42 U.S.C. § 1983, seeking relief from the imposition of sanctions.** The sanctions included exclusion from football and basketball tournaments for one school year. Section 1983 is a federal civil rights statute that contains no substantive rights, but provides for the vindication of civil rights guaranteed by other federal laws and the U.S. Constitution. Because § 1983 requires that the underlying civil rights violation result from some action "under color of state law," courts first consider whether there has been "state action" before proceeding to substantive issues. The district court ruled that the TSSAA was a state actor that had violated Brentwood's First Amendment rights. The TSSAA appealed to the U.S. Court of Appeals, Sixth Circuit, arguing that it was a private organization immune from § 1983 claims. The Sixth Circuit reversed, and Brentwood petitioned the Supreme Court for review.

The Court held that state action exists where there is a close nexus between the state and the challenged action, so that the action is fairly attributable to the state itself. TSSAA's governing legislative council and board of control were made up entirely of public school principals, assistant principals and superintendents from member schools. Each TSSAA official was elected by representatives of the member schools. TSSAA employees were eligible to participate in the state's retirement system. The relationship between Tennessee and the TSSAA was confirmed by the state's willingness to allow student participation in TSSAA-sanctioned sports to satisfy state physical education requirements. **The TSSAA had a public character and was capable of state action for the purposes of Brentwood's § 1983 claims**, according to the Court. The Sixth Circuit decision was reversed and the case remanded for further proceedings. *Brentwood Academy v. Tennessee Secondary School Athletic Association*, 531 U.S. 288, 121 S.Ct. 924, 148 L.Ed.2d 807 (2001).

♦   A Montana private school student wished to participate in a public school's sports program for social purposes such as friendship and team camaraderie. **The school board refused to allow her to join the program, since participation was limited to students enrolled fulltime in the public school**. Her parents filed suit on her behalf against the board in state court, alleging that the board policy was unconstitutional and requesting a preliminary injunction allowing her to play volleyball on the public school team. The court granted the injunction and both parties filed summary judgment motions. The court upheld the constitutionality of the school board's policy, granted the board's motion and dissolved the preliminary injunction. The parents appealed to the Supreme Court of Montana.

The parents argued that under the Montana Constitution each resident of the state is guaranteed an equal educational opportunity. Finding that the right to participate in extracurricular activities is not a fundamental right, the court applied a middle tier analysis and needed only to determine if the classification based on public school enrollment was reasonable and if the school's interests outweighed the student's interests in participating in extracurricular activities. Considering the state's heavy emphasis on the concept of an educational system, the court held that the enrollment classification was reasonable. **The court stated that the established integration of academic and extracurricular activities within the public school system did not lend itself to participation by nonenrolled students**. The court affirmed the lower court's decision. *Kaptein v. Conrad School Dist.*, 931 P.2d 1311 (Mont.1997).

♦   An Indiana student attended a public high school until the middle of her junior year and then transferred to a Catholic school. **She played on the varsity volleyball team at the public school and wanted to play on the private school's varsity team but was found ineligible to play** under the Indiana High School Athletic Association (IHSAA) transfer rule. Under the rule, if a transfer does not involve a parental change of residence, the student must fall under one of 13 exceptions to be eligible to participate in school athletics. The rule does not prohibit all participation, but only that at the varsity level. The student's parents had not moved, and the student claimed that she transferred because she had recently converted to Catholicism and wanted to take certain advanced courses not offered at the public school. Because this reason did not fall under any of the exceptions, the student was denied eligibility to play varsity volleyball, but she was allowed to play on the subvarsity team. The student appealed the decision but the IHSAA upheld the one-year denial of eligibility. The student appealed to the U.S. District Court for the Southern District of Indiana, requesting a preliminary injunction allowing her to play.

The student argued that the transfer rule burdened parents' and students' rights to the free exercise of their religion. **The court held that for there to be an undue burden, there must be grave interference with significant religious tenets**. Here, the student presented no evidence of this. Although the transfer rule is based on the theory that when a transfer occurs without a corresponding parental change of residence, athletic considerations are often involved, the court noted that the rule can deny eligibility to students who do not transfer for an athletic reason. Despite this fact, the court found that the rule could not be considered irrational. The student also failed to show that she would be irreparably harmed by the rule. It did not prevent her from fully practicing her religion, from attending the school she wished to attend or from participating in subvarsity athletics. **Because she failed to show a likelihood of success on the merits and irreparable harm, the court denied the preliminary injunction**. *Robbins v. Indiana High School Athletic Ass'n, Inc.*, 941 F.Supp. 786 (S.D.Ind.1996).

C. Breach of Contract

1. Educational Programs

◆   A student applied for admission to a private university's graduate school, and was admitted as a probationary special student, which allowed the taking of graduate level courses but would not lead to a master's degree. An associate dean met with the student and explained to him that his admission was probationary because he lacked the requisite academic background or coursework in computer science. **She told him that to be admitted to the degree program, he would need to successfully complete coursework in the computer science department and obtain a faculty advisor**. However, the university's graduate school catalog specifically provided that offers of admissions had binding force only when made by the school in writing. The student obtained a letter from a professor which stated that he would be working under the professor's supervision for his master's project. Subsequently, the university informed the student that his special student status was discontinued and that he had not been admitted into the master's program. The student sued the university for breach of contract in a Rhode Island federal district court, and the judge granted judgment as a matter of law to the university.

The student appealed to the U.S. Court of Appeals, First Circuit, asserting that the district court judge had improperly taken the case from the jury. He asserted that he reasonably expected that if he satisfactorily performed his coursework and obtained a sponsor for his master's project, he would be admitted as a master's degree candidate based on the statement of the associate dean. The court, however, noted that the graduate school catalog divested faculty members of any authority to promise admission or to determine the necessary prerequisites for admissions. **Even if the associate dean had the authority to offer admission to the student, she could not do so except by a signed writing**. Further, the letter from the student's advisor did not qualify as a faculty recommendation. Accordingly, the student's breach of contract claim failed. The district court decision was affirmed. *Mangla v. Brown Univ.*, 135 F.3d 80 (1st Cir.1998).

◆   A high school senior attended a private preparatory school in Georgia since kindergarten. One afternoon, she was taking a make-up math test in a study hall when another student showed her how to do a problem correctly. While the student was receiving the correct answer, a staff member and a math teacher caught both students cheating. **The senior was permanently expelled from school**, even though she was within days of taking her final exams before graduation. In the Honor Council proceedings that led to her expulsion, the school justified its action by noting that during the prior year, the student had been found guilty of an honor code violation regarding an "intent to cheat." The student and her parents brought an action against the school in a Georgia trial court for intentional infliction of emotional distress, breach of fundamental fairness and due process, and breach of contract. The court granted the school's motion for summary judgment, and the student appealed to the Court of Appeals of Georgia.

The court reviewed a Georgia Supreme Court case, *Woodruff v. Ga. State Univ.*, 304 S.E.2d 697 (1983), which held that it would not review a teacher's academic assessment of a student's work. The court of appeals found that the case applied to this situation. Cheating is a fundamental breach of trust by the student. The student and her parents had contracted with the school to impliedly do four things essential to the student-school relationship: diligently seek to learn and perform as a good student; be honest and responsible; maintain reasonable discipline and self-discipline in the academic setting; and pay fees, tuition, and expenses. Failure to render any one at any time was such a fundamental breach of the contract as to result in termination of the student's relationship with the school. The court agreed that there was a total failure of consideration and breach of contract; however, the breach of contract was on the part of the student and her parents. **The expulsion was not arbitrary or capricious, but a reasonable exercise of administrative and academic discretion**. Therefore, there was no violation of fundamental fairness in the treatment of the student. The court affirmed the judgment of the lower court. *Blaine v. Savannah Country Day School*, 491 S.E.2d 446 (Ga.App.1997).

◆   A Florida couple enrolled their children in a Catholic school that taught a family life course at all grade levels, kindergarten through eighth. Because portions of the course dealt with human sexuality, they objected to their children having to take the course. The school excused the children from having to take the course in the 1994-95 school year, but notified the parents that their children would no longer be exempt in the following year. However, after the parents threatened a lawsuit, the children were exempted from the course in the following year. After a number of disputes between the parents and the school, **the school notified the parents that their children would not be accepted for the 1997-98 school year**. The parents sued the school in a Florida trial court for breach of contract and intentional infliction of emotional distress as well as for injunctive relief to keep their children in the school. The trial court entered a temporary injunction ordering the school to allow the children to attend for the remainder of the academic year and to hold spaces for them for the next year. The school appealed to the District Court of Appeal of Florida, Fourth District.

On appeal, the school argued that the trial court had violated the Establishment Clause of the First Amendment by involving itself in an ecclesiastical matter. The court noted that it did not need to address this issue because the contract between the parents and the school was one for personal services that was not enforceable by injunction. **If the school were compelled to educate the children until they graduated from eighth grade, the trial court would be involved throughout the rest of their schooling.** Since courts are unable to supervise contracts for personal services, the lower court had improperly issued the injunction. The court reversed the trial court's decision. *Glass v. Anderson*, 704 So.2d 697 (Fla.App.4th Dist.1997).

♦ **A Washington technical college developed a real estate appraising program that fulfilled the educational requirements of the state licensing statute,** but made no statements that the course fulfilled the statute's experience requirements. A number of students signed up for the program and their instructor orally represented that the realistic training and experience could be counted towards the hours of experience required by the statute. The instructor was later fired and replaced. The new instructor stated that the program would meet the educational requirements for licensure but not the experience requirements, and all of the students finished the course. Although they had the required educational hours, they had no work experience hours. They filed suit against the college in state court, alleging, among other claims, breach of contract. The court found for the college and the students appealed to the Court of Appeals of Washington.

The students argued that they would not have taken the course had they known that it would not provide any work experience hours. The court of appeals noted that to show the existence of a contract, the students had to prove mutual assent between the contracting parties. **The court held that in all of the written materials regarding the program, the college stated that the course objective was to qualify students for entry-level employment in the appraising industry.** It never stated that the program would meet the state licensure requirements. The students argued that their first instructor was an agent of the college and that he orally represented that the program would provide work experience hours, but the court found no authority stating that an instructor could create a contract between students and a school through oral representations. The students also failed to show that the instructor had the authority to legally bind the school. Finding no evidence of a contract between the students and the school, the court affirmed the trial court's decision. *Ottgen v. Clover Park Technical College*, 928 P.2d 1119 (Wash.App.Div.2 1996).

2. Tuition

A private school filed a complaint for breach of contract and unjust enrichment against a parent for his failure to pay his three sons' tuition for

the 1993-1994 academic school year. The trial court entered a default judgment against the parent when he continually failed to appear for a settlement conference. An attorney trial referee then conducted a hearing on damages and granted the school reimbursement for the deficient tuition payments plus interest totaling $68,819.66 as well as $26.11 per day if the parent failed to pay the tuition within two days of the judgment. The parent filed a motion to open the default and another objecting to the attorney referee's report. Both motions were denied, and the parent appealed to the Appellate Court of Connecticut.

The appellate court stated that a trial court can proceed with a case even if a defendant fails to appear in court. Although the parent had been diagnosed with hypertension, a letter explaining his poor health was not filed on record until the day the trial court entered judgment against him. **The court upheld the judgment against the parent. However, it then determined that the amount of the judgment was improper**. The school's complaint sought recovery of tuition for one academic year, but the attorney trial referee granted tuition reimbursement for two years. In addition, the amount of interest had been miscalculated. The matter was remanded to the trial court for a reconsideration of the amount of damages. *Brunswick School, Inc. v. Hutter*, 730 A.2d 1206 (Conn.App.1999).

◆   A Missouri nursing school graduated its first class of students in 1984. The school was accredited by the Missouri State Board of Nursing. It was also a "candidate for accreditation" with the North Central Association for Colleges and Schools (NCA). However, the school's brochure actually stated that the school "has ... been granted [NCA] candidacy for review status" and that "accreditation for [the school] is expected in 1983." In 1981, a letter from the student services coordinator restated the above-quoted information to the class of 1984. The students were not apprised of the NCA accreditation status prior to their graduation and the school was not formally accredited until 1987. This accreditation status did not apply retroactively to the class of 1984. **Several members of the class of 1984 filed suit in a Missouri trial court, alleging that the school intentionally misrepresented its accreditation status which limited their job prospects, advanced education possibilities and future earning power**. The trial court granted the school's motion for summary judgment, and the students appealed to the Missouri Court of Appeals.

The students contended that the school's affirmative statement regarding the likelihood of achieving accreditation legally bound it to disclose all material facts related to its receipt of NCA accreditation. Consequently, they argued, the school's silence on this issue was intentional misrepresentation. The court of appeals rejected the students' appeal. **Although misrepresentation of a material fact by silence may amount to actionable fraud, the students failed to show that they relied on the school's allegedly fraudulent statements** in enrolling or remaining enrolled in the program. Because the students failed to establish the reliance element of fraud, the court refused to address the issue of whether the school had a duty to disclose all material facts related to the anticipated accreditation. The holding of the trial court was affirmed. *Nigro v. Research College of Nursing*, 876 S.W.2d 681 (Mo.App.W.D.1994).

D. Discipline, Suspension and Expulsion

◆   After a hearing before a board of school officials, **a student was expelled from the college preparatory military high school he attended for physically attacking his roommate**. The student, whose roommate was Hispanic and Catholic, admitted that the attack was racially motivated. On appeal, the school superintendent upheld the student's expulsion. The student then filed suit against officials at the school, alleging he was denied his constitutional right to due process and equal protection. He claimed he was not given adequate notice of the charges against him before the hearing. A federal district court granted the school's summary judgment motion. The student appealed to the U.S. Court of Appeals, Tenth Circuit.

The circuit court first examined the alleged violation of Watson's due process rights, and cited the U.S. Supreme Court's ruling in *Goss v. Lopez*, 419 U.S. 565 (1975), which set the due process standard for short-term school suspensions. The *Goss* court determined that students are entitled to written or oral notice of the charges against them, an explanation of the evidence obtained by authorities and a chance to present their side of the story. The Tenth Circuit noted that the Supreme Court has never established a due process standard for long-term or permanent suspensions, so the circuit court decided to use the *Goss* standard as a guide. The circuit court found **the student was well aware of the allegations against him since he had received verbal notice of the hearing regarding the assault**. His argument that he was not informed of the charge of racism against him failed because the board determined "racism" to be a motivating factor in the assault, but it was not an independent charge brought against him. The record showed the student was expelled for the assault, not because he was racist. The student's claim that the school violated his equal protection rights also failed. He claimed that other local schools would have given him written notice, but the defendants maintained that the difference in procedure was related to the school's military nature. The Tenth Circuit agreed with the school. "The principle difference between a military school and other schools is the degree of discipline imposed on students.... This difference is a fundamental ingredient of a military education." The district court's grant of summary judgment in favor of the school was upheld. *Watson v. Beckel et al.*, 242 F.3d 1237 (10th Cir. 2001).

◆   An eighth-grade parochial school student, Sean, sold his broken BB gun to a classmate, "Paul," for $17 and a social studies outline. A few months later, Paul brought the gun to school to sell to a third student. Before the sale, Sean and Paul went to Sean's house during lunch to fix the gun. Although they could not repair the gun, Paul sold it when he returned to school. The boy who purchased the gun later used it to threaten a classmate. The principal investigated and learned that Paul obtained the gun from Sean. The principal approached Sean about his involvement, but Sean merely stated that he gave the gun to Paul. She approached Sean several more times and held a meeting with Sean, his parents, the pastor and the school's attorney. Sean eventually admitted selling the gun and turning in Paul's social studies outline as his own. **The principal notified the parents of Sean, Paul and the two boys involved in the incident that they would have to withdraw from school within a week or else the students would be expelled**. The school cited its "zero-tolerance" weapons policy as the reason for expulsion. All of the students but Sean voluntarily removed themselves from school. Sean's parents filed a suit, alleging that the expulsion was a breach of contract and a violation of their son's due process rights. A trial court granted summary judgment to the school, finding the decision to expel Sean was consistent with the rules set forth in the school handbook.

The parents appealed to the Ohio Court of Appeals, arguing that the trial court erred by upholding Sean's expulsion and by not considering the testimony of the former principal of the school, who said the gang activity policy was not a formal adoption of a zero-tolerance weapons policy. After reviewing Ohio case law, the appellate panel stated that courts should only intervene in a private school's disciplinary decision if the evidence demonstrates that the private school clearly violated the terms of the contract; or the private school clearly abused its discretion by applying its disciplinary standards in such a way that it departs from the purpose of the educational contract and therefore breaches the contract. **The appellate court ruled that the school did not abuse its discretion when it expelled Sean, because it was well within the terms and purpose of the handbook's disciplinary policy,** which says that students will be asked to withdraw if the principal or pastor feels that the student is a danger to others; expulsion is used as a last resort. The court found Sean's actions violated the behavioral norms set by the school in the handbook by initially lying about the gun sale and plagiarizing a social studies outline. In addition, he facilitated Paul's misconduct. In light of these actions, the appellate court ruled that the trial court did not err by overlooking the testimony of the former principal who disputed the "zero-tolerance" weapons policy because Sean's lying, cheating and disregard of parental permission requirements were a violation of other disciplinary standards in the handbook. The court of appeals also rejected the parents' defamation claim since they could not show that the letter sent to all parents contained false statements. The panel affirmed the trial court's decision in full and granted attorneys' fees to the school. *Riley et al. v. St. Ann Catholic School et al.*, No. 78129, 2000 WL 1902430 (Ohio App. 2000).

♦   Just prior to the start of his senior year, a parochial school student and his parents were informed that the student was being placed on disciplinary probation for the first semester. During the fall semester, the student was suspended once. In February, the student was suspended again. Shortly thereafter, two classmates told the assistant principal that the student was using and selling steroids, and bragging about relieving himself in lockers. At a meeting between the student, his parents and the assistant principal, the student was informed that he was suspended indefinitely. The school's disciplinary committee determined that the student should be dismissed from school and made that recommendation to the principal. When the student refused to withdraw, he was dismissed. **The student** then **sued the school in state court, claiming his dismissal violated the due process clauses of the U.S. and New Jersey Constitutions**. The school unsuccessfully sought to dismiss the case.

On appeal to the Superior Court of New Jersey, Appellate Division, the court reversed, finding that the school complied with due process requirements. Because the school was a private parochial school, it could not be considered a state actor (as required to establish a federal due process violation) even though it received state aid. For the same reasons, the court held that the due process provisions of the New

Jersey Constitution were not implicated. The court then noted that no New Jersey court had yet addressed the procedural requirements applicable to private school expulsions. While the protections required when expelling a public school student or a college student were well established, those required for private high school students were uncertain. **The court developed a two-part test, which first required schools to follow their established procedures for dismissal/expulsion, and to ensure that those procedures were "fundamentally fair."** In applying the test to the facts of this case, the court concluded that the school followed its procedures before expelling the student. The second step was also met, as the school notified the student of the allegations against him, gave him an opportunity to defend himself, and allowed him to appeal his suspension and dismissal to the school director. Under these circumstances, the dismissal was fundamentally fair. *Hernandez v. Don Bosco Preparatory High,* 322 N.J.Super. 1, 730 A.2d 365 (N.J.Super.A.D.1999).

◆   After a private student admitted improperly grabbing and touching other students, an administrator imposed a three-day suspension and advised his parents that he could not remain at the school unless he received counseling. Instead of enrolling their son in counseling, the parents withdrew him from school and sued for personal injuries arising from the discipline. The court granted pretrial judgment to the school, and the family appealed to the Court of Appeals of Ohio. The appellate court rejected the student's assertion that the school and administrator had breached a contract created by the school handbook in imposing discipline on him. **The investigation of his misconduct, the recommendation for counseling, and the suspension were consistent with handbook language prohibiting sexual harassment and violence by students**. The student had admitted to acts of sexual violence that implicated school discipline and eventually gave rise to criminal proceedings.

Under Ohio law, private schools are vested with broad discretion in student disciplinary matters. Ohio courts do not interfere in these cases in the absence of a clear abuse of discretion by the school's governing board. The court also rejected the student's claim that the administrator had breached a duty to him that was created by the handbook. There was no merit to the argument that she had failed to act on the student's own complaints that other students had tied him up during a recess period. There was no legal cause of action for holding a school administrator liable for failing to punish students in an equal manner. The court affirmed the trial court judgment. *Iwenofu v. St. Luke School,* 724 N.E.2d 511 (Ohio App.8th Dist.1999).

E. Students with Disabilities

◆   A student was diagnosed with Down Syndrome and mental retardation when he was two-months old. He began his schooling in an early intervention program at a Catholic school, but switched to public school for the first grade. His local school district offered him a free appropriate public education and developed an individual education plan in accordance with the Individuals with Disabilities Education Act. Due to the student's distress at being separated from his brothers and friends who attended the Catholic school, his parents voluntarily removed him from the public school and reinstated him at the Catholic school. The local intermediate unit (IU) customarily provides disabled students attending the parochial school with one day per week of speech language lessons, two days per week of remediation services, one day per week of counseling and psychological and diagnostic services, as needed. In addition to these services, the parents requested speech therapy, occupational therapy, itinerant teaching services and a teacher's aide. **The IU agreed to provide these services to the student in the public school setting, but denied the parents' request to provide the additional services at the Catholic school.** The parents filed suit in the U.S. District Court for the Eastern District of Pennsylvania seeking a permanent injunction requiring the IU to provide the requested services.

The court found that § 504 of the Rehabilitation Act and the IDEA alone did not require the IU to provide the requested services; however, state law governing the role of intermediate units obliged the IU to offer the student such services. The IDEA requires that states provides a free appropriate public education to all disabled students according to the educational standards set by each state. **Pennsylvania law, 24 Pa. Cons. Stat. § 13-1372[4], requires intermediate units to offer "proper education training for all exceptional children who are not enrolled in classes or schools maintained and operated by school districts or who are not otherwise provided for."** The district court found that the student was an exceptional child covered by the statute. Since he could not receive a "proper education" in the public school, because of his need to be with his brothers and friends, the court ruled that the local IU was required to provide the student with a proper education at the parochial school—which included the requested special services. The court granted the requested injunction. *John T. et al v. The Delaware County Intermediate Unit et al.*, 2000 U.S. Dist. LEXIS 6169 (E.D. Pa. 2000).

◆   The parents of a student with attention deficit hyperactivity disorder sued the student's parochial school, claiming the school violated § 504 of the Rehabilitation Act by failing to accommodate the student's disability. The school filed a motion to dismiss the suit, claiming it was not a recipient of federal funds under the Rehabilitation Act. **A federal district court denied the school's motion to dismiss, finding the school was a recipient of federal funds through grants it received from the local school board.** Accordingly, the suit could proceed. *Dupre, et al. v. The Roman Catholic Church of the Diocese of Houma-Thibodaux et al.,* 1999 U.S. Dist. LEXIS 13799 (E.D. La. 1999).

◆   A sixth grade student attending regular education classes at a private school in Puerto Rico was indefinitely suspended for serious disciplinary violations. He frequently disrupted classes, used obscenities, fought with other students and walked out of classes. The school's headmaster estimated that he spent 30 percent of his time dealing with the student's behavior problems. Following the suspension, the student's family had a psychologist examine the student. The student was diagnosed as having oppositional defiant disorder, childhood depression and attention deficit hyperactivity disorder. The family filed a federal district court action against the school for violations of the Americans with Disabilities Act (ADA) and the Rehabilitation Act. The court required the school to readmit the student. **The student's disruptive behavior continued when he returned to school, and**

school officials refused to re-enroll him for the seventh grade. The family brought a contempt motion which the district court denied. However, the court extended the order requiring the school to enroll the student in seventh grade and alter its disciplinary code with respect to the student.

The school appealed to the U.S. Court of Appeals, First Circuit, where it argued that the district court had erroneously ordered the student's reinstatement. **The court agreed, noting that the ADA does not require educational institutions to fundamentally alter their programs. The school was not required to suspend the application of its disciplinary code to accommodate the student**. Since the ADA did not require the school to fundamentally modify its program, and there was significant evidence that the student did not conform his behavior to the code, the district court should not have ordered the school to enroll the student. *Bercovitch v. Baldwin School, Inc.*, 133 F.3d 141 (1st Cir.1998).

♦   Boston University, one of the largest private universities in the U.S., gained a reputation as a leader in providing comprehensive services to students with learning disabilities. It established a program of accommodation that included in-class notetakers, extra time for tests and course substitutions for required classes in foreign languages and mathematics. Prior to the 1995-1996 school year, a university administrator determined that course substitutions should cease immediately based on his belief that "hundreds of thousands of children" were improperly diagnosed as having learning disabilities and that the requested accommodations threatened the university's academic integrity. **During the academic year, several students were forced to substantiate their learning disabilities**, and three of them were required to undergo retesting for disabilities shortly before their final examinations. **Other students were informed that course substitutions for required classes in mathematics and foreign languages were no longer possible**. The university took these actions despite the lack of a written policy on the retesting of admitted students with disabilities. Some students received conflicting versions of the university's new requirements from administrators. The university then reorganized its learning disabilities support services office and revised certain academic policies.

A number of university students with attention deficit hyperactivity disorder, attention deficit disorder, and other disorders filed a federal district court action against the university under the Americans with Disabilities Act (ADA), § 504 of the Rehabilitation Act and analogous state laws, seeking declaratory and injunctive relief and compensatory damages for discrimination. The court found evidence of discrimination in the administrator's outspoken public stance, which expressed doubt about the legitimacy of requests for accommodations by students with learning disabilities. It also found that **the university's inconsistent policies had a discriminatory effect on some students**, in particular the three who had been forced to undergo retesting just prior to their academic examinations. **The university could not lawfully impose requirements that unnecessarily screened out persons with disabilities**. The three students were entitled to recover their reevaluation costs plus additional amounts for emotional distress. **The class was entitled to certain requested injunctive relief, including the cessation of the required retests for students with learning disorders where they already had current evaluations by qualified evaluators**. The university was ordered to propose a deliberative procedure for considering modification of its policy for course substitution in foreign languages, but not mathematics. *Guckenberger v. Boston Univ.*, 974 F.Supp. 106 (D.Mass.1997).

◆   A Missouri elementary school student suffered from severe asthma which was determined to be potentially life threatening. Her doctor discovered that exposure to some scents and some animals triggered her asthma. The student attended a private, Catholic school through the fifth grade and the school provided a voluntary scent-free classroom for the student. However, **when the student reached the sixth grade, her mother demanded that the school provide a mandatory, rather than voluntary scent-free environment**, prohibiting the wearing of all perfumes and colognes, among other accommodations. School officials met with the student's doctor, who informed them that the student's condition required a mandatory scent-free classroom. After the meeting, **the officials determined that they could not provide such an environment at the school and notified the student that she would no longer be able to attend**. The student sued the school in a Missouri federal district court, alleging that it had violated § 504 of the Rehabilitation Act, which prohibits discrimination because of disability.

The district court first determined that because the private school received federal funds through Title I and the National School Lunch Program and School Breakfast Program, it was subject to the dictates of the Rehabilitation Act. The court also determined that the student was a handicapped individual under the act because of her asthma and because the school regarded her as having an impairment. However, **the court then found that the student was not otherwise qualified because she could not succeed despite all appropriate accommodations**. The regulations interpreting the Rehabilitation Act did not require private schools to make reasonable accommodations for students. Rather, **the school was only required to make a minor adjustment to accommodate her**. The voluntary scent-free classroom more than met the definition of a minor adjustment. Because the school met its responsibilities under the Rehabilitation Act, and because the school's accommodation was not sufficient to safeguard the health of the student, she was not otherwise qualified to attend. The court entered judgment for the school. *Hunt v. St. Peter School*, 963 F.Supp. 843 (W.D.Mo.1997).

For additional cases involving private schools and students with disabilities, see Chapter Twelve.

IV. PUBLIC AND PRIVATE SCHOOL COOPERATION

Any cooperation between public and private schools must pass stringent constitutional examination. Cooperative efforts must avoid the appearance of government approval of religion and must not constitute government aid to, or excessive entanglement with, religious organizations. Several U.S. Supreme Court cases address a variety of cooperative efforts, particularly in the area of direct government payments to private schools.

A. Textbook Loans and Other Materials

◆   The provision of textbooks by the state to private and parochial school students is permissible under the First Amendment. In *Cochran v. Louisiana State Bd. of Educ.*, 281 U.S. 370, 50 S.Ct. 335, 74 L.Ed.2d 1929 (1930), the U.S. Supreme Court upheld a state law which authorized the purchasing and supplying of textbooks to all school children, including parochial school children, on the basis of what is now called the "child benefit" doctrine. **The Court held that the textbook loan statute was constitutional because the legislature's purpose in enacting the statute was to benefit children and their parents, not religious schools**.

◆   Nearly 40 years later, the U.S. Supreme Court reaffirmed the validity of the child benefit doctrine in a case involving a New York textbook loan statute. This statute required local school districts to lend textbooks free of charge to all children in grades seven through twelve. Parochial school students were included. The Court observed that the textbooks loaned to parochial school children were the same nonreligious textbooks used in the public schools. **The loaning of textbooks was permissible here because the parochial school students used them for secular study**. Thus, there was no state involvement in religious training. The state of New York was merely providing a secular benefit to all school children *Bd. of Educ. v. Allen*, 392 U.S. 236, 88 S.Ct. 1923, 20 L.Ed.2d 1060 (1968).

◆   In 1973, the U.S. Supreme Court ruled that **private schools with racially discriminatory admissions policies may not benefit from textbook loan programs**. This ruling was based on the principle that the state may not give assistance to acts of racial discrimination. Textbooks were "a basic educational tool," said the Court, and to permit racially discriminatory private schools to benefit from state textbook loans would be to allow the state to accomplish indirectly what it could not accomplish directly: a state-funded racially segregated school system. *Norwood v. Harrison*, 413 U.S. 455, 93 S.Ct. 2804, 37 L.Ed.2d 723 (1973).

◆   Also in 1973, the U.S. Supreme Court struck down another form of state funding of instructional services. The case involved a New York program which granted annual lump-sum disbursements to parochial schools to help pay the costs of administering state-required student testing and record keeping activities. The tests, which were prepared by parochial school personnel, were characterized by the U.S. Supreme Court as "an integral part of the teaching process." **The Court concluded that it was likely that the tests would, "unconsciously or otherwise, ... inculcate students in the religious precepts of the sponsoring church."** *Levitt v. Comm. for Pub. Educ. & Religious Liberty*, 413 U.S. 472, 93 S.Ct. 2814, 37 L.Ed.2d 736 (1973).

◆   However, the New York legislature responded to the *Levitt* decision by reenacting the reimbursements for teacher-prepared tests but adding a requirement that the funds be audited to ensure that no state subsidizing of religion would occur. The U.S. Supreme Court upheld the plan and found that **the state audits did not excessively entangle the state in the affairs of parochial schools**. *Comm. for Pub. Educ. & Religious Liberty v. Regan*, 444 U.S. 646, 100 S.Ct. 840, 63 L.Ed.2d 94 (1980).

♦   **A group of Louisiana citizens sued the Jefferson Parish School Board in 1985 for violating the First Amendment, alleging that the board improperly provided Chapter Two funds to parochial schools to acquire library materials and media equipment.** The group asserted that expenditures for books, computers, software and other audiovisual equipment violated the Establishment Clause, since 41 of the 46 participating private schools were religiously affiliated. The district court agreed, granting summary judgment to the group because the funding failed the religious advancement test from *Lemon v. Kurtzman*, 403 U.S. 602 (1971). The court held that the loan of materials to sectarian schools constituted direct government aid under *Meek v. Pittenger*, 421 U.S. 349 (1975), and *Wolman v. Walter*, 433 U.S. 229 (1977). Two years later, the district court reversed itself in post-judgment activity, citing the intervening U.S. Supreme Court decision in *Zobrest v. Catalina Foothills School District*, 509 U.S. 1 (1993). The citizens appealed to the U.S. Court of Appeals, Fifth Circuit, which also held that the Chapter Two grants were unconstitutional under *Meek* and *Wolman*. The U.S. Supreme Court agreed to review the decision.

The court stated that it has consistently applied the principle of neutrality in funding cases, upholding aid that is offered to a broad range of recipients without regard to religion. According to the Court, the issue was not one of diversion of public assistance for religious use, but whether the assistance itself had an impermissible religious content. **Where assistance was suitable for use in public schools, it was also suitable for private school use. The court found less concern for attributing religious indoctrination to the government where its assistance lacked any specific content.** Applying this reasoning, the court found no basis for ruling that the school board's use of Chapter Two funds had the effect of advancing religion. The use of Chapter Two funds by private schools did not result in government indoctrination because eligibility was determined on a neutral basis and through private choices by parents. **Chapter Two had no impermissible content and did not define its recipients by reference to religion.** The distribution of Chapter Two funds did not create an improper incentive for parents to select religious schools for their children. A broad array of schools was eligible for assistance without regard to religious affiliation. **The program was neutral with regard to religion, and private decision making controlled the allocation of funds to private schools.** Students who attended schools receiving Chapter Two funds were the ultimate beneficiaries of the assistance, even though the schools used the funds to purchase computers, software, books and other equipment. The court upheld the board's use of Chapter Two funding and held that the parish did not need to exclude sectarian schools from its program. *Mitchell v. Helms*, 530 U.S. 793, 120 S.Ct. 2530, 147 L.Ed.2d 660 (2000).

♦   A 1997 Wisconsin law created the Technology for Education Achievement (TEACH) Board, which administered the Education Telecommunications Access program. **The TEACH board approved access for data lines and video links under a heavily subsidized program in which both public and private schools participated.** A taxpayer group objected to the program on constitutional grounds because $58,873 of the program's annual total of over $1.9 million was awarded to nine religiously affiliated Wisconsin schools and private colleges. The taxpayers filed a federal district court action against state education officials, including the

TEACH board. The court held that the program as a whole did not violate the Constitution, but found that unrestricted cash grants to private, sectarian schools violated the Establishment Clause's prohibition on state support of religion.

The parties appealed unfavorable aspects of the decision to the Seventh Circuit. The taxpayers dismissed their appeal concerning the constitutionality of the full program in view of the U.S. Supreme Court's intervening decision in *Mitchell v. Helms*, above. The Seventh Circuit proceeded to the question of grants to religious schools under the Wisconsin law, noting that the test for evaluating the constitutionality of private school funding remains the one devised by the Supreme Court in *Lemon v. Kurtzman*, 403 U.S. 602 (1971), as modified by *Agostini v. Felton*, 521 U.S. 203 (1997). The *Agostini* court relied upon the three primary criteria of the *Lemon* test by evaluating whether government aid has the effect of advancing religion, but casting the inquiry somewhat differently. The Seventh Circuit summarized the *Agostini* inquiry as asking whether the program or statute results in governmental indoctrination, defines its recipients by reference to religion or creates excessive entanglement between the government and religion. The court sought to resolve the question of whether the cash grants to the religious schools directly advanced religion. **The Wisconsin law violated the third *Agostini* criteria, because in the absence of any restriction on the expenditure of public funds by the schools, the expenditures had a primary effect that advanced religion**. The subsidies could easily be used for maintenance, chapels, religious instruction, or connection time to view religious websites. The law did not bar schools from using the grants for these and other constitutionally impermissible purposes. Because direct aid from the government to a sectarian institution in any form is invalid, the court affirmed the district court's finding that the provision of direct subsidies to religious schools was unconstitutional. *Freedom From Religion Foundation Inc. v Bugher*, 249 F.3d 606 (7th Cir. 2001).

B. Transportation

◆   The principle that transportation may be provided to parochial school students without violating the First Amendment was established in a 1947 U.S. Supreme Court case. This case involved a New Jersey law that allowed reimbursement to parents of children attending nonprofit religious schools for costs incurred by the children in using public transportation to travel to and from school. The law's purpose was to provide transportation expenses for all school children regardless of where they attended school, as long as the school was nonprofit. The Court analogized free transportation to other state benefits such as police and fire protection, connections for sewage disposal, and public roads and sidewalks, which also benefited parochial school children. **It was not the purpose of the First Amendment to cut off religious institutions from all government benefits. Rather, the state was only required to be neutral toward religion**. *Everson v. Bd. of Educ.*, 330 U.S. 1, 67 S.Ct. 504, 91 L.Ed.2d 711 (1947).

However, use of state funds to reimburse private schools for transportation for field trips was declared unconstitutional by the U.S. Supreme Court in *Wolman v. Walter*, above. There was no way public officials could monitor the field trips to assure that they had a secular purpose. Even if monitoring by the state *was* feasible, the monitoring would be so extensive that the state would become entangled in religion to an impermissible degree.

◆   Under Wisconsin law, public high school districts must provide private school students with transportation to and from their schools. Elementary districts may elect to provide those services instead of the high schools. One of the methods elementary districts may use to provide transportation is by contracting directly with the parents/guardians of students. The parents of students who attended Providence Catholic School contracted with the public elementary districts to provide transportation and were paid by the public districts. The parents then turned the transportation money over to Providence, which used the money to pay for buses. When the amount provided to the parents became less than the cost of providing transportation, Providence requested additional money from the districts. When this request for additional money was refused, the parents filed an action in state court, seeking various forms of relief, including an injunction requiring the public districts to provide transportation to the parochial school. The trial court denied various motions brought by the parties, and appeals followed. After concluding the trial court had jurisdiction over the dispute and resolving several other procedural matters, **the appeals court concluded that the public districts were statutorily allowed to contract with the parents of private school students regarding transportation**. The parents' assertion that state law barred these contracts and required the provision of transportation services was rejected, as state law gave the public districts assorted options for providing transportation to private school students. One of these options was contracting directly with the parents. *Providence Catholic School et al. v. Bristol Sch. Dist. No. 1 et al.,* 231 Wis.2d 159, 605 N.W.2d 238 (Wis. App. 1999).

◆   The Jefferson County, Kentucky, Fiscal Court passed a resolution that provided for busing of private and parochial school children paid for by transportation subsidies. The subsidies were paid directly to the local board of education, not to the schools. A resident and taxpayer challenged the resolution, arguing that it illegally aided private and parochial schools. The Supreme Court of Kentucky noted that **the resolution in its intended and practical application provided safe transportation for elementary school children attending nonpublic schools. The children constituted the primary beneficiaries of the subsidies**. Any incidental benefit to the nonpublic schools did not make the resolution illegal. The funds allocated under its provisions flowed directly to the providers of the transportation, thus providing only an indirect, remote or incidental benefit to the nonpublic schools. *Neal v. Fiscal Court, Jefferson County, Kentucky,* 986 S.W.2d 907 (Ky.1999).

◆   For six years, a West Virginia school board provided transportation for children residing within the county to a private, religious school in a nearby county. The school district then began to experience severe financial difficulties, and eliminated a number of activities and jobs including two bus driver positions. The district could no longer afford to transport students to the private school. **Thirty-two students were affected by this decision and the father of two of them requested that the board either resume bus service to the private school or furnish a**

stipend for their transportation costs. The board refused and the father sought a court order from the Supreme Court of Appeals of West Virginia to compel the board to provide transportation or a stipend. The father argued that because the board had transported the students for six years, it could not later withdraw the service without violating his equal protection and religious freedom rights. **The court held that the board had no legal duty to transport the students, and had not acted arbitrarily or capriciously in terminating its discretionary bus service for private school students**. It had withdrawn the service as a response to extreme financial difficulties and had also been forced to cut many other services and job positions. Because the father had failed to present any evidence contradicting the board's financial difficulties, the court denied the requested order. *State of West Virginia v. Bd. of Educ. of Summers County*, 478 S.E.2d 341 (W.Va.1996).

◆   A Massachusetts school district provided transportation to students who attended private schools located in a neighboring district. However, the district voted to discontinue this service during the 1991-1992 school year. The school district also declined to provide transportation to any student attending a public school outside the district. Although the private schools were located within a regional vocational school district, that district refused to transport the students. The parents filed suit in a Massachusetts superior court seeking to compel one of the districts to provide transportation to the private school. The superior court granted summary judgment to the school districts, and the parents appealed to the Appeals Court of Massachusetts, Worcester. The parents contended that the school committees were obligated to provide transportation to all students who attended private schools outside school district boundaries located no further than the public school they were entitled to attend. The appeals court disagreed. **School committees were generally obligated to provide such transportation to students attending an approved private school within the boundaries of the school district. A school committee must also provide transportation to private school students outside the school district if it provides such transportation to public school students**. Here, since the committee did not provide transportation to students attending public schools outside the district, it was not required to provide transportation to the private school children. Further, none of the children were enrolled in a private school with a comparable vocational curriculum. Consequently, the regional vocational school committee was not obligated to provide the students with transportation. *Garon v. Dudley-Charlton Reg'l School Comm.*, 633 N.E.2d 1051 (Mass.App. 1994).

C. Personnel Sharing

◆   Title I of the Elementary and Secondary Education Act of 1965 provides federal funding through the states to local educational agencies for remedial education, guidance and job counseling to at-risk students and students residing in low-income areas. **Title I requires that funding be made available for all eligible students, including those attending private schools**. Local agencies retain control over Title I funds and materials. The New York City Board of Education attempted to implement Title I programs at parochial schools by allowing public employees to instruct students on private school grounds during school hours. The U.S. Supreme

Court agreed with a group of taxpayers that this violated the Establishment Clause in *Aguilar v. Felton*, 473 U.S. 402, 105 S.Ct. 3232, 87 L.Ed.2d 290 (1985).

On remand, **a federal district court ordered the city board to refrain from using Title I funds for any plan or program under which public school teachers and counselors appeared on sectarian school grounds**. In response to *Aguilar*, local education boards modified their Title I programs by moving classes to remote sites including mobile instructional units parked near sectarian schools. However, a new group of parents and parochial school students filed motions seeking relief from the permanent order.

The district court denied the motions and the U.S. Court of Appeals, Second Circuit, affirmed the decision. On further appeal, the U.S. Supreme Court agreed with the city board and students that recent Supreme Court decisions required a new ruling on the question of government aid to religious schools. For example, the provision of a sign language interpreter by a school district at a private school was upheld in *Zobrest v. Catalina Foothills School Dist.*, 509 U.S. 1 (1993), see Chapter Twelve, § III. The Court held that it would no longer presume that the presence of a public school teacher on parochial school grounds creates an unconstitutional symbolic union between church and state. The provision of Title I services at parochial schools resembled the provision of the sign language interpreter in *Zobrest* under the Individuals with Disabilities Education Act. **New York City's Title I program was constitutionally permissible because it did not result in government indoctrination, define funding recipients by reference to religion or create excessive entanglement** between education officials and religious schools. The Court reversed the lower court judgments. *Agostini v. Felton*, 521 U.S. 203, 117 S.Ct. 1997, 138 L.Ed.2d 391 (1997).

◆   In *Lemon v. Kurtzman*, the U.S. Supreme Court invalidated Rhode Island and Pennsylvania statutes that provided state money to finance the operation of parochial schools. **The Rhode Island statute provided a 15 percent salary supplement to parochial school teachers who taught nonreligious subjects also offered in the public schools using only public school teaching materials. The Pennsylvania statute authorized payment of state funds to parochial schools to help defray the cost of teachers' salaries, textbooks and other instructional materials**. Reimbursement was limited, however, to the costs of secular subjects that were also taught in the public schools. Applying a three-part test to the two state programs in question, the Court held that the legislative purpose of the programs was a legitimate, secular concern with maintaining high educational standards in both public and private schools. "First, the statute must have a secular legislative purpose; second, its principal or primary effect must be one that neither advances nor inhibits religion, ... finally, the statute must not foster 'an excessive government entanglement with religion." The Court did not reach the second inquiry under the three-part test because it concluded that the state programs failed to pass muster under the third inquiry.

The Rhode Island salary supplement program excessively entangled the state with religion because of the highly religious nature of the Roman Catholic parochial schools that were the primary beneficiaries of the program. The teachers who received the salary supplements provided instruction in classrooms and buildings containing religious symbols such as crucifixes. Similar defects were found in the Pennsylvania program. The Court also observed that in order to ensure that the state-funded parochial school teachers did not inject religious dogma into their instruction, the state would be forced to extensively monitor the parochial school classrooms. This would result in excessive state entanglement with religion. Consequently, the salary supplement programs were held to violate the First Amendment. *Lemon v. Kurtzman*, 403 U.S. 602, 91 S.Ct. 2105, 29 L.Ed.2d 745 (1971).

D. School Facilities and Property

◆   The Michigan Economic Development Corporation Act was enacted to allevi- ate unemployment by encouraging and assisting local industrial and commercial endeavors. The statute created "economic development corporations" in each of the state's municipalities, which are authorized to borrow money and issue revenue bonds to finance various construction and improvement projects. In 1995, the Academy of Sacred Heart sought tax-exempt bond financing from the EDC of Oakland County. The school was interested in constructing an addition to one of its buildings, renovating its science wing and revamping other resources. **The EDC approved financing for the project. To do so, it issued revenue bonds and loaned the $3.5 million in bond proceeds to the academy**. The EDC bonds were exempt from taxes, which resulted in a fairly low interest rate on the school's loan. A local taxpayer objected to the loan and asserted that it injured taxpayers because the bond's tax-exempt status deprived the Michigan treasury of approximately $64,400 in additional revenue. The taxpayer filed a suit claiming the loan to the academy violated the Establishment Clause, but a federal district court granted summary judgment to the EDC. The taxpayer appealed to the U.S. Court of Appeals, Sixth Circuit.

The Sixth Circuit examined the taxpayer's Establishment Clause claim and rejected his initial assertion that any state aid to sectarian elementary and secondary schools is unconstitutional. The circuit court also discredited the argument that a tax exemption is equivalent to a direct subsidy. The court then examined the Economic Development Corporation Act under the *Lemon* test. The circuit court found the act passed all three prongs of the *Lemon* test. The statute clearly had a secular purpose in stimulating the local economy and inhibiting unemployment. It neither hindered nor advanced religion because the EDC financed many projects for non-religiously affiliated organizations under the same criteria. In addition, the loan only covered renovation of secular school resources. Lastly, **since the Academy of Sacred Heart has a non-religious educational purpose and the loan was used for secular improvements, the issuance of the tax-exempt bonds in this case did not create excessive government entanglement with religion**. The Sixth Circuit concluded that neither the Economic Development Corporation Act nor the issuance of tax-exempt bonds on behalf of the school violated the Establishment Clause. The district court's grant of summary judgment to the EDC was affirmed. *Johnson v. Economic Development Corporation of the County of Oakland*, 241 F.3d 501 (6th Cir. 2001).

◆   Under a Montgomery County, Maryland, zoning ordinance, all businesses and organizations must obtain a special exception in order to build a non-residential structure on land designated for residential use. The county's appeals board will only grant a petition for special exception after determining, through a public hearing, that the new building will not disrupt the surrounding community. **The ordinance exempts lots owned or leased by religious organizations from having to obtain a special exception**. The U.S. District Court for the District of Maryland examined the constitutionality of the exemption after residential neighbors of the Connelly School of the Holy Child, a parochial school, objected to the school's construction of a new building. The district court found the exemption unconstitutional under the test established in *Lemon v. Kurtzman*, 403 U.S. 602 (1971), because it favored religious schools over other nonprofit schools and constituted an excessive government entanglement with religion.

The Connelly School appealed the district court decision to the Fourth Circuit. The circuit court applied the *Lemon* test and found that **the exemption met the first prong of the test because it had the secular purpose of allowing the county to prevent government interference with the religious mission of various organizations** and avoided creating a forum during special exception hearings in which anti-religious views might be expressed. The exemption also satisfied the second prong of the *Lemon* test because it neither advanced nor inhibited religion. The county merely relieved religious schools from the burden of applying for a special exception. "Any advancement of religion that follows would be the result of the religious schools' own acts in light of the exemption," according to the court. Finally, the circuit court found that the third prong was satisfied because the exemption did not foster an excessive entanglement with religion. This part of the *Lemon* test is confined to cases where direct financial subsidies are paid to parochial schools. Because all three prongs of the Lemon test were satisfied, the ordinance was deemed constitutional, as it did not violate the Establishment Clause. The district court decision was reversed. *Renzi et al. v. Connelly School of the Holy Child Inc.*, 224 F.3d 283 (4th Cir. 2000).

◆   For 20 years, a New York school district transported students from an elementary school to released time religious classes at a local church. The district also leased buses to the church at a fair market rate for transportation of the students to church. **The board then adopted guidelines for released time religious education under which it discontinued the leasing of buses for students being transported from public schools to the church**. The church filed a declaratory judgment action in a New York trial court, seeking an order that the change in policy violated state law, the New York Constitution and the U.S. Constitution. The New York Supreme Court, Madison County, considered the church's summary judgment motion. The district argued that it could not lease its buses to an entirely religious entity. The church maintained that it was entitled to lease buses under a state statute allowing districts in rural counties to lease buses to nonprofit organizations for educational purposes. Accordingly, the failure to continue leasing buses constituted discrimination on the basis of religion. **The court agreed with the church, finding that it was a nonprofit organization engaged in education**. No state funds were provided to the church, and the arrangement did not advance religion in any way. Refusal to rent buses to the church would violate the Establishment Clause by treating the church differently from nonreligious entities. *St. James Church v. Bd. of Educ. of the Cazenovia Central School Dist.*, 621 N.Y.S.2d 486 (N.Y. Sup.– Madison County 1994).

◆   The Los Angeles Community College District sought to generate additional revenue by sale or lease of its surplus real property. Notice of a surplus land sale was given with a listed minimum price, but no offers were received and the property was not sold. The district then mailed notices to people on its real property mailing list of its intention to lease the property. During the bidding process, only one bid was received by the district, which it accepted. **A religious organization agreed to pay over $3 million for 75 years and planned to develop a temple, meeting rooms and housing during the term of the lease**. A homeowner's organization sought to invalidate the lease and sued in a California trial court, asserting that the lease would involve the district in the unconstitutional establishment of a religious enterprise. The trial court upheld the lease, and the homeowners appealed to the California Court of Appeal, Second District. The court of appeal noted that the primary purpose of the district's lease was secular. Also, **there was no evidence that the lease resulted in government sponsorship or promotion of the organization's religious objectives**. Both religious and secular groups had received an equal opportunity to obtain the government benefit of the long-term lease. The court held that the administrative power of the district over the religious organization did not create an impermissible entanglement in the organization's religious affairs. The court affirmed the trial court's decision. *Woodland Hills Homeowners Organization v. Los Angeles Community College Dist.*, 266 Cal.Rptr. 767 (Cal.App.2d Dist. 1990).

E. Release Time Programs

The courts generally will uphold release time programs only where the religious education takes place off public school grounds.

◆   **The first type of release time program to be declared unconstitutional by the U.S. Supreme Court was a Champaign, Illinois, program in which public school students were given religious instruction in public schools**. Although the groups supplied the religious education teachers at no cost to the school district, the superintendent of schools exercised supervisory powers over them. A taxpayer in the Champaign school district sued the school board claiming that the release time program violated the Establishment Clause of the First Amendment. The U.S. Supreme Court agreed. "This is beyond all question a utilization of the tax-established and tax-supported public school system to aid religious groups," said the Court. "[T]he First Amendment has erected a wall between Church and State which must be kept high and impregnable." *McCollum v. Bd. of Educ.*, 333 U.S. 203, 68 S.Ct. 461, 92 L.Ed.2d 649 (1948).

◆   However, four years later the U.S. Supreme Court upheld a different kind of release time program. In this New York program, **students could be released from public school classes during the school day for a few hours in order to attend religious education classes**. However, unlike the program in the *McCollum* case, students in the New York release time program received their religious instruction off the public school grounds. Church officials made out weekly attendance reports and sent the reports to public school officials, who then checked to assure that the released students had actually reported for their off-school-grounds religious instruction. **The Court approved the New York program largely because the** religious instruction took place off school grounds. **There was no religious indoctrination taking place in the public school buildings nor was there any expenditure of public funds on behalf of religious training**. Also, there was no evidence of any subtle or overt coercion exerted by any public school officials to induce students to attend the religious classes. The public schools were merely accommodating religion, not aiding it. The Court declined to invalidate the New York release time program, saying, "We cannot read into the Bill of Rights such a philosophy of hostility to religion." *Zorach v. Clauson*, 343 U.S. 306, 72 S.Ct. 679, 96 L.Ed.2d 954 (1952).

V.   STUDENT FINANCIAL ASSISTANCE

The most common forms of state financial assistance to private school students include grants, loans, and tax credits or deductions. In order to be constitutionally permissible, the financial assistance must seek to primarily benefit the students, not their schools. Additionally, federal funding of programs and activities requires compliance with federal statutes such as Title VI, Title IX, the Rehabilitation Act, the Americans with Disabilities Act and the Age Discrimination in Employment Act. Thus, students receiving Basic Educational Opportunity Grants, National Direct Student Loans, and other federal grants will be deemed to be receiving assistance for federal law purposes. A recent trend in education involving financial assistance to students has been the enactment of voucher programs, which provide state funds to public school students who choose to attend private schools. For cases involving these programs, see Chapter II, Section IV.

◆   Maryland's Joseph A. Selinger program gives public aid to private colleges within the state. Qualifying colleges receive direct annual payments from the state to be used for secular purposes. In 1990, Columbia Union College applied for Selinger funds, but the Maryland Higher Education Commission denied the application because it believed the college was too sectarian. A few years later, the school sought reconsideration of its application in view of *Rosenberger v. Rector and Visitors of the University of Virginia*, 515 U.S. 819 (1995), which emphasized the importance of neutral criteria in determining eligibility for public aid. The commission maintained that it would continue rejecting the school's application. In 1996, **Columbia Union applied for Selinger aid to specifically fund its math, computer science, clinical laboratory science, respiratory care and nursing programs, but again the request was denied**. The school filed suit in federal district court, alleging constitutional and statutory violations. The district court ruled in favor of the commission. On appeal, the U.S. Court of Appeals, Fourth Circuit, reversed and remanded, finding that although *Roemer* was the appropriate reasoning to follow, there was an issue of material fact as to whether Columbia Union is "pervasively sectarian." The district court then conducted a lengthy bench trial and concluded Columbia Union was not pervasively sectarian, therefore it was eligible for Selinger funds.

The commission appealed, arguing that the district court wrongly concluded the school was not pervasively sectarian. Columbia Union countered that whether an institution is pervasively sectarian is no longer relevant when determining an institution's eligibility for public aid, in light of *Mitchell v. Helms*, 530 U.S. 793 (2000). In *Mitchell*, the Supreme Court upheld the constitutionality of a state aid program that helped parochial schools acquire computers, televisions, and laboratory equipment. The Supreme Court used the test outlined in *Agostini v. Felton*, 521 U.S. 203 (1997), examining whether the program had a secular purpose and whether it had the primary effect of inhibiting or advancing religion. The Fourth Circuit evaluated the case under both the *Mitchell* and *Roemer* analyses. Under *Mitchell*, **the panel reasoned that giving Selinger funds to Columbia Union had a secular purpose and did not advance religion because the program stipulates that the aid must be used for secular purposes**. The program's requirement that the funds be used for secular purposes adequately safeguards against the school diverting the funds for religious purposes in the future, the circuit court determined. Under *Roemer*'s "pervasively sectarian" analysis, the panel reaffirmed that it was not unconstitutional to give Selinger funds to Columbia Union. According to the district court, although Columbia Union had a mandatory worship policy, it applied only to a minority of students. The lower court also reasoned that the college's traditional liberal arts classes were not taught with the primary objective of religious indoctrination. Although the district court noted the Seventh-day Adventist Church had a strong influence over college affairs and the college preferred to hire and admit members of that faith, these factors by themselves were not enough to make the college pervasively sectarian. Relying on the district court's conclusions, the Fourth Circuit determined that Columbia Union passed the *Roemer* analysis. *Columbia Union College v. Oliver et al.*, 254 F.3d 496 (4th Cir. 2001).

◆   **The Arizona legislature passed a bill authorizing a $500 tax credit for charitable contributions to school tuition organizations**. A school tuition organization was defined as a charitable entity that allocated at least 90 percent of its revenue to educational scholarships or tuition grants to allow students to attend any qualified school selected by their parents. The statute also established a tax credit of $200 for parents of public school students who paid extracurricular fees. A group of organizations and individuals challenged the $500 credit, claiming it violated the federal and Arizona constitutions.

The Arizona Supreme Court applied the *Lemon* test to the tax credit and concluded it was constitutional. **The credit had a secular purpose of facilitating the state's overall educational goals**. Encouraging private school attendance was characterized as a part of the state's recent expansion of educational options, such as charter schools and open enrollment. **The tax credit did not have the primary effect of furthering sectarian schools**, as it was only one of many credits available to taxpayers under the state code. The credit did not directly benefit private schools because any benefit to such institutions relied on the intervening choices of individual parents. The court also rejected the plaintiffs' assertion that the credit violated the Arizona constitution. *Kotterman v. Killian*, 193 Ariz. 273, 972 P.2d 606 (Ariz. 1999).

◆   The parents of three Georgia students enrolled in nonsectarian private schools filed suit in state court against the state, the Board of Education and others for the enforcement of the state Tuition Grant Act. The act provided for direct grants of money, under specified conditions, to the parents of students attending grades K-12 in nonsectarian private schools. **The parents alleged that they were denied these grants which, in turn, denied them the equal protection of the law** since students in pre-kindergarten and post-12th grade programs at private schools had state funds available to them. The parents requested that the court order the defendants to implement and enforce the act. The defendants filed a dismissal motion which the trial court granted and the parents appealed to the Supreme Court of Georgia.

The supreme court noted that to establish an equal protection claim, a plaintiff must show that he or she is similarly situated to members of the class who are treated differently. Although the two groups in this case were treated differently with regard to educational funding, they were not similarly situated. Children in K-12 had a constitutional right to an education at state expense and were required to attend school. However, the group of children in pre-kindergarten and post-12th grade had no constitutional right to education and were not required to be enrolled in educational programs. Public education for the K-12 students was supported by taxation but the funding for the other students resulted not only from taxation but also from lottery proceeds. **The court held that the disparate entitlements and obligations of the two groups prevented them from being similarly situated**. It refused to grant the writ and affirmed the trial court's decision. *Lowe v. State of Georgia*, 482 S.E.2d 344 (Ga.1997).

◆   A private, not-for-profit technical school in Indiana participated in the Guaranteed Student Loan (GSL) program authorized by Title IV of the Higher Education Act. **The program required the school to make refunds to the lender if a student withdrew from school during a term**. If the school failed to refund loans to the lender, the student would be liable for the full amount of the loan. The treasurer of the school conferred with the school's owners and initiated a practice of not making GSL refunds. As a result, the school owed $139,649 in refunds. After the school lost its accreditation, a federal grand jury indicted the treasurer for "knowingly and willfully misapplying" federally insured student loan funds in violation of 20 U.S.C. § 1097(a). A federal district court dismissed the indictment because it lacked an allegation that the treasurer intended to injure or defraud the United States. The U.S. Court of Appeals, Seventh Circuit, reinstated the prosecution, and the U.S. Supreme Court granted review. The Supreme Court held that § 1097(a) did not require the specific intent to injure or defraud. **If the government can prove that the defendant misapplied Title IV funds knowingly and willfully, that is sufficient to show a violation of § 1097(a)**. The Court affirmed the court of appeals' decision to reinstate the prosecution against the treasurer. *Bates v. U.S.*, 522 U.S. 23, 118 S.Ct. 285, 139 L.Ed.2d 215 (1997).

◆   A provision of Title IV of the Higher Education Act, 20 USC 1091b(a), requires college and post-secondary vocational training schools that receive federal funds for student financial aid programs to establish a fair and equitable policy for refunding unearned tuition and other costs when a student receiving such aid fails to enter or prematurely leaves the intended program. Subsection (b) declares that an institution's refund policy shall be considered fair and equitable if the refund is at least the largest of the amounts provided under state law, the institution's nationally recognized accrediting agency formula, or the statutorily described formula for pro rata refunds. **A regulation issued by the Secretary of Education—34 CFR § 668.22(b)(4)—provided that schools had to deduct "any unpaid charges owed by the student for the period of enrollment for which the student has been charged."** Former regulations had put the risk of student nonpayment on the government. A coalition of vocational training schools in New York sought a federal district court injunction against the operation of the regulation. The U.S. Court of Appeals, Second Circuit, stated that § 668.22(b)(4) represented a reasonable interpretation of the statute. *Coalition of New York State Career Schools Inc. v. Riley*, 129 F.3d 276 (2d Cir.1997).

◆   The U.S. Supreme Court unanimously ruled that the First Amendment to the U.S. Constitution did not prevent the state of Washington from providing financial assistance directly to a disabled individual attending a Christian college. The plaintiff, a blind person, sought vocational rehabilitative services from the Washington Commission for the Blind pursuant to state law. The law provided that visually impaired persons were eligible for educational assistance. However, **because the plaintiff was a student at a Christian college intending to pursue a career of service in the church, the Commission for the Blind denied him assistance**. The Washington Supreme Court upheld this decision on the ground that the First Amendment to the U.S. Constitution prohibited state funding of a student's educa-tion at a religious college. The U.S. Supreme Court took a less restrictive view of the First Amendment and reversed the Washington court. **The operation of Washington's program was such that the Commission for the Blind paid money directly to students, who could then attend the schools of their choice.** The fact that the student in this case chose to attend a religious college did not constitute state support of religion because "the decision to support religious education is made by the individual, not the state." The First Amendment was therefore not offended. *Witters v. Washington Dep't of Services for the Blind*, 474 U.S. 481, 106 S.Ct. 748, 88 L.Ed.2d 846 (1986).

On remand, the Washington Supreme Court reconsidered the matter under the Washington State Constitution, which is far stricter in its prohibition on the expenditure of public funds for religious instruction than the U.S. Constitution. **Vocational assistance funds for the student's religious education violated the state constitution because public money would be used for religious instruc-tion**. The commission's action was constitutional under the Free Exercise Clause because there was no infringement of the student's constitutional rights. The court reaffirmed its denial of state funding for the student's tuition. *Witters v. State Comm'n for the Blind*, 771 P.2d 1119 (Wash.1989).

◆   In 1973, the U.S. Supreme Court invalidated a New York program which: 1) provided $50-$100 in direct money grants to low income parents with children in private schools, and 2) authorized income tax credits of up to $1,000 for parents with children in private schools. **The program had the primary effect of advanc-ing religion and thus was constitutionally invalid. The Court characterized the tax credits as akin to tuition grants** and observed that they were really cash giveaways by the state on behalf of religious schools. *Committee for Public Educ. & Religious Liberty v. Nyquist*, 413 U.S. 756, 93 S.Ct. 2955, 37 L.Ed.2d 948 (1973).

❖   However, the U.S. Supreme Court upheld a Minnesota program which involved tax deductions (as opposed to tax credits) that were available to parents of public and private school children alike. The Minnesota program allowed state income tax deductions for tuition, nonreligious textbooks and transportation. In upholding the program, the Court observed that the state had a legitimate interest in assuring that all its citizens were well educated. Also, the tax deductions in question were only a few among many other deductions such as those for medical expenses or charitable contributions. Unlike the program in the *Nyquist* case, the Minnesota program was part of a bona fide income tax deduction system available to parents of all school children. The Court held that the First Amendment was not offended by the Minnesota tax deduction program. *Mueller v. Allen*, 463 U.S. 388, 103 S.Ct. 3062, 77 L.Ed.2d 721 (1983).

❖   In *Hunt v. McNair*, the U.S. Supreme Court upheld a South Carolina plan that allowed both private and public colleges to use the state's authority to borrow money at low interest rates. The case involved a Baptist college that used this money to finance the construction of a dining hall. The college had no religious test for either its faculty or students and the student body was only about 60 percent Baptist, the same percentage found in the surrounding community. The Court found that the college was not "pervaded by religion." Unlike the situation commonly found in K-12 parochial schools, religiously-affiliated colleges and universities are often not dominated by a religious atmosphere. The Court concluded that both the purpose and effect of the state's borrowing program was secular and thus constitutional. The argument that aid to one (secular) portion of a religious institution makes it free to spend more money on religious pursuits was rejected as unpersuasive and irrelevant. If that were the case, the Court noted that police and fire protection for religious schools would have to be cut off as well. *Hunt v. McNair*, 413 U.S. 734, 93 S.Ct. 2868, 37 L.Ed.2d 923 (1973).

❖   A 1971 case involved the federal Higher Education Facilities Act of 1963. This federal funding program offered assistance to both public and private colleges in constructing academic facilities. Although the program mandated that any building constructed with federal assistance be used by private colleges only for nonreligious purposes, it stated that after 20 years the buildings could be put to religious uses if the private college so desired. The U.S. Supreme Court upheld most of this program against constitutional challenges. The Court, however, invalidated the portion of the program that would have lifted the religious uses provision after 20 years. *Tilton v. Richardson,* 403 U.S. 672, 91 S.Ct. 2091, 29 L.Ed.2d 790 (1971).

❖   The state of Maryland enacted a program which authorized annual, noncategorical grants to religiously affiliated colleges. The program was challenged by taxpayers who alleged that state money was being put to religious uses by the schools, which had wide discretion in spending the funds. The U.S. Supreme Court began its analysis of the Maryland program with the following observation: "*Hunt v. McNair* requires (1) that no state aid at all go to institutions that are so 'pervasively sectarian' that secular activities cannot be separated from sectarian ones, and (2) that if secular activities *can* be separated out, they alone may be funded." The colleges involved in this case were not found to be pervasively sectarian even though they were affiliated with the Roman Catholic Church. **The Court held that the "secular side" of the colleges could be separated from the sectarian, and found that state aid had only gone to the colleges' secular side**. It was admittedly somewhat difficult to ensure that the colleges and the Maryland Council for Higher Education would take care to avoid spending state funds on religious activities, but the Court expressed its belief that those entities would spend the money in good faith and avoid violating the First Amendment. *Roemer v. Bd. of Pub. Works*, 426 U.S. 736, 96 S.Ct. 2337, 49 L.Ed.2d 179 (1976).

CHAPTER FOURTEEN

Interscholastic Athletics

I. HIGH SCHOOL ATHLETICS

Interscholastic high school athletics are regulated by state athletic associations, which impose eligibility, transfer and academic rules and standards upon participating schools and students. Schools and school districts typically have behavior and academic rules for student athletes that are stricter than those regulating the conduct of general student populations. Courts have upheld even-handed rules holding athletes to a higher standard of conduct due to the representative role played by student athletes and their diminished expectations of privacy.

A. Eligibility Rules

1. Drug Testing

Drug testing by urinalysis constitutes a search under the Fourth Amendment to the U.S. Constitution. Courts have frequently found drug testing of general student populations in conflict with constitutional requirements of individualized suspicion. Some of those cases appear in Chapter Four. This section considers testing of students who wish to participate in interscholastic athletics. Testing limited to potential interscholastic sports participants has met with court approval where the tests are limited in scope, provide for student privacy and clearly state the consequences of positive tests.

◆   An Oregon school district responded to increased student drug use by instituting a random drug testing policy for all students wishing to participate in varsity athletics. Each student athlete was to submit a consent form authorizing a test at the beginning of the season and weekly random testing thereafter. The policy provided for progressive discipline leading to suspension for the current and following athletic seasons. Students who refused were suspended from sports for the rest of the season. **A seventh grader who wanted to play football refused to sign the drug testing consent form and was suspended from sports for the season.** His parents sued, arguing that the testing policy violated their son's rights under the Fourth Amendment and the Oregon Constitution. A federal district court upheld the policy.

The parents appealed to the Ninth Circuit. The court held that participation in interscholastic sports did not diminish a high school athlete's reasonable expectation to be free from compelled, suspicionless urinalysis. The government interest in maintaining school discipline was not as strong as in other federal cases upholding random drug tests in high security or high-risk areas. **The policy violated both the U.S. and Oregon Constitutions, and the circuit court reversed and remanded the case.** The district appealed to the U.S. Supreme Court.

The Supreme Court stated that under its prior cases, the reasonableness of a search under the Fourth Amendment required balancing the interests between the government and individual. Prior decisions of the Court indicated that **students had a lesser expectation of privacy than the general populace, and that student-athletes had an even lower expectation of privacy in the locker room.** The invasion of privacy in this case was no worse than what was typically encountered in public restrooms. Positive test results were disclosed to only a limited number of school employees. **The insignificant invasion of student privacy was outweighed by the school district's important interest in addressing drug use by students who risked physical harm while playing sports.** The Court vacated and remanded the decision of the court of appeals. *Vernonia School Dist. 47J v. Acton*, 515 U.S. 646, 115 S.Ct. 2386, 132 L.Ed.2d 564 (1995).

◆   **A school district adopted a policy requiring all students who wished to participate in extracurricular activities to submit to drug testing.** The policy required random testing in any year in which a student participated in an activity, and reasonable suspicion testing for extracurricular participants. A student who participated in show choir, marching band and academic team challenged the policy.

The court awarded summary judgment to the district, ruling that the policy did not violate the Fourth Amendment's prohibition on unreasonable searches and seizures. The student appealed to the Tenth Circuit.

The circuit court examined recent school and non-school drug-testing cases involving the "special needs" exception to the Fourth Amendment. The U.S. Supreme Court developed the "special needs" exception allowing drug testing in the absence of reasonable suspicion of drug use when the government identifies a special need that makes adherence to the normal warrant and probable cause requirements of the Fourth Amendment improper. In the school context, the existence of a "drug culture" led by student-athletes was held to justify a random testing program of student-athletes in *Vernonia School District v. Acton*, above. Applying the *Vernonia* test, the circuit court found that student drug use in the Oklahoma district was far from epidemic or an immediate crisis. Because the evidence indicated that drug use among extracurricular activities participants was negligible, the district failed to show that there was a need to test all prospective participants for drug use through a random testing policy. The district policy tested too many students who were apparently at little risk of drug abuse by selecting only extracurricular activities participants. Concern for safety and degree of school supervision over these students also did not justify random testing. **Without a demonstrated drug-abuse problem in the group being tested, the policy violated the *Vernonia* balancing test and the U.S. Constitution**. The Tenth Circuit reversed and remanded the district court judgment. *Earls et al. v. Board of Education of Tecumseh Public School District*, 242 F.3d 1264 (10th Cir. 2001).

◆   All middle and high school students or their parents were required by their school district to sign a contract consenting to drug and alcohol testing by breath, urine and blood tests throughout the school year as a prerequisite for participation in extracurricular activities and school driving/parking privileges. There was no provision for reporting unlawful activity for law enforcement or school disciplinary purposes. Parents or students could elect to opt out of activities or participate in mandatory drug/alcohol assistance programs in order to continue the activity. Repeat offenders could be barred from extracurricular activities and school parking/driving privileges. **Students and parents who objected to the policy sued** the school district in a Pennsylvania trial court, **asserting violations of the search and seizure provisions of the U.S. and Pennsylvania constitutions**. The court upheld the policy and the students and parents appealed to the Pennsylvania Commonwealth Court.

The court observed that Article I, Section 8 of the Pennsylvania Constitution requires that a search be based on a compelling government interest and that the state interest be justified by the purpose of the search in order to avoid a gratuitous invasion of personal privacy. Students do not have unlimited privacy rights while at school and the school has an interest in protecting the health of all students. This case could be distinguished from other school search cases because it singled out a select group of students. It also did not call for criminal prosecution and possible surrender of extracurricular or school parking/driving privileges. The U.S. Supreme Court has held that schools must show a special need for selective testing of students without individualized suspicion. The court disagreed with the school district's assertion that just by exercising a privilege, a student's privacy expectation in school was reduced.

The district could not condition participation in an activity just because the activities were optional. **The school district was required to state a special need to test only those students who sought to engage in optional activities when compared with the general student population. The district's sweeping policy without stating a reason for singling out this group infringed student privacy rights**. This part of the trial court decision was vacated and remanded for further proceedings. *Theodore et al. v. Delaware Valley School District*, 761 A.2d 652 (Pa. Commw. 2000).

◆   **A rural Indiana school board adopted a policy requiring high school students to consent to random urinalysis testing for drugs, alcohol or tobacco prior to participating in extracurricular activities** or receiving permission to drive to school. Students failing an initial test were allowed to take an additional test. A second test failure resulted in the loss of permission to participate in extracurricular activities or drive to school. However, unlike the school's reasonable suspicion testing policy, failure of a random drug or alcohol test could not lead to student discipline. A group of students and parents filed a federal district court action against the school district, asserting constitutional rights violations. The court granted summary judgment to the district and officials, and the complaining parties appealed to the U.S. Court of Appeals, Seventh Circuit.

The court reviewed the case in view of the U.S. Supreme Court's decision in *Vernonia School Dist. 47J v. Acton*, 515 U.S. 646 (1997), above. In that case, the Court upheld the random, suspicionless urine testing of students participating in interscholastic athletics in a rural school district where a growing drug problem existed. In this case, there was a strong school interest in testing students who were involved in extracurricular activities and driving to school. Like athletics, these activities are privileges in high school. **The testing program applied only to students voluntarily participating in these activities and was primarily intended to protect student health**. The district had a compelling interest in deterring drug use by students to protect their health, and the court affirmed the judgment. *Todd v. Rush County Schools*, 133 F.3d 984 (7th Cir.1998).

2.   Age and Time Limits

School districts or state high school athletic associations are generally allowed to impose rules which limit athletic competition to eight consecutive semesters and which begins to toll either upon the completion of the eighth grade or upon the commencement of the ninth grade. They may also impose a rule limiting competition beyond a certain age: usually, 19.

◆   An Arizona high school student was a member of his school basketball team. However, he became dependent on alcohol, cocaine and marijuana during his sophomore year. He dropped out of high school and fled to California to escape drug-related debt. He later returned to Arizona and committed burglary to satisfy the debts. He then confessed to the burglary and was incarcerated at a school where he became rehabilitated. He returned to the high school, achieved good grades and did not return to drug use. **He sought an exception to the state interscholastic association's eight-consecutive-semester eligibility rule in order to participate on the**

basketball team. He hoped to qualify under an exception to the rule that allowed participation where the student was unable to attend school because of disabling illness or injury, met academic requirements and had a doctor's statement. The association denied the student's petition for an exception, determining that the student was incarcerated and not disabled and that his reform school medical reports were not statements from an attending physician under its rules. The student filed a complaint in an Arizona trial court, which granted his application for a temporary injunction, permitting him to participate on the basketball team. The court ruled that the decision of the athletic association had been arbitrary. The association appealed to the Arizona Court of Appeals, which vacated the trial court's decision. The student appealed to the Arizona Supreme Court. The supreme court agreed to hear the case even though the student had completed participation on the basketball team for the season. It agreed with the trial court that the student's drug and alcohol dependency had caused his absence from school. **The association had arbitrarily refused to consider the student's medical reports as they had clearly shown that he suffered from a disabling illness**. The supreme court affirmed the trial court's preliminary order. *Clay v. Arizona Interscholastic Ass'n,* 779 P.2d 349 (Ariz. 1989).

3. Transfer Students

Eligibility rules requiring a sit-out period for athletes transferring into a district, either from a neighboring school district or from out of state, may be enforced if it can be shown that the rules are reasonably related to the prevention of recruiting student athletes.

◆   A student attended private school until his parents separated and initiated divorce proceedings. He participated in varsity cross-country and track during his freshman and sophomore years. His mother became unable to pay the private school tuition, and the student transferred to a public school that was one of the private school's leading rivals. **He sought an exemption from the Indiana High School Athletic Association's transfer rule, which provided for ineligibility for one year if a student transferred primarily for athletic reasons**. The IHSAA denied the student's request for a full exemption, allowing him to only participate on the junior varsity team. It found that he did not meet the necessary conditions for a hardship exemption because the transfer was motivated by athletic reasons and was not beyond the control of himself and his family. The student obtained a temporary restraining order from a state trial court allowing him to run cross-country on the public school's varsity team. The court made the order permanent, finding that he met all the conditions of the hardship rule by showing a significant change in financial circumstances.

The IHSAA appealed to the Indiana Court of Appeals, which stated that the hardship rule was designed for situations when a change in financial condition was permanent, substantial and significantly beyond the control of the student or the student's family. The trial court had properly found that IHSAA decisions were subject to reversal if they were arbitrary and capricious. The **IHSAA had no power to deny hardship exceptions where a student met the rule's listed criteria, as had occurred in this case. There was no evidence of athletic motivation or "school jumping"** in this case, but there was contrary evidence that the family's financial difficulties had motivated the transfer. The hardship rule required a showing of change in financial condition, not proof of poverty. Because no reasonable person could fail to conclude that the student's family had undergone undue hardship, the court affirmed the judgment. *Indiana High School Athletic Association Inc. v. Durham et al.*, 748 N.E.2d 404 (Ind. App. 2001).

♦   A learning disabled 10th-grade student transferred from a Christian school to a metropolitan public school. The executive director of the Tennessee Secondary Schools Athletic Association (TSSAA) ruled that the student was ineligible to participate in interscholastic sports for a period of 12 months. The student submitted an appeal asking that the TSSAA grant a hardship request, which was denied. The student appealed to a number of authorities, but all his appeals were denied. After the first four games, the student's parents filed suit in a federal district court claiming that the student's ineligibility for participation in athletics deprived him of his rights under the Individuals with Disabilities Education Act (IDEA). **The court concluded that a student who transfers from one school to another for the purpose of receiving special education could not be prohibited from participating in extracurricular activities since such a prohibition would amount to discrimination based on disability**. *Crocker v. Tennessee Secondary School Athletic Ass'n,* 735 F.Supp. 753 (N.D.Tenn.1990).

4. Academic Standards

♦   A Kentucky high school student sued his school for not allowing him to compete in interscholastic wrestling. The school had a grade point requirement of 2.0 in order to participate in interscholastic sports, which the student had been unable to achieve. The trial court dismissed the case and the student appealed. **The Court of Appeals of Kentucky stated that the student's interest in wrestling was not a property right and therefore the grade point requirement was not unconstitutional**. The student did not have a fundamental right to participate in extracurricular activities. The school board's policy of excluding students from activities based on grades did not exceed the reasonable and legitimate interest of the school system. *Thompson v. Fayette County Public Sch.*, 786 S.W.2d 879 (Ky.App.1990).

B. Other Rules and Restrictions

♦   **An Iowa high school basketball player enjoyed no First Amendment protection to circulate a letter to teammates complaining about her coach's failure to promote her to the varsity team.** The letter was insubordinate and the coach reasonably required her to apologize for circulating it as a condition for participating on the team, according to the Eighth Circuit. While students have First Amendment rights, there is no absolute right to express opinions on school grounds. School officials have the authority to prohibit public expressions of vulgarity and teach civility and sensitivity in the expression of opinions. There was a distinction between being in a classroom and participating on an athletic team that further diminished the student's expectations of protected speech. The school district maintained a student conduct handbook, as did the basketball program, which both stated that the coach had the discretion to take disciplinary action for disrespect and insubordination. The circuit court rejected the student's argument that there was no specific evidence of material disruption of a school activity. The school did not interfere with her education by requiring her to apologize for the letter. Coaches deserved a modicum of respect from athletes, and the coach's action was reasonable in view of the student's insubordinate letter. *Wildman v. Marshalltown School District*, 249 F.3d 768 (8th Cir. 2001).

◆   Police officers ticketed a student for possessing an alcoholic beverage at a party. The school temporarily suspended him from the school's baseball team and a coach assigned him the task of performing forward and backward rolls across a field. The student refused to do the rolls and was removed from the team. The school board affirmed the action, and **the student sued the school district and its trustees in a Texas district court for damages and an order reinstating him to the team**. The court granted the student a temporary order disallowing his removal from the team.

The district and trustees appealed to the state court of appeals, which noted that the trial court had scheduled a final hearing long after the baseball season ended and after the student's scheduled graduation date. By postponing the hearing, the trial court had effectively decided the case in favor of the student. The court had also preempted the ability of school officials to enforce disciplinary rules and to punish the student for his alleged misconduct. Since school districts have the obligation and the right or privilege to control and discipline students, the trial court should have scheduled a final hearing on the dispute at a time that would have better protected the rights and interests of the parties. The trial court had erroneously found that the school's proposed discipline threatened the student's college baseball career. Evidence indicated that he had only modest talent and did not stand to gain a college baseball scholarship. He had only sought admission to one college and had made little effort to inquire into available scholarships. **Since the student's claim to irreparable harm in the absence of a temporary order was based on unsupported speculation that he would receive a college baseball scholarship, the trial court order was erroneous** and the court reversed and remanded the preliminary injunction. *Friona Independent School District v. King*, 15 S.W.3d 653 (Tex. App. 2000).

◆   A school maintained a zero tolerance policy providing for the 30-day suspension of students from all school sponsored extracurricular activities for violating student citizenship standards. The policy prohibited students from possessing or being under the influence of alcohol and extended to off-campus incidents. **The principal learned that two football players had been drinking alcohol** at the beach over a long weekend. After obtaining statements from one of the students and some witnesses, the principal suspended the students from the football team for two days. She rescinded the suspensions as premature and they rejoined the team pending an investigation and written notification to the parents. Both students admitted either drinking or possessing alcohol. The principal issued both students notices of suspension from all school-sponsored extracurricular activities for 30 days. The students appealed to the school board and received hearings, which they attended with their parents, witnesses and attorneys. The board issued notices of suspension for 30 days from extracurricular activities, credited for the two-day suspensions previously imposed by the principal. The students appealed to a state trial court, asserting that they had constitutionally protected property interests in extracurricular activities and could not be disciplined for off-campus conduct unrelated to a school event.

The court did not rule on the question of school authority to issue discipline for conduct arising off campus. However, it held that students have no constitutionally protected right to participate in interscholastic activities. **Participation in extracurricular activities is a privilege, and the Constitution protects only liberty and property interests that are of sufficient dignity to warrant due process protection**. The court agreed with the majority of federal courts that have considered the question and held that the students had no protected interest in extracurricular activities. Even though the principal deviated from the citizenship standard procedures, she substantially complied with its investigative procedures and the students received full hearings. The court affirmed the school board suspension orders. *L.P.M. and J.D.T. v. School Bd. of Seminole County, Florida*, 753 So.2d 130 (Fla.App.5th Dist. 2000).

◆   A high school football player admitted alcohol consumption to police when they encountered him in a convenience store parking lot when responding to a 911 call at 3:00 a.m. The officers reported the admission to school officials under a reciprocal reporting agreement with the school. **The school's assistant principal determined that the student had violated a school policy and suspended him from participation in athletics for the entire football season**. The school activity council affirmed the suspension, and the school superintendent refused to overturn the decision after meeting with the student, a stepparent, the student's attorney and police officers. Instead of appealing to the board, the family commenced a state court action against the school board, claiming that the discipline violated the Constitution and had been arbitrary and capricious. The court held for the board and the student appealed.

An Illinois appellate court observed, "courts have repeatedly held that there is no property or liberty interest in taking part in interscholastic athletics." **Playing football is a privilege, not a right. Even though the student claimed that he had attracted college recruiters and expected a scholarship, this was a contingency that did not create a constitutional right to interscholastic sports participation**. The student had no protectable interest in a scholarship and was not entitled to a hearing prior to his suspension. According to the court, recognition of a due process claim to participate in extracurricular activities would amount to a rule of judicial intervention in school disciplinary cases. Contrary to the student's argument, the state School Code did not create a hearing process for football players who violated their commitments to avoid using alcohol and drugs. "School officials can administer discipline for zero-tolerance conduct code violations without formal notice and hearing," held the court. Even though police had released confidential information to school officials under the reciprocal reporting agreement, the officials had acted in good faith when they received the police report. They were not precluded from acting on the information and in this case were obligated to do so in view of a prior alcohol violation by the student. *Jordan v. O'Fallon Township High School Dist. No. 203 Bd. of Educ.*, 706 N.E.2d 137 (Ill.App.5th Dist.1999).

◆   While West Virginia law provided for home schooling as an exemption to compulsory school attendance, the state athletic association excluded home-schooled students from eligibility for interscholastic sports competition. The association affirmed a decision by local school officials to deny a home-schooled student's request to try out for the cross-country team of a school in his area. The family sued the association in a state trial court and obtained a temporary order allowing the student to compete for a junior high team during the ninth grade. **After completion of the ninth grade season, the court dissolved the temporary order and held that the association did not violate the rights of home-schooled students by barring them from competition**. It agreed that the association rule was permissible to prevent the use of home schooling as a way to avoid academic requirements such as maintaining a C average to remain eligible for competition. The student then became a regular student in the public school system and competed in cross-country during his tenth grade year. Meanwhile, his appeal reached the Supreme Court of Appeals of West Virginia, which found the absence of a live controversy between the parties. The court noted that the family did not suggest that they wanted to home school the student at any point in the future. Accordingly, the case was moot and subject to dismissal. *Gallery v. West Virginia Secondary Schools Activities Comm.*, 205 W.Va. 364, 518 S.E.2d 368 (W.Va.1999).

◆   The Virginia High School League is a nonprofit corporation that supervises athletic competition and student activity among public high schools in Virginia. Its legislative council includes the principals of its member high schools. Its bylaws create classifications for high schools based upon student attendance, with separate classes for schools with 500 or less students, 501 to 1,000 students and 1,001 or more students. Its bylaws establish procedures for redistricting on the basis of study committee recommendations and requests by schools in the same general area. **The league's legislative council developed a redistricting and reclassification plan for all member schools**. Because of time constraints, a study committee used school attendance data from the prior year for students in ninth through 11th grades, instead of attendance figures for the current year for students in tenth through twelfth grade as required by league bylaws.

The proposed reclassification and redistricting resulted in reclassification of one school and placement of it in a different district. The high school filed a Virginia circuit court action against the league, seeking an order to prohibit the reclassification and transfer to the new district. The court granted the requested order and the league appealed to the Supreme Court of Virginia. **The court found the league bylaws to be unambiguous and held that the league was without authority to act in contravention of them**. Despite the presence of time constraints, the committee was bound to act according to the bylaws, and its actions were invalid. The court affirmed the trial court judgment. *Virginia High School League, Inc. v. J.J. Kelly High School*, 493 S.E.2d 362 (Va.1997).

◆   The Kansas State High School Activities Association (KSHSAA) is a voluntary nonprofit corporation organized under a state law that regulates interscholastic athletics and other extracurricular activities in the state. **A group of students who wanted to play on interscholastic basketball teams objected to KSHSAA rules** restricting their ability to compete in school-sponsored basketball camps, prohibiting them from playing on non-school teams during the basketball season, and prohibiting their attendance at private clinics during the basketball season. A Kansas trial court agreed with the students and held that KSHSAA rules were void as an unconstitutional delegation of legislative power. The KSHSAA appealed to the Supreme Court of Kansas, which observed that the Kansas Constitution prohibits the delegation of legislative power to a private group or association. Although the KSHSAA was a nonprofit corporation, state law expressly required the state board of education to supervise the KSHSAA and approve any changes to its bylaws. Because the KSHSAA was a voluntary association of high schools, its rules were created by contract and not by a legislative delegation of power. The court reversed the trial court decision concerning the constitutionality of KSHSAA powers, but remanded to the trial court other questions concerning whether the KSHSAA had jurisdiction to adopt and implement the challenged rules and whether the rules were arbitrary, capricious and unreasonable. *Robinson v. Kansas State High School Activities Ass'n, Inc.*, 917 P.2d 836 (Kan.1996).

II. INTERCOLLEGIATE ATHLETICS

Major colleges and universities participate in the National Collegiate Athletic Association (NCAA), which regulates competition and eligibility. Individual colleges and universities typically institute their own rules and regulations, which must be administered in a reasonable manner.

◆   **Four African-American students filed a class action lawsuit against the National Collegiate Athletic Association (NCAA) challenging Proposition 16, one of the eligibility rules for participating in college athletics.** Proposition 16 increased the number of required high school core courses from 11 to 13, and established an initial eligibility index regarding the standardized testing requirements for freshman college students who will be participating in interscholastic sports. According to the suit, the requirements had a disproportionate effect on college-bound African-American students. A federal district court initially determined that the NCAA was susceptible to a lawsuit under Title VI, which prohibits racial discrimination by recipients of federal funds. The NCAA was an indirect recipient of federal funds, therefore Title VI applied. The court reviewed evidence that a statistically relevant number of college-bound African-American students failed to meet the Proposition 16 testing requirements. The NCAA argued that Proposition 16 was designed to raise the graduation rates of African-American students and close the gap between graduation rates of white and African-American students. The court rejected the NCAA's assertion, characterizing it as an attempt to reframe the lawsuit. The court stated that the students had successfully demonstrated racial discrimination. The NCAA was unable to overcome this showing with evidence that Proposition 16 was justified by educational necessity, and it was further unable to show that any particular test score was a valid predictor of graduation rates. **While raising the graduation rate of student athletes was a legitimate educational goal, the NCAA's attempt to redress the gap in white and African-American graduation rates was not. There was no evidence this goal was behind the**

adoption of Proposition 16. The students' motion for summary judgment was granted.

The NCAA appealed to the Third Circuit, which found that the district court had based its decision on two incorrect theories of Title VI liability. The Third Circuit rejected each of the students' theories for subjecting the NCAA to a disparate impact claim under Title VI regulations. **According to the Third Circuit, the NCAA did not receive federal funds either directly or indirectly** based on its relationship with member institutions. There was insufficient evidence to establish that the National Youth Sports Program, an NCAA-affiliate that received federal funds, was the alter ego of the NCAA under the direct funding recipient theory. Title VI regulations are by their terms program specific, and it was not alleged that NCAA programs and activities themselves had a disparate impact on African-Americans. Therefore, the **Third Circuit found that the action could not be based on the theory that the NCAA was an indirect receipt of federal funding through the NYSP**. The court also rejected the theory that the NCAA was a federal funding recipient by virtue of its authority over member schools that received federal funds. The U.S. Supreme Court has held that the NCAA does not control its members through their delegation of authority over intercollegiate athletics. The Third Circuit determined that the ultimate decision-making power for freshman athletic participation remained with member schools. The threat of NCAA sanctions, although undesirable to colleges, did not result in NCAA control. Because NCAA member institutions retained their authority, the court found that each of the students' arguments for Title VI liability failed. The court reversed the district court judgment for the students and remanded the case. *Cureton v. NCAA*, 198 F.3d 107 (3d Cir. 1999).

In response to the Third Circuit's decision, attorneys for the plaintiffs filed a motion in the district court seeking to amend their original complaint with a claim alleging intentional discrimination. The judge denied the motion, finding the plaintiffs had waited too long to amend the complaint, that allowing the amendment would result in impermissible prejudice to the NCAA, and that the amendment would be futile. On appeal, the Third Circuit upheld the district court decision, agreeing that the amended complaint was filed too late. According to the circuit court, allowing the plaintiffs to proceed under the amended complaint would be "burdensome" to the NCAA. *Cureton et al. v. NCAA*, No. 00-1559 (3d Cir. 2001).

✦   **A student with a learning disability who was deemed ineligible to play Division I football during his freshman year sued the NCAA, two universities that stopped recruiting him once he was declared ineligible and the ACT/Clearinghouse, claiming the NCAA "core course" requirement violated the Rehabilitation Act and the Americans with Disabilities Act.** The court denied the NCAA's motion for summary judgment, finding evidence that its blanket exclusion of all courses taught "below the high school's regular instructional level (*e.g.*, remedial, special education or compensatory)" from consideration as core courses was not facially neutral and was premised on a specified level of academic achievement that persons with disabilities were less capable of meeting. The court determined that the student should receive a trial to determine whether the NCAA was liable for monetary damages and should be granted full athletic eligibility. The court held that his claim based on the alleged deprivation of a chance to play professional football was too speculative to survive pre-trial dismissal. Further, the court determined he was without legal standing to challenge NCAA initial eligibility rules because he would never again be subject to them.

The NCAA moved the court for reargument, noting that the court had presumed that the student could never regain his full allotment of four years of athletic eligibility. The NCAA argued that its rules had been changed as the consequence of a 1998 consent decree between it and the U.S. Department of Justice. Under current NCAA regulations, partial and nonqualifying student athletes could eventually gain a fourth year of athletic eligibility. Since the student had not lost any athletic eligibility, the NCAA argued that his claim for injunctive relief was now moot. It further alleged that the student lacked standing to seek injunctive relief because he could not prove that he lost any years of eligibility due to its discriminatory conduct. The court agreed with the NCAA that the prior order had presumed that the student had forever lost a year of eligibility under pre-1998 NCAA rules. Under the current rules, he could regain a fourth year of athletic eligibility. The court granted the NCAA's motion for reargument and held that the student no longer had standing to seek injunctive relief against the NCAA. It amended its order to dismiss the claims seeking injunctive relief under the ADA and Rehabilitation Act. **The student was otherwise entitled to proceed with his ADA claims against the universities as well as his Rehabilitation Act claims against the universities and the NCAA** as described in the prior order. *Bowers v. National Collegiate Athletic Association et al.*, 130 F.Supp.2d 610 (D.N.J. 2001).

◆   An all-state varsity basketball player who was highly recruited by Division I universities became dissatisfied with an class that was on the NCAA's list of approved core English courses. A guidance counselor suggested that he take a course called "Technical Communications" instead, a new offering that year. The counselor advised the student that the class would be approved by the NCAA as a core course. However, the district failed to include the course on a list of classes submitted to the NCAA for approval. The student received a full scholarship from a Division I university. After he enrolled, the NCAA Clearinghouse notified him that Technical Communications did not satisfy its core course requirement. The student was unable to compete in the basketball program and lost his scholarship. **He sued the NCAA and school district in an Iowa court for claims including negligent misrepresentation**. The claim against the NCAA was voluntarily dismissed and the court awarded summary judgment to the school district.

The student appealed to the Iowa Supreme Court, which noted that courts must refrain from rejecting "all claims that arise out of a school environment under the umbrella of educational malpractice." The case instead arose under the tort cause of action for negligent misrepresentation. **Guidance counselors** assumed an advisory role and were aware that students would rely on the information they provided. They **owed students a duty of reasonable care when supplying information** and the district was not entitled to summary judgment on the claim for negligent misrepresentation. However, the trial court had properly awarded summary judgment to the district on the claim that the school had negligently failed to submit the Technical Communications course to the NCAA for approval. The district had no duty to submit this information, and the court remanded the case to the trial court. *Sain v. Cedar Rapids Community School District*, 626 N.W.2d 115 (Iowa 2001).

◆   A group of student athletes at a west coast university sued the NCAA, contending that its drug testing program violated their rights to privacy under the California Constitution. **Student athletes seeking to participate in NCAA-sponsored competition are required to sign a consent form agreeing to allow the association to test them for banned drugs. Failure to sign the form renders the student ineligible.** Drug testing is conducted at NCAA athletic events by urinalysis. All student athletes in championship events for postseason bowl games are potentially subject to testing. Particular athletes are chosen for testing according to plans that may include random selection or other selection criteria such as playing time, team position, place of finish or suspicion of drug use. Upon a written notice following his or her participation in an athletic event, the selected athlete is required to report promptly to a collection station. The sample is then given in the presence of an NCAA official monitor.

The trial court concluded that the NCAA's drug testing program violated the state constitutional privacy rights of the student athletes. The court permanently enjoined any testing of student athletes whether inside or outside the state of California. The NCAA appealed to the Court of Appeal of California which affirmed the trial court's judgment, including the permanent injunction. The NCAA appealed this decision to the Supreme Court of California.

The supreme court reversed the decisions of the lower courts. Although the court rejected the NCAA's assertions that the right of privacy did not govern the conduct of private nongovernmental entities, it found nonetheless that student athletes had a lower expectation of privacy than the general student population. Observation of urination obviously implicated privacy interests. However, by its nature, participation in highly competitive postseason championship events involves close regulation and scrutiny of the physical fitness and bodily condition of student athletes. **Required physical examinations (including urinalysis) and the special regulation of sleep habits, diet, fitness and other activities that intrude significantly on privacy interests are routine aspects of a college athlete's life not shared by other students** or the population at large. Athletes frequently disrobe in the presence of one another as well as their athletic mentors and assistants in locker room settings where private bodily parts are readily observable by others of the same sex. They also exchange information about their physical condition and medical treatment with coaches, trainers, and others who have a need to know. The court noted that drug testing programs involving student athletes have routinely survived Fourth Amendment privacy challenges. Finally, the court concluded that the NCAA had an interest in protecting the health and safety of student athletes involved in NCAA-regulated competition. *Hill v. NCAA*, 26 Cal.Rptr.2d 834 (Cal.1994).

◆   The University of Colorado conducted a drug testing program for intercollegiate athletes that entailed a urine test at each annual physical with random tests thereafter. A program amendment substituted random rapid eye examinations for urinalysis, and **the university prohibited any athlete refusing to consent to the testing from participating in intercollegiate athletics**. The program called for progressive sanctions ranging from required participation in rehabilitation programs to permanent suspension from athletics. A group of athletes filed a class action suit against the university in a Colorado trial court seeking declaratory and injunctive relief. The court ruled for the athletes. The Colorado Court of Appeals affirmed this decision, and the university appealed to the Supreme Court of Colorado. The supreme court observed that the program did not ensure confidentiality and was mandatory inasmuch as refusal to participate disqualified students from participating in university athletic programs. **The university was unable to articulate an important governmental interest for the program. Unlike cases involving high school athletes, college students did not have a diminished expectation of privacy under the Fourth Amendment** that justified government searches in the absence of an important governmental interest. Random, suspicionless urinalysis was unconstitutional. University student athletes did not consent to participation in the program because there could be no voluntary consent where the failure to consent resulted in denial of a governmental benefit. *Univ. of Colorado v. Derdeyn*, 863 P.2d 929 (Colo.1993).

◆ Following a lengthy investigation of allegedly improper recruiting practices by the University of Nevada, Las Vegas (UNLV), the NCAA found 38 violations, including ten by the school's head basketball coach. The NCAA proposed a number of sanctions and threatened to impose more if the coach was not suspended. Facing an enormous pay cut, **the coach sued the NCAA under 42 U.S.C. § 1983 for violating his due process rights**. The Nevada Supreme Court held that the NCAA's conduct constituted state action for constitutional purposes. It upheld a Nevada trial court's dismissal of the suspension and award of attorneys' fees. The NCAA appealed to the U.S. Supreme Court, which held that the NCAA's participation in the events that led to the suspension did not constitute state action within the meaning of § 1983. The NCAA was not a state actor on the theory that it misused the power it possessed under state law. **UNLV's decision to suspend the coach in compliance with the NCAA's rules and recommendations did not turn the NCAA's conduct into state action**. This was because UNLV retained the power to withdraw from the NCAA and establish its own standards. The NCAA could not directly discipline the coach, but could threaten to impose additional sanctions against the school. It was the school's decision and not the NCAA's to suspend the coach. *NCAA v. Tarkanian*, 488 U.S. 179, 109 S.Ct. 454, 102 L.Ed.2d 469 (1988).

◆ A student at Brown University spent his first two semesters of college at the University of Nebraska. The student, a talented wrestler, failed a course during his first semester at Nebraska and did not repeat the course. **The NCAA notified him that he would be prohibited from wrestling during the following academic year because he had not successfully repeated the course**. The student sued in federal court seeking an injunction to restrain the NCAA from preventing him from wrestling. The federal district court denied the injunction since the student was not likely to succeed on the merits of his case. NCAA regulations prevent athletic participation for one year after transfer. There is an exception to the one-year abstinence rule for students in good academic standing who would have been eligible to participate had they remained at their previous institution. **Since he had failed the course, he would have been ineligible at Nebraska, so he was ineligible at Brown**. In addition, the student could not bring constitutional claims since the NCAA is a private actor, not a state agent. *Collier v. NCAA*, 783 F.Supp. 1576 (D.R.I.1992).

III. DISCRIMINATION AND EQUITY

Federal civil rights laws forbid discrimination based on sex, race or disability in federally funded school athletic programs. All public school districts must also comply with the Equal Protection Clause.

A. Gender Equity

Title IX of the Education Amendments of 1972 prohibits sex discrimination in any "program or activity" receiving federal financial assistance. The U.S. Department of Education's Title IX regulations, 34 CFR Part 106, provide more explicit guidance than the words of Title IX itself. Under the regulations, a school may operate separate teams for male and female athletes if selection for the team is based on competitive skill or the sport is a contact sport (defined as "boxing, wrestling, rugby, ice hockey, football, basketball and other sports the purpose or major activity of which involves bodily contact"). For noncontact sports, female athletes must be allowed to try out for traditionally male teams if there is no such team for females. Further, funding levels and other resource allocations must provide members of both sexes with "equal athletic opportunity." Although Title IX allows schools to maintain single sex teams for contact sports, several court decisions have questioned whether this practice is constitutional.

◆   **A federal jury awarded a female place-kicker $3 million in damages on her Title IX claims against Duke University, deciding that Duke football coaches discriminated against the kicker and that athletic department officials were indifferent to the discrimination**. According to the kicker, the head coach did not permit her to attend summer camp, refused to allow her to dress for games or sit on the sidelines during games, and gave her fewer opportunities to participate in practices than other walk-on kickers. She also alleged that the head coach made a number of offensive comments to her and later dropped her from the team. This conduct lead to the lawsuit, which, after various court proceedings, went to trial. After the verdict was announced, Duke sought to set aside the $2 million in punitive damages, arguing that even if the evidence supported the judgment, there is no clear-cut legal authority stating that punitive damages are allowable under Title IX. In addition, Duke claimed that the evidence did not support a finding that the university acted with any malice or reckless indifference to the kicker's rights. Duke asked the court to either rescind or reduce the punitive damages, or at the very least, grant a new trial. The trial court rejected Duke's arguments, upheld the award and ordered the university to pay the kicker's attorneys' fees. *Mercer v. Duke University et al.*, No. 97-CV-959 (M.D.N.C. 2001).

◆   In 1994, two groups of female athletes filed suits against Louisiana State University, claiming it violated Title IX by denying them an equal opportunity to participate in intercollegiate athletics and receive athletic scholarships, denying them equal access to the services provided to the school's varsity athletes, and discriminating against women in relation to athletic scholarships and paid compensation to coaches. The suits were consolidated, and the district court granted summary judgment to LSU on the claims for equal treatment in areas such as coaches' salaries and budgets because the plaintiffs could not demonstrate that they had been injured by programs in which they were not seeking to participate. The district court entered an order provisionally certifying a class of plaintiffs, including all female LSU students since 1993 who wanted to participate on a varsity sports team, but were denied the opportunity because LSU failed to establish such teams. Subsequently, the district court decertified the class. **The district court ultimately decided that LSU violated Title IX, but did not do so intentionally; therefore, the school was not liable for monetary damages.** LSU was required to implement a compliance plan. The plaintiffs appealed to the U.S. Court of Appeals, Fifth Circuit, claiming the district court erred by decertifying the class and holding that LSU did not intentionally violate Title IX. LSU moved to dismiss the suit because the Eleventh Amendment granted the school sovereign immunity. The district court denied the motion to dismiss and LSU appealed.

The Fifth Circuit vacated the district court order decertifying the class. In light of the potential number of female students in Louisiana who may seek to attend and play varsity soccer or softball at LSU, the numerosity requirement to certify a class was satisfied. The panel also rejected the district court's ruling that the plaintiffs who objected to LSU's lack of a female varsity soccer team did not have standing to file suit. Although the plaintiffs may not have had the athletic skills required to make the soccer team, they still had standing. Despite its finding that the plaintiffs had standing to assert effective accommodation claims under Title IX, the circuit court found they did not have standing to assert claims for unequal treatment. The panel affirmed the district court holding that since none of the plaintiffs were varsity athletes, they could not say they were treated unequally in relation to male varsity athletes. The Fifth Circuit rejected LSU's argument that it had sovereign immunity from the suit, finding that the university waived sovereign immunity by accepting federal funds under Title IX. The panel affirmed the district court's finding that LSU had violated Title IX, and stated that the violations were intentional. The university's ignorance of Title IX violations did not preclude a finding that the violations were intentional. **The court held that LSU's "archaic" view that women have less of an interest in athletic opportunities than men constituted intentional discrimination. Because LSU was found to have intentionally violated Title IX, the plaintiffs' claims for monetary damages could proceed** in district court. *Pederson et al. v. Louisiana State University et al.*, 213 F.3d 858 (5th Cir. 2000).

◆   Female students constituted 64 percent of a California university's student population, but only 39 percent of athletic team rosters. Female teams received only 32 percent of available athletic scholarship money, prompting a lawsuit by the National Organization of Women. The matter was settled under a consent decree mandating target percentages for female athletic participation. The university attempted to comply with the decree by reducing the size of male athletic teams. **After the men's wrestling team roster was capped, team members filed a federal district court lawsuit alleging gender discrimination in violation of Title IX and the Equal Protection Clause.** The court initially granted the team's request for an order preventing team reductions and concluded that the university's action violated Title IX. It did not rule on the Equal Protection issue and rejected the assertion that the Title IX compliance test created a "safe harbor" for schools to achieve substantial proportionality between the percentage of athletes of one gender and percentage of students of that gender.

University trustees appealed to the Ninth Circuit, which evaluated the language and intent of Title IX and its regulations. According to the court, Congress enacted Title IX with the understanding that male athletes had an enormous head start over female athletes for athletic resources. The intent of the act was to level the playing field and encourage female athletic participation. This undercut the team members' argument that males were more interested in sports than females and thus entitled to a greater share of funding. Increasing numbers of female participants would gradually increase demand for funding, and the percentage of female athletes had risen from 15 to 37 from 1972 to 1998. This increase was at least in part attributable to Title IX. **Title IX permits universities to reduce athletic opportunities for male athletes in order to bring participation into line with opportunities available for females**. Policy interpretations of the Office for Civil Rights were entitled to deference by the courts, and the "safe harbor" interpretation did not violate Equal Protection rights. The policy interpretation furthered the important objectives of avoiding the use of federal funds to support discriminatory practices and providing individuals with effective protection against discrimination. The court reversed the judgment and vacated the preliminary injunction for the team members. *Neal v. Bd. of Trustees of California State Universities*, 198 F.3d 763 (9th Cir. 1999).

◆   Male student enrollment at Illinois State University was only 45 percent, but the athletic participation rate for male students was 66 percent. **A university gender equity commission concluded that the disparity was inequitable to females and the university considered 10 options to achieve Title IX compliance. The university decided to focus on the goal of substantial proportionality in athletic participation as a means of complying with Title IX** policy interpretations published by the Office for Civil Rights. After the university decided to make these adjustments, female athletic participation rate rose to almost 52 percent, while the male rate slipped to 48. Former members of the men's soccer and wrestling teams sued the university regents in a federal district court, asserting that elimination of the programs under the gender equity plan had been based on their sex and therefore violated Title IX. They also asserted constitutional rights violations under 42 U.S.C. §§ 1983 and 1985(3). The court awarded summary judgment to the university on the Title IX claim, and found that the constitutional claims were preempted by the availability of a cause of action under Title IX.

The male student-athletes appealed to the Seventh Circuit, which rejected their argument that the university could not eliminate male programs when the decision was motivated by sex-based considerations. In this case, financial considerations were also a part of the decision. The Office for Civil Rights policy interpretations were entitled to deference, and clearly stated that **Title IX compliance may be shown where there is proof that female athletic participation is substantially proportionate to female enrollment. After the male programs were eliminated, male athletic participation remained within three percentage points of male enrollment**. There was no merit to the claim that this interpretation of Title IX violated the Equal Protection Clause, since the purpose of Title IX was to increase athletic opportunities for women in furtherance of the elimination of sex-based discrimination in federally funded educational programs. Moreover, the existence of a cause of action under Title IX precluded any action by the male students for civil rights violations under 42 U.S.C. §§ 1983 and 1985(3). The court affirmed the district court decision for the university regents. *Boulahanis v. Bd. of Regents, Illinois State Univ.*, 198 F.3d 633 (7th Cir.1999).

◆   A college graduate who had played intercollegiate volleyball at a private college for two years before enrolling in postgraduate programs at other colleges sought a waiver of the NCAA's Postbaccalaureate Bylaw. Under the Postbaccalaureate Bylaw, postgraduate student-athletes can compete in intercollegiate sports only at the institution from which they received an undergraduate degree. **When the NCAA denied the student's request for a waiver, she filed suit in a federal district court, claiming the NCAA's decision discriminated against her on the basis of gender in violation of Title IX.** The complaint also alleged that the NCAA granted more waivers to male students than female students. The district court dismissed the case, and denied the student's request to add as parties to her suit the two colleges that she had attended after receiving her undergraduate degree. Both colleges received Title IX funds. The U.S. Court of Appeals, Third Circuit, allowed the student to bring the colleges into the suit, ruling that the student had made a legally sufficient claim that the NCAA received Title IX funds through the dues paid by member institutions, such as the two colleges.

The Supreme Court disagreed with the circuit court, holding that entities receiving federal assistance are covered by Title IX, but those that only benefit economically from federal assistance are not. While entities that receive federal assistance in a direct or indirect manner may be sued under Title IX, **the NCAA did not receive federal funds through its receipt of dues from member institutions. The NCAA only received an indirect economic benefit, which did not trigger Title IX coverage.** The Supreme Court limited its decision to the question of whether an entity which receives dues payments from recipients of federal funding is considered a recipient of federal funds for Title IX applicability purposes, refusing to address the student's other arguments regarding the applicability of Title IX to the NCAA. The circuit court decision was vacated and remanded to the district court for further proceedings. *National Collegiate Athletic Ass'n v. Smith*, 525 U.S. 872, 119 S.Ct. 924, 142 L.Ed.2d 929 (1999).

◆   An eighth grade Kansas student was the only girl on her junior high school wrestling team. Although she compiled a record of five wins and three losses for the junior high school team, **she was prohibited from joining the high school team as a freshman based on a decision by the superintendent** of schools. The superintendent anticipated parental objections, sexual harassment lawsuits, student safety problems and school disruption. He also noted that regulations under Title IX of the Education Amendments of 1972 classified wrestling as a contact sport and thus did not require her participation. The student filed a lawsuit against the school board, district and superintendent in the U.S. District Court for the District of Kansas, which considered her motion for a preliminary order allowing her participation.

The court agreed with the school officials that because wrestling is a contact sport under Title IX regulations, the Title IX claim would likely be dismissed at a trial. However, it rejected the officials' argument that Title IX established a comprehensive remedial scheme that precluded the student's constitutional claims. Sex-based discrimination by a government agency could only be justified where the discrimination was substantially related to important governmental objectives. In this case, school officials had identified no important governmental objective. **Parental objections and the inconvenience of providing separate locker room facilities were not important governmental objectives,** and there was no evidence that the student's participation was likely to result in great danger. The court granted her request for a preliminary order. *Adams by and through Adams v. Baker,* 919 F.Supp. 1496 (D.Kan.1996).

◆   A Pennsylvania university with an undergraduate population that was 56 percent female fielded an equal number of male and female varsity athletic teams. However, male teams had more athletes and were better funded. The university cut men's tennis and soccer and women's gymnastics and field hockey teams because of budget problems. **Three female athletes sued the university** in the U.S. District Court for the Western District of Pennsylvania **under Title IX of the 1972 Education Amendments, seeking an order to force the university to reduce the disparity between men's and women's varsity athletics,** and to reinstate women's gymnastics and field hockey. The court granted a preliminary injunction and certified a class. It then held that the university was not in compliance with Title IX regulations and ordered reinstatement of the gymnastics and field hockey programs. The university filed a motion to modify the injunction to allow replacement of the gymnastics team with a women's soccer team. The court refused to modify the injunction and the university appealed to the U.S. Court of Appeals, Third Circuit. The court observed that modification of an injunction is appropriate only when there has been a change of circumstances making the original order inequitable. There was no such change in circumstances in this case. The district court had not abused its discretion in ordering the temporary preservation of athletic programs. **The university's proposal for a women's soccer program as a replacement for the women's gymnastic team would result in a net reduction in funding for women's athletics that was in contravention of Title IX goals.** *Favia v. Indiana Univ. of Pennsylvania,* 7 F.3d 332 (3d Cir.1993).

The protections of Title IX apply equally to males and females. However, due to the "contact sports" limitation in Title IX and the fact that the Equal Protection Clause does not require that the schools be "sex blind," this does not mean that males will automatically be allowed to play on female teams.

◆   **A male Rhode Island high school student desired to compete as a member of his school's girls' field-hockey team**. However, the regulations of the Rhode Island Interscholastic League forbade boys from participating on girls' athletic teams. A federal district court refused the student's request for an injunction based on the Fourteenth Amendment's Equal Protection Clause. The student then sued the league in a Rhode Island state court seeking an injunction based on the state constitution's equal protection provisions. The trial court granted the request, noting that the state constitution required stricter scrutiny of gender classifications than the U.S. Constitution. It granted the injunction and the league appealed to the Rhode Island Supreme Court. The state supreme court stated that the trial court had applied the wrong standard. **Gender classifications under the state constitution need only serve important governmental objectives and be substantially related to** the achievement of those objectives. Safety concerns and physical differences between the sexes justified the rule. The injunction was vacated and the action remanded. *Kleczek v. Rhode Island Interscholastic League, Inc.*, 612 A.2d 734 (R.I.1992). See also *Williams v. School Dist. of Bethlehem*, 998 F.2d 168 (3d Cir.1993), where the U.S. Court of Appeals, Third Circuit, overturned a district court decision allowing a Pennsylvania boy to compete on a girls' field hockey team.

B.   Students with Disabilities

Section 504 of the Rehabilitation Act of 1973 provides that an otherwise qualified individual with a disability may not, by reason of his or her disability, be excluded from participation in, be denied the benefits of, or be subjected to discrimination under any program or activity receiving federal financial assistance. The phrase "otherwise qualified" means a person who is qualified to participate in spite of the disability. The Americans with Disabilities Act of 1990 also provides protection against discrimination.

◆   A Kentucky school district maintained a no-cut policy for ninth-grade students wishing to play junior varsity basketball. A few days after the team started practicing, a student's coach was advised to investigate medical records to see if it was appropriate for him to play. The coach reviewed a physical form stating that the student should not engage in activities that would put him at increased risk of physical injury and indicating that he had hemophilia and hepatitis B. **The school principal then instructed the coach to put the student's status on "hold" and seek further medical information**. The student was forced to sit on the sidelines during certain drills in team practices and was asked to serve as the team's manager. The coach, principal and others determined that the student should remain on hold status until they received a statement from a physician on the appropriateness of his participation. The physician faxed a letter to school officials, but the coach was unsatisfied with the vagueness of the letter. Within 10 days, the principal advised the coach to allow the student to practice and play with the team.

Before the principal's decision was communicated to the family, the student decided that he no longer wanted to play. The family commenced a federal district court action against the school district, board and school officials, asserting violations of § 504 of the Rehabilitation Act and the Americans with Disabilities Act. The district court entered judgment for the school district and officials, and the family appealed to the U.S. Court of Appeals, Sixth Circuit. The court noted that **under either § 504 or the ADA, a person with disabilities may be excluded from a program if participation presents a direct threat to the health and safety of others**. In this case, the school district was attempting to determine whether the student's participation on the junior varsity basketball team presented a serious health risk to others. Congress created a narrow exception to the broad prohibition against discrimination contained in the ADA in cases where an individual with disabilities presents a direct threat to the health and safety of others. School officials had never removed the student from the team but had placed him on hold status while awaiting medical advice. The action was appropriate in view of the potential liability faced by the school if a competitor became infected as a result of his participation. It appeared that the student had chosen not to participate on the team of his own volition, and there was no violation of his rights under either § 504 or the ADA. *Doe v. Woodford County Board of Education*, 213 F.3d 921 (6th Cir. 2000).

◆ The Michigan High School Athletic Association (MHSAA) regulates interscholastic high school athletics in Michigan. Its handbook makes ineligible for interscholastic sports competition any student who has been enrolled in grades 9-12 for more than eight semesters. It also declares that a school using an ineligible player must forfeit individual or team records where a court order allowing participation is subsequently vacated, stayed or reversed. A student who had to repeat his eleventh grade year due to academic problems began his senior year with eight semesters of high school experience. As he entered his senior year, he was diagnosed as having attention deficit hyperactivity disorder and a seizure disorder. **He requested a waiver from MHSAA rules on the basis of his disabilities. The MHSAA denied the waiver**, and the student filed a federal district court action against it under the Americans with Disabilities Act (ADA), § 504 of the Rehabilitation Act and Michigan law. The court issued a preliminary order allowing him to participate in varsity basketball during his senior year. The MHSAA appealed to the U.S. Court of Appeals, Sixth Circuit.

The court found that in order to demonstrate violations of the ADA and § 504, the student would have to show that the MHSAA's actions had been taken because of his disability. This could be demonstrated either by proving that the MHSAA took learning disabilities into consideration in the formulation of the eight-semester rule or that it had unreasonably denied a requested accommodation. **Because the student had not shown that the MHSAA rule was motivated by the intent to prevent students with learning disabilities from playing sports, there was no evidence of discrimination in the drafting of the rule**. The court also found that the request for a waiver was unreasonable since many case-by-case waiver requests could potentially inundate the MHSAA and the inclusion of many older students in interscholastic sports would be a fundamental alteration in the MHSAA program. The rule had an important purpose in regulating high school sports, and allowing the student to participate was not a reasonable accommodation under the ADA. The court found that the district court order should be vacated and that the athletic records compiled by the student and the high school should be forfeited. *McPherson v. Michigan High School Athletic Ass'n, Inc.*, 119 F.3d 453 (6th Cir.1997).

◆ Students who turn 19 on or before September 1 of any school year are prohibited by the Michigan High School Athletic Association (MHSAA) from competing in interscholastic high school sports. Two Michigan students with histories of learning disabilities experienced two-year delays in their school progress due to their disabilities. Both of them participated in cross-country and track during their first three years of high school, but turned 19 at the close of their junior years. **When the MHSAA refused to waive its age limit for the students, they obtained a preliminary order** from the U.S. District Court for the Eastern District of Michigan **which allowed them to participate in cross-country and track as a reasonable accommodation** under § 504 of the Rehabilitation Act and the Americans with Disabilities Act (ADA). The MHSAA appealed to the U.S. Court of Appeals, Sixth Circuit.

The court stated that since both students had graduated by the time argument reached the court, the question of their participation in interscholastic sports was moot. However, their interest in preserving team and personal victories remained a live controversy. Under both the Rehabilitation Act and the ADA, a complaining party must demonstrate that there has been discrimination solely by reason of a disability. In this case, any discrimination by the MHSAA had occurred because of the age limitation, and therefore could not have been caused solely by reason of a disability. Regardless of their disabilities, both students were barred from interscholastic sports by the age regulation, and neither the Rehabilitation Act nor the ADA prohibited a neutral rule that incidentally disqualified a disabled person. **The demand to waive the age restriction did not constitute a reasonable accommodation because it would result in a hardship to the schools and the MHSAA**. The district court had also erroneously determined that the MHSAA qualified as a public accommodation, and its decision was reversed and remanded. *Sandison v. Michigan High School Athletic Ass'n*, 64 F.3d 1026 (6th Cir.1995).

IV. ISSUES IN COACHING

A. Employment

1. Hiring

Coaches generally receive a salary supplement and school districts frequently consider the position severable from teaching contracts. Positions may be assigned or terminated with less restrictions than for regular teaching assignments because coaches do not have a property interest in the position of coach or tenure as a coach.

◆   An Ohio school district employed a high school teacher with a supplemental contract to coach the girls' basketball team. The board adopted a resolution to terminate all supplemental contracts at the conclusion of the school year. It later conducted a roll call vote to issue over 80 supplemental contracts for the following school year. **The basketball coach's supplemental contract was rejected, and he filed a complaint in an Ohio court, seeking an order to compel the board to issue the supplemental contract**. The court dismissed the case and the coach appealed to the Supreme Court of Ohio. The court rejected the coach's argument that the board's failure to enter votes on the record and abide by Robert's Rules of Order violated state law. Supplemental contracts, unlike regular teacher employment contracts, were not subject to conditional voting by resolution, and a roll call vote was not required. **There was no uncertainty concerning the voting and the coach had no legal right to the supplemental contract**. Parliamentary rules adopted by a school board were intended to assist the board in the orderly conduct of business, and failure to abide by them did not create a legal cause of action. The court affirmed the board's action. *State ex rel. Savarese v. Buckeye Local School Dist. Bd. of Educ.*, 74 Ohio St.3d 543, 660 N.E.2d 463 (1996).

◆   A California school district opened a new high school and advertised openings for several basketball coaching positions. **A tenured, credentialed teacher who was employed at a district junior high school applied for several of the**

positions but was not hired. One of the coaches selected for a position did not have a state teaching credential, and the junior high school teacher filed a lawsuit against the school district in a California superior court, asserting violation of a state law concerning limited assignments for athletic activities. The court denied the teacher's petition, but the California Court of Appeal reversed its decision. The school board appealed to the Supreme Court of California. The court reviewed the statute, which provides that limited assignment coaching positions "shall first be made available to teachers presently employed by the district." The teacher asserted that this language gave him a right of first refusal over noncredentialed candidates and candidates who were not employees of the district. The board argued that the statute simply required that it post notices so that district employees had knowledge of a vacancy. **The supreme court agreed with the teacher that a credentialed, district employee was entitled to a limited employment preference over nondistrict employees**. However, it agreed with the board that a teacher applying for a coaching position must meet employment qualifications established by the school district. Because the superior court had not determined whether the teacher met district qualifications, the case was remanded for further proceedings. *California Teachers Ass'n v. Governing Bd. of Rialto Unified Sch. Dist.*, 59 Cal.Rptr.2d 671, 927 P.2d 1175 (Cal.1997).

2. Termination and Defamation

♦   A Georgia high school teacher received a salary supplement of $7,400 for serving as the school's head football coach. The school district was a member of the Georgia High School Association (GHSA), a voluntary association of public and private high schools that enforces eligibility rules for interscholastic sports. A student who wanted to play on the football team was found ineligible. The coach arranged for testing of the student and a determination was made that he had a learning disability. When this information was communicated to some of the student's teachers, four of the student's grades were changed and the school declared the student eligible to play football. **The Professional Practices Commission** (PPC), a state agency authorized to investigate alleged violations of state education rules and regulations, **recommended suspension of the coach's teaching certificate, and within one week, the county school board, without holding a hearing, terminated his coaching duties**. The coach submitted a resignation letter. He sued the school district, GSHA, PPC, and various school officials in the U.S. District Court for the Middle District of Georgia.

The district court granted summary judgment in favor of the school superintendent on the teacher's equal protection and libel claims. The PPC and its officials argued that the Eleventh Amendment barred any suit against them in federal court. The district court rejected their summary judgment motion and remanded the head coach's claims against the PPC and its officials to a Georgia trial court. The court determined that while Georgia tenure laws extended to written teaching contracts, there was no evidence that the tenure law should protect unwritten coaching contracts. Accordingly, the head coach had no property interest in the coaching position and was not entitled to a pretermination hearing. *Brewer v. Purvis*, 816 F.Supp. 1560 (M.D.Ga.1993).

The court remanded the case to the Clarke County Superior Court, which held that the PPC and its officials were not entitled to summary judgment on the state law or constitutional claims. **The PPC and officials appealed to the Court of Appeals** of Georgia, which determined that the superior court had improperly denied them summary judgment on the basis of official immunity for the constitutional claims. However, they were not entitled to summary judgment on the state law claims for libel and slander, and this part of the superior court decision was affirmed. *Professional Practices Comm'n v. Brewer*, 466 S.E.2d 651 (Ga.App.1995).

◆   A Texas newspaper reported on a brawl occurring among players after a football game. **It published an article which was sharply critical of the head football coach of one school**, who was also the school's athletic director and a classroom teacher. The article faulted the coach for "turning his back on the situation" and implied that his team played "dirty football." The coach and his wife sued the newspaper and one of its sportswriters in a Texas trial court, which granted the newspaper's summary judgment motion. The coach and his wife appealed to the Court of Appeals of Texas, Amarillo. The coach argued that he was not a public official and that he only needed to show negligence by the newspaper to prevail in his libel suit. The newspaper argued that the coach was a public official, whose greater recognition required a showing of actual malice in order for there to be any liability. The court of appeals noted that the coach was by his own admission a very well known individual in the area, and therefore a public official. **Because there was no evidence that the newspaper had made a false and defamatory statement with reckless disregard for the truth, the coach failed to show actual malice.** Accordingly, the trial court's summary judgment ruling was correct and its decision to dismiss the lawsuit was affirmed. *Johnson v. Southwestern Newspapers Corp.*, 855 S.W.2d 182 (Tex.App.–Amarillo 1993).

B. Liability

Generally, coaches remain free from liability for injuries received from faulty athletic equipment absent a showing of wilful or wanton misconduct.

◆   **A high school football player fell while attempting a tackle during a game and struck his head on the ground. He felt dizzy and disoriented**, but stayed in the game for a few plays, then took himself out. Coaches observed that he was short of breath, but attributed his dizziness to hyperventilation, not a head injury. Because the student made normal eye contact with an assistant coach and had normal speech and movement, no medical attention was sought. When the student asked to return to the game during the next quarter, coaches allowed him to do so, observing that he seemed normal and did not complain of a headache. Although family members reported that the student suffered a headache the entire weekend, there was conflicting evidence that he shared this information with the coaching staff the following week. He was allowed to practice with the team and suffered a closed-head traumatic brain injury.

He sued the school district in a Nebraska trial court for personal injuries. The suit was dismissed on grounds that the school was not negligent. The student appealed to the state supreme court, which stated that the trial court should not have discredited testimony by the student's expert witnesses, who were certified athletic trainers. The trainers, who taught state-required courses for obtaining coaching endorsements, testified that Nebraska high school coaches should be aware that headache, dizziness and disorientation are symptomatic of a concussion. Instead of relying on this testimony, the trial court improperly relied on testimony by a high school coach, believing that local community standards governed the conduct of coaches. The Nebraska Supreme Court held that **the standard of care applicable to high school coaches did not vary among districts, but was instead that of a "reasonably prudent person holding a Nebraska teaching certificate with a coaching endorsement."** Because the trainers instructed the courses taken by coaches seeking endorsement, they were competent to testify about this standard. The court remanded the case to the trial court. *Cerny v. Cedar Bluffs Junior/Senior Pub. Sch.*, 262 Neb. 66, 628 N.E. 2d 697 (Neb. 2001).

◆   During softball tryouts, a ninth grader who was trying out for catcher used only a glove, not a facemask. The student signaled the pitcher to throw a straight fastball, but the pitcher threw a curve ball, which tipped the edge of the catcher's mitt and struck her in the face. As a result, the catcher suffered a concussion and a broken nose. **The catcher sued the coaches and school officials, claiming she should have been provided with a face mask**. At trial, a jury found the catcher 40 percent liable for her injuries and the district defendants 60 percent liable.

The defendants appealed, arguing that "customary practice" did not require catchers to wear a mask and helmet during warm-ups and practice sessions when no batter is present. The appeals court noted that the catcher's expert witness opined at trial that the association that governs softball requires players engaged in pitcher warmups to wear a mask and helmet. In addition, he testified that **it was a "customary practice" in most New York schools to require a catcher to wear protective equipment during warm-ups and practice sessions when no batter is present**. In reviewing the arguments, the appeals court cited case law, which supported the notion that the defendants' failure "constituted a breach of sound coaching practice, which enhanced the risk of injury normally associated with the activity." Accordingly, the court upheld the jury's verdict. *Zmitrowitz v. Roman Catholic Diocese of Syracuse*, No. 85038 (A.D. 2000).

◆   A 110-pound eighth grade Louisiana student played for his elementary school football team. In a game played against another elementary school team, a 270-pound eighth grade player from the opposing team tackled the student, causing a fracture of the student's leg. There was no penalty called on the play. **The student and his parents sued the coaches of both football teams and the insurer of one of the coaches, claiming that they should be held liable for the injury**. It was claimed that the accident was caused by allowing smaller elementary school students to scrimmage and play against larger students. The coaches and insurer filed a motion for summary judgment in a Louisiana trial court, claiming that there was no duty by the coaches to prevent players from being injured in supervised, refereed interschool football games and that the tackling was neither unexpected nor unsportsmanlike. The court granted the summary judgment motion and the student and his parents appealed to the Court of Appeal of Louisiana, First Circuit. **The court of appeal found that there was no duty imposed upon coaches to protect players against the potential risk of injury from playing football games with players of different weights**. Even though the Louisiana Supreme Court had abolished the doctrine of assumption of risk several years previously, the absence of any duty to protect players precluded a finding of liability. The summary judgment decision of the trial court was affirmed. *Laiche v. Kohen*, 621 So.2d 1162 (La.App. 1st Cir. 1993).

APPENDIX A

United States Constitution

Provisions of Interest to Educators

ARTICLE I

Section 1. All legislative Powers herein granted shall be vested in a Congress of the United States, which shall consist of a Senate and House of Representatives.

* * *

Section 8. The Congress shall have Power To lay and collect Taxes, Duties, Imposts and Excises, to pay the Debts and provide for the common Defence and general Welfare of the United States; but all Duties, Imposts and Excises shall be uniform throughout the United States:

To borrow money on the credit of the United States;

To regulate Commerce with foreign Nations, and among the several States, and with the Indian Tribes;

To establish an uniform Rule of Naturalization, and uniform Laws on the subject of Bankruptcies throughout the United States;

* * *

To promote the Progress of Science and useful Arts, by securing for limited Times to Authors and Inventors the exclusive Right to their respective Writings and Discoveries;

* * *

To make all Laws which shall be necessary and proper for carrying into Execution for the foregoing Powers, and all other Powers vested by this Constitution in the Government of the United States, or in any Department or Office thereof.

* * *

Section 9. * * * No Bill of Attainder or ex post facto Law shall be passed.

Section 10. No State shall * * * pass any Bill of Attainder, ex post facto Law, or Law impairing the Obligation of Contracts, or grant any Title of Nobility.

* * *

ARTICLE II

Section 1. The executive Power shall be vested in a President of the United States of America.

* * *

ARTICLE III

Section 1. The judicial Power of the United States, shall be vested in one Supreme Court, and in such inferior Courts as the Congress may from time to time ordain and establish. The Judges, both of the supreme and inferior courts, shall hold their Offices during good Behaviour, and shall, at stated Times, receive for their Services a Compensation, which shall not be diminished during their Continuance in Office.

Section 2. The judicial Power shall extend to all Cases, in Law and Equity, arising under this Constitution, the Laws of the United States, and Treaties made, or which shall be made; under their Authority; to all Cases affecting Ambassadors, other public Ministers and Consuls; to all Cases of admiralty and maritime Jurisdiction, to Controversies to which the United States shall be a party to Controversies between two or more States; between a State and Citizens of another State; between Citizens of different States; between Citizens of the same State claiming Lands under the Grants of different States, and between a State, or the Citizens thereof, and foreign States, Citizens or Subjects.

* * *

ARTICLE IV

Section 1. Full Faith and Credit shall be given in each State to the public Acts, Records and judicial Proceedings of every other State.* * *

Section 2. The Citizens of each State shall be entitled to all Privileges and Immunities of Citizens in the several States.

* * *

Section 4. The United States shall guarantee to every State in this Union a Republican Form of Government, and shall protect each of them against Invasion; and on Application of the Legislature, or of the Executive (when the Legislature cannot be convened) against domestic Violence.

ARTICLE V

The Congress, whenever two thirds of both Houses shall deem it necessary, shall propose Amendments to this Constitution, or, on the Application of the Legislatures of two thirds of the several States, shall call a Convention for proposing Amendments, which, in either Case, shall be valid to all Intents and Purposes, as part of this Constitution, when ratified by the Legislatures of three fourths of the several States, or by Conventions in three fourths thereof, as the one or the other Mode of Ratification may be proposed by the Congress; Provided that no Amendment which may be made prior to the Year One thousand eight hundred and eight shall in any Manner affect the first and fourth Clauses in the Ninth Section of the first Article; and that no State, without its Consent, shall be deprived of its equal Suffrage in the Senate.

ARTICLE VI

* * *

This Constitution, and the Laws of the United States which shall be made in Pursuance thereof; and all Treaties made, or which shall be made, under the Authority of the United States, shall be the Supreme Law of the Land; and the Judges in every State shall be bound thereby, any Thing in the Constitution or Laws of any State to the Contrary notwithstanding.

The Senators and Representatives before mentioned, and the Members of the several State Legislatures, and all executive and judicial Officers, both of the United States and of the several States, shall be bound by Oath or Affirmation, to support this Constitution; but no religious Test shall ever be required as a Qualification to any Office or public Trust under the United States.

* * *

AMENDMENT I

Congress shall make no law respecting an establishment of religion, or prohibiting the free exercise thereof; or abridging the freedom of speech, or of the press; or the right of the people peaceably to assemble, and to petition the Government for a redress of grievances.

* * *

AMENDMENT IV

The right of the people to be secure in their persons, houses, papers, and effects, against unreasonable searches and seizures, shall not be violated, and no Warrants shall issue, but upon probable cause, supported by Oath or affirmation, and particularly describing the place to be searched, and the persons or things to be seized.

AMENDMENT V

No person shall be held to answer for a capital, or otherwise infamous crime, unless on a presentment or indictment of a Grand Jury, except in cases arising in the land or naval forces, or in the Militia, when in actual service in time of War or public danger; nor shall any person be subject for the same offence to be twice put in jeopardy of life or limb; nor shall be compelled in any criminal case to be a witness against himself, nor be deprived of life, liberty, or property, without due process of law; nor shall private property be taken for public use, without just compensation.

AMENDMENT VI

In all criminal prosecutions, the accused shall enjoy the right to a speedy and public trial, by an impartial jury of the State and district wherein the crime shall have been committed, which district shall have been previously ascertained by law, and to be informed of the nature and cause of the accusation; to be confronted with the witnesses against him; to have compulsory process for obtaining witnesses in his favor, and to have the Assistance of Counsel for his defense.

AMENDMENT VII

In Suits at common law, where the value in controversy shall exceed twenty dollars, the right of trial by jury shall be preserved, and no fact tried by jury, shall be otherwise re-examined in any Court of the United States, than according to the rules of the common law.

AMENDMENT VIII

Excessive bail shall not be required, nor excessive fines imposed, nor cruel and unusual punishments inflicted.

AMENDMENT IX

The enumeration in the Constitution, of certain rights, shall not be construed to deny or disparage others retained by the people.

AMENDMENT X

The powers not delegated to the United States by the Constitution, nor prohibited by it to the States, are reserved to the States respectively, or to the people.

AMENDMENT XI

The Judicial power of the United States shall not be construed to extend to any suit in law or equity, commenced or prosecuted against one of the United States by Citizens of another State, or by Citizens or Subjects of any Foreign State.

* * *

AMENDMENT XIII

Section 1. Neither slavery nor involuntary servitude, except as a punishment for crime whereof the party shall have been duly convicted, shall exist within the United States, or any place subject to their jurisdiction.

Section 2. Congress shall have power to enforce this article by appropriate legislation.

AMENDMENT XIV

Section 1. All persons born or naturalized in the United States, and subject to the jurisdiction thereof, are citizens of the United States and of the State wherein they reside. No State shall make or enforce any law which shall abridge the privileges or immunities of citizens of the United States; nor shall any State deprive any person of life, liberty, or property, without due process of law; nor deny to any person within its jurisdiction the equal protection of the laws.

* * *

Section 5. The Congress shall have power to enforce, by appropriate legislation, the provisions of this article.

APPENDIX B

Subject Matter Table of
Education Cases Decided by the
United States Supreme Court

Note: Please see the Table of Cases (located at the front of this volume) for Supreme Court cases reported in this Volume.

Academic Freedom
> Univ. of Pennsylvania v. EEOC, 493 U.S. 182, 110 S.Ct. 577, 107 L.Ed.2d 571 (1990).
> Epperson v. Arkansas, 393 U.S. 97, 89 S.Ct. 266, 21 L.Ed.2d 228 (1968).
> Meyer v. Nebraska, 262 U.S. 390, 43 S.Ct. 625, 67 L.Ed.2d 1042 (1923).

Aliens
> Toll v. Moreno, 458 U.S. 1, 102 S.Ct. 2977, 73 L.Ed.2d 563 (1982)
> Plyler v. Doe, 457 U.S. 202, 102 S.Ct. 2382, 72 L.Ed.2d 786 (1982).
> Ambach v. Norwick, 441 U.S. 68, 99 S.Ct. 1589, 60 L.Ed.2d 49 (1979).
> Vlandis v. Kline, 412 U.S. 441, 93 S.Ct. 2230, 37 L.Ed.2d 63 (1973).

Collective Bargaining
> Chicago Teachers Union v. Hudson, 475 U.S. 292, 106 S.Ct. 1066, 89 L.Ed.2d 232 (1986).
> Minnesota State Board for Community Colleges v. Knight, 465 U.S. 271, 104 S.Ct. 1058, 79 L.Ed.2d 299 (1984).
> Perry Education Association v. Perry Local Educators' Association, 460 U.S. 37, 103 S.Ct. 948, 74 L.Ed.2d 794 (1983).
> City of Madison Joint School District v. WERC, 429 U.S. 167, 97 S.Ct. 421, 50 L.Ed.2d 376 (1976).

Compulsory Attendance
> Wisconsin v. Yoder, 406 U.S. 205, 92 S.Ct. 526, 32 L.Ed.2d 15 (1972).
> Pierce v. Society of Sisters, 268 U.S. 510, 45 S.Ct. 571, 69 L.Ed. 1070 (1925).

Continuing Education
> Austin ISD v. U.S., 443 U.S. 915, 99 S.Ct. 3106, 61 L.Ed.2d 879 (1979).
> Harrah ISD v. Martin, 440 U.S. 194, 99 S.Ct. 1062, 59 L.Ed.2d 248 (1979).

Corporal Punishment
> Ingraham v. Wright, 430 U.S. 651, 97 S.Ct. 1401, 51 L.Ed.2d 711 (1977).

Desegregation
> Missouri v. Jenkins, 515 U.S. 70, 115 S. Ct. 2038, 132 L.Ed.2d 63 (1995).
> U.S. v. Fordice, 505 U.S. 717, 112 S.Ct. 2727, 120 L.Ed.2d 575 (1992).

Freeman v. Pitts, 503 U.S. 467, 112 S.Ct. 1430, 118 L.Ed.2d 108 (1992).

Bd. of Educ. of Oklahoma City Public Schools v. Dowell, 498 U.S. 237, 111 S.Ct. 630, 112 L.Ed.2d 715 (1991).

Missouri v. Jenkins, 495 U.S. 33, 110 S.Ct. 1651, 109 L.Ed.2d 31 (1990).

Crawford v. Bd. of Educ., 458 U.S. 527, 102 S.Ct. 3211, 73 L.Ed.2d 948 (1982).

Washington v. Seattle School Dist. No. 1, 458 U.S. 457, 102 S.Ct. 3187, 73 L.Ed.2d 896 (1982).

Board of Education v. Superior Court, 448 U.S. 1343, 101 S.Ct. 21, 65 L.Ed.2d 1166 (1980).

Columbus Board of Education v. Penick, 443 U.S. 449, 99 S.Ct. 2941, 61 L.Ed.2d 666 (1979).

Bustop v. Board of Education, 439 U.S. 1380, 99 S.Ct. 40, 58 L.Ed.2d 88 (1978).

Vetterli v. U.S. District Court, 435 U.S. 1304, 98 S.Ct. 1219, 55 L.Ed.2d 751 (1978).

Dayton Board of Education v. Brinkman, 433 U.S. 406, 97 S.Ct. 2766, 53 L.Ed.2d 851 (1977).

Milliken v. Bradley, 433 U.S. 267, 97 S.Ct. 2749, 53 L.Ed.2d 745 (1977).

Pasadena City Board of Education v. Spangler, 427 U.S. 424, 96 S.Ct. 2697, 49 L.Ed.2d 599 (1976).

Milliken v. Bradley, 418 U.S. 717, 94 S.Ct. 311, 41 L.Ed.2d 1069 (1974).

Bradley v. School Board of City of Richmond, 416 U.S. 696, 94 S.Ct. 2006, 40 L.Ed.2d 476 (1974).

Keyes v. School District No. 1, 413 U.S. 189, 93 S.Ct. 2686, 37 L.Ed.2d 548 (1973).

Drummond v. Acree, 409 U.S. 1228, 93 S.Ct. 18, 34 L.Ed.2d 33 (1972).

U.S. v. Scotland Neck City Board of Education, 407 U.S. 484, 92 S.Ct. 2214, 33 L.Ed.2d 75 (1972).

Wright v. Council of City of Emporia, 407 U.S. 451, 92 S.Ct. 2196, 33 L.Ed.2d 51 (1972).

Winston-Salem/Forsyth County Board of Education v. Scott, 404 U.S. 1221, 92 S.Ct. 1236, 31 L.Ed.2d 441 (1971).

Dandridge v. Jefferson Parish School Board, 404 U.S. 1219, 92 S.Ct. 18, 30 L.Ed.2d 23 (1971).

Guey Heung Lee v. Johnson, 404 U.S. 1215, 92 S.Ct. 14, 30 L.Ed.2d 19 (1971).

North Carolina State Board of Education v. Swann, 402 U.S. 43, 91 S.Ct. 1284, 28 L.Ed.2d 586 (1971).

McDaniel v. Barresi, 402 U.S. 39, 91 S.Ct. 1287, 28 L.Ed.2d 582 (1971).

Davis v. Board of School Commissioners, 402 U.S. 33, 91 S.Ct. 1289, 28 L.Ed.2d 577 (1971).

Swann v. Charlotte-Mecklenburg Board of Education, 402 U.S. 1, 91 S.Ct. 1267, 28 L.Ed.2d 554 (1971).

Northcross v. Board of Education, 397 U.S. 232, 90 S.Ct. 891, 25 L.Ed.2d 246 (1970).

Dowell v. Board of Education, 396 U.S. 269, 90 S.Ct. 415, 24 L.Ed.2d 414 (1969).

Carter v. West Feliciena Parish School Bd., 396 U.S. 290, 90 S.Ct. 608, 24 L.Ed.2d 477 (1970).

Alexander v. Holmes County Board of Education, 396 U.S. 19, 90 S.Ct. 29, 24 L.Ed.2d 19 (1969).

U.S. v. Montgomery County Board of Education, 395 U.S. 225, 89 S.Ct. 1670, 23 L.Ed.2d 263 (1969).

Monroe v. Board of Commissioners, 391 U.S. 450, 88 S.Ct. 1700, 20 L.Ed.2d 733 (1968).

Raney v. Board of Education, 391 U.S. 443, 88 S.Ct. 1697, 20 L.Ed.2d 727 (1968).

Green v. New Kent County School Board, 391 U.S. 430, 88 S.Ct. 1689, 20 L.Ed.2d 716 (1968).

Rogers v. Paul, 382 U.S. 198, 86 S.Ct. 358, 15 L.Ed.2d 265 (1965).

Bradley v. School Board, 382 U.S. 103, 86 S.Ct. 224, 15 L.Ed.2d 187 (1965).

Griffin v. County School Bd., 377 U.S. 218, 84 S.Ct. 1226, 12 L.Ed.2d 256 (1964).

Goss v. Bd. of Educ., 373 U.S. 683, 83 S.Ct. 1405, 10 L.Ed.2d 632 (1963).

U.S. v. State of Louisiana, 364 U.S. 500, 81 S.Ct. 260, 5 L.Ed.2d 245 (1960).

Cooper v. Aaron, 358 U.S. 1, 78 S.Ct. 1401, 3 L.Ed.2d 5 (1958).

Brown v. Board of Education (II), 349 U.S. 294, 75 S.Ct. 753, 99 L.Ed. 1083 (1955).

Bolling v. Sharpe, 347 U.S. 497, 74 S.Ct. 693, 98 L.Ed. 884 (1954).

Brown v. Board of Education (I), 347 U.S. 483, 74 S.Ct. 686, 98 L.Ed. 873 (1954).

Disabled Students

Cedar Rapids Community School Dist. v. Garret F. by Charlene F., 526 U.S. 66, 119 S.Ct. 992, 143 L.Ed.2d 154 (1999).

Lane v. Pena, 518 U.S. 187, 116 S.Ct. 2092, 135 L.Ed.2d 486 (1996).

Florence County School Dist. v. Carter, 510 U.S. 7, 114 S.Ct. 361, 126 L.Ed.2d 284 (1993).

Zobrest v. Catalina Foothills School Dist., 509 U.S. 1, 113 S.Ct. 2462, 125 L.Ed.2d 1 (1993).

Dellmuth v. Muth, 491 U.S. 223, 109 S.Ct. 2397, 105 L.Ed.2d 181 (1989).

Honig v. Doe, 484 U.S. 305, 108 S.Ct. 592, 98 L.Ed.2d 686 (1988).

Honig v. Students of Cal. School for the Blind, 471 U.S. 148, 105 S.Ct. 1820, 85 L.Ed.2d 114 (1985).

Burlington School Committee v. Department of Education, 471 U.S. 359, 105 S.Ct. 1996, 85 L.Ed.2d 385 (1985).

Smith v. Robinson, 468 U.S. 992, 104 S.Ct. 3457, 82 L.Ed.2d 746 (1984).

Irving Independent School District v. Tatro, 468 U.S. 883, 104 S.Ct. 3371, 82 L.Ed.2d 664 (1984).

Board of Education v. Rowley, 458 U.S. 176, 102 S.Ct. 3034, 73 L.Ed.2d 690 (1982).

University of Texas v. Camenisch, 451 U.S. 390, 101 S.Ct. 1830, 68 L.Ed.2d 175 (1981).

Southeastern Community College v. Davis, 442 U.S. 397, 99 S.Ct. 2361, 60 L.Ed.2d 980 (1979).

Discrimination Generally

Reeves v. Sanderson Plumbing Products, 530 U.S. 133, 120 S.Ct. 2097, 147 L.Ed.2d 15 (2000).

Kimel v. Florida Bd. of Regents, 528 U.S. 62, 120 S.Ct. 631, 145 L.Ed.2d 522 (2000).

Murphy v. United Parcel Service, Inc., 527 U.S. 516, 119 S.Ct. 2133, 144 L.Ed.2d 484 (1999).

Sutton v. United Airlines, Inc., 527 U.S. 471, 119 S.Ct. 2139, 144 L.Ed.2d 450 (1999).

Bragdon v. Abbott, 524 U.S. 624, 118 S.Ct. 2196, 141 L.Ed.2d 540 (1998).

U.S. v. Virginia, 518 U.S. 515, 116 S.Ct. 2264, 135 L.Ed.2d 735 (1996).

Jett v. Dallas Indep. School Dist., 491 U.S. 701, 109 S.Ct. 2702, 105 L.Ed.2d 598 (1989).

Carnegie-Mellon Univ. v. Cohill, 484 U.S. 343, 108 S.Ct. 614, 98 L.Ed.2d 720 (1988).

School Board of Nassau County v. Arline, 480 U.S. 273, 107 S.Ct. 1123, 94 L.Ed.2d 307 (1987).

Hazelwood School Dist. v. U.S., 433 U.S. 299, 97 S.Ct. 2736, 53 L.Ed.2d 768 (1977).

DeFunis v. Odegaard, 416 U.S. 312, 94 S.Ct. 1704, 40 L.Ed.2d 164 (1974).

Monell v. Dep't of Social Serv., 436 U.S. 658, 98 S.Ct. 2018, 56 L.Ed.2d 611 (1978).

Due Process

Gilbert v. Homar, 520 U.S. 924, 117 S.Ct. 1807, 138 L.Ed.2d 120 (1997).

University of Tennessee v. Elliot, 478 U.S. 788, 106 S.Ct. 3220, 92 L.Ed.2d 635 (1986).

Memphis Community School District v. Stachura, 477 U.S. 299, 106 S.Ct. 2537, 91 L.Ed.2d 249 (1986).

Cleveland Board of Education v. Loudermill, 470 U.S. 532, 105 S.Ct. 1487, 84 L.Ed.2d 494 (1985).

Perry v. Sindermann, 408 U.S. 593, 92 S.Ct. 2694, 33 L.Ed.2d 570 (1972).

Board of Regents v. Roth, 408 U.S. 564, 92 S.Ct. 2701, 33 L.Ed.2d 548 (1972).

Elections

Reno v. Bossier Parish School Bd., 528 U.S. 320, 120 S.Ct. 866, 145 L.Ed.2d 845 (2000).

Texas v. U.S., 523 U.S. 296, 118 S.Ct. 1257, 140 L.Ed.2d 406 (1998).

Reno v. Bossier Parish School Bd., 520 U.S. 471, 117 S.Ct. 1491, 137 L.Ed.2d 730 (1997).

Dougherty County Bd. of Educ. v. White, 439 U.S. 32, 99 S.Ct. 368, 58 L.Ed.2d 269 (1978).

Mayor of Philadelphia v. Educ. Equality League, 415 U.S. 605, 94 S.Ct. 1323, 39 L.Ed.2d 630 (1974).

Kramer v. Union Free School Dist. No. 15, 395 U.S. 621, 89 S.Ct. 1886, 23 L.Ed.2d 583 (1969).

Sailors v. Board of Education, 387 U.S. 105, 87 S.Ct. 1549, 18 L.Ed.2d 650 (1967).

Federal Aid

Traynor v. Turnage, 485 U.S. 535, 108 S.Ct. 1372, 99 L.Ed.2d 618 (1988).

Selective Service System v. MPIRG, 468 U.S. 841, 104 S.Ct. 3348, 82 L.Ed.2d 632 (1984).

Bell v. New Jersey and Pennsylvania, 461 U.S. 773, 103 S.Ct. 2187, 76 L.Ed.2d 312 (1984).

Valley Forge Christian College v. Americans United for Separation of Church and State, 454 U.S. 464, 102 S.Ct. 752, 70 L.Ed.2d 700 (1982).

Board of Education v. Harris, 444 U.S. 130, 100 S.Ct. 363, 62 L.Ed.2d 275 (1979).

Wheeler v. Barrera, 417 U.S. 402, 94 S.Ct. 2274, 41 L.Ed.2d 159 (1974).

Tilton v. Richardson, 403 U.S. 672, 91 S.Ct. 2091, 29 L.Ed.2d 790 (1971).

Financing

Camps Newfound/Owatonna, Inc. v. Town of Harrison, Maine, 520 U.S. 564, 117 S.Ct. 1590, 137 L.Ed.2d 852 (1997).

Papasan v. Allain, 478 U.S. 265, 106 S.Ct. 2932, 92 L.Ed.2d 209 (1986).

Bennett v. New Jersey, 470 U.S. 632, 105 S.Ct. 1555, 84 L.Ed.2d 572 (1985).

Bennett v. Kentucky Department of Education, 470 U.S. 656, 105 S.Ct. 1544, 84 L.Ed.2d 590 (1985).

Lawrence County v. Lead-Deadwood School Dist. No. 40-1, 469 U.S. 256, 105 S.Ct. 695, 83 L.Ed.2d 635 (1985).

Grove City College v. Bell, 465 U.S. 555, 104 S.Ct. 1211, 79 L.Ed.2d 516 (1984).

San Antonio v. Rodriguez, 411 U.S. 1, 93 S.Ct. 1278, 36 L.Ed.2d 16 (1973).

Freedom of Religion (see also Religious Activities)

Edwards v. Aguillard, 482 U.S. 578, 107 S.Ct. 2573, 96 L.Ed.2d 510 (1987).

Ansonia Board of Education v. Philbrook, 499 U.S. 60, 107 S.Ct. 367, 93 L.Ed.2d 305 (1986).

Freedom of Speech

Board of Regents of Univ. of Wisconsin System v. Southworth, 529 U.S. 217, 120 S.Ct. 1346, 146 L.Ed.2d 193 (2000).

Rosenberger v. University of Virginia, 515 U.S. 819, 115 S.Ct. 2510, 132 L.Ed.2d 700 (1995).

Bd. of Educ. of Westside Community School. v. Mergens, 496 U.S. 226, 110 S.Ct. 2356, 110 L.Ed.2d 191 (1990).

Bd. of Trustees of the State Univ. of New York v. Fox, 492 U.S. 469, 109 S.Ct. 3028, 106 L.Ed.2d 388 (1989).

Hazelwood School Dist. v. Kuhlmeier, 484 U.S. 261, 108 S.Ct. 562, 98 L.Ed.2d 592 (1988).

Bethel School District v. Fraser, 478 U.S. 675, 106 S.Ct. 3159, 92 L.Ed.2d 549 (1986).

Board of Education v. Pico, 457 U.S. 853, 102 S.Ct. 2799, 73 L.Ed.2d 435 (1982).

Givhan v. Western Line Consolidated School District, 439 U.S. 410, 99 S.Ct. 693, 58 L.Ed.2d 619 (1979).

Mt. Healthy City School v. Doyle, 429 U.S. 274, 97 S.Ct. 568, 50 L.Ed.2d 471 (1977).

Papish v. Board of Curators, 410 U.S. 667, 93 S.Ct. 1197, 35 L.Ed.2d 618 (1973).

Grayned v. City of Rockford, 408 U.S. 104, 92 S.Ct. 2294, 33 L.Ed.2d 222 (1972).

Police Dept. v. Mosley, 408 U.S. 92, 92 S.Ct. 2286, 33 L.Ed.2d 212 (1972).

Tinker v. Des Moines, 393 U.S. 503, 89 S.Ct. 733, 21 L.Ed.2d 733 (1969).

Pickering v. Board of Education, 391 U.S. 563, 88 S.Ct. 1731, 20 L.Ed.2d 811 (1968).

Keyishian v. Board of Regents, 385 U.S. 589, 87 S.Ct. 675, 17 L.Ed.2d 629 (1967).

Adler v. Bd. of Educ., 342 U.S. 485, 72 S.Ct. 380, 96 L.Ed. 517 (1952).

Labor Relations

Christensen v. Harris County et al., 529 U.S. 576, 120 S.Ct. 1655, 146 L.Ed.2d 621 (2000).

Central State University v. American Ass'n of Univ. Professors, Central State Univ. Chapter, 526 U.S. 124, 119 S.Ct. 1162, 143 L.Ed.2d 227 (1999).

Lehnert v. Ferris Faculty Ass'n, 500 U.S. 507, 111 S.Ct. 1950, 114 L.Ed.2d 572 (1991).

Fort Stewart Schools v. Federal Labor Relations Authority, 495 U.S. 641, 110 S.Ct. 2043, 109 L.Ed.2d 659 (1990).

Minnesota State Board for Community Colleges v. Knight, 465 U.S. 271, 104 S.Ct. 1058, 79 L.Ed.2d 299 (1984).

NLRB v. Yeshiva University, 444 U.S. 672, 100 S.Ct. 856, 63 L.Ed.2d 115 (1980).

NLRB v. Catholic Bishop of Chicago, 440 U.S. 490, 99 S.Ct. 1313, 59 L.Ed.2d 533 (1979).

Abood v. Detroit Bd. of Educ., 431 U.S. 209, 97 S.Ct. 1782, 52 L.Ed.2d 261 (1977).

Loyalty Oaths

Connell v. Higgenbotham, 403 U.S. 207, 91 S.Ct. 1772, 29 L.Ed.2d 418 (1971).

Whitehill v. Elkins, 389 U.S. 54, 88 S.Ct. 184, 19 L.Ed.2d 228 (1967).

Elfbrandt v. Russell, 384 U.S. 11, 86 S.Ct. 1238, 16 L.Ed.2d 321 (1966).

Baggett v. Bullitt, 377 U.S. 360, 84 S.Ct. 1316, 12 L.Ed.2d 377 (1964).

Cramp v. Bd. of Educ., 368 U.S. 278, 82 S.Ct. 275, 7 L.Ed.2d 285 (1961).
Slochower v. Bd. of Higher Educ., 350 U.S. 551, 76 S.Ct. 637, 100 L.Ed. 692 (1956).

Maternity Leave

Richmond Unified School Dist. v. Berg, 434 U.S. 158, 98 S.Ct. 623, 54 L.Ed.2d 375 (1977).
Cleveland Board of Education v. La Fleur, 414 U.S. 632, 94 S.Ct. 791, 39 L.Ed.2d 52 (1974).
Cohen v. Chesterfield, 414 U.S. 632, 94 S.Ct. 791, 39 L.Ed.2d 52 (1974).

Private Schools

Brentwood Academy v. Tennessee Secondary School Athletic Ass'n, 531 U.S. 288, 121 S.Ct. 924, 148 L.Ed.2d 807 (2001).
Mitchell v. Helms, 530 U.S. 793, 120 S.Ct. 2530, 147 L.Ed.2d 660 (2000).
Bates v. U.S., 522 U.S. 23, 118 S.Ct. 285, 139 L.Ed.2d 215 (1997).
Agostini v. Felton, 521 U.S. 203, 117 S.Ct. 1997, 138 L.Ed.2d 391 (1997).
Farrar v. Hobby, 506 U.S. 103, 113 S.Ct. 566, 121 L.Ed.2d 494 (1992).
Corp. of the Presiding Bishop of the Church of Jesus Christ of Latter-day Saints v. Amos, 483 U.S. 327, 107 S.Ct. 2862, 97 L.Ed.2d 273 (1987).
St. Francis College v. Al-Khazraji, 481 U.S. 604, 107 S.Ct. 2022, 97 L.Ed.2d 749 (1987).
Witters v. Washington Department of Services for the Blind, 474 U.S. 481, 106 S.Ct. 748, 88 L.Ed.2d 846 (1986).
Aguilar v. Felton, 473 U.S. 402, 105 S.Ct. 3232, 87 L.Ed.2d 290 (1985).
Grand Rapids School District v. Ball, 473 U.S. 373, 105 S.Ct. 3216, 87 L.Ed.2d 267 (1985).
Grove City College v. Bell, 465 U.S. 555, 104 S.Ct. 1211, 79 L.Ed.2d 516 (1984).
Mueller v. Allen, 463 U.S. 388, 103 S.Ct. 3062, 77 L.Ed.2d 721 (1983).
Bob Jones University v. United States, 461 U.S. 574, 103 S. Ct. 2017, 76 L.Ed.2d 157 (1983).
Valley Forge Christian College v. Americans United for Separation of Church and State, 454 U.S. 464, 102 S.Ct. 752, 70 L.Ed.2d 700 (1982).
St. Martin Evangelical Lutheran Church v. South Dakota, 451 U.S. 772, 101 S.Ct. 2142, 68 L.Ed.2d 612 (1981).
Committee v. Regan, 444 U.S. 646, 100 S.Ct. 840, 63 L.Ed.2d 94 (1980).
NLRB v. Catholic Bishop of Chicago, 440 U.S. 490, 99 S.Ct. 1313, 59 L.Ed.2d 533 (1979).
New York v. Cathedral Academy, 434 U.S. 125, 98 S.Ct. 340, 54 L.Ed.2d 346 (1977).
Wolman v. Walter, 433 U.S. 229, 97 S.Ct. 2593, 53 L.Ed.2d 714 (1977).
Runyon v. McCrary, 427 U.S. 160, 96 S.Ct. 2586, 49 L.Ed.2d 415 (1976).
Roemer v. Board of Public Works, 426 U.S. 736, 96 S.Ct. 2337, 49 L.Ed.2d 179 (1976).
Meek v. Pittenger, 421 U.S. 349, 95 S.Ct. 1753, 44 L.Ed.2d 217 (1975).
Wheeler v. Barrera, 417 U.S. 402, 94 S.Ct. 2274, 41 L.Ed.2d 159 (1974).
Sloan v. Lemon, 413 U.S. 825, 93 S.Ct. 2982, 37 L.Ed.2d 939 (1973).

Committee for Public Education and Religious Liberty v. Nyquist, 413 U.S. 756, 93 S.Ct. 2955, 37 L.Ed.2d 948 (1973).

Hunt v. McNair, 413 U.S. 734, 93 S.Ct. 2868, 37 L.Ed.2d 923 (1973).

Levitt v. Committee for Public Education and Religious Liberty, 413 U.S. 472, 93 S.Ct. 2814, 37 L.Ed.2d 736 (1973).

Early v. Di Censo, 403 U.S. 602, 91 S.Ct. 2105, 29 L.Ed.2d 745 (1971).

Lemon v. Kurtzman, 403 U.S. 602, 91 S.Ct. 2105, 29 L.Ed.2d 745 (1971).

Board of Education v. Allen, 392 U.S. 236, 88 S.Ct. 1923, 20 L.Ed.2d 1060 (1968).

Flast v. Cohen, 392 U.S. 83, 88 S.Ct. 1942, 20 L.Ed.2d 947 (1968).

Zorach v. Clauson, 343 U.S. 306, 72 S.Ct. 679, 96 L.Ed. 954 (1952).

McCollum v. Board of Education, 333 U.S. 203, 68 S.Ct. 461, 92 L.Ed. 649 (1948).

Everson v. Board of Education, 330 U.S. 1, 67 S.Ct. 504, 91 L.Ed. 711 (1947).

Farrington v. Tokushige, 273 U.S. 284, 47 S.Ct. 406, 71 L.Ed. 646 (1927).

Racial Discrimination

Texas v. Lesage, 528 U.S. 18, 120 S.Ct. 467, 145 L.Ed.2d (1999).

St. Francis College v. Al-Khazraji, 481 U.S. 604, 107 S.Ct. 2022, 97 L.Ed.2d 749 (1987).

Wygant v. Jackson Board of Education, 476 U.S. 267, 106 S.Ct. 1842, 90 L.Ed.2d 260 (1986).

Runyon v. McCrary, 427 U.S. 160, 96 S.Ct. 2586, 49 L.Ed.2d 415 (1976).

Lau v. Nichols, 414 U.S. 563, 94 S.Ct. 786, 39 L.Ed.2d 1 (1974).

Norwood v. Harrison, 413 U.S. 455, 93 S.Ct. 2804, 37 L.Ed.2d 723 (1973).

Religious Activities in Public Schools

Santa Fe Independent School District v. Doe, 530 U.S. 290, 120 S.Ct. 2266, 147 L.Ed.2d 295 (2000).

Bd. of Educ. of Kiryas Joel Village v. Grumet, 512 U.S. 687, 114 S.Ct. 2481, 129 L.Ed.2d 546 (1994).

Lamb's Chapel v. Center Moriches Union Free School District, 508 U.S. 384, 113 S.Ct. 2141, 124 L.Ed.2d 352 (1993).

Lee v. Weisman, 505 U.S. 577, 112 S.Ct. 2649, 120 L.Ed.2d 467 (1992).

Karcher v. May, 484 U.S. 72, 108 S.Ct. 388, 98 L.Ed.2d 327 (1987).

Bender v. Williamsport Area School District, 475 U.S. 534, 106 S.Ct. 1326, 89 L.Ed.2d 501 (1986).

Wallace v. Jaffree, 472 U.S. 38, 105 S.Ct. 2479, 96 L.Ed.2d 29 (1985).

Widmar v. Vincent, 454 U.S. 263, 102 S.Ct. 269, 70 L.Ed.2d 400 (1981).

Stone v. Graham, 449 U.S. 39, 101 S.Ct. 192, 66 L.Ed.2d 199 (1980).

Epperson v. Arkansas, 393 U.S. 97, 89 S.Ct. 266, 21 L.Ed.2d 228 (1968).

Chamberlin v. Dade County Board of Public Instruction, 377 U.S. 402, 84 S.Ct. 1272, 12 L.Ed.2d 407 (1964).

Abington School District v. Schempp, 374 U.S. 203, 83 S.Ct. 1560, 10 L.Ed.2d 844 (1963).

Engel v. Vitale, 370 U.S. 421, 82 S.Ct. 1261, 8 L.Ed.2d 601 (1962).

McCollum v. Bd. of Educ., 333 U.S. 203, 68 S.Ct. 461, 92 L.Ed. 649 (1948).

West Virginia Board of Education v. Barnette, 319 U.S. 624, 63 S.Ct. 1178, 87 L.Ed. 1628 (1943).

Residency

> Martinez v. Bynum, 461 U.S. 321, 103 S.Ct. 1838, 75 L.Ed.2d 879 (1983).
>
> Elgins v. Moreno, 435 U.S. 647, 98 S.Ct. 1338, 55 L.Ed.2d 614 (1978).

School Liability

> Clark County School Dist. v. Breeden, 532 U.S. 268, 121 S.Ct. 1508, 149 L.Ed.2d 509 (2001).
>
> Gebser v. Lago Vista Indep. School Dist., 524 U.S. 274, 118 S.Ct. 1989, 141 L.Ed.2d 277 (1998).
>
> Regents of Univ. of California v. Doe, 519 U.S. 337, 117 S.Ct. 900, 137 L.Ed.2d 55 (1997).
>
> Bradford Area School Dist. v. Stoneking, 489 U.S. 1062, 109 S.Ct. 1333, 103 L.Ed.2d 804 (1989).
>
> Smith v. Sowers, 490 U.S. 1002, 109 S.Ct. 1634, 104 L.Ed.2d 150 (1989).
>
> Deshaney v. Winnebago County DSS, 489 U.S. 189, 109 S.Ct. 998, 103 L.Ed.2d 249 (1989).

Sex Discrimination

> Davis v. Monroe County Board of Educ., 526 U.S. 629, 119 S.Ct. 1661, 143 L.Ed.2d 839 (1999).
>
> National Collegiate Athletic Ass'n v. Smith, 525 U.S. 84, 119 S.Ct. 924, 142 L.Ed.2d 929 (1999).
>
> Burlington Industries, Inc. v. Ellerth, 524 U.S. 742, 118 S.Ct. 2257, 141 L.Ed.2d 633 (1998).
>
> Faragher v. City of Boca Raton, 524 U.S. 775, 118 S.Ct. 2275, 141 L.Ed.2d 662 (1998).
>
> Oncale v. Sundowner Offshore Offshore Services, Inc., 523 U.S. 75, 118 S.Ct. 998, 140 L.Ed.2d 201 (1998)
>
> Franklin v. Gwinnett County Public Schools, 503 U.S. 60, 112 S.Ct. 1028, 117 L.Ed.2d 208 (1992).
>
> Ohio Civil Rights Commission v. Dayton Christian Schools, 477 U.S. 619, 106 S.Ct. 2718, 91 L.Ed.2d 512 (1986).
>
> Mississippi University for Women v. Hogan, 458 U.S. 718, 102 S.Ct. 3331, 73 L.Ed.2d 1090 (1982).
>
> Rendell-Baker v. Kohn, 457 U.S. 830, 102 S.Ct. 2764, 73 L.Ed.2d 418 (1982).
>
> Cannon v. Univ. of Chicago, 441 U.S. 677, 99 S.Ct. 1946, 60 L.Ed.2d 560 (1979).
>
> Bd. of Trustees v. Sweeney, 439 U.S. 24, 99 S.Ct. 295, 58 L.Ed.2d 216 (1978).

Striking Teachers

> Hortonville Joint School District v. Hortonville Education Association, 426 U.S. 482, 96 S.Ct. 2308, 49 L.Ed.2d 1 (1976).

Student Searches

> Vernonia School Dist. 47J v. Acton, 515 U.S. 646, 115 S. Ct. 2386, 132 L.Ed.2d 564 (1995).
>
> New Jersey v. T.L.O., 469 U.S. 325, 105 S.Ct. 733, 83 L.Ed.2d 720 (1985).

Student Suspensions

Regents v. Ewing, 474 U.S. 214, 106 S.Ct. 507, 88 L.Ed.2d 523 (1985).

Board of Education v. McCluskey, 458 U.S. 966, 103 S.Ct. 3469, 73 L.Ed.2d 1273 (1982).

Carey v. Piphus, 435 U.S. 247, 98 S.Ct. 1042, 55 L.Ed.2d 252 (1978).

Bd. of Curators v. Horowitz, 435 U.S. 78, 98 S.Ct. 948, 55 L.Ed.2d 124 (1978).

Wood v. Strickland, 420 U.S. 308, 95 S.Ct. 992, 43 L.Ed.2d 214 (1975).

Goss v. Lopez, 419 U.S. 565, 95 S.Ct. 729, 42 L.Ed.2d 725 (1975).

Teacher Termination

Patsy v. Bd. of Regents, 457 U.S. 496, 102 S.Ct. 2557, 73 L.Ed.2d 172 (1982).

Chardon v. Fernandez, 454 U.S. 6, 102 S.Ct. 28, 70 L.Ed.2d 6 (1981).

Delaware State College v. Ricks, 449 U.S. 250, 101 S.Ct. 498, 66 L.Ed.2d 431 (1980).

Beilan v. Board of Public Education, 357 U.S. 399, 78 S.Ct. 1317, 2 L.Ed.2d 1414 (1958).

Textbooks

Norwood v. Harrison, 413 U.S. 455, 93 S.Ct. 2804, 37 L.Ed.2d 723 (1973).

Board of Education v. Allen, 392 U.S. 236, 88 S.Ct. 1923, 20 L.Ed.2d 1060 (1968).

Cochran v. Louisiana State Board of Education, 281 U.S. 370, 50 S.Ct. 335, 74 L.Ed.2d 1929 (1930).

Transportation Fees

Kadrmas v. Dickinson Pub. Schools, 487 U.S. 450, 108 S.Ct. 2481, 101 L.Ed.2d 399 (1988).

Use of School Facilities

Ellis v. Dixon, 349 U.S. 458, 75 S.Ct. 859, 99 L.Ed. 1231 (1955).

Weapons Control

U.S. v. Lopez, 514 U.S. 549, 115 S. Ct. 1624, 131 L.Ed.2d 626 (1995).

The Judicial System

In order to allow you to determine the relative importance of a judicial decision, the cases included in *Deskbook Encyclopedia of American School Law* identify the particular court from which a decision has been issued. For example, a case decided by a state supreme court generally will be of greater significance than a state circuit court case. Hence a basic knowledge of the structure of our judicial system is important to an understanding of school law.

Almost all the reports in this volume are taken from appellate court decisions. Although most education law decisions occur at trial court and administrative levels, appellate court decisions have the effect of binding lower courts and administrators so that appellate court decisions have the effect of law within their court systems.

State and federal court systems generally function independently of each other. Each court system applies its own law according to statutes and the determinations of its highest court. However, judges at all levels often consider opinions from other court systems to settle issues which are new or arise under unique fact situations. Similarly, lawyers look at the opinions of many courts to locate authority which supports their clients' cases.

Once a lawsuit is filed in a particular court system, that system retains the matter until its conclusion. Unsuccessful parties at the administrative or trial court level generally have the right to appeal unfavorable determinations of law to appellate courts within the system. When federal law issues or constitutional grounds are present, lawsuits may be appropriately filed in the federal court system. In those cases, the lawsuit is filed initially in the federal district court for that area.

On rare occasions, the U.S. Supreme Court considers appeals from the highest courts of the states if a distinct federal question exists and at least four justices agree on the question's importance. The federal courts occasionally send cases to state courts for application of state law. These situations are infrequent and in general, the state and federal court systems should be considered separate from each other.

The most common system, used by nearly all states and also the federal judiciary, is as follows: a legal action is commenced in district court (sometimes called trial court, county court, common pleas court or superior court) where a decision is initially reached. The case may then be appealed to the court of appeals (or appellate court), and in turn this decision may be appealed to the supreme court.

Several states, however, do not have a court of appeals; lower court decisions are appealed directly to the state's supreme court. Additionally, some states have labeled their courts in a nonstandard fashion.

In Maryland, the highest state court is called the Court of Appeals. In the state of New York, the trial court is called the Supreme Court. Decisions of this court may be appealed to the Supreme Court, Appellate Division. The highest court in New York is the Court of Appeals. Pennsylvania has perhaps the most complex court system. The lowest state court is the Court of Common Pleas. Depending on the circumstances of the case, appeals may be taken to either the Commonwealth Court or the Superior Court. In certain instances the Commonwealth Court functions as a trial court as well as an appellate court. The Superior Court, however, is strictly an intermediate appellate court. The highest court in Pennsylvania is the Supreme Court.

While supreme court decisions are generally regarded as the last word in legal matters, it is important to remember that trial and appeals court decisions also create important legal precedents. For the hierarchy of typical state and federal court systems, please see the diagram below.

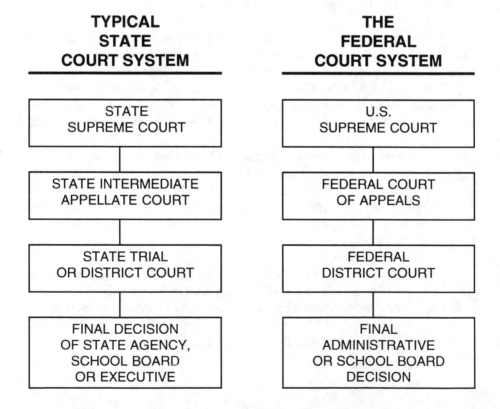

TYPICAL STATE COURT SYSTEM	THE FEDERAL COURT SYSTEM
STATE SUPREME COURT	U.S. SUPREME COURT
STATE INTERMEDIATE APPELLATE COURT	FEDERAL COURT OF APPEALS
STATE TRIAL OR DISTRICT COURT	FEDERAL DISTRICT COURT
FINAL DECISION OF STATE AGENCY, SCHOOL BOARD OR EXECUTIVE	FINAL ADMINISTRATIVE OR SCHOOL BOARD DECISION

Federal courts of appeals hear appeals from the district courts which are located in their circuits. Below is a list of states matched to the federal circuits in which they are located.

First Circuit	— Maine, Massachusetts, New Hampshire, Puerto Rico, Rhode Island
Second Circuit	— Connecticut, New York, Vermont
Third Circuit	— Delaware, New Jersey, Pennsylvania, Virgin Islands
Fourth Circuit	— Maryland, North Carolina, South Carolina, Virginia, West Virginia
Fifth Circuit	— Louisiana, Mississippi, Texas
Sixth Circuit	— Ohio, Kentucky, Michigan, Tennessee
Seventh Circuit	— Illinois, Indiana, Wisconsin
Eighth Circuit	— Arkansas, Iowa, Minnesota, Missouri, Nebraska, North Dakota, South Dakota
Ninth Circuit	— Alaska, Arizona, California, Guam, Hawaii, Idaho, Montana, Nevada, Northern Mariana Islands, Oregon, Washington
Tenth Circuit	— Colorado, Kansas, Oklahoma, New Mexico, Utah, Wyoming
Eleventh Circuit	— Alabama, Florida, Georgia
District of Columbia Circuit	— Hears cases from the U.S. District Court for the District of Columbia
Federal Circuit	— Sitting in Washington, D.C., the U.S. Court of Appeals, Federal Circuit, hears patent and trade appeals and certain appeals on claims brought against the federal government and its agencies

How to Read a Case Citation

Generally, court decisions can be located in case reporters at law school or governmental law libraries. Some cases can also be located on the Internet through legal Web sites or official court websites.

Each case summary contains the citation, or legal reference, to the full text of the case. The diagram below illustrates how to read a case citation.

case name (parties) case reporter name and series court location

Mangla v. Brown Univ., 135 F.3d 80 (1st Cir. 1998).

volume number first page year of decision

Some cases may have two or three reporter names such as U.S. Supreme Court cases and cases reported in regional case reporters as well as state case reporters. For example, a U.S. Supreme Court case usually contains three case reporter citations.

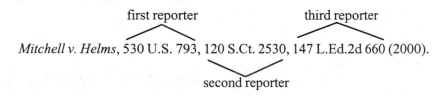

first reporter third reporter

Mitchell v. Helms, 530 U.S. 793, 120 S.Ct. 2530, 147 L.Ed.2d 660 (2000).

second reporter

The citations are still read in the same manner as if only one citation has been listed.

Occasionally, a case may contain a citation which does not reference a case reporter. For example, a citation may contain a reference such as:

case name year of decision first page year of decision

Porta v. Klagholz, No. 98-2350, 1998 WL 598385 (D.N.J.1998).

court file number WESTLAW[1] court location

The court file number indicates the specific number assigned to a case by the particular court system deciding the case. In our example, the U.S. District Court for the District of New Jersey has assigned the case of *Porta v. Klagholz* the case

---

[1] WESTLAW® is a computerized database of court cases available for a fee.

number of "No. 98-2350" which will serve as the reference number for the case and any matter relating to the case. Locating a case on the Internet generally requires either the case name and date of the decision, and/or the court file number.

Below, we have listed the full names of the regional reporters. As mentioned previously, many states have individual state reporters. The names of those reporters may be obtained from a reference law librarian.

P.	**Pacific Reporter**	
	Alaska, Arizona, California, Colorado, Hawaii, Idaho, Kansas, Montana, Nevada, New Mexico, Oklahoma, Oregon, Utah, Washington, Wyoming	
A.	**Atlantic Reporter**	
	Connecticut, Delaware, District of Columbia, Maine, Maryland, New Hampshire, New Jersey, Pennsylvania, Rhode Island, Vermont	
N.E.	**Northeastern Reporter**	
	Illinois, Indiana, Massachusetts, New York, Ohio	
N.W.	**Northwestern Reporter**	
	Iowa, Michigan, Minnesota, Nebraska, North Dakota, South Dakota, Wisconsin	
S.	**Southern Reporter**	
	Alabama, Florida, Louisiana, Mississippi	
S.E.	**Southeastern Reporter**	
	Georgia, North Carolina, South Carolina, Virginia, West Virginia	
S.W.	**Southwestern Reporter**	
	Arkansas, Kentucky, Missouri, Tennessee, Texas	

F.   **Federal Reporter**
The thirteen federal judicial circuits courts of appeals decisions. *See, The Judicial System, p. 639* for specific state circuits.

F.Supp. **Federal Supplement**
The thirteen federal judicial circuits district court decisions. *See, The Judicial System, p. 639* for specific state circuits.

U.S.   **United States Reports**
S.Ct.   **Supreme Court Reporter** ⟩ U.S. Supreme Court Decisions
L.Ed.   **Lawyers' Edition**

GLOSSARY

Age Discrimination in Employment Act (ADEA) - The ADEA, 29 U.S.C. § 621 *et seq.*, is part of the Fair Labor Standards Act. It prohibits discrimination against persons who are at least 40 years old, and applies to employers that have 20 or more employees and that affect interstate commerce.

Americans with Disabilities Act (ADA) - The ADA, 42 U.S.C. § 12101 *et seq.*, went into effect on July 26, 1992. Among other things, it prohibits discrimination against a qualified individual with a disability because of that person's disability with respect to job application procedures, the hiring, advancement or discharge of employees, employee compensation, job training, and other terms, conditions and privileges of employment.

Bona fide - Latin term meaning "good faith." Generally used to note a party's lack of bad intent or fraudulent purpose.

Class Action Suit - Federal Rule of Civil Procedure 23 allows members of a class to sue as representatives on behalf of the whole class provided that the class is so large that joinder of all parties is impractical, there are questions of law or fact common to the class, the claims or defenses of the representatives are typical of the claims or defenses of the class, and the representative parties will adequately protect the interests of the class. In addition, there must be some danger of inconsistent verdicts or adjudications if the class action were prosecuted as separate actions. Most states also allow class actions under the same or similar circumstances.

Collateral Estoppel - Also known as issue preclusion. The idea that once an issue has been litigated, it may not be re-tried. Similar to the doctrine of *Res Judicata* (see below).

Due Process Clause - The clauses of the Fifth and Fourteenth Amendments to the Constitution which guarantee the citizens of the United States "due process of law" (see below). The Fifth Amendment's Due Process Clause applies to the federal government, and the Fourteenth Amendment's Due Process Clause applies to the states.

Due Process of Law - The idea of "fair play" in the government's application of law to its citizens, guaranteed by the Fifth and Fourteenth Amendments. Substantive due process is just plain *fairness*, and procedural due process is accorded when the government utilizes adequate procedural safeguards for the protection of an individual's liberty or property interests.

Education for All Handicapped Children Act (EAHCA) - [see Individuals with Disabilities Education Act (IDEA).]

Education of the Handicapped Act (EHA) - [see Individuals with Disabilities Education Act (IDEA).]

Employee Retirement Income Security Act (ERISA) - Federal legislation which sets uniform standards for employee pension benefit plans and employee welfare benefit plans. It is codified at 29 U.S.C. § 1001 *et seq.*

Enjoin - (see Injunction).

Equal Pay Act - Federal legislation which is part of the Fair Labor Standards Act. It applies to wage discrimination which is based on gender. For race discrimination, employees paid unequally must utilize Title VII or 42 U.S.C. § 1981. Unlike many labor statutes, there is no minimum number of employees necessary to invoke the act's protection.

Equal Protection Clause - The clause of the Fourteenth Amendment which prohibits a state from denying any person within its jurisdiction equal protection of its laws. Also, the Due Process Clause of the Fifth Amendment which pertains to the federal government. This has been interpreted by the Supreme Court to grant equal protection even though there is no explicit grant in the Constitution.

Establishment Clause - The clause of the First Amendment which prohibits Congress from making "any law respecting an establishment of religion." This clause has been interpreted as creating a "wall of separation" between church and state. The test frequently used to determine whether government action violates the Establishment Clause, referred to as the *Lemon* test, asks whether the action has a secular purpose, whether its primary effect promotes or inhibits religion, and whether it requires excessive entanglement between church and state.

Ex Post Facto Law - A law which punishes as criminal any action which was not a crime at the time it was performed. Prohibited by Article I, Section 9, of the Constitution.

Exclusionary Rule - Constitutional limitation on the introduction of evidence which states that evidence derived from a constitutional violation must be excluded from trial.

Fair Labor Standards Act (FLSA) - Federal legislation which mandates the payment of minimum wages and overtime compensation to covered employees. The overtime provisions require employers to pay at least time-and-one-half to employees who work more than 40 hours per week.

Federal Employers' Liability Act (FELA) - Legislation enacted to provide a federal remedy for railroad workers who are injured as a result of employer or co-employee negligence. It expressly prohibits covered carriers from adopting any regulation, or entering into any contract, which limits their FELA liability.

Federal Tort Claims Act - Federal legislation which determines the circumstances under which the United States waives its sovereign immunity (see below) and agrees to be sued in court for money damages. The government retains its immunity in cases of intentional torts committed by its employees or agents, and where the tort is the result of a "discretionary function" of a federal employee or agency. Many states have similar acts.

42 U.S.C. §§ 1981, 1983 - Section 1983 of the federal Civil Rights Act prohibits any person acting under color of state law from depriving any other person of rights protected by the Constitution or by federal laws. A vast majority of lawsuits claiming constitutional violations are brought under § 1983. Section 1981 provides that all persons enjoy the same right to make and enforce contracts as "white citizens." Section 1981 applies to employment contracts. Further, unlike § 1983, § 1981 applies even to private actors. It is not limited to those acting under color of state law. These sections do not apply to the federal government, though the government may be sued directly under the Constitution for any violations.

Free Exercise Clause - The clause of the First Amendment which prohibits Congress from interfering with citizens' rights to the free exercise of their religion. Through the Fourteenth Amendment, it has also been made applicable to the states and their sub-entities. The Supreme Court has held that laws of general applicability which have an incidental effect on persons' free exercise rights are not violative of the Free Exercise Clause.

Handicapped Children's Protection Act (HPCA) - [see also Individuals with Disabilities Education Act (IDEA).] The HPCA, enacted as an amendment to the EHA, provides for the payment of attorneys' fees to a prevailing parent or guardian in a lawsuit brought under the EHA (and the IDEA).

Hearing Officer - Also known as an administrative law judge. The hearing officer decides disputes that arise *at the administrative level*, and has the power to administer oaths, take testimony, rule on evidentiary questions, and make determinations of fact.

Incorporation Doctrine - By its own terms, the Bill of Rights applies only to the federal government. The Incorporation Doctrine states that the Fourteenth Amendment makes the Bill of Rights applicable to the states.

Individualized Educational Program (IEP) - The IEP is designed to give children with disabilities a free, appropriate education. It is updated annually, with the participation of the child's parents or guardian.

Individuals with Disabilities Education Act (IDEA) - Also known as the Education of the Handicapped Act (EHA), the Education for All Handicapped Children Act (EAHCA), and the Handicapped Children's Protection Act (HPCA). Originally enacted as the EHA, the IDEA is the federal legislation which provides for the free, appropriate education of all children with disabilities.

Injunction - An equitable remedy (see Remedies) wherein a court orders a party to do or refrain from doing some particular action.

Jurisdiction - The power of a court to determine cases and controversies. The Supreme Court's jurisdiction extends to cases arising under the Constitution and under federal law. Federal courts have the power to hear cases where there is diversity of citizenship or where a federal question is involved.

Labor Management Relations Act (LMRA) - Federal labor law which pre-empts state law with respect to controversies involving collective bargaining agreements. The most important provision of the LMRA is § 301, which is codified at 29 U.S.C. § 185.

Mainstreaming - Part of what is required for a free appropriate education is that each child with a disability be educated in the "least restrictive environment." To the extent that disabled children are educated with nondisabled children in regular education classes, those children are being mainstreamed.

National Labor Relations Act (NLRA) - Federal legislation which guarantees to employees the right to form and participate in labor organizations. It prohibits employers from interfering with employees in the exercise of their rights under the NLRA.

Negligence per se - Negligence on its face. Usually, the violation of an ordinance or statute will be treated as negligence per se because no careful person would have been guilty of it.

Occupational Safety and Health Act - Federal legislation which requires employers to provide a safe workplace. Employers have both general and specific duties under the act. The general duty is to provide a workplace which is free from recognized hazards that are likely to result in serious physical harm. The specific duty is to conform to the health and safety standards promulgated by the Secretary of Labor.

Overbroad - A government action is overbroad if, in an attempt to alleviate a specific evil, it impermissibly prohibits or chills a protected action. For example, attempting to deal with street litter by prohibiting the distribution of leaflets or handbills.

Placement - A special education student's placement must be appropriate (as well as responsive to the particular child's needs). Under the IDEA's "stay-put" provision, school officials may not remove a special education child from his or her "then current placement" over the parents' objections until the completion of administrative or judicial review proceedings.

Preemption Doctrine - Doctrine which states that when federal and state law attempt to regulate the same subject matter, federal law prevents the state law from operating. Based on the Supremacy Clause of Article VI, Clause 2, of the Constitution.

Prior Restraint - Restraining a publication before it is distributed. In general, constitutional law doctrine prohibits government from exercising prior restraint.

Rehabilitation Act - Section 504 of the Rehabilitation Act prohibits employers who receive federal financial assistance from discriminating against otherwise qualified individuals with handicaps solely becuase of their handicaps. An otherwise qualified individual is one who can perform the "essential functions" of the job with "reasonable accomodation."

Related Services - As part of the free, appropriate education due to children with disabilities, school districts may have to provide related services such as transportation, physical and occupational therapy, and medical services which are for diagnostic or evaluative purposes relating to education.

Remand - The act of an appellate court in returning a case to the court from which it came for further action.

Remedies - There are two general categories of remedies, or relief: legal remedies, which consist of money damages, and equitable remedies, which consist of a court mandate that a specific action be prohibited or required. For example, a claim for compensatory and punitive damages seeks a legal remedy; a claim for an injunction seeks an equitable remedy. Equitable remedies are generally unavailable unless legal remedies are inadequate to address the harm.

Res Judicata - The judicial notion that a claim or action may not be tried twice or re-litigated, or that all causes of action arising out of the same set of operative facts should be tried at one time. Also known as claim preclusion.

Section 1981 & Section 1983 - (see 42 U.S.C. §§ 1981, 1983).

Sovereign Immunity - The idea that the government cannot be sued without its consent. It stems from the English notion that the "King could do no wrong." This immunity from suit has been abrogated in most states and by the federal government through legislative acts known as "tort claims acts."

Standing - The judicial doctrine which states that in order to maintain a lawsuit a party must have some real interest at stake in the outcome of the trial.

Statute of Limitations - A statute of limitation provides the time period in which a specific cause of action may be brought.

Summary Judgment - Also referred to as pretrial judgment. Similar to a dismissal. Where there is no genuine issue as to any material fact and all that remains is a question of law, a judge can rule in favor of one party or the other.

In general, summary judgment is used to dispose of claims which do not support a legally recognized claim.

Supremacy Clause - Clause in Article VI of the Constitution which states that federal legislation is the supreme law of the land. This clause is used to support the Preemption Doctrine (see above).

Title VII, Civil Rights Act of 1964 (Title VII) - Title VII prohibits discrimination in employment based upon race, color, sex, national origin, or religion. It applies to any employer having fifteen or more employees. Under Title VII, where an employer intentionally discriminates, employees may obtain money damages unless the claim is for race discrimination. For those claims, monetary relief is available under 42 U.S.C. § 1981.

U.S. Equal Employment Opportunity Commission (EEOC) - The EEOC is the government entity which is empowered to enforce Title VII (see above) through investigation and/or lawsuits. Private individuals alleging discrimination must pursue administrative remedies within the EEOC before they are allowed to file suit under Title VII.

Vacate - The act of annulling the judgment of a court either by an appellate court or by the court itself. The Supreme Court will generally vacate a lower court's judgment without deciding the case itself, and remand the case to the lower court for further consideration in light of some recent controlling decision.

Void-for-Vagueness Doctrine - A judicial doctrine based on the Fourteenth Amendment's Due Process Clause. In order for a law which regulates speech, or any criminal statute, to pass muster under the doctrine, the law must make clear what actions are prohibited or made criminal. Under the principles of the Due Process Clause, people of average intelligence should not have to guess at the meaning of a law.

Writ of Certiorari - The device used by the Supreme Court to transfer cases from the appellate court's docket to its own. Since the Supreme Court's appellate jurisdiction is largely discretionary, it need only issue such a writ when it desires to rule in the case.

INDEX